Strategically Created Treaty Conflicts and the Politics of International Law

Treaty conflicts are not merely the contingent or inadvertent by-products of the increasing juridification of international relations. In several instances, States have deliberately created treaty conflicts in order to catalyse changes in multilateral regimes. Surabhi Ranganathan uses such conflicts as context to explore the role of international law, in legal thought and practice. Her examinations of the International Law Commission's work on treaties and of various scholars' proposals on institutional action, offer a fresh view of 'mainstream' legal thought. They locate in a variety of writings a common faith in international legal discourse, built on liberal and constructivist assumptions. Ranganathan's three rich studies of treaty conflict, relating to the areas of seabed mining, the International Criminal Court, and nuclear governance, furnish a textured account of the specific forms and practices that constitute such a legal discourse, and permit a grounded understanding of the interactions that shape international law.

Surabhi Ranganathan is an Assistant Professor of Law at the University of Warwick. She was previously a Junior Research Fellow at the Lauterpacht Centre for International Law and King's College, Cambridge. She is the Assistant Editor of the *Cambridge Companion to International Law* (2012) edited by James Crawford and Martti Koskenniemi.

CAMBRIDGE STUDIES IN INTERNATIONAL AND COMPARATIVE LAW

Established in 1946, this series produces high quality scholarship in the fields of public and private international law and comparative law. Although these are distinct legal sub-disciplines, developments since 1946 confirm their interrelations.

Comparative law is increasingly used as a tool in the making of law at national, regional and international levels. Private international law is now often affected by international conventions, and the issues faced by classical conflicts rules are frequently dealt with by substantive harmonisation of law under international auspices. Mixed international arbitrations, especially those involving state economic activity, raise mixed questions of public and private international law, while in many fields (such as the protection of human rights and democratic standards, investment guarantees and international criminal law) international and national systems interact. National constitutional arrangements relating to 'foreign affairs', and to the implementation of international norms, are a focus of attention.

The series welcomes works of a theoretical or interdisciplinary character, and those focusing on the new approaches to international or comparative law or conflicts of law. Studies of particular institutions or problems are equally welcome, as are translations of the best work published in other languages.

A list of books in the series can be found at the end of this volume.

Strategically Created Treaty Conflicts and the Politics of International Law

Surabhi Ranganathan

CAMBRIDGE
UNIVERSITY PRESS

CAMBRIDGE
UNIVERSITY PRESS

University Printing House, Cambridge CB2 8BS, United Kingdom

Cambridge University Press is part of the University of Cambridge.

It furthers the University's mission by disseminating knowledge in the pursuit of education, learning and research at the highest international levels of excellence.

www.cambridge.org
Information on this title: www.cambridge.org/9781107043305

First published 2014

A catalogue record for this publication is available from the British Library

Library of Congress Cataloging-in-Publication Data
Ranganathan, Surabhi, author.
Strategically created treaty conflicts and the politics of international law / Surabhi Ranganathan.
pages cm – (Cambridge studies in international and comparative law ; 113)
ISBN 978-1-107-04330-5 (hardback)
1. International law. 2. Treaties. I. Title.
KZ3410.R36 2014
341–dc23

2014019425

ISBN 978-1-107-04330-5 Hardback

Contents

Foreword

International legal scholarship tends to address the political substrate of international law in one of two extreme modes: either by not dealing with it at all and engaging only with the doctrinal surface; or by being entirely consumed with it and reducing doctrinal form to insignificance. In Dr Ranganathan's chosen field of inquiry – treaty conflict – these modes involve either the fixed assumption that treaty conflicts are inadvertent by-products of the increasing numbers of treaties, to be resolved by application of formal rules and procedures; or that treaty conflicts merely confirm the epiphenomenal character of international law.

Dr Ranganathan challenges both these approaches. Arguing that treaty conflicts are often strategically created by States for the purpose of catalysing changes in multilateral legal regimes, she builds upon, and finesses, existing understandings in four respects.

First, she departs from a long tradition of argument over the appropriate definition of the concept of 'treaty conflict' (does it include only instances where treaties provide for mutually exclusive obligation, or also those of incompatibilities between rights and obligations?), showing that from the perspective of their impact upon international relations there is no distinction between the two. A conflict between a right granted by one treaty and an obligation provided under another may, depending upon the context, involve a greater challenge to the stability and coherence of an existing legal regime than an outright conflict of obligations. Denying to the former the status of a treaty conflict properly so-called makes little difference. Dr Ranganathan, instead, calls attention to other features of treaty conflicts that may be more important: the strategic context; the lack of identity between their parties, bringing into play the doctrinal restrictions of the *pacta tertiis* rule; and the possibility, through a cleverly leveraged conflict, of challenging a hard-won multilateral treaty regime through a bilateral or 'small-group' treaty.

Second, she shows that treaty conflicts that display these characteristics are not fully or adequately addressed through current legal rules, whether those provided in the Vienna Convention on the Law of Treaties or those suggested, in numerous works, as rules of thumb for reconciling or allocating priority between conflicting treaties. The problem does not lie with the rules themselves. Dr Ranganathan, following Jan Klabbers (*Treaty Conflicts and the European Union*, Cambridge University Press, 2009) argues that legal rules *cannot* address such conflicts unless they depart from foundational principles of treaty law. Alternative proposals, by Hersch Lauterpacht amongst others, infringe or ignore the *pacta tertiis* rule, the rule that treaties between different parties are *res inter alios acta*, and States' freedom to enter into treaties.

That legal doctrine cannot offer satisfactory solutions to a variety of treaty conflicts may lead to the conclusion that there is little point in further analysis, that international law can contribute little to regulating a phenomenon that nonetheless challenges its own systemic character and, worse still, that we must accept the critique that international law is reduced to a form of 'managerialism'. Dr Ranganathan's further contribution lies in challenging these conclusions.

Third, by way of detailed studies of treaty conflicts strategically created in order to challenge, respectively, the deep seabed mining regime under the UN Convention on the Law of the Sea, the International Criminal Court established by the Rome Statute, and the nuclear-governance regime underpinned by the Nuclear Non-Proliferation Treaty, she shows that international law is neither purely epiphenomenal nor purely instrumental to politics. In truth, legal forms play a role in framing the scope and terms of the conflict, mediating interactions and moderating outcomes. She is careful not to suggest that the limits introduced by international legal practices are necessarily for the good – they may indeed be obstructive to some interests and from some perspectives – but she does maintain that they are real, significant and not easily wished away; reminders that there is indeed a 'system' of international law, that becomes visible precisely in the moments of challenge that arise from treaty conflicts. The three studies encompass a range of socio-legal materials, and offer rich analyses of three distinct and topical issues.

Dr Ranganathan, finally, uses treaty conflicts as a prism to explore the conceptions of international law underlying a range of scholarship that she describes as 'mainstream': writings in the context of the International Law Commission's efforts to identify an appropriate conflict rule, and works on treaty implementation – from Lauterpacht and Rosenne's doctrine of approximate application to the compliance scholarship of the US academy, to recent work on regime interaction (for instance, Margaret Young, *Saving Fish, Trading Fish*, Cambridge University Press, 2011). These works are dispersed in time and tradition, but, as she shows, they have in common their engagement with the politics of international law and their ultimate conception of law, not as rules or procedures, but as a discourse anchored in both. She argues that this conception is founded on liberal and constructivist assumptions about international law; on this view, engaging in a legal discourse has (or at least can have) the effect of advancing the rule of law by moderating positions and outcomes; the very experience of engaging through law can strengthen respect for the rule of law. She is largely sympathetic with, though occasionally sceptical of, the liberal assumption; she rightly does not seek to prove or disprove constructivist positions. But her reading finesses summary judgments, whether of naïve idealism or rigid doctrinalism, often visited upon international law's mainstream.

In these ways, her work aims to get to the heart of what makes international law, in legal thought and in the practice of international relations. It will be for readers to judge its success; but it is on any view a fine first achievement by a promising scholar.

James Crawford
Lauterpacht Centre for International Law
University of Cambridge
7 April 2014

Preface

It is difficult – for anyone, I imagine – to reconstruct the process by which one comes to write the book that one writes. Many factors shape the choice of a project and the way one goes about developing it. I *think* the early trigger for this book was my desire to explore the paradoxes revealed by one event: the India–US Nuclear Deal. But that exercise grew into a much larger exploration of strategically created treaty conflicts and what they might teach us about the politics of law.

The Nuclear Deal was announced in 2005, revealed in specific bilateral form in August 2007, and pronounced nearly dead a few weeks later. In the course of these developments, it had made some news in the United States, where I was then based, and had a compelling hold on public debate back home, in India, where it was variously regarded as a major foreign policy triumph (in his January 2014 exit interview, the two-term Indian Prime Minister, Manmohan Singh, identified it as his greatest moment in office), and as a foreign policy disaster that had signed away India's autonomy in international relations to the United States. In a country dogged by massive corruption scandals, rocketing inflation, fierce debates over social and economic spending, and controversies relating to the deployment of the military in Kashmir, the northeast, and against Maoists, the Nuclear Deal was the *only* issue on which the government was challenged through a no-confidence motion.

The delirium surrounding the Deal was to a large extent connected to expectations that, energy benefits aside, it would boost India's nuclear weapons programme and imply US, and international, acceptance of the same, paving the way perhaps for that sixth seat on the UN Security Council. But here was the paradox. While neutralising domestic opposition entailed emphasising, in India, these aspects of the Deal, the bid for international acceptance was based on the claim that the Deal was unconnected to India's nuclear weapons programme and left unaffected the international legal regime for nuclear non-proliferation and disarmament, underpinned by the Nuclear Non-Proliferation Treaty (NPT).

I became interested in the question whether there *was* indeed, legally speaking, a treaty conflict between the Deal and the NPT – it seemed to me that I could build a strong argument both in favour, and against (and indeed some of these arguments were being made in public debate) – and, if so, whether there was any particular legal solution that could be applied to it. Gradually, the complexities in answering both questions became apparent: the 'conflict' was less a matter of determination than perception and representation, but, even accepting that there was a conflict, there was no easy way of getting around the attributes that made it legally intractable: it was a strategic conflict, and one State party to one treaty (the Deal) – India – could claim to have no legal obligation to respect the other (the NPT). What kind of legal 'solution' could be proposed for such a situation? Even if one was proposed, would it be regarded by the relevant parties?

I began to see, also, that the small question, of treaty conflict between the Deal and the NPT, actually provided a context in which to explore many other questions, and anxieties, that no doubt all students of international law feel from time to time, and most of all when faced with the fragility of, and political subtext to, legal rules: what actually *is* international law? Is it really *law*, if States simply replace rules with others when it suits them to? How does it work? Why have so many believed it is for so long? And then more specifically: What happens when States seem to replace one treaty by another? Particularly when only some States party to one treaty replace it with another in their dealings with each other, or with third States? Is there an appropriate definition of treaty conflict? Are there effective legal solutions to such conflicts? How else are treaties to be protected? Why does the Vienna Convention on the Law of Treaties (VCLT) take the approach it does? Does the VCLT approach have any relevance to practice? And to square the circle: What is the practice of treaty conflicts? Does it tell us anything about the role and influence of international law?

These questions form the subject of this book. I do not pretend to have provided *the* answers to them, but I have offered *my* answers, in the hope of perpetuating that broad conversation that – I have suggested – sustains and enriches international law. There are many people who guided and helped me in developing both questions and answers, and in completing this work, and I owe them my sincerest thanks.

First, and above all, to James Crawford. James supervised the PhD thesis on which this book is based with exceptional patience and encouragement, and continued to advise on the development of the book. Without his careful scrutiny of my writing and his exhortations to 'finish!', I would not have reached the point of writing this preface.

Several others also played a role in guiding my thoughts, on the book as a whole, or on specific sections of it. I owe thanks, in particular, to Jan Klabbers, Martti Koskenniemi and Guglielmo Verdirame, for generous discussions on the project as a whole, and for very insightful comments on specific chapters. Many friends provided careful assessments of specific portions: no doubt, if and when they read this book, Douglas Guilfoyle, Jessie Hohmann, Sarah Nouwen, Federica Paddeu, Tiina Pajuste, Mieke van der Linden and Sara Wharton, will recognise portions where their comments have joined the text. In addition to James, Rohit De and T. C. A. Ranganathan read through the full manuscript and provided valuable feedback on the argument as a whole. Sumati Dwivedi's edits were a marvel; her several hundred comments, suggestions and corrections, for each chapter, have shaped both language and substance.

Many more gave generously of their time. I am very grateful to the late R. P. Anand (who met me despite his failing health and gave both advice and books), Ben Batros, Giovanni Bassu, P. R. Chari, B. S. Chimni, P. S. Das, Matthew Heaphy, David Koller, Sunil Pal, Rod Rastan, Manpreet Sethi, O. P. Sharma, Yogesh Tyagi, Siddharth Varadarajan, John Washburn, and a few others who prefer to remain unnamed, for their advice on both conceptual and factual matters.

While a book takes shape in the mind, it needs material conditions to flourish. My doctoral research and travel were made possible by the Gates Trust, the J. C. Hall Scholarship at St John's College, and an Overseas Research Scholarship, and by the excellent working and living environments provided by the Cambridge Faculty of Law and St. John's College. My post-doctoral time at King's College, and at the Lauterpacht Centre for International Law, has been absolutely fantastic: each has provided both intellectual stimulation and companionship, and very generously accommodated the disturbances caused by my book writing. I especially owe thanks to Eva Nanopoulos for relieving me from admissions work, my office-mate Tiina for monitoring my progress, and Karen Fachechi and Anita Rutherford for providing administrative guidance and support at various points.

I have benefitted enormously from presentations and discussions at workshops in America, Europe and India. The book draws upon these conversations, and on publications that grew from them, and I am extremely grateful to all who contributed to both. Among others, and in addition to those already named, Eyal Benvenisti, Samantha Besson, Lucas Lixinski and Michael Waibel provided instructive chats on specific conceptual points, and Sophie Chapman, Mirina Grosz, Paula Haas, Nayanika Mathur and Pallavi Raghavan provided perspectives from the vantage point of their own disciplines. I also owe thanks to Lorenzo Cassini, Simon Chesterman, Angelina Fisher, the late Thomas Franck, Kirsty Gover, Benedict Kingsbury and Euan Macdonald for development of the early research proposal while I was at NYU, and for their mentorship. Gauri and Gittu Modi in New York, Anubhuti Agrawal and Avirup Nag, Sumona Bose and Ashwin Bishnoi, Shivani Mathur, and Kriti Kapila in London, provided house room and home comforts on several research trips.

This book would not exist at all if it had not been for the stellar support given by Cambridge University Press. I am extremely grateful to Finola O' Sullivan, Elizabeth Spicer, Elizabeth Davey, Gillian Dadd, Martin Gleeson, Richard Woodham and others for encouraging the work and accommodating delays.

Without Rohit's arguments, encouragement and very good cooking, the process of research and writing would have lacked sparkle. Without my family's affection, support and humour, the book could not have been completed. I am grateful to my nana and nani, Yashbir and Nirmal Das, for cheerfully tolerating the many times I shut myself up to work during my (and their trips) to Bombay, and to my father Ranganathan, my mother Namita and my brother Jayant for putting up with all my grouching and hair-tearing in Bombay *and* Delhi. This book is dedicated, with my love, to them, and to 15C Shanaz, where it had its start and its end.

Abbreviations

123 Agreement	Bilateral agreement for nuclear cooperation concluded by the United States
ASIL	American Society of International Law
ASP	Assembly of States Parties
ASPA	American Servicemembers' Protection Act
AU	African Union
BIA	Bilateral immunity agreement
CACJ	Central American Court of Justice
CAR	Central African Republic
CICC	Coalition for the ICC
CJEU	Court of Justice of the European Union
CTBT	Comprehensive Test Ban Treaty
Deal	India–US Nuclear Deal
DRC	Democratic Republic of the Congo
EC	European Community
ECJ	European Court of Justice
EES	Group of Eastern European States
ENDC	Eighteen Nation Committee on Disarmament
EU	European Union
Euratom	European Atomic Energy Community
FMCT	Fissile Materials Cut-off Treaty
FRG	Federal Republic of Germany
G8	Group of 8
G77	Group of 77
GAL	Global Administrative Law
GAOR	General Assembly Official Records
GATT	General Agreement on Tariffs and Trade
GNEP	Global Nuclear Energy Partnership

IAEA	International Atomic Energy Agency
ICC	International Criminal Court
ICJ	International Court of Justice
ILC	International Law Commission
ILM	International Legal Materials
INFCIRC	Information Circular
Interim Agreement	Agreement concerning Interim Arrangements relating to Polymetallic Nodules of the Deep Seabed
ISA	International Seabed Authority
ISSA	India-Specific Safeguards Agreement
ITER	International Thermonuclear Experimental Reactor
LOSC	United Nations Convention on the Law of the Sea
LRA	Lord's Resistance Army
MTCR	Missile Technology Control Regime
NATO	North Atlantic Treaty Organization
NGO	Non-governmental organisation
NIEO	New International Economic Order
NNWS	Non-nuclear-weapons States
NPT	Nuclear Non-Proliferation Treaty
NSG	Nuclear Suppliers Group
NSSP	Next Steps in Strategic Partnership
NWS	Nuclear-weapons States
OSPAR Convention	Convention on the Protection of the Marine Environment of the North-East Atlantic
OTP	Office of the Prosecutor
Part I Guidelines	NSG Guidelines for Nuclear Transfers
Part II Guidelines	NSG Guidelines for Transfer of Nuclear-Related Dual Use Equipment, Materials, Software, and Related Technology
PCIJ	Permanent Court of International Justice
PrepCom	Preparatory Commission
Provisional Understanding	Provisional Understanding Regarding Deep Seabed Matters between Belgium, France, Germany, Italy, Japan, the Netherlands, the United Kingdom and the United States
PSI	Proliferation Security Initiative
PTC	Pre-Trial Chamber

Rome Statute	Rome Statute of the International Criminal Court
RSR	Reciprocating States Regime
SCN	Special Commission
SIPRI	Stockholm International Peace Research Institute
SOFA	Status of Forces Agreement
TRIPs	Trade-Related Aspects of Intellectual Property Rights
UAE	United Arab Emirates
UNCLOS III	Third United Nations Conference on the Law of the Sea 1973–82
UNEP	United Nations Environmental Programme
UNGA	United Nations General Assembly
UNSC	United Nations Security Council
UNTS	United Nations Treaty Series
UPDF	Ugandan People's Defense Forces
USSR	Union of Soviet Socialist Republics
UST	United States Treaties and Other International Agreements
VCLT	Vienna Convention on the Law of Treaties
WHO	World Health Organization
WTO	World Trade Organization

Table of cases and procedural documents

Table of treaties and other international instruments

Treaties and Final Acts

Declarations, joint statements and decisions

Introduction

1 Strategically created treaty conflicts

On treaty conflict and the questions that follow

'Strategically created treaty conflicts' – a notion introduced in this monograph – may seem an odd choice of subject-matter for a book. 'How many can there be, and are they even a category?', has been a common response to my presentations of the topic. Yet such conflicts are fairly common, and have catalysed changes in various legal regimes. Moreover, they provide a fruitful context for a dual analysis of the relationship between international law and politics. Firstly, they offer a straightforward illustration of key themes in critical legal literature: the limits of a formal conception of international law, the legal field's turn to managerial solutions, and the ultimate co-option of both legal forms and managerial processes by powerful actors. In other words, strategically created treaty conflicts reveal international law as contingent upon, or instrumental to politics, and legal doctrine's inability to transcend these features of international law. But, secondly, such conflicts also complicate the conclusions reached in the first analysis: they call into question the existence of any purely formal or managerial account of international law, and illuminate the complex assumptions and conceptions that underlie key doctrinal turns. Most importantly, they show the various ways in which international legal practices enable but also limit international politics (and not always for the better). This chapter expands upon these points, beginning with an overview of the incidence and key features of strategically created treaty conflicts.

The challenged Court, and other stories

The International Criminal Court (ICC or 'Court') is now over a decade old, and many regard it as an established component of the international legal landscape. But the situation was different only a few years ago: in its early years, particularly between 2002 and 2005, the Court was fiercely opposed by the United States. The United States was concerned that the Court might attempt to exercise jurisdiction over US nationals, including government and military officials; its participation in peacekeeping missions and in the armed conflict in Afghanistan seemed to afford the requisite opportunities. It was not convinced by provisions of the Rome Statute – the Court's founding treaty – that limited the Court's jurisdiction in situations where a State was able and willing to conduct its own investigations and trials.

The United States manifested its hostility to the Court in a number of ways: public criticism, blocking funds to the Court from the United Nations, even deleting references to it from international documents. The centre-piece of its 'campaign'[1] against the Court was its conclusion of bilateral immunity agreements (BIAs) with 102 other States, stipulating non-surrender of US persons to the Court even where the Court had made a request for such surrender. These agreements were concluded both with States that were party and non-party to the Rome Statute, and often couched in reciprocal terms – that is, providing also for the non-surrender of that other State's persons to the Court. The agreements were backed by US legislation.

Many signatories to these BIAs claimed that these treaties were consistent with the Rome Statute. They cited Article 98(2) of the Statute, which requires the Court not to press a State to surrender a person sent to its territory by another State without that State's consent where the first State is under a treaty obligation to seek consent from the other State; the preambles of most BIAs refer to this provision. However, members of the European Union and commentators,[2] disputed the claim of consistency, arguing that the BIAs not only sought protection for a broader category of persons than Article 98(2) allowed, but also undermined the Rome Statute's object of 'no impunity' by failing to make reference to specific alternative procedures for investigation and

[1] P. Sands, *Lawless World: America and the Making and Breaking of Global Rules* (London, Penguin 2005) 48.

[2] Council Conclusions on the International Criminal Court, 30 September 2002, www.consilium.europa.eu/uedocs/cmsUpload/ICC34EN.pdf. See also J. Crawford *et al.*, Joint Opinion in the Matter of the Statute of the International Criminal Court and in the Matter of Bilateral Agreements Sought by the United States under Article 98(2) of the Rome Statute, 5 June 2003, www.iccnow.org/documents/SandsCrawfordBIA14June03.pdf.

prosecution of the persons sought by the Court. Amnesty International termed the BIAs 'impunity agreements'.[3]

The BIAs were treaties in conflict with another treaty, the Rome Statute. Now, treaty conflicts as such are not remarkable occurrences in the international legal system: there are (at least) 193 States and several international organisations capable of entering into treaties with each other and they do so on all manner of issues - to the extent that some argue international law suffers from 'treaty congestion'.[4] In such a context, overlap between treaties is only to be expected, though it may lead to considerable confusion and uncertainty as to the rules applicable to particular States and the requirements of specific legal regimes.[5] Jan Klabbers observes:

> Chances are that those who negotiate a trade agreement are so focused on trade, that possible environmental ramifications or human rights ramifications do not enter their minds - something that will be strengthened by the fact that, typically, trade agreements will be the work of trade experts.[6]

In other words, treaty conflicts may often be contingent and inadvertent by-products of the increasing juridification of international relations.

However, the conflict between the BIAs and the Rome Statute was not inadvertent, or the result of an oversight or a misreading of the Statute. The BIAs were concluded to restrict the Court's access to possible suspects and to limit the assistance offered by States. Against the regime for

[3] Amnesty International, Letter to the EU Presidency, 30 August 2002, www.amnesty.eu/en/press-releases/human-rights-in-the-eu/police-and-judicial-co-operation/u-s-agreements-violate-international-court-treaty-0075.

[4] C. Borgen, 'Resolving Treaty Conflicts' (2005) 37 *George Washington International Law Review* 573, 574; B. L. Hicks, 'Comment: Treaty Congestion in International Environmental Law: The Need for Greater International Coordination' (1998–9) 32 *University of Richmond Law Review* 1643, 1644; G. Handl, 'Compliance Control Mechanisms and International Environmental Obligations' (1997) 5 *Tulane Journal of International and Comparative Law* 29. See also K. Alter and S. Meunier, 'The Politics of International Regime Complexity', Framing Paper, Conference on the Politics of International Regime Complexity, Princeton University, 1 March 2007, www.princeton.edu/~smeunier/AlterMeunierFramingPiece2.pdf.

[5] The International Law Commission has highlighted several concerns including 'the erosion of general international law, emergence of conflicting jurisprudence, forum-shopping and loss of legal security': 'Fragmentation of International Law: Difficulties Arising from the Diversification and Expansion of International Law', Report of the Study Group of the International Law Commission (chaired by M. Koskenniemi), A/CN.4/L.682 (2006), 12.

[6] J. Klabbers, *Treaty Conflicts and the European Union* (Cambridge University Press 2009) 12.

cooperation set out in the Rome Statute, the BIAs outlined provisions on non-cooperation. Through them, the United States aimed to impede the effective functioning of the Court, possibly even to undermine the Court altogether. Claims that the BIAs were compatible with Article 98(2) of the Statute were window-dressing.

In sum, the United States, a non-party to the Rome Statute, used BIAs as an expedient to influence the functioning of the Court. The conflict between the Rome Statute and the BIAs was not merely a treaty conflict, but one strategically created to challenge the legal regime established by the Statute. It consisted in the use of one legal form (a series of bilateral treaties) to limit the operation of another (a multilateral treaty).

Nor by any means was it the only example of such a practice. Consider the following examples.[7]

(1) In 1990, the United States and the European Union withdrew from the Uruguay Round on the expansion of the 1947 General Agreement on Tariffs and Trade (GATT). They concluded, bilaterally, a modified trade agreement, which they 'invited' other States to join. This grew into the World Trade Organization (WTO), including the 1994 GATT.[8]

(2) More recently, the United States and the European Union have pressed developing countries to sign bilateral 'TRIPs-plus' agreements whose standards of intellectual property protection exceed those provided in the 1994 Agreement on Trade Related Aspects of Intellectual Property Rights, and, *inter alia*, seriously limit access to affordable medicine.[9]

(3) The 1982 United Nations Convention on the Law of the Sea (LOSC) provided for a regime for deep seabed mining based on the principle that the seabed and its resources were the common heritage of mankind. This was immediately challenged by eight States (the United States, the United Kingdom, France, Germany, the Netherlands, Belgium, Japan and Italy), which concluded an alternative treaty regime which described seabed mining as a freedom of the high seas.[10]

(4) Some years earlier, the movement for a New International Economic Order had seen the adoption of the 1976 Bogotá Declaration by eight

[7] These are also listed in S. Ranganathan, 'Responding to Deliberately Created Treaty Conflicts', in C. Tams *et al.* (eds.), *Research Handbook on the Law of Treaties* (Cheltenham, Edward Elgar 2014) Chapter 15.

[8] See E. Benvenisti and Downs, 'The Empire's New Clothes: Political Economy and the Fragmentation of International Law' (2007) 60 *Stanford Law Review* 595, 616.

[9] See L. Helfer, 'Regime Shifting: The TRIPs Agreement and the New Dynamics of Intellectual Property Lawmaking' (2004) 29 *Yale Journal of International Law* 1, 24.

[10] See R. R. Churchill and A. V. Lowe, *Law of the Sea* (3rd edn, Manchester University Press 1999) Chapter 12. See also Chapter 4 of this book.

developing equatorial States (Brazil, Colombia, Congo, Ecuador, Indonesia, Kenya, Uganda and Zaire). These States claimed sovereignty over the geostationary orbit, and asserted that the conflicting 1967 Outer Space Treaty 'cannot be considered as a final answer to the problem of the exploration and use of outer space, even less when the international community is questioning all the terms of international law which were elaborated when the developing countries could not count on adequate scientific advice and were thus not able to observe and evaluate the omissions, contradictions and consequences of the proposals which were prepared with great ability by the industrialized powers for their own benefit.'[11]

(5) In 2005, the United States and India announced plans to conclude a civil nuclear cooperation agreement under which the United States would supply nuclear fuel and technology to India. India maintains a nuclear weapons programme but, unlike the United States, is not a party to the 1968 Nuclear Non-Proliferation Treaty (NPT). The NPT recognises the United States as a nuclear weapons State but does not endorse India's programme. Moreover, its provisions on nuclear energy assistance seem to exclude the sort of nuclear cooperation envisaged by the two States in 2005 and finalised in a 2007 bilateral agreement.[12]

These cases relate to a wide range of subjects. But they have in common that, in each, the alternative treaty (or treaties) sought to displace, compete with, carve exceptions from, or alter, the regime established by the existing treaty. Drawing on the description of fragmentation by the International Law Commission (ILC), as conflicts of treaty rules, institutions and regimes,[13] these cases may be described as the *strategic* fragmentation of international law.[14]

Two further parallels may be drawn between such cases of treaty conflict. First, in each case, the alternative, conflicting treaty took the form of a bilateral treaty, a series of bilateral treaties, or a small-group treaty, while the challenged treaty was a multilateral one. Second, in many of these examples, the small treaty included a few States not party

[11] Conclusion 4, Declaration of the First Meeting of Equatorial Countries, Bogotá, Colombia, 3 December 1976. In his book, space law expert Ricky Lee treats the Bogotá Declaration as a treaty, using provisions of the 1969 Vienna Convention on the Law of Treaties to assess its implications: R. Lee, *Law and Regulation of Commercial Mining of Minerals in Outer Space* (London, Springer 2012) 172.

[12] See S. Ranganathan, 'Visions of International Law: Lessons from the 123 Agreement', Special Issue on India, the 123 Agreement and Nuclear Energy: Issues of International Law (2011) 51(2) *Indian Journal of International Law* 146. See also Chapter 6 of this book.

[13] ILC, 'Report of Study Group on Fragmentation', 10–11.

[14] See also Benvenisti and Downs, 'The Empire's New Clothes.

to the multilateral treaty. India was not a party to the NPT, while the United States was. The United States was not party to the Rome Statute, but some of its bilateral co-signatories were. Brazil, Colombia and Ecuador were parties to the Outer Space Treaty, the other five were not. France and the Netherlands were party to the LOSC, the other States were not. In other words, the conflicting treaties in most of the above cases had 'non-identical' parties.

We might call the first of the two parallel features the small treaty/large treaty dynamic. The second parallel feature denotes a specific category of treaty conflicts: those between treaties with non-identical parties – or treaties with some common and some distinct parties – referred to, in shorthand, as AB/AC conflicts (the letters indicate common (A) and distinct (B and C) parties to the treaties; conflicts between treaties with identical parties may be called AB/AB conflicts).

As the next section explains, both features contribute to the success of the strategy of challenging or changing existing legal regimes by means of treaty conflict.

Legal doctrine on treaty conflict

To begin with, the two features exploit key tenets of international law that flow from the idea that it is a horizontal system between formally equal States. Founded on this idea, international law places all treaties at par: it does not consider a multilateral treaty more important than a bilateral one, nor – but for the UN Charter, which enjoys primacy[15] – does it endorse any other hierarchy between treaties. It demands that all treaties be taken seriously as sources of legal rights and obligations for the states parties. In general, it does not forbid States from creating new treaties, even if such treaties conflict with existing ones. Nor does international law impose particular solutions in case of treaty conflicts. The last two points are relevant *a fortiori* for conflicts between treaties with non-identical parties.

These fundamental characteristics of international law may be seen in the 1969 Vienna Convention on the Law of Treaties (VCLT).[16] The VCLT includes rules to protect all treaties: Article 26 restates the principle of *pacta sunt servanda*, that agreements must be observed in good faith; while other provisions direct the sanction of invalidity only at exceptional cases of treaty conflict – where a treaty conflicts with a peremptory norm,[17] and *possibly* where one of the two treaties is an

[15] See Article 103, Charter of the United Nations, 1945; Art. 30(1), VCLT.
[16] 8 ILM 679. [17] Article 53, VCLT.

inter se agreement between some parties to the other treaty, and is prohibited by that treaty, infringes upon rights or obligations of other parties to that treaty, or is inimical to its object and purpose.[18] Article 30 deals with the other cases of treaty conflict. For AB/AB conflicts, it provides that, in the absence of more specific rules regulating the relationship of the two treaties, the later of the two should prevail over the earlier. For AB/AC conflicts, it merely notes that each treaty remains effective between its parties, though a State may be responsible for any breach of obligation resulting from the conflict; this rule neither blocks States from concluding new treaties, nor specifies which treaty takes precedence.

Legal doctrine outside of the VCLT goes only a little further. Silent on strategically created treaty conflicts,[19] and minimally attentive to AB/AC conflicts,[20] it embraces two conflict-solving techniques – 'reconciliation' and 'priority'.[21] However, these techniques are not ordinarily applicable to AB/AC conflicts, and in any event their use only gives ballast to the

[18] Article 41, VCLT. Article 41 is stated as a permissive rule:

Agreements to modify multilateral treaties between certain of the parties only

1. Two or more of the parties to a multilateral treaty may conclude an agreement to modify the treaty as between themselves alone if:
   (a) the possibility of such a modification is provided for by the treaty; or
   (b) the modification in question is not prohibited by the treaty and:
      (i) does not affect the enjoyment by the other parties of their rights under the treaty or the performance of their obligations;
      (ii) does not relate to a provision, derogation from which is incompatible with the effective execution of the object and purpose of the treaty as a whole.

[19] Only one article offers an examination of 'strategic fragmentation': Benvenisti and Downs, 'The Empire's New Clothes'. A very few other works refer to strategic regime shifting – i.e. pushing discussions of an international issue from one international regime to another, more favourable one: see Helfer, 'Regime Shifting'; see also N. Krisch, 'International Law in Times of Hegemony' (2004) 16 *European Journal of International Law* 369.

[20] We only find two book-length studies on such conflicts between treaties with non-identical parties: G. Binder, *Treaty Conflict and Political Contradiction: The Dialectic of Duplicity* (New York, Praeger 1989); Klabbers, *Treaty Conflicts and the European Union.* The first of these, i.e. Binder's, finds no mention in many later works, including J. Pauwelyn, *Conflict of Norms in Public International Law: How WTO Law Relates to Other Rules of International Law* (Cambridge University Press 2003); R. Wolfrum and N. Matz, *Conflicts in International Environmental Law* (London, Springer 2003); and S. A. Sadat-Akhavi, *Methods of Resolving Conflict between Treaties* (Leiden, Martinus Nijhoff 2003).

[21] A selection of the literature on treaty conflicts includes: Q. Wright, 'Conflicts between International Law and Treaties' (1917) 11 *American Journal of International Law* 566; C. Rousseau, 'De la compatibilité des normes juridiques contradictoires dans l'ordre

strategy of creating treaty conflict in order to alter an existing legal regime.

First, I will take up the latter point, that is, the ballast given by techniques of reconciliation and priority to the strategy of creating treaty conflicts. The literature on treaty conflict reveals an overwhelming preference for reconciling conflicting treaties by means of interpretation, and draws distinctions between 'true' and 'false' conflicts. True conflicts are described as those where the treaties have irreconcilable, mutually incompatible obligations; all other cases fall into the category of false conflicts. False conflicts, then, include situations where a State's rights under one treaty clash with obligations under another, or two treaties deal with the same subject from different perspectives, or one treaty embodies more far-reaching obligations than another. Such conflicts are seen as less serious because they do not necessitate the breach of an obligation by a State. Instead, the treaties may be interpreted in harmony, or a State may simply forgo its rights for the sake of its obligations, or recourse may be had to practical principles of coordination, effectiveness, and mutual support.[22] While the trend of distinguishing true and false conflicts was probably initiated by Wilfred Jenks' landmark 1953 article;[23] it has since been taken up in a vast

international' (1932) 39 *Revue Générale de Droit International Public* 153; J. Garner, 'Harvard Research in International Law: Draft Convention on the Law of Treaties' (1935) 29 *American Journal of International Law Supplement* 1024; H. Aufricht, 'Supersession of Treaties in International Law' (1951–2) 37 *Cornell Legal Quarterly* 698; C. W. Jenks, 'The Conflict of Law-Making Treaties' (1953) 30 *British Yearbook of International Law* 401; A. D. McNair, *Law of Treaties* (Oxford, Clarendon Press 1961); M. Zuleeg, 'Vertragskonkurrenz in Völkerrecht. Teil I: Verträge zwischen souveränen Staaten' (1977) 20 *German Yearbook of International Law* 246; W. Czapliński and G. Danilenko, 'Conflicts of Norms in International Law' (1990) 21 *Netherlands Yearbook of International Law* 12; W. Karl 'Conflicts between Treaties', in R. Bernhardt (ed.), *Encyclopedia of Public International Law*, Vol. VII (1984) 468; J. Mus, 'Conflicts between Treaties in International Law' (1998) 15 *Netherlands International Law Review* 214; Pauwelyn, *Conflict of Norms in Public International Law Wolfrum and Matz, Conflicts in International Environmental Law*) Sadat-Akhavi, Methods of Resolving Conflict between Treaties; Borgen, 'Resolving Treaty Conflicts' 574; C. Borgen, 'Treaty Conflicts and Normative Fragmentation', in D. B. Hollis (ed.), *The Oxford Guide to Treaties* (Oxford University Press 2012) 448–70. Numerous works also address treaty conflict as part of wider explorations of the law of treaties, fragmentation of international law, norm conflicts, regime collisions and dispute settlement.

[22] Such calls appear, for instance, in Mus, 'Conflicts between Treaties in International Law'; Karl, 'Conflicts between Treaties'; Wolfrum and Matz, *Conflicts in International Environmental Law*; Sadat-Akhavi, *Methods of Resolving Conflict between Treaties.*

[23] Jenks, 'Conflict of Law-Making Treaties', 425–7.

number of subsequent works,[24] and was implicit in the International Court of Justice's decision in *FYR Macedonia* v. *Greece*, which did not find Greece's rights under a previous treaty to have implications for its obligations under its 1995 Interim Accord with the former Yugoslav Republic of Macedonia.[25]

Joost Pauwelyn suggests that legal scholars press the distinction between true and false conflicts because, to them, a conflict of norms implies an imperfection of the legal system.[26] Describing many conflicts as false – because capable of reconciliation – allows the impression that these imperfections are rare. But, in many cases, attempts at reconciling treaties may in effect substantially limit or alter one of the treaties, bypassing formal procedures for its amendment. Indeed, that may be their very purpose. Such cases make it evident that legal doctrine's emphasis on reconciliation allows strategic creation of treaty conflicts to be a productive endeavour; for to create a new, conflicting, treaty is to create a new starting point for reconciliation.

In cases where reconciliation is ruled out – such as when two treaties set out mutually exclusive obligations – legal doctrine suggests attention to priority principles, on the basis of which one treaty may be applied in preference to the other. Such principles include: *lex posterior* or priority to the treaty later in time;[27] *lex specialis* or priority to the treaty containing the more specific obligation;[28] *lex prior* or priority to the treaty

[24] Other examples include Mus, 'Conflicts between Treaties in International Law'; Karl, 'Conflicts between Treaties'; Pauwelyn, *Conflict of Norms in Public International Law*; Wolfrum and Matz, *Conflicts in International Environmental Law*; Sadat-Akhavi, *Methods of Resolving Conflict between Treaties*; Borgen, 'Resolving Treaty Conflicts'. As Chapter 2 will discuss, even the drafters of the Vienna Convention on the Law of Treaties placed emphasis on distinguishing true and false conflicts. The ILC's 2006 Fragmentation Report, however, was not persuaded of the distinction: its definition of treaty conflicts includes situations where treaties frustrate each others' goals or possess different background justifications, emerge from different legislative policies or aim at divergent ends: ILC, 'Report of Study Group on Fragmentation', 24.

[25] *Application of the Interim Accord of 13 September 1995 (former Yugoslav Republic of Macedonia* v. *Greece)*, Judgment of 5 December 2011 (2011) ICJ Rep 644, para. 109. For a comment see A. Tzanakopoulos, 'Legality of Veto to NATO Accession: The ICJ's Decision in the Dispute between FYR Macedonia and Greece', *European Journal of International Law: Talk!*, 7 December 2011.

[26] Pauwelyn, *Conflict of Norms in Public International Law*, 172.

[27] The *lex posterior* principle is probably the best established and is recognised in all of the treaty conflict literature cited above. It makes an appearance in Article 30(3) and 4(a) of the VCLT: see Chapter 2.

[28] *Lex specialis*, though not mentioned in the VCLT, is well accepted in scholarly literature and judicial decisions: see A. Lindroos, 'Conflicts in a Fragmented Legal System: The

earlier in time and prohibiting later inconsistent *inter se* agreements;[29] *lex superior* or priority to the treaty involving application of a higher order norm[30] or otherwise subject to its own regime of interpretation and application (such as the constituent instrument of an international organisation).[31] There is no settled hierarchy between these principles: their application remains a matter for argument in each case although, in practice, *lex posterior* and *lex specialis* are the most commonly used.[32] Judicial institutions may choose to follow several of these principles: as Klabbers shows, the Court of Justice of the European Union (CJEU) has found European Union Treaties to prevail over both previous and subsequent treaties entered into by their member States.[33] In any event, allocating priority to the later or more specific treaty, may permit a strategically created conflicting treaty effectively to limit an existing one.

Moreover, the application of priority principles to AB/AC conflicts may transgress two foundational legal principles: *res inter alios acta* (each agreement is only effective as between its parties); and, related to it, *pacta tertiis nec nocent nec prosunt* (no treaty may interfere with the rights and obligations of a third State without its consent).[34] Together

Doctrine of Lex Specialis' (2005) 74 *Nordic Journal of International Law* 30, 37–8. Lindroos also notes that, at the Vienna Conference on the Law of Treaties, Sir Humphrey Waldock, the Expert Consultant (and ILC Special Rapporteur) on the topic, noted that, in certain cases, one could rely on the principle of *generalia specialibus non derogant. ibid.* The application of this principle may be traced in *Mavrommatis Palestinian Concessions* (1924) PCIJ Series A, No. 2, 6.

29 *Lex prior* was the preferred principle in canonical international law scholarship, including works by Grotius, Pufendorf and Vattel and in early twentieth century jurisprudence of the Central American Court of Justice: see ILC, 'Report of Study Group on Fragmentation', 122–3, paras. 236 and 239. A detailed discussion may be found in Binder, *Treaty Conflict and Political Contradiction*, 22–4, 40–2. The application of *lex prior* may also be traced in some PCIJ cases: *Oscar Chinn* (1934) PCIJ Series A/B, No. 63, 65; *European Commission of the Danube* (1927) PCIJ Series B, No. 14, 6; *Austro-German Customs Union* (1931) PCIJ Series A/B, No. 41, 37. In the VCLT, Article 41 may perhaps be taken as an application of the *lex prior* principle.

30 *Lex superior* finds mention in Article 30 (1) of the VCLT, which recognises the priority of the UN Charter. It also finds indirect reference in Article 53 on 'Treaties conflicting with a peremptory norm of general international law'. Besides these categories, there are few accepted examples of *lex superior*.

31 VCLT Article 5 provides that the Convention 'applies to any treaty which is the constituent instrument of an international organization and to any treaty adopted within an international organization without prejudice to any relevant rules of the organization'. See also the ILC's observations on self-contained regimes: ILC, 'Report of Study Group on Fragmentation', 65 *et seq.*

32 ILC, 'Report of Study Group on Fragmentation', 36.

33 Klabbers, *Treaty Conflicts and the European Union*, Chapters 6 and 9.

34 *ibid.*, 99–100.

these principles imply that, where the parties to conflicting treaties are not identical, one treaty cannot be given preference over another treaty if this would infringe upon the rights and obligations of a State party only to that other treaty. The same holds for reconciling the two treaties.[35] Thus, while particular institutions may have addressed AB/AC conflicts via techniques of reconciliation and priority,[36] their decisions cannot be the final word on the conflicts. For, such decisions cannot bind States which are not parties to the treaty enforced, nor otherwise subject to the jurisdiction of, the institution in question. The CJEU's finding that EU Treaties prevail over its members' treaties with third States is not binding upon those third States. In the early example of *Costa Rica* v. *Nicaragua* (1917), the Central American Court of Justice (CACJ) found that it could not invalidate a Nicaragua–US treaty incompatible with an earlier Nicaragua–Costa Rica treaty for lack of jurisdiction over the United States.[37] It could only find that there was a conflict between the two that entailed a breach of Nicaragua's obligation. In short, conflicts between treaties with non-identical parties exacerbate the difficulties of legal solution that pertain to all treaty conflicts.

There may of course be some scope for practical resolution of such conflicts. The ILC's 2006 Report on Fragmentation offered a finely graded evaluation of different approaches, noting that, while priority principles like *lex specialis* and *lex posterior* were 'irrelevant' and 'not meaningful' in conflicts between treaties with non-identical parties,[38] a coordination approach could serve where the treaties were linked by parallel objectives and common institutions.[39] Perhaps these links may also assist in cases of strategically created treaty conflicts (which the Report did not consider). However, the efficacy of a coordination approach is a matter of context and diplomacy; international institutions cannot enforce coordination as a matter of *law*. As the ILC Report noted (and as the CACJ found in 1917), institutions may do no more than uphold the subjective rights provided by the conflicting treaties.[40] This conclusion echoes VCLT Article 30.

[35] These points are more fully developed in Chapter 2.

[36] For rich analyses of institutional approaches, see Pauwelyn, *Conflict of Norms in Public International Law*; Klabbers, *Treaty Conflicts and the European Union*.

[37] *Costa Rica* v. *Nicaragua*, CACJ, Judgment of 30 September 1916 (1917) 11 *American Journal of International Law* 181; Borgen, 'Resolving Treaty Conflicts', 591–5.

[38] ILC, 'Report of Study Group on Fragmentation', 62 (para. 113) and 125 (para. 243).

[39] *ibid.*, 166, para. 323. [40] *ibid.*

The political economy of treaty conflict

Let us return now to the small treaty/large treaty dynamic. This dynamic – given that smaller treaties are more easily concluded – indicates that a treaty conflict may be an effective way of challenging existing multilateral regimes. In the case of the Rome Statute–BIA conflict, for instance, a multilateral treaty drafted in consultation with 160 States, 30 international organisations and UN agencies, and 140 non-governmental organisations from all parts of the world, based on a text prepared by the ILC, drawing upon forty years of aspiration, and finally adopted by a vote of 120 to 7, was vulnerable to challenge by just one powerful State.[41] The same applies to the multilateral treaties in some of the other examples.

Those persuaded of the defective character of these specific multilateral treaties may welcome treaty conflicts as challenges to them and as likely catalysts for their reform. Nevertheless, that one or a few States may destabilise a multilateral treaty regime by the expedient of concluding another treaty should cause some disquiet. Not least, for all the difficulties international lawyers have faced in creating adequate taxonomies of treaty types,[42] it is evident that many treaties have purposes other than specifying the rights and obligations owed between States: treaties for foreign aid confer privileges, human rights treaties implicate interests of individuals, environmental treaties and the NPT address matters of concern to all, and treaties like the Framework Convention on Climate Change establish regimes for future discussions. The application of these instruments should not be dependent upon the will of a few of their States parties.

This is particularly because, as Benvenisti and Downs observe, the turn to bilateral or small-group treaties is a means co-opted by powerful States, to advance their interests and maintain their relative hegemony in the international system.[43] Bilateralism, including serial

[41] These numbers are derived from the lists attached to the Final Act of the United Nations Diplomatic Conference of Plenipotentiaries on the Establishment of an International Criminal Court, done at Rome on 17 July 1998, UN Doc. A/CONF.183/10*.

[42] The most useful taxonomies are based on the character of the obligations in the treaties. For instance, Crawford distinguishes between obligations of bilateral and multilateral types: ILC, Third Report on State Responsibility by J. Crawford, Special Rapporteur, UN Doc. A/CN.4/507, 10 March 2000, paras. 90–116. Taxonomies based on the subject-matter of treaties are less useful: see ILC, 'Report of Study Group on Fragmentation', 17–18, paras. 21–3.

[43] Benvenisti and Downs, 'The Empire's New Clothes', 610–11, 614–19.

bilateralism, allows powerful States to negotiate on a one-to-one basis with less powerful States, which reduces opportunities for coalition-building and collective bargaining by the latter. Powerful States can also tailor the commitments undertaken (and the *quid pro quo* offered) to particular States. Examples of serial bilateralism include TRIPs-plus agreements and BIAs; Benvenisti and Downs note that serial bilateralism occurs also in the fields of drug pricing and foreign investment.

Bilateral or small-group agreements may also be a way of regime or venue 'shifting', that is, marginalising one forum by centring another. Such shifting

> most frequently takes place when a particular agreement is initially negotiated or during the renegotiations that have been convened to deal with a new problem or political crisis. Typically, one or more powerful states become dissatisfied with the trajectory of negotiations and decide to exit the negotiations and exploit their agenda-setting power to set up a parallel and competing set of negotiations with other powerful states. Once they have created the alternative venue and reached a consensus among themselves about the character of the agreement they desire, they approach weaker states with a proposal to restart negotiations. This simple two-step maneuver or some closely related variant has enabled the powerful states to break the coordinated resistance of the weaker parties during several multilateral negotiations.[44]

Examples include the GATT and LOSC-related conflicts discussed above (the latter more fully in Chapter 4). The example of the NPT–Nuclear Deal conflict is also relevant; indeed, Chapter 6 on that conflict shows that venue-shifting may also be used to redistribute decision-making authority within a regime that has subsisted for a significant period and is not being renegotiated.

Of course, similar strategies may be used by less powerful States to counter more powerful ones. For instance, Laurence Helfer notes developing States' efforts to counter the 'TRIPs-plus' agreements by raising concerns about intellectual property rights at other international forums, with the result that

> [i]ntellectual property issues are now at or near the top of the agenda in intergovernmental organizations such as the World Health Organization and the Food and Agriculture Organization, in international negotiating fora such as the Convention on Biological Diversity's Conference of the Parties and the Commission on Genetic Resources for Food and Agriculture, and in expert and political bodies such as the United Nations Commission on Human Rights and

[44] *ibid.*, 615.

its Sub-Commission on the Promotion and Protection of Human Rights. In some of these venues, 'intellectual property lawmaking' involves the negotiation of new treaties; in others, such lawmaking occurs through the reinterpretation of existing agreements and the creation of new nonbinding declarations, guidelines, recommendations, and other forms of 'soft law'.[45]

At these forums, developing States have been able to assert their numerical superiority, or invoke the forum's own objects and purposes. But they have been less successful in promoting changes to multilateral treaty regimes when acting in small groups. For example, of all the cases of treaty conflict discussed above, there was only one in which the later treaty entirely failed to achieve its object. This was the Bogotá Declaration, which had sought to challenge the Outer Space Treaty. The participants to this Declaration were eight developing States, and their claim to the geostationary orbit enjoyed no support from the powerful States of the time. Indeed, the United States and the Soviet Union had already installed their satellites in this orbit.[46] In all the other cases, the United States was one of the parties to the bilateral or small-group treaties and, in most cases (except for the seabed mining conflict), at a time when it was the *only* superpower, and was accompanied by other established or emerging powers. In these cases, the treaty conflict did have an impact upon the multilateral treaty regime. Strategically created treaty conflicts may thus be particularly the weapon of the most powerful States.

Law and politics in confluence

This analysis of the role that political power plays in shaping treaty regimes brings us to the question of the role of law in international affairs. While treaties are products of political bargaining, their 'law-creating' capacity owes much to the fact that as formal agreements, or even as disagreements reduced to writing,[47] they offer relatively stable bases for interactions between their parties. In other words, though emerging from political processes, in ordinary cases they seem to operate at a remove from politics. The rise in their numbers is one of

[45] Helfer, 'Regime Shifting', 5–6.

[46] The United States had launched a geo-stationery satellite, Syncom 3, into orbit in August 1964; the USSR followed in 1974.

[47] The description of treaties as 'disagreements reduced to writing' is borrowed from P. Allott, 'The Concept of International Law' (1999) 10 *European Journal of International Law* 31, 43, para. 35.

the grounds upon which legal scholars speak of the juridification, or legalisation, of international relations.

But treaty conflicts reveal to us the fragility of treaties, including agreements establishing multilateral legal regimes. That it is relatively easy for States to create conflicting bilateral or small-group treaties with non-identical parties, which are amenable to few legal solutions, seems to reinforce one of two views of international law. The first holds that international law is purely contingent on politics, particularly the political preferences of powerful States. The second view that States (and other actors) seek to co-opt the authority of international law to advance their interests. In other words, international law is not just a product of politics but also its tool.

Either view must, and in these times does, give rise to concern. As the next section will outline, the post-Cold War era has seen international law pass from being the subject of anticipation (in the early 1990s) to one of anxiety. While critical thought on international law has a long trajectory, the late 1990s, and especially the 2000s, have seen, in some sense, a mainstreaming of this thought. The claim that international law is political appears everywhere; the differences lie in perceptions of the character and modes of its politics, and of how they relate to international politics *per se*.

As the next section argues, strategically created treaty conflicts offer context in which to evaluate these different perceptions. They are also a useful context in considering further questions. Chiefly, on what basis, and with what motives, have scholars of international law for long regarded international law as a force for good in international relations? Surely, if easily instrumentalised, international law is only a force for coercion of the less powerful by the more powerful? And further still: do we indeed see the subordination of law, or are there more complex dynamics at work? Does international law also constrain politics? And what may all of this tell us about the role of international law in international relations? These inquiries form the underlying subject of this book.

Between epiphenomenality and lawfare

This section paves the way for the dual analysis undertaken in the following chapters, by making the argument that our perception of what international law *is* both shapes and is shaped by how we regard its presence in international politics. It introduces two influential critical views of international law: either as contingent to politics, or as a mode of politics. These views espouse particular understandings of international law, and represent two of today's predominant anxieties about its function. The section suggests that both may find their expression *and* their limits in the study of strategically created treaty conflicts.

One reformulation of that question about international law

It is common to speak of the early to mid 1990s as a period of high optimism for international law. Amongst other things, these years seemed to have disposed of the question that has troubled legal scholars for decades: whether international law is truly 'law'. The introductory lecture of Thomas Franck's 1993 Hague General Course announced that 'international law has entered its post-ontological era. Its lawyers need no longer defend the very existence of international law.'[48]

But this only opened the way for other questions that have now come to dominate legal scholarship. Many of these, too, were articulated by Franck (reflecting, we might say, his 'uncanny ability to see around corners'[49]). Franck observed that 'emancipated from the constraints of defensive ontology, international lawyers are now free to undertake a critical assessment of its content'; to ask, in other words: 'is international law effective? Is it enforceable? Is it understood? And, the most important question: Is international law fair?'[50]

In a neat twist, these very questions have become the basis of a renewed 'lawness' test of international law in the 2000s. These years of the spread of terror, violence and economic crises have provoked much thinking over what international law actually does – its function in the present-day world. The answers naturally depend upon, and feed into, assumptions of what international law *is* (and should be). We haven't quite retired the ontological debate.

No doubt the terms of the debate have changed. The concern is not whether there is a body of rules which displays enough formal hallmarks of 'law'. Challenges from the Austinian standpoint (lacking a sovereign,

[48] T. Franck, *Fairness in International Law and International Institutions* (Oxford, Clarendon Press 1995) 6. Or see T. Franck, 'Fairness in the International Legal and Institutional System', General Course on Public International Law (1993) 240 *Recueil des Cours* 9, 25. See also I. Scobbie, 'Tom Franck's Fairness' (2002) 13 *European Journal of International Law* 909.

[49] D. Kennedy, 'Tom Franck and the Manhattan School' (2003) 35 *NYU Journal of International Law and Politics* 397, 398.

[50] Franck, *Fairness in International Law*, 6.

therefore not law properly so called) as well as the Hartian (lacking well-developed secondary rules, therefore not a system) are almost routinely rebutted on the basis that domestic analogies are inappropriate and that international law is its own system, populated by a doctrine of sources, constitutive principles, accepted procedures, established institutions and rules of validity and responsibility. We might today dispense with Austin's and Hart's formal critiques by directing the former to New York or Geneva and the latter to Geneva or The Hague. As Franck, again, observed in 2009 (in one of his last public addresses):

> [I]f one follows the international treaty practice of states, the decisions of international tribunals and compliance with those decisions by the states that are party to the litigation, one must have some sense that there's obviously something out there that looks an awful lot like law, sounds a lot like law, has an awful lot of institutions that have names that seem to resonate in legal practice.[51]

But there remain questions about the purposes served by an international law that is thus formally conceived. What is its purchase against political power? Does it constrain more powerful States against less powerful ones, or *vis-à-vis* other actors? In David Rieff's evocative framing: what does it 'actually accomplish . . . for people in need of justice, or aid, or mercy, or bread . . . has [it] kept a single jackboot out of a single human face'?[52] And, what would it take for international law to have such an impact?

The poles[53] of this debate are represented by two leading works published in the mid-2000s: Jack Goldsmith and Eric Posner's *The Limits of International Law*,[54] which reinforces this formal conception in order to argue that international law is simply contingent to power politics; and David Kennedy's *Of War and Law*,[55] which argues that international law is a powerful mode of politics – the mark of legitimacy in international affairs – but this is accompanied by a near complete loss of a formal concept of legality. The two works seem to suggest that

[51] T. Franck, 'Remarks: In What Sense Is International Law Law' (2009) 103 *ASIL Proceedings* 161.

[52] D. Rieff, *A Bed for the Night: Humanitarianism in Crisis* (London, Vintage 2002) 15.

[53] It may seem odd to describe two books published within the same (US) academy, and written in the same halls (Harvard) as the polar positions of a debate, yet the works are significant for their sharp and distinct positions as to the relationship between international law and politics; they are also representative of a wider literature. The chapters that follow focus on many of the works that fall somewhere in between these positions, or take a different view entirely.

[54] Oxford University Press 2005. [55] Princeton University Press 2006.

international law must be the one or the other: a rigorous, technical, determinate and limited system of marginal importance; or a politically engaged practice of critique and advocacy, central to international relations, but reduced to being the vehicle for clashes of values, rationales and sensibilities, with no core of its own. The fate of international law, to borrow the title of Martti Koskenniemi's 2007 essay, teeters 'between technique and politics'.[56]

Epiphenomenality

Goldsmith and Posner's *Limits*, though criticised,[57] is undoubtedly a leading work of the 2000s: speaking at Cambridge in July 2008, Koskenniemi observed that it was the most widely distributed international law book of its time.[58] Its challenge to international law has been as influential as it is blunt; drawing its conception of international law from the very scholarship it describes as improbably doctrinal and idealistic,[59] *Limits* claims that international law is only epiphenomenal to the interests of powerful States.[60]

Limits asserts that international law, that is treaties and custom, emerges entirely from 'states acting rationally to maximize their interests, given their perceptions of the interests of other states and the distribution of state power'.[61] Goldsmith and Posner take State interests as given – prior to and not shaped by international law – and identifiable by looking at the preferences of States' political leadership.[62] They exclude the possibility that States may have a non-instrumental preference for complying with international law,[63] for such an explanation 'says nothing interesting about when and why States act consistently with international law', and 'provides no basis for understanding

[56] M. Koskenniemi, 'The Fate of Public International Law: Between Technique and Politics' (2007) 70 *Modern Law Review* 1.

[57] See, for instance, P. S. Berman, 'Review Essay: Seeing Beyond the Limits of International Law' (2006) 84 *Texas Law Review* 1265; D. M. Golove, 'Leaving Customary International Law Where It Is: Goldsmith and Posner's The Limits of International Law' (2005–6) 34 *Georgia Journal of International and Comparative Law* 333; A. van Aaken, 'To Do Away with International Law? Some Limits to "The Limits of International Law"' (2006) 17 *European Journal of International Law* 289.

[58] M. Koskenniemi, 'The Lauterpacht Tradition and its Successors: Towards Theory?', in J. Crawford and M. Young (eds.), *The Function of Law in the International Community: An Anniversary Symposium* (2008), Proceedings of the 25th Anniversary Conference of the Lauterpacht Centre for International Law, http://moot.law.cam.ac.uk/Media/25_anniversary/Lauterpacht_Tradition_paper.pdf.

[59] Goldsmith and Posner, *Limits*, 3. [60] *ibid.*, 13. [61] *ibid.*, 3. [62] *ibid.*, 6. [63] *ibid.*, 9.

variation in, and violation of, international law'.[64] Instead, they consider that State behaviour can usually be explained as one, or a combination, of four 'models' of inter-State relations: coincidence of interest, coordination, cooperation and coercion.[65] Each of these models operates within bilateral relationships: to Goldsmith and Posner, multilateral relationships are, usually, only aggregates of bilateral relationships.

In Goldsmith and Posner's account, doctrine may identify what the law provides at any given time, but this cannot ensure that it is actually complied with by States. Rather, depending on the relative power of the States, their actions may serve to modify the law itself. They make this claim particularly emphatically *vis-à-vis* customary international law: while insisting that they do not deny its existence,[66] they do in effect deny the concept any value. In their explanation, there is nothing 'customary' or 'law'-like about customary international law; such law is no more than patterned regularities in (usually) bilateral interactions resulting from a stable configuration of State interests and relative power. When interests and power change, behaviour will also change so that an existing 'custom' is violated. To Goldsmith and Posner, the description of customary international law as 'universal state practices followed from a sense of legal obligation' makes little sense.[67]

Their dismissal of customary international law as having no influence upon State behaviour extends also to treaty law, but they consider treaties have more of a purpose. For treaties are expressed and as such serve as formal means by which States may communicate with each other, and provide information that can enhance their cooperation.[68] Goldsmith and Posner note that treaties have 'an implicit two-step logic: in step 1, States come together and negotiate common terms; in step 2, States cooperate (or not) *in pairs*, with each State in a pair complying with the common terms as long as the other State in the pair does.'[69] But treaties do not otherwise influence State behaviour: Goldsmith and Posner reject the view that treaties can be normatively strengthened to increase their 'compliance-pull';[70] State compliance has only to do with the underlying configuration of State interests and power.

Goldsmith and Posner also explain the 'legalistic' quality of international discourse in terms of international law's communicative utility. Legal language, because formal and abstract, may be comprehended by audiences that share little community with the speaker. Invoking the

[64] *ibid.*, 10. [65] *ibid.*, 13. [66] *ibid.*, 43. [67] *ibid.*, 42. [68] *ibid.*, 84. [69] *ibid.*, 87.
[70] *ibid.*, 83–4.

law is thus a convenient way for States to clarify their preferences, explain their actions and protest against the actions of other States.[71] But such invocations carry no particular charge *vis-à-vis* those States' political preferences. Indeed, other languages, such as of religion or morality, may serve similar ends and more persuasively, but, being less formal and abstract, their comprehensibility is conditional upon a certain degree of community between the speaker and the audience.[72]

According to Goldsmith and Posner, the purely epiphenomenal character of international law has escaped the attention of mainstream legal scholars.[73] They claim that mainstream scholarship lacks the sophistication displayed by the international relations subfield of political science: led by the belief that States comply with international law for non-instrumental reasons, mainstream scholars – 'law professors' – remain tied to a doctrinal research agenda of identifying the 'black letter' of international law irrespective of actual behaviours. At most, they might also explain the conditions under which international law exerts compliance-pull. Underlying this agenda is the idea that States are drawn towards compliance with international law because such compliance is 'morally right or legitimate'. Goldsmith and Posner, however, do not attach any moral weight to 'international legality'. To them, the morality or immorality of international law is exhausted by its content;[74] therefore, 'we cannot condemn a State merely for violating international law. The question is whether by violating international law a State is likely to change international law for the better from a moral perspective.'[75] And this is usually only established after the fact.

It must be said that, despite their critique of doctrinal scholarship, Goldsmith and Posner do not themselves depart from a doctrinal approach to identifying international law. Indeed, to them, it is only the 'objective' appeal of the conclusions (about what the rules provide) reached via doctrinal techniques that gives international law value as a means of communication. As a shared concept, international law permits each State to evaluate the actions of other States as aligned with or contrary to law, as well as whether these actions have the effect of altering the law. International law is not a basis upon which to judge State behaviour; we may only note whether the law has been followed,

[71] *ibid.*, 184. [72] See *ibid.*, 182–3. [73] *ibid.*, 14–15. [74] *ibid.*, 197. [75] *ibid.*, 199.

not followed, or altered by that behaviour. It is therefore purely formal and purely incidental to international relations.

Lawfare

In *Of War and Law*, David Kennedy offers an alternative critical narrative of law as a powerful, but coopted, force in international relations. He observes that 'law has become a mark of legitimacy – and legitimacy has become the currency of power'.[76] In present times, when 'transnational activities of all sorts, including warfare', is conducted on a strategic terrain of background legal regulations,[77] law has also become 'a vocabulary for judgment, for action, for communication'.[78] But, this exalted position has come at great cost to the very idea of law, stripping it of its distinctiveness and depriving it of its separation from 'political, economic – and military – reality'.[79]

Kennedy observes that, in earlier times, international law maintained a distinct identity from politics, initially because it was grounded in ethics and later because it took on a formal, rule-oriented character:

> Eighteenth-century international law *was* rooted in ethics and visions of natural justice. Nineteenth-century international law *was* formal and rule-oriented. It *was* abstract; legal scholars did try to elaborate a 'scientific' doctrinal system, linking all the rules to a few general principles.[80]

As such, international law was also marginal. Kennedy notes, in the context of the relationship between law and use of force, that, 'when law saw *itself* as an autonomous discipline, external to the institutions it regulated, it was more difficult for legal ideas and rules to infiltrate the military professions, or to become the political vocabulary for assessing the legitimacy of strategy and tactic'.[81]

International law thus had little role in regulating the use of force, or other aspects of international relations. This, indeed, had been Hans Morgenthau's experience of international law in the inter-war years, and informed the sharp criticism of his 1940 essay. International law, Morgenthau claimed, was too detached from politics and subject to an 'inveterate tendency to stick to [its] assumptions and to suffer constant defeat from experience rather than to change [its] assumptions in the

[76] Kennedy, *Of War and Law*, 44. [77] *ibid.*, 10.
[78] *ibid.*, 44. More recently Goldsmith has echoed this view: J. Goldsmith, 'Mea Culpa: Lawfare', *Lawfare*, 8 September 2011.
[79] Kennedy, *Of War and Law*, 44. [80] *ibid.* [81] *ibid.*, 9. Emphasis in the original.

light of contradicting fact'.[82] It would have a greater influence on international relations if it took into account the core ideals and ethical principles of international society as well as 'the sociological context of economic interests, social tensions and aspirations for power which were the motivating forces' that 'gave rise to the factual situations forming the raw material for regulation by international law'.[83] In sum, he considered a functional theory of international law a precondition for the fulfilment of the 'ethical and political desire to improve international relations by means of the law'.[84] He did not elaborate further, turning instead to the study of international relations as a *political* science, but the description in *Of War and Law* suggests that a functional approach has been embraced by many, including military and humanitarian actors in the context of armed conflict.

Kennedy argues that, for some time now, international law 'has been in revolt against formalism, and has sought in every possible way to become a practical vocabulary for politics'.[85] The concept of international law as clear legal rules has been replaced by a conception which accommodates principles and standards, broad exceptions, and disputed interpretations. International law's vocabulary is 'fluid and pluralistic';[86] in it can be found traces of all its epochs:

> [T]here are ethical innovations and considerations of policy reminiscent of the preclassical period, sharp doctrinal boundaries and images of absolute sovereign power reminiscent of the classical, as well as more continuous institutions and fluid standards of behavior that blur the boundaries between war and peace, or legal and political action.[87]

This allsorts vernacular permits the invocation of international law arguments towards various ends.

But it adds to the indeterminacy of international law. Indeed, Kennedy presents a picture of international law's indeterminacy as rooted in

[82] H. Morgenthau, 'Positivism, Functionalism and International Law' (1940) 34 *American Journal of International Law* 260. Of course, in 1940, the law of armed conflict – the subject of Kennedy's work – was not even a major subject for international law.

[83] *ibid.*, 269.

[84] *ibid.*, 284. For a detailed discussion of Morgenthau's 'turn', see O. Jütersonke, *Morgenthau, Law and Realism* (Cambridge University Press, 2010); see also J. Crawford, 'Chance, Order, Change: The Course of International Law', General Course on Public International Law (2013) 365 *Recueil des Cours* 9, 33–5.

[85] Kennedy, *Of War and Law*, 44–5. [86] *ibid.*, 42.

[87] *ibid.*, 47. Kennedy's periodisation in pre-classical and classical eras maps loosely on to his earlier observations about international law in the eighteenth and nineteenth century.

messier dynamics than those noted by Koskenniemi in *From Apology to Utopia*.[88] Koskenniemi focused upon argumentation in the context of dispute settlement before international courts and tribunals, showing that the substantive open-endedness of legal arguments was bounded by a rigorous formal mode of production in which any invoked position had to be shown to satisfy requirements of both normativity and concreteness.[89] This is an impossible balance, making international legal argument always vulnerable to charges of apology and utopia. But, as Kennedy points out, in the deformalised, highly pluralistic contexts in which international law arguments are advanced and evaluated – the 'court of public opinion', or where 'international norms [are] enforced through decentralized processes [by the] "international community"'[90] – even these constraints on making 'legal' arguments may be lost. 'Legal argument' ranges across the search for functional solutions, efficient outcomes, ethical absolution and so on. In short, it is often not very much about legality in the formal sense.

Kennedy makes this point crisply in discussing the different registers of international legal discourse. The 'classical' register, still significant in the conversations of 'legal elites', is of *validity*. In this,

> [s]omething is legal if it complies with a valid norm. A norm is valid if it is promulgated by the appropriate authority using the authorized procedure, or if it can be deduced from first principles by recognized professional canons of deduction and interpretation. If the norm is valid, it should be followed. In the world of validity, the law is the law – you should follow it because it is valid.[91]

This discourse can operate as the *sole* register only within formal dispute settlement processes. In the less formal and more plural contexts of international law, where there is little scope for authoritative determination of the validity of norms and interpretations, legal discourse operates much more in the register of *persuasiveness*. Actors follow norms if they are 'persuaded' they should: this may be because they perceive the norm to be valid, but it may also be because the norm dictates a course of conduct that appears 'wise or ethically compelling', 'encapsulates best practice', or due to fear of 'the consequences of not following it'. Indeed, notes Kennedy, the more 'legal elites' begin to adopt the register of persuasiveness, the more they come to see persuasiveness as the criterion for validity as well: a norm appears valid only if

88 M. Koskenniemi, *From Apology to Utopia: The Structure of International Legal Argument* (reissue with new epilogue, Cambridge University Press 2005).
89 *ibid.*, 17–19, 66–7, 562. 90 Kennedy, *Of War and Law*, 91. 91 *ibid.*

it turns out 'to *have been* persuasive'.[92] Thus, validity suffers a double blow, becoming only the rhetoric of persuasion, and being itself evaluated in terms of persuasiveness. We might see in this international law's descent into managerialism, with experts deciding on the course of action that is the most efficient, or ethical, or possessed of whichever other value their expertise represents.[93]

Moreover, the register of persuasion permits much to be asserted, challenged and defended in legal terms; 'the law becomes a strategic asset . . . used differently by those with divergent strategic objectives'.[94] And, importantly, it becomes *recognisably* just that – a strategic asset, used by either side, both aware (or considering themselves aware) of the instrumental quality of the other's so-called formal legal argument. Thus, paradoxically, 'as we use the discourse more, we believe it less'.[95] Over time, the purely strategic use of law may lead to a loss of confidence in it as the mark of legitimacy.[96]

In the lawfare thesis, international law is thus an important factor in international relations – constituting the categories in which we perceive situations, and providing the language in which we make and justify decisions, and determine which action is appropriate and which is not. But it becomes such a factor, first, by losing a sharp conception of itself (as more and more is absorbed into the concept of legality) and, gradually, by the erosion of the sense that making a legal argument signifies anything more than strategy.

With his focus on the law in the use of force, Kennedy offers sharp images of the implications of this manner of legal discourse. He reminds us that both military and humanitarian professionals turn to the law with the desire to limit violence through its application. But the very process of using the law in this endeavour – determining which targets may be fired at, for instance, or where collateral damage is acceptable – dissolves into a wide-ranging discussion encompassing both practical and moral considerations, which legitimates what is not proscribed, and normalises actions that would otherwise be abhorrent. Central to decision-making about, and in, war, law is also complicit in its outcomes. In the striking phrase used by China Miéville: '[t]he chaotic and bloody world around us *is the rule of law*'.[97]

[92] *ibid.*, 92–3. [93] See Chapter 3. [94] Kennedy, *Of War and Law*, 116. [95] *ibid.*, 135.
[96] *ibid.*, 135–6.
[97] C. Miéville, *Between Equal Rights: A Marxist Theory of International Law* (Leiden and Boston, Brill 2005) 319.

It is important to note that Kennedy does not call for a return to a formalistic approach to international law. Indeed, such a return would be neither plausible nor productive: critical international legal scholarship, of which Kennedy is a leading voice, has challenged and exposed the ways in which doctrinalism was co-opted by, and served to perpetuate, serious inequalities and disadvantage. However, he has now also usefully pointed out that an escape from doctrinalism is not emancipation from the maladies of international law.

Indeed, these arguments of epiphenomenality and lawfare suggest that something is rotten in the state of international law. Either it is formalistic and only a reflection of international relations; or it is important but lacking precise identity. Yet, one might argue that it is precisely the seeking and finding of a balance between these two poles that preserves international law's distinctiveness and authority. The effort may be detected in (some strands of) international legal thought, as well as in practice. This book will develop this argument by focusing upon strategically created treaty conflicts, because *prima facie* such conflicts exemplify the narratives of epiphenomenality and lawfare.

Which?

On the one hand, as discussed earlier, strategically created treaty conflicts exemplify the epiphenomenal character of international law. Their incidence seems to support Goldsmith and Posner's claim that treaties are no more than a formal expression of the underlying configuration of State power and interests: when this configuration changes, new treaties may appear even in blithe contradiction of the old; when it does not change (as in the case of the Bogotá Declaration), the co-option of a legal form may have few consequences.

Yet, the epiphenomenality thesis is almost too neat. The significant fact about treaty conflicts is not just the substitution of old treaties and alliances by new ones; it is the privileging of treaties – new ones – rather than other means of challenging or changing the existing treaty regimes. By strategically creating treaty conflicts, States seek to leverage the law's own power, using treaties as vehicles for their interests. Not least, they take full advantage of international legal doctrine's permissive and legitimating effects to accomplish their ends. They rely also on the rhetoric of law to exhort compliance with their preferred treaty regime.

Perhaps, then, the lawfare thesis is the more astute. However, though lawfare may serve as an explanatory account, it raises several questions. First, of course, is whether using law instrumentally necessarily requires a complete break from its formal trappings; or is Kennedy's observation in that respect contingent to the specific field of his study? Second, and related, does using international law instrumentally necessarily rob it, in time, of its authority; or is that too a contingent observation?

A study of strategically created treaty conflicts may offer some answers.

The argument of this book

A dual analysis

As mentioned, the book undertakes a dual analysis. First, and already in the foregoing sections of this chapter, it problematises the idea of legal resolution of treaty conflicts. The chapters that follow explore in more detail some rules-based and institutional approaches directed at regulating treaty conflicts, and the ways in which such conflicts have shaped specific legal regimes.

The second analysis emerges from the first. Strategically created treaty conflicts, while not necessarily resolved by international law, offer an excellent context in which to explore its role in international relations, as well as the ways in which this role has been conceived (in other words, to assess the epiphenomenality and lawfare theses on legal doctrine and on the operation of international law).

Key findings

In the next two chapters, the book examines a number of ways in which legal scholars have sought to regulate treaty conflicts, proposing either appropriate conflict rules, or institutional actions to secure effective operation of multilateral treaty regimes. It elects to focus on proposals that fulfil two criteria: they deal with treaty conflict or implementation and, in doing so, provide insight into the relevant scholar's conception of international law; and two, they are linked to a practice context, and in that respect fall within international law's mainstream. Accordingly, the chapters examine the International Law Commission's work in drafting the Law of Treaties, a task shared between several preeminent legal scholars of the 1950s and 1960s. They also explore the idea of 'approximate application of treaties' advanced by Hersch Lauterpacht; the 'managerial' approach espoused by Abram and Antonia Chayes, and suggestions for treaty coordination and regime interaction outlined in some recent works.

These examinations cut across a broad swathe of mainstream legal scholarship. To the extent that they may be taken as representative of such scholarship (and this can only be a qualified claim of course) they show that mainstream scholars rarely make a strict distinction between formal and functional (or managerial) approaches. Nor do they see international law's integrity as mutually exclusive with its instrumental use. Rather, we see in all the works discussed a strikingly similar notion, of international law operating as a broadly conceived discourse between various actors, that accommodates formal and functional elements yet remains distinctively 'legal' in character. This view of international law, moreover, is supported by liberal and constructivist assumptions: liberal in that most of these scholars believe that engaging in a legal discourse advances the rule of law; constructivist in that they believe that even an instrumental engagement with international law will gradually reinforce its authority, amongst States and other actors.

The three following chapters then undertake studies of specific strategically created treaty conflicts, with a view to mapping the operation of legal discourse. The three conflicts selected are those relating to seabed mining, the ICC and the India–US Nuclear Deal (all mentioned above). These conflicts share some common characteristics: a small treaty/large treaty dynamic, non-identical parties, and their strategic creation in order to challenge or force change in a multilateral treaty regime. Of course, there are also important differences: subject matter; the stage of the multilateral regime in question (ranging from a long-existing in case of the nuclear-governance regime, to newly entered into force in case of the ICC, to awaiting entry into force in case of the LOSC); and the eras in which they emerged. Moreover, they emerged for different reasons, and had different protagonists. For these reasons, comparisons can only be made with caution. But, the chapters do point to a number of similar practices that make up the discourse observed in each case.

One practice is what this book calls 'document-rattling': the serial production of a variety of documents by all principal stakeholders in each conflict. These documents range from the formal to the quasi formal in character, and are produced as a matter of competitive strategy and tactic; either seeking to leverage the treaty conflict for their desired ends, or aiming to mitigate the impact of other documents. The *treaties* in conflict are therefore only a part of the story of each treaty conflict; they are embedded within a network of related documents and processes of production of these other documents. A second practice is that of the making of 'legality claims' by various stakeholders, aimed at leading the conflict to their desired outcomes. Thus, we see a give and take of arguments focused on validity and interpretation of various documents; various actors' competence to conclude them and to participate in the processes for their production; and the distinctions between 'technical' exercises of competence and 'political' assertions of power in making, interpreting, challenging and implementing these documents. These claims are certainly made for instrumental purposes, but they do not draw upon functional reasoning alone; they are constantly challenged to justify themselves according to generalisable formal criteria.

All in all, the dual analysis undertaken in this book suggests that, while it is misleading to evaluate international law in terms of whether or not it authoritatively solves treaty conflicts – it cannot solve strategically created ones – it is also misleading to suppose that such conflicts signify the 'limits' or absence of international law. Treaty conflicts, including strategically created ones, are perpetuated through the practices of legal discourse, and also constrained in their effects by the formal and routinising demands of the relevant discursive practices. These constraints may be for better or worse – we must not forget that different actors, including different States, have different capacities for participating in and (even more so) leveraging legal discourse – but they are real, and manifest themselves even in the more instrumental invocations of international law.

The book may be seen as embracing Kennedy's account of lawfare to a significant extent (certainly in preference to the epiphenomenality thesis) but also as complicating that account in several ways. While it supports Kennedy's view of international law as an influential and instrumental discourse that encompasses rules, processes and more, it raises some doubts as to the suggestion that such invocations lead to substantial fluidity in the concept of legality, so as to render it indistinct in concept, and ultimately bereave it of normative authority. It presents a number of explorations of legal thought and of specific treaty conflicts that suggest, instead, that 'legality' remains a distinctive, if contested, quality; and offer an entirely different prognosis of its role in international relations. The book in short, aims at a textured account of lawfare, at least as it manifests in the particular contexts under study.

The next section is a brief digression that seeks to unpack some key ideas introduced above: the idea of law as a broadly conceived legal discourse; and the liberal and constructivist assumptions that support the mainstream idea of international law as a distinctive and influential mode of engagement in international relations.

Unpacking ideas

Locating legality in discursive practices

The idea of international law as a broadly conceived legal discourse stands apart from two other, more common ideas of international law: either, a set of rules of specific content determined by a given shared framework for ascertainment, interpretation and application; *or*, a process, with less determinate content, circumscribed by previous decisions and formal decision-making criteria. Obviously, to some extent, both content and context matter: a conversation in a novel that rigorously expounds legal rules is not *of* international law, for its speakers and context are too far removed. Equally, an emotional discussion by a duly appointed lawyer at the International Court of Justice would not seem to conform to legal discourse, should it be too far removed from the forms that dictate how law is identified and used.[98] Even so, the preponderance of the one allows some relaxation of the other: doctrinal scholarship, though produced outside the context of a formal process, can be an authoritative guide to what international law is. Similarly, a court might indulge in some 'progressive development' of the law matching legal considerations with policy ones.

This latter possibility is most clearly articulated by Rosalyn Higgins. Reformulating the policy science scholarship of Myers McDougal and Harold Lasswell, Higgins explained that we should think of international law in terms of a decision-making process in which authority and power coincide in the hands of an appropriate decision-maker.[99] According to her, where 'decisions are made by authorized persons or organs, in appropriate forums, within the framework of certain established practices and norms, then what occurs is *legal*

[98] Koskenniemi recalls that Bosnia was compelled to replace its initial American counsel because of the style of presentation he elected to use. See M. Koskenniemi, 'Letter to the Editors of the Symposium', Symposium on Method in International Law (1999) 93 *American Journal of International Law* 351.

[99] R. Higgins, *Problems and Process: International Law and How We Use It* (Oxford, Clarendon Press 1994). See also R. Higgins, 'International Law and the Avoidance, Containment and Resolution of Disputes', General Course on Public International Law (1991) 230 Recueil des Cours 9–342.

decision-making'.[100] This approach 'rejects the notion of law merely as the impartial application of rules'.[101] International law is the entire decision-making process, and not just the trend of past decisions which are termed 'rules'.[102] Rules *are* relevant, but, as 'there is no avoiding the essential relationship between law and policy', the authorised decision-maker must 'systematically and openly' take into account both rules and policy factors, making choices that are 'open to public scrutiny and discussion'.[103] Thus, with an authorised decision maker at the helm, it is possible to steer away from a consideration of legal rules alone.

The idea of international law as a discursive practice, however, takes a broader view of both content and context; recognising that invocations of 'international law' may both diverge from the formal grammar of rules and are made outside of formal, authorised, decision-making processes. This raises the question of how to locate the 'legal' in such usage.

In answering this question assistance may perhaps be had from Friedrich Kratochwil's view of the legal as a specific mode of reasoning? In *Rules, Norms and Decisions*,[104] Kratochwil asserts that law

> can be understood neither as a static system of norms nor as a set of rules which all share some common characteristic such as sanctions; in the same vein [it is] . . . mistaken to depict law simply as a process in which claims and counter-claims are made. Rather, law is a choice-process characterized by the principled nature of *norm-use* in arriving at a decision through reasoning.

Kratochwil explains this mode of reasoning as a specific *style* of norm-use,[105] distinguishing it from policy and moral reasoning. The comparison reveals that legal rules are more specific in setting out the conditions of validity of an action, the relevance of the actor's intention and the evidence that may be used to determine 'truth'. Legal decision-making, moreover, is 'characterized by the need to come to a final decision'.[106] What legal decision-making shares with moral decision-making is that both must be carried out in a principled way – 'not only can one not make legal rules as one goes along, even

[100] *ibid.*, 2, quoting from a previous work: R. Higgins, 'Policy Considerations and the International Judicial Process' (1968) 17 *International and Comparative Law Quarterly* 58.
[101] *ibid.* [102] *ibid.* [103] *ibid.*, 5.
[104] F. Kratochwil, *Rules, Norms and Decisions: On the Concept of Practical and Legal Reasoning in International Relations and Domestic Affairs* (Cambridge University Press 1999).
[105] *ibid.*, 205. [106] *ibid.*, 206–7.

if such decisions were to command substantial majoritarian support, but "legality" requires the even-handed application of rules in "like" situations in the future'.[107] To illustrate what he means by principled reasoning, he refers to the ways in which advocates plead before courts:

> The advocate in international law, like his partner in the domestic arena, faces either previous decisions or other pronouncements of varying authoritative quality. Typically, the opponent will also have a particular reading of the legal landscape. Consequently, the skill of advocacy will consist in turning attention to the features of the case which, in a plausible fashion, buttress one's own side. Conversely, a variety of avoidance techniques are available to weaken authoritative decisions favouring the other side: faulty application of legal rules, fundamental incompatibility of the facts at hand, lack of clarity as to the scope of the rule enunciated in the decision, changed conditions, inconsistent subsequent practice, etc. These are some of the standard devices to inhibit adherence to the opponent's argument.[108]

In building these arguments, the advocate relies less on deductive or inductive logic, than on rhetoric.[109] Kratochwil is particularly interested in the role of *topoi* – commonplaces – in establishing the 'starting-points' for arguments, by framing actions within a specific narrative: imposing particular characterisations upon actions and locating the issues at stake in a substantive set of common understandings. He considers the advocate to rely on both general and legal *topoi*. General *topoi* reflect common-sense understandings, and are persuasive in developing the overall non-technical narrative; legal *topoi*, derived from procedural rules and settled practices, guide the more specific appraisal of the issues. Kratochwil lists four typical legal *topoi*: the question of whether the literal meaning or the ascertainable will of the legislator shall be decisive; the possibility of inconsistent or contradictory legal prescriptions; unclear or ambiguous formulations of the law; and incompleteness of the legal order making necessary the closing of gaps. Each in turn leads on to other topical considerations. He observes that '[t]he enumeration of legal *topoi* ... provides not only instructions as to how a practitioner is to go about a case, but also assurances that in the process, a case is looked at from different angles'.[110] That is to say, competing interests and interpretations are highlighted, and taken into account or rebutted. This process of

[107] *ibid.*, 208. [108] *ibid.*, 209. [109] *ibid.*, 209–10. [110] *ibid.*, 228.

reasoning through *topoi* culminates in 'the "authoritative" decision which establishes the holding by either subsuming the case under a certain norm, or by stating the applicability of rule of *stare decisis* (together with relevant facts and *obiter dicta*)'. Kratochwil notes that such a decision 'depends for its persuasiveness largely upon a careful weaving, into one strand of thought, of legal and common-sense arguments'.[111]

The above is a truncated account of Kratochwil's argument, but conveys two features of it. First, it *is* useful at illuminating distinctive features of legal reasoning, particularly the role of *topoi*. But, second, it remains closely bound to the manner in which arguments unfold in a formal dispute settlement process, and might rule out several invocations of 'international law' as being in the legal style.

But, if this conclusion is available to a theorist of international relations, it is not one that has appealed to international law scholars. Koskenniemi, for instance, would agree with Kratochwil that there is a distinctive style to making legal argument; moreover, and as Balakrishnan Rajagopal points out, *From Apology to Utopia* did proceed as if international legal practice consisted solely of techniques of public international lawyering by legal advisors to governments, usually before courts or in other rigorously formal settings.[112] But his later book, *The Gentle Civilizer of Nations*, recognises international legal practice as more broad-ranging, including not only legal advocacy, negotiation and mediation, but also 'law-talk' at the popular level and much in between.[113]

Gentle Civilizer, then, offers a view of international 'law' as a practice of decision-making that is bounded by but not limited to formal rules and procedures. It speaks of a 'culture of formalism' (distinguished from a 'culture of dynamism'):

> a practice that builds on formal arguments that are available to all under conditions of equality. It seeks to persuade the protagonists (lawyers, decision-makers) to take a momentary distance from their preferences and to enter a terrain where these preferences should be justified, instead of taken for granted, by reference to standards that are independent from their particular positions or interests.[114]

[111] *ibid.*

[112] B. Rajagopal, 'Martti Koskenniemi's From Apology to Utopia: A Reflection' (2006) 7(12) *German Law Journal* 1089.

[113] M. Koskenniemi, *The Gentle Civilizer of Nations: The Rise and Fall of International Law 1870–1960* (Cambridge University Press 2001) 494–509.

[114] *ibid.*, 502.

This is a view of 'law' as a practice of legal justification – by discourse amongst 'protagonists'. The discourse is conducted in the language of legal rules and principles and may be carried out in large part through one or more legal processes. Its subject-matter includes differences over the characterisation of a matter, the interpretation and application of various rules, and over the processes followed; it has a rigour that is missing from discussions that are purely about what either side considers the better outcome. Such a discourse need not take particular rules, principles or processes as given: the protagonists may critique these too – as not well established, or as only reflecting particular interests and inappropriate to the ideal of a truly universal international law[115] – but these are immanent critiques of law.

Koskenniemi offers, in short, a more expanded account of legal discourse: as a discourse about the justification of actions by reference to independent standards, and about the generalisability of such justifications; and as a discourse attentive to the procedural conditions that determine who gets to offer and receive these justifications.[116] This view finds echoes in the various strands of legal thought explored in this book.

The liberal assumption

This book suggests that, in privileging legal discourse, mainstream scholars rely on liberal assumptions. These assumptions explain not only why law-in-itself is seen as a valuable constituent of society but, moreover, why law even shorn of many of its formal trappings is accorded the same importance. For, in itself, the notion of law as legal discourse is a bit hazy: a discourse may be more or less legally rigorous; particular procedures or forums may be more influential, more deliberative and/or more biased; some actors may have less capacity to effectively participate in discourse; and a discussion in terms of rules and principles may be weighted more towards the *status quo* rather than reform (it is always harder to argue for altering a rule than for following it) – these are all important critiques of specific instances of legal discourse.

[115] *ibid.*, 504–7. Koskenniemi clarifies that 'universality' cannot be defined in the absolute: we cannot say what is universal; but can contest particular rules, processes, goals, outcomes, or blueprints for international community as falling short of being so.

[116] *ibid.*, 501.

To understand the value placed on legal discourse, we might turn again to Koskenniemi, who acknowledges that all the above critiques are plausible. But he notes that a legal discourse also levels the playing field in various ways: it regulates all particular demands by requiring them to be justified in general terms; further, even rules and principles invoked in support of particular interests have a formal logic of their own, and are thus available for 'capture' by other actors too. The same might not be true of other types of justifications, in 'technical languages of effectiveness, optimization, compliance'.[117] For Koskenniemi, legal discourse equates to a culture of formalism:

> a culture of resistance to power, a social practice of accountability, openness, and equality whose status cannot be reduced to the political positions of any one of the parties whose claims are treated within it.[118]

In the same vein, he continues:

> [L]ike any culture, formalism may often have become bureaucratic and worked as a smokescreen for apathy and disinterest. It may have frequently failed to live up to its promises and it has certainly sometimes been used to support dubious or outright abominable causes. None of this, however, abolishes the value of the political message that its rituals, traditions and documents express sometimes more, sometimes less adequately ... that there must be limits of the exercise of power, that those who are in positions of strength must be accountable and that those who are weak must be heard and protected, and that when professional men and women engage in an argument about what is lawful and what is not, they are engaged in politics that imagines the possibility of a community overriding particular alliances and preferences and allowing a meaningful distinction between lawful constraint and the application of naked power.[119]

Embedded in this statement is an argument relating to the role of lawyers – professional men and women – as flag-bearers of legal discourse, and as monitors who ensure that it does take place in the terms outlined by Koskenniemi. He goes on to observe that something of this idea about legal discourse – a common *feel* about the role of law – emerges at different points in the history of international relations since 1873.[120] As this book will show, it is also reflected in legal thought relating to treaty conflict.

As he outlines these claims, Koskenniemi cautions that his idea of a culture of formalism should not be mistaken for a statement of support

[117] *ibid.*, 496. [118] *ibid.*, 500. [119] *ibid.*, 502. [120] *ibid.*, 502–3.

for the 'Rule of Law' ideal, at least to the extent that that ideal is attached to the fulfilment of particular rules or procedures – for in this sense '[t]he Rule of Law hopes to fix the universal in particular, positive space (a law, a moral or procedural principle, an institution). A culture of formalism resists such fixation.'[121] Similarly, he describes as academic hubris the attachment of various lawyers to specific jurisprudential positions, 'suggesting that international problems could only be resolved after the adoption of one or another theory as the "basis" for one's legal practice'.[122]

But Koskenniemi's argument *is* a variant of a rule of law argument, in which attachment to a broadly conceived legal discourse substitutes for affinity to particular rules or principles. Robert Cryer claims that *Gentle*'s exhortation in favour of a culture of formalism recalls E. P. Thompson's 'apostatical avowal of the rule of law'.[123] In the final pages of *Whigs and Hunters*, Thompson observed (in the context of domestic law):

> [L]aw when considered as institutions (the courts, with their class theatre and class procedures) or as personnel (the judges, the lawyers, the Justices of Peace) may be very easily assimilated to those of the ruling class. But all that is entailed in 'the law' is not subsumed in these institutions. The law may also be seen as ideology, or as particular rules and sanctions which stand in a definite and active relationship (often a field of conflict) to social norms; and finally, it may be seen simply in terms of its own logic, rules, and procedures – that is, simply as *law*.[124]

Moreover, to Thompson, while law could be 'seen instrumentally as mediating and reinforcing existent class relations and, ideologically, as offering to these a legitimation',[125] it was not reducible to a mere representation of these relations: 'For class relations were expressed, not in any way one likes, but *through the forms of law*; and the law . . . has its own characteristics, its own independent history and logic of evolution'.[126] This supplied the basis for a strong appeal in favour of the rule of law:

> [T]here is a difference between arbitrary power and the rule of law. We ought to expose the shams and inequities which may be concealed beneath this law. But the rule of law itself, the imposing of effective inhibitions upon power and the defense of the citizen from power's all-intrusive claims, seems to me an

[121] *ibid.*, 507. [122] *ibid.*, 504.
[123] R. Cryer, 'Déjà Vu in International Law' (2002) 65 *Modern Law Review* 931, 946.
[124] E. P. Thompson, *Whigs and Hunters: The Origin of the Black Act* (London, Allen Lane 1975) 260.
[125] *ibid.*, 262. [126] *ibid.* Emphasis in the original.

unqualified human good. To deny or belittle this good is, in this dangerous century when the resources and pretensions of power continue to enlarge, a desperate error of intellectual abstraction. More than this, it is a self-fulfilling error, which encourages us to give up the struggle against bad law and class-bound procedures, and to disarm ourself before power. It is to throw away a whole inheritance of struggle *about* law, and within the forms of law, whose continuity can never be fractured without bringing men and women into immediate danger.[127]

Similar themes resonate in Koskenniemi's own support of a culture of formalism. Moreover, in the context of treaty conflicts at least, this book will suggest that several scholarly proposals are less evidence of academic hubris than they are efforts to steer such conflicts onto the terrain of legal discourse. Of course, the law may not prove an adequate medium for the articulation of all perspectives; the chapters on practice will reflect upon the possibilities that adopting a legal mode forecloses even as it advances others.

So this was the liberal assumption – the idealisation of international legal discourse as begetter of the rule of law, coupled with the faith that there is something distinctive about *legal* argument – which comes through even in works by a critical legal studies scholar and a Marxist historian. The book finds this assumption reflected in the works of legal scholars discussed in the following chapters.

Two constructivist understandings

This book also suggests that the view of international law as a broadly conceived legal discourse is supported by constructivist assumptions. It is important not to overstate the constructivist leanings of the scholars whose work is discussed in Chapters 2 and 3, for the application of constructivist theory to international relations and international law came later than many of their works[128] and usually with the warning

[127] *ibid.*, 266.

[128] Leading works include: Kratochwil, *Rules, Norms and Decisions*; N. Onuf, *World of Our Making: Rules and Rule in Social Theory and International Relations* (University of South Carolina Press 1989); N. Onuf, 'The Constitution of International Society' (1994) 5 *European Journal of International Law* 1; E. Adler, 'Seizing the Middle Ground: Constructivism in World Politics' (1997) 3 *European Journal of International Relations* 319; A. Wendt, *Social Theory of International Politics* (Cambridge University Press 1998); J. G. Ruggie, 'What Makes the World Hang Together? Neo-Utilitarianism and the Social Constructivist Challenge' (1998) 52 *International Organization* 855; N. Onuf, 'Constructivism: A User's Manual', in V. Kubálková *et al.* (eds.), *International Relations in a Constructed World* (New York, M. E. Sharpe 1998). Recent works explicitly applying

that there is a vast difference between the impact of their rather dense social relationships upon individuals, and the limited international society upon States.[129] For the same reason, the book does not explore whether these constructivist leanings were justified. Rather, it argues for the possibility that it was by espousing two related understandings, which we might now think of as constructivist, that the scholars examined were able to support their liberal assumption of the importance of legal discourse.

The *first* understanding, to echo Nicholas Onuf's claim about international society, was of the international legal order as both 'a thing *and* a process', such that both (thing and process) act upon each other.[130] Onuf makes an argument for a continuous, two-way process of the mutual constitution of agents and structures: existing structures of social and legal rules constitute actors as agents, who simultaneously and consistently renegotiate those structures.[131] At any time it is possible to take a 'snapshot' of society – but with the dual awareness that the picture is evolving throughout, and that the manner of evolution is tempered by the preceding conditions. Similarly, international legal order: on the one hand its rules constitute States as the key subjects and clarify their rights and obligations at any given time (as well as the capacities of other actors); on the other hand, these rules are constantly renegotiated by the actions of States. Change is continuous, but usually incremental.[132]

This view is reflected in Jutta Brunnée and Stephen Toope's interactional theory of international law,[133] which draws upon Lon Fuller's work.[134] Brunnée and Toope speak of legal norms as 'built, maintained, and sometimes destroyed through a continued *practice* of legality' – a view of agents negotiating and renegotiating structures. But they see existing structures as also determining the capacities of the agents, and

constructivist theory to international law include: A. C. Arend, *Legal Rules and International Society* (Oxford University Press 1999); J. Brunnée and S. Toope, *Legitimacy and Legality in International Law: An Interactional Account* (Cambridge University Press 2010); and A. Sinclair, *International Relations Theory and International Law: A Critical Approach* (Cambridge University Press 2010). The earliest works among these come two decades after the adoption of the Vienna Convention on the Law of Treaties.

129 For instance, Wendt, *Social Theory of International Politics*, 2; Onuf, *A User's Manual*, 62; perhaps also Kratochwil, *Rules, Norms and Decisions* 66–7.

130 Onuf, 'The Constitution of International Society', 1.

131 See also Onuf, *A User's Manual*; Onuf, *World of Our Making*.

132 Onuf, 'The Constitution of International Society', 18–19.

133 Brunnée and Toope, *Legitimacy and Legality*.

134 L. Fuller, *The Morality of Law* (revised edn, Yale University Press 1969); L. Fuller, 'Positivism and Fidelity to Law' (1957) 71 *Harvard Law Review* 630.

controlling which practices are practices of *legality*, in particular by requiring agents to reason about the rules in terms of eight criteria of legality: generality, promulgation, prospectivity, clarity, coherence, stability, not demanding the impossible, and congruence between official action and the declared rules.[135] Theirs, too, then is a view of international law as a thing – verifiable legal rules, identified agents of rule-making, accepted criteria of legality – as well as a process in which agents support and critique the rules by applying these criteria of legality. Of course, over time, both agents and criteria of legality may also undergo change. In Chapters 2 and 3, we will see the espousal of a similar approach by scholars, while Chapters 4 to 6 will show these mutually constitutive effects in practice, elaborating upon the practices that agents draw upon, and engage in, in using and changing international law.

This first understanding should not be taken to reflect a too dynamic view of international legal order, for the *second* constructivist understanding is of the reinforcement of structures amidst change. In Chapters 2 and 3, this translates into the view that using legal discourse as the means for change fosters a culture of respect for international law.

Let me explain this again by reference to Onuf, who offers an anatomy of the constructivist process.[136] He explains that rules – social and legal – provide the link between agents and society: they constitute society and tell us who the agents are and their respective capacities. The ways in which agents deal with rules – follow, adapt, change them – are called practices. Agents undertake these practices to achieve certain outcomes; and, as they do, rules and related practices frequently form stable patterns which we recognise as institutions. As they come into being, institutions further influence agents, for they constitute the environment within which agents decide on their actions. Of course, agents also act upon institutions, 'collectively changing . . . institutional features, and themselves, in the process. Nevertheless, from any agent's point of view, society consists of diverse institutions that seem, for the most part, to be held in place by rules linking them to other institutions.'[137] Finally, 'in a complex world, agents often make choices that have consequences, for themselves and others, that they had not anticipated or do not care very much about. Unintended consequences frequently form stable patterns with respect to their effect on agents. Any stable pattern of rules, institutions, and unintended consequences gives

[135] Brunnée and Toope, *Legitimacy and Legality*, Chapter 1.
[136] Onuf, 'A User's Manual', 59–61. [137] *ibid.*, 61.

society a structure, recognizable as such to any observer.'[138] While all this seems abstract, Onuf is here suggesting that discrete practices take on a pattern and that pattern perpetuates itself by conditioning the responses of agents. Moreover, we might explain how practices develop by referring to the role of ideology – prevailing ideas guide agents in determining their actions;[139] as the ideas become institutionalised, their force is even more determining. The change that happens normally happens within these structures.

Brunnée and Toope's re-articulation of Fuller's concept of 'fidelity' to law may be read as reflecting this understanding. Their emphasis is actually on fidelity to legality – that is, on an attachment to reasoning with norms in terms of the eight criteria that were first listed by Fuller as the desiderata of the inner morality of law.[140] In other words, the process of norm modification by agents (and *vice versa*) is continuous, but the idea that the appropriate practice is to reason with norms in terms of particular criteria becomes entrenched, indeed becomes the structure within which change is sought.

Outline of the chapters

With that, let us turn to the specific chapters. As already mentioned, Chapters 2 and 3 discuss several scholarly proposals to regulate treaty conflict either by way of conflict rules or through institutional action.

Chapter 2 examines the International Law Commission's efforts to draft suitable treaty conflict rules for inclusion in the law of treaties. Focusing on the commentaries and contemporary writings of the main ILC Special Rapporteurs for the topic, Lauterpacht, Gerald Fitzmaurice and Humphrey Waldock, and recalling attention to the particular challenges posed to the codification enterprise in the ILC's early years, the chapter argues that the resulting, much-criticised formula incorporated in Article 30 of the VCLT may be understood actually as part of a project to promote international law by drawing States into legal discourse over the implementation and application of treaties.

[138] *ibid.*

[139] For a discussion of the importance of ideas even in the international system, see Wendt, *Social Theory of International Politics*, Chapters 1 and 3.

[140] Brunnée and Toope, *Legitimacy and Legality*, 21; Fuller, *The Morality of Law*, 46–91.

Chapter 3 explores three proposals as to how international institutions may implement multilateral treaties facing challenges such as those posed by strategically created treaty conflicts. These proposals – Lauterpacht's doctrine of 'approximate application' outlined in his 1956 *South West Africa* separate opinion; Abram and Antonia Chayes' managerial approach set out in their book *The New Sovereignty*; and recent blueprints for treaty coordination and regime interaction advanced by, respectively, Rüdiger Wolfrum and Nele Matz, and Margaret Young, make the similar suggestion that institutions may modify multilateral treaties, without resort to formal processes of amendment, if required in order to effectively implement them. The chapter argues that, despite the obvious differences in time, context and scholarly traditions that characterise these proposals, and their different conceptions of State consent and institutional competence, they too reveal a common view of international law as a discursive practice, and subscribe to liberal and constructivist assumptions.

The three following chapters, 4, 5 and 6, explore the operation of legal discourse in three instances of strategically created treaty conflicts, paying attention to the practices of document rattling and making of legality claims described earlier. Conveniently, these chapters also loosely map on to the modes of institutional action outlined in Chapter 3, allowing further bases for evaluation of those modes.

Chapter 4 examines the conflict between the respective seabed mining regimes embedded in the LOSC, and in the 'Reciprocating States Regime' (RSR) established by eight States in the early 1980s. This conflict, in some sense a tussle over the proper elaboration of the concept of 'the common heritage of mankind', was characterised by deep ideological oppositions between developed and developing, and capitalist and socialist States. It was gradually mediated by exertions of a few States, the LOSC Preparatory Commission, a set of informal consultations convened by the UN Secretary-General and a few key individuals. Relying upon a variety of rarely visited materials – records of the Preparatory Commission and the UN Secretariat, the *travaux préparatoires* of LOSC, G77 records, and records of the US and other governments – the chapter reconstructs the dynamics of the legal discourse over seabed mining around two key moments: the conclusion of the 1987 Midnight Agreement which created a bridge between the two regimes by way of approximate application of the LOSC regime, and the 1994 Implementation Agreement which in effect substantially altered the LOSC regime.

Chapter 5 discusses the Rome Statute/BIAs conflict, drawing upon legal and policy documents produced by various ICC organs, US government materials, materials of the Coalition for the ICC (CICC) and other NGOs, speeches and evaluations of leading scholars who played a major role both in creating and critiquing the ICC, UN records, and interviews conducted with officials from each key organ of the Court and the Legal Advisors of CICC and the American Coalition for the ICC. It offers an account of how ICC organs, and particularly the Office of the Prosecutor, have responded discursively to the challenge posed to the Court by the United States, in two key phases: an initial phase in which they sought to bring the Court into operation by acquiring their first cases; and a later phase following the referral of Darfur, Sudan, in which they sought to respond to the critiques of the policies that had so far been followed. There are parallels between the role played by the Court organs and the managerial approach outlined by Chayes and Chayes.

Chapter 6 explores the conflict between the India–US Nuclear Deal and the NPT-based nuclear-governance regime, locating the Deal as falling initially within a broader US-led effort to decentre the NPT in the nuclear-governance regime in favour of informal networks, but being gradually adapted – in the course of long (though ad hoc) discursive process of seeking approvals from the International Atomic Energy Agency (IAEA), the Nuclear Suppliers Group (NSG), the US Congress and the Indian Parliament – in ways that brought it in greater coordination with the NPT regime. In making this argument, Chapter 6 draws on NPT preparatory materials and records of its Review Conferences; primary materials relating to the Deal; IAEA and NSG records; US and Indian government documents; policy analyses, news reports and NGO reports; and interviews with people connected with the US–India strategic dialogue and with the former editor of a leading Indian newspaper who had personally covered the passage of the Deal.

Chapter 7, finally, draws together the discussion in the foregoing chapters, and returns to the question of how we might use strategically created treaty conflicts as context in which to explore the politics of international law.

PART I
International law thought

2 Writing the 'principle of political decision' into the law of treaties

> Even if the view is to be accepted – and it may be readily accepted – that the social ideal is not law, but justice, there still remains the fact that ultimately law is the more effective guarantee of securing that end.
>
> In order to endow law with the maximum of effectiveness it is necessary to provide means for the change of law . . . [I]n a large number of cases it is through law that the change of law will be most conveniently effected.
>
> Hersch Lauterpacht[1]

Introduction

The International Law Commission ('Commission' or ILC) commenced its work in April 1949, and drafted the Vienna Convention on the Law of Treaties (VCLT) in its early phase, that is, in the 1950s and 1960s. These years were times of both expectation and anxiety. On the one hand, the Commission was established in the context of the re-emerging idea that international relations must be founded on law. The UN Charter, adopted in 1945, outlawed the use of force and stipulated peaceful settlement of international disputes. The establishment of the Bretton Woods monetary system and the General Agreement on Tariffs and Trade juridified – or at least institutionalised – economic relations between States. Various efforts were initiated to outline new obligations for States in areas such as the use of the high seas, atomic energy and nuclear weapons, prevention and punishment of war crimes and crimes against humanity, to name a few. The Commission, drawing upon the recommendations of the UN

[1] H. Lauterpacht, *The Function of Law in the International Community* (Oxford University Press 2011 [1933]) 354.

Secretariat,[2] undertook to codify and progressively develop the law on several fundamental topics: treaties, State responsibility, immunities of States and diplomats, nationality, *et cetera*. Its work on these 'essential building blocks'[3] was in seeming fulfilment of the expectation that international lawyers could supply the 'fifth element' – the *quintessence* – of the post-war international legal system in the form of 'a well-developed body of law'.[4]

On the other hand, there were looming memories of legal overreach in the inter-war period, including failure of the Hague Codification Conference; the context of the Cold War contributed to doubts about the possibility of addressing difficult political issues through international law; it was feared that the Commission could do no more than reproduce, to the disservice of international law, the rigidity and hyper-formalism that had characterised international law doctrine in previous years.[5] The establishment of the Commission was accompanied by suggestions that it be disbanded; more moderate advice was that it should focus on some 'easy and unimportant' topic, like 'piracy'.[6]

The law of treaties was not such a topic: it was important and difficult; despite earlier codification efforts,[7] there was little clarity on several matters. The issue of treaty conflict, demanding conceptual and empirical engagement with the relationship between international law and politics, was amongst the most prominent unresolved questions. As this chapter will explain, the Commission recognised that a number of conflicts involved treaties with non-identical parties, as also that many were strategically created by States. The Commission's materials convey that it perceived the difficulties of legally regulating these conflicts. But it

[2] 'Survey of International Law in Relation to the Work of Codification of the International Law Commission: Preparatory Work Within the Purview of Article 18, Paragraph 1, of the Statute of the International Law Commission', Memorandum submitted by the UN Secretary-General, A/CN.4/1/Rev.1, 1949.

[3] T. Franck and M. ElBaradei, 'The Codification and Progressive Development of International Law: A UNITAR Study of the Role and Use of the International Law Commission' (1982) 76 *American Journal of International Law* 630, 631.

[4] C. Hurst, 'A Plea for the Codification of International Law on New Lines' (1946) 32 *Transactions of the Grotius Society* 135, 136–7. See the section entitled 'International law as an ILC project', below.

[5] For discussion and references, see the section entitled 'International law as an ILC project', below.

[6] R. Y. Jennings, 'The Progressive Development of International Law and its Codification' (1947) 24 *British Yearbook of International Law* 301, 324–5.

[7] For instance, J. Garner, 'Harvard Research in International Law: Draft Convention on the Law of Treaties' (1935) 29 *American Journal of International Law Supplement* 1024.

perceived, too, the impossibility of ignoring them. Beginning with the second Special Rapporteur on treaties, Hersch Lauterpacht, ILC members considered it imperative for international law's authority that it effectively regulate even politically charged treaty conflicts. Further, it was requisite that the method of regulation take into account the competing pressures of stability and change. The various proposals that ILC members developed to this end reveal much about their conceptions of international law, and about its proper, and possible, role in international relations.

Outline of the argument

The ILC's final formulation appears as VCLT Article 30, which states:

Article 30 Application of successive treaties relating to the same subject matter

1. Subject to Article 103 of the Charter of the United Nations, the rights and obligations of States parties . . . shall be determined in accordance with the following paragraphs.
2. When a treaty specifies that it is subject to, or that it is not to be considered as incompatible with, an earlier or later treaty, the provisions of that other treaty prevail.
3. When all the parties to the earlier treaty are parties also to the later treaty . . . the earlier treaty applies only to the extent that its provisions are compatible with those of the later treaty.
4. When the parties to the later treaty do not include all the parties to the earlier one:
   a. as between States parties to both treaties the same rule applies as in paragraph 3;
   b. as between a State party to both treaties and a State party to only one of the treaties, the treaty to which both States are parties governs their mutual rights and obligations.
5. Paragraph 4 is without prejudice to article 41, or to any question of the termination or suspension of the operation of a treaty under article 60 or to any question of responsibility which may arise for a State from the conclusion or application of a treaty, the provisions of which are incompatible with its obligations towards another State under another treaty.

Several legal scholars have described this provision as a disappointing and 'mechanistic' rule which provides little meaningful guidance on resolving treaty conflicts.[8] This chapter offers a more nuanced reading

[8] See G. Fox, 'International Organizations: Conflicts of International Law' (2001) 95 *ASIL Proceedings* 183, 186.

of its promise and limits, and of what the ILC sought to achieve through this formulation. It recognises that, as a set of rules to *resolve* treaty conflict, Article 30, especially paragraphs (4) and (5) on treaties with non-identical parties, is indeed inadequate. But it may be misleading to evaluate these provisions as conflict rules. They serve other purposes: at the simplest, they are closure rules, that is, they paper over a possible gap in law relating to the consequences of treaty conflict for rights and obligations of States party to the treaties.[9] More impressively – and some ILC members supported this view – they may operate as steering provisions, that is, provisions that encourage States to resort to legal discourse to calibrate their rights, interests, expectations and obligations. Read historically, they may be perceived as part of an ILC effort to build respect for international law. In this sense, these rules reveal a 'project' of international law that informed the work of the early ILC.

The chapter makes the above points through a layered analysis of the textual, conceptual and historical dimensions of Article 30. The latter two complicate the evaluation suggested by textual analysis alone. On a first reading, the text of Article 30 suggests a reductive view of treaty conflict in which significance is attached only to the breach of treaty obligations owed to States. Moreover, in practice it may only benefit (powerful) States that deliberately use the device of treaty conflict to challenge or change an existing legal state of affairs. Yet, this provision was not adopted in a hurry: the ILC finalised it after several iterations and deliberations over nearly two decades, and with attention to the difficulties of regulating politically charged treaty conflicts. This alone would beg closer engagement with the conceptual and historical influences upon the Commission's thought.

A conceptual exploration is accomplished in Jan Klabbers' recent monograph, *Treaty Conflict and the European Union.*[10] In this book, Klabbers describes Article 30(4)(b) as 'the principle of political decision',[11] a phrase he translates from Manfred Zuleeg's 1977 work.[12] This provision, Klabbers argues, is the only possible response to conflict between treaties with non-identical parties, because alternative formulae

[9] I am grateful to Professor Guglielmo Verdirame for suggesting the phrase 'closure rules'.

[10] J. Klabbers, *Treaty Conflicts and the European Union* (Cambridge University Press 2009).

[11] *ibid.*, 88.

[12] M. Zuleeg, 'Vertragskonkurrenz in Völkerrecht Teil I: Verträge zwischen souveränen Staaten' (1977) 20 *German Yearbook of International Law* 246.

are incompatible with fundamental principles of international order. Moreover, Article 30 is also the most appropriate provision, for it provides space for 'responsive politics'.[13] But Klabbers does not fully develop this argument, for he does not clarify whether he considers that the provision merely permits 'responsive politics' or also influences the dynamics of treaty conflict. This chapter develops the argument between these two possibilities, noting ways in which Article 30 might promote responsive politics.

The conceptual explanation, however, is only part of the story, for there are several explanations of the purpose that Article 30 was intended to serve. Guyora Binder's excellent and overlooked 1989 study implies that, by the mid-1960s, the Commission members did not wish to provide a more determinate conflict rule because their philosophy of international law differed from that of their predecessors.[14] In Binder's view, a comparison of Article 30 with previous drafts evidences their respective authors' differing conceptions of the appropriate relationship between State sovereignty and international order. He states that Article 30 is a 'licence to breach' that emanates from the value some ILC members placed upon State autonomy, and from their doubts about the efficacy and legitimacy of international law. But this may be a misreading of the ILC's work. This chapter offers a different explanation for the rule finally adopted. It draws upon the Commission's materials on treaty conflict, particularly commentaries prepared by the three ILC Special Rapporteurs on the topic, Sir Hersch Lauterpacht, Sir Gerald Fitzmaurice and Sir Humphrey Waldock. Based on these materials, read with contemporaneous writings by Lauterpacht, Fitzmaurice and Waldock, it argues that ILC members preferred a provision enabling States to restate their treaty claims in legal terms to one that would definitively decide the outcomes of treaty conflict. Further, it proposes as the ground for this preference the early Commission's opinion that the former would steer States towards legal discourse while an overly decisive provision might simply be disregarded.

[13] Klabbers, *Treaty Conflicts and the European Union*, 90.

[14] G. Binder, *Treaty Conflict and Political Contradiction: The Dialectic of Duplicity* (New York, Praeger 1989). Major works on treaty conflict that do not cite Binder include: J. Pauwelyn, *Conflict of Norms in Public International Law: How WTO Law Relates to Other Rules of International Law* (Cambridge University Press 2003); R. Wolfrum and N. Matz, *Conflicts in International Environmental Law* (London, Springer 2003); and S.A. Sadat-Akhavi, *Methods of Resolving Conflict between Treaties* (Leiden, Martinus Nijhoff 2003).

The chapter then argues that this opinion of the early Commission reflects its embrace of liberal and constructivist assumptions. The constructivist assumption is implicit in their expectation that encouraging States to engage via legal discourse would gradually promote acceptance of international law as the appropriate medium for pursuit of various interests. The liberal assumption is implicit in the view that such encouragement would promote the rule of law in international relations, and lead to more appropriate outcomes to treaty conflict. Drawing upon Michel de Certeau's strategy/tactics distinction,[15] the chapter argues that Article 30 may be evaluated as part of an ILC strategy for building respect for international law.

This alternative explanation of the Commission's choices and the assumptions implicit in them is a challenge to Binder's in several respects. In contrast to Binder's focus on the difference in the approaches adopted by groups of ILC members, it points to their shared project and similar embrace of liberal and constructivist assumptions. Unlike Binder's explanation of the various ILC proposals being founded upon their authors' differing philosophical standpoints on the proper relationship between State sovereignty and international law, the alternative explanation roots these proposals in a common historical context of anxiety and expectation about the *possible* role of international law. Finally, departing from Binder's evaluation of Article 30 as a 'licence to breach', it suggests that Article 30 was grounded on a subtle conception of the ways in which international law infiltrates international politics. With that, let us turn to the first, textual, reading.

VCLT Article 30 and its discontents

On a textual reading, paragraphs (1) and (2) of VCLT Article 30 provide for the overriding priority of the UN Charter and of *non-obstante* provisions that may be found in either of the conflicting treaties. The third paragraph deals with situations of treaty conflict in which all the parties to the earlier treaty (say A, B and C) are also party to the later (becoming, say, A, B, C and D). For these, it recommends the application of the *lex posterior* principle, that is, for the treaty later in time to prevail. Paragraph 4(a) relates to treaty conflicts where parties to the later treaty (A and B) are a subset of the parties to the earlier (A, B and C). Normally,

[15] M. de Certeau, *The Practice of Everyday Life* (S. Randall (trans.), University of California Press 1984) xix, 34–9.

in such cases too, between that subset of parties (A and B), the *lex posterior* rule applies, unless the earlier treaty had forbidden its parties from entering into an inconsistent later treaty, or unless the later treaty would infringe on the rights of other parties (C) to the earlier treaty, or derogate from a provision essential to the earlier treaty's object and purpose.[16] Paragraph(4)(b) addresses conflicts between treaties with non-identical parties (A, B and A, C) providing, in effect, that each treaty remains valid and effective between its parties.

The implication of Article 30(4)(b) is that a State (A) party to two conflicting treaties may find it necessary to determine how best to comply with its commitments to both; when this is not possible, it would 'simply have to choose which one to honour'.[17] The decision would not be without cost to such State for, as paragraph (5) recognises, State responsibility will arise in case the conclusion or application of one treaty results in a breach of obligations towards another State under another treaty. By referring to Article 60, paragraph (5) also notes the possibility of termination or suspension of one or both of the treaties.

Article 30 can be criticised on two grounds: first, that it takes a reductive view of treaty conflict; and, second, that it does not offer any direction on which of the conflicting treaties should take priority.

A reductive view of treaty conflict

Article 30 takes a reductive view of treaty conflict in that it seems concerned only with situations where a State's conclusion or application of one treaty leads to breach of its obligation towards another State under another treaty. Paragraph (5), in referring to State responsibility, ignores breaches of obligations owed to, or infringements of rights conferred upon other actors. It also excludes situations where one treaty impairs the object and purpose of another without breaching any specific obligation.

May Article 30(5) be read more expansively to include the latter situation? The ILC Articles on State Responsibility merely indicate that there is a breach of obligation when an act is 'not in conformity with what is required … by that obligation';[18] they do not demand that the

[16] This follows from the reference to Article 41 in Article 30(5).
[17] Klabbers, *Treaty Conflicts and the European Union*, 88.
[18] Article 12, Articles on Responsibility of States for Internationally Wrongful Acts, 2001, annexed to UNGA Res. 56/83 (12 December 2001). See also J. Crawford, *The International Law Commission's Articles on State Responsibility: Introduction, Text and Commentaries* (Cambridge University Press 2002) 124–30, 191–241, 254–63, 276–80.

obligation must be one specifically undertaken in a treaty. Is it worth considering whether an argument can be made that conduct not breaching a specific treaty obligation may still violate the treaty's object and purpose, thus breaching a more general obligation of good faith (spelt out in VCLT Articles 18, 26 and 31)?

The International Court of Justice's (ICJ) jurisprudence in *Nicaragua* suggests this argument would not receive much encouragement. Though the Court attributed such a claim to Nicaragua without clarifying their view of it,[19] Judges Oda and Jennings rejected this possibility. Judge Oda argued that the VCLT's references to 'object and purpose' related to the duty not to breach a specific provision essential to the fulfilment of the treaty's object and purpose. Therefore, the Court could not 'scrutinize any act remotely describable as inimical to the object and purpose of the treaty in question'.[20] Judge Jennings was blunt in his agreement: 'Either [the] acts are breaches of some provision ... or they have nothing to do with the [t]reaty. The "object and purpose" of a treaty cannot be a concept existing independently of any of its terms.'[21]

There may, however, be conflicts where the contradiction lies precisely between the objects and purposes of the treaties, even if this contradiction does not translate into a necessary breach of a specific obligation owed to another State under either treaty. This situation may arise where one of the treaties is only concluded to provide a specific right or establish a regime, or to promote a goal – objects and purposes which may not obligate a State (and may be set aside in favour of other treaty obligations), but which may have great contextual significance. The UN Framework Convention on Climate Change is one such example: since it does not impose specific obligations on States, its parties may continuously subordinate it to their other treaty obligations, but that would hardly be a desirable outcome.

Even Judge Oda, in denying that legal consequences can follow even if there is no breach of a treaty provision, noted that he did not 'condon[e] or minimiz[e] the gravity of any action which does in fact thwart the purpose of a treaty'.[22] A more expansive view of treaty conflict, then, is appropriate, but does not find expression in Article 30.

[19] *Military and Paramilitary Activities in and against Nicaragua (Nicaragua v. United States)* (1986) ICJ Rep 14, para. 270.

[20] *Nicaragua*, Dissenting Opinion of Judge Oda (1986) ICJ Rep 212, para 80.

[21] *Nicaragua*, Dissenting Opinion of Judge Jennings (1986) ICJ Rep 528, 542.

[22] *Nicaragua*, Dissenting Opinion of Judge Oda, para 82.

No fetters on the exercise of political decision

A second criticism is that Article 30(4)(b) offers no direction on which of the conflicting treaties should have priority. In this respect, it is unlike the VCLT provisions for conflict between treaties with identical parties or where one treaty is concluded between a subset of the parties to the other. For instance, Article 41(1) provides that a subset of the States party to one treaty may conclude another treaty between themselves (*inter se*) to modify the first only if this is permitted by the first treaty or, if not provided for, is not prohibited and does not affect the rights enjoyed by other parties under that treaty nor derogate from its object and purpose. While there is some ambiguity about the legal consequences that will follow if the *inter se* treaty fails these conditions – is it thereby invalidated or merely subordinated? – the suggestion that such a treaty's effectiveness is contingent, not absolute, remains an affirmation of the earlier treaty.

Omitting such specific directions, Article 30(4)(b) also does not adopt any legal principle that weights the choice in favour of either treaty by making one contingent on the other, or by distinguishing them by the gravity of the interests they protect. Nor does it endorse as generally preeminent any principle connected to the time of conclusion of treaties (*lex prior*, *lex posterior*) or subject-matter (*lex specialis*).[23] In all fairness, there is no accepted hierarchy between these principles in general international law. They provide arguments in favour of one or the other of the treaties, but may also work at cross-purposes. Ultimately, the choice to be made by a State party to the conflicting treaties is unguided by principle, and is thus a political choice.[24]

Given this lack of guidance, to describe political decision-making as a 'principle', like Klabbers does, may seem a legal sleight-of-hand, reminiscent of formalistic arguments against gaps in international law. In *Lotus*,[25] the Permanent Court of International Justice (PCIJ) suggested the logical impossibility of gaps because 'whatever is not prohibited by

[23] In any case, it is not clear how *lex posterior* or *specialis* would apply in conflicts between treaties with non-identical parties. See ILC, 'Report of Study Group on Fragmentation', 62 (para. 113), 125 (para. 243).

[24] The exception is where one treaty contains *jus cogens* principles that are affected by the treaty conflict. In such a case, the State must honour this treaty, and the other will be regarded as void.

[25] *SS Lotus (France* v. *Turkey)* (1927) PCIJ Series A, No. 10, 4.

international law is permitted',[26] thus transforming the absence of a rule into the presence of a closure rule: if the law does not regulate, it permits, not just as a matter of fact but of principle; the legal system is therefore complete.[27] Is the description of Article 30(4)(b) as the principle of political decision similarly based on a formalistic approach?[28]

That, however, is not the substance of Klabbers' defence of this provision.

Explaining the principle of political decision

Klabbers offers three justifications for Article 30(4)(b). The first is that the rule adopted in this provision is the only one compatible with basic principles of the international order. The second is that the rule deserves respect because of its inclusion in the VCLT. The third is the most interesting, and suggests that Article 30(4)(b) offers a platform for responsive politics.

Compatibility with fundamental principles

Klabbers outlines four relevant fundamental principles of international legal order: States' freedom to contract with each other; *pacta sunt servanda*, or that States should observe their agreements in good faith; *res inter alios acta*, or that each agreement is only effective as between its parties; and *pacta tertiis nec nocent nec prosunt*, or that no treaty may create obligations for a third State without its consent.[29] These principles tend

[26] P. Weil, 'Non Liquet Revisited' (1998) 36 *Columbia Journal of Transnational Law* 109, 112.

[27] This 'logical' approach to completeness is different from the view in which the international legal system is complete as 'an *a priori* assumption about every system of law, not a prescription of positive law': Lauterpacht, *The Function of Law in the International Community*, 72. According to Lauterpacht, while there may be gaps in statutory or customary law, there are no gaps in the legal system as a whole. In the absence of clear rules, a judge is bound to decide cases before him using analogies, general principles of law, balancing and teleological interpretation. See also M. Koskenniemi, 'The Function of Law in the International Community: 75 Years After' (2008) 79 *British Yearbook of International Law* 353, 359–60.

[28] However, it would be unfair to compare the principle of political decision to a formal dismissal of '*non liquet*', if *non liquet* was what the ICJ pronounced in its *Nuclear Weapons* Advisory Opinion. There, the Court felt unable to decide whether it would, ultimately, be lawful or unlawful for a State to use nuclear weapons 'in an extreme circumstance of self-defense' ((1996) ICJ Rep 226, 263, 266). Article 30(5) does not put the unlawfulness of a State's assuming conflicting obligations in doubt; though this does not imply that either treaty is invalidated as a result.

[29] Klabbers, *Treaty Conflicts and the European Union*, 99–100.

to contradict each other when applied to conflicts between treaties with non-identical parties.

While States' freedom to contract is an aspect of their sovereignty, *pacta sunt servanda* (per Hans Kelsen) is the basic customary norm that underpins the legally binding character of treaties.[30] Citing this norm, the VCLT provides in Article 26 that 'Every treaty in force is binding upon the parties to it and must be performed by them in good faith'. However, this does not imply that States must restrict their treaty-making capacities in deference to existing treaties; the VCLT also gives expression to the *pacta tertiis* and *res inter alios acta* principles, which are both aspects of the concept of privity. *Pacta tertiis* implies that a State may not cite its treaty commitments under one treaty as a reason for altering or abridging its commitments under another. *Res inter alios acta* guarantees that each treaty is valid between the States party to it. Thus, a conflict rule can only provide, as Article 30(5) does, that States party to one treaty can invoke State responsibility if that treaty is breached as the result of the conclusion or application of another treaty.

Indeed, as also noted in Chapter 1, even a provision encouraging harmonious interpretation of two conflicting treaties could violate the *pacta tertiis* and *res inter alios acta* principles. As Klabbers explains, by reference to Zuleeg's work, 'harmonisation'

> will normally entail that one treaty will be brought into line with the other. But on what basis can an objective decision be made to interpret treaty A so as to accommodate treaty B, rather than the other way round? Doing so goes (in abstract, at any rate) against the interests of parties to A that are not parties to B, and therewith stumbles, once again, on the idea that treaties are ever so many *res inter alios acta*.[31]

Thus, Klabbers says 'the resort to the principle of political decision is well-nigh inescapable'.[32]

Imprimatur of the VCLT

Klabbers' second justification is that the principle of political decision is 'after all, the Vienna Convention's formula, and for that reason alone is

30 H. Kelsen, *Pure Theory of Law* (M. Knight (trans.), University of California Press 1967) 216.
31 Zuleeg, 'Vertragskonkurrenz in Völkerrecht', in Klabbers, *Treaty Conflicts and the European Union*, 89.
32 Klabbers, *ibid.*, 98.

authoritative ... [I]t carries the stamp of approval which inclusion in the Convention entails.'[33]

This is unsatisfactory at first sight. If the principle is criticised because it does not provide a solution to treaty conflict, then to argue that it deserves respect because of inclusion in the VCLT appears too formalistic. Klabbers himself refers to Sir Ian Sinclair's view that Article 30 'is in many respects not entirely satisfactory', but '[p]erhaps little harm has been done so long as the Convention rules are regarded as residuary in character'.[34] Sinclair thus suggests that Article 30 can be regarded positively so long as it is not actually taken as authoritative. Gregory Fox too has described Article 30(4)(b) as an 'approach out of place in a world of proliferating legislative treaties', unable to comprehend 'the issues actually involved in conflict' and 'the interests evident (or not evident) in both treaty regimes in having their rules applied'.[35] Should such a rule be accorded respect only because it appears in a key formal document?

Despite the arguments in these chapters against the above proposition, the principle does acquire a certain resonance from its context and background, as I will discuss. Given his own discussion of the history of Article 30, perhaps Klabbers too is pointing us towards appreciation of the same.

A space for responsive politics

Klabbers' third justification is the most interesting. Contrary to Fox, who describes Article 30(4)(b) as 'a mechanistic rule that wholly ignores the substantive claims at issue', Klabbers argues that it appeals because it 'avoids all the drawbacks of a single, more determinate rule'. *Lex posterior* 'risks sacrificing normative instruments on the altar of later departures'; *lex prior* 'does the same in reverse, and interferes ... with the progressive development of international law'; and, as to *lex specialis*, 'the distinction between special versus general treaties is itself hopelessly uncertain'. In contrast, the principle of political decision

> allows states and in particular decision-makers (think of judges) to choose the treaty they deem the most worthy in the circumstances ... What is more, it allows others to pressure the state or the tribunal concerned into making the right choice: human rights advocates, for example, may use the principle of political

33 *ibid.*, 89–90.

34 I. Sinclair, *The Vienna Convention on the Law of Treaties* (Manchester University Press 1984) 98.

35 Fox, 'International Organizations', 186.

decision in advocating that in a conflict between a human rights convention and another treaty, the state concerned ought to give preference to the human rights treaty ... [I]t is precisely the indeterminacy of the principle of political decision that allows for flexible and responsive politics and makes it possible for society at large ... to participate in international decision-making processes.[36]

One calls to mind Shabtai Rosenne's observation that in many cases, '[t]he most that the law might be able to do would be to ... give diplomacy and political acumen the necessary breathing space'.[37] Klabbers seems to suggest that Article 30(4) may be read as a provision doing precisely this.

The key question is whether the justification is that the article merely permits 'flexible and responsive politics', or whether it facilitates such politics in response to treaty conflict. This is an important distinction. If it merely permits, then we return to the objection that it is no more than a closure rule. The principle has greater normative value if it can be argued that it exercises some influence on the mediation of treaty conflict.

The basis for such a claim deserves consideration. It may be argued that the principle is to be justified primarily because, against attempts to 'finally' 'resolve' conflicts by judicial balancing, or institutional compromise, it confirms a continuing 'right of contest' of States party to both treaties on the premise of both treaties having validity and effective applicability. This is important because it reminds us of legal entitlements that may be overlooked in practice. For instance, Klabbers shows that the European Court of Justice (ECJ, now the Court of Justice of the European Union, or CJEU) disregards the principle of political decision, so that in a conflict between European Union Treaties and other treaties concluded with non-members, the EU Treaties always prevail.[38] In contrast, Article 30(4) reminds us that an ECJ decision is not a final pronouncement on the rights of all parties to both treaties. Parties to the non-EU treaty retain the capacity to insist upon its performance, perhaps even to go to another court to secure normative backing for its priority. In sum, Article 30(4) is a reminder that, in international law, there cannot be an *ex parte* determination of the rights and duties of States.

Article 30(4) may also have a role in the context of treaty harmonisation.[39] While parties to conflicting treaties may be pressured to agree to

[36] Klabbers, *Treaty Conflicts and the European Union*, 90.

[37] S. Rosenne, *Breach of Treaty* (Cambridge, Grotius 1985) 107.

[38] Klabbers, *Treaty Conflicts and the European Union*, 226.

[39] For instance, Wolfrum and Matz, *Conflicts in International Environmental Law*. See also Chapter 3.

all sorts of compromises in practice, in law they are not obliged to give consideration to a conflicting treaty. This formal guarantee may be significant in the course of their negotiations. Underlying a move for compromise will be the awareness that treaty parties could instead insist upon performance of commitments owed to them (or compensation, or termination of the treaty); to some extent, this formal guarantee places treaty parties on a level playing field, where the games of coordination can unfold.

Article 30(4) has implications, ultimately, for the integrity of treaties. It preserves a core substantive validity of each treaty. In its absence, all conflicting treaties could only have relative validity, depending upon the current relative importance of *leges posterior*, *prior*, *specialis* and *superior* as normative ordering principles; and their own relative later, earlier, special or superior qualities. The effect of Article 30(4) is to limit these 'principles' to policy arguments.

Much of this is implicit in Klabbers' work though absent in his overt discussion. The reason, probably, is that Klabbers deals with this principle in a sequential way, considering it activated as a residual rule, failing the application of heuristic devices such as 'the more favourable provision' or 'maximum effectiveness',[40] or practices of coordination or assurance,[41] or avoidance strategies such as conflict clauses, or judicial techniques to define conflicts away. However, the intrinsic substantive validity confirmed by this provision may regulate even the application of these devices. They are invoked and applied in the knowledge that they cannot overcome the legal entitlements of States parties to such treaties; and any move for reconciliation, coordination or avoidance can thus only have traction if presented in a legally significant way. These factors might then contribute to a more flexible and responsive politics.

A caveat on stability and change

Apart from providing for State responsibility for breaches of obligation, Article 30 does not dictate the manner of exercise of political decision. It is thus outcome-neutral, indicating no preference for the substantive values contained in the treaties.

Against appearances, however, Article 30 carries embedded elements of change and stability that reflect the substantive implications of treaty conflict. The dynamic element of Article 30(4) is its recognising as valid a

[40] For a discussion, see Sadat-Akhavi, *Methods of Resolving Conflict between Treaties*.

[41] Discussed in Borgen, 'Resolving Treaty Conflicts'.

treaty which conflicts with an earlier treaty. In other words, it accepts that the international legal order is constantly in flux, continuously open to renegotiation. Its integral element consists in the confirmation that each treaty continues to govern the rights and obligations of its parties, and must thus be carried out in good faith. This may level the playing field for political negotiation.

But Article 30 does not necessarily preserve the effective application of the earlier treaty in the face of a new-made conflicting legality. The impact of the two elements of the Article – the dynamic and the integral – is thus not equal. In some sense, while Article 30 stems the decay of existing treaties, it legitimates (and gives a fillip to) new ones; therefore, perhaps it is not quite neutral when it comes to a choice between the values of stability and change.

Competing philosophies of international law?[42]

This section explores two explanations of how and why the ILC came to adopt the current formulation of Article 30. The first explanation is that advanced by Binder. The second offers an alternative explanation.

The section begins with an overview of the variety of treaty conflict rules that were developed by ILC members, especially the second, third and fourth Special Rapporteurs on treaties – Lauterpacht, Gerald Fitzmaurice and Humphrey Waldock. Waldock also served as 'Expert Consultant' to the Vienna Conference (convened to adopt the Commission's draft of the VCLT) and its Committee of the Whole. The ILC's first Special Rapporteur on treaties, J. L. Brierly, did not take up the issue of treaty conflict. In the course of their discussions other ILC members also expressed their views on the proper scope of Article 30. Altogether, the Commission's records reveal how difficult it was to achieve an appropriate formula for treaty conflicts, particularly those involving non-identical States parties.

Previous formulations

Lauterpacht, Fitzmaurice and Waldock presented multiple reports on the issue of treaty conflicts, and they each outlined more than one formula for dealing with that issue. The ILC intensively debated

[42] A version of the argument developed in this section and the next appears in S. Ranganathan, 'Between Philosophy and Anxiety? The Early International Law Commission, Treaty Conflict and the Project of International Law' (2012) 83 *British Yearbook of International Law* 82.

Waldock's proposal, which the Drafting Committee further modified before recommending it to the UN Conference on Treaties. Detailed summaries of these proposals may be found elsewhere.[43] My discussion focuses on the links between these proposals, in terms of the challenges they all recognised treaty conflicts as posing.

Lauterpacht wrote two reports, in which he provided a general 'invalidity' rule but – and the second report tends more to this – with a heavily qualified application.[44] He suggested that a treaty was *voided* where its 'performance involves a breach of a treaty obligation previously undertaken by one or more of the contracting parties', but only if the breach would 'interfere seriously with the interests of the other parties to that treaty or seriously impair an essential aspect of the original purpose of the treaty'.[45] He believed that many treaty conflicts would be deliberate, and provided that a party to solely the later treaty would be entitled to damages only if it were unaware of its treaty's conflict with any earlier treaty undertaken by its co-parties. Lauterpacht also recognised that his invalidity clause should not impede multilateralism – and included several exceptions that confirmed the validity of multilateral treaties even if these were in serious conflict with previous treaties.

Fitzmaurice substituted Lauterpacht's invalidity rule with a 'priority' rule that favoured the earlier treaty.[46] Less certain than Lauterpacht about the preponderance of deliberate treaty conflicts, he shifted the burden of proof for compensation: States party to the later treaty would be entitled to compensation *unless* aware of the conflict with the earlier. He distinguished situations where the later treaty was an *inter se* agreement amongst some parties to the earlier treaty from situations where the later treaty included States not party to the earlier treaty. In the former case, the later treaty would be invalidated where the earlier treaty prohibited conclusion of inconsistent treaties or where the later treaty required parties to take 'action in direct breach of their

[43] See, for instance, Klabbers, *Treaty Conflicts and the European Union*; Borgen, 'Resolving Treaty Conflicts'; Binder, *Treaty Conflict and Political Contradiction*.

[44] See ILC, First Report on the Law of Treaties by H. Lauterpacht, Special Rapporteur, A/CN.4/63 (1953) *ILC Yearbook*, Vol. II, 156; ILC, Second Report on the Law of Treaties by H. Lauterpacht, Special Rapporteur, A/CN.4/87 and Corr.1 (1954) *ILC Yearbook*, Vol. II, 133.

[45] ILC, Second Report on the Law of Treaties by H. Lauterpacht, Special Rapporteur, A/CN.4/87 and Corr.1 (1954) *ILC Yearbook*, Vol. II, 133.

[46] ILC, Third Report on the Law of Treaties by G. Fitzmaurice, Special Rapporteur, A/CN.4/101 (1958) *ILC Yearbook*, Vol. II, 27.

obligations under the earlier one'.[47] The latter case would be governed by the priority rule, unless it involved a 'special' treaty. Fitzmaurice distinguished two types of 'special' treaties from the general category of 'reciprocal' ones. While reciprocal treaties were conglomerates of bilateral obligations, special treaties were either *integral*, in which 'the force of the obligation is self-existent, absolute and inherent for each party, and not dependent on a corresponding performance by the others'; or *interdependent*, in which 'a fundamental breach ... by one party will justify a corresponding non-performance generally by the other parties, and not merely a non-performance in their relations with the defaulting party'.[48] He suggested that a treaty which conflicted in a material particular with such special treaties would be void.

Waldock further refined Fitzmaurice's priority thesis. Revising his own initial proposal,[49] he suggested that as between a State party to both treaties and a State party only to the earlier treaty, the earlier treaty should prevail; as between States parties to both treaties, the later treaty should prevail; and, as between a State party to both treaties and a State party only to the later treaty, the later treaty should prevail, unless that State was aware that the earlier treaty was in force.[50] In this case (where a State party to the later treaty was aware of its conflict with an earlier one), the later treaty should not be invalidated, but its members should not be entitled to demand its specific enforcement or damages for non-performance. Thus, Waldock entirely omitted the invalidity rule.

Later, based on discussions of the plenary, he removed the good-faith clause pertaining to the knowledge of earlier treaty, as also the suggestion that either treaty 'prevails' with respect to the other,[51] bringing us to the current formula in VCLT Article 30.

Indicative of complete philosophies of international law ...

These formulations reveal a pattern of departures between the approach of each Special Rapporteur and his immediate predecessor. Lauterpacht, for instance, took a different view from that articulated in

[47] *ibid.*, 27 (Article 18). [48] *ibid.*, 27 (Article 19).

[49] ILC, Second Report on the Law of Treaties by H. Waldock, Special Rapporteur, A/CN.4/156 and Add.1–3 (1963) *ILC Yearbook*, Vol. II, Article 14, 53.

[50] ILC, Third Report on the Law of Treaties by H. Waldock, Special Rapporteur, A/CN.4/167 and Add.1–3 (1964) *ILC Yearbook*, Vol. II, Article 65, 34.

[51] Summary Record of the 755th Mtg of the ILC, A/CN.4/SR.755 (30 June 1964) 2.

James Garner's 1935 Harvard Draft,[52] and in scholarly papers by Hans Aufricht,[53] and Wilfred Jenks,[54] that were published around the same time as his first report. Fitzmaurice departed from the position taken by Lauterpacht. Waldock departed from Fitzmaurice's position. The ILC adopted a rule that was, again, different. This was despite claims by all that they furthered the logic of their predecessors, and despite their reliance on the same sources: nineteenth and early twentieth-century scholarship and a few judicial decisions.[55] How can we account for these departures? Binder offers one explanation:

> The [view that the later treaty is void] is derived from a conception of treaties as a source of property rights, while the second view [that the earlier treaty takes priority] derives from a conception of treaties as a source of more limited liability rights. These opposed conceptions of treaty rights emanate in turn from contradictory conceptions of the relationships between sovereignty and the international legal order. If treaty rights are rooted in a transcendent international legal order, then they may constrain sovereignty; if, however, they are dependant on the will of the signatories, they may at most create obligations. The former view is generally associated with the claim that sovereignty is conferred on states by the international legal order; the latter view is generally associated with the view that sovereignty is created by particular communities.[56]

Binder suggests that each Special Rapporteur was influenced by his own view of the appropriate relationship between international law and State sovereignty. In other words, discrete, philosophically complete visions of international order underlay, and explain, their formulations. Accordingly, while Lauterpacht retained faith in a transcendent international order, Fitzmaurice was more convinced of the primacy of State

52 Garner, 'Harvard Research in International Law: Draft Convention on the Law of Treaties'. Garner proposed in Article 22 a priority rule favouring the earlier treaty.

53 H. Aufricht, 'Supersession of Treaties in International Law' (1951–2) 37 *Cornell Legal Quarterly* 698. His focus, broadly speaking, was on the application of the *lex posterior* principle.

54 C. W. Jenks, 'The Conflict of Law-Making Treaties' (1953) 30 *British Yearbook of International Law* 401, 425–7.

55 PCIJ: *Oscar Chinn* (1934) Series A/B, No. 63, 65; *European Commission of the Danube* (1927) Series B, No. 14 6; *Mavrommatis Palestinian Concessions* (1924) Series A, No. 2, 6; *Austro-German Customs Union* (1931) Series A/B, No. 41, 37. Central American Court: *Costa Rica* v. *Nicaragua* (1917) 11 *American Journal of International Law* 181; *El Salvador* v. *Nicaragua* (1917) 11 *American Journal of International Law* 674. On these two cases, see also Q. Wright, 'Conflicts between International Law and Treaties' (1917) 11 *American Journal of International Law* 566.

56 Binder, *Treaty Conflict and Political Contradiction*, 4.

will. Binder directs harsh criticism at Waldock,[57] and at the ILC,[58] seeing the culmination of their work in the complete subordination of international law to State interest. He explains that this was because Waldock and the other ILC members regarded 'good faith' and 'progressive development of international law' as conflicting values, and gave preference to the latter. In their conception, allowing States complete freedom to conclude new treaties in line with changing interests would allow for more robust development of international law in line with the hegemonic interests of the most powerful States.

In fact, Binder suggests that, at least from Fitzmaurice onwards, the ILC's positions reflected Hegelian thought, according to which treaty relations served the ends of both association and exploitation between States. Moreover, which of the two ends they served depended upon States' calculations of their interests and relative power. In keeping with this, it was natural for States to both enter into and breach treaties, and for their treaties to conflict. Significantly, the ILC considered these processes should be welcomed because they promoted the progress of individual States, and of the international order. In this view, it was neither possible nor desirable to imagine a world without conflict, or a perfectly universal equality; for exploitation and conflict would always be essential drivers of progress. Based on such thinking, Binder argues, ILC members saw their proper response to treaty conflict as two alternatives: either to provide (as Fitzmaurice did) for a liability rule which would pay some heed to the principle of good faith in treaty relations while preserving State autonomy to conclude new treaties, or to entirely embrace the idea of progress, by providing for a licence to breach treaties (as Waldock did).[59]

The above is of course a truncated account of Binder's deconstruction of the ILC commentaries on treaty conflict, but it suffices to make the point (which was also Binder's point) that there was much more underlying the different proposals on Article 30 than is granted in standard criticisms of its 'mechanical' character and of mainstream doctrinalism more generally.[60] At the very least, Binder's reading makes evident

[57] For instance, p. 59: 'Where Fitzmaurice merely questioned the efficacy of international law, Waldock and his supporters seemed to question its legitimacy.'

[58] For instance, p. 60: 'By the end of this process, the [ILC] is no longer convinced that duplicity and connivery should be discouraged.'

[59] Binder, *Treaty Conflict and Political Contradiction*, 80–5. Binder mainly relies on G. Hegel, *Hegel's Philosophy of Right* (T Knox (trans.), Oxford University Press 1967).

[60] For instance, J. Goldsmith and E. Posner, *The Limits of International Law* (Oxford University Press 2005) 3, 15–16.

Article 30's microcosmic reflection of international law's enduring politics of philosophy (and, in the reference to Hegel, its philosophy of politics).

... or crises of confidence (but not lack of faith)?

But we cannot stop there. Binder's reading, for all its insights, is perhaps too neat an explanation of Article 30 and of the factors that shaped the Commission's work in its early phase. As the next section will argue, the Commission's work on treaty conflict reveals not so much the ILC members' certainties about the appropriate relationship between sovereignty and international law, as their anxiety about the possibility of (the rule of) law in international relations, joined to a determination to promote international legal order and the respect for international law. Their proposals illuminate how they believed this overarching goal could feasibly be achieved. The explanation proceeding from this argument allows comprehension of the extent to which reflection about the function of international law has been about the 'art of the possible' – and in this way political.

Binder's error is in mistaking the vein of realism in the Commission's thought – for instance, their loss of faith in States' respect for the authority of existing institutions[61] – as the full expression of their *idealism*. His recognition of the influence of the ILC's immediate historical context upon its work is overshadowed by his insistence on viewing the Commission members (particularly the Special Rapporteurs) as inheritors of distinct currents of intellectual thought, with correspondingly distinct views of international law's proper relationship with sovereignty. He fails to perceive the liberal and constructivist assumptions that shaped their common project of international legal order, and particularly misreads Waldock's suggestions as prescriptions in favour of sovereignty.

Between philosophy and anxiety

To get at the crux of the thought underlying the ILC's early work, we might profitably start with Shabtai Rosenne's assessment of the considerations leading to Article 60 VCLT on breach of treaty. Rosenne, who

[61] For instance, he notes that the retreat from the property view was consistent with loss of faith in States' respect for the authority of existing institutions: Binder, *Treaty Conflict and Political Contradiction*, 49–51.

served on the ILC from 1962 to 1971, notes the reluctance in major works such as the Harvard Draft or Lauterpacht's writings to devote much attention to breach of treaty.[62] He explains that the formula that only *material* breaches may lead to the termination of a treaty was also a 'deliberate approach' reflecting the ILC's reluctance towards greater exposition on the topic:

> Underlying this obviously deliberate approach, one can detect a broad aspiration … to protect and preserve the integrity of treaty relations, breach notwithstanding … [While] there is no fundamental reason why the right [to terminate the treaty] should be limited to 'material breach' … it is only by some form of *appropriate* reparation … coupled with the reinstatement of the performance of the treaty in its existing or in a new interpretation, that the internationally wrongful act constituted by the breach … can be redressed … It is doubtful if the statement of principle can be taken much further than that, and it may be a disservice to international law in general, and to the stability and integrity of treaty relationships in particular, to attempt to give greater precision both to the concept of breach, and to the methods of redressing [its] undesirable consequences.[63]

Clearly, this assessment is at odds with Binder's suggestion that the ILC was quite comfortable providing for a licence to breach. But, more than that, it illuminates how the ILC dealt with questions that, on the one hand, it felt compelled to address (because not doing so would implicitly concede that *political* matters like treaty breach and conflict lay outside the limits of regulation by international law), but that on the other hand could not solve simply by prescription. In such cases, the ILC used restrained formulae (in Rosenne's words, refraining from giving 'greater precision') to dispel challenges to the authority of international law and the legal relations authenticated by it, avoiding more decisive but possibly counter-productive responses. One might see the continuation of this theme in the discussions on treaty conflict.

Lauterpacht

It is necessary to start with Lauterpacht's ILC commentaries, read also in light of his other writings. In an article in 1936 and later in his first ILC report, Lauterpacht pointed out the challenge that treaty conflicts posed for international law:

> Treaties, woven into the structure of customary international law, are the substance of the growing and changing law of nations. International law cannot

[62] Rosenne, *Breach of Treaty*, 123–4. [63] *ibid.*, 124.

recognize and it must actively discourage a state of affairs in which the law-creating faculty of states is abused for violating existing law as laid down in valid agreements. Governments cannot be permitted to discredit international law and to render it unreal by filling it with mutually exclusive obligations and by reducing treaties to conflicting makeshifts of political expediency.[64]

Lauterpacht asserted that international law must regulate treaty conflict, as much for the sake of its own authority, as for effective accomplishment of the objects and purposes of the treaties in question. His discussion reflects three aims: that legal regulation should strike a balance between stability and change; that it should advance (and protect advances in) multilateralism; and that Courts should play a central role in resolving treaty conflicts.

It is apparent that Lauterpacht was attentive to the competing doctrinal and policy justifications for stability and change. In favour of stability, he noted 'if parties to a treaty bind themselves to act in a manner which is a violation of the rights of a party under a pre-existing treaty, they commit a legal wrong which taints the subsequent treaty with illegality'.[65] While emphasising the need to preserve States' rights under existing treaties, Lauterpacht also emphasised the coherence of the legal system, arguing that it was 'as a general rule, incompatible with the unity of the law for the courts to enforce mutually exclusive rules of conduct laid down in a treaty, a statute, or a contract'.[66] Moreover, unlike individual contracts, treaties were 'relatively few and a matter of general knowledge'; thus a later conflicting treaty posed a greater shock 'to the sentiment of the unity of the law'.[67]

But Lauterpacht also recognised the importance of legal change. His reports, while extensively citing other portions of his 1936 article, omitted to reproduce the following, categorical, passage:

The necessity of discouraging such a state of affairs is so compelling that it is imperative to disregard the theoretical possibility of maintaining both treaties, for instance, when the injured contracting party fails to protest or when the offending state obtains release from the former treaty. States which deliberately choose to bind themselves to act in a manner contrary to obligations which they

64 H. Lauterpacht, 'The Covenant as Higher Law' (1936) 17 *British Yearbook of International Law* 54, 63–4. Also quoted in ILC, First Report on the Law of Treaties by Lauterpacht, 158, Note.

65 ILC, First Report on the Law of Treaties by Lauterpacht, 156, para. 2.

66 *ibid.*, 158, Note; Lauterpacht, 'The Covenant as Higher Law', 63–4.

67 ILC, First Report on the Law of Treaties by Lauterpacht, 158; Lauterpacht, 'The Covenant as Higher Law', 63–4.

have undertaken, as well as states which induce such conduct, must know that the new treaty does not create a legal bond and that courts will refuse to enforce it.

...

[T]he rule postulating the invalidity of treaties conflicting with previous treaty obligations is a necessary deduction from law-making effects of treaties in general and must be regarded as a beneficent principle calculated to enhance the authority of the Law of Nations and to safeguard its unity as a system of law.[68]

That is, Lauterpacht's ILC reports retreated from his previous, much broader, invalidity rule. He now extended to all treaties the view that he had earlier embraced with respect to *inter se* agreements: affirming their necessary and frequent occurrence to revise previous treaties and noting that it was 'impossible to accept the view that the provisions of a multilateral treaty cannot be modified ... unless with the consent of all other contracting parties'.[69] Instead of this view, he took recourse to a distinction based on the gravity of conflict. Where treaty conflicts did not challenge an essential aspect of the object and purpose of the earlier treaty, his focus was on allocating priority between them:

[U]nless the inconsistency is so gross, irremediable and raising the issue of good faith as to call urgently for the application ... of invalidity, the problem is one of resolving the conflict by application of principles appropriate to the case.[70]

Additionally, Lauterpacht provided three exceptions that confirmed, in all cases, the validity of 'legislative' treaties. These could be treaties 'partaking of a degree of generality which imparts to them the character of legislative enactments', which he claimed was a recognised category in the *Reparation* case;[71] treaties concluded in the international interest, which was a *lex ferenda* category, but unavoidable in a progressive and developing international society, even if it interfered with the legal rights of States;[72] and, finally, treaties revising multilateral conventions, 'one of the most important aspects of the international legislative process'.[73]

These exceptions reflect his equation of multilateralism with progress. This is also evident in that, while prefiguring Fitzmaurice's distinction between 'reciprocal' and 'special' treaties, Lauterpacht placed

[68] *ibid.*, 65.
[69] H. Lauterpacht, 'The Oscar Chinn Case' (1935) 16 *British Yearbook of International Law* 164; see also ILC, Second Report on the Law of Treaties by Lauterpacht, 136, para. 7.
[70] ILC, Second Report on the Law of Treaties by Lauterpacht, 136, paras. 7–8.
[71] ILC, First Report on the Law of Treaties by Lauterpacht, 157, para. 5.
[72] ILC, Second Report on the Law of Treaties by Lauterpacht, 139, para. 14.
[73] *ibid.*, 139, para. 16.

greater emphasis on the general interest of all parties in the observation of 'most – or perhaps all – multilateral conventions' by other parties, whether or not they included integral obligations. For one, this would promote 'smoothness' and 'uniformity' in international relations.[74] Moreover, he considered multilateral treaties, in most cases, as concluded for different purposes than bilateral ones; they were not merely contracts. This opposition between multilateral and bilateral instruments, and concern with preserving the effective operation of the former, pervaded his proposals.[75]

Lauterpacht believed that his proposals on treaty conflicts would be ultimately implemented by courts. Although he did not rule out the role of inter-party or institutional diplomacy, where diplomacy failed, recourse could be had to a tribunal, which had to provide a solution even if by 'assigning the same treaties and provisions a hierarchical priority of importance by reference to the character and objects of the treaties in question'.[76]

It may appear that he was far too sanguine about the possibility that courts would get the opportunity to pronounce upon treaty conflicts. Certainly, in much of Lauterpacht's writing, the role of courts appears as an article of faith: essential for international law's power to control the manner of its change, and thereby its effectiveness. This was a central thesis of his seminal 1933 work, *The Function of Law in the International Community*, in which he had asserted the importance of judicial bodies for 'disposing of disputes by developing and adapting the law of nations, within the orbit of existing law, to the new conditions of international life through a process of equitable judicial interpretation and reasoning'.[77]

It must also be remembered, however, that, of all the Special Rapporteurs, Lauterpacht was perhaps the most convinced of the strategic background to most treaty conflicts; his faith in law (and multilateralism) did not obscure his recognition of their politics.[78] Rather, he emphasised that his proposal *enabled* States to approach courts: it enabled parties to the earlier treaty to approach a tribunal for specific enforcement of their treaty and to have the later treaty declared invalid (here Lauterpacht overlooked *pacta tertiis*); it also enabled a tribunal to

[74] *ibid.*, 135, para. 5.
[75] On this, see also Jenks, 'The Conflict of Lawmaking Treaties', 443.
[76] ILC, Second Report on the Law of Treaties by Lauterpacht, 136–7, para. 8.
[77] Lauterpacht, *Function of Law in the International Community*, 254.
[78] See ILC, First Report on the Law of Treaties by Lauterpacht, 156, para. 3.

harmonise the treaties, or declare the later treaty invalid in response to a request for specific enforcement made by a party to the later treaty.[79]

The crux of his proposal was the assumption that, by reconciling the demands of stability and change, judicial bodies could crystallise law's position at the heart of the international system. They could show – as his book had asserted – that 'in a large number of cases it is through law that the change of law will be most conveniently effected'.[80]

Lauterpacht's approach, in short, combined qualities which may be called *integrity* (particularly condemning States' misuse of their law-creating faculty) and *instrumentality* (avoiding blind constraint of States' actions, and prescribing an enabling invalidity rule). Such an approach, his reports suggest, would permit effective legal regulation of treaty conflicts by providing an incentive for States to take their disputes to court; and, moreover, was appropriate to the mutually constitutive relationship between international law and international community. Lauterpacht regarded international law as fostering international community, which in turn would promote further development of international law.[81] Thus, his proposal oscillated between asserting international law's authority and providing a basis for its consolidation.

Fitzmaurice

Fitzmaurice redefined the ILC's task as that of providing an expository code on treaties which, he explained, enabled him to deal with the subject in a discursive way. He could include appropriate principles, highly tailored rules, and declaratory and explanatory material in the body of the code, whereas in drafting a convention he would be confined to a strict statement of obligation.[82] He was also at greater liberty to unpack considerations associated with different categories of treaties instead of striving for uniformly applicable rules, and thus to do justice to the substantive interests involved.[83]

[79] *ibid.*, 156, para. 4; ILC, Second Report on the Law of Treaties by Lauterpacht, 136, para. 8.

[80] Lauterpacht, *Function of Law in the International Community*, 354.

[81] H. Lauterpacht, 'The International Community and the Universality of International Law', in E. Lauterpacht (ed.), *International Law: Being the Collected Papers of Hersch Lauterpacht*, Vol. 1 (Cambridge University Press 1970).

[82] ILC, First Report on the Law of Treaties by G. Fitzmaurice, Special Rapporteur, A/CN.4/101 (1956) *ILC Yearbook*, Vol. II, 106–7.

[83] *ibid.*

Fitzmaurice's discussion reveals an attempt to find a *via media* between integrity and instrumentality (or flexibility), which he, like Lauterpacht, saw as the two bases of 'authority' of international law. In a short article contemporaneous with his tenure as ILC Special Rapporteur, he sought to disentangle law's authority from its 'binding force'.[84] He asserted that international law is binding as a matter of form. Its enforcement, or lack thereof, has nothing to do with the obligation to obey. However, its authority – the quality that caused its subjects to obey it in fact – depends on more than just legal form. Enforcement is one factor, but more important is 'the general assent or tolerance of the community . . . that the States making up the international society recognise it as binding upon them . . . as members of that society, irrespective of their individual wills'.[85] This recognition was based on the fact that law is the hallmark of society – *ubi societas ibi jus* – the necessity of the 'international (or any other) order'.[86] Also apparent in this article was Fitzmaurice's belief that law is the instrument of justice – justice achieved indirectly through 'order, stability, certainty and elimination of the subjective element that cannot fail to enter into any attempt to apply justice directly, and which often vitiates it'.[87] Thus, integrity (order, stability, certainty and elimination of subjectivity) and instrumentality (responsiveness to felt social necessity) are both necessary to the authority of international law.

His Hague Lectures, delivered during his ILC tenure, discussed the paradox of legal change in the vein of integrity and instrumentality as well. Fitzmaurice argued that on the one hand, a State's departure from a legal rule is a breach, and it would be 'impossible . . . without fatal injury to the whole structure and binding force of international law, to regard departures from an admitted rule as anything else . . . than violations of international law'. On the other hand, such departures, condoned by other States, provide the basis for a State's prescriptive right to be lawfully exempt from a rule; and for a group of States, the basis for a new rule.[88] Evidently, international law must recognise the original departure as unlawful, but also admit the legal consequences of a prescriptive case in favour of an exception, or a new rule.

[84] G. Fitzmaurice, 'The Foundations of Authority of International Law and the Problem of Enforcement' (1956) 19 *Modern Law Review* 1.

[85] *ibid.*, 8. [86] *ibid.*, 8, 11. [87] *ibid.*, 12.

[88] G. Fitzmaurice, 'The General Principles of International Law considered from the Standpoint of the Rule of Law' (1957) 92[II] *Recueil des Cours* 5, 113–14.

In the same spirit, Fitzmaurice's ILC commentaries reflect the view that international law must not unduly restrict the rights of States to conclude treaties; conflict rules must conform to structural principles of legal order and protect actions performed in good faith; and States must be encouraged not to disregard conflict rules in favour of extra-legal options more conducive to their interests.

These dual considerations explain the doctrinal ambiguities in his formula, including why he adopted a 'priority' rule. At first sight, it is not apparent that a priority rule serves any purpose. While Fitzmaurice presented it as necessary to protect the rights to compensation of innocent parties to the later treaty (since their treaty would still be valid, though subordinated),[89] Lauterpacht had associated compensation for innocent parties with the invalidity rule as well. Moreover, Fitzmaurice recognised that the priority rule may not be followed in practice, for a State might perform the later treaty rather than the earlier; while there was no 'right of election' in international law, 'in the existing state of international organization, it may not be possible to prevent a *power* of election from being in fact exercised'.[90] In such a case, the election would be effective; should the 'guilty' State in fact carry out its obligations under the later treaty, the other party to the later treaty must carry out its own obligations.[91] So how did a priority rule, as opposed to a rule of election, matter? The answer for Fitzmaurice was that the priority rule struck a more precise balance (than a general invalidity rule) between integrity and instrumentality: it expressed disapproval of the subversion of existing treaties via new ones, and accepted that all the treaties have legal consequences.

His concern for reconciling integrity with instrumentality also explains Fitzmaurice's exceptional application of the invalidity rule in conflicts involving integral or interdependent treaties. Perhaps his commentaries may be taken to indicate that this exception was motivated by the distinction between *jus cogens* and *jus dispositivum* rules.[92] Fitzmaurice described *jus cogens* rules as mandatorily binding upon all States, for they involved considerations of morals and international good order, and applied the invalidity rule against treaties in conflict with *jus cogens* rules. On the other hand, *jus dispositivum*, which constituted 'a very large part of international law', merely furnished 'rules for

[89] ILC, Third Report on the Law of Treaties by Fitzmaurice, 41–2, para. 83.
[90] *ibid.*, 42, para. 85. [91] *ibid.*, 42, paras. 83–5. [92] *ibid.*, 40, para. 76.

application in the absence of any other agreed regime'.[93] Conflicts involving *jus dispositivum* rules could trigger State responsibility, but would not lead to the invalidity of either treaty. While Binder draws on this distinction between *jus cogens* and *jus dispositivum* to argue that the ILC members placed greater emphasis on the breach of good morals than on the breach of good faith in the philosophy of treaty conflict,[94] that reason alone cannot fully explain Fitzmaurice's formula. Certainly, Fitzmaurice (rightly) gave a special status to 'good morals' norms (in particular, integral treaties instituted for the protection of individuals). But he also prescribed invalidity for treaties conflicting with interdependent treaties. These, it may be recalled, were in his view multilateral treaties with extremely contingent membership, such that breach by one State would destabilise the entire treaty. Such treaties, for instance disarmament treaties, are not *jus cogens*; they fall within *jus dispositivum*. Fitzmaurice's exceptional provision for invalidity is better interpreted in the same way as Lauterpacht's: especially protecting treaties that represent an advancement of 'international good order' (as he called it).

Fitzmaurice had referred to the *res inter alios acta* principle as a key reason to apply the priority rule to conflicts between reciprocal treaties, for each treaty would be effective only between its parties and could not create effects for non-parties. He recognised that this was true only in a formal sense:

> [A]ny impairment of the obligation under the earlier treaty ... will be in the factual ... sense, and it can of course be maintained ... that in practice such action tends to weaken, and indirectly to injure, the position of the non-participating countries.[95]

But this could not be addressed via legal rules, for in certain cases one treaty must also be permitted to have an impact upon another. For instance, *inter se* agreements were, to him, a means of overcoming collective action problems to change the existing legal *status quo* established by a multilateral treaty. Thus, he spoke of the *right* of States acting *inter se* to modify a multilateral treaty. Similarly, even while speaking of the absolute character of the obligations in integral and interdependent agreements, he noted that, in case of such treaties too, in practice, if parties

> agree not to insist, so far as they are concerned, on the performance of it by one another, this may weaken the force of the treaty, and may be inconsistent with

[93] *ibid.*, 40–1, para. 76. [94] Binder, *Treaty Conflict and Political Contradiction*, 37.
[95] ILC, Third Report on the Law of Treaties by Fitzmaurice, 43, para. 89(b).

the spirit of it, but it is not in direct conflict with the treaty so long as they do not agree actually not to perform the treaty obligations. Since it is in fact always open to parties to a treaty not to insist on performance by other parties . . . such an agreement can hardly be invalid – or if it is, its invalidity makes no difference and cannot affect the situation.[96]

Without analysing his work in terms of pragmatism as well as philosophy, we could not explain the application of the above reasoning, at least to integral treaties. As Klabbers notes, the point of his classification between integral treaties and ordinary 'reciprocal' treaties was that obligations under the latter could not be bilateralised; yet with the suggestion that invalidity may be avoided if other parties decide not to insist on performance, bilateralism crept back into the analysis.[97] Already there is a glimpse of what James Crawford observes of the VCLT approach: 'it looks at multilateral treaties from the perspective of bilateral treaties . . . Only peripherally does it deal with the "public order" aspects of multilateral treaties, and then usually indirectly. *That may even have been part of the secret of its diplomatic success.*'[98]

Indeed, Fitzmaurice was acutely aware of these considerations: he noted that treaty conflicts may not be brought before any international tribunal,[99] and may be subject to States' power of election; perhaps this also motivated his choice of formulating an expository code that might grow in 'authority'.

Waldock

Binder directs harsh criticism at Waldock. His book proposes that Waldock's view, that treaty conflicts should be addressed in terms of 'the application of treaties' rather than invalidity, implied that he gave preference to State autonomy over good faith and the protection of treaty rights. Binder argues that Waldock considered these values antithetical to the development of international institutions that would, in fact, be dominated by a few 'Western powers'.[100] This goal required that States remained free to conclude newer treaties in accord with their evolving interests, checked only by political objections from other States. Binder concludes that '[w]here Fitzmaurice merely questioned the efficacy of international law, Waldock and his supporters seemed to

96 *ibid.*, 44–5, para. 94. 97 Klabbers, *Treaty Conflicts and the European Union*, 77.

98 J. Crawford, 'Responsibility to the International Community as a Whole' (2001) 8 *Indiana Journal of Global Legal Studies* 303, 311 (emphasis added).

99 Fitzmaurice, Third Report on Treaties, 42, 85.

100 Binder, *Treaty Conflict and Political Contradiction*, 100–1.

question its legitimacy'.[101] Thus, while Fitzmaurice resorted to compromises, Waldock offered a licence to breach.

But how accurate is this reading of Waldock's project? Waldock's own commentary, being extensive but veiled, at first sight provides little indication of any project at all. The commentary sets out a summary of his predecessors' proposals, an examination of their sources, a range of arguments for their proposals being inadequate, and an explanation why his proposal accorded with judicial practice. On first impression, Waldock's formulation appears to be a result of careful pruning of the more radical elements of the previous proposals – driven more by doctrine than policy. However, policy considerations having to do with the authority of international law were clearly important, which is revealed in his repeated references to 'the current state of international organization'. For instance, '[t]he imperfect state of international organization and the manifold uses to which treaties are put seem to make it necessary for the Commission to be cautious in laying down rules which brand treaties as illegal and void'.[102] While it might be possible to develop complex rules to address different categories of treaties, 'it seems safer for the Commission, in the present state of the development of international law to abide by a more flexible rule'.[103] At one ILC meeting, he admitted to finding invalidity attractive from an academic perspective, but questioned 'whether it could be admitted at the present stage of development'.[104] He reiterated that to adopt a priority rule instead of an invalidity rule

> is not to condone the conclusion of a treaty the effect of which is to violate obligations under an earlier treaty; nor is it to authorise departures from the rules concerning [revision, but] in the present condition of international law the matter is to be resolved on the plane of the legal responsibility and not of the competence of the offending State.[105]

These statements reflect a prudential concern that the ILC should not undermine international law's authority by espousing norms that will not be followed in practice. Binder views such espousal as cynical encouragement to international lawyers to 'cut their coat to suit their

[101] *ibid.*, 59–60.
[102] ILC, Second Report on the Law of Treaties by Waldock, 56, para. 14.
[103] *ibid.*, 60, para. 29.
[104] Summary Record of the 703rd Mtg of the ILC, A/CN.4/SR.703 (19 June 1963) para. 75. See also para. 5.
[105] ILC, Third Report on the Law of Treaties by Waldock, 44, para. 34.

cloth'.[106] Waldock would probably deny the charge of cynicism but would not be disturbed by the criticism that he was indeed adopting a practical approach. In his General Course at the Hague Academy in 1962, during his tenure on the ILC, he discussed the lack of recourse to international judicial dispute settlement:

> The short answer is that States have not yet fully accepted subjection to the rule of law in their international relations. This fact may be unpalatable, but it is no good deceiving ourselves about it, or we shall not understand the conditions in which international law has to work.[107]

Binder errs in ascribing to Waldock the view that the international legal order lacks the legitimacy to constrain sovereign autonomy.[108] Waldock certainly agreed that international law lacked *capacity* to enforce compliance, and its compliance-pull was often of the gentlest kind.[109] But he was critical of those who sought to 'imply that sovereignty is a quality inherent in all States which makes it impossible for them to be fully subordinated either to the rule of law or control by any international authority'.[110] His Hague lectures included a biting criticism of Marxist theory as the 'new ally' of the doctrine of sovereignty, concluding that:

> [t]he unwillingness of States to submit themselves to international adjudication – an unwillingness by no means confined to Marxist States – may have to be accepted during the present period of acute tension; but to admit that a State, by reason of its sovereignty, is incapable of being fully subordinated to law on the international plane is to deny the possibility of an international legal order.[111]

All of this suggests that Waldock was concerned that it was States that did not consider constraints imposed by international law as legitimate, and that overreaching conflict rules would undermine the respect for international law. Binder, however, reads Waldock himself as being unconvinced that international law should significantly constrain State sovereignty. He says, '[f]or Waldock, the key advantage of a liability rule lay not in its capacity to compensate innocent victims of treaty conflict but in its capacity to empower perpetrators of treaty

[106] Binder, *Treaty Conflict and Political Contradiction*, 99.

[107] H. Waldock, 'General Course on Public International Law' (1962) 106[II] *Recueil des Cours* 5, 107.

[108] Binder, *Treaty Conflict and Political Contradiction*, 59.

[109] Waldock, 'General Course on Public International Law', 7–9. See especially the reference to the UN as government by persuasion.

[110] *ibid.*, 157. [111] *ibid.*, 159.

conflict'.[112] This leads Binder to conclude that 'Waldock and his supporters' were not concerned with equity but only with State autonomy and systemic flexibility.[113]

Certainly, flexibility was important for Waldock. He espoused Fitzmaurice's argument that *inter se* agreements could be conduits for change in multilateral treaties, recommending 'the safest course for the Commission to adopt is not to prescribe nullity'.[114] This does not imply that he was unconcerned with good faith or equity. To take a general example, his provisions on treaty revision included extensive commentary on the right of consultation enjoyed by each party.[115] In the context of treaty conflict his Third Report included the proviso that the later treaty would not prevail if parties to it knew of the conflict with an earlier treaty.[116] Moreover, his commentary suggested that in such case the party to the later treaty would not be entitled to damages, not just – as Binder claims – that the later treaty would not be specifically enforceable.[117]

Overall, Waldock is best understood as following the same approach as Fitzmaurice: resting international law's claims to authority upon both integrity and instrumentality. In affirmation of integrity, he offered condemnation of acts of bad faith and a liability rule ascribing State responsibility for breach of treaty, and outlined the possibility that membership in international organisations could restrict the capacity of States to undertake new treaties.[118] With respect to instrumentality, he noted the many roles that treaties performed in international society and cautioned against rules that could impede these roles. On a prudential assessment of the current state of international organisation, he opted for simple rules that would neither overreach nor entail complex nuances.

It is true that, in doing away with complexity, Waldock entirely excluded the enhanced protections that Lauterpacht and Fitzmaurice, respectively, had provided for legislative multilateral treaties and for special (integral or interdependent) multilateral treaties. Indeed, his formula, the basis for the present draft of Article 30, does not respond to the possibility that treaty conflicts may undermine the integrity of such treaties even in the absence of a breach. However, Waldock was

[112] Binder, *Treaty Conflict and Political Contradiction*, 59. [113] *ibid.*, 60, 99–100.
[114] ILC, Second Report on the Law of Treaties by Waldock, 58, para. 20.
[115] ILC, Third Report on the Law of Treaties by Waldock, 47–52 (Articles 67–69).
[116] *ibid.*, 40–1, para. 22. [117] Binder, *Treaty Conflict and Political Contradiction*, 58.
[118] ILC, Second Report on the Law of Treaties by Waldock, 54, paras. 4–5 (Article 14(3)(a)).

convinced of the equal normative force held by all treaties and considered a conflict involving a *jus cogens* norm the only appropriate context for invalidity. Thus, to apply invalidity to all integral and interdependent treaties would be over-inclusive[119] – using selected examples, he showed that conflicts involving some such treaties would not create the sort of effects for which they must be safeguarded by an invalidity rule. Indeed, he turned Fitzmaurice's argument on its head, arguing that many *inter se* agreements were actually agreements concluded with a view to change interdependent treaties.

In short, for Waldock, the key consideration was the current State of development of international organisation.[120] However, he did not, as Binder alleged, seek to promote progressive development by writing in a Darwinian scheme (survival of the fittest treaties!). Rather, his work pointed to the absence of legal machinery for making principled distinctions between more and less important norms and enforcing the former. His emphasis on the effective validity of treaties was on the basis that this would permit States parties to either or both treaties to insist upon the performance of these treaties (or on reparations), and thus guard against *ex parte* 'solutions' that used an invalidity or priority rule to set aside one of the conflicting treaties. This is also evident in his contributions to the ILC discussions.

The ILC

Waldock's third report was not the final word on Article 30. Having discussed his initial proposal over three meetings at its fifteenth session in 1963,[121] the ILC reviewed his revised proposal over two meetings at the sixteenth session, in 1964,[122] then once more following the Drafting Committee's adoption of a text.[123] The ILC then made its report to the UN General Assembly and invited comments from States.[124] Waldock reported a summary of these comments along with his own views once again to the ILC, at its eighteenth session, in 1966; and the ILC once more

119 *ibid.*, 59, paras. 25–6. 120 *ibid.*, 60, para. 29.

121 Summary Record of the 685th Mtg of the ILC, A/CN.4/SR.685 (22 May 1963); Summary Record of the 687th Mtg of the ILC, A/CN.4/SR.687 (27 May 1963); Summary Record of the 703rd Mtg of the ILC.

122 Summary Record of the 742nd Mtg of the ILC, A/CN.4/SR.742 (10 June 1964); Summary Record of the 743rd Mtg of the ILC, A/CN.4/SR.743 (11 June 1964).

123 Summary Record of the 755th Mtg of the ILC.

124 ILC, Report to the UN General Assembly on the Law of Treaties, A/5809 (1964) *ILC Yearbook*, Vol. II, 177, 185–92.

discussed the article, in two meetings.[125] It recommended a revised draft to the Drafting Committee, which proposed a text which was reviewed and adopted at a further meeting of the ILC members.[126] The provision was then briefly discussed during finalisation of the ILC Report to the General Assembly,[127] setting out the proposed text and commentaries.[128] The General Assembly again invited comments from member States and treaty depositories, before convening the UN Conference on the Law of Treaties in 1967.[129] At the UN Conference, the 'Committee of the Whole' discussed the proposed text over three meetings, spread over 1968 and 1969,[130] following which its draft was approved at the thirteenth plenary meeting of the Conference. This was on 6 May 1969;[131] the Conference adopted the VCLT as a whole on 22 May 1969.

A comparison between Waldock's proposal and Article 30 reveals the following differences: in Article 30, there is no suggestion of a priority rule, while Waldock's draft had referred to one treaty prevailing over the other; further, in Article 30 there is no suggestion that a party to the later treaty which knew of its conflict with an earlier one could not invoke its rights against a party to both. Thus, the lack of good faith in creating the treaty conflict would not lead to special consequences; instead, Article 30 refers to the *res inter alios acta* principle, and the possibility of application of State responsibility.

Naturally, ILC discussions are the key to understanding how these alterations came about. There were many twists and turns to the process, but the notion prevailed throughout that international law (through the VCLT) should signify its disapproval of intentionally created treaty conflicts. The ILC members maintained a tenacious grip on the language of priority,[132] even as one member pointed out that priority did not quite

[125] Summary Record of the 857th Mtg of the ILC, A/CN.4/SR.857 (24 May 1966); Summary Record of the 858th Mtg of the ILC, A/CN.4/SR.858 (25 May 1966).

[126] Summary Record of the 875th Mtg of the ILC, A/CN.4/SR.875 (22 June 1966).

[127] Summary Record of the 893rd Mtg of the ILC, A/CN.4/SR.893 (18 July 1966).

[128] ILC, Draft Articles on the Law of Treaties with Commentaries (1966) *ILC Yearbook*, Vol. II, 187, 214–17.

[129] UNGA Res. 2166 (XXI) (5 December 1966); UNGA Res. 2287 (XXII) (6 December 1967).

[130] Summary Record of the 31st Mtg of the Committee of the Whole, A/CONF.39/C.1/SR.31 (19 April 1968); Summary Record of the 85th Mtg of the Committee of the Whole, A/CONF.39/C.1/SR.85 (10 April 1969); Summary Record of the 91st Mtg of the Committee of the Whole, A/CONF.39/C.1/SR.91 (19 April 1969).

[131] Summary Record of the 13th Mtg of the Plenary, A/CONF.39/SR.13 (6 May 1969).

[132] Discussion at the 742nd Mtg of the ILC. Priority remained a normatively attractive device for expressing disapproval long after it was recognised that it does not preclude the exercise of a 'power of election'. For instance, Jiménez de Aréchaga, 743rd Mtg of

square with either the principle of invalidity or the principle of liability.[133] They also repeatedly debated the inclusion of an invalidity rule, or at least a rule directing States to terminate the conflicting treaty where interdependent or integral treaties were involved.[134] They continued to worry about seeming to condone treaties concluded with the intention of violating previous ones, and several times considered provisos suggesting that such treaties would not be enforceable.[135] These efforts were underlined by statements of the need to promote the sanctity of treaties.

These arguments were balanced against considerations of the application of the *res inter alios acta* and *pacta tertiis* principles,[136] and of State autonomy,[137] but also, significantly, of the absence of judicial institutions to declare invalidity[138] and of international law's current inability to distinguish welcome and unwelcome conflicts,[139] to determine how a rule based on good faith would be administered,[140] or to ensure that a priority rule would be observed by a State party to two conflicting treaties.[141]

Ultimately, the moral sanction against attempts to undermine existing treaties was expressed in two ways: it was combined with the legal sanction in article 30(5)[142] – at least some ILC members thought that the

the ILC, 130, para. 46. The idea that the earlier treaty must be accorded 'priority' – even if only in a formal sense – began to be questioned only during the eighteenth session: see Ago, 857th Mtg of the ILC, 102, paras. 90–2.

133 Jiménez de Aréchaga, 742nd Mtg of the ILC, 123, paras. 44–5.

134 This continued right up to the adoption of the ILC Draft Articles on the Law of Treaties: see ILC, Draft Articles on the Law of Treaties with Commentaries, 217, paras. 12–13.

135 For instance, the amendment proposed by Jiménez de Aréchaga and Pal, 703rd Mtg of the ILC, 196, para. 4. Waldock offered a proviso to this effect in his Third Report. A similar amendment was again proposed by Jiménez de Aréchaga, 857th Mtg of the ILC, 96, para. 15. This was received favourably by many, even though Waldock's proposal had not found its way into the provision.

136 For instance, de Luna, 687th Mtg of the ILC, 89, para. 28, 857th Mtg of the ILC, 102, para. 93.

137 Waldock, 742nd Mtg of the ILC, 121, para. 22 ('[t]here was a definite tendency in the Commission not to admit limitations by treaties on the treaty-making capacity of States').

138 For instance, Reuter, 743rd Mtg of the ILC, 127, para. 9.

139 Tabibi, 703rd Mtg of the ILC, 201, para. 63 ('[m]any old treaties belonged to the colonial era and should not be given precedence over more recent ones'); Bartoš, 742nd Mtg of the ILC, 126, para. 82; Ago, 857th Mtg of the ILC, 102, para. 91.

140 Briggs, 742nd Mtg of the ILC, 123–4, para. 51; Rosenne, 742nd Mtg of the ILC, 124, para. 58.

141 De Luna, 857th Mtg of the ILC, 102, para. 95.

142 For instance, Reuter, 743rd Mtg of the ILC, 127, para. 10 ('It would be better to refer to the theory of State responsibility ... by some form of words such as "subject to the application of the rules concerning international responsibility". In that way the

ILC's work on responsibility, once concluded, would provide appropriate remedies for intentional creation of treaty conflict.[143] Additionally, the title of the article was changed from one referring to 'conflict' or 'incompatibility' of treaty provisions to 'Application of successive treaties relating to the same subject-matter'.[144] Though there was some discussion of including a reference to *pacta sunt servanda* in the opening clause,[145] this was ultimately thought superfluous.

But the arguments in favour of Article 30 were not made only in terms of what it could not aspire to; in response to the criticism that the proposed text only stated truisms, Waldock argued that it performed an 'extremely important' function in clarifying

> whether, as between two States, one of them could invoke the fact that it was already a party to a prior treaty with another State as a ground for non-performance of the later treaty. That in essence was the problem of the relativity of treaties, and it had real practical significance in the case of a conflict between treaty obligations.[146]

In other words, Waldock provided a defence similar to that discussed earlier in the chapter with respect to justifying the element of 'principle' in the principle of political decision.

International law as an ILC project

In offering their respective proposals on treaty conflict, the ILC Special Rapporteurs all claimed merely to have furthered the logic of their predecessors, even if by departing from their specific provisions. If we adopt

Commission would show its awareness of the fact that there were cases in which the conclusion of the later treaty was a wrong, not only because it infringed an earlier treaty, but because it contravened rules of general conduct.'). See also Waldock, 858th Mtg of the ILC, 103, para. 8 ('the desire to produce a text which did not appear to condone possible cases of breach . . . had led the Commission to frame paragraph 5 in the form of a comprehensive reservation to the effect that the rules set out in the preceding paragraphs concerning the relative priority of treaty obligations . . . would not affect the responsibility that might be incurred as a result of acts by the parties').

143 For instance, Reuter, 857th Mtg of the ILC, 97, para. 31; Yasseen, 857th Mtg of the ILC, 102, para. 89.

144 To 'avoid any risk of . . . being interpreted as sanctioning the conclusion of a treaty incompatible with obligations undertaken towards another State under another treaty': ILC, Draft Articles on the Law of Treaties with Commentaries, 214, para. 1.

145 El-Erian, 857th Mtg of the ILC, 101, para. 82; Talalaev, 31st Mtg of the Committee of the Whole, 164, para. 5. See also Bevan, 31st Mtg of the Committee of the Whole, 166, para. 23 (explaining why it should not be specifically alluded to).

146 Waldock, 857th Mtg of the ILC, 99, para. 59.

Binder's reading of their philosophical differences, then such assertions can only be regarded as empty courtesy. But this view would disregard the fact of each Rapporteur's report citing the same few judicial decisions and scholarly works. Moreover, for all their superficial differences, and the various labels they used – invalidity, priority, license – the proposals were not very different in their envisaged operation. As discussed above, in each case, concern about the practical limits of international law and the determination to promote legal regulation of treaty conflict informed rules that combined integrity and instrumentality. Despite their differences, the Special Rapporteurs (and some other Commission members) were, arguably, united by a common project of international law.

This section examines that project, starting with a review of the historical context of the ILC's work in which its codification enterprise was greeted both with expectations from its success and fear of the consequences of its failure. It then discusses whether we should view the ILC's work as a series of *tactical* compromises to secure acceptance of the VCLT, or if it is possible to read in a more comprehensive *strategy*. My argument is that it is possible to read the various ILC members' commentaries as partaking of common liberal and constructivist assumptions about international law and its influence.

The fifth element

In October 1946, Sir Cecil Hurst gave a lecture to the Grotius Society titled 'A Plea for the Codification of International Law on New Lines'. A former judge of the Permanent Court of International Justice, he began by drawing a distinction between the situation that existed 'two years ago' and 'today'. Two years before, that is, in 1944, the Second World War was still going on: the Allied forces had just about defeated Germany, but Japan continued to fight; the San Francisco Conference, which led to the UN Charter, had yet to be convened. Without expressly listing these events, Hurst observed that:

> At that time a wave of scepticism prevailed as to whether international law could be said to exist at all. It was due no doubt to the success with which the enemy appeared to be ignoring the obligations which it was believed that international law imposed upon him, and which led men to wonder whether international law was anything more than the pious aspirations of the professors.[147]

[147] Hurst, 'A Plea for the Codification', 135.

However, today (that is, in 1946), 'the position ha[d] changed'. In a hopeful vein, Hurst noted the growing interest in international law, and acceptance of its existence and binding force. 'There is no one', he argued, 'at our meeting today, who will question the proposition that international law constitutes a legal system the rules of which it is incumbent upon all States to observe.'[148] Nevertheless, there was a gulf between the recognition of international law as law by members of the Grotius Society and its effective operation on the international plane. He called upon 'international lawyers of all countries' to act together to breach this gulf.

Hurst noted that there were five elements to a well-developed and sound legal system. Four of these – a legislature to change the law in light of current needs and new ideas, skilled and impartial courts to administer the law, an incorruptible police force to enforce the law, and professors to teach and expound the law – could either be realised only by States or (in case of the last) fell within their national spheres. But the fifth element, 'a well developed body of law', was up to international lawyers.[149]

Hurst considered it the duty of international lawyers 'to contribute what they can to the work of discussing and of formulating in broad outline the rules and principles of international law so that ultimately there may emerge universal agreement on the subject'.[150] It would be this work, that is, 'patient and continual research and effort on the part of international lawyers',[151] that would promote the development of international law.

Developing the quintessence of international law, then, was the duty of international lawyers. Hurst was firm that international law's development could not be left to international law courts or State practice alone. The former hardly received cases of such volume as would enable them to play a role corresponding to that of common law courts; the latter required interpretation and contextualisation by the international lawyer. Loath to leave the development of international law 'to progress spontaneously and automatically',[152] Hurst heavily emphasised the constructive role of codification in the evolution of international law.

But the high hopes attached to codification were accompanied by deep anxiety about the consequences that would follow its failure. While successful codification would go a long way towards establishing

[148] *ibid.* [149] *ibid.*, 136–7. [150] *ibid.*, 138. [151] *ibid.*, 153. [152] *ibid.*

the credentials of international law as a proper legal system, and facilitate the development of international organisation to ensure its effectiveness, failure would

> not only prevent any further efforts in the same direction but it would render it almost impossible to persuade what we call the man in the street that international law is a legal system capable of constituting the foundation of the law and order on which the new world is to be based.[153]

Hurst's lecture therefore focused in large measure on the proper design and elaboration of aims of a successful codification enterprise.

Similar themes appear in much (like the ILC Special Rapporteurs, particularly Anglo-American) writing on codification during the late-1940s and 1950s. Hurst's view on the consequences of failure was cited in 1948–49 by J. L. Brierly[154] and in 1957 by Julius Stone.[155] Brierly, Stone, Lauterpacht[156] and Sir Robert Jennings[157] also offered substantive meditations on the proper scope of the ILC's codification enterprise. Like several other scholars,[158] they reflected on the ILC's potential to contribute to the development of international law in a difficult political environment.

These scholars discussed which topics were the most suitable for codification, the acceptable degree of progressive development, and, importantly, the outcomes that the ILC should pursue. Their work reflected two preoccupations: the success of the ILC's work, and its salience. A perceptible fear was that the two did not necessarily match – success, in terms of States' acceptance of the Commission's work, could necessitate focusing on issues of low salience and on the elaboration of principles or codes, not on draft treaties.[159] For some, the

[153] *ibid.*, 140.

[154] J. L. Brierly, 'The Codification of International Law' (1948–9) 47 *Michigan Law Review* 2, 6.

[155] J. Stone, 'On the Vocation of the International Law Commission' (1957) 57 *Columbia Law Review* 16, 21 n. 15.

[156] H. Lauterpacht, 'Codification and Development of International Law' (1955) 49 *American Journal of International Law* 16.

[157] Jennings, 'Progressive Development and Codification', 301.

[158] S. Rosenne, 'The International Law Commission, 1949–59' (1960) 36 *British Yearbook of International Law* 104; M. Bartoš, *Medjunarodno javno pravo*, Vol. 1 (Beograd, Cultura 1954) 155–6, quoted in Rosenne, *ibid.*, 156–7. See also, on codification *per se*, C. de Visscher, *Theory and Reality in International Law* (Princeton University Press 1957) 144–8.

[159] See, for instance, Jennings, 'Progressive Development and Codification', 324–5, suggesting that the ILC open its work by focusing on some 'easy and unimportant'

elaboration of broad principles or codes was also the safer approach, given concerns that international law would be 'strangulated' by reduction into concrete legal forms.[160] This segued into yet another debate, one over the relative merits of certainty and flexibility in the law. We see, for instance, criticisms of the 'excessive regard for certainty'; for too-certain rules could prejudice justice in actual cases, and invite State rejection:

> It is to be observed, moreover, that even an unclear rule constitutes a certain means of social control, moderating the claims of States to the extent of keeping them within the range of debated alternatives. An unclear rule is not necessarily a mere nullity in its impact on State conduct. This is a capital fact to be remembered when considering enthusiastic codification programs which may have the effect merely of substituting rules that, though clear and certain, have little prospect of State acceptance. The superficial virtues of clarity, certainty, and neatness of rules may, even when they fail of State acceptance, constitute a serious blow to international law as a means of social control. They substitute for the real though amorphous influence of unclear and uncertain old rules clear new formulae which are devoid of influence as a means of social control.[161]

A number of factors contributed to the apprehension that there was no avoiding the trade-off between success and salience. There was, to begin with, the looming memory of the failure of legal overreach during the inter-war period. A significant portion of each of the above-mentioned works is devoted to analysing the failure of the 1930 Hague Codification Conference, called under the aegis of the League of Nations. The positions adopted on the proper scope of the ILC's work seem to be particularly guided by the desire to avoid repeating the errors made during that time. While Hurst cautioned against a *second* failure of codification,[162] to some others abandoning codification altogether offered the best hope for the success of international law.[163]

The difficulties attached to codification were magnified by two other ongoing and vital developments – the Cold War and decolonisation – both of which presented challenges for the legitimacy of the codification

topic, like 'piracy'; Stone, 'On the Vocation of the ILC', 44, on the difficulties of securing 'multital' acceptance for treaties; Hurst, 'A Plea for Codification', 140 *et seq*; Brierly, 'The Codification of International Law', 6–8.

160 Brierly, 'The Codification of International Law', 8–9; Stone, 'On the Vocation of the ILC', 32–3.

161 Stone, *ibid*., 18.

162 Hurst, 'A Plea for Codification', 140.

163 Stone, 'On the Vocation of the ILC', 46 *et seq*; de Visscher, *Theory and Reality*, 147–8.

enterprise.[164] As Rosenne notes, the central criticism related to the perception that codification was focused on the preservation of Western political interests, to the cost of both the Soviet bloc and the newly independent, developing States. There were doubts about the appropriateness of the very idea of codifying laws that were European in origin and developed for imperialist and colonialist purposes; there were questions whether the choice of issues on the ILC's agenda was in keeping with the changing political and technological landscape. To Rosenne, these charges indicated the desirability of drafting conventions rather than codes, for the former would ensure that the ILC's work was subjected to a political test.[165] But, as noted above, it was precisely the political test that was feared by several other scholars; and the threshold for success at a multilateral treaty conference was considered impossibly high.

All of this is important context for the drafting of the VCLT. The convention on treaties, listed amongst the 'building blocks in the development of the post-war international legal system' that were achieved by the ILC in its early phase of operation,[166] was a topic of no small importance. Moreover, as Lauterpacht – who maintained faith in the idea of codification, but described the achievements of the ILC as limited – noted, there were pronounced differences of view on various issues relating to the topic, and the issue of treaty conflict was especially contested.[167] And, of course, while Fitzmaurice had for a period turned the ILC's focus to the drafting of an expository code on treaties, in Waldock's tenure the Commission resumed its original intention of drafting a convention, thus clearly anticipating the political test of a multilateral treaty conference (which it successfully passed in 1969).

Consider the obvious implications of all these factors for the attitude that the ILC members could take towards addressing treaty conflicts. It is evident from the discussion in the previous section that all members were aware of the difficulties of formulating a suitable rule. They recognised that treaty conflicts could be deliberately created. They also appreciated the dilemmas associated with such conflicts – of stability and change, and of respect for treaty commitments and State autonomy. Indeed, contrary to Binder's argument that from

[164] See Rosenne, 'The International Law Commission', 155 *et seq.* [165] *ibid.*, 159.

[166] Franck and ElBaradei, 'The Codification and Progressive Development of International Law', 631.

[167] Lauterpacht, 'Codification and Development of International Law', 19.

Lauterpacht's time to Waldock's there was a slide from a 'property view' to a 'licence to breach', reflecting a shift that privileged positivism and State autonomy, it is apparent that each Special Rapporteur found it appropriate to balance these competing considerations. In this context, they paid particular attention to the additional doctrinal complications of conflicts involving treaties with non-identical parties. Moreover, as expressed most clearly in Fitzmaurice's famous passage on the distinction between a right of election and a power of election,[168] the ILC members also anticipated that States' attitudes towards specific treaties, and *vis-à-vis* resolving treaty conflicts, would be driven by political considerations. These factors made it difficult to specify the outcomes that would result in all cases of treaty conflict, by means of a general rule.

Therefore, as described in the previous section, the Special Rapporteurs, and in later stages the ILC, proposed different variations on the principle of political decision, that is, a rule combining integrity and instrumentality by providing a baseline against which treaty conflicts could be discursively addressed by the States involved. They chose different ultimate results, and to that extent their suggestions *may* indicate different sensibilities as to what rule would be both appropriate and effective. But these different results were specified towards a similar purpose, of enabling some of the States involved in a treaty conflict to approach a court in order to have their claims upheld. For Lauterpacht, then, the invalidity rule provided the appropriate baseline by ultimately protecting the rights of States party to the earlier treaty; for Waldock, in contrast, the invalidity rule 'though attractive from the academic point of view',[169] was not workable in practice, for courts would rarely take it upon themselves to invalidate treaties involving States that were not before them. Validity, on the other hand, would provide a basis for ordering specific enforcement or compensation. Moreover, it would be the more acceptable formulation for States. We might say that Lauterpacht's firm view that courts should form the heart of the system of international dispute settlement continued to be influential, but it was tempered with a more pragmatic understanding of how courts could rule on treaty conflicts.

This discussion of the context of the ILC's work suggests the need for a nuanced appreciation of what was, and was felt by the Commission

[168] ILC, Third Report on the Law of Treaties by Fitzmaurice, 42, para. 85.
[169] Waldock, 703rd Mtg of the ILC, para. 75.

members to be, at stake in drafting treaty conflict rules. And this brings up the further question of whether the ILC members were guided essentially by what they felt would pass the test of multilateral acceptance, or if they regarded their approach as having additional, intrinsic, merits.

A long view?

This question may perhaps be illuminated by reference to de Certeau's distinction between 'strategy' and 'tactics'.[170] In de Certeau's view, 'strategy' describes actions, or calculations, by a subject which can distance itself from its immediate temporal context, and use its own 'place' to establish particular and stable relationships with (and we might say between) its others:[171]

> I call a 'strategy' the calculus of force-relationships which becomes possible when a subject of will and power ... can be isolated from an 'environment'. A strategy assumes a place that can be circumscribed as proper (*propre*) and thus serve as the basis for generating relations with an exterior distinct from it ... Political, economic and scientific rationality has been constructed on this strategic model.[172]

A 'tactic', on the other hand, is a momentary subversion; the user of a tactic may lack a separate 'place' from which to act towards establishing a stable relationship with an *other*. The user might, however, 'on the wing', seize opportunities, or manipulate an event into an opportunity, for a temporary victory over the other by turning to advantage the tools or techniques of the other.[173] A tactic is 'an art of the weak', and tactical gains are ephemeral.[174]

Might this difference be relevant to understanding the approach of the early ILC? It must be acknowledged that the Commission may seem removed from the contexts of 'everyday life' for which de Certeau

[170] de Certeau, *The Practice of Everyday Life*. [171] *ibid.*, xix, 34–9.

[172] *ibid.*, xix. In a later section, de Certeau elaborates further: 'I call a *strategy* the calculation (or manipulation) of power relationships that becomes possible as soon as a subject with will and power (a business, an army, a city, a scientific institution) can be isolated [from an "environment"]. It postulates a *place* that can be delimited as its *own* and serve as the base from which relations with an *exteriority* composed of targets or threats (customers or competitors, enemies, the country surrounding the city, objectives and objects of research, etc.) can be managed. As in management, every "strategic" rationalization seeks first of all to distinguish its "own" place, that is the place of its own power and will, from an "environment." A Cartesian attitude, if you wish: it is an effort to delimit one's own place in a word bewitched by the invisible powers of the Other. It is also the typical attitude of modern science, politics, and military strategy.' *ibid.*, 35–6.

[173] *ibid.*, xix, 34–9. [174] *ibid.*, 37.

outlined these two modes of action. But the distinction between these two modes does illuminate the ILC's work. On the one hand, we might recognise the Commission's relative powerlessness and uncertain position, particularly in the early phase of its operation. We might say the same of international law's own status in international relations.[175] From this perspective, the ILC's effort to provide a formula that balanced integrity and instrumentality appears a tactical compromise that States could be persuaded to accept. Further, this view of VCLT Article 30 makes sense of both its achievements and its limits. In one sense it is a small victory, for the ILC, of law over politics; the restatement of an almost intractable political question in terms of a legal principle. At the same time, it is also proof of the insubstantial character of the victory, since it does not quite address all the complicated issues surrounding treaty conflict. The ILC may be seen as having merely accomplished, in de Certeau's terms, the introduction of a Brownian movement in the system[176] – that is, added to the political landscape of treaty conflict one other element that could potentially impact upon the conflict dynamics. The resolution of the conflict could now at least be construed as being addressed, or even resolved by law, even if this law was only a thin veneer for politics.

On the other hand, this view of the ILC's work as tactics does not quite account for the tone of the ILC's reports and discussions. Certainly, the ILC members were well aware of their complicated context. But there was equal concern that the 'victory' achieved should be substantial, not momentary, and should more firmly establish the place of international law and international institutions. As Lauterpacht asserted:

Although account must be taken of the attitude of governments, there is little or no merit in proposals of codification which anticipate, to the extent of regarding it as decisive, the possible opposition of governments and which are couched in terms of the lowest common denominator of probable general acceptance. Governments are composed of human beings and they must be credited with the capacity for being influenced by the intrinsic merits of the drafts as finally

[175] Moreover, as Oliver Jütersonke has recently noted in his intellectual biography of Hans Morgenthau, international law writings of that period were overwhelmingly concerned with 'power politics' and the corresponding limits of international law: O. Jütersonke, *Morgenthau, Law and Realism* (Cambridge University Press, 2010) 179–80.

[176] de Certeau, *The Practice of Everyday Life*, xx. 'Brownian movement', in physics, is the random moving of particles suspended in a a liquid or a gas, as a result of bombardment by the fast-moving molecules of that medium. Discovered by Robert Brown in 1827, the phenomenon was explained by Albert Einstein in 1905.

elaborated ... [O]nce the codifying agency ... has reached the conclusion that a draft is desirable and dictated by the interests of the international community, of the rationally conceived interests of states and the requirements of a progressive development of international law as an instrument of international co-operation and as the protector of the rights of the individual conceived as the ultimate subject and beneficiary of all law, then it must take the risk that the General Assembly will do no more for the time being than take note of the report which has been published. A report, adopted after mature consideration and after taking into account the views expressed by governments, is bound to exercise and influence and to rally around it the support of enlightened states.[177]

This statement of Lauterpacht's is a neat summary of the expectations that the ILC members, for all their differences, held in common: as we saw, Fitzmaurice and Waldock, too, were keen to draft rules that would strengthen the authority of international law, and considered it possible to persuade States to accept and take recourse to international law. The work of the early ILC can thus be described as strategy – that is, a strategy for its members to provide the fifth element of the international legal system by formulating workable conflict rules that would promote the development of international legal order, using the position of expertise accorded to them.

This brings us to the ILC's liberal and constructivist assumptions. Important with respect to both assumptions was the ILC's emphasis on constituting States party to the conflicting treaties as *claimants* in international law, able to approach courts for protection of their subjective rights. Underlying this was the expectation that the status of 'claimant' would nudge States towards a legal discourse of justification, exemption and reparation, whether before or outside judicial forums; and that this would lead to more principled outcomes.

The ILC's liberal assumption is expressed in their faith in multilateralism, and their sense that acting through law to address treaty conflicts – whether to modify or terminate treaties, determine reparations, or carve out exceptions – would lead to better outcomes. Could the ILC members have set out a more substantive approach, calling for investigation into why the conflicts were created in the first place, and whether they signalled the need for changing existing treaties? Binder notes that an alternative threshold could have been for treaties to be modified or terminated on the basis of 'substantive criteria of fairness': such criteria had been favoured by national liberation movements but

177 Lauterpacht, 'Codification and Development of International Law', 35.

countered by ILC members such as de Luna, the delegate from 'fascist Spain'.[178] To Binder, the ILC's approach revealed a preference for the 'naked power' of some States. Yet, the ILC discussions suggest that the various members did not take the view that they had provided a threshold of naked power; rather, they seemed to consider substantive criteria unnecessary. Indeed, it is not a foregone conclusion that a fairness criterion would have levelled the playing field between States; as a criterion that at least at the time had little content, 'fairness' might indeed have lent itself more easily to 'naked power'. But it is significant that the ILC members took the view that recourse to legal process, and even the possibility of recourse to legal process, by generating responsive politics, would ensure appropriate outcomes even without the oversight of some substantive value.

As to the Commission's constructivist assumptions, whilst we should be careful in attributing to ILC members ideas that were explicitly (and cautiously) advanced in connection with international relations and international law only much later,[179] it is possible to see two major constructivist propositions in their proposals.

The first is the view of international law as both 'a thing and a process'[180] – and correspondingly, reading treaty conflict in terms of the mutual constitution of international law and sovereignty. This is expressed in the ILC members' recognition of the changes in law catalysed by treaty conflict, coupled with the belief that international law as

[178] Binder, *Treaty Conflict and Political Contradiction*, 100.

[179] As Chapter 1 notes, the earliest works applying constructivist theory to international relations and international law came two decades after the adoption of the VCLT. These include: F. Kratochwil, *Rules, Norms and Decisions* (Cambridge University Press 1989); N. Onuf, *World of Our Making: Rules and Rule in Social Theory and International Relations* (University of South Carolina Press 1989); N. Onuf, 'The Constitution of International Society' (1994) 5 *European Journal of International Law* 1; E. Adler, 'Seizing the Middle Ground: Constructivism in World Politics' (1997) 3 *European Journal of International Relations* 319; A. Wendt, *Social Theory of International Politics* (Cambridge University Press 1998); J. G. Ruggie, 'What Makes the World Hang Together? Neo-Utilitarianism and the Social Constructivist Challenge' (1998) 52 *International Organization* 855; N. Onuf, 'Constructivism: A User's Manual', in V. Kubálková *et al.* (eds.), *International Relations in a Constructed World* (New York, M. E. Sharpe 1998). Recent works explicitly applying constructivist theory to international law include: A. C. Arend, *Legal Rules and International Society* (Oxford University Press 1999); J. Brunnée and S. Toope, *Legitimacy and Legality in International Law: An Interactional Account* (Cambridge University Press, 2010); and A. Sinclair, *International Relations Theory and International Law: A Critical Approach* (Cambridge University Press 2010).

[180] Onuf, 'The Constitution of International Society', 1–2.

it stood should also govern these changes. Thus, they sought rules that expressed both law's integrity (as an institution structuring State autonomy) and its instrumentality (being shaped by States).

The second, related, idea is of subjects internalising the institution of law as a result of using it.[181] Jutta Brunnée and Stephen Toope have traced this view in Lon Fuller's work on 'fidelity to law' as the result of it being possible to 'reason' with it – to *use* law.[182] For Fuller, this is the case in any legal system that has a certain inner morality, that is, if its laws satisfy eight conditions: generality, promulgation, prospectivity, clarity, coherence, stability, not demanding the impossible, and congruence between official action and declared rules. Brunnée and Toope also observe that international law structures the practice of building, maintaining and destroying particular norms, on the basis that it is possible to achieve these ends *through* law.[183]

The ILC commentaries reflect the same sense: that appropriately formulated rules would promote recourse to legal discourse as a means of settling competing claims. International law could therefore provide the transactional medium even if it could not quite support strong and compulsory institutions. This would, in addition, strengthen respect for the idea of international law in international affairs. This understanding indicates that the ILC indeed took a long view of the potential contribution of its own work.

Eddies in the mainstream

Contrary to accounts of the early ILC that would reduce its work – as they would reduce mainstream scholarship more generally – to a simple doctrinalism or concession to power politics, the ILC reports on treaty conflict and the writings of its individual members reveal a vision of international law that blends philosophy, politics, anxiety and strategy. The Commission was asked to provide appropriate rules on an issue (treaty conflict) that tested the limits of international law, and had to do so at a time when both international law and the ILC itself had only a fragile presence in international relations. The Commission took the view that Article 30, enabling States to press for performance of their

[181] On which, see Onuf, *World of Our Making*, 9–61.
[182] L. Fuller, *The Morality of Law* (revised edn, Yale University Press 1969), 40–1; see also L. Fuller, 'Positivism and Fidelity to Law' (1957) 71 *Harvard Law Review* 630, 632 *et seq.*
[183] Brunnée and Toope, *Legitimacy and Legality*, Chapter 1.

treaties in legal terms, would work better than a provision setting out a detailed scheme on the outcomes of treaty conflict in various situations. They considered that the former would encourage States to engage through the medium of international law, while the latter's very decisiveness might lead States to resist mediating treaty conflicts through international law.

In essence, the ILC members viewed immediate challenges (here, treaty conflict) in the context of conceptual and social theories of international law and its relationship to politics, without succumbing to the trap either of pure realism or of rigid formalism. Their work reveals the presence of liberal and constructivist assumptions that informed, albeit in different ways, a project of strengthening international law. The liberal assumption lay in the idea that an appropriately crafted provision would encourage recourse to a legal discourse between States, which in turn would promote better outcomes of treaty conflict. The constructivist assumption lay in the idea that steering States towards a legal discourse would ultimately strengthen respect for international law as a transactional medium.

While there is scope for a more elaborate critique of liberal and constructivist assumptions about international law, it is important to note that the ILC's subtle understanding of international law's role resonates with many of us international lawyers today. In the face of near-existential critiques that international law is an epiphenomenon or (at the same time) complicit with power politics, it is a similar sense of the 'integrity amidst instrumentality' of international law's processes that provides the basis for our continued faith in it. This sense may also be seen to pervade institutional proposals for altering multilateral treaties challenged by treaty conflict, discussed next.

3 The idea of effective implementation of treaties

> If a treaty regime is to endure and continue to serve its basic purpose over time, it must be adaptable to inevitable changes in technology, shifts in substantive problems, and economic, social and political developments ... [T]reaty lawyers have developed ways to deal with the problem of adaptation without seeking formal amendment.
>
> A. Chayes and A. H. Chayes[1]

Three variations on a theme

The previous chapter discussed the International Law Commission's efforts to address treaty conflict by way of a legal rule that would reconcile the disruptive and dynamic implications of treaty conflict for international legal order; this culminated in their strategic adoption of the principle of political decision. The present chapter continues the exploration of mainstream international legal thought, but now in the context of the mainstream's application of a different lens to treaties and treaty conflicts.

Viewed through this lens, the most prominent feature of a treaty conflict is not the conflict itself, but the challenge that it poses to the effective operation of one or more of the relevant (especially, multilateral) treaties. Indeed, treaty conflict is but one of a number of ways in which multilateral treaties may be challenged: the three strands of legal thought examined in this chapter are also concerned with other practices of 'lawfare' including refusals to accept the treaties in question as legitimate, and attempts to (re)describe their scope through interpretation and practice. Common to these strands is the focus on effective

[1] A. Chayes and A. H. Chayes, *The New Sovereignty: Compliance with International Regulatory Agreements* (Harvard University Press 1998) 225–6.

implementation of the treaties facing such challenges; each contemplates that this may call for the *institutional modification* (as distinct from formal amendment) of specific terms of those treaties. The chapter examines the bases upon which these strands justify institutional modification, and what these justifications reveal of their proposers' conceptions of international law. Moreover, explaining that the approach taken in each of the three strands may be described as managerialist, the chapter also offers a layered view of managerial thought in international law.

The first strand, typified in Sir Hersch Lauterpacht's doctrine of approximate application,[2] reflects a quasi-constitutionalist view of international legal order as a framework of treaties, custom and general principles, inclining towards universal community, stewarded by judicial expertise. According to this doctrine, a court might alter a multilateral treaty for the sake of its effective implementation if it finds that the treaty had been intended to establish an objective regime. The chapter explores the context in which Lauterpacht outlined this doctrine, his justifications, and later iterations of the doctrine in the work of Shabtai Rosenne,[3] and in the *Gabčíkovo-Nagymaros Project* case.[4]

The second strand explored in the chapter is the compliance-management approach that has been especially visible in international law and international relations discourses in the United States. Under this approach, it is up to international institutions, especially treaty bodies affiliated to multilateral treaties, to promote compliance; mainly through various persuasive and monitoring mechanisms, but also by adapting the treaties to their members' capacities to comply. The chapter interrogates this approach through an analysis of Abram Chayes and Antonia Chayes' 1995 book, *The New Sovereignty*.

The third strand, still emerging in literature, reconceives treaties as not merely formal legal instruments, but also as vehicles for specific projects of international order. In this view, treaty conflict provides opportunities for reviewing these projects, and modifying them in light of the critiques generated or revealed by their conflicts with other projects. Treaty 'conflict', then, is no more than a call for 'treaty coordination' or 'regime interaction'. The chapter explores two works, Rüdiger Wolfrum and Nele Matz's book on treaty

[2] *Admissibility of Hearings of Petitioners by the Committee on South West Africa*, Separate Opinion of Sir Hersch Lauterpacht (1956) ICJ Rep 35.

[3] S. Rosenne, *Breach of Treaty* (Cambridge, Grotius 1985).

[4] *Gabčíkovo-Nagymaros Project (Hungary/Slovakia)*, Judgment (1997) ICJ Rep 7.

coordination,[5] and Margaret Young's monograph on regime interaction,[6] that provide the most detailed commentaries on this mode of implementing multilateral treaties.

This chapter cuts into a vast body of international literature: scholarship produced in different periods, at different places and within highly differentiated scholarly traditions and schools. While possibly all the works explored draw upon their authors' contemporaneous location in, or experience of, practice, their practitioner contexts are also different: Lauterpacht's doctrine comes from a sitting judge of the International Court of Justice (ICJ or 'Court'); the Chayeses, and Abram Chayes in particular, played a role in shaping US foreign policy; Wolfrum served in German and international advisory positions and as judge on the International Tribunal for the Law of the Sea; Young had a stint at the WTO. Most importantly, these works do not speak to each other; cross-references are rare.[7] With all these differences, there is little to gain from a *comparative* exercise – that could only result in misleading or bland conclusions about the varied scope of each approach (which hardly needs pointing out). So, the purpose of the chapter is not as such to compare or contrast, but to present a number of perspectives on effective implementation of treaties.

The chapter does trace common currents in the three perspectives it examines: institutional modification of treaties, justified on 'recourse to law' assumptions. To the extent that these currents can be deduced in each of the three, it offers the tentative suggestion that the broad church of mainstream scholarship is united in its liberal and constructivist assumptions about international law. The suggestion must be tentative, for the chapter seeks a precarious balance between breadth and depth of engagement with relevant literature. In order to present a variety, its reviews are necessarily brief; but, equally, its selection is not exhaustive.[8] Despite this, I hope that enough is presented to illuminate

5 R. Wolfrum and N. Matz, *Conflicts in International Environmental Law* (London, Springer 2003).

6 M. Young, *Trading Fish, Saving Fish: The Interaction between Regimes in International Law* (Cambridge University Press 2011).

7 Young's book, which is the most recent, briefly notes a resonance with Chayes and Chayes' view that 'adherence to international law is based on active management by parties and actors' (185), but does not amplify this; it does not cite Wolfrum and Matz. Wolfrum and Matz do not cite Chayes and Chayes or the doctrine of approximate application; Chayes and Chayes do not consider the doctrine of approximate application.

8 Missing in particular is an examination of the New Haven policy science approach. It would be quite impossible to do justice to a fourth strand in one short chapter.

several different modes of treaty implementation and to justify the conclusions drawn.

The chapter also addresses itself to a further, descriptive aim, related to the rise of managerialism in international law. This rise is highlighted particularly in Martti Koskenniemi's writings,[9] neatly critiqued and summarised in Fleur Johns' recent book.[10] Johns notes that, for Koskenniemi, managerialism represents

> a 'view' or 'mindset' concerned with coordinating relations amongst transnational 'regimes' or fields of expertise while 'faithfully' refining and reproducing the logic of the regime or field of expert knowledge with which one primarily identifies. Its gestures are those of 'contextual deal-striking', balancing and adjusting. Its reading of freedom is as strategic-interest realisation. Its preference is for 'informal "regimes"' rather than 'the formal aspects of the legal craft that it often sees as an obstacle for effective action'. Its fantasy is to counsel the prince towards 'concrete results' without much regard for normative analysis of those results; for managerialism, 'the objectives of institutional action are given'. In managerialists' hands ... international law has become a set of 'rules of thumb or soft standards that refer to the best judgment of the experts in the [subdisciplinary] box' from which they emanate.[11]

Johns suggests that in advancing these observations, Koskenniemi retreats from a more complex understanding of the 'manoeuvres, mannerisms and multivalence' of international law's 'disciplinary voice', such as that which he had advanced in *From Apology to Utopia*.[12] In that book, he had noted international lawyers' 'characteristically modern appeals to politics, policies and ideals' and their '"constant movement"

[9] M. Koskenniemi, 'The Fate of Public International Law: Between Technique and Politics' (2007) 70 *Modern Law Review* 1; M. Koskenniemi, 'International Law: Constitutionalism, Managerialism and the Ethos of Legal Education' (2007) 1 *European Journal of Legal Studies* 1; M. Koskenniemi, 'The Politics of International Law – 20 Years Later' (2009) 20 *European Journal of International Law* 7.

[10] F. Johns, *Non-Legality in International Law: Unruly Law* (Cambridge University Press 2013) Chapter 1.

[11] *ibid.*, 16 (citations omitted; they refer to the works listed in footnote 2, above). Johns notes that Koskenniemi ascribes the fall of classical international law to the influence of late-nineteenth to mid-twentieth-century French thought concerning international social administration, inter-war emigré lawyers' efforts to entrench a professionally administered cosmopolitan legal system modelled on the institutions of the liberal state; and the convergence of law and instrumentalism in the United States in the aftermath of the Second World War: *ibid.*, 14. The most detailed account is M. Koskenniemi, *The Gentle Civilizer of Nations: The Rise and Fall of International Law 1870–1960* (Cambridge University Press 2001).

[12] M. Koskenniemi, From Apology to Utopia: The Structure of International Legal Argument (reissue with a new epilogue, Cambridge University Press 2005).

between these positions', as well as their propensity to 'look "beyond modern (liberal) doctrines" by reference to notions of justice or equitableness and to appeal to particular descriptions of social fact'; though he had said much less about international lawyers' 'techniques of calibration and prediction'.[13] Koskenniemi's account of the turn to managerialism flattens this rich texture of legal argumentation by presenting it as simply a turn to deformalised decision-making by experts seeking to advance this or that policy goal, signifying international law's fall and its need for rescue by the return to a 'culture of formalism'.[14]

Johns challenges the usefulness of the formal versus anti-formal distinction as the basis for understanding the dynamics and stakes of contemporary international legal work; and in several quasi-ethnographic studies offers detailed 'maps' of the managerialist technique of legal professionals. In agreement with her project of unpacking international legal managerialism, this chapter offers a complementary though less detailed account of managerial thought in the context of institutional implementation of multilateral treaties. The three strands it explores all reflect traces of what Koskenniemi describes as managerialism: Chayes and Chayes consciously describe their approach as managerial; and Young, whose approach, like Wolfrum and Matz's, promotes balancing and adjusting and informal regimes, describes the risks of managerialism as constantly present in contexts of regime interaction. Even the classic international lawyer, Lauterpacht, cannot resist managerial metaphors in explaining the scope of permissible approximate application. Yet, in each case, the managerial element is shot through with complex understandings of the concept and role of international law, which the chapter explores.

Approximate application of treaties

'Approximate application' has had a limited articulation in international law, being confined to one separate opinion, one scholarly investigation and one plea before the ICJ. Moreover, these articulations do not quite agree on the nature, or content, of the concept. The first to discuss it, Sir Hersch Lauterpacht's 1956 Separate Opinion in *Admissibility of Hearings of Petitioners*, did not use the term 'approximate application'. The only monograph to engage with it, Shabtai Rosenne's

[13] Johns, *Non-Legality in International Law*, 16–17.
[14] Term introduced in Koskenniemi, The Gentle Civilizer of Nations, 500.

1985 *Breach of Treaty*, referred to it as a 'theory'. In *Gabčíkovo–Nagymaros Project*, Slovakia stoutly asserted a 'doctrine' of approximate application that departed in its content from both Lauterpacht and Rosenne's conceptions of it.

Nevertheless, the concept is interesting in that, to Lauterpacht, it offered a plausible basis for a *court* to alter the terms of a multilateral treaty. He defended approximate application as principled, commonsensical and appropriate in situations where a State's non-compliance could not be adequately addressed by rules on termination, or on State responsibility for breach of obligation. As discussed in Chapter 1, many strategically created treaty conflicts give rise to such situations. This section will unpack the concept of approximate application, and the rationale that animates it.

Lauterpacht and South-West Africa

Admissibility of Hearings was one amongst a string of cases related to South-West Africa (present-day Namibia) that occupied the ICJ's docket during the 1950s and 1960s. South-West Africa, a former German colony, was classified by the League of Nations as a Mandate territory to be administered by South Africa (then a British dominion) under supervision of the League Council. With the termination of the League in 1946 arose the question of whether the Mandate too had come to an end, or whether it could continue under the aegis of the United Nations. South Africa, which had since achieved full independence from Britain, claimed that, with the dissolution of the League, the Mandate had lapsed.[15] It proposed to integrate South-West Africa into its own territory. However, the Court, asked by the UN General Assembly for an advisory opinion on this question, concluded that the Mandate continued and the General Assembly could take on the League Council's supervisory powers,[16] on the condition that

> [t]he degree of supervision to be exercised by the General Assembly should not ... exceed that which applied under the Mandates System, and should conform as far as possible to the procedure followed ... by the [League Council].[17]

[15] South Africa's position was spelt out in its oral submissions: see Statement by Dr Steyn, Minutes of the Public Sittings Held at the Peace Palace, The Hague from May 16th to 23rd, and on July 11th 1950, CR 1950, 273–317, www.icj-cij.org/docket/files/10/8935.pdf.

[16] *International Status of South-West Africa*, Advisory Opinion (1950) ICJ Rep 128.

[17] *ibid.*, 138.

The General Assembly duly established a Committee to supervise South Africa's administration of South-West Africa, but found South Africa unwilling to cooperate.[18] Given South Africa's attitude, the Committee began to explore creative ways of fulfilling its supervisory functions, and the General Assembly made several references to the ICJ for advice on the consistency of these measures with the limitative clause laid down in its earlier Opinion.[19] In *Admissibility of Hearings*, which came during Lauterpacht's tenure on the bench, the Court was asked whether it was 'consistent with [its 1950 Opinion] for the Committee ... to grant oral hearings to petitioners on matters relating to the territory of South West Africa?'[20] Oral hearings had never been granted by the League Council, so the issue was whether, in doing so, the Committee would exceed the degree of supervision exercised under the Mandates System.

In deciding the case, the Court and Lauterpacht came to the same answer – that it was permissible for the Committee to grant oral hearings – but for different reasons. The Court held that it was consistent with its previous Opinion for the Committee to grant oral hearings, because these would not 'add to the obligations of the Mandatory and thus lay upon it a heavier burden than it was subject to under the Mandates System'.[21] The Court noted that it must be guided by the paramount purpose of safeguarding the 'sacred trust of civilization' through effective international supervision of the Mandate; and especially given the practical difficulties caused to the Committee by South Africa's non-cooperation, direct oral hearings might enable it to better judge the merits of each petition.[22]

Lauterpacht, however, argued that oral hearings did imply a more stringent degree of supervision and the Committee could *not* have granted them if South Africa had not been uncooperative.[23] For him, the essential concern was overcoming South Africa's non-cooperation to maintain effective supervision of the Mandate regime. This, he concluded, could only be accomplished by some modification of the terms

[18] UNGA Res. 749A (28 November 1953).

[19] The others, in addition to the opinion discussed in this chapter, were: *Voting Procedure*, Advisory Opinion (1955) ICJ Rep 67; *Legal Consequences for States of the Continued Presence of South Africa in Namibia (South West Africa)*, Advisory Opinion (1971) ICJ Rep 16. The Court also decided two contentious cases: *South West Africa cases (Ethiopia* v. *South Africa; Liberia* v. *South Africa)*, Preliminary Objections (1962) ICJ Rep 319; and *Second Phase*, Judgment (1966) ICJ Rep 6.

[20] *Admissibility of Hearings*, Advisory Opinion (1956) ICJ Rep 23, 24.

[21] *ibid.*, 30.

[22] *ibid.*, 27–8.

[23] *Admissibility of Hearings*, Separate Opinion of Judge Lauterpacht, 39.

of the regime, which could be made by the Court itself. Rosenne describes this decision as 'the doctrine of approximate application'.[24]

This was a significant doctrine for Lauterpacht to embrace, for it amounted to the argument that the *Court*, rather than the *parties* to a legal instrument (to which he likened the Mandate), could legally alter its terms; this marked a qualification of the principle of State consent. Therefore, it is important to understand why Lauterpacht considered its use to be justified.

Lauterpacht's principal reason was that to modify the terms of the Mandate was in keeping with its very scheme. He asserted that the Mandate regime expounded in the 1950 Opinion was

> a régime in the nature of an objective law which is legally operative irrespective of the conduct of the Union of South Africa ... [and] must be given effect except in so far as its application is rendered impossible, in terms of its general purpose, having regard to the attitude adopted by the Union. To that extent there are permissible such modifications in its application as are necessary to maintain – but no more – [its] effectiveness.[25]

Analogising the regime laid out in the 1950 Opinion to a treaty, Lauterpacht explained:

> It is a sound principle of law that whenever a legal instrument of continuing validity cannot be applied literally owing to the conduct of one of the parties, it must, without allowing that party to take advantage of its own conduct, be applied in a way approximating most closely to its primary object. To do that is to interpret and to give effect to the instrument, not to change it.[26]

This followed from the fact that the regime 'like any other legal text', must be read as a whole, that is, 'not merely with regard to its individual clauses but in relation to its major purpose'. Because South Africa's non-fulfilment of its Mandate obligations had destroyed the conditions under which the limitative clause of the 1950 opinion (specifying the permissible degree of supervision) could operate, it was 'unreasonable to uphold fully and literally the limitations of a rule after the possibility of giving effect to the rule itself has disappeared'.[27] A conflict had arisen, 'as the result of the action of a party, between the overriding purpose of the instrument and its individual provisions and limitations'.[28] In such a case, the Court could not permit particular rules to thwart the overall purpose.

[24] Rosenne, *Breach of Treaty*, 95–101.

[25] *Admissibility of Hearings*, Separate Opinion of Judge Lauterpacht, 46. [26] *ibid.*

[27] *ibid.*, 45. [28] *ibid.*

This, then, was Lauterpacht's view of approximate application. Lauterpacht clarified that it did not have a punitive purpose. Indeed, measures of approximate application 'would not be permissible if they were attempted not because of . . . real need but as an expression of the disapproval'.[29] The key justification was the essence of a regime-creating multilateral instrument:

> [T]heir validity continues notwithstanding changes in the attitudes, or the status, or the very survival of individual parties or persons affected. Their continuing validity implies their continued operation and the resulting legitimacy of the means devised for that purpose by way of judicial interpretation and application of the original instrument. The unity and the operation of the régime created by them cannot be allowed to fail because of a breakdown or gap which may arise in consequence of an act of a party or otherwise.[30]

Therefore, for Lauterpacht, the basis for approximate application was the Mandate's similarity to *special* (interdependent and integral) multilateral treaties, whose continuing validity he had defended as an ILC member.[31] Moreover, *good faith* and *common sense* would support the Court's decision to substitute 'a measure of supervision or an act of performance for one repudiated or frustrated by the party affected by the instrument in question'.[32] The same basic principles of good faith and common sense underpinned the related principles of 'estoppel'; that 'a State cannot benefit from its own wrong'; and that a State cannot rely on 'the non-fulfilment of an obligation imposed on it by an international engagement'.[33]

We see that Lauterpacht considered approximate application a justified exercise of judicial authority in service of multilateral regimes. The intermixing of the factual assertion and the normative prescription that had guided him as an ILC member was also obvious here:[34] Lauterpacht simultaneously claimed that certain multilateral instruments *remain* valid despite breach, non-performance or other challenge, and that the regimes they establish *should not be* allowed to fail. Thus, the Court may act as he suggested.

However, judicial authority in this respect was not unlimited. Lauterpacht carefully outlined three conditions upon which the Court might justifiably make use of approximate application. The first of these, as discussed, was that the treaty in question should have

[29] *ibid.*, 53. [30] *ibid.*, 48. [31] See Chapter 2.
[32] *Admissibility of Hearings*, Separate Opinion of Judge Lauterpacht, 47–8, 55. [33] *ibid.*
[34] See the discussion in Chapter 2 on Lauterpacht's work on treaty conflict.

established an objective regime of continuing validity. Lauterpacht used the *Interpretation of Peace Treaties (Second Phase)*[35] case as an example of a situation in which the Court may not use approximate application: in that case the parties to the peace treaties had failed 'not accidentally, *but by design*' to endow the dispute settlement clauses with a 'full measure of effectiveness'.[36]

The second condition also concerned the non-cooperative attitude of States party to the treaty. Though approximate application was not a punitive measure, and though Lauterpacht generally embraced an evolutionary approach to multilateral treaties, preferring to adapt rather than terminate them,[37] he felt his specific suggestions in this particular case were legitimated by South Africa's conduct. South Africa's actions in rejecting the continuation of the League Mandate under UN supervision, and its refusal to cooperate with the UN General Assembly's Committee for South West Africa, reconciled for him the systemic imperative driving approximate application with the sovereign right of a State upon which – in this case – it imposed an additional burden.

The third condition seemed to refer not to the Court's authority, but to its expertise. Lauterpacht insisted that the modifications must be precisely calibrated: made only to the extent needed to maintain the effective operation of the regime. In fact, he used various metaphors of technical competence to emphasise this point, describing the modifications as analogous to 'removing a clog or filling a lacuna or adopting an alternative device in order to prevent a standstill of the entire system on account of a failure in any particular link or part'.[38]

Overall, Lauterpacht's discussion implies that approximate application may be used in situations other than where literal application of a treaty is made impossible by a State party, for instance, due to a fundamental change of circumstances. However, in these situations, the variations would have to be more respectful of the States' sovereign rights; and, in any case, made only to the extent necessary to maintain effective operation of the regime.

After Lauterpacht

The doctrine was named and further developed by Rosenne. While building on Lauterpacht's formulation and conditions, Rosenne imported two features into it. First, that the doctrine may, in fact,

[35] Advisory Opinion (1950) ICJ Rep 221. [36] *ibid.* (emphasis added).
[37] *Admissibility of Hearings*, Separate Opinion of Judge Lauterpacht, 49. [38] *ibid.*, 48.

demand the active participation of States in the process. And, second, that it may be applied not just by courts, but also by competent non-judicial organs:

> [F]aced with a situation of established breach ... the parties themselves in the first instance, renegotiate and apply the treaty in good faith and where they are not successful in doing this themselves, then acting through or with the assistance of a competent international organ, whether judicial or not are legally obliged to take steps to redraft the treaty or reformulate the subsystem so as to ensure its continued effective application.[39]

The first of these additional features, that is, the legal obligation of States to renegotiate treaties, had been partly implied in Lauterpacht's explanation, for he assumed that States would have to *accept* the modifications made by a court, but did not indicate a duty upon them to participate in renegotiating the treaty. The second was simply an expansion, for Lauterpacht had concerned himself solely with what the Court might do. Possibly, Rosenne was actuated by the expectation that non-judicial international organs could more proactively use the concept, and could be relied on to make the exact calibrations demanded by Lauterpacht:

> With the growing complexity of international treaty-making and a rapidly changing general international situation, formal amendment of treaties is becoming increasingly [difficult]. As a counterpart to this, when a treaty applied as its authors originally intended comes under strain, it is easy to proclaim breach ... [However, the doctrine of approximate application] if skilfully used may serve as a prod to the renegotiation, reinterpretation or readaptation of a treaty which in its general lines remains desirable to all parties but which in its details cannot stand up to the wear and tear of daily life. The doctrine is thus a constructive contribution to the general stability of juridical relations which are to be coupled in appropriate cases with a *carefully controlled dose of peaceful change and adaptation*.[40]

Rosenne was persuaded that the doctrine fell within the general approach of the law of treaties 'which found expression in Article 60 of the [VCLT] and in the discussions which preceded it ... which was not inclined to regard breach of a treaty as automatically putting an end to the existence of the treaty obligation, and which placed overriding importance on the maintenance and stability of international treaty relationships'.[41]

39 Rosenne, *Breach of Treaty*, 100.
40 *ibid.* (emphasis added; the last phrase, 'carefully controlled dose', is yet another allusion to technical expertise).
41 *ibid.* See also *Admissibility of Hearings*, Separate Opinion of Judge Lauterpacht, 55–6.

Rosenne's additions to the doctrine sketched out by Lauterpacht, though minor, set in motion various misreadings which either claimed or challenged the doctrine of approximate application as signifying a *unilateral* measure that could be imposed by one State upon another. Pierre-Marie Dupuy, for instance, in a short essay in 1998, insisted that Rosenne's formulation should be read as indicating a narrow remit for the doctrine, as merely requiring parties to negotiate with each other to overcome impediments to the literal application of a treaty.[42] He added that there was no suggestion in VCLT Article 60 that would permit a State to unilaterally invoke the doctrine: '[n]o trace of such a principle is ... to be found in the only provision dealing with the conduct to be adopted by one party to a treaty on account of breach by another party, which is Article 60.'[43] Dupuy also suggested that the activation of the doctrine could only be an exceptional measure, for the purpose of safeguarding the continuance of a 'sacred trust of civilization'. On the basis of a passage taken from the Court's opinion in *Admissibility of Hearings*, rather than Lauterpacht's Separate Opinion, he claimed that this exceptional character was at the 'core' of Lauterpacht's position.[44] However, Dupuy's reasoning errs on all counts: Lauterpacht's reasoning had little to do with sacred trusts or other adjectival qualities of the Mandate; and Rosenne had not outlined the possibility that parties might unilaterally redraft a treaty. Rosenne's focus was on their joint legal obligation to take the assistance of an international organ. That would be in keeping with the *approach* of Article 60. Nevertheless, Dupuy's criticisms are illuminating, for they were shaped in response to the grosser misreading of the doctrine that Slovakia advanced in *Gabčíkovo-Nagymaros*, where Dupuy had been counsel for Hungary.

Misreadings in Gabčíkovo-Nagymaros

In *Gabčíkovo-Nagymaros*, Slovakia had attempted to considerably broaden the scope of the doctrine, equating it with its own unilateral entitlement to modify its bilateral agreement with Hungary, following Hungary's breach of the same.[45] Slovakia ignored the fact that Lauterpacht had outlined the doctrine in terms of what a court might do to safeguard treaties it judged to be of continuing validity. Indeed, Slovakia

[42] P.-M. Dupuy, 'On the "Doctrine" of Approximate Application of Treaties in International Law', in G. Hafner *et al.* (eds.), *Liber Amicorum: Ignaz Siedl-Hohenveldern – In Honour of His 80th Birthday* (The Hague, Kluwer 1998) 97, 102.

[43] *ibid.*, 102. [44] *ibid.*, 100. In footnote 10, Dupuy cites p. 28 of the Court's Opinion.

[45] *Gabčíkovo-Nagymaros*, Slovakia's Memorial, Vol. I (2 May 1994) 285, para. 7.21.

suggested that the doctrine was not limited to treaties establishing regimes *in rem*, for the 'underlying reasons of principle and policy' supported the protection of all types of treaty relations:

> [T]o refuse the ability of the injured party to put the treaty into best effect, merely because the other party has refused to perform its part, is ... to widen the tolerated circumstances for non-performance and to put in jeopardy the stability of treaty relations ... [N]o proper satisfaction for breach of treaty can be achieved save through an approximate measure of performance and a State may not benefit from its wrongdoing.[46]

Slovakia also claimed that the treaty in question was essential to the safety of its inhabitants.[47] Slovakia's reasons were phrased similarly to Rosenne's, but its conception of approximate application departed significantly from the formulations of both Lauterpacht and Rosenne. Neither Lauterpacht nor Rosenne would have upheld the view that the doctrine could be used unilaterally by a State, or to modify an ordinary bilateral treaty breached by one of its parties. Slovakia claimed that its proposed modifications complied with Lauterpacht's condition that they be 'such ... as are necessary to maintain – but no more – the realisation of the objectives'.[48] But they were, in fact, substantial; the ICJ noted that they fell outside the limits of the treaty.[49]

The *Gabčíkovo–Nagymaros* case is a good example of the subversion of a framework (founded on a complex of treaty law principles, judicial authority and analogies to technical expertise) to purely instrumental reasoning (intended to advance Slovakia's desired goal, the Danube dam). For, even as it cited the 'doctrine' of approximate application, Slovakia proceeded to reformulate each of its accompanying conditions with reference to extra-legal imperatives or loose purposive justifications ('community interest in the protection of all treaties').

This subversion perhaps is what Judge Bedjaoui responded to in the sharp criticism of the doctrine recorded in his Separate Opinion in the case. Bedjaoui stated that 'because of its dangers, this theory [of approximate application] deserved wholehearted censure'.[50] He was concerned that any State which undertook a specific obligation would be

> free to fulfil another, which it would be cunning to present as very close to the first obligation. The State would only have to observe that its

[46] *ibid.*, 285–6, paras. 7.22–7.24. [47] *ibid.*, 288, para. 7.30. [48] *ibid.*, 285, para. 7.21.

[49] *Gabčíkovo–Nagymaros*, Judgment, 50, para. 76.

[50] *Gabčíkovo–Nagymaros*, Separate Opinion of Judge Bedjaoui (1997) ICJ Rep 120, 127, para. 30.

> '*approximate application*' was allowed since, according to it, the conduct of the other party placed it in the impossibility of performing its obligations under the treaty and since it had no other remedy. All breaches of the obligations of the State would thus run the risk of being presented as an '*approximate application*'.[51]

Bedjaoui indicated that the lack of a reliable criterion for measuring the 'tolerable degree of "proximity" or "approximation" . . . [which] is left to the subjective evaluation of the State',[52] allowed effective 'reinterpretation' of a treaty without the consent of all States-parties.[53] This concern was anticipated in Lauterpacht's careful explanation, offering several conditions to regulate the exercise of judicial discretion. Bedjaoui's criticisms reveal an overall anxiety as to the thin line between principled and purely instrumental uses of approximate application, which Slovakia crossed.

Hungary made a detailed challenge to Slovakia's reasoning, promptly demanding evidence for the 'so-called' doctrine that 'Slovakia presents . . . as if it were a well-established and self-evident rule of positive international law. This is certainly not the case.'[54] Hungary's rejection was essentially directed at Slovakia's reading, and it seemed to concede that approximate application may be a relevant concept in more limited cases, such as in the situation confronting Lauterpacht.[55] Hungary insisted that Slovakia had failed to establish a legal basis for the doctrine that could support its expansive reading, which extended to unilateral measures. Hungary's Counter Memorial asserted that there was no rule of approximate application in the law of treaties, though Slovakia had tried to locate it 'under the auspices of "*pacta sunt servanda*" . . . as the counterpart of . . . "a State cannot benefit from its own wrongdoing"'. These ideas were of long pedigree which made it remarkable that '"approximate application" [was] virtually unheard of'.[56] The VCLT provided specific and exhaustive avenues of conduct available to a State facing a breach by another State.[57] Similarly, the law of State responsibility, and specifically its provisions on countermeasures, did not permit States to 'rewrite treaty provisions so as to give effect to them in an "appropriate" way'.[58]

[51] *ibid.*, 127–8, para. 31. [52] *ibid.*, 128, para. 31. [53] *ibid.*, 128, para. 32.
[54] *Gabčíkovo-Nagymaros*, Hungary's Counter Memorial, Vol. I (5 December 1994) 240, 241, para. 6.84.
[55] *ibid.*, 242–5. See especially para. 6.97. [56] *ibid.*, para. 6.85. [57] *ibid.*, para. 6.87.
[58] *ibid.*, 242, para. 6.88.

Slovakia, it appeared, had overextended a 'virtually unknown' doctrine, discussed only by Lauterpacht and Rosenne and missing from leading textbooks like Oppenheim's.[59] Approximate application, Hungary further claimed, could not be regarded as a customary rule or a general principle of international law. It found support 'neither in the practice of States nor in the jurisprudence of the [ICJ] or of any arbitral tribunal'. Curiously, Hungary referred to its non-use in the *Interpretation of Peace Treaties Case* in support of this claim[60] – Lauterpacht, it may be recalled, had used that case as an example of when a Court should not use the doctrine. However, Hungary was correct in its assessment of Slovakia's overly broad reading of the doctrine.

Slovakia appeared to recognise this, at least to the extent of accepting that there was a distinction to be made between ordinary bilateral treaties and treaties creating rights *in rem*. It claimed in its Reply that its treaty with Hungary (previously indicated as an ordinary bilateral treaty) fell into the latter category.[61] But its overall statement of the doctrine was no more coherent than before, for it now sought to assert that the doctrine was founded on the principle of restitution.[62] Restitution is not the basis for the doctrine; the doctrine is applied to secure the effective operation of a regime, not the mutual rights and obligations of States. For this reason, Hungary's insistence on the consent of all States parties was also misplaced.[63] Lauterpacht had taken onboard the consent argument to the extent of specifying that the regime in question must have been one of continuing validity, but believed that thereafter it would be up to a court to secure its effective operation by making the necessary modifications. As the next section will discuss, he seemed to consider carefully calibrated modifications by a judicial body a possible basis for renewed interactions between States, and other actors.

Approximate application and international law

Lauterpacht's expression of approximate application, therefore, remains the most carefully considered and the most strictly conditioned. It now remains to explore the role performed by this concept. To begin with, what is its legal status? Was Hungary correct in its claim that approximate

[59] *ibid.*, para. 6.89. [60] *ibid.*, para. 6.86.

[61] *Gabčíkovo-Nagymaros*, Slovakia's Reply, Vol. I (20 June 1995) 126, para. 6.19.

[62] *ibid.*, para. 6.20.

[63] *Gabčíkovo-Nagymaros*, Hungary's Counter Memorial, 246, para. 6.101.

application cannot be described as 'a principle of international law and a general principle of law',[64] or can the doctrine guide international courts or other organs in their decision-making? In *Gabčíkovo-Nagymaros*, the Court chose not to enter into this discussion, simply stating:

> It is not necessary . . . to determine whether there is a principle of international law or a general principle of law of 'approximate application' because, even if such a principle existed, it could by definition only be employed within the limits of the treaty in question.[65]

Academic commentary has received this statement in different ways. Some view the Court's holding as indicating its 'willingness to adopt the new concept if need should arise', as setting out a definite scope for its operation, that is, 'within the limits of the treaty in question', and as proof that 'the codifying character of the [VCLT] does not exclude the reception of new legal trends within its scope'.[66] Others view the judgment as having 'decisively rejected Slovakia's novel argument that international law recognised some doctrine of "approximate application" of treaties'.[67] Still others prefer to read neither affirmation nor rejection in the Court's opinion.[68]

Perhaps approximate application may be seen as a species of 'evolutive interpretation', though it would more accurately represent an extension of the same, since evolutive interpretation draws upon States' intention, expressed in the text, that the meaning of a treaty term should evolve over time,[69] while approximate application focuses on the fact that the treaty, overall, is one that seems to establish an objective regime. Moreover, evolutive interpretation cannot be used to impose additional obligations on States,[70] but in *Admissibility of Hearings*,

[64] *Gabčíkovo-Nagymaros*, Judgment, 53, para. 75. [65] *ibid.*, 53, para. 76.

[66] D. Reichert-Facilides, 'Down the Danube: The Vienna Convention on the Law of Treaties and the Case Concerning the Gabcikovo-Nagymaros Project' (1998) 47(4) *International and Comparative Law Quarterly* 837, 848.

[67] P. Okowa, 'Case Concerning the Gabcikovo-Nagymaros Project (Hungary/Slovakia) (Unreported, 1997) (ICJ)' (1998) 47(3) *International and Comparative Law Quarterly* 688, 694.

[68] M. Fitzmaurice and O. Elias, *Contemporary Issues in the Law of Treaties* (Utrecht, Eleven International Publishing 2005) 368.

[69] See J. Arato, 'Subsequent Practice and Evolutive Interpretation: Techniques of Treaty Interpretation over Time and Their Diverse Consequences' (2010) 9 *The Law and Practice of International Courts and Tribunals* 443.

[70] M. Fitzmaurice, 'Dynamic (Evolutive) Interpretation of Treaties and the European Court of Human Rights', in A. Orakhelashvili and S. Williams (eds.), *Forty Years of the Vienna Convention on the Law of Treaties* (London, BIICL 2010) 55, 93.

approximate application was Lauterpacht's basis for imposing a greater burden on South Africa.[71] But, even if approximate application *is* viewed as related to the principle of evolutive interpretation, this does not clarify its legal status: as Malgosia Fitzmaurice notes, the acceptability of evolutive interpretation is itself evolving.[72]

It is also difficult to claim that approximate application echoes a general principle of law recognised within municipal legal systems. While Rosenne found 'faint echoes' of the common law doctrine of *cy-près*[73] and Slovakia argued the similarity to common and civil law governing construction contracts,[74] these share only faint family resemblances with approximate application. Indeed, Slovakia's attempts to explain the doctrine through analogies only highlighted its failure to appreciate the rationale underlying approximate application.

Therefore, it is hard to offer a positive conclusion as to the legal status of approximate application. However, while not explicitly named or espoused, 'approximate application' is how international courts and other institutions (sometimes) respond where changes in context, or the actions of particular States, prevent the literal application of a treaty. Its echoes may be found in 'living tree' approaches to 'constitutional' treaties.[75] Indeed, as Slovakia pointed out (with greater merit than many of its other arguments), 'in all the cases concerning South Africa, commencing with the Advisory Opinion of 1950, the Court itself ... did in fact seek to secure an approximate application of the mandate treaty, in the face of South Africa's refusal to perform its obligations thereunder'.[76]

Moreover, despite Malgosia Fitzmaurice's observation that an evolutive approach, '(at the early stages of its development) must have been an unacceptable (if not shocking) violation of the sacred principles of

71 Though, as discussed, this was because the impediment to the literal application of the treaty was also provided by South Africa.

72 M. Fitzmaurice, 'Dynamic (Evolutive) Interpretation', 92 *et seq.*

73 Rosenne, *Breach of Treaty*, 100.

74 *Gabčíkovo-Nagymaros*, Slovakia's Reply, 129–31, paras. 6.28–6.33.

75 Tom Franck notes with respect to the UN Charter: 'What emerges from the vast legacy of recorded debates and decisions of principal political organs is that they tend to treat the Charter not as a static formula, but as a constitutive instrument capable of organic growth ... the Charter is "a living tree"': T. Franck, *Recourse to Force: State Action against Threats and Armed Attacks* (Cambridge University Press 2002) 6. Chapter 4 of this book will describe the role of the UN Law of the Sea Convention's Preparatory Commission in terms of approximate application.

76 *Gabčíkovo-Nagymaros*, Slovakia's Reply, 125, para. 6.14.

international law for classical international lawyers such as [Gerald] Fitzmaurice',[77] it is certainly the case that Lauterpacht (and Rosenne) invoked approximate application and considered it to be an application of the principle of effective interpretation. Indeed, the initial portions of Lauterpacht's Separate Opinion were a classic display of legal reasoning: he wove together arguments from common sense and reasonableness to point to well-founded if unexplored distinctions between types of treaties; indicated that justice demanded that the unity and operation of regimes established by multilateral treaties 'cannot be allowed to fail' due to the acts of particular States; drew analogies with principles such as 'estoppel', 'no State must benefit from its own wrong', or 'avail itself of an objection which would amount to relying on the non-fulfilment of an obligation imposed by an international engagement', which the Court had applied in other cases; and referred to conditions that governed the Court's use of approximate application. These included the character of the regime and the attitude of participating States, and stressed the precisely determined scope of the modifications to be made. In Lauterpacht's view, all of these factors provided a basis for the Court's exercise of its judicial authority to apply approximate application, for they ensured that the Court would do no more than give a proper interpretation to its 1950 Opinion.

In addition, Lauterpacht offered a further, subtle, reason in support of the Court's use of approximate application, which had to do with the function that it served. He pointed out that the *Admissibility of Hearings* case had emerged from the UN General Assembly's request for an Advisory Opinion. The General Assembly possessed the capacity to simply alter the Mandate supervision regime established by the Court's 1950 Opinion, but had *chosen* to seek the Court's advice on the propriety of introducing oral hearings. That is, through its reference, the General Assembly had initiated a *legal* discourse on the proper scope of a legal instrument (the 1950 Opinion), aimed at giving effect to its provisions. The Court had a duty to participate in and promote this discourse.

Lauterpacht observed that, while the Court would naturally have to remain unconcerned with the political effects of its decisions, it should 'as a matter of international public policy … bear in mind the indirect consequences of any pronouncement which, by giving a purely literal interpretation of the [1950 Opinion], would have rendered it impotent in face of obstruction by one party'.[78] Approximate application, by

[77] M. Fitzmaurice, 'Dynamic (Evolutive) Interpretation', 92.

[78] *Admissibility of Hearings*, Separate Opinion of Judge Lauterpacht, 57.

contrast, he implied, would preserve the instrument's potency; and moreover, reinforce the central place of law in deciding the consequences of South Africa's rejection of the Mandate.

In other words, Lauterpacht asserted that, given the opportunity to bring considerations of legal principle to bear upon a difficult political situation, the Court had the responsibility to show that international law could, and did, afford a medium to address that situation. This, then, is an additional justification for the doctrine: as a manifestation of the duty of a judicial or other international organ to participate in and promote a legal discourse between various actors on a particular issue, in this case on the effective operation of an international regime. This justification, like his previous work on treaty conflicts, evidences the liberal and constructivist strains in Lauterpacht's thought: he assumes that recourse to law should be promoted in order to achieve more appropriate outcomes; and that recourse to law would be so promoted by the Court's action in embracing a legal solution that combined integrity and instrumentality.[79]

Compliance management

Compliance-management literature sits within a broad field of 'compliance studies' that seek to explain 'why nations behave'.[80] It focuses on the role of organs affiliated to treaties in promoting compliance with those treaties.

Compliance studies' explanations are generally based on a combination of theoretical expectation and empirical observation. For instance, Thomas Franck focuses on the compliance-pull of legitimately generated international rules,[81] while Jack Goldsmith and Eric Posner argue that States only comply with treaties to the extent that the benefits of doing so exceed the costs.[82] Others point to

[79] See the section entitled 'Between philosophy and anxiety' in Chapter 2.

[80] The phrase is from J. Alvarez, 'Foreword, Why Nations Behave: A Symposium on Implementation, Compliance and Effectiveness' (1998) 19 *Michigan Journal of International Law* 303. Alvarez, in turn, draws upon Louis Henkin's book *How Nations Behave* (2nd edn, Columbia University Press 1979), especially famous for its observation that '[i]t is probably the case that almost all nations observe almost all principles of international law and almost all of their obligations almost all of the time' (47).

[81] T. Franck, *The Power of Legitimacy Among Nations* (Oxford University Press 1990).

[82] J. Goldsmith and E. Posner, *The Limits of International Law* (Oxford University Press 2005).

domestic politics,[83] or transnational politics,[84] or governmental networks,[85] or assert that international relations must be analysed as an iterated game.[86] Some constructivist theories suggest that compliance is also a function of the self-perception of States as law-abiding members of an international legal system.[87] Regime theory adds that 'institutions' foster cooperation because they 'provide information, reduce transaction costs, make commitments more credible, establish focal points for coordination, and in general facilitate the operation of reciprocity'.[88] While all these explanations occasionally persuade, none satisfies all its interlocutors, or prevents emergence of yet other explanations. Though the foregoing references may suggest otherwise, the field of compliance studies is neither new, nor solely concentrated in the United States; in a detailed review, Harold Koh has traced the recurring patterns of compliance explanations from scholars of antiquity to the present.[89]

The compliance-management literature draws upon some of the above explanations, but makes one additional point to explain how multilateral treaties are effectively implemented: institutions, particularly treaty-affiliated administrative bodies, actively encourage States to comply with their treaty commitments, including, if necessary, by adjusting specific treaty terms.

The 'new sovereignty' and the managerial approach

One of the most influential accounts of compliance management is offered in Chayes and Chayes' *The New Sovereignty*. Chayes and Chayes found their managerial theory on the presumption that States have a

[83] K. Raustiala, 'Refining the Limits of International Law' (2006) 34 Georgia Journal of International and Comparative Law 423; A. Moravcsik, 'Taking Preferences Seriously: A Liberal Theory of International Politics' (1997) 51 International Organization 513.

[84] R. Keohane and J. Nye, 'Transgovernmental Relations and International Organizations' (1974) 27 *World Politics* 39.

[85] A.-M. Slaughter, *A New World Order* (Princeton University Press 2004); A.-M. Slaughter, 'Sovereignty and Power in a Networked World Order' (2004) 40 *Stanford Journal of International Law* 283.

[86] J. Setear, 'An Iterative Perspective on Treaties: A Synthesis of International Relations Theory and International Law' (1996) 37 *Harvard International Law Journal* 139.

[87] A. C. Arend, 'Do Legal Rules Matter? International Law and International Politics' (1998) 38 *Virginia Journal of International Law* 107.

[88] R. Keohane and L. Martin, 'The Promise of Institutionalist Theory' (1995) 20 *International Security* 39.

[89] H. Koh, 'Review Essay: Why Do Nations Obey International Law?' (1997) 106 *Yale Law Journal* 2599.

propensity to comply with their treaty obligations for three reasons: efficiency, interest and the normative force of the treaty obligations. Compliance is often efficient, because decision-making involves costs; it may be less costly for States to comply with rules than to calculate an alternative course of action.[90] Moreover, the treaties may be in keeping with their interests – treaty negotiations do permit States to insist upon the fulfilment of their particular interests, and 'parties not only weigh the benefits and burdens of commitment, but also explore, redefine and sometimes discover their interests . . . [I]f the agreement is well-designed . . . compliance problems . . . are likely to be manageable.'[91] Chayes and Chayes also marshal empirical and academic analyses to show that social communities tend to develop and abide by norms; that norms provide 'a reason for action'; and define the international discourse through which States seek to justify their actions. Norms thus provide an independent basis for conforming behaviour.[92]

When, despite these factors, States fail to comply, it only rarely signals a 'premeditated and deliberate violation of treaty obligation'.[93] Instead, non-compliance may be attributed to the indeterminacy of treaty language, offering a 'considerable range within which parties may reasonably adopt differing positions as to the meaning of the relevant terms', making the very fact of non-compliance contestable.[94] Or the States may lack the regulatory, fiscal, bureaucratic, scientific or technical capacity to comply.[95] Alternatively, a treaty may envisage full compliance only over a period of time (particularly where compliance entails the making of significant socio-economic changes), so that a cross-sectional view of any given moment may mislead the observer.[96] Chayes and Chayes recognise that a State may strategically 'take advantage of the indeterminacy of treaty language to justify its preferred course of action'[97] – but point out that this is distinct from a deliberate violation.

At the core of these explanations is the 'new sovereignty', which consists not in 'the freedom of States to act independently, in their perceived self-interest, but in membership in good standing in the regimes that make up the substance of international life'. Therefore,

> [t]o be a player, a state must submit to pressures that international regulations impose. Its behaviour in any single episode is likely to affect future relationships not only within the particular regime involved but in many others as well, and

[90] Chayes and Chayes, *The New Sovereignty*, 4. [91] *ibid.*, 4–5, 7. [92] *ibid.*, 8.
[93] *ibid.*, 9–10. [94] *ibid.*, 10. [95] *ibid.*, 12. [96] *ibid.*, 15. [97] *ibid.*, 12.

perhaps its position within the international system as a whole. When nations enter into an international agreement, therefore, they tend to alter their mutual expectations and actions over time, in accordance with its terms ... [S]overeignty, in the end, is status.[98]

Building on this, Chayes and Chayes present a framework within which international institutions, especially treaty bodies, may (and do) harness the incentives generated by this new sovereignty to promote compliance by defining what standards of behaviour are acceptable, and by using strategies of persuasion to induce States to hold to these standards.

Chayes and Chayes argue that compliance is not an on/off phenomenon, as most regimes allow an acceptable margin of 'what would be strictly speaking non-compliance'.[99] A treaty body may thus calibrate an appropriate margin for its relevant treaty, based on its character, context, State behaviour, capacity to comply, urgency of the problem, *et cetera*. Chayes and Chayes specify that the accepted level of calibration will reflect 'the perspectives and interests of the participants in an ongoing political process rather than some external, scientifically or market-validated standard'. They find that, in general, 'the level of acceptable compliance rises over the life of the treaty'. In sum, treaty bodies should facilitate the political process through which the level of acceptable compliance is determined and 'mobiliz[e] the political impetus for a higher level of compliance'.

Chayes and Chayes are not alone in claiming that compliance cannot be determined in black and white; Benedict Kingsbury argues that 'the concept of "compliance" with law does not have, and cannot have, any meaning except as a function of prior theories of the nature and operation of the law to which it pertains'.[100] He traces the different conceptions of compliance provided by rule- and process-based theories, rationalist and behavioural theories, and directive and non-directive theories about the international legal system. Moreover, he asserts the need to study 'regulatory strategies and compliance-related operations of international legal institutions, particularly bodies established to implement regulatory treaties', taking the example of the Montreal Protocol on Substances that Deplete the Ozone Layer.[101] The Protocol's

[98] *ibid.*, 27. [99] *ibid.*, 18–20.

[100] B. Kingsbury, 'The Concept of Compliance as a Function of Competing Conceptions of International Law' (1998) 19 *Michigan Journal of International Law* 345, 346.

[101] *ibid.*, 364–8.

Implementation Committee assesses compliance in terms relative to the capacity of various States and the possibility of building long-term relations. Kingsbury observes that in practice 'even the narrow "legal" concepts of "compliance" and "non-compliance" are more completely described in terms of a process involving relevant international institutions, the regulated states, and other states'.[102] Chayes and Chayes similarly suggest that, often, the acceptable level of compliance will be determined by scrutiny of a State's justifications for non-compliance in a broad discursive process managed by treaty-affiliated administrative bodies.

In addition, treaty bodies may use various strategies of persuasion: (i) due to the benefits that accrue from regimes, including a greater flow of information, treaty bodies may clarify expected standards of behaviour and provide information on the actions of other States; (ii) because interactions within a regime may foster a spirit of compliance, treaty bodies may foster an 'iterative process of discourse among the parties, the treaty organization and the wider public';[103] and (iii) they may employ measures of 'active' management. These measures include providing forums for deliberation, agenda-setting, and reviewing States' justifications for non-compliance; reporting, data collection, verification, monitoring, policy review, capacity-building and dispute settlement; and, importantly, adjusting treaty terms. Chayes and Chayes present illustrative 'anecdata'[104] of situations where such strategies facilitate compliance.

The New Sovereignty has received much attention, and, in some quarters, wide acclaim.[105] It has provided the platform for later and more detailed work on the role of administrative bodies. The book's unusual location in the domain of legal scholarship, rather than that of international relations, enabled it to transcend the theoretical divides (such as that between rational instrumentalism and constructivism) that characterise the latter discipline, and also – while building on empirical observation – to focus its attention on the distinctive application of *legal* (treaty) norms. International relations literature, in contrast, often fails to distinguish legal norms from others, or to account for why the former *should* have distinct application. Nevertheless, Chayes and Chayes' managerial approach has been questioned on three fronts, and its scope may be better understood in the course of addressing these questions.

[102] *ibid.*, 367. [103] Chayes and Chayes, *The New Sovereignty*, 25.
[104] Term borrowed from Kingsbury, 'Concept of Compliance', 346.
[105] For instance, Slaughter, *New World Order*, xiii.

Two critiques relate to whether managerial strategies sufficiently account for State compliance. First, is there no role for enforcement? Chayes and Chayes suggest as much:

> [A]s a practical matter, coercive economic – let alone military – measures to sanction violations cannot be utilised for the routine enforcement of treaties in today's international system, or in any that is likely to emerge in the foreseeable future. The effort to devise and incorporate such sanctions in treaties is largely a waste of time.[106]

Critics argue, however, that the presumption of States' propensity to comply, upon which this dismissal of sanctions is founded, does not hold true when there is a requirement for 'deep cooperation', that is, when States are asked to significantly depart from what they would have done in the absence of the treaty.[107] Here, enforcement is necessary. It is also pointed out that Chayes and Chayes' managerial approach is in fact an amalgam of managerial and 'social enforcement' strategies, social enforcement being

> a process of discourse that uses information generated by reporting requirements and NGO efforts to persuade, cajole, and shame states into compliance. The process works most powerfully when it leverages the conditions of the New Sovereignty: increased interdependence among international actors and complex global issue areas that create a demand for more law. As these conditions intensify, social enforcement will become an ever more powerful element of regime strategy and will be especially effective for those regimes supported by international organizations vested with authority and resources sufficient to play an active role.[108]

The second critique relates to whether Chayes and Chayes' approach, focusing on discourse, says much 'that is truly material about when such discourse does or does not have an impact on behavior, or about the conditions and boundaries of its effectiveness'?[109] This criticism is not merely that Chayes and Chayes fail to achieve the parsimony that is the hallmark of various rationalist explanations of State behaviour, because they do not effectively unbundle managerial strategies from

[106] Chayes and Chayes, *The New Sovereignty*, 2.
[107] G. Downs *et al.*, 'Is the Good News about Compliance Good News about Cooperation?' (1996) 50 *International Organization* 379, 383; K. Danish, 'Book Review: The New Sovereignty' (1997) 37 *Virginia Journal of International Law* 789, 801–2.
[108] Danish, 'Book Review', 809.
[109] Kingsbury, 'Concept of Compliance', 359 ('citing the rationalist objection').

enforcement mechanisms.[110] It is also that they fail to sufficiently elaborate the conditions and causal pathways for discourse to lead to compliance. Their work does not, for instance, engage with scholarship on deliberation and argumentation that reflects on the theatres and patterns that may foster persuasion through discourse.[111] Nor – beyond stating the constitutive impact of the 'new sovereignty'[112] – do they explore the sociological or psychological reasons for which States may be amenable to persuasion in particular instances. As a result of these omissions, many of their case-studies only serve as possible illustrations, amenable to alternative explanation. More recent scholarship has sought to address these issues by describing and modelling the process- or propensity-based frameworks through which States come to obey international commitments.[113]

The third question is perhaps the most important in the context of Chayes and Chayes' suggestion that treaty bodies may adapt or tailor specific provisions. Under what conditions, and in what contexts, may they justifiably do so? The question is particularly significant because Chayes and Chayes' approach has both descriptive and prescriptive components. To the extent that they seek to describe how international regulatory regimes 'in the real world go about it, for the most part',[114] the principled or unprincipled role played by treaty bodies is not essential to their analysis; however, to the extent that they *prescribe* that treaty bodies may alter treaties, it is necessary to examine the bases for treaty bodies to do so. Here, Chayes and Chayes' discussion of the role of legal discourse proves significant.

110 Criticism of lack of parsimony is directed at, for instance, behavioural theories of compliance. See C. Jolls *et al.*, 'A Behavioural Approach to Law and Economics', in C. Sunstein (ed.), *Behavioural Law and Economics* (Cambridge University Press 2000) 13, 20.

111 For instance, C. Perelman and L. Olbrechts-Tyca, *The New Rhetoric: A Treatise on Argumentation* (University of Notre Dame Press 1968); M. Setala, 'Rhetoric and Deliberative Democracy', *Redescriptions: Yearbook of Political Thought, Conceptual History and Feminist Theory* (2009) 61; J. Habermas, *Between Facts and Norms: Contributions to a Discourse Theory of Law and Democracy* (W. Rehg (trans.), MIT Press 1996).

112 Chayes and Chayes, *The New Sovereignty*, 118–27.

113 For instance, H. Koh, 'Transnational Legal Process' (1996) 75 *Nebraska Law Review* 181; H. Koh, 'Bringing International Law Home: The Frankel Lecture' (1998) 35 *Houston Law Review* 623; R. Goodman and D. Jinks, 'How to Influence States: Socialization and International Human Rights Law' (2004) 54 *Duke Law Journal* 621; T. Risse, 'Let's Argue!: Communicative Action in World Politics' (2000) 54 *International Organization* 1.

114 Chayes and Chayes, *The New Sovereignty*, 28.

Treaty adaptation

In explaining why treaty bodies may adopt various managerial strategies, Chayes and Chayes first point out that the focus of all these strategies must be on promoting the effective operation of that treaty. Despite discussing the factors that determine the legitimacy of legal norms, they do not raise the question of whether securing compliance with a treaty is itself desirable.[115] The treaty is a given. For a treaty body, its '*raison d'être* is the treaty. At least presumptively, it will be committed to treaty compliance'.[116] Therefore, the purpose of applying managerial strategies is clarified at the outset; it does not include a critical evaluation of the treaty itself, but only of the difficulties that States might face in complying with it.

Chayes and Chayes then suggest that the normative force of a treaty compels from its parties a 'general sense of obligation to comply with a legally binding prescription in the absence of strong countervailing considerations'. This sense of obligation can be bolstered by requiring States to justify departures from the treaty's provisions.[117] In many cases, treaty bodies may promote dialogue between States, requiring them to persuade each other of the validity of their proposed actions in almost 'Socratic fashion', through which 'egoists learn to cooperate [by] reconstructing their interests in terms of shared commitments to social norms'.[118]

In addition, however, Chayes and Chayes also contemplate adaptation of treaty terms by treaty bodies, where this becomes necessary to promote compliance. Chayes and Chayes' defence of this element of the managerial approach relies, primarily, on State consent and the formal competence of international organisations. As to State consent, they again point to the central role of legal discourse. They claim that the adaptation of treaty terms is worked out in a process of justification and scrutiny. Of particular importance is the 'participation of the state whose conduct is challenged', in order to clarify the obstacles to its compliance; this is reviewed and countered by other relevant actors. Accordingly, 'the essence of the international legal process is a dialectic that, by emphasizing assent at every stage, operates to generate pressure for compliance'.[119]

[115] On this point, see also Koh, 'Review Essay', 2641.
[116] Chayes and Chayes, *The New Sovereignty*, 274. [117] *ibid.*, 110. [118] *ibid.*, 123.
[119] *ibid.*, 110–12.

However, this dialectic process may in fact involve the substitution of an organisational decision to adapt treaty terms (*vis-à-vis* the recalcitrant State) for the specific consent of other States parties to a treaty. Chayes and Chayes defend this as legitimate on the basis of the embedded competence of the relevant organisation:

> An international organization is a creature of law. It is typically established by a constitutive treaty that identifies the limits and powers of the organization and its subparts, specifying the range of matters over which each can act. It prescribes the terms and conditions of membership. It lays out the procedures and decision rules that each of the organs must follow to take legally effective action. And it defines the formal relations, hierarchical and otherwise, among the constituent parts. In consequence, organizational decision making necessarily has a heavy legal component.[120]

In other words, international organisations, especially treaty bodies, can stand in for State consent where this is in exercise of their delegated powers. Chayes and Chayes do recognise that, in practice, this is not an easy determination to make. They anticipate the arguments later developed by Finnemore and Barnett,[121] acknowledging that States have 'developed a deep skepticism about bureaucracies', in part because 'they have the defects of other bureaucracies', and in part because, 'like other bureaucracies, they generate a degree of autonomy that impinges on the States' freedom of action'.[122] For this reason, administrative due process is important:

> Much of the debate and discussion seems to go not to the merits of a proposed action but to matters of interpretation, jurisdiction, and procedural regularity. These issues should not be dismissed as procedural technicalities, however. Since compliance with substantive norms depends in significant degree on their perceived validity and legitimacy, the functioning of these institutional rules can be crucial for the compliance problem.[123]

Moreover, Chayes and Chayes avoid a detailed discussion of the claim that, in applying 'instruments of active management', such as 'adaptation and modification' of the treaty,[124] treaty bodies alter treaties through practice; they focus, rather, on 'authoritative or semi-authoritative *interpretation* by a designated body of the organization, often the secretariat or

[120] *ibid.*, 125.

[121] M. Barnett and M. Finnemore, 'The Politics, Power, and Pathologies of International Organizations' (1999) 53 *International Organization* 699.

[122] Chayes and Chayes, *The New Sovereignty*, 111, Chapter 12.

[123] *ibid.*, 125.

[124] *ibid.*, Chapter 9.

a legal committee'.[125] But alteration is implied in 'tailoring' the application of treaties. In such cases, institutional rules may not fully address concerns about the substantive decisions made by treaty bodies: a significant feature of the managerial approach is that, in seeking to effectively implement their relevant treaty, treaty bodies must take their cue from the challenges posed to it, whether by recalcitrant States or by conflicting treaties. In such cases, procedural criteria may not sufficiently constrain their exercise of discretion; particularly where the challengers are powerful States, an administrative body may concede greater modifications.

This is, after all, the criticism advanced against a procedural 'global administrative law' (GAL).[126] A body of scholarship that emerged after the publication of *The New Sovereignty*, GAL posits that much institutional activity may be understood as administrative, and evaluated in terms of its concordance with appropriate principles of administrative action, including accountability, transparency, participation, review, reason-giving, *et cetera*. It acknowledges the possibility that such measures might only be leveraged by powerful actors or co-opted by the relevant institutions to legitimate their actions.[127] However, it also points out that viewing institutional activity in administrative terms expands the platform for its critique.

Even if administrative concepts may be best leveraged by powerful actors, or co-opted by treaty bodies, 'framing global regulation in traditional terms of administration and regulation exposes its character and extent more clearly than the use of vague terms such as governance'.[128] Koskenniemi, despite his strong criticism of managerialism, notes:

> I totally approve of the political move to re-define the managerial world of inter national institutions through constitutional or administrative vocabularies ... for the critical challenge they pose to today's culture of a-political expert rule, and perhaps for the appeal of the (Kantian) perfectibility that they set up as a regulative goal for human institutions.[129]

[125] *ibid.*, 209 (emphasis added).

[126] For instance, B. S. Chimni, 'Cooption and Resistance: Two Faces of Global Administrative Law' (2006) 37 *NYU Journal of International Law and Politics* 799. See also S. Marks, 'Naming Global Administrative Law' (2005) 37 *NYU Journal of International Law and Politics* 995. In Marks' words, 'progressive concepts can become pacifying ideologies'.

[127] B. Kingsbury *et al.*, 'The Emergence of Global Administrative Law' (2005) 68 *Law and Contemporary Problems* 15, 52.

[128] *ibid.*, 27.

[129] M. Koskenniemi, 'The Politics of International Law – 20 Years Later' (2009) 20 *European Journal of International Law* 7, 17.

The suggestion here is that administrative vocabulary, with its attendant focus on due process, adds a layer of complexity to managerialism that at least offers weaker actors (States or other), relevant non-instrumental criteria with which to challenge institutional decisions. This vocabulary, however, is also internal to Chayes and Chayes' managerial approach.

Expectations of law

In addition to Chayes and Chayes' primary defense of State consent and organisational competence, we must take note of their constant return to the idea that treaty bodies' actions are justified when they serve to promote, and are the result of, legal discourse between relevant actors. In fact, Chayes and Chayes claim, ultimately, that the managerial approach promotes discursive engagement between States (and other actors) by 'intensif[ying] the legal content of the discourse'.[130] This forces States to justify their actions in terms that can be evaluated by other actors. Other (non-legal) grounds for justification have characteristic problems:

> Arguments invoking the other parties' interests and broadly utilitarian appeals face the familiar difficulties of divining subjective preferences and aggregating utilities ... Alternatively, justification of questioned conduct often relies on broadly accepted background principles rooted in practical experience and common sense: rough fairness, the *status quo*, precedent and custom ... In most situations however, there will be more than one plausible objective criterion, and none of them will be neutral.[131]

According to Chayes and Chayes, the legal vocabulary is the most appropriate for evaluating a State's compliance or non-compliance with its treaty commitments. Moreover, they suggest that it is hard for any party, having debated seriously and at length *via* legal norms, to dismiss them as unimportant: the managerial approach thus consolidates respect for international law.

Here, Chayes and Chayes reveal the liberal and constructivist currents of their approach. On the one hand, the managerial approach is justified because it operates through legal discourse. This discourse takes as its starting point the relevant multilateral treaty and as its vocabulary, legal norms, especially the justifications and excuses for non-compliance provided in these norms. While Chayes and Chayes do not

[130] Chayes and Chayes, *The New Sovereignty*, 125. [131] *ibid.*, 120.

fully develop their view of the conditions under which legal discourse can be fair or persuasive, they suggest its procedural conditions will be specified in the institutional rules of treaty bodies and – perhaps – refined through concepts associated with administrative due process. This discourse, their work suggests, legitimises the alteration of a treaty's terms for the sake of its effective implementation as a whole. On the other hand, the very fact of the managerial approach bringing States and other actors to participate in legal discourse, and employing a legal vocabulary as the means for arguing about their preferences, is expected also to promote the importance of international law.

Of course, Chayes and Chayes recognise that States may participate in legal discourse in an instrumental way:

> It is almost always an adequate explanation for an action, at least *prima facie*, that it follows the legal rule. It is almost always a good argument for an action that it conforms to the applicable legal norms, and against, that it departs from them. The argument may not persuade, but there is no doubt where the burden of proof lies. It is almost always a ground for disapproval that an action violates the norms.[132]

Arguments of *legality* may thus be made strategically by all sides. This brings us back to the discussion in the first chapter of whether legal discourse can then generate any constraint. However, Abram Chayes has argued that the so-called indeterminacy of international legal argument is overstated. In his account of the US government's decision-making during the Cuban Missile Crisis (during which he was Legal Advisor to the US State Department), he has claimed that even at the height of the crisis, some legal arguments (such as self-defence) were not advanced because they would 'trivialize the whole effort at legal justification'.[133] The purpose in developing a legal justification was not simply to muscle through a preferred course of action, but to offer a sustainable precedent. Thus, he concluded, the need to provide justification did serve as a constraint.

As with approximate application, the expectations of the role of law that underlie the managerial approach bear further scrutiny. Chapter 5, on the International Criminal Court, explores treaty adaptation by a treaty body, the ICC's Office of the Prosecutor, faced with the challenge of implementing the Rome Statute in view of the strong opposition to it.

[132] *ibid.*, 119.

[133] A. Chayes, *The Cuban Missile Crisis: International Crises and the Role of Law* (Oxford University Press 1974) 65.

Accommodation via treaty coordination or regime interaction

The concept of regime 'coordination' or 'interaction' builds on a complex view of the practice of treaty conflict, noting that efforts to *resolve* conflicts in a definitive way, via application of conflict rules, often give rise to institutional conflict. The more effective course of action for international institutions, suggest Young,[134] and Wolfrum and Matz,[135] is to find ways of accommodating the conflicting regimes in a common framework of understanding. This may transform the conflict into an opportunity for mutual learning and enrichment between the conflicting regimes.

These suggestions can appear as problematic, for they advance the view that the implementation of a treaty must be contingent not simply on its own terms as interpreted according to well-established rules but also on conflicting treaties and their related norms, institutions and practices. While to some extent the rules of treaty interpretation, specifically the principle of systemic integration, do provide for reference to 'any relevant rules of international law applicable in the relations',[136] this may, at most, only apply to other treaties of which all the (relevant[137]) States-parties to the first treaty are members; this does not include treaties with non-identical parties. To adopt a 'coordination' or 'interaction' approach may then appear to sideline the formal process of interpretation and application, and be seen as an unpalatable reminder that legal change can be forced by means of a conflicting treaty. However, the authors of these suggestions indicate that it is possible to construct a principled account of coordination/interaction on the basis of normative criteria of ends (pluralism) and means (due process). Their justification (conditions of international order that merit accommodationist responses and principles that undergird their legitimacy) ultimately rests on the recourse to legal discourse; a reminder of the pervasiveness of liberal and constructivist presumptions in international law.

This section will explore the coordination/interaction approach. It will begin with a short overview of the difficulties of resolving treaty conflict, followed by a discussion of the approach and its justifications.

[134] Young, *Trading Fish, Saving Fish*. See also M. Young, 'Regime Interaction in Creating, Implementing and Enforcing International Law', in M. Young (ed.), *Regime Interaction in International Law: Facing Fragmentation* (Cambridge University Press 2012).

[135] Wolfrum and Matz, *Conflicts in International Environmental Law*.

[136] Article 31(3)(c), VCLT.

[137] In the event that a multilateral treaty's structure of obligations is bilateral.

Beyond resolution: from treaty conflict to institutional conflict

The International Law Commission's (ILC) Report on Fragmentation explains that treaty conflict is relevant from a systemic perspective because each treaty necessarily alters the normative environment in which the others must operate.[138] Therefore, any approach that merely concerns itself with the implementation of one treaty cannot adequately respond to concerns raised by fragmentation. A judicial or administrative body may secure the effective implementation of one treaty, but where each treaty is affiliated to an administrative body or international institution, a conflict of norms may translate into a conflict between institutions.

The ILC discusses this in connection with the *Mox Plant* case,[139] where three treaties addressed the same facts: the UN Convention on the Law of the Sea (LOSC); the Convention on the Protection of the Marine Environment of the North-East Atlantic (OSPAR Convention); and the European Community and European Atomic Energy Community (Euratom) Treaties. The matter was correspondingly raised in three institutional procedures: the OSPAR compulsory dispute settlement procedure, the Court of Justice of the European Union (then the European Court of Justice), and an Arbitral Tribunal set up under Annex VII of the LOSC.

In response to an objection to its jurisdiction on the ground that the same matter was also pending at two other forums, the LOSC Tribunal ruled that 'even if the OSPAR Convention, the EC Treaty and the EURATOM treaty contain rights or obligations similar to or identical with the rights set out in [the LOSC], the rights and obligations under these agreements have a separate existence from those under [the LOSC]'.[140] Declaring itself concerned solely with implementing the LOSC, it refused to cede jurisdiction to the other relevant institutions, even as it pointed out that 'the application of even the same rules by different institutions might be different owing to the "differences in the respective context, object and purpose, subsequent practice of parties and *travaux préparatoires*"'.

Other cases may be even more complex, with subject-matter evidently pertaining to different regimes, such as trade versus environment conflicts. In such cases, as Christopher Borgen points out:

[138] ILC, 'Report of Study Group on Fragmentation', 127, 208–21, 239–42.
[139] *ibid.*, 12, 13. [140] *ibid.*, 13.

> [i]f states party to both treaty regimes disagree as to which treaty applies in a given case, which treaty's dispute resolution mechanism should apply? . . . This issue presents a second level of treaty conflict: when the conflicting treaties themselves have different – and possibly conflicting – modes of dispute resolution.[141]

This may often be the case, given that most treaty organs simply focus on furthering the logic of their treaties: as previously noted, Klabbers shows that in a conflict between European Union Treaties and members' treaties with non-members, the EU Treaties always prevail.[142] For the EU non-members party to the conflicting treaty, this might only be incentive to approach a more favourable forum that will uphold that treaty.

Treaty interaction

As an alternative to this vision of institutional conflict, Young, and Wolfrum and Matz, suggest that treaty conflict may be better addressed by efforts to 'coordinate the implementation, interpretation and development' of treaties.[143] Wolfrum and Matz document forms of cooperation '(1) between the organs of international environmental agreements; and (2) between the agreements and responsible international organizations and institutions'.[144] They cooperate in three ways: by facilitating information exchanges between parties to all treaties through creation of joint institutions, harmonisation of reporting requirements and development of joint networks to facilitate exchange of experiences; by adopting memoranda of understanding on how the treaties should be implemented (such memoranda are not legally binding on States, but serve to place their relations on a quasi-formal basis); and, by establishing joint programmes of action on the relevant provisions of each treaty and forums in which various stakeholders can coordinate their activities. Wolfrum and Matz's analysis encompasses roles played by Conferences of States Parties, Secretariats, and Scientific and Technical subsidiary organs. It also extends to cross-cutting institutions such as the UN General Assembly and UN Environmental Programme (UNEP) that are

[141] C. Borgen, 'Resolving Treaty Conflicts' (2005) 37 *George Washington International Law Review* 573, 614–15. See also S. Safrin, 'Treaties in Collision? The Biosafety Protocol and the World Trade Organization' (2002) 56 *American Journal of International Law* 606.

[142] Klabbers, *Treaty Conflicts and the European Union*, 226.

[143] Wolfrum and Matz, *Conflicts in International Environmental Law*, 163.

[144] *ibid.*, 163 *et seq.*

forums for negotiating and implementing agreements, policy-making, decision-making *et cetera*.

Wolfrum and Matz focus on treaty coordination as an ongoing process of cooperation, to which individual treaties or provisions may be subordinated. They suggest, in other words, that a distinctly functional attitude prevails among certain treaty bodies and institutions and accounts for their cooperation. This gives rise to two questions: how and why is this attitude fostered? And, more importantly, how and why is it justified?

Wolfrum and Matz do not fully answer the first question, noting only that some treaties expressly direct their organs to cooperate with organs of other treaties and international institutions.[145] More generally, they note that the main impediment to cooperation 'is the perception on the part of States that institutional cooperation will erode [their] national sovereignty'.[146] On the whole, they simply seem to assume that treaty organs and institutions view coordination as the best means to accomplish their treaty objectives. Thus, where sufficiently empowered, they will coordinate. Perhaps their explanation hinges on the nature of the issues and disputes that they study: environmental matters. Wolfrum and Matz underline 'the international community's will to actively collaborate on an interstate level' on such issues.[147]

Young explores factors that promote or impede 'regime interaction' in greater detail.[148] Her concept of regime interaction is based on case-studies of fisheries management. By 'regime', she refers to 'norms, decision-making procedures and international organisations coalescing around functional issue areas'.[149] She suggests that 'interaction' encompasses collaboration between institutions as well as the 'cross-fertilization' of norms.[150] The inclusion of the latter is implicit rather than explicit in Wolfrum and Matz's work.

Young recognises that institutions may act outside of a State-consent framework, driven by the 'practical necessity for learning and understanding' between regimes;[151] that is, that institutional actors appreciate that a treaty conflict points to a need for further study of the relevant issue. In other words, they recognise that, if there is conflict, there is

[145] *ibid.*, 167. [146] *ibid.*, 163. [147] *ibid.* [148] Young, *Trading Fish, Saving Fish*, 249–66.
[149] Young, 'Regime Interaction', 86.
[150] Young, *Trading Fish, Saving Fish*, 22. See also M. Young, 'Regime Interaction in Creating, Implementing and Enforcing International Law', Conference Paper, Lauterpacht Centre for International Law, Cambridge, 26–27 June 2009, 8.
[151] Young, *Trading Fish, Saving Fish*, 253.

usually a reason. Non-State actors and epistemic communities may promote awareness of this.[152] This is a reminder of Koh's view of 'norm entrepreneurs' in the 'transnational legal process'.[153] Young also says that regime interaction may be bolstered by application of resources by States, institutions and independent non-State actors.[154]

Critically, Young suggests that legal criteria for application of treaties may act as 'barriers' to a cooperative approach.[155] Regime interaction is impeded by 'attempts to limit or deny the role of one regime *vis-à-vis* another through questioning the competence of the forum'; by 'lack of transparency and openness within regimes' that limits opportunities for participation and information exchange; and by 'fixation on the need for parallel membership of regimes' so that interaction is only permitted with another regime that has identical parties. That is, factors that we would consider essential to a formal treaty analysis – subject-matter, operational provisions, and impact on third parties – are here viewed as obstructive.

In all fairness, Young recognises that, because her approach rejects these formal criteria, she must offer a different legal basis for regime interaction, one which justifies subordination of particular treaty guarantees to a larger process of engagement. In the following sections, the chapter unpacks various elements of the possible justification sketched by her and partly echoed by Wolfrum and Matz (though Wolfrum and Matz focus more on describing regime coordination than analysing it). The chapter uses *coordination* and *interaction* interchangeably, and, where not inappropriate, substitutes *treaty* for *regime* to clarify the application of this approach to treaty conflicts. Obviously, a regime includes norms and institutions besides treaties; but treaty conflicts too often manifest in dynamic confrontations between the norms, institutions and various interests relating to each treaty.

Justification for treaty interaction

What justifies treaty interaction if it takes place at the cost of the formal implementation of particular treaty provisions and despite considerations of competence and privity? Obviously, a justification must go beyond the descriptive element that it does take place, for its proponents, Young and Wolfrum and Matz, clearly view it as desirable. In the following five subsections, I focus on three aspects of the possible

[152] *ibid.*, 255. [153] Koh, 'Bringing International Law Home'.
[154] Young, *Trading Fish, Saving Fish*, 256–7. [155] *ibid.*, 258–66.

justification that is sketched out in their analysis. These are, first, the agents of coordination: these scholars suggest that treaty bodies and institutions can bring conflicting agreements within a common framework. What entitles them to do so, if not State consent? Second, why is *interaction* more appropriate than conflict *resolution*? These aspects overlap: the authority of various institutions and treaty bodies is held to be based on the fact that they promote interaction; conversely, doubts about interaction (as opposed to treaty implementation or conflict resolution) are laid to rest on the basis that it is carried out by appropriate institutions. The third aspect – the propriety of the process of interaction – fulfils an additional criteria of legitimacy, but also provides a basis for evaluating the legality of interaction under the aegis of particular institutions.

Pluralism: within and without authorised forums

Young, and Wolfrum and Matz, agree that institutional attempts to implement treaties in isolation from their broader normative environment only perpetuate conflict. To them, treaty interaction is justified because it takes place in contexts where institutions *should* engage with each other so as to better address a particular issue. Most importantly, as Young indicates, institutions should engage with treaties, not solely as *legal instruments*, but as *vehicles for ideas*. To her, what is important is not the normative authority of conflicting treaties, but their presentation of diverse perspectives. She implies that a specific treaty conflict is only a starting point for obtaining a richer diversity of views; one might further take into account other instruments and perspectives. Thus, she says, commentators support NGO participation in the WTO's decision-making, 'to ensure the inclusion of ideas that are "overlooked or undervalued by governments"'.[156]

There is a flavour of the 'law as process' approach here. When Wolfrum and Matz assert that '[a]ny approach involving the cooperation between States, treaty organs, organizations and other institutions cannot be based on a one-time event but must involve a continuous process',[157] they appear to echo Rosalyn Higgins' claim that '"rules" are just accumulated past decisions ... if international law was just "rules", then [it] would indeed be unable to contribute to, and cope with, a changing

[156] *ibid.*, 275, quoting S. Charnovitz, 'WTO Cosmopolitics' (2002) 34 *NYU Journal of International Law and Politics* 299, 343.

[157] Wolfrum and Matz, *Conflicts in International Environmental Law*, 159.

political world'.[158] Higgins' further assertion that there is no avoiding the relationship between law and policy, and thus decision-makers must take into account, systematically and openly, the full range of relevant policy factors,[159] is echoed in Young's claim that it is functionally necessary for institutions to take account of 'multiplicious interests' of States and non-State actors, because ignoring these leads to flawed decisions.[160]

However, Higgins provides a clear blueprint for *legal* decision-making: 'by authorized persons or organs, in appropriate forums, within the framework of certain established practices and norms'.[161] She expects such decision-makers to appropriately consider policy factors. By focusing on duly authorised decision-makers, Higgins is able to avoid having to defend the propriety of taking policy factors into account when implementing and applying rules; in particular, she can assert that there is no reason to believe that the stability of current norms will be entirely contingent on such extraneous factors – '[t]rends of past decisions still have an important role to play in the choices to be made, notwithstanding the importance of both context and desired outcome'.[162]

Young's, and Wolfrum and Matz's, conceptions of interaction are not premised solely on the duly authorised treaty bodies and international institutions, nor do they contemplate it solely within the framework of 'certain established practices and norms'. To them, interaction is an umbrella term, which may refer not to one authoritative process but to a range of localised processes between various actors and institutions. If bodies which serve as decision-making forums are viewed as authoritative, it might merely be because they have, in many cases, constituted themselves as such. This is particularly likely where conflicting relevant treaties do not have identical parties and so no body at all enjoys the consent of all parties to both treaties.[163] Young, and Wolfrum and Matz, must thus defend the propriety of interaction *per se*, even when it takes place in the absence of State consent, through the agency of institutions and treaty bodies that lack specific authority for this purpose.

Creative bases of consent

First, to circumvent the issue of consent, Young suggests that the legal basis for treaty interaction via institutional collaboration resides in the

[158] R. Higgins, *Problems and Process: International Law and How We Use It* (Oxford, Clarendon Press 1994) 3.
[159] *ibid.*, 5. [160] Young, *Trading Fish, Saving Fish*, 273.
[161] Higgins, *Problems and Process*, 2. [162] *ibid.*, 6.
[163] This is discussed in Young, *Trading Fish, Saving Fish*, 270–1.

implicit powers of such institutions. Institutions 'such as the WTO may have the implied power to take account of external sources because it is necessary for them to do so as part of their functions'.[164] She draws on the *Reparation* case,[165] in which the Court found that 'the rights and duties of an entity like the UN "must depend upon its purposes and functions as specified or implied in its constituent documents and developed in practice"'.[166] Similarly, in environmental matters, institutions may be functionally required to take into account diverse interests. Wolfrum and Matz also suggest this, though in a more veiled way: '[e]ven if cooperation with other institutions is not expressly mentioned in a treaty, it is likely that the authority to cooperate could be based upon a general competence to deal with issues necessary for better implementation of an agreement'.[167]

The implied powers argument foregrounds a treaty (the constituent document of the relevant institution) as the basis for interaction. If the relevant institution is a treaty body of one of the conflicting treaties, then that treaty becomes the basis. However, it is not clear that 'implied powers' is a sufficient substitute for consent in all cases: where the relevant institution is a treaty body, its implied powers might indeed justify interaction even if this affects particular treaty rights of member States; but, in other cases, where the relevant institution is not one established by either conflicting treaty and shares only partial membership with each, implied powers could not justify actions that have an impact on other States' treaty rights.

Young's example after all relates to the UN where, arguably at least, there is little question of partial membership. But, even here, it is worth reflecting on the different approaches taken by the ICJ in the two cases Young cites. In *Reparation*, the Court employed the test of necessity to find that 'members of the UN had endowed it with the capacity to bring international claims "when necessitated by discharge of its functions"'.[168] The Court found it necessary for the UN to be able to claim reparations for injury caused to its agents; this was an easy conclusion, for the UN's mandate to undertake the function that led to the injury was not in question. However, as Young herself points out, in *Use of Nuclear Weapons in Armed Conflict*,[169] the Court found the World Health

[164] *ibid.*, 272. [165] *UN Reparation Case*, Advisory Opinion (1949) ICJ Rep 174.
[166] Young, *Trading Fish, Saving Fish*, 272 (footnote omitted).
[167] Wolfrum and Matz, *Conflicts in International Environmental Law*, 167.
[168] Young, *Trading Fish, Saving Fish*, 272. [169] Advisory Opinion (1996) ICJ Rep 66.

Organization (WHO) not competent to address the legality of use of nuclear weapons 'even in view of their health and environmental effects'.[170] The Court here considered that the WHO's implied powers were subject to the principle of speciality of international organisations;[171] the WHO could not, therefore, simply constitute itself as the relevant body to address the legality of nuclear weapons. This fine distinction highlights why it may be difficult for an institution, apart from a treaty body, to legitimately lead a process of treaty interaction on the basis of functional necessity. And Young, and Wolfrum and Matz, do not limit their analysis to treaty bodies. Wolfrum and Matz urge *States* to provide a legal platform for coordination in environmental matters by enhancing the UNEP's coordinating functions or by convening a harmonisation conference as a common forum to coordinate conflicting treaties.[172] Young goes further, suggesting that we need to view international law through a different optic altogether, in which State consent is not privileged over a pluralistic accommodation of diverse perspectives.

However attractive this idea seems, we must consider how far it can be developed, and on what basis. Should we view institutional pluralism as an end in itself? Or as a means of achieving value pluralism? Should we think of accommodation of diverse interests as an ideal result or only as a stepping stone to consensus? And do these questions open the way to legal criteria for guiding interaction? These are difficult questions, and are only partially explored in the two works discussed in this section; the following subsections will develop the hints given in these works by reference to a broader range of writings on these issues.

Institutional pluralism as an end in itself

It is empirically accepted that every field of international affairs is populated by a plurality of institutions, but there is less agreement on what makes an institution relevant to any particular issue. Koskenniemi and Päivi Leino note that this is often a matter of its representation as such – the result of a politics of description and characterisation, that lies at the heart of fragmentation.[173] For instance, it is not unusual to find the same situation characterised as a human rights issue by one actor and as a trade issue by another. Some actors

[170] Young, *Trading Fish, Saving Fish*, 273. [171] *ibid.*

[172] See Wolfrum and Matz, *Conflicts in International Environmental Law*, 209–13.

[173] M. Koskenniemi and P. Leino, 'Fragmentation of International Law? Postmodern Anxieties' (2002) 15 *Leiden Journal of International Law* 553, 575.

even go a step beyond, to describe human rights as being in service of larger goals of liberty represented by free trade, or free trade as being in service of larger goals of equality represented by human rights.[174] Koskenniemi and Leino believe this is normatively defensible; after all, 'no overall solution – a single hierarchy – is available. The ICJ, a human rights body, a trade regime or a regional exception may each be used for good and for ignoble purposes and it should be a matter of debate and evidence, and not of abstract "consistency," as to which institution should be preferred in a particular situation'.[175]

Nico Krisch describes this 'pluralization of authority' as the arrogation of decision-making by a variety of institutions,[176] but suggests it is regulated in a pragmatic way by a two-level demand for accountability from each institutional claimant. First, accountability to the constituency on the basis of which it makes its claim to decision-making authority. Second, the need to justify its claim against competing claims by other institutions. Thus, ironically, institutional conflicts may safeguard the legitimacy of treaty interaction, while a treaty-interaction approach may bolster pluralism amongst international institutions. Krisch suggests that pluralisation allows the inclusion of views of a broad range of constituencies: national constituencies represented by individual States; international constituencies represented by groups of States; and cosmopolitan constituencies represented by the global civil society. Conversely, a constitutional model in which authority is delineated might exclude some constituencies.

This view has, of course, been challenged. Eyal Benvenisti and George Downs note that such analysis partakes of incorrect assumptions:

> [T]he implicit assumption that fragmentation represents a major advance over hierarchy because the multiplicity that it embodies is inherently pluralistic which, in turn, is a harbinger of the emergence of a more democratic international legal order [and] the assumption ... that the fragmentation of international law is either an unintended side effect of the natural evolution of the international system or the result of judicial creativity in the face of change.[177]

[174] See Klabbers, *Treaty Conflicts and the European Union*, 42–3.

[175] Koskenniemi and Leino, 'Fragmentation: Postmodern Anxieties', 578.

[176] N. Krisch, 'The Pluralism of Global Administrative Law' (2006) 17 *European Journal of International Law* 247, 266.

[177] E. Benvenisti and G. Downs, 'The Empire's New Clothes: Political Economy and the Fragmentation of International Law' (2007) 60 *Stanford Law Review* 595, 603–4.

They claim that a larger number of institutions does not lead to more representation of diverse interests. On the contrary, institutional pluralisation may be a strategy of powerful States to maintain their dominance by impeding opportunities for weaker States to coalesce into strong bargaining coalitions within any one institution.[178]

Krisch recognises the force of this objection. He notes, '[p]luralist approaches ... have long had to face the objection that some groups in society possess superior organizational capabilities and, in general, more power than others, so that relying on their free interplay will merely favour the powerful at the expense of the weak'. Even so,

> [i]t is open to question whether a pluralist landscape would be much different in this respect from a classical, hierarchically ordered, unitary structure ... [Moreover] power disparities may be more effectual when the regulatory process leads to one final decision; incentives for capture are biggest in a concentrated decision-making process. The dominant influence of powerful actors on the final decision will then reinforce these actors' power and legitimize its exercise. In contrast, recognizing the provisional and contestable nature of regulatory decisions limits their claim to legitimacy and may open up space for less powerful actors to articulate their position. Their contestation can remain visible and is not submerged in a process that claims to produce a decision reflecting the 'common good'.[179]

Accommodation as an end: value pluralism in the international system

Treaty interaction may also be justified on the basis of the type of outcome it seeks. Young suggests it leads to 'pluralistic accommodation of diverse perspectives'. This could be supported for two different reasons: either as a step towards better-informed and more robust coherence, or as an end in itself. Some scholars have taken the first view, claiming that treaty proliferation 'is either an unavoidable minor problem in a rapidly transforming international system, or even a rather positive demonstration of the responsiveness of legal imagination to social change ... [D]ifferent approaches adopted in relation to the same subject may only represent a healthy "level of experimentation in a collective effort to find the best rule to serve the international community as a whole".'[180]

[178] *ibid.*, 604. [179] Krisch, 'Pluralism of Global Administrative Law', 275–6.

[180] Koskenniemi and Leino, 'Fragmentation: Postmodern Anxieties', 575. The quote is from J. Charney, 'International Law and Multiple International Tribunals' (1998) 271 *Recueil des Cours* 145, 354–5. Koskenniemi and Leino are not themselves enamoured of this idea.

But several others, in contrast, deprecate coherence where there is radical divergence of values; for such coherence may simply be hegemonic. Notably, philosophers from John Rawls to John Gray have focused on intermediate outcomes between conflict and consensus, such as '*modii vivendi*',[181] 'negotiated conflictuality'[182] and 'overlapping consensus'[183] as legitimate ends. Without going into details, it may be useful to take note of what, for instance, *negotiated conflictuality* entails:

> [Negotiated conflictuality] has nothing to do with the abandonment or the mere denial of conflictuality, but rather concerns a change in the form(s) of conflictuality. It is not 'peace' in the Kantian sense of suppression of any cause of future conflict ... [T]here remains lurking tension which coexists with the apparently reasonable outcome ... [i]ndividuals and groups can construct some kind of agreement, if they can agree to disagree, as long as they understand that rationality and conflictuality are not mutually incompatible ... Conflict is not necessarily an all or nothing issue, it can be a matter of degree, some conflicts may be acceptable within a business-as-usual framework.[184]

This has obvious application to treaty interaction as a means of securing effective operation of conflicting treaties, rather than as the final resolution of the conflict in favour of one or other treaty. It is thus worth exploring the normative defence for such intermediate outcomes. John Horton usefully outlines and responds to several objections that might be made to intermediate outcomes (that he terms *modii vivendi*).[185] Relevant amongst these are that they may be unstable; indeterminate; and unjust or immoral. Horton argues that the charge of instability, that is, that *modii vivendi* remain at the mercy of a balance of interests, does not ring true empirically. Conceivably,

[181] J. Gray, 'Where Plurals and Liberals Part Company' (1998) 6(1) *International Journal of Philosophical Studies* 17; J. Horton, 'John Gray and the Political Theory of Modus Vivendi' (2006) 9(2) *Critical Review of International Social and Political Philosophy* 155.

[182] C. Arnsperger and E. Picavet, 'More Than Modus Vivendi, Less Than Overlapping Consensus: Towards a Political Theory of Social Compromise' (2004) 43(2) *Social Science Information* 167.

[183] J. Rawls, 'The Idea of Overlapping Consensus' (1987) 7(1) *Oxford Journal of Legal Studies* 1.

[184] Arnsperger and Picavet, 'More Than Modus Vivendi', 169, 175.

[185] Horton, 'Modus Vivendi', 162–6. It should be noted that the scholars cited here use different terms to describe similar outcomes of compromise while confusingly using the same term – *modus vivendi* – to signify different things: mere coexistence as well as a more substantial degree of mutual accommodation. For a discussion of two possible conceptions of *modus vivendi* in international relations, see T. Pogge, 'From Modus Vivendi to Value Overlap', in *Realizing Rawls* (Cornell University Press 1989) 218–39.

[e]xperiencing the value of *modus vivendi* may have beneficial impact on political motivations, it may encourage a political culture of negotiation, compromise, flexibility, of accepting limits to what can be changed and of seeking only the practically feasible.

He also asserts that *modii vivendi* appeal to 'more minimal and less exclusive' values, and are thus more likely to be stable. He answers the corresponding charge, that a 'political settlement based on the *modus vivendi* will always be circumstantial and contingent, not keyed to any definite set of principles or institutions towards which political actions should aim', with the assertion that general normative theory cannot determine which settlement is better. For Horton, the decision on what outcome is acceptable and how to attain it must be left to political agents, who will apply notions (like prudence, judgment, compromise and bargaining) that are only weakly normative and should be contextually determined.

Horton recognises that this leads to the third objection, that any outcome at all may be legitimated under the colour of being a *modus vivendi* that represents a move beyond full *conflictuality*.[186] He recognises the seriousness of this charge, which, however, may be partly alleviated by the application of two qualitative criteria: first, the *modus vivendi* must be consistent with a 'uniform minimum morality' (following Gray, he claims its content 'overlaps with that of liberal morality in that both proscribe such practices as genocide or slavery; but it underdetermines liberal morality in that it does not dictate distinctive liberal freedoms of the press, religion or autonomous choice'[187]); and, second, it must be acceptable to all parties, and not take the form of a ruthless imposition by one party on another. While the outcome may be regarded as more expedient than just, and the acceptance may be grudging, wary, or reluctant, it must be present.

Horton, here, essentially emphasises the idea of a normatively girded discourse, which rules out certain outcomes (as falling outside of the universal minimum morality) and expects parties to reach a solution which, if not ideal, is also not simply imposed. This could easily be taken

[186] This recalls arguments that progress narratives are used in international relations to subvert formal guarantees. For instance, Binder notes, 'in the context of treaty law, the "progressive development of international law" seems to entail the complete ... subordination of treaty expectations of some nations to the goal of preserving and developing international institutions ... For the [ILC] such domination would be the price of international progress.' Binder, *Treaty Conflict and Political Contradiction*, 100.

[187] Gray, 'Where Plurals and Liberals Part Company', 33.

for the idea of legal discourse that pervades so much of international law scholarship: there is even a striking overlap between the content of Horton's universal minimum morality and the *jus cogens* prohibitions of international law. For the rest, as Chapter 1 has discussed, the emphasis in international legal scholarship is not on blind observance of rules, but on taking them seriously as starting points for argument and decision-making. By its very logic this demands openness towards the opposite point of view.

The above argument is also a partial response to a final objection that Horton considers: that the idea of a *modus vivendi* privileges a narrow and contestable conception of value, that is, peace and stability.[188] Horton here responds with the argument that 'the pursuit of *modus vivendi* is not a quest for some kind of super-value ... The end of *modus vivendi* is not some supreme good – even peace.' A *modus vivendi* is the best way forward '*if* people want to live together in a civil manner, without resort to tyranny or persistent violent struggle, and in a way that at least extends a measure of toleration to diverse ways of life'. As such, '*modus vivendi* is not an inspiring ideal. It lacks the theoretical glamour ... of more ambitious forms of liberal theory. But in a world where civil disorder and violence are much more likely a prospect than a realization of our highest ideals, there is much to be said for it.' All this might also go to explaining Wolfrum and Matz's, and especially Young's, embrace of regime interaction, but it must be noted that they place their ambitions higher – to them, a *modus vivendi* achieved on the basis of the discursive process referred to above, might reflect a richer appreciation of diverse perspectives.

The importance of right process

We come, finally, to the importance of accountability in regime interaction. According to Young, this is the main safeguard against the abuse of treaty interaction in terms of 'a "technicalisation" of international affairs, where managerial procedures and decision-making by unseen experts begins to control global politics'.[189] For, she notes, 'where law is envisaged "beyond the state", and as an "instrument for particular values, interests, preferences", there is a grave risk of managerialism'.[190]

This risk can be alleviated by adopting a 'framework of contestation and inter-regime engagement ... to ensure a range of perspectives are

[188] Horton, 'Modus Vivendi', 166–7. [189] Young, *Trading Fish, Saving Fish*, 276.
[190] *ibid.*, 302 (citations omitted).

included'.[191] 'Legitimacy in international law', Young suggests, 'rests, at various moments of regime interaction, on the capacity for stakeholder participation and deliberation rather than on the consent of States.'[192] Young emphasises a discursive process to which the primary participants are institutions (treaty bodies and international organisations); these also serve as the sites for dialogue. She relies on these institutions to play a gatekeeper role *vis-à-vis* external norms: they should scrutinise the '"sources" of external regimes (the norms themselves, including the degree to which they are supported internationally) and the "sources of the external sources", including NGOs that wish to gain access to the relevant regimes'.[193] Moreover, she turns to 'process norms' such as transparency and reason-giving, and review and open deliberation, that recent GAL literature has also identified as crucial to accountable and legitimate law-making and implementation.[194] Indeed, Young suggests the possibility of a principle of 'good governance', comprising openness, transparency, participation and review in regime interaction, as a source of international law alongside traditional consent-based sources.[195]

This reliance on process norms recalls Chayes and Chayes' managerial approach, though there are important differences between the two. Chayes and Chayes focus on effective implementation of one treaty by its treaty body, relying to a greater extent on State consent than treaty interaction which more highly values a plurality of norms and institutions. But their conceptions of legal discourse are similar: both view institutions as participants in and sites for discourse, and rely on such institutions to structure the discourse by references to legal norms and procedures, in particular the principles of right process. As such, both embrace the principles now described as GAL, as essential to the accountability of institutions and to the legitimacy of the outcomes reached. Both, then, may attract the criticisms that are often directed at GAL, beginning with the charge that it lacks comprehensive normative and positive political theories,[196] which makes it difficult to precisely identify which administrative law principles and standards are relevant in evaluating the activities of institutions operating within the 'global administrative space'.[197] How, for instance, can we claim that interaction fostered by any particular body is appropriate because of the

[191] *ibid.*, 303. [192] *ibid.*, 287. [193] *ibid.*, 277. [194] See, for instance, *ibid.*, 278–87.
[195] *ibid.*, 301. [196] See Kingsbury *et al.*, 'The Emergence of Global Administrative Law'.
[197] *ibid.*, 26.

institution's accountability, if we do not have a full conception of the different interests that it should be accountable to, or the mechanisms that make it most effectively accountable? We also lack a well-developed understanding of the ideal conditions for discourse: the formal and procedural prerequisites for institutions to ensure that they not only allow participation of all relevant interests but also do so in an effective manner.[198] There is no point in proclaiming a process inclusive because it brings diverse interests into a single meeting-room, if it only provides a pulpit for a powerful few to preach to the rest; yet, how do we evaluate a process in which various interests have a say, but not in a format that allows them much impact? Structures, forms and formats of discourse are all important, but we lack theories about these through which to assess claims made by institutions fostering treaty interaction. Nor, indeed, is it clear that we can achieve general theories to this end. This theme will be taken up again in Chapter 6, on nuclear governance.

To return to the concern recognised by Krisch and Horton, the pluralisation of authority, and accommodation, may only represent opportunities for a powerful few to advance their interests. This is an inescapable charge, though, as both point out, it is probably equally salient for formal unified authority, and would also apply to formal resolution of treaty conflict or institutional focus on the effective implementation of any one of the conflicting treaties.

Conceptions of international law

The three strands discussed in the previous sections are quite different in their scope and justification, though they all recommend the modification of treaty terms by international institutions. The doctrine of approximate application pursues a 'rule of law' sensibility, visible in Lauterpacht's conviction that 'the unity and the operation of the régime created by [legal instruments of continuing validity] cannot be allowed to fail because of a breakdown or gap which may arise in consequence of an act of a party or otherwise'.[199] Therefore, in an enactment of a species of the effectiveness principle, courts may modify specific treaty terms. This idea of the continuing validity of the instrument reconciles judicial modification with the principle of State consent. Compliance management, taking off from a belief in States' propensity to comply with

[198] See in this context C. Sunstein, *Infotopia* (Oxford University Press 2006).
[199] *Admissibility of Hearings*, Separate Opinion of Judge Lauterpacht, 48.

treaty commitments unless impeded by too-demanding terms or other factors, locates State consent in the delegated powers of the treaty body and/or in the continuing discourse through which a treaty body works out the modifications to be made. Chayes and Chayes avoid detailed consideration of the discretion that treaty bodies may exercise in making modifications; to the extent that they acknowledge this discretion, they look to procedural safeguards to ensure accountability. Regime interaction distances itself from a view of legitimacy premised solely on State consent. Instead, it gives importance to the participation of States and non-State actors, as representatives of interest groups affected by a particular issue and as sources for new ideas, in a discourse towards the establishment of a more inclusive legal framework. Young foresees the need for some regulation of this discourse and relies on institutions, which act as sites of interaction, to provide such regulation. As with Chayes and Chayes, she expects such institutions to apply GAL principles and to themselves be regulated by these principles.

Despite the different motives that drive each strand (effectively implementing treaties, overcoming obstacles to compliance, developing more inclusive frameworks), they have in common their support for a discourse framed in terms of international law. They rely on a legal discourse to guarantee the appropriateness of the modifications made; but they also justify the approach of making modifications because it promotes legal discourse – and eventually, respect for international law. Regime interaction and compliance management suggest it is appropriate to work out alterations via discourse among relevant actors, which for regime interaction are institutions, States and a variety of non-State actors, and for compliance management, international institutions/treaty bodies and States. Both proposals envisage treaty bodies as playing a dual role: as *sites* for legal discourse and as *participants* in it. With respect to approximate application, we see that Lauterpacht, too, cites the ICJ's responsibility to participate in a legal discourse initiated by the General Assembly to promote the maintenance and stability of treaty relations by clarifying how the Mandate regime may be modified. The Court, here, is intended to participate in and promote a distinctively legal dialogue on the fate of South-West Africa, by showing that the issue at hand can be properly addressed via international law.

While there is a pragmatic element to each approach, and a shift of focus away from a finding of breach or allocation of State responsibility, this pragmatism is tinged with the sense that international relations should be filtered through the legal rules and procedures, and that acting through law conditions the attitudes of States and non-State actors so that they come to act in more community-regarding ways. As described in previous chapters, this sense may be taken as a manifestation of liberal and constructivist assumptions about the role of international law and the way to develop the international legal order.

Of course, there is no common ideal of the international legal order: approximate application appears to be directed towards a constitutionalist order of flourishing 'objective' multilateral treaty regimes stewarded by courts; compliance management seems attached to the idea of deep cooperation between States informed by recognition of the 'new sovereignty'; and regime interaction favours pluralism and emphasises continuous contestation and accommodation.

However, there is a common conception of international law being, in its operation, something like what Kingsbury and Megan Donaldson have called 'inter-public' law:

> [A] law between 'public entities' (primarily, but not limited to, States), these public entities being subject to public law and thus to basic public law principles, including legality, rationality, proportionality, rule of law, and fundamental rights, as well as to an additional quality of 'publicness' inherent in law, one that is difficult to define but nevertheless crucial. As described by Jeremy Waldron, this public character of law lies in 'the fact that law presents itself not just as a set of commands by the powerful [or] a set of rules recognized among an elite, but as a set of norms made publicly and *issued in the name of the public . . . that ordinary people can in some sense appropriate as their own, qua members of the public*'.
>
> In this vision of international law as inter-public law, it is the law itself that functions as the vessel for normativity . . . [I]t need not depend on any consensus as to *a priori* principles of morality or the normative ends of international life, and there may be no coherent pre-legal international community or community interest. Rather, it is the existence of law that both creates a certain kind of society in its own right, through the practice of seeking law-governed relationships, and allows other communities – or publics – to come into being and assert their interests, by making available certain institutional mechanisms to satisfy public law principles of rationality and rule of law, and by creating rhetorical possibilities for demands that the law respond to the felt needs of a particular public.[200]

[200] B. Kingsbury and M. Donaldson, 'From Bilateralism to Publicness in International Law', New York University Institute for International Law and Justice, Public Law and Legal Theory Research Paper, No. 11-07 (January 2011) 79, 83–4; see also B. Kingsbury, 'International Law as Inter-Public Law', in H. Richardson and M. Williams (eds.), *Nomos XLIX: Moral Universalism and Pluralism* (New York University Press 2009) 167, 172–5.

While this conception may be subjected to several questions – such as what constitutes a public entity (what about auto-constitution?), what is an appropriate public, which publics are relevant to an issue, which public law principles must be satisfied[201] – the endless basis these questions offer for review of institutional practice is perhaps the added complexity that belies the idea of pure managerialism in any of the strands discussed in this chapter.

Conclusion

The chapter unpacks the various elements of three recipes for institutional action in response to challenges to treaties, *inter alia* in the form of treaty conflict. It follows the discussion of the previous chapter in suggesting that, despite their differences, the three strands share liberal and constructivist assumptions about the role of international law and the development of international legal order that manifest in their common references to the recourse to legal discourse. This recourse is presented both as a justification and as a desirable end in the three strands of approximate application, compliance management, and regime interaction.

This dual presentation of the recourse to legal discourse complicates the claims that, by adopting gestures of deal-making, balancing, adjusting and optimising by citations of non-legal data and technical expertise, scholars and institutions fall prey to a culture of managerialism pure and simple. In fact, the managerialist techniques promoted in the three strands discussed here are pervaded by a sense that in some degree equates to what Koskenniemi (the source of strong critiques against managerialism) has called the culture of formalism.[202] This brings us back to Johns' point that,

> in international law and in other legal fields, extra-legal normative codes (political, moral, religious, expedential, etc.) and related arguments have long been understood, at least some of the time, 'as . . . fully "inside" the practice of legal interpretation, rather than as external'.[203]

The sense of the fall of international law due to a turn to managerialism may, therefore, be exaggerated.

[201] Kingsbury and Donaldson, 'From Bilateralism to Publicness in International Law', discuss some of these questions.

[202] Koskenniemi, *Gentle Civilizer of Nations*, 502. For a discussion of Koskenniemi's culture of formalism, see Chapter 1.

[203] Johns, *Non-Legality in International Law*, 21 (citations omitted).

Yet, Koskenniemi is right to draw attention to the politics of international legal argument and claim-making, and instrumental applications of international law, that rely on and perpetuate its immanent structural biases but lie concealed in assertions of expertise and external necessities. The next three chapters take their cue from this, to examine more closely the dynamics of legal discourse and practices of lawfare in the context of three instances of deliberately created treaty conflict. This will reveal, I hope, how international law may be both constraint and leverage, shield and sword, such that there can be no simple summation or dismissal of its place in international affairs.

PART II

Treaty conflicts in practice

4 Notions of ocean: the dispute over deep seabed mining

> It would clearly be in the interests of nonsignatories to the Law of the Sea Convention to set up an alternate treaty of their own. Then, if an international tribunal were called upon to assess the legal consequences of two conflicting multilateral treaties on the law of deep seabed mining, at least the parties to the alternate treaty would have a valid international instrument of their own to cite against the Convention.
>
> Moreover, they would argue that there is no principle of majority rule in international law that would make the Convention more significant than their own alternate treaty. And they would add that there is no principle of priority in time that would favor the Convention because it was concluded first.
>
> Anthony D'Amato, April 1983[1]

Back to the future?

In February 2013, a report appeared on the website of the International Seabed Authority (ISA), the institution established by the 1982 UN Convention on the Law of the Sea (LOSC)[2] to regulate activities in the 'Area', that is, the portion of the seabed outside the limits of national jurisdiction. This report, 'Technical Study No. 11', is titled 'Towards the Development of a Regulatory Framework for Polymetallic Nodule Exploitation in the Area'.[3] It is a reminder that, even though the rest of the world may have moved on from a controversy that held its attention

[1] A. D'Amato, Editorial Comment: 'An Alternative to the Law of the Sea Convention' (1983) 77 *American Journal of International Law* 281, 283.

[2] 21 ILM 1261. Opened for signature 10 December 1982, entered into force 16 November 1994.

[3] A. Clark *et al.*, 'Towards the Development of a Regulatory Framework for Polymetallic Nodule Exploitation in the Area', ISA Technical Study No. 11, 26 February 2013, www.isa.org.jm/files/documents/EN/Pubs/TStudy11.pdf.

for almost a quarter of a century, international institutions can continue to carry out their mandate with extraordinary tenacity.[4] For this report once again attempts to initiate the construction of a legal framework on the recovery of deep seabed polymetallic nodules. It speaks of nodule mining as an 'impending reality'[5] – a conviction reminiscent of that which catalysed the LOSC negotiations in the 1970s. Four decades later, we are back to viewing deep seabed minerals as resources of the imminent future.

In a note prepared for consideration by the ISA Council at the ISA's nineteenth annual session (July 2013), the ISA Secretariat attributes the 'renewed interest' in seabed mining to various factors, including 'dramatic' increases in the demand for and price of metals, the decline of land-based deposits, high profitability of mining companies, and 'technological advances'.[6] While the technical report concedes that 'much of the technology is unproven under real-life operation',[7] the ISA note (omitting this concession) takes inspiration from the fact that in 2011, a private company, Nautilus Minerals Inc., obtained a licence from Papua New Guinea to mine for minerals in its territorial sea: it concludes that the private sector must have some inkling of the commercial viability of seabed mining.[8] Different ISA bodies are now actively engaged in reviewing and developing the ISA's legal regulatory framework on the exploitation of nodules – a process they hope to fulfil in the short term of three to five years.

Irrespective of the ISA's tenuous claim to technological feasibility, the reinvigoration of efforts for international legal regulation of the seabed mining is also in keeping with the resurgence of the 'global commons' as a 'political and philosophical concept'.[9] As Sundhya

[4] Harrison offers a succinct account of the ISA's activities since the time it came into operation in 1994. This includes developing regulations on protection of the marine environment, and restating the LOSC provisions in the form of regulations on the exploration (not exploitation) of polymetallic nodules. The ISA is also considering how to adapt these regulations to poly metallic sulphides and cobalt-rich crusts which require application of different technology. See J. Harrison, *Making the Law of the Sea: A Study in the Development of International Law* (Cambridge University Press 2011) Chapter 5.

[5] Clark *et al.*, 'Towards the Development of a Regulatory Framework', 7, 77.

[6] 'Towards the Development of a Regulatory Framework for Polymetallic Nodule Exploitation in the Area', Note by the ISA Secretariat, ISBA/19/C/5, 25 March 2013, www.isa.org.jm/files/documents/EN/19Sess/Council/ISBA-19C-5.pdf.

[7] Clark *et al.*, 'Towards the Development of a Regulatory Framework', 11.

[8] See ISA Secretariat Note, 1, para. 1.

[9] S. Pahuja, 'Conserving the World's Resources?', in J. Crawford and M. Koskenniemi, *The Cambridge Companion to International Law* (Cambridge University Press 2012) 398, 400.

Pahuja notes, the reconceived idea of the commons marries 'economic and environmental justice', and extends both to common resources (the seabed, the high seas, the polar regions and outer space) and common concerns (climate change, the atmosphere). The quest for international legal regulation has followed as a corollary of imagining these spaces and phenomena as resources and/or concerns, and common ones at that: intensive treaty-making also took place between the late 1950s and 1970s, when the moon, the seabed and Antarctica came (or, due to Cold War misinformation, seemed) within technological reach.[10]

But the relationship between international law and the commons is not linear: on the one hand, international law is a medium to advance equitable (and, to a more limited extent, sustainable) use of the commons, but, on the other, it is also the means through which ideas counter to that of the commons are asserted. There is no better example of this than seabed mining, where, while the LOSC was concluded to give expression to an expanded conception of the seabed as the 'common heritage of mankind', a strategically created treaty conflict in the 1980s was also the basis for dilution of this concept. The example of seabed mining reveals international law as a terrain of treaty politics over the global commons.

The ISA's injection of fresh momentum into its project of building a legal framework to regulate seabed mining compels us all the more to examine the texture of the politics – and correspondingly the role of international law – that was illuminated by the treaty conflict pertaining to the LOSC. That this conflict occurred, and that it served to alter the LOSC regime, supports the concerns relating to epiphenomenality and lawfare discussed in Chapter 1. But the conflict also tells us something about the lingering consequences of resort to international law's forms and processes, which might assuage some of those concerns (while giving rise to fresh ones). Let us turn then to the conflict.

An overview of the conflict

The conflict in question, persisting through the long 1980s, was between the LOSC deep seabed mining regime and the Reciprocating

[10] On outer space: Outer Space Treaty, 1967, 6 ILM 386; Rescue Agreement, 1968, 7 ILM 149; Liability Convention, 1975, 11 ILM 1; Registration Convention, 1975, 15 ILM 43; Moon Treaty, 1979, 17 ILM 1434. On Antarctica: Antarctic Treaty, 1959, 402 UNTS 71; Agreed Measures for Conservation of Antarctic Fauna and Flora, 1964, 17 UST 992; Convention on the Conservation of Antarctic Seals, 1972, 11 ILM 251; Convention on the Conservation of Antarctic Marine Living Resources, 1980, 19 ILM 837.

States Regime (RSR) established by the United States, the United Kingdom, France, Italy, the Netherlands, Belgium, Germany (FRG) and Japan.

The LOSC's seabed mining regime, negotiated over the 1970s, was founded on the principle that the seabed was the common heritage of mankind. It envisaged exploitation of the seabed's rich polymetallic resources for the equal benefit of all nations, regardless of their capacity to conduct mining. This regime was an artefact of a then-vibrant movement for a New International Economic Order (NIEO),[11] which sought substantive equality between developed and developing States. The initial years of its negotiation were a time of optimism about the imminent transformation of relations between developed and developing States and progress towards a more just world under international law.[12] Developing States viewed the Third UN Conference on the Law of the Sea 1973–82 (UNCLOS III), at which the LOSC was drafted, as 'a microcosm of the possibilities the future held and the inauguration of a new era in international relations'.[13] The seabed regime was to be important evidence of this new era.

While LOSC negotiations began in 1973 in a spirit of optimism, they were overtaken by the Cold War-era suspicion between 'Eastern' and 'Western' States. The optimistic beginnings had paved the way for an elaborate regime for deep seabed mining, but several Western States were suspicious that its centralised authority structures heralded a 'socialist' economic order.[14] These States were concerned that the LOSC mechanisms would obstruct efficient recovery of seabed resources and resented provisions that imposed high costs on them for some dubious collective benefit. Led by the United States, some refused to sign the LOSC; others did sign but expressed dissatisfaction with its

[11] See Declaration on the Establishment of a New International Economic Order, UNGA Res. S-6/3201 (1 May 1974); Programme of Action on the Establishment of a New International Economic Order, UNGA Res. S-6/3202 (1 May 1974); Charter on Economic Rights and Duties of States, UNGA Res. 29/3281 (12 December 1974). See also M. Bedjaoui, *Towards a New International Economic Order* (London, Holmes and Meier 1979).

[12] B. S. Chimni, 'International Law Scholarship in Post-colonial India: Coping with Dualism' (2010) 23 *Leiden Journal of International Law* 23, 35–41.

[13] *ibid.*, 38. Schmidt notes that the idea of common heritage was unnecessarily burdened by its linkage to NIEO: M. G. Schimdt, *Common Heritage or Common Burden* (Oxford, Clarendon Press 1989).

[14] See J. Malone, 'The United States and the Law of the Sea after UNCLOS III' (1983) 46(2) *Law and Contemporary Problems* 29. Malone was Chairman of the US delegation to UNCLOS III.

seabed mining regime. These States did not contest the idea that the seabed was the common heritage of mankind, but considered this idea lacked precise legal content. They asserted that, at least until the LOSC's entry into force, exploitation of the seabed would be governed by the principle of freedom of the high seas, outlined in the 1958 High Seas Convention.[15] Between 1980 and 1985, many of them enacted domestic laws enabling them to license the exploration and exploitation of the seabed on this basis. They agreed to recognise each other's licences and drafted procedures for resolving overlapping claims to mining sites. These international agreements and domestic laws constituted the RSR.

There was evident tension between the LOSC regime and the RSR. The LOSC regime was stipulated as solely applicable and universally accepted; the RSR refuted this. Developing States considered the RSR invalid, because it was 'outside the framework of and inconsistent with [the LOSC]'.[16] But, this view was complicated by the fact that the LOSC did not come into force until 1994 – and so was not binding at the time the RSR was floated. RSR States claimed their legislation was temporary and would cease to have effect once the LOSC entered into force for them.

However, this distinction between the LOSC's 'entry into force' and 'entry into force for certain developed States' was read cynically by developing States who believed Western States would never become party to the LOSC. Developing States relied upon two Resolutions (I and II) annexed to the Final Act of UNCLOS III to argue that the LOSC's adoption precluded alternative regimes.[17] These Resolutions directed a Preparatory Commission (PrepCom) to establish an international seabed authority (in effect, the ISA) and to govern pioneer activities relating to seabed mining. An integral part of the LOSC, these Resolutions instituted an authoritative regime that was effective prior to its entry into force. But many RSR States paid no attention to the PrepCom, conducting their mining activities outside its aegis.

This state of affairs continued for several years, despite multiple efforts – some more successful than others – to find a *modus vivendi* between the two regimes. Gradually, with the waning of the Cold War and spread of economic liberalisation, the impracticability and commercial non-viability of seabed mining became the most relevant considerations; the issue lost its political importance. In 1994, via consultations led by the UN Secretary-General, a number of States

[15] 450 UNTS 82. [16] Declaration of the Group of 77, LOS/PCN/5, 11 April 1983.
[17] 21 ILM 1245.

agreed upon an Implementation Agreement.[18] This Agreement heavily modified Part XI, and paved the way for additional accessions to the LOSC. The new parties included most RSR States,[19] except the United States, which signed the Implementation Agreement but remains a non-party to the LOSC.[20]

This chapter examines this conflict between the LOSC and the RSR as well as the stages in which it was mediated through the exertions of the PrepCom, the UN Secretary-General's Informal Consultations, and some States caught between the two regimes, up to the conclusion of the Implementation Agreement. It traces the role(s) that international law played in this process, arguing that, while there was no scope for formal dispute settlement, legal forms and arguments were central - overriding, and even excluding claims based on efficiency and equity. The chapter also uses the work of the PrepCom to illuminate the prospects and limits of the doctrine of approximate application, which was discussed in Chapter 3.

The chapter now proceeds as follows: the next three sections describe the LOSC and RSR mining regimes, and explain why their relationship can be viewed as an example of deliberately created treaty conflict, setting out the practical and ideological underpinnings of this conflict. Following this, it introduces two significant moments of mediation between the two regimes: the 1987 Midnight Agreement and Exchange of Notes[21] and the 1994 Implementation Agreement. The chapter excavates the dynamics through which these were achieved and analyses the role of international law in this process.

The conventional regime

Background to the LOSC

Part XI and Annexes III and IV of the LOSC lay out its framework on seabed mining. The expansive scope of the regime is indicated by the number of provisions in these parts: Part XI contains fifty-nine articles,

[18] 33 ILM 1309.

[19] Accessions: Germany 1994, UK 1997. Ratifications: Italy 1995, France 1996, the Netherlands 1996, Belgium 1998, Canada 2003. Russia also ratified the LOSC in 1997.

[20] On US policy, see J. Duff, 'The United States and the Law of the Sea Convention: Sliding Back from Accession and Ratification' (2006) 11 *Ocean and Coastal Law Journal* 1; J. Noyes, 'US Policy and the UN Convention on the Law of the Sea' (2007) 39 *George Washington International Law Review* 621.

[21] 26 ILM 1502.

including principles, policies for the development of seabed resources, institutional provisions for the establishment of the ISA, and dispute settlement. Annex III comprises twenty-two articles, which provide basic conditions for prospecting, exploring and exploiting the seabed. Annex IV contains thirteen articles which constitute the ISA Statute.

There is reason underlying this detail. The LOSC was negotiated at a time of changing international relations. While Okafor cautions us against claims of 'newness' in world order, the 1960s, as a period in which many Asian and African States gained independence, indeed represented a new era.[22] The increase in the number of States was accompanied by the NIEO movement, which sought substantive equality and just redress of the disparities between developed and developing States. They considered these aims achievable partly through wider distribution of gains from technological progress, which appeared to offer access to previously unattainable resources of the global commons. In debates on the most equitable way to utilise these resources, the 'common heritage' idea gained popularity. Commentators agree that the catalyst for the LOSC was Maltese Ambassador Arvid Pardo's 1967 speech at the United Nations,[23] elaborating upon these themes of his Note Verbale:

> The time has come to declare the seabed and the ocean floor a common heritage of mankind and that immediate steps should be taken to draft a treaty embodying, *inter alia*, the following principles ... [no national appropriation, exploration consistent with purposes and principles of the UN Charter, use and exploitation undertaken with the aim of safeguarding the interests of mankind]. The net financial benefits derived from the use and exploitation of the seabed and of the ocean floor shall be used primarily to promote the development of poor countries.[24]

Pardo's speech was followed by much UN activity. In 1967, it established an 'Ad-Hoc Committee to Study the Peaceful Uses of the Seabed', to

[22] O. Okafor, 'Newness, Imperialism, and International Legal Reform in Our Time: A TWAIL Perspective' (2005) 43 *Osgoode Hall Law Journal* 171, 189.

[23] The full speech is available in UN GAOR 22nd Sess., First Committee, 1515th and 1516th Meetings, General Debate, 1 November 1967, UN Doc. A/C.1/PV.1515 and A/C.1/PV.1516 (1967). On its catalysing effect, see E. D. Brown, *The International Law of the Sea* (Aldershot, Dartmouth 1994) 10; C. Joyner, *International Law in the 21st Century: Rules for Global Governance* (Lanham, MD, Rowman and Littlefield 2005) 230; E. Egede, *Africa and the Deep Seabed Regime: Politics and International Law of the Common Heritage of Mankind* (London, Springer 2011) 11.

[24] See Note Verbale of 17 August 1967 from Malta to UN Secretary-General, UN GAOR, 22nd Sess., UN Doc. A/6695 (1967), in E. D. Brown, *Seabed Energy and Minerals: The International Legal Regime*, Vol. 3 (The Hague, Martinus Nijhoff 2001) 37.

explore 'practical means of promoting international cooperation in the exploration, conservation and use of the seabed'.[25] This was reincarnated as the 'Committee on the Peaceful Uses of the Seabed' in 1968,[26] and remained in operation until UNCLOS III convened in 1973.

In 1970, the UN General Assembly adopted the 'Declaration of Principles Governing the Seabed'.[27] The Declaration reiterated that the seabed and ocean floor, beyond the limits of national jurisdiction, are the common heritage of mankind. Echoing Pardo, the Declaration called for international regulation of '[a]ll activities regarding the exploration and exploitation of the resources of the [seabed]', through 'an international treaty of universal character, generally agreed upon'. It outlined governing principles for such a treaty: non-appropriation, particular consideration of the needs and interests of developing countries, and equitable sharing of benefits. The Declaration was adopted by vote, with 108 States voting in favour, none against and 14 abstaining (including the United States).

The PrepCom and developing States later cited this overwhelming vote in favour of the Declaration to argue that it authoritatively clarified that the LOSC (an international treaty of universal character, generally agreed upon) could be the 'only regime for exploration and exploitation of the [seabed] and its resources'.[28] While the Declaration could support such a claim with respect to a treaty in force, it is not clear that it did so with respect to the LOSC prior to its entry into force in 1994. Robin Churchill and Vaughan Lowe note that the Declaration is ambiguously worded, open to interpretations ranging from that supporting open access to seabed resources until the relevant international treaty entered into force, to that supporting a moratorium on the unilateral exploitation of seabed resources pending the establishment of an international regime.[29] A previous 'Moratorium' Resolution[30] had been introduced with the aim of crystallising the latter interpretation; but it was adopted with only sixty-two developing States voting in favour, twenty-eight (developed Western States) voting against and

[25] UNGA Res. 22/2340 (18 December 1967).
[26] UNGA Res. 23/2467 (21 December 1968).
[27] UNGA Res. 25/2749 (17 December 1970).
[28] Declaration adopted by the Preparatory Commission (August 30), LOS/PCN/72, 2 September 1985.
[29] R. R. Churchill and A. V. Lowe, *Law of the Sea* (3rd edn, Manchester University Press 1999) 228.
[30] UNGA Res. 24/2574 (15 December 1969).

twenty-eight abstentions. Given the slim majority in its support, it could not be evidence of generally accepted practice.[31]

UNCLOS III negotiations were conducted against this background of opposition between developed and developing States. Developing States' interests coalesced into a demand for comprehensive regulation of seabed mining to give effect to the common heritage principle; developed States were keen to secure as much autonomy and flexibility as possible. This divergence of positions extended to other issues. It was therefore agreed early in the drafting process that negotiations would be comprehensive (covering all ocean-related issues) and conducted on the understanding that compromise must be sought between varied interests; all States would honour the eventual treaty on the basis that it was a 'package deal', whereby, if they lost some, they also won some.[32]

The Part XI regime

Where developing States appeared to have won was in the regime initially secured for seabed mining.[33] Part XI contained key features that gave content to the idea of common heritage. These are well encapsulated in Article 155 (2), which provides for a review conference fifteen years from the commencement of commercial production to consider

> maintenance of the principle of the common heritage of mankind, the international regime designed to ensure equitable exploitation of the resources … for the benefit of all countries, especially the developing States, and an Authority to organize, conduct and control activities … [M]aintenance of the principles laid down in [Part XI:] exclusion of claims or exercise of sovereignty … rights of States and their general conduct … participation in activities … in conformity with [the LOSC], prevention of monopolization of activities … use … exclusively for peaceful purposes, economic aspects of activities … marine scientific research, transfer of technology, protection of the marine environment, protection of human life, rights of coastal States, the legal status of the waters superjacent … and that of the air space above those waters and accommodation

[31] Churchill and Lowe, *Law of the Sea*, 227.

[32] See UNCLOS III, Second Session, Caracas, 19th Plenary Meeting, A/Conf.62/SR.19, 27 June 1974. See also H. Caminos and M. Molitor, 'Progressive Development of International Law and the Package Deal' (1985) 79 *American Journal of International Law* 871.

[33] Churchill and Lowe, *Law of the Sea*, 228, note 'a steady movement away from the position of the western States and towards that of the Group of 77'. But 'third world' scholars evidently felt otherwise: B. S. Chimni, 'Imperialism All the Way' (1982) 17 *Economic and Political Weekly* 407, argued that several lacunae such as on production policies and technology sharing made the draft unpalatable to developing States.

between activities in the [seabed] and other activities in the marine environment.

Part XI's scheme comprises two segments. The first is a list of principles to govern seabed mining, including characterisation of the seabed beyond national jurisdiction, and its resources, as the common heritage of mankind (Article 136), and stipulation that seabed-related activities should be carried out for the benefit of mankind as a whole with particular consideration given to the needs and interests of developing States (Article 140 (1)). This segment also provides for non-appropriation of the seabed and its resources (Article 137); State responsibility for acts of nationals and persons under their effective control (Article 139); and equitable sharing of financial and other economic benefits (Article 140(2)). Further, the segment includes specific benefits for developing States: Article 148 calls for promotion of their effective participation in mining; and Article 144 mandates transfer of technology and scientific knowledge to them. Finally, the segment also stipulates cooperation in marine scientific research (Article 143) and protection of the marine environment (Articles 145 and 147).

The second segment of Part XI, together with Annexes III and IV, set out specific policies intended to flesh out the principles of the first segment. E. D. Brown neatly summarises these policies under the following five heads:[34]

(1) *Parallel system and site banking*: the ISA would both license mining by State or private enterprises, and conduct mining through an organ called the 'Enterprise'. Applicants for licences would have to identify two areas of equal value; one of these would be 'banked' for use by the Enterprise or by developing States.
(2) *Financial and technological aid to the Enterprise*: via funds provided to ISA by member States; licence fees, annual fees and production charges paid by licensees; and technology transfer by licensees, who would ensure the availability of any technology they used to the Enterprise and to developing States.
(3) *Production policies*: including an annually calculated production ceiling, production quota for the Enterprise, and compensation to land-based producers of the same minerals.
(4) *Qualifications of applicants*: they would be required to be States party to the LOSC, or their state enterprises or nationals, or persons under their effective control; with the relevant financial and technical capacity.
(5) *Review*: on a five-yearly basis by the ISA Assembly, and a more detailed review after the first fifteen years.

[34] Brown, *The International Law of the Sea*, 448.

Appendix 1 to this book offers a detailed overview of these provisions.

Part XI also set out the composition, powers and functions of the ISA. Of importance was the division of powers and functions between the ISA Assembly and Council (its principal organs, along with the Secretariat and the Enterprise). The ISA Assembly would include all LOSC parties, each having one vote. The ISA Council would have restricted membership, determined by criteria indicated in Appendix 1. In substance, developed States would have greater proportionate representation on the Council, and developing States would have numerical majority in the Assembly. The former accordingly sought greater decision-making powers for the Council: Natalie Klein notes that they preferred to limit the Assembly's role to approving broad policy guidelines, leaving a wide executive role to the Council.[35] Developing States wanted expanded powers for the Assembly, to make it the 'truly supreme decision making organ'.[36] Ultimately, under Article 160, the LOSC effected a division that allowed the Council to advise the Assembly on many issues, such as equitable sharing of benefits, but left final decision to the Assembly. Article 162 authorised the Council to approve plans of work submitted by States or private entities and by the Enterprise.

Developed (Western) States considered these provisions to be overly bureaucratic, burdensome and disabling to their effective participation: 'nothing less than a new socialist international economic order'.[37] Shortly before the tenth session of UNCLOS III negotiations - seven years after the Conference had convened - the United States announced that it would undertake a detailed review of 'the serious problems raised by the Draft Convention'.[38] At the eleventh session, in 1982, it suggested 'hundreds of amendments' that, according to the chairman of the Australian delegation, would have displaced the entire negotiating text.[39] The Conference could not come to consensus, and decided

[35] N. Klein, 'Dispute Settlement in the International Law of the Sea' (Cambridge University Press 2005) 325.

[36] *ibid.*

[37] A. S. Anand, 'Common Heritage of Mankind: Mutilation of an Ideal', in *Studies in International Law and History: An Asian Perspective* (Leiden, Martinus Nijhoff 2004) 180, 188.

[38] US Department of State, Press Release, 2 March 1981, cited from B. H. Oxman, 'The Third United Nations Conference on the Law of the Sea, The Tenth Session (1981)' (1982) 76 *American Journal of International Law* 1.

[39] K. Brennan, 'The United Nations Conference on the Law of the Sea' (1982) 76 *ASIL Proceedings* 107, 108–9.

to vote on the adoption of the LOSC. The United States was one of 4 States that voted against, while 17 States abstained and 130 States voted in favour.

Pioneer investor provisions

At the eleventh session, negotiators also agreed to establish the PrepCom, to prepare the legal and operational framework for the ISA, which could begin functioning once the LOSC entered into force. By this session, potential challenges to the universal acceptance of the LOSC, and specifically its seabed regime, had become evident. But, without some sort of international framework, States – lacking security of tenure over mining sites – would be unable to persuade private investment into seabed mining. Thus, an interim regime was provided through Resolution II, to safeguard pioneering investment activities. The PrepCom was given the added charge of administering this regime.[40]

Resolution II provided a scheme for licensing exploratory activities by pioneer investors (exploitation, that is, commercial recovery, could only commence by licence from the ISA, once the LOSC entered into force; pioneer investors would get priority). It named several States and entities that could apply for one exploratory licence each: India, Japan, the USSR, France and four certified consortia from Belgium, Canada, Germany, Italy, Japan, the Netherlands, the United Kingdom and the United States (once these States signed the LOSC). These States and entities would have to fulfil certain necessary financial conditions by 1 January 1983. The Resolution also permitted LOSC-signatory developing States to apply for pioneer investor licences if they fulfilled the same financial conditions by 1 January 1985.

Under Resolution II, pioneer investors would be allotted sites following the site-banking provisions of Part XI, and they would have to progressively relinquish these sites over several years. They would also have to ensure that sites requested in their applications did not overlap with those already allotted or applied for by other States. Once registered, the investors would have to pay licence fees and annual fees, maintain a minimum level of investment in the sites and, at the PrepCom's request, undertake various other activities such as exploring a reserved site (on a costs-plus 10 per cent basis), transferring technology, and training personnel. Licensee States (including States certifying

[40] Res. I, para. 5(h).

licensed entities) would also have to provide funds to the Enterprise. Appendix 2 of this book offers details on these obligations.

Despite this list of obligations, commentators point out that the interim regime completely rewrote the Convention's rules in favour of pioneer investors.[41] Certainly, its provisions offered concessions to Western States, recognising activities that had taken place pursuant to their unilateral legislation (which had been declared illegal at UNCLOS III[42]). Even so, the regime was not accepted amongst these States, which established their own interim regime in the form of the RSR.

The common heritage principle in Part XI and Resolution II

Part XI and Resolution II crystallised States' duties under the common heritage principle in a concrete and limited way. Part XI's first segment set out general principles, derived from the 1970 Declaration; its second segment, and Resolution II, elaborated institutional provisions. According to these, the common heritage principle comprised the following:

(1) *Non-appropriation/non-alienation of the seabed*: Article 137 of Part XI offered the general principle that no State could claim sovereignty over the seabed, nor appropriate any part of it; the rights over seabed resources were vested in mankind as a whole. However, under the institutional provisions of Part XI and Resolution II, this principle was realised in a partial way, for they allowed particular States or consortia to bring large portions of the seabed under their exclusive control for significant periods, and also permitted (eventually, upon the LOSC's entry into force) mining large quantities of minerals, even denuding the sites. Seabed resources were thus only formally non-appropriable.

(2) *Equitable sharing*: this was perhaps the most essential aspect of the LOSC's common heritage framework. Part XI in fact contemplated both *effective sharing* of benefits derived from seabed mining (Article 140) and *effective participation* in mining activities (Article 148). As a corollary, these principles required special consideration for the needs of developing and geographically disadvantaged States.

    The means for effectively sharing benefits were not fully spelt out, but clearly entailed transfer of financial gains from developed States to the ISA. Article 160 also tasked the ISA Assembly with formulating suitable rules, and Article 162 required the ISA Council to offer its recommendations for this purpose.

[41] Churchill and Lowe, *Law of the Sea*, 230.

[42] B. S. Chimni, 'Law of the Sea: Winners Are Losers' (1982) 17 *Economic and Political Weekly* 987, 989 (quoting the Sierra Leone delegate at UNCLOS, A/Conf.62/L.146, 29 April 1982).

Means of effective participation included building developing States' capacity in seabed mining through training personnel, transferring technology and reserving sites. Developing States were thus encouraged to enter the field. While the LOSC did not exclude a 'first come first served' approach (which benefitted developed States),[43] this was not a permanent barrier as new applicants would have priority in each round of authorisations.[44] Meanwhile, site-banking would prevent early mover developed States from grabbing all the best sites.[45] Also, an exception was provided for the Enterprise, which could be authorised to mine at any time, in concert with developing States. This ensured that there was always a small opportunity for an interested developing State to join in seabed mining.

Another aspect of effective participation was in the administration of seabed mining: the LOSC provided for developed and developing States to govern the ISA, through Council and Assembly. This was important for the NIEO context in which the LOSC was concluded: a new order required that developing States could no longer remain merely passive recipients of marginal benefits from the exploitation of common property resources.

(3) *The no harm principle*: this third element of the common heritage principle was elaborated in three types of provisions: the Article 141 general principle that the seabed must be used exclusively for peaceful purposes; policies (production limits, compensation) to ensure that land-based (developing State) producers of minerals were not economically harmed; and, in LOSC Article 145 and 147, provisions to preserve the marine environment.

Developed States were not alone in their dissatisfaction with these provisions. Even Pardo felt that the LOSC provisions were too burdensome. In a speech delivered in 1983, he noted that 'the viability of the future international regime for the seabed beyond national jurisdiction and economic realities were largely forgotten by the contending parties in the almost theological debate'.[46] He suggested that developing States had pressed for compromises that would preserve the integrity of their ideological position on common heritage, at the cost of a regime that could actually allow seabed resources to be used for the equal benefit of all nations. His speech noted several ways in which the regime thus fell short of developing States' own interests: it excluded living resources;

[43] Art. 151(2)–(7), LOSC; Res. II, para. 9. [44] Res. II, para. 9(c).

[45] Importantly, the number of tenable sites was soon found to be small: C. Sanger, *Ordering the Oceans: The Making of the Law of the Sea* (University of Toronto Press 1987) 165.

[46] A. Pardo, 'Before and After' (1983) 46 *Law and Contemporary Problems* 95, 102.

its focus was limited to manganese nodules, excluding other mineral resources; the ISA, while possessing detailed rulemaking authority, was substantively too weak and structurally too complex to be workable; the composition and decision-making procedures of the ISA Council were too complex to allow timely and effective decisions on important matters; and the regime imposed unrealistic production limitations, heavy bureaucratic controls and onerous payments upon those granted production authorisations. The result was to impede any meaningful implementation of the common heritage principle.[47]

Pardo suggested, moreover, that the United States' opposition to the LOSC was an expression of frustration with developing States' loud proclamations in favour of the common heritage principle, which it rejected at the ideological level. Certainly, in establishing the RSR, the United States and other Western States endorsed a contrary principle, the freedom of the high seas.

The Reciprocating States Regime

Domestic legislation

The first instrument of the RSR was the US Deep Seabed Hard Mineral Resources Act of 1980,[48] providing 'an interim procedure for the orderly development of hard mineral resources in the deep seabed, pending adoption of an international regime'. The Act explained that much time could elapse before UNCLOS III negotiations were concluded, and *would* elapse before an international regime was operational, but research and development of mining technology, a multi-year commitment, could not await the LOSC's entry into force. Some legal regulation was necessary to encourage potential investors to invest resources in the same.

In addition to this economic rationale, the Act also provided legal justification. It noted the United States' support for the common heritage principle, but claimed that this principle lacked precise legal content. It asserted that one of the purposes of the Act was 'to encourage the successful conclusion of a comprehensive Law of the Sea Treaty, which will give legal definition to the principle that the hard mineral resources of the deep seabed are the common heritage of mankind, and which will assure, among other things, nondiscriminatory access to such resources for all nations'. The Act also claimed that it had anticipated

[47] *ibid.*, 103–4. [48] Public Law 96-283, 19 ILM 1003 (1980).

the likely provisions of such a treaty by requiring the United States to establish an international fund to share mining revenue amongst the international community once the LOSC entered into force. Meanwhile, it was the 'legal opinion' of the United States that mining was 'a freedom of the high seas, subject to a duty of reasonable regard to the interests of other States in their exercise of that and other freedoms recognised by general principles of international law'.[49]

The Act provided a scheme for regulation of seabed mining, *inter alia* forbidding exploration or commercial recovery of minerals unless licensed by the United States or a 'reciprocating' State, or permitted by an international agreement in force for the United States. It designated a reciprocating State as such if it regulated seabed mining in a manner compatible with the Act, recognised licences issued under the Act and prohibited exploration or commercial production in conflict with that authorised under the Act. The Act also forbade US citizens from interfering with seabed-mining licences issued by reciprocating States. It reiterated the claim that seabed mining was a freedom of the high seas and required reasonable regard for interests of other States. It also included provisions on the environment, conservation of natural resources, and safety of life and property from dangers posed by seabed mining.

Similar legislation was adopted by other States. Germany adopted the Act of Interim Regulation of Deep Seabed Mining 1980 (amended 1982);[50] the United Kingdom adopted the Deep Sea Mining (Temporary Provisions) Act 1981;[51] France adopted the Law on the Exploration and Exploitation of the Mineral Resources of the Deep Sea-Bed 1981;[52] Japan adopted the Law on Interim Measures for Deep Sea-Bed Mining 1982;[53] and Italy adopted the Regulations on the Exploration and Exploitation of the Mineral Resources of the Deep Sea-Bed 1985.[54] (The USSR enacted the 1982 Edict on Provisional Measures to Regulate Soviet Enterprises for the Exploration and Exploitation of Mineral Resources,[55] but did not participate in the RSR.)

The UK, French, German, Italian and Japanese Acts provided similar regimes for the domestic regulation of seabed mining and offered reciprocal recognition to licences granted by each other. Like the US Act, they claimed that seabed mining was a freedom of the high seas. According to Brown, all the Acts had three common motives: to ensure non-discriminatory access for their nationals to seabed resources,

[49] Section 2(a)(12), US Seabed Act. [50] 20 ILM 393. Amended version at 21 ILM 832.
[51] 20 ILM 1217. [52] 21 ILM 808. [53] 22 ILM 102. [54] 24 ILM 983. [55] 21 ILM 551.

leading to secure national access to supplies of minerals; to promote investment in research and development towards technology for seabed mining; and to ensure that their nationals were not at a competitive disadvantage *vis-à-vis* nationals of other States that had adopted interim legislation.[56]

None of the Acts expressly opposed the LOSC – indeed, they claimed to be of temporary duration and to give way before a valid treaty duly entered into force. Even so, the United States, the United Kingdom and Germany did not sign the LOSC when it was opened for signature in 1982; the others did sign (Italy and Belgium only did so in December 1984) but did not ratify it until the conclusion of the 1994 Implementation Agreement. Moreover, in signing the LOSC, France and Italy made declarations that Part XI contained 'considerable deficiencies and flaws', which the PrepCom must rectify.[57]

International agreements

The unilateral laws were crystallised into a regime via two international agreements. First, in 1982, France, Germany, the United Kingdom and the United States concluded the Agreement concerning Interim Arrangements relating to Polymetallic Nodules of the Deep Seabed ('Interim Agreement'),[58] to facilitate resolution of their overlapping claims to mining sites. The Interim Agreement provided for consultations between parties and voluntary resolution of conflicting claims, with recourse to arbitration if necessary.

In 1984, the Interim Agreement was replaced by the Provisional Understanding Regarding Deep Seabed Matters between Belgium, France, Germany, Italy, Japan, the Netherlands, the United Kingdom and the United States ('Provisional Understanding').[59] The Provisional Understanding provided for notification and consultations to avoid overlapping claims to mining sites, and for binding arbitration. Additionally, it required its member States to harmonise their application requirements and operating standards.[60] A Memorandum for Implementation spelt out the standards to be enforced by each State, including: reasonable regard for interests of other States parties (in furtherance of the principle of freedom of the high seas); non-interference with activities

[56] E. D. Brown, *Seabed Energy and Minerals: The International Legal Regime*, Vol. 2 (The Hague, Martinus Nijhoff 2001) 247.
[57] www.un.org/Depts/los/convention_agreements/convention_declarations.htm.
[58] 21 ILM 950. [59] 23 ILM 1354. [60] Art. 8, Provisional Understanding.

licensed by another State party; protection of the environment and prevention of waste; sustainable exploitation to preserve future mining opportunities; and protection of life and property at sea.[61]

Churchill and Lowe note that the cautious terminology used in titling the Provisional Understanding reflected the insistence on the RSR being a purely interim scheme.[62] Even so, the Provisional Understanding was a step beyond the Interim Arrangement, for it gave multilateral articulation to substantive principles – in particular, the high seas principle – governing seabed mining.

Conflict between the LOSC and the RSR

A treaty conflict?

This section will argue that, with the conclusion of the Provisional Understanding, the differences between the LOSC and the RSR crystallised into a treaty conflict. It will consider and rebut the arguments made by several RSR States that there was no conflict with the LOSC because the LOSC had not entered into force and the RSR was only an interim regime; and because the RSR was compatible with the spirit of the LOSC regime.

This section will make the point that, even though the LOSC itself was not in force, its key integral components – the PrepCom and the pioneer investor regime – were, and they made operational (at least the core principles constituting) the LOSC's seabed mining regime even prior to 1994. Moreover, this regime excluded alternatives: the very text of LOSC Article 137(2) provided: '[t]he minerals recovered . . . may only be alienated in accordance with . . . Part [XI] and the rules, regulations and procedures of [the ISA]'. This was, *prima facie*, a denial of the RSR's validity. It informed the PrepCom's initial stance:

> 1. . . . (a) The only regime for the exploration and exploitation of the [seabed] and its resources is that established by the [LOSC] and related resolutions . . . (b) Any claim, agreement or action . . . which is incompatible with [the LOSC] and its related resolutions shall not be recognized.
> 2. . . . such claim, agreement or action [is rejected] as a basis for creating legal rights and [regarded] as wholly illegal.[63]

[61] 23 ILM 1358. [62] Churchill and Lowe, *Law of the Sea*, 233.
[63] PrepCom Declaration, LOS/PCN/72, 2 September 1985.

The section will open with a brief summary of the key substantive differences between the LOSC and the RSR; it is already clear that they embraced different administrative frameworks. It will then explore the RSR States' argument that there was no conflict because the LOSC was not in force. Finally, it will assess the claim that the RSR was compatible with the spirit of the LOSC.

Divergences between the LOSC and the RSR

The RSR emerged as a result of developed States' reservations about the seabed regime which was taking shape at UNCLOS III. Klein suggests that one purpose of these States' domestic legislation was to influence the course of negotiations by demonstrating clearly what was acceptable to them.[64] The domestic laws diverged from the LOSC in several respects, including their production levies (which were half of that provided in the LOSC), the absence of a site-banking provision, and the lack of technology-transfer requirements.[65]

There were also other differences. While the LOSC, in Article 152, had provided for non-discrimination by the ISA in granting mining licences, the domestic laws envisaged more favourable regimes for RSR nationals. Unlike LOSC Annex III Article 6, no limit was imposed on the number or total area of mining sites that could be licensed. Unlike LOSC Article 151, no provisions were made for the protection of land-based producers. Besides preambular statements, there were few concrete commitments in the domestic legislations to the establishment of an international revenue sharing fund.

The multilateral treaties, particularly the Provisional Understanding, exacerbated these differences, first, by describing the duty of the RSR States as simply one of reasonable regard for the interests of other States, and, second, by envisaging more favourable treatment for other RSR States in according mutual recognition to each other's licences. The Provisional Understanding also set out substantive standards for RSR States, but these did not include any provisions corresponding to the above-discussed LOSC provisions.

The situation in the 1980s

It is true that, when some of the domestic legislation was enacted, the LOSC had not even been adopted. Moreover, once adopted (in 1982), it

64 Klein, 'Dispute Settlement in the International Law of the Sea', 339.

65 Churchill and Lowe, *Law of the Sea*, 233.

did not enter into force until 1994. Some RSR States argued that, during the intervening period, they could only be governed by the High Seas Convention,[66] as the admonition in LOSC Article 137(2) could have no effect before its entry into force. These RSR States could even have invoked VCLT Article 28, which provides for the non-retroactivity of treaties, such that

> [u]nless a different intention appears from the treaty or is otherwise established, its provisions do not bind a party in relation to any act or fact which took place or any situation which ceased to exist before the date of the entry into force of the treaty with respect to that party.

This provision would support their argument that, as an interim regime, which was intended to be terminated upon the LOSC's entry into force, the RSR was not contrary to the LOSC.

Against this, however, it can be argued that the seabed mining regime of the LOSC *was* legally effective from its adoption in 1982. In particular, Part XI had been largely finalised by 1980 (when the US enacted its Seabed Mining Act) and by 1982 most States appeared to view it as an appropriate crystallisation of the 1970 Declaration of Principles adopted by the UN General Assembly. The Declaration, which *recognised* that the high seas principle did not provide a substantive basis for seabed mining and *declared* the seabed beyond national jurisdiction the common heritage of mankind, had received overwhelming support.[67] As such, it may be taken as evidence of *opinio juris* on the principles governing the seabed.[68] Moreover, though its operative provisions were only broadly sketched and thus were divergently interpreted by States, one element of its conception of the common heritage principle was clear enough: that seabed mining must be administered by a universal international regime. The UNCLOS III was convened to establish this regime, in the form of the LOSC, which set out specific provisions building on the Declaration. It was signed by 119 delegations on the day it opened for

66 Brown, *Seabed Energy and Minerals*, Vol. 2, 456–7; Klein, 'Dispute Settlement in the International Law of the Sea', 338.

67 T. Kronmiller, *The Lawfulness of Deep Seabed Mining*, Vol. I (London, Oceana Publications 1980) 283, notes that the statement that the Area was the common heritage of mankind was not at all challenged.

68 For instance, *Nuclear Weapons*, Advisory Opinion (1996) ICJ Rep 226, para. 70: 'The Court notes that General Assembly resolutions, even if they are not binding, may sometimes have normative value. They can, in certain circumstances, provide evidence important for establishing the existence of a rule or the emergence of an *opinio juris*.'

signature.[69] By August 1985, the number of signatories stood at 159:[70] an overwhelming majority of States, including RSR States (though these took care to record their dissatisfaction with Part XI). The LOSC's adoption with the support of a huge majority, read with the Declaration, is suggestive of its normative significance even prior to its entry into force.

Moreover, even according to the VCLT, a treaty need not be in force in order to create obligations for signatories: Article 18 provides for the good-faith obligation to refrain from acts that would defeat the object and purpose of the treaty. This provision by itself was sufficient to prevent LOSC signatories from concluding alternative regimes that defeated its common heritage aspirations.[71]

Most importantly, it could be argued that the LOSC did indicate the 'different intention' mentioned in VCLT Article 28. Resolutions I and II were integral components of the LOSC, and provided for the operation of a PrepCom and an investment protection regime prior to the LOSC's entry into force. Signatories to the LOSC were thus committed to the scheme provided in Resolution II. This is supported by VCLT Article 24, which provides: 'The provisions of a treaty regulating . . . matters arising necessarily before the entry into force of the treaty apply from the time of the adoption of its text'. Moreover, Resolution II proclaimed that the ISA would 'recognize and honour the rights and obligations arising from this resolution and [PrepCom decisions] taken pursuant to it'.[72] While it did not expressly state that the ISA could recognise *only* those rights and obligations that arose from Resolution II and PrepCom decisions (and not those resulting from RSR), this was a certain enough implication, which was bolstered by the PrepCom's decided stance that the LOSC provided the 'only regime for the exploration and exploitation of the [seabed]'.[73] This linkage between the ISA, and Resolution II and the PrepCom lends further weight to the argument that the normative framework (if not the precise institutional architecture) of the UN seabed mining regime had come into force upon the adoption of the LOSC.

Indeed, scholars writing in the 1980s did not see the RSR as 'interim' and the LOSC as 'not in force', but as competing regimes. In 1983, D'Amato considered how the International Court of Justice, or another

69 Anand, 'Common Heritage of Mankind', 190.

70 Statement by the Chairman of the Group of 77, LOS/PCN/L.5, 20 March 1985.

71 This was also asserted by the EES: Statement by the Chairman of the Group of East European Socialist Countries (August 13), LOS/PCN/49, 17 August 1984.

72 Res. II, para. 13. 73 PrepCom Declaration, LOS/PCN/72, 2 September 1985.

tribunal, may decide a case between the two, suggesting that the mining practice under each could be the deciding factor:

[T]he Court . . . might place considerable weight on the practice of states under the two treaties. If, for example, an American firm engaged in deep seabed mining according to [RSR] . . . and there were no other mining activities by any of the countries party to [the LOSC], the very practice of such a firm would tend to reinforce the norms of [the RSR]. Conversely, if deep seabed mining activities were first begun by states party to [the LOSC], then it would tend to be reinforced by the practice . . . A future tribunal, therefore, might accord great weight to whichever treaty is first implemented by actual mining practice.[74]

Significantly, RSR States that had signed the LOSC also seemed to treat it as already effective. For instance, upon concluding the Provisional Understanding, France and the Netherlands sent letters to the PrepCom Chairman explaining that the Understanding was not contrary to the LOSC, or Resolution II, but, in fact, 'fulfil[led] in part the requirement of Resolution II to resolve overlapping claims'.[75]

Principles underpinning the RSR and the LOSC

France and the Netherlands sought to justify the Provisional Understanding on the basis that it furthered the scheme provided in Resolution II, particularly in paragraph 5:

(a) Any State which has signed [the LOSC] and which is a prospective certifying State shall ensure, before making applications to [PrepCom] under paragraph 2, that areas in respect of which applications are made do not overlap one another or areas previously allocated as pioneer areas. The States concerned shall keep [PrepCom] currently and fully informed of any efforts to resolve conflicts with respect to overlapping claims and of the results thereof.

. . .

(c) The prospective certifying States, including all potential claimants, shall resolve their conflicts . . . by negotiations within a reasonable period.

The two States argued that the Provisional Understanding was a mechanism to enable them to identify and avoid potential conflicts over mining sites. They also asserted that, in concluding the Provisional Understanding, they had only undertaken obligations of self-restraint,

[74] D'Amato, 'An Alternative to the Law of the Sea Convention', 284.

[75] Letter from the Government of the Netherlands to the PrepCom Chairman (August 3), LOS/PCN/46, 16 August 1984; Letter from the Chairman of the French delegation to the PrepCom Chairman (August 3), LOS/PCN/47, 16 August 1984.

to avoid claiming sites that overlapped with those claimed by other States, but their participation did not 'entail the recognition of any claims whatsoever from the enterprises [of other RSR States]'. In short, they claimed that the Understanding did not bind them to admit as legally enforceable claims to mining sites allocated outside the LOSC regime. Indeed, their certified entities would submit applications for registration as pioneer investors by the PrepCom once their conflicting claims to mining sites were resolved. For these reasons, they considered the Provisional Understanding 'fully compatible with the obligation ... to undertake deep sea-bed activities within the framework of resolution II'.

This argument, of the Provisional Understanding's compatibility with the LOSC, was rejected by various LOSC signatories, including the Group of 77 States (G77) and the Group of Eastern European States (EES).

The G77 viewed the Provisional Understanding, together with the domestic laws, as an attempt 'to arrogate to [its parties] the powers of [the ISA] to authorise seabed operations'. 'Furthermore', it pointed out, 'the Provisional Understanding goes beyond the resolution of conflicts arising from overlapping claims, by including provisions regarding exploration and exploitation of the seabed resources, outside of [the LOSC]'.[76]

The EES, for their part, considered the Understanding a 'mini-treaty'

> to establish a regime for the exploitation of the resources of the Area that is completely contradictory to [the LOSC]. Indeed, it seeks, as is clear from the [Memorandum of Implementation], to substitute for the rules, regulations and procedures for activities ... that have been elaborated in detail in [the LOSC] and are to be rendered more specific by the [PrepCom] its own 'standards' permitting western consortia to act without control in exploring and exploiting the resources of the deep seabed.[77]

The USSR claimed that the 'obvious purpose' of the Provisional Understanding was to undermine the LOSC and the PrepCom.[78] It urged the PrepCom to commence the registration of pioneer investors as soon as possible, in order to give effect to the LOSC. The PrepCom was itself hostile to the RSR. It espoused all the above claims

[76] Statement by the G77 Chairman to the Preparatory Commission (August 13), LOS/PCN/48, 16 August 1984.

[77] Statement by the EES Chairman, LOS/PCN/49, 17 August 1984.

[78] Letter from the Acting Permanent Representative of the USSR (June 10), LOS/PCN/64, 1 July 1985.

in its declaration that the LOSC provided the *only* regime for exploration and exploitation of the seabed.[79]

Thus, while France and the Netherlands had sought a *via media* that would enable their continued adherence to both regimes, their strategy of presenting the Provisional Understanding as compatible with Resolution II was unsuccessful. Indeed, in claiming that they were merely acting in pursuance of paragraph 5 of Resolution II, they did not account for their domestic legislation and its 'freedom of the high seas' underpinnings, which were echoed in the Provisional Understanding.

Another strategy consisted in the claim of RSR States that, while they accepted the idea of common heritage in principle, they considered it lacking in precise legal content. This claim, it must be said, was much better made in later scholarship than by the RSR States at the time. The RSR States simply asserted that the principle suffered from this lack, and asserted that their own laws were sufficiently in tune with its general idea – for these laws precluded claims of sovereignty over the seabed and its resources, expressed support for an appropriate universal treaty, envisaged revenue-sharing and even the provision of funds to a suitable seabed authority, once it was operational.

Brown notes that the RSR States could have further claimed that their own objections to Part XI made it evident that the LOSC administrative scheme was not the only possible means to realise the common heritage principle.[80] This view had support in the scheme of the LOSC itself, which placed seabed mining principles and institutional provisions into distinct – and logically severable – segments.[81] Indeed, Part XI's institutional provisions referred to entities not in existence prior to 1994, while the adoption of Resolution II showed how its principles could be fleshed out (if temporarily) by different institutional provisions. Thus, arguing that the common heritage principle was not bound to any particular institutional provisions, RSR States could assert that the RSR conformed to the 'spirit' of the LOSC.

In fact, Brown notes, they could have argued in even stronger terms: that it was unrealistic to foist onto the common heritage principle 'an ambitious and untried system of central planning which was

[79] PrepCom Declaration, LOS/PCN/72, 2 September 1985.

[80] France, Italy and Belgium made declarations of dissatisfaction with Part XI and 'hoped' the PrepCom would address its shortcomings.

[81] This is also argued by J. Morell, *The Law of the Sea: The 1982 Treaty and its Rejection by the United States* (Jefferson, NC, McFarland 1992) 164.

alien to those whose role it would be to supply the initial capital and technology'.[82]

However, even these claims could not overcome the fact that the RSR, too, failed to uphold key attributes of the common heritage principle that had been articulated in the 1970 Declaration of Principles and in the LOSC principles segment. The RSR, biased as it was towards nationals of reciprocating States, did not fulfil the principle of non-discrimination. It did not aim at effective participation of developing States: it made no provision to prevent occupation of mining sites on a 'first come first served' basis, which would exclude latecomer (developing) States, nor for capacity-building of developing States. It took a narrow view of the principle of equitable sharing of benefits as extending only to revenue-sharing, according to a scheme determined by the RSR States alone. It ignored a major element of the 'do no harm principle' by failing to provide for production limits to safeguard land-based producers. The RSR States could have rejected the LOSC and its conceptualisation of the common heritage principle altogether (as the United States did[83]), but they could not claim accord with the spirit of the LOSC.

Ultimately, the RSR States' espousal of 'the freedom of the high seas' principle was clear proof of the RSR's underlying philosophical conflict with the LOSC. The high seas principle and the common heritage principle are diametrically opposed. The former allows unilateral use by any State, so long as it maintains a reasonable regard for the rights of other States to also use the resource. This naturally excludes duties to preserve opportunities for, or help capacity-building in developing States. The latter makes the use of a common heritage resource contingent upon a number of obligations that promote substantive equality in the use of that resource by all States. A regime predicated on the former principle is thus not reconcilable in spirit with the latter.

[82] Brown, *Seabed Energy and Minerals*, Vol. 2, 278.

[83] See Malone, 'The United States and the Law of the Sea after UNCLOS III', 32. Malone, Chairman of the US delegation to UNCLOS III, explained that the United States could not sign the LOSC because of how the LOSC had conceptualised the common heritage principle: 'The "common heritage" is certainly a noble phrase. Unfortunately, the phrase became severely distorted in its meaning during the long LOS negotiations. It became a guise under which the seabed's wealth was to be governed, regulated, and allocated under the false assumption that every nation has an undivided property interest in the deep seabed, and therefore, each is automatically entitled to its proportionate share of the fruits from those whose efforts produce wealth from what would otherwise be economically valueless.'

In this context, James Morell has made an interesting suggestion that the underlying basis of both principles is, in fact, the doctrine of *res communis*.[84] Morell argues that the application of *res communis* must be determined by the nature of the resource. Where the resource is abundant and renewable and its use is not to the detriment of others with similar rights to use, it can be used freely. Where the resource is limited and – we could argue – more difficult for some to exploit than for others, *res communis* demands application of the common heritage principle. Since polymetallic nodules are a common property resource that is non-renewable, and extremely difficult to mine, the latter approach would be the more appropriate.

However, the RSR States had not simply embraced the wrong emanation of *res communis*, relying on false assumptions about the abundance and renewability of seabed minerals, and the ease of their recovery. Their position, like the position of the States opposing them, was guided by ideology. And, ironically, when finally all these States came to acknowledge that seabed minerals were difficult to mine and not abundantly recoverable, their response was to retreat from the common heritage principle.

Conflict to compromise: two key moments

States parties to the LOSC and RSR regimes were obviously keen to implement them effectively, but also recognised that the competition between them threatened the security of tenure over mining sites. To overcome this, the RSR States aimed at reform of the LOSC regime. For their part, LOSC signatories (except those also parties to the RSR) and the PrepCom initially took the position of denying the validity of the RSR, but gradually came to accept the need for compromise with that regime.

This section introduces two key moments of compromise – the conclusion of the Midnight Agreement and Exchange of Notes on 14 August 1987; and the adoption of the Implementation Act of 1994. It suggests that, while the Midnight Agreement was a *modus vivendi* between the two regimes, the Implementation Agreement was a substantial modification of the LOSC regime. The next section explores the dynamics that led to each.

[84] Morell, *The Law of the Sea*, 176–8.

The Midnight Agreement and Exchange of Notes, 1987

The Midnight Agreement was concluded in 1987 as a pragmatic arrangement to identify and resolve overlapping claims to mining sites between LOSC signatories and RSR States. It was a key achievement for both regimes, because prior to its conclusion the lack of a common process to resolve overlapping claims had created many practical problems.

Take the example of the four mining consortia established by entities from Belgium, Canada, Germany, Italy, Japan, the Netherlands, the United Kingdom and the United States: Ocean Minerals Company (OMCO), Ocean Management Inc. (OMI), Ocean Mining Associates (OMA) and the Kennecott Consortium (KCON).[85] On the basis of the RSR, the United States, the United Kingdom and Germany had issued them licences to explore sites in the nodule-rich Clarion–Clipperton Zone of the Pacific, after resolving potential overlaps with sites claimed by Japanese and French State enterprises.[86] But the USSR, also prospecting in the Clarion–Clipperton Zone, rejected the validity of these licences.[87] The USSR asserted that exploration could only take place under PrepCom licences, and that it was not obliged to recognise the exclusive tenure of these four consortia to any mining site. This was obviously a matter of concern for these consortia and their licensing States.

But the USSR's own security of tenure was also contingent upon the assent of RSR States. Four of these States – Belgium, Italy, Japan and the Netherlands – had signed the LOSC and were entitled to participate in the PrepCom. As potential applicants for pioneer investor licences under Resolution II, these States could block a PrepCom licence to the USSR on the basis that it conflicted with the sites claimed by them.[88] Thus, a situation was created in which no one enjoyed any certainty of exclusive rights over any portion of the Clarion–Clipperton Zone.

This situation was finally overcome by the Midnight Agreement and Exchange of Notes concluded between the RSR States and relevant LOSC signatories. LOSC signatories Belgium, Canada, Italy, the Netherlands and the USSR signed the Agreement at a midnight ceremony on

[85] For details of their respective holdings, see Sanger, *Ordering the Oceans*, 161–7.

[86] L. Kimball, 'Introductory Note on the Midnight Agreement' (1987) 26 ILM 1502.

[87] Letter from the Acting Permanent Representative of the USSR, LOS/PCN/64, 1 July 1985.

[88] Kimball, 'Introductory Note on the Midnight Agreement', 1502–3.

14 August 1987; and they each exchanged bilateral notes with the United States, the United Kingdom and Germany reiterating the terms of the Agreement.[89]

The Midnight Agreement recorded an apportionment of mining sites amongst its parties. These States agreed not to act, either on their own or in concert with third parties, to block PrepCom licences *vis-à-vis* the apportioned sites. While this was obviously a pro-USSR measure, the USSR also made a concession: the Midnight Agreement provided that its parties would not support seabed mining or PrepCom licences that were incompatible with the 'respect for areas' apportioned under it. The parties to the Midnight Agreement also agreed to ensure that their entities did not physically interfere with mining operations in the relevant sites, nor to create additional practical problems. They committed to mutual consultations when necessary for the implementation of the Midnight Agreement.

The Exchange of Notes between the USSR and the United States, the United Kingdom and Germany extended the above provisions of the Midnight Agreement on a bilateral basis. Notes exchanged between the three LOSC non-signatories and Italy, France, Belgium and the Netherlands, provided that these States would not terminate the Midnight Agreement and Notes exchanged with the USSR except by previous agreement between themselves.

The Implementation Agreement, 1994

The Implementation Agreement paved the way for near-universal accession to the LOSC. Brown notes the 'pretence' implicit in the title, for the Agreement substantially amends Part XI, though both its title and text avoid using terms that categorically say so.[90] Instead, the Implementation Agreement is projected as an integral part of the LOSC. Thus, Article 4 provides that, after the adoption of the Agreement, 'any instrument of ratification or formal confirmation of or accession to the Convention shall also represent consent to be bound by this Agreement'. Correspondingly, a State cannot establish its consent to be bound by the Implementation Agreement without ratifying or acceding to the LOSC. Moreover, Article 2(1) provides that the Implementation Agreement is to be interpreted and applied together with Part XI as a single instrument.

[89] As prototypes: Exchange of Notes between USA and USSR, 26 ILM 1506; Exchange of Notes between USA and the Netherlands, 26 ILM 1508.

[90] Brown, *The International Law of the Sea*, 471.

However, this suggestion of harmony is diluted in the very next sentence, which provides that '[i]n the event of any inconsistency between this Agreement and Part XI, the provisions of this Agreement shall prevail'.

The Implementation Agreement responded to the major demands of developed States. It reduced their financial obligations to the ISA, and allowed them greater control over that body. It expanded the Council's powers and maintained the United States' *de facto* permanent seat on it. It removed Part XI's technology-transfer obligations and production limitations and subsidies, and underlined that seabed resources should be developed in accordance with commercial principles rather than those of equity and no-harm. It reduced the application fee for mining licences. It also placed the Enterprise on the same commercial footing as other contractors, removing the several functional privileges envisaged in the LOSC. Finally, it provided that, instead of a review conference, the ISA Assembly would review the regime's operation upon advice of the ISA Council. Appendix 3 of this book offers a more detailed assessment of the changes made.

It is evident that the Implementation Agreement significantly altered the LOSC. Indeed, among the provisions altered by it were several that were integral to the common heritage principle as conceptualised in the LOSC. These included provisions on equitable sharing of benefits, no-harm and the right of all States to participate equally in decision-making. R. P. Anand, a prominent critical voice in favour of the NIEO, argues that it 'mutilated' the common heritage principle, for the seabed 'will not be explored and exploited in the future as common property "primarily in the interests of mankind and with particular regard to the needs of poor countries ...". [It] will now be exploited on commercial terms, irrespective of the needs and interests of the weaker members of the international community.'[91]

In contrast to Anand's view, voices from the developed world considered the Agreement to be in keeping with the realities of the time: Louis Sohn described it as an 'excellent example of adapting international law to new circumstances'.[92] These circumstances included, of course, the end of the Cold War and the faltering of the ideologies of both socialism and the NIEO. The same circumstances also permitted acknowledgment of the practical barriers to seabed mining – the issue as a whole began to

[91] Anand, 'Common Heritage of Mankind', 196. Emphasis omitted.

[92] L. B. Sohn, 'International Law Implications of the 1994 Agreement' (1994) 88 *American Journal of International Law* 696, 704–5.

be seen as irrelevant and as an unnecessary impediment to the universal ratification of the LOSC.

Dynamics of compromise

The Midnight Agreement and the Implementation Agreement mark distinct phases in the conflict between the LOSC and the RSR. The Midnight Agreement, which created a *modus vivendi* between the two regimes, may be seen as an example of approximate application (discussed in Chapter 3) of the LOSC regime by the PrepCom. The PrepCom modified the process and conditions for registration of pioneer investors and their rights and duties with a view to ensuring effective implementation of the LOSC regime given the practical obstructions posed by the RSR. The Implementation Agreement represented a more substantial amendment of the LOSC regime, through a process of informal consultations convened by the then UN Secretary-General. The PrepCom, as a creature of the LOSC, could not have accomplished these changes, which were desired by the RSR States: indeed, recognising this, the United States did not even participate in its work.[93] Possibly, the changes made may be seen as illustrating the regime interaction approach, also discussed in Chapter 3. This section will discuss the dynamics of these two phases in turn.

Under the PrepCom: 1983–9

The PrepCom's powers, functions and approach

Resolution I set out the PrepCom's mandate, which was to undertake various activities necessary to establish the ISA. These included: drafting rules of procedure for the ISA Assembly and Council, a budget for the ISA's first financial period and rules on financial management and internal administration; making recommendations relating to the establishment of the ISA Secretariat, the relationship between the ISA and various international organisations, and the problems encountered by land-based minerals producers; and practical arrangements for establishment of the International Tribunal of the Law of the Sea. The PrepCom was also to administer the Resolution II interim regime for pioneer investors,[94] that is – according to Resolution II – decide on pioneer investor applications, register qualifying applicants, and

[93] Malone, 'The United States and the Law of the Sea after UNCLOS III', 32.
[94] Res. I, para. 5(h).

oversee their activities. Additionally, the PrepCom was to create a Special Commission that would facilitate the Enterprise's early entry into operation,[95] and could also establish other subsidiary bodies as needed for its functions.

Resolution I also provided for the PrepCom's composition and duration. The PrepCom would include representatives from all LOSC parties and signatories, while States which had signed the Final Act would be entitled to participate in its deliberations (but not its decisions). It would remain in existence until the first session of the ISA Assembly, at which it would present a final report on all matters within its mandate. Subsequently, its property and records would be transferred to the ISA. The PrepCom would be financed by the United Nations and would enjoy the legal capacity necessary for its functions.

At its first session in 1983, the PrepCom decided to allocate the functions relating to seabed mining amongst a Plenary and three Special Commissions (SCNs).[96] The Plenary, its principal organ, would undertake tasks related to the overall implementation of Resolution II, including registration and oversight of pioneer investors. Its executive arm would be a General Committee, composed of officers of the Plenary and SCNs, and chaired by the PrepCom chairman. SCN I would examine problems of land-based producers and SCN II would perform tasks necessary for the Enterprise's early entry into effective operation. SCN III's mandate derived from a broad interpretation of paragraph 5(g) of Resolution I, which states that the PrepCom

> shall prepare draft rules, regulations and procedures, as necessary, to enable [the ISA] to commence its functions, including draft regulations concerning ... financial management and ... internal administration.

The PrepCom interpreted this as a directive to prepare a seabed mining code, that is, 'rules, regulations and procedures for exploration and exploitation'.[97] Paragraph 5(g) does not specifically demand such a code, though it has relevance for elaborating regulations for financial management and internal administration. Nevertheless, in deciding to prepare a code, the PrepCom clearly took a flexible approach to interpreting its mandate.

95 Res. I, para. 8. Res. II, para. 12, provided pioneer investors would assist the Enterprise to explore reserved areas; train personnel and transfer technology; and contribute to its budget.

96 Suggestions by the PrepCom Chairman, Annex I, LOS/PCN/27, 8 September 1983.

97 *ibid.*, Annex I, Section I(1)(c).

This matched the expectations of some developed States. The Italian representative to the PrepCom, Tullio Treves, noted in a public lecture:

> The adaptations Part XI . . . will probably require in order to become more widely acceptable, and permit the universal acceptance of [the LOSC], might be pursued by States within PrepCom or at the margins of it. PrepCom seems the forum that gives the best guarantees for avoiding reopening for discussion also the aspects of [the LOSC] that are different from seabed mining.[98]

Treves was here echoing hopes expressed by France, Italy and Japan, that PrepCom would play a transformational role in improving Part XI. At the last session of UNCLOS III, France had desired the PrepCom to modify technology-transfer and financial-support obligations of Western States, Italy had pushed for a pragmatic attitude, Norway had claimed that the PrepCom's role would be crucial for achieving universal application of the LOSC and Japan had stated that its decision to ratify the LOSC would depend on the PrepCom's work.[99]

As the PrepCom settled into a routine of meeting twice a year, in March and August, it realised that it would be difficult to build consensus on the more controversial issues pertaining to seabed mining. So it decided to bracket all 'hard-core' issues – particularly rules for internal administration and financial and budgetary matters of the ISA itself – and to focus on matters where it could make rapid progress, that is, the implementation of the pioneer investor regime. It returned to some hard-core issues in later years, but only in a cursory way.[100]

Some scholars claim that the PrepCom's failure to address hard-core issues led to a general feeling of malaise amongst States *vis-à-vis* the LOSC regime.[101] But, viewed in the context of the obstacles it faced at the time, its work does not appear so insignificant. After all, it was tasked with cementing the relevance of the LOSC regime in a period where it was not in force, and was challenged by an alternative regime preferred by most States actually capable of engaging in mining. Today it is easy to view the LOSC as the main seabed regime and the RSR as its

[98] T. Treves, 'The Role of Universal International Organizations in Implementing the 1982 UN Law of the Sea Convention', in A. H. A. Soons (ed.), *Implementation of the Law of the Sea Convention through International Institutions* (Honolulu, The Law of the Sea Institute 1989) 14, 28.

[99] UN Press Release SEA/515, 9 March 1983.

[100] See Progress Report by the PrepCom Chairman, LOS/PCN/L.103, 7 July 1992, paras. 47–50.

[101] D. Anderson, 'Efforts to Achieve Universal Participation in the UN Convention on the Law of the Sea' (1993) 42 *International and Comparative Law Quarterly* 644, 645.

incompatible alternative, but the situation in the 1980s was more ambiguous. Neither treaty enjoyed clear pre-eminence. As we have already seen from D'Amato's 1983 article, the International Court of Justice (or any other tribunal), if called upon, would likely examine the relevant practice of both regimes before allocating priority among them, rather than exclusively upholding the LOSC regime.[102] The PrepCom thus had to implement the pioneer investor regime as a matter of priority.

Moreover, as Elizabeth Riddell-Dixon notes, the PrepCom's decision to focus on the effective implementation of Resolution II proved significant in three ways: it facilitated a scheme for resolving overlapping claims, and registering pioneer investors; it kept seabed issues on the international agenda; and it provided a framework and an institutional memory for future negotiations.[103] The PrepCom, notably, was able to keep all types of States – developed and developing, capitalist and socialist, LOSC signatories and RSR parties – engaged in its consensus-building process, and thereby engaged with the LOSC regime. This was difficult enough to do without considering the hard-core issues.

Brokering the Midnight Agreement

The PrepCom facilitated the Midnight Agreement as a pragmatic arrangement to break the impasse between LOSC signatories (the USSR and India), RSR parties signatory to the LOSC, and RSR parties not signatory to the LOSC. While the Agreement did not resolve the basic incompatibility between the LOSC and the RSR, it did cement the former's authority by enabling effective implementation of its pioneer investor regime.

Prior to the Midnight Agreement, the PrepCom could not issue a single licence; the pioneer investor regime existed only as an abstraction. This was in contrast to the RSR, under which the United States, the United Kingdom and Germany had issued several mining licences. However, once the Midnight Agreement was formalised, the PrepCom was able to register four pioneer investors – India, the USSR, France and Japan – in rapid succession, and also to address other issues relating to Resolution II. The PrepCom's actions in facilitating the Midnight Agreement highlighted its centrality as the forum for raising and

[102] D'Amato, 'An Alternative to the Law of the Sea Convention', 284.
[103] E. Riddell-Dixon, 'Individual Leadership and Structural Power' (1997) 30 *Canadian Journal of Political Science* 257, 269.

resolving concerns relating to seabed mining, which contributed to the LOSC's normative authority.

The dynamics leading up to the Midnight Agreement spanned two short phases. In the first phase, between 10 December 1982 and 9 December 1984, States were entitled to sign the LOSC without ratifying it. The second phase was from December 1984 to 13 August 1987 (the date of the Midnight Agreement). In an additional, third phase, up to August 1990, PrepCom took further creative decisions to clarify the rights and obligations of pioneer investors.

Phase I: bringing States to the negotiating table

Paragraph 5 of Resolution II required States certifying pioneer investor applicants to ensure that 'areas in respect of which applications are made do not overlap one another or areas previously allocated as pioneer areas'. It also set out a timeline for identifying and resolving overlapping claims: States could negotiate until 1 March 1983; if these negotiations failed to reach an outcome, binding arbitration would commence by 1 May and conclude by 1 December 1983. But, during Phase I, the LOSC signatory/non-signatory distinction remained nebulous, since the treaty could be signed at any time up to 9 December 1984; non-signatories like the United States, the United Kingdom, Germany, and for a time Italy and Belgium, could not be ruled out as potential certifying States. Thus, during Phase I, it was not settled which States would ultimately qualify as certifying States, and so must be consulted in order to resolve overlapping claims. The prescribed timeline for negotiations only led to confusion, and contributed to claims of over- and under-inclusiveness of the various processes initiated towards this end.

Canada and the USSR both initiated such processes, accompanied by objections from other States. Canada's multilateral negotiations, begun in July 1982, were open to all 'potential claimants'.[104] Initially, all RSR States and the USSR took part, but the USSR soon withdrew, expressing dissatisfaction with Canada's decision to include LOSC non-signatories as 'potential claimants'.[105] The USSR not only objected to the interests of LOSC signatories and non-signatories being linked; it was also concerned that the RSR States would collusively apportion the most promising sites amongst themselves before allowing the Canadian process to

[104] Letter from the Alternate Representative of the Delegation of Canada (April 11), LOS/PCN/40, 11 April 1984.

[105] Letter from the Chairman of the USSR Delegation (April 3), LOS/PCN/36, 5 April 1984.

progress. The conclusion of the Interim Agreement on 2 September 1982 must have further fuelled its suspicions. The USSR initiated its own process on 6 April 1983.

The USSR extended invitations to consult only to other LOSC signatories.[106] It proposed a cut-off date of 1 May 1983 by which interested States had to indicate intent to negotiate. Only India agreed to this proposal.[107] Other States responded angrily, denying the USSR's right to unilaterally set deadlines: States that were RSR parties as well as LOSC signatories argued that the Canadian process was more efficacious, for it enabled comprehensive identification and resolution of overlapping claims between all potential mining States;[108] while several LOSC non-signatories argued that, while the LOSC remained open for signature, they could qualify at any time as certifying States, and therefore the USSR could not exclude them from consultations.[109]

The stand-off between the USSR and the participants in the Canadian initiative continued for several months, broken only when the USSR and India filed for the registration of their enterprises as pioneer investors.[110] France and Japan were immediately concerned, for, like the USSR, they had interests in the Clarion–Clipperton Zone, and as LOSC signatories were keen to apply for similar licences. They now communicated their willingness to consult with the USSR,[111] but were also unable to dissociate themselves from the Canadian initiative at this

[106] Letter from the Chairman of the USSR Delegation (April 6), LOS/PCN/4, 8 April 1983.

[107] Note Verbale from the Permanent Representative of India to the United Nations (April 24), LOS/PCN/7, 26 April 1983.

[108] Letter from the Permanent Representative of France to the United Nations, LOS/PCN/8, 27 April 1983; Letter from the Permanent Representative of Japan to the United Nations, LOS/PCN/11, 28 April 1983; Letter from the Permanent Representative of Canada to the United Nations (April 28), LOS/PCN/15, 29 April 1983; Letter from the Permanent Representative of the Netherlands to the United Nations (April 27), LOS/PCN/18, 3 May 1983.

[109] Note Verbale from the Permanent Representative of the Federal Republic of Germany to the United Nations (April 27), LOS/PCN/9, 28 April 1983; Letter from the Representative of the United Kingdom to the United Nations (April 27), LOS/PCN/13, 29 April 1983. Italy and Belgium made like claims, but signed the LOSC: Letter from the Permanent Representative of Italy to the United Nations (April 28), LOS/PCN/10, 28 April 1983; Letter from the Permanent Representative of Belgium to the United Nations (April 27), LOS/PCN/14, 29 April 1983.

[110] Letter from the Permanent Representative of the USSR to the United Nations (July 20), LOS/PCN/30, 24 October 1983; Receipt of Application from India for Registration as a Pioneer Investor under Resolution II of UNCLOS III, LOS/PCN/32, 14 February 1984.

[111] Letter from the Chairman of the Delegation of Japan, LOS/PCN/34, 29 March 1984; and Letter from the Chairman of the Delegation of France, LOS/PCN/35, 2 April 1984.

late stage. They wrote a letter to the PrepCom jointly with Canada, Italy, the Netherlands, Belgium, Germany and the United Kingdom, desiring the PrepCom to recognise the compatibility of the Canadian initiative with Resolution II.[112]

While the USSR agreed to consult bilaterally with France and Japan, it continued to suspect – despite denials[113] – collusive apportionment of mining sites between these two States and other RSR States.[114] Assertions by non-signatories like Germany that they too should be permitted to participate in the USSR's consultations[115] made it more suspicious.[116] The USSR remained unwilling to link the interests of non-signatories and signatories.

The August 1984 Provisional Understanding complicated matters by committing the RSR States to precisely such a link.[117] The USSR and the EES perceived this Understanding as evidence that the RSR States had effected a 'seizure and division of the most promising sections of the international seabed'.[118]

Meanwhile, Japan and France submitted applications for the registration of their enterprises as pioneer investors;[119] their claimed sites remained in conflict with the USSR.

This is when the PrepCom Chairman, Joseph Warioba, stepped in for the first time, taking the initiative to convene effective consultations

[112] Letter from the Representatives of the Delegations of Belgium, France, the Federal Republic of Germany, Italy, Japan, the Netherlands and the United Kingdom, LOS/PCN/41, 12 April 1984.

[113] France, Japan and Canada wrote to the PrepCom rejecting that they had acted contrary to Res. II and denied any separate agreement carving up the seabed between them. See Letter from the Alternate Representative of the Delegation of Canada, LOS/PCN/40, 11 April 1984; Letter from the Chairman of the Delegation of Japan, LOS/PCN/42, 12 April 1984; Letter from the Chairman of the Delegation of France, LOS/PCN/44, 12 April 1984.

[114] Letter from the Chairman of the USSR Delegation, LOS/PCN/36, 5 April 1984.

[115] Letter from the Chairman of the Delegation of Federal Republic of Germany to the United Nations, LOS/PCN/37, 6 April 1984.

[116] Letter from the Chairman of the USSR Delegation (April 9), LOS/PCN/38, 10 April 1984.

[117] Article 5(1)(b) provided that parties should consult 'with regard to any arrangements between one or more Parties and another State or States for the avoidance of overlapping in deep seabed operations'.

[118] Statement by the EES Chairman, LOS/PCN/49, 17 August 1984.

[119] Receipt of Application from Japan for Registration of the Japanese Enterprise 'Deep Ocean Resources Development Co. Ltd' as a Pioneer Investor under Resolution II of UNCLOS III, LOS/PCN/50, 22 August 1984; Receipt of Application from France for Registration of AFERNOD as a Pioneer Investor under Resolution II of UNCLOS III, LOS/PCN/51, 23 August 1984.

between the USSR, France and Japan. On 31 August 1984, he reported that two 'Understandings' had been reached.[120] The first, on the 'Resolution of Conflicts Among Applicants for Registration as Pioneer Investors', referred to a 'first group' of applicants, comprising States which had submitted applications prior to 9 December 1984; the applications of this first group would be considered *en banc* at the 1985 session of PrepCom and registered once all overlapping claims had been resolved. The group would meet to identify conflicts on 17 December 1984. According to the second Understanding on the 'Procedure for Conflict Resolution', at this meeting, the first-group States would exchange the geographical coordinates of their mining sites and ascertain if there were any overlaps. They would resolve conflicts via negotiations commencing in January, and concluding by 4 March 1985. Their registration would not prejudice the right of other States to apply for registration, but these other States would have to avoid overlaps with the sites allocated to the first group or designated as reserved areas. This responded to the USSR's concern of collusive early apportionment of sites between the RSR States.

The PrepCom stated that the consultations over these two Understandings had extended to all interested States, including LOSC non-signatories, and the Understandings had taken into consideration their various legal and practical arguments. The two Understandings had also taken on board the point that, until 9 December 1984, the category of qualified certifying States would not be settled, and accordingly had recalibrated the timeline provided in Resolution II.

However, the RSR States, the United Kingdom, the Netherlands, Italy and Belgium, as well as Canada, disclaimed any impact of these two Understandings upon themselves.[121] They refused to recognise that their claimed mining sites would now be subject to compatibility with those allocated to the first group. All (except the UK) argued that the PrepCom had overstepped its mandate, as 'the matter of resolution of

[120] Statement of PrepCom Chairman regarding the Understanding on Resolution of Conflicts among Applicants for Registration as Pioneer Investors, LOS/PCN/L.8, 31 August 1984; see also Statement by PrepCom Chairman, LOS/PCN/L.13, 4 September 1984.

[121] Letter from the Chairman of the Delegation of United Kingdom (September 4), LOS/PCN/54, 24 September 1984; Letter from the Chairman of the Delegation of the Netherlands (March 28), LOS/PCN/60, 26 April 1985; Letter from the Chairman of the Delegation of Belgium (April 2), LOS/PCN/61, 26 April 1985; Letter from the Chairman of the Delegation of Italy (April 2), LOS/PCN/62, 26 April 1985; Letter from the Chairman of the Delegation of Canada (April 3), LOS/PCN/63, 26 April 1985.

conflicts among applicants for pioneer investors does not form part of [its] functions'.[122] They also emphasised that conflicts could only be satisfactorily resolved by a multilateral process that included them, for they were specifically named in Resolution II. As Phase I drew to a close, they also began to argue that the 9 December 1984 deadline was irrelevant, for they had a sovereign right to accede to the LOSC at any time.

Phase II: Creative interpretation of Resolution II

Phase II commenced after 9 December 1984, when the LOSC signatory/non-signatory status of various States was finally determined. By this time, the PrepCom's initiative had paved the way for discussions between the USSR, France and Japan, who were all part of the first group together with India (whose claims, being limited to the Indian Ocean, did not overlap with the others).

Following consultations, the USSR's overlap with Japan was easily resolved, but that with France proved too extensive. In March 1985, the USSR and France turned again to the PrepCom for help, informing it that they were unable to reach a solution that would allow them each to submit two equivalent sites, of which one could be designated as a reserved area.[123] Mindful of the criticism levelled at the PrepCom Chairman's initiatives during the first phase, they also offered justification for its intervention at this stage: France, now pursuing different interests from the other RSR States, argued that the Chairman's intervention was in necessary implementation of the provisions of Resolution II.[124] The USSR relied on the Chairman's observance of due process in the first phase, pointing out that he had consulted with a range of participants including the RSR States, and had allowed them all the chance to join the first group by filing an application before 9 December 1984.[125]

The USSR also underlined the strategic importance of the PrepCom's intervention: expeditious registration of pioneer investors was essential to cementing the LOSC regime. The urgency for this was provoked by the United States, the United Kingdom and Germany issuing licences

[122] For instance, Letter from the Netherlands, LOS/PCN/60, 26 April 1985.
[123] Letter from France, Japan and the USSR (February 28), LOS/PCN/56, 12 March 1985.
[124] Letters from the Chairman of the Delegation of France (July 31), LOS/PCN/67–70, 16 August 1985.
[125] Letters from the Acting Permanent Representative of the USSR (June 28), LOS/PCN/65–66, 8 July 1985.

under the RSR. The PrepCom and its member States had responded angrily to these licences, particularly since they saw these as in breach of the UK's and Germany's participation in the PrepCom. Between July and September 1985, the USSR, China and then the PrepCom categorically condemned these licences as illegal and invalid.[126] This was not well received by the United Kingdom and Germany, which now joined the United States in openly challenging the PrepCom's authority.[127] They argued that the PrepCom's actions were not conducive to mediating compromises between States. They also claimed that its condemnation of the RSR licences violated international law, for it gave legal effect to (LOSC) provisions that were not yet in force, could not even when in force bind them as non-parties, and did not enjoy the status of customary international law. They also argued that the PrepCom could not rely upon the 1970 Declaration of Principles, because its reference to 'an international treaty of universal character generally agreed upon' was not yet true of the LOSC.

During all this time, even as the bilateral consultations between the USSR and France achieved no result, the PrepCom Chairman offered periodic encouragement, and advised that for a sustainable result the negotiations should reflect the interests of the first-group States as well as those of the ISA and potential applicants.[128] In February 1986, Chairman Warioba, now also the Prime Minister of Tanzania, took the further step of inviting the first group for talks in Arusha.[129] Here, three days of negotiation achieved a result that accommodated the first group's and the ISA's interests. That is, the 'Arusha Understanding' resolved the deadlock between the USSR and France in a way that would also preserve the site-banking concept. Building on this Understanding, the Chairman undertook further consultations with the first group, potential applicants, G77 States and other interest

[126] PrepCom Declarations, LOS/PCN/72, 2 September 1985 and LOS/PCN/78, 21 April 1986; Letters from the Acting Permanent Representative of the USSR (June 10), LOS/PCN/64, 1 July 1985 and LOS/PCN/76, 27 March 1986; Letter from the Chairman of the Delegation of China (August 15), LOS/PCN/71, 20 August 1985.

[127] Letter from the Chairman of the Delegation of the Federal Republic of Germany (October 25), LOS/PCN/73, 9 January 1986; Letter from the Chairman of the Delegation of United Kingdom (November 4), LOS/PCN/74, 9 January 1986.

[128] Statement made by the Acting Chairman of the PrepCom, LOS/PCN/L.41, 5 September 1986.

[129] Report by the PrepCom Chairman regarding the Resolution of Conflicts among Applicants for Registration as Pioneer Investors, LOS/PCN/L.28, 21 March 1986; Statement by the Acting Chairman of the PrepCom, LOS/PCN/L.34, 10 April 1986.

groups, to arrive at the 'New York Understanding' of August 1986. This also accommodated the interests of potential applicants.[130]

The innovation brokered by the Chairman was to creatively link the provisions of paragraphs 1(e) and 3(a) of Resolution II. Paragraph 3(a) was the site-banking provision. Paragraph 1(e) provided for a scheme by which pioneer investors would gradually relinquish 50 per cent of their initially allotted 150,000-square-kilometre sites to the ISA. The new Understanding allowed France, Japan and the USSR to immediately relinquish 50 per cent of their allotted sites upon their registration as pioneer investors, thus receiving an effective allotment of 75,000 square kilometres. In parallel, the PrepCom would designate equally reduced areas of 75,000 square kilometres as reserved sites contributed by each of these States. Now that they would effectively be seeking smaller allotments, there was a greater capacity for the USSR and France to resolve their overlapping claims.

Moreover – making effective allotment of a reduced area more attractive – each applicant could now specify a 'core area' of 52,300 square kilometres which would be necessarily included in the site allotted to it. Applicants with overlapping claims could also indicate which portions of the overlapping areas, up to 52,300 square kilometres, must be incorporated into sites reserved for the Enterprise. In a nod to potential applicants' concerns, other portions of the relinquished areas would be reserved for their consideration (and they would follow a similar immediate relinquishment plan as the first group).

The Understanding also permitted developing States, and one EES applicant, to seek pioneer investor status at any time before the LOSC's entry into force; that is, it removed the previous cut-off date of 1 January 1985.

The PrepCom clarified that it had devised the Arusha Understanding to overcome practical difficulties arising from the unforeseen concentration of claims within the Clarion–Clipperton Zone.[131] And the Arusha and New York Understandings certainly paved the way for productive consultations over the following year between the USSR and the RSR States:[132] on 3 August 1987, these States reported that they had concluded

[130] Statement by PrepCom Chairman (August 22), 1986, LOS/PCN/L.36, 2 September 1986; Statement made by the Acting Chairman of the PrepCom, LOS/PCN/L.41/Rev.1, 11 September 1986.

[131] Statement by the Acting Chairman of the PrepCom, LOS/PCN/L.34, 10 April 1986.

[132] Letter from the Delegation of the USSR (March 19), LOS/PCN/81, 24 March 1987; Letter from the Representatives of the Delegations of Belgium, Canada, Italy, and the Netherlands (March 30), LOS/PCN/83, 30 March 1987.

the Midnight Agreement and Exchange of Notes to apportion their claims.[133]

Modifying the rights and obligations of pioneer investors

UN Secretary-General Javier Pérez de Cuéllar described the Midnight Agreement as 'one of the most significant developments in the Law of the Sea since the adoption of the Convention'.[134] Certainly, it sparked off a period of rapid progress in the PrepCom's work. In quick succession, it registered India, the USSR, France and Japan as pioneer investors. Following the Arusha Understanding, these States had agreed to withhold their revised applications till a process for settlement of overlapping claims was also agreed with other potential pioneer investors.[135] They submitted these revised applications soon after the New York Understanding was adopted.[136] India was registered as a pioneer investor in October 1987,[137] and registration of the USSR, France and Japan followed in 1988.[138]

The PrepCom also made progress in other areas. It established a consultative group to discuss various issues relating to implementation

[133] Letter from the Delegations of Belgium, Canada, Italy, the Netherlands and the USSR, LOS/PCN/90, 3 August 1987; Letter from the Chairman of the Delegation of the United Kingdom (August 5), LOS/PCN/92, 6 August 1987; Letter from the Chairman of the Delegation of Germany (August 5), LOS/PCN/93, 6 August 1987.

[134] UN Press Release SEA/845, 6 August 1987.

[135] Letter from the Delegations of France, India, Japan and the USSR (March 19), LOS/PCN/82, 24 March 1987.

[136] Statement of Understanding on the Implementation of Resolution II made by PrepCom Chairman (April 10), LOS/PCN/L.43/Rev.1, 15 April 1987; Receipt of a Revised Application from Japan for Registration of the Japanese Enterprise 'Deep Ocean Resources Development Co. Ltd' as a Pioneer Investor under Resolution II of UNCLOS III, LOS/PCN/86, 23 July 1987; Receipt of a Revised Application from India for Registration as a Pioneer Investor under Resolution II of UNCLOS III, LOS/PCN/87, 23 July 1987; Receipt of a Revised Application from the USSR for Registration of the Soviet Enterprise 'Yuhzmorgeologia' as a Pioneer Investor, LOS/PCN/88, 23 July 1987; Receipt of a Revised Application from France for Registration as a Pioneer Investor under Resolution II of UNCLOS III, LOS/PCN/89, 23 July 1987.

[137] Decision of the General Committee on the Application of India for Registration as a Pioneer Investor under Resolution II, LOS/PCN/94, 9 October 1987.

[138] Decision of the General Committee of the PrepCom on the Application of France for Registration as a Pioneer Investor under Resolution II (December 17), LOS/PCN/97, 6 January 1988; Decision of the General Committee of the PrepCom on the Application of Japan for Registration as a Pioneer Investor under Resolution II (December 17), LOS/PCN/98, 6 January 1988; Decision of the General Committee of the PrepCom on the Application of the USSR for Registration as a Pioneer Investor under Resolution II (December 17), LOS/PCN/99, 6 January 1988.

of Resolution II, including exploration of reserved sites; payment of registration and annual fee; training of personnel; technology transfer; funds for the Enterprise; reporting to the PrepCom; States' expenditures on mining sites; and protection of the marine environment.[139]

In August 1990, following consultations with the first group, the PrepCom produced the Understanding on the Fulfilment of Obligations by the Registered Pioneer Investors and their Certifying States.[140] The Understanding reformulated some Resolution II obligations to reduce costs to certifying States and mining enterprises. States' duty to ensure availability of funds to the Enterprise would now be implemented only upon the LOSC's entry into force. While mining enterprises would still be asked to undertake preparatory and initial exploratory work on one mine site for the Enterprise at their own expense, the PrepCom would waive their US$1 million annual fee. The PrepCom would also recommend to the ISA that it continue waiving this fee until commercial production became likely.

This August 1990 Understanding provided a basis for the negotiation of contracts also with other pioneer investor applicants from China,[141] and from the EES.[142]

Towards a new framework: 1989–90

However, the 1990 Understanding was a brief Indian summer for the PrepCom; already by the end of the 1980s, the momentum was shifting away from it. Indeed, seabed mining was losing its ideological relevance. In 1989, the United States and the USSR declared the end of the Cold War; and Germany found itself on the brink of reunification. At this time, and through the early 1990s, ideas of economic liberalisation were ascendant: many developing States embraced pro-market reforms, and the administrative structure proposed for the ISA had started to look dated. The NIEO movement had made few advances in the 1980s, and came to an end as its proponent States embraced neo-liberal policies.

In the seabed context, 1989 was marked by a change in the tone of communication. Speaking at the PrepCom's seventh session, the G77 spokesperson issued a remarkable invitation:

139 Statement by PrepCom Chairman, LOS/PCN/L.62, 7 April 1988; Statement by PrepCom Chairman, LOS/PCN/L.67, 1 September 1988.

140 Statement by PrepCom Chairman, LOS/PCN/L.87, 30 August 1990.

141 Statement by PrepCom Chairman, LOS/PCN/L.102, 13 March 1992.

142 Statement by PrepCom Chairman, LOS/PCN/L.108, 20 August 1992.

> Any delegation, or group of delegations, be they currently involved in the work of PrepCom or not, whether signatories or non-signatories to [the LOSC], are welcome to open a dialogue with [G77] ... without any preconditions, other than ... a positive approach to serious and meaningful talks.[143]

This was in striking contrast to the G77's previous condemnatory attitude, which the spokesperson now tried to disown, claiming that the G77 had always taken the above approach, but 'for unexplained reasons ... it has not been fully appreciated'. He also clarified with respect to the ISA that 'a false impression has been ... perpetuated' that G77 wanted a large bureaucratic structure; they favoured a cost-effective, functionally determined structure. This statement met with a warm response from other States, including RSR parties.[144]

Similarly, the UN General Assembly produced an annual resolution[145] that omitted the thinly veiled criticisms of the RSR included in previous resolutions.[146] The 1989 resolution offered scope for more flexible interpretation of the LOSC, in keeping with the needs of the time. In particular, operative paragraph 5 now called upon States to 'safeguard the unified character of the Convention and related resolutions therewith and to apply them in a manner consistent with that character and with their object and purpose'. This was a loosening of the direction in the corresponding paragraph in previous resolutions, which asked States to 'safeguard the unified character of the Convention and related resolutions therewith'.[147] The PrepCom Chairman, Jose Luis Jesus, who introduced the draft, explained that such changes were intended to reflect a positive approach.[148]

Two concerns informed the General Assembly meetings in which the 1989 resolution was reviewed and adopted: the LOSC's now imminent

143 Statement by Zambia on behalf of the G77 (1 September 1989), 15 *Law of the Sea Bulletin*, May 1990.

144 Statements by Denmark on behalf of the Friends of the Group of Eleven, France on behalf of the European Economic Community, Bulgaria on behalf of the Group of Eastern European States, Italy on behalf of the Group of Six (UK, the Netherlands, Belgium, Japan, Italy, and Germany), and Canada on behalf of Potential Applicants (1 September 1989), 15 Law of the Sea Bulletin, May 1990.

145 Law of the Sea, UNGA Res. 44/26 (20 November 1989).

146 Statement of Mr Pickering, US Delegate, Provisional Verbatim Record, UNGA 61st Mtg, 44th Sess. (November 20), A/44/PV.61, 28 November 1989. A previously used clause, asking states to 'desist from taking actions which undermine the Convention', was deleted.

147 Law of the Sea, UNGA Res. 43/18(1 November 1988) para. 4.

148 Statement of Mr Jesus, PrepCom Chairman, Provisional Verbatim Record, UNGA 61st Mtg, 44th Sess. (November 20), A/44/PV.61, 28 November 1989.

entry into force (it only awaited a few more ratifications); and the doubt whether the PrepCom could secure a seabed regime acceptable to all.[149]

If the LOSC entered into force unsupported by developed States, developing States would be faced with the costs of sustaining the ISA. For developed States, the LOSC's entry into force would challenge the RSR's stability. More importantly, in not acceding to the LOSC because of concerns over Part XI, they would forgo the benefit of other LOSC provisions, which they could not invoke unless they subscribed to the LOSC package. Moreover, it would be a dismal prospect for the 'constitution of the oceans' to enter into force when lacking universal acceptance. Treves underlined this point, arguing that the LOSC already influenced maritime practices so as to '[form] an essential element in the maintenance of legal order in the seas and oceans', which made it imperative to secure universal adherence to it as it entered into force.[150] According to Treves,

> [a] convention in force to which important sectors of the international community could not become parties might involve certain risks for the orderly development of international relations. The world would get divided between states upon which it was binding, and states for which it would constitute mere guidance ... The way would be opened for divergent practice and for an evolution of the law that would not be the same for every State.

He warned that the LOSC 'might not, in that situation, be able to continue to fulfil the function that it is fulfilling now, pending its entry into force'.

The impetus for universal adherence was also provided by other factors, not least the 'historic changes occurring in the world' acknowledged in a fulsome speech by the USSR delegate.[151] By 1989, States were also willing to recognise that the commercial outlook for seabed mining was bleak. Australia had submitted a paper to this effect in January 1986,[152] pointing out that, for seabed mining to be commercially viable, metal prices would have to increase to twice their current levels, and

[149] Provisional Verbatim Record, UNGA 44th Sess., 61st Mtg (November 20), A/44/PV.61, 28 November 1989; Provisional Verbatim Record, UNGA 44th Sess., 62nd Mtg (November 20), A/44/PV.61, 1 December 1989.

[150] Statement of Mr Treves, Italian Delegate, Provisional Verbatim Record, UNGA 61st Mtg, 44th Sess. (November 20), A/44/PV.61, 28 November 1989.

[151] Statement of Mr Bykov, USSR Delegate, Provisional Verbatim Record, UNGA 62nd Mtg, 44th Sess. (November 20), A/44/PV.62, 1 December 1989.

[152] Economic Viability of Deep Seabed Mining of Polymetallic Nodules, LOS/PCN/SCN.2/WP.10, 14 January 1986.

also noting that no reliable technology had been developed, so that mining remained a high-risk venture, making it difficult to attract capital.[153] In February 1988, the PrepCom Secretariat also presented a paper noting that two of the three basic mining technologies had been abandoned or temporarily shelved, while the third required long-term testing to prove its reliability.[154] For a long time, the deliberations within the PrepCom had proceeded oblivious to these economic and technological analyses but by 1989 this was no longer the case.

Thus, by 1989, it was clear that seabed mining must not be a sticking point for universal ratification of the LOSC. The General Assembly invited all States 'to make renewed efforts to facilitate participation in the Convention'.[155] But how the regime should be modified, and through what process, still remained matters for debate. The PrepCom Chairman claimed that the 'effectiveness of [the LOSC] goes hand-in-hand with the work of [the PrepCom]'.[156] However, States had begun to express doubts. The United States had of course always disregarded the PrepCom, and reiterated that 'fundamental reform is a task that exceeds [the PrepCom]'.[157] Even Brazil, a G77 member, acknowledged that the PrepCom's achievements were uneven, though it blamed Western States' attitudes for this,[158] arguing that, each time the PrepCom adopted a flexible stance, they claimed it had acted outside its competence. But it recognised that the PrepCom had made limited progress on matters apart from the implementation of Resolution II. At the PrepCom's 1991 session, even the G77 claimed that, on hard-core issues, the PrepCom had 'simply wasted its time'.[159]

While developing States were aware of seabed mining's increasingly illusory promise, they were also wary of moves to comprehensively renegotiate Part XI. This informed their continued support for the PrepCom's limited mandate. Even in 1989, Brazil asserted that Part XI was not open to fundamental revision, and 'universal participation must be sought within the purview of [the LOSC] itself and the legal

153 *ibid.*
154 'Current Status of Deep Seabed Exploration and Mining Technology', Paper Prepared by PrepCom Secretariat, LOS/PCN/L.56, 23 February 1988.
155 UNGA Res. 44/26, 20 November 1989.
156 Statement of Mr Jesus, A/44/PV.61, 28 November 1989.
157 Statement of Mr Pickering, A/44/PV.61, 28 November 1989.
158 Statement of Mr Perri, Brazilian Delegate, Provisional Verbatim Record, UNGA 62nd Mtg, 44th Sess. (November 20), A/44/PV.62, 1 December 1989.
159 'PrepCom Hears Calls for Resolution of "Hard Core" Issues, Statement by Thailand on Behalf of the G77', UN Press Release SEA/1285, 30 August 1991.

framework provided by PrepCom and would be achieved following universal participation in the work of PrepCom'.[160] The G77 held this position for several months.[161] But the impetus had swung away from the PrepCom. Even as it continued to implement the Understanding on Rights and Obligations of Pioneer Investors, calls had begun for an early conclusion to its work.[162]

Its decreasing importance was manifested in its shortened meetings. At the conclusion of 1991's August session, it was decided to hold only an eighteen-day session the following March, instead of the customary four weeks.[163] At the time, it was claimed that this decision did not preclude reinstating the four-week period in the following year, but the sessions were only further shortened thereafter, to between four and fourteen days.[164] The focus was now on preparing a final account of the PrepCom's activities; no further progress was made on the hard-core issues.

The making of the Implementation Agreement

In August 1990, UN Secretary-General Pérez de Cuéllar launched informal consultations to resolve deadlocks over Part XI, which his successor Boutros Boutros Ghali continued to conclusion in the form of the Implementation Agreement in 1994. The consultations were launched in order to make substantial changes to Part XI. Even so, it remained an influential idea that various parties were seeking accommodation of new developments within the LOSC, rather than its complete revision. The Secretary-General insisted that there was no mandate for the renegotiation of Part XI.[165] Indeed, many States, including the G77,

160 Statement of Mr Perri, A/44/PV.62, 1 December 1989.

161 'PrepCom Hears Calls for Resolution of "Hard Core" Issues, Statement by Thailand on Behalf of the G77', UN Press Release SEA/1285, 30 August 1991. See also 'Statements by Jamaica, and France for India, Japan and the USSR', UN Press Release SEA/1193, 31 August 1990.

162 UN Press Release SEA/KIN/32, 13 March 1992.

163 UN Press Release SEA/1285, 30 August 1991.

164 The spring 1992 session was twelve days compared to eighteen in the previous year; the spring 1993 session was twelve days, the summer session was not convened. In spring 1993, it was decided that a two-week annual session would remain the pattern until the LOSC entered into force. Ultimately, PrepCom met twice, four days in February 1994 and two weeks in August 1994, to make final preparations for the first session of the ISA.

165 'Information note concerning the Secretary-General's Informal Consultations (December 10, 1992)' (1992) 8 *International Organizations and the Law of the Sea Documentary Yearbook* 246.

were hostile to the idea that principles underpinning Part XI could be revised at all.[166] The consultations were thus carried out on the basis of the shared myth that they would only recalibrate the institutional provisions of Part XI; this was evident in the discussion over the 'form' that the outcome should take.

The question of form

The discussion on form was initiated in April 1993, with the UN Secretary-General outlining four possibilities:

(1) a protocol formally amending Part XI;
(2) an interpretative agreement;
(3) an agreement to establish a nuclear ISA and Enterprise with provision for a later conference to establish a definitive mining regime once commercial production became feasible; and
(4) an agreement 'additional' to the LOSC and forming an integral part of it, which would establish a nuclear ISA but enable its evolution as needed in response to the changing context of commercial production of seabed minerals.[167]

The difference between options three and four was that four allowed seamless transition from when seabed mining was not viable to when it became viable; a fresh conference to negotiate a mining regime would not be necessary. Option three envisaged express agreement relating to some issues and 'golden principles' to address others, leaving it to the ISA to implement these principles as circumstances demanded.

The Secretary-General pointed out that option one would run contrary to the claim that Part XI was not being renegotiated, and would cause difficulties with respect to States that had already ratified the LOSC. Indeed, it could motivate them to withdraw their ratifications. Option two would least interfere with the integrity of the LOSC as originally negotiated, but the solutions discussed for some of the outstanding issues could not be described as simply 'interpretative'. Options three and four seemed more pragmatic, and better suited to express the compromises being hammered out during the consultations. However, they ran into objections because it was initially felt

[166] H. Valle, 'Adjustments to Part XI: United Nations Efforts (The Negotiation Process)', in M. H. Nordquist and J. N. Moore (eds.), *Entry into Force of the Law of the Sea Convention: Rhodes Papers* (Leiden, Martinus Nijhoff 1994) 47, 49–51.

[167] 'Information Note concerning the Secretary-General's Informal Consultations (April 8, 1993)' (1993) 9 *International Organizations and the Law of the Sea Documentary Yearbook* 431.

that both options would have the effect of deleting Part XI, or of allowing States to enter reservations to Part XI, which was not permitted by the LOSC.[168] The form of the 'Implementation Agreement' finally agreed on would draw upon options three and four, but squarely base itself on Part XI.

Following this, in drafting substantive provisions, the delegates to the consultations were careful to avoid suggestions that the Implementation Agreement provisions 'replaced' Part XI provisions; they were stated to 'apply instead' of Part XI provisions that were 'no longer applicable'. There is no difference in legal effect between these formulations, but Treves points out that there is a difference in appearance: 'Provisions replacing others could only be seen as amendments. Provisions introduced at the side of others that are declared to be inapplicable could be seen as having an implementing nature.'[169] The overall impression sought to be conveyed was that the originally negotiated provisions were being updated or adjusted, not revised.

Some participants in the consultations have asserted that the agreement on form followed agreement on substance. However, the chosen form also controlled the substantive changes made. Even though the discussion on form was only taken up in 1993, at the time substantive provisions had not actually been drafted. Treves notes that, during consideration of various options on form, 'the key point delegations had in mind ... was the fate of Part XI in case one or another of these options were adopted',[170] and, of course, certain formal options permitted more expansive (reading of) alterations than others.

The process of consultation

The substance of the 'adjustments' to Part XI was discussed over several rounds of consultation. Brown suggests these rounds can be organised into three phases.[171] Phase one ran from 1990 to 1991, and included six rounds attended by thirty States invited by the Secretary-General. These included the three major LOSC non-signatories, the United States, the United Kingdom and Germany. The Brazilian delegate to the consultations recalls that these rounds proceeded in a deliberate manner, by way of unilateral statements rather than open discussion.[172] He says this was

[168] T. Treves, 'The Agreement Completing the UN Law of the Sea Convention: Formal and Procedural Aspects', in M. H. Nordquist and J. N. Moore (eds.), *Entry into Force of the Law of the Sea Convention: Rhodes Papers* (Leiden, Martinus Nijhoff 1994) 99, 102.

[169] *ibid.*, 105. [170] *ibid.*, 102. [171] Brown, *The International Law of the Sea*, 462.

[172] Valle, 'Adjustments to Part XI', 48.

felt necessary to avoid derailment of a fledgling process; 'dramatics at the outset . . . could have led to more frustration'. The main achievement of this phase was to identify nine 'areas of concern to some States': costs of the ISA; operation of the Enterprise; ISA decision-making; Review Conference; technology transfer; production limitations; compensation fund; financial terms of contracts; and environmental considerations. Many States - developing States in particular - were disappointed by the limited numbers of participants and by the format followed.[173] At the end of this phase, it was decided to extend these consultations to other interested States and follow an open-ended format.

The second phase included double the number of delegations. It consisted of three rounds, two in 1992 and one in January 1993. During these, participating States agreed to drop 'environmental considerations' from the agenda, for this was not an impediment to ratification. On the other eight issues, they agreed that relatively detailed solutions could be offered on costs, operation of the Enterprise, decision-making, Review Conference, and technology; while general principles could be framed for the other three to be elaborated when commercial production became viable.[174] At the end of the phase it was felt that 'the stage had been reached when a text based on more operational approach [to mining] should be prepared in a form which could be the basis of an agreement'.[175] It was at this time that the Secretary-General was asked to outline various options on form.

Phase three consisted of five rounds between April 1993 and June 1994. It was informed by two important documents. The first was an updated version of the Secretary-General's Information Note of April 1993, which outlined various choices of form and also set out an 'operationally directed formulation' of agreements reached in phases one and two. It provided, in draft agreement format, arrangements for the ISA: setting out the scope of the mining regime immediately following entry into force of the LOSC and enabling its evolution as mining became commercially viable.[176]

The second document, popularly called the 'Boat Paper', was a composite document prepared in consultation between several developing

[173] *ibid.*, 50.

[174] See 'Consultations of the Secretary-General on Outstanding Issues: Report of the UN Secretary-General (9 June 1992)' (1994) 10 *International Organizations and the Law of the Sea Documentary Yearbook* 76, 77.

[175] *ibid.* [176] *ibid.*, 78. The updated Information Note was released on 4 June 1993.

and developed States in August 1993, following the end of round one of phase three.[177] The Boat Paper contained a draft UN General Assembly resolution, a draft implementation agreement for Part XI and two annexes containing agreed conclusions as to adjustments to be made to Part XI. The Paper indicated that it did not necessarily reflect the position of any of the (unidentified) delegations involved in its drafting, but that they all considered it provided a useful basis for negotiation.[178] And it did serve as a useful basis, forming the template for the final text of the Implementation Agreement.

While these two documents gave phase three its momentum, Guyana's ratification of the LOSC in November 1993 also provided impetus for final agreement.[179] This ratification brought the total up to the threshold number of sixty ratifications required for the LOSC's entry into force, confirming that this would take place in November 1994. Thus, the Informal Consultations now had an external cut-off date, of summer 1994, to allow the PrepCom to take the final necessary steps to convene the ISA Assembly's first session.[180]

The Implementation Agreement and the common heritage principle

It was noted earlier that commentators from developed and developing States made different assessments of the Implementation Agreement: Sohn described it as an 'excellent example of adapting international law to new circumstances';[181] while Anand argued that its effect had been to 'mutilate' the common heritage principle.[182] Anand pointed to the fact that a number of modifications were directly responsive to the United States' demands: greater powers to the ISA Council, and a guaranteed seat on it for the United States; deletion of technology-transfer provisions, production ceilings and annual fees; grant of sites to US-led multinational consortia on terms as favourable

[177] 'Boat Paper (August 3, 1993)' (1993) 9 *International Organizations and the Law of the Sea Documentary Yearbook* 440; 'Boat Paper (Amended), Report of the Secretary-General, UN Doc. A/48/950 (June 9, 1994), Annex II: "Draft Resolution and Draft Agreement Relating to the Implementation of Part XI of the United Nations Convention on the Law of the Sea of 10 December 1982"' (1994) 10 *International Organizations and the Law of the Sea Documentary Yearbook* 76.

[178] Brown, *The International Law of the Sea*, 468.

[179] Report of the UN Secretary-General, Addendum, A/48/527/Add.1, 30 November 1993.

[180] *ibid.* [181] Sohn, 'International Law Implications of the 1994 Agreement', 704–5.

[182] Anand, 'Common Heritage of Mankind'.

as those granted to registered pioneer investors; and the restructuring of the Enterprise as a purely commercial entity.[183]

It is true that the Implementation Agreement dropped many provisions most favourable to developing States, and retreated from the LOSC's elaborate common heritage framework. But it is worth examining whether it so altered the LOSC regime as to completely detach it from the very idea of the Area as the common heritage of mankind.

The Agreement did retain some of the key principles – though not their elaborated forms – which characterised the LOSC framework. It catered to each of the three key ideas of non-appropriation, equitable sharing and no-harm. *Non-appropriation* had a formal but practically limited application even in the LOSC, and this was not altered in the Implementation Agreement. The two components of *no-harm* from the Part XI 'principles' segment (exclusive use for peaceful purposes, and preservation of the marine environment) were not affected. The third component, specific policies to prevent harm to land-based producers, was affected: production ceilings were deleted, and the Agreement now provides that seabed resources should be recovered according to commercial principles and traded according to the General Agreement on Tariffs and Trade. But it offers protections to land-based producers: it disallows subsidies for seabed production of minerals, and provides for assistance to land-based producers seriously affected by loss of export earnings.

The major changes have been with respect to the *equitable sharing* principle. Its first component, equitable sharing of benefits through transfer of financial gains from mining to the ISA, was not directly affected: the only modification was the establishment of a Finance Committee to offer recommendations to the ISA Assembly and Council on '[r]ules, regulations and procedures ... [for] equitable sharing',[184] based on the claim that this was in furtherance of a particular LOSC provision (Article 162(2)(y)). But the second component, effective participation in the exploitation of the seabed, was significantly modified. Unlike the LOSC scheme for participation of developed and developing States in the administration of seabed mining, the ISA now has a more limited structure, and the balance of power has shifted from the Assembly to the Council. Moreover, the LOSC scheme for capacity-building among developing States – such as via technology transfer – has been weakened. Provisions to cater to their interests do remain, but

[183] *ibid.*, 195. [184] Annex Section 9, Implementation Agreement.

there is a basis for critics to conclude that their needs have not been adequately met.[185]

Ultimately, how the Implementation Agreement is evaluated depends upon the commentator's context – as we have seen. Possibly, viewed on its own (not in contrast to Part XI), the Agreement would seem to advance the common heritage principle to a certain extent. But, of course, its history does not permit such an isolated view.

The Implementation Agreement and the RSR

The Implementation Agreement enabled several RSR accessions and ratifications of the LOSC: the United Kingdom and Germany acceded, while Belgium, Canada, Italy, the Netherlands, France and Japan ratified it (as did Russia). With this, these States took on the full range of LOSC obligations. The United States provisionally signed the Implementation Agreement, which allowed it to participate in the work of the ISA for some time. But this signature has now lapsed following its failure to ratify the LOSC.

For its part, the Agreement validated activities that took place pursuant to the RSR. It now permits multinational consortia controlled by RSR States to apply for exploration permits on terms as favourable as those applicable to the LOSC pioneer investors. And it provides that the ISA Council, in framing provisions for exploitation, must treat the RSR States on a par with pioneer investors.

While RSR instruments were intended to be of an interim nature, they have not become defunct in all cases. Yet, they have lost practical relevance. We can see this in the case of the United Kingdom.

The United Kingdom's Deep Sea Mining (Temporary Provisions) Act 1981 remains in force, even though section 18 had permitted its administrative repeal upon the LOSC's entry into force. The government explains:

> Further legislation may be needed in due course to give effect to the new deep sea mining regime, but details of the regime have yet to be worked out by [the ISA]. Deep seabed mining is still years away from being a reality and for the time being the prohibition [against unlicensed mining] in [the UK Act] is sufficient to enable the United Kingdom to fulfil its obligations to give effect

[185] Egede, *Africa and the Deep Seabed Regime*, 76–114, sets out this position in detail. See also Appendix 2 for a summary of the changes wrought by the Implementation Agreement.

to the mining regime under Part XI of the [LOSC] and the 1994 implementing agreement.[186]

In 1996 and 2000, the United Kingdom issued successive versions of the ISA (Immunities and Privileges) Order, which recognises its authority and legal personality. Beyond this, the government position is that, in the absence of concrete prospect of mining, amendment of existing legislation is not essential. Moreover, the only licence issued under the UK Act was surrendered before the United Kingdom's accession. David Anderson suggests that fresh legislation in fulfilment of LOSC provisions would become desirable if a British company became interested in seabed mining.[187] In the absence of this practical interest, seabed mining legislation is simply not a matter of priority.

International law and the dynamics of compromise

In several ways, international law was central to the explication and mediation of the LOSC/RSR conflict – 'legality' was, in fact, both a key weapon and a prize. This was probably inevitable, given that for much of the duration of the conflict the seabed was conceived more as a *normative* resource than an *economic* one. The shape that developing States sought for the LOSC regime reflected that they valued the NIEO for more than the mere flow of financial advantages to them. It embodied the aspiration of these States, mostly newly independent entities, to participate on equal footing with their former colonisers in shaping the framework that would govern their choices. The seabed, literally *and* legally uncharted territory, became the natural focus of this aspiration; on most other issues, the NIEO advocates were forced to accommodate pre-existing legal regimes. The seabed's commercial advantages were thus far outstripped by its symbolic function. For developed States, divided along Eastern and Western lines, the seabed represented a new frontier over which to advance their preferred ideologies: defining the ruling legality would, they expected, also define the shape of the political. Thus, international law was for all States the means of propagating and reinforcing ideology.

But international law was also a technique of communication; a medium in which assertions not only provoked responses, but were

[186] Quoted in D. Anderson, 'British Accession to the UN Convention on the Law of the Sea' (1997) 46 *International and Comparative Law Quarterly* 761, 780.
[187] *ibid.*

also receptive to them. That interests were couched in legal form made them effective but also subjected them to accepted modes of interpretation and rebuttal: they came within the system of legal discourse. Later, as ideological opposition between States receded, the common heritage principle's normatively significant but materially indeterminate character permitted pragmatic adjustments to the LOSC regime.[188]

This section will trace the role of international law, focusing on the importance of formal actions and key moves in legal discourse. It will also offer a brief analysis of the PrepCom's work and the UN Secretary-General's Consultations in terms of the models of institutional action discussed in Chapter 3.

Document-rattling: the importance of legal forms

The dispute over seabed mining was shaped at different points by formal documentary acts of the parties. In fact, an assembly of the formal documents produced during the 1980s and the early 1990s results in quite a comprehensive narrative of the developments. This is not to say that the developments themselves were limited to formal actions: there were political, economic, technological and ideological changes aplenty. But these were filtered into the production of various legal (and soft-legal) documents, such as treaties, PrepCom-led Understandings, exploration licences, UN resolutions and mock drafts. These documents were the *loci* of communication between the parties; various developments proved influential only when expressed through them.

The relevant example is of technological and economic developments. Even though there was much evidence of the practical non-viability of seabed mining by the early 1980s, and Australia had also presented this evidence to the PrepCom in January 1986, it was not given any attention. The PrepCom Secretariat noted (in February 1998) that there were no tested technologies available to conduct seabed mining, but this too remained a margin note: as a mere technical paper, it was not able to influence the normative discourse. The PrepCom was finally able to factor this evidence into its decisions only following the 1989 General Assembly resolution, inviting discussions on necessary modifications to the LOSC regime.

[188] See M. Koskenniemi and M. Lehto, 'The Privilege of Universality: International Law, Economic Ideology and Seabed Resources' (1996) *Nordic Journal of International Law* 533, 554.

On the other hand, the legal documents that were produced served as 'unlocking' devices – they triggered sharp responses, including dramatic changes of position by various parties. Here I briefly recount some examples of the effects catalysed by legal documents.

The obvious example is of the domestic laws adopted by the United States (1980), Germany (1980), France (1981), the United Kingdom (1981) and Japan (1982), and the Interim Agreement (1982). These instruments made it clear that there was no easy way to overcome the objection of Western States to the LOSC regime and achieve consensus, and triggered the decision to bring the UNCLOS III negotiations to a close by way of a vote. It also led to the adoption, at the last minute, of the pioneer investor regime, as a substantial concession, *contra* Part XI, in favour of the RSR.

Another example is the initial applications for exploration licences filed before the PrepCom by the USSR and India in early 1984. These applications provoked a rift within the RSR, for they made France and Japan anxious to resolve overlapping claims with the USSR and apply for PrepCom licences. While initially they wrote to the PrepCom in an effort to reconcile their LOSC and RSR commitments, their position was complicated by the United States' grant of exploration licences to four consortia.[189] The timing of these licences suggests that they were a response to the Indian and USSR applications. As we saw earlier, they in turn provoked angry responses from China, the USSR and the PrepCom, and catalysed the 1984 Understandings between the 'first group' applicants. Moreover, though the United States claimed to have already solved overlaps with France and Japan, there evidently remained problems: the other RSR States wrote to the PrepCom claiming that the 1984 Understandings failed to take into account the sites claimed by the consortia. This crystallised the rift with France and Japan. France now wrote to the PrepCom asserting that

> to maintain that registration by the [PrepCom] of applications from the first [group] is dependent upon resolution of any overlapping with the consortia is tantamount to asserting that, henceforth, the decisions the Commission will be called upon to take will be subject to the goodwill of private commercial

[189] United States National Oceanic and Atmospheric Administration, 'Deep Seabed Mining Report to the US Congress in compliance with Section 309 of the Deep Seabed Hard Mineral Resources Act (PL 96-283)', December 1989, www.gc.noaa.gov/documents/gcil_dsm_89_20110607085546.pdf.

undertakings which were unable to or unwilling to benefit from the rights introduced by [the Pioneer Investor regime].[190]

Thus, the licences (even the filing of licence applications) proved to be consequential acts, triggering a chain of responses – verbal and actual – by each side, aimed at the production of yet more documents to redeem their position.

We may note some other examples from the PrepCom era: the Midnight Agreement was an immediate product of the Arusha and New York Understandings, and despite its awkward form provided a stable *modus vivendi* allowing the PrepCom to finally issue exploration licences. The 1989 UN General Assembly resolution, even with its cosmetic changes of language, altered the common sense amongst parties on how the LOSC should be interpreted. The PrepCom's conclusion of the Understanding on the Fulfilment of Obligations by the Registered Pioneer Investors and their Certifying States in August 1990, reformulating several provisions of the pioneer investor regime, gave it an Indian summer of relevance at a time when momentum had begun to swing away from it.

We also saw that the decision on the form of the outcome document of the Secretary-General's Consultations proved important to bring the Consultations to a speedy close: an 'Implementation Agreement' offered an appropriate compromise between a mere interpretative agreement and a far-reaching amending protocol. Moreover, the Consultations were facilitated by documents that were not 'legal' documents as such but organised in that form. The Boat Paper, for instance, although the product of an informal process between unidentified authors, had all the appropriate trappings, including (in draft form) the necessary UN General Assembly resolution, the Implementation Agreement for Part XI, and two annexes containing the agreed conclusions as to adjustments to Part XI. These became the templates for the final outcome documents adopted soon thereafter.

In short, in different ways, the production of legal documents and of documents bearing that form was essential to the dispute over seabed mining, and shaped the conflict dynamics. It is then unsurprising that the language of legality was the other core element of the efforts by the various parties to bolster their own regime and challenge the other.

[190] Letter from the Chairman of the Delegation of France, LOS/PCN/67 (– 70), 16 August 1985.

Key moves in making legal claims

That the language of legality would play an important role was not apparent at the outset. Some groups, like the G77, had certainly embraced it early on, justifying their position and challenging that of the RSR States purely in legal terms.[191] But the RSR States and the EES had initially expressed their preferences in different terms. At the time the PrepCom commenced its work, RSR States called upon it to display the necessary 'realism' and 'pragmatism' to alter the LOSC seabed mining provisions.[192] The EES initially used a combination of legal and political arguments against the RSR, describing it as:

> more than an attempt to legalize the separate understanding concerning the seizure and division of the most promising sections of the international sea-bed area [between] the world's leading eight capitalist States ... in fact a 'mini treaty' ... [that was] blatant evidence of the hegemonistic, imperialistic policy of the current United States administration, which is aimed against equitable cooperation among States.[193]

This, they claimed, was incompatible with the LOSC and with the good faith obligation that the VCLT imposed upon signatory States. They rejected as illegal this 'deliberate challenge to the Preparatory Commission and to the entire international community'. This statement was delivered on 13 August 1984. In striking contrast, a draft PrepCom declaration proposed by the EES a mere week later, on 21 August 1984, omitted reference to US hegemony, imperialism and the undermining of equity, to instead focus purely on the illegality of the RSR mining regime.[194] Its language now came closer to that of the G77.

And so followed a rigorous discourse on legality, which may be summarised in terms of three sets of moves and counter-moves. Admittedly, this summary schematises a set of arguments as made either by LOSC States or RSR States, while there also existed much dissonance within these groups: France and Japan came to take positions contrary to other RSR States and the USSR often stood apart from other LOSC signatories in its view of the PrepCom, expressing impatience at its delays,[195] while the other signatories showered enthusiastic

[191] For instance, Statement by the G77 Chairman, LOS/PCN/48, 16 August 1984.
[192] UN Press Release SEA/515, 9 March 1983.
[193] Statement by the EES Chairman, LOS/PCN/49, 17 August 1984.
[194] Letter from the Head of Bulgarian Delegation and Chairman of the Group of Eastern European States (August 21), LOS/PCN/L.7/Rev.1, 21 August 1984.
[195] UN Press Release SEA/821, 27 July 1987.

acclaim upon it.[196] Moreover, on technology transfer, the USSR supported the views of RSR States.[197] But, such differences notwithstanding, the general trends in discourse may be mapped in terms of LOSC claims and RSR claims.

The first move, by various groups of LOSC signatories, noted above, was to interpret the RSR – particularly as represented by the 1984 Provisional Understanding – as conflicting with the LOSC, and therefore illegal. The RSR States countered this by way of a narrow interpretation of the Provisional Understanding, to insist that the two regimes were not incompatible.

According to the G77, the EES, the USSR and some other States, the LOSC was the culmination of a legal process underlined by the 1970 Declaration of Principles. The Declaration had established that the Area was the common heritage of mankind and was to be exploited only pursuant to a universal regime, which was concretised in the LOSC. The ISA and, prior to the LOSC coming into operation, the PrepCom, were thus the only competent bodies to authorise activities relating to seabed mining. The RSR agreements were contrary to the LOSC's letter and spirit: the 1984 Provisional Understanding was in fact a 'mini-treaty' that went 'beyond the resolution of conflicts arising from overlapping claims, by including provisions regarding exploration and exploitation of seabed resources, outside the [LOSC]'.[198] The RSR, thus, was not a basis for creating legal rights: it was 'wholly illegal'.

The RSR counter-argument was that the Provisional Understanding 'in no way' contained an alternative to the LOSC. It was merely concerned with conflict resolution, in line with the 'basic principle' of international law that States should resolve their disputes by peaceful means. The obligation imposed on each state by the Provisional Understanding was one of 'self-restraint', and not of recognition or support for any particular claim of the other States. It fulfilled the requirement of the UN pioneer investor regime to resolve overlapping

[196] For instance, Statement by the Chairman of the Group of 77 (March 11), LOS/PCN/L.15, 20 March 1985.

[197] UN Press Release SEA/KIN/37, 29 March 1988.

[198] Statement by the G77 Chairman, LOS/PCN/48, 16 August 1984; Statement by the EES Chairman, LOS/PCN/49, 17 August 1984; Letter from the Head of Bulgarian Delegation and EES Chairman, LOS/PCN/L.7/Rev.1, 21 August 1984; Statement by the G77 Chairman, LOS/PCN/L.15, 20 March 1985; Letter from the Acting Permanent Representative of the USSR, LOS/PCN/64, 1 July 1985; Letter from China, LOS/PCN/71, 20 August 1985; PrepCom Declaration, LOS/PCN/72, 2 September 1985.

claims.[199] Moreover, in response to the claim that the RSR was 'wholly illegal', Germany asserted that prior to its entry into force the LOSC could not create rights and obligations for any States, and, even when it did come into force, it could not bind non-parties. Therefore, 'the claim that the [LOSC] ha[d] established a regime for deep sea-bed activities [was] without legal foundation'. Germany dismissed the PrepCom declaration rejecting the legality of the RSR as being 'essentially political in nature'.[200]

The second move related to defining the category of States that were entitled to have their claims to mining sites considered by the PrepCom, and by each other. There were several rounds of claims and counterclaims on this issue.

Initially, in July 1982, Canada had initiated a process open to all 'potential claimants', that is, including all RSR States and the USSR, while the USSR had claimed that it was under no obligation to consult with LOSC non-signatories.[201] The LOSC non-signatories of the time had claimed that, since it remained possible for them to sign the LOSC until 9 December 1984, they could not be excluded from consultations until this date.[202] Later, when the PrepCom produced its two 1984 Understandings relating to the registration of the first group, it was met with objections by various RSR States that they

199 Letter from the Netherlands, LOS/PCN/46, 16 August 1984; Letter from France, LOS/PCN/47, 16 August 1984; Statement by the Netherlands, on behalf of Belgium, France, Germany, Italy, Japan and the United Kingdom (August 14), LOS/PCN/52, 24 August 1984. See also Letter from Canada, LOS/PCN/40, 11 April 1984; Letter from Belgium, France, the Federal Republic of Germany, Italy, Japan, the Netherlands and the United Kingdom, LOS/PCN/41, 12 April 1984; Letter from Japan, LOS/PCN/42, 12 April 1984; Letter from France, LOS/PCN/44, 12 April 1984.

200 Letter from the Federal Republic of Germany, LOS/PCN/73, 9 January 1986.

201 Letter from the USSR Delegation, LOS/PCN/4, 8 April 1983; Letter from the USSR, LOS/PCN/17, 2 May 1983; Letter from the USSR, LOS/PCN/36, 5 April 1984; Letter from the USSR, LOS/PCN/38, 10 April 1984.

202 For rebuttals of the USSR's claims, see: Letter from France, LOS/PCN/8, 27 April 1983; Note Verbale from the Federal Republic of Germany, LOS/PCN/9, 28 April 1983; Letter from Italy, LOS/PCN/10, 28 April 1983; Letter from Japan, LOS/PCN/11, 28 April 1983; Letter from the United Kingdom, LOS/PCN/13, 29 April 1983; Letter from Belgium, LOS/PCN/14, 29 April 1983; Letter from Canada, LOS/PCN/15, 29 April 1983; Letter from the Federal Republic of Germany to the United Nations, LOS/PCN/37, 6 April 1984; Letter from Canada, LOS/PCN/40, 11 April 1984; Letter from Belgium, France, Germany, Italy, Japan, the Netherlands and the United Kingdom, LOS/PCN/41; Letter from Japan, LOS/PCN/42; Letter from France, LOS/PCN/44, 12 April 1984; Letter from Japan, LOS/PCN/45, 16 August 1984; Letter from the Netherlands, LOS/PCN/46, 16 August 1984; Letter from France, LOS/PCN/47, 16 August 1984.

had not been included in the settlements. The PrepCom observed that it had *consulted* with them, but could not admit their claims to mining sites unless they filed for PrepCom registration.[203] The RSR States insisted that they could not be affected by a settlement to which they were not party.[204] As noted earlier, by this time France and Japan had departed from the stance of the other RSR States; France challenged the RSR's arguments as aiming to condition the PrepCom's work on 'the goodwill of private commercial undertakings', that is, the RSR mining consortia.[205]

The third move was to draw distinctions between 'technical' and 'political' initiatives in order to justify and challenge, respectively, developments in the LOSC and RSR regimes.

The RSR States criticised the 1984 PrepCom Understandings as having exceeded the PrepCom's legal competence. The PrepCom and the first-group States responded to these charges by presenting the Understandings as being within the PrepCom's overall mandate of implementing the pioneer investor regime, and as merely technical adjustments directed towards its proper implementation.[206] At the same time as they challenged the PrepCom's initiatives, the RSR States also sought to justify their own 1984 Provisional Understanding as merely in technical implementation of the UN regime, and characterised the PrepCom's rejection of it as a political act. LOSC signatories responded with the claim that the RSR's Provisional Understanding was more than a technical agreement, and was in fact an attempt to usurp the PrepCom's functions and substitute for the UN regime another regime based on different principles.

Perhaps in response to these earlier exchanges, the PrepCom took care to describe its later adjustments to the UN pioneer investor regime as devised purely in order to overcome the practical difficulties in the implementation of the LOSC regime, and not amounting to an

203 Statement of PrepCom Chairman regarding the Understanding on Resolution of Conflicts among Applicants for Registration as Pioneer Investors, LOS/PCN/L.8, 31 August 1984; Statement by PrepCom Chairman, LOS/PCN/L.13, 4 September 1984; Letter from the USSR, LOS/PCN/65 (– 66), 8 July 1985.

204 Letter from the United Kingdom, LOS/PCN/54, 24 September 1984; Letter from the Netherlands, LOS/PCN/60, 26 April 1985; Letter from Belgium, LOS/PCN/61, 26 April 1985; Letter from Italy, LOS/PCN/62, 26 April 1985; Letter from Canada, LOS/PCN/63, 26 April 1985.

205 Letter from France, LOS/PCN/67 (– 70), 16 August 1985.

206 *ibid.*; LOS/PCN/65–66, 8 July 1985.

amendment of that regime.[207] The PrepCom held this position through several Understandings: Arusha and New York in 1986, and the Midnight Agreement in 1987.

Much later, the Secretary-General's Informal Consultations were also carried out on the basis that they were only recalibrating the practical provisions of Part XI, not fundamentally revising it; therefore, there was no need for fresh consent from States that had signed on to the original LOSC regime. This also determined the choice to title the final outcome the *Implementation* Agreement.

In sum, the dispute over seabed mining boiled down to a discourse focused on the proper interpretation of legal instruments; the normative force of the common heritage principle according to treaty and customary law; the rights of different States as LOSC parties, signatories, potential signatories and non-signatories; and the changes possible by way of technical modifications of either regime. We should not focus too much on the quality of these arguments; they were, to a large extent, simply asserted rather than carefully proved. What is interesting is that the language of legality came to substitute for claims of equity and efficiency *simpliciter*. For, this espousal of legality exposed the limits of the various positions: the RSR States had to recognise that they could not base their regime solely on its interim character, and tried to read the RSR as compatible with the LOSC in various ways. The LOSC signatories and the PrepCom too had to recognise that they could not simply dismiss the RSR as illegal: they did continue to distinguish between LOSC signatories and non-signatories but also recognised the legal effect of acts performed in pursuance of the RSR. This was implied in the PrepCom's consultations with the RSR States for the Arusha and New York Understandings, and evidently stated in the Implementation Agreement.

The Secretary-General's Consultations also exemplify the lasting effect of formulating preferred positions in legal terms. Though the provisions of the Implementation Agreement considerably watered down Part XI's practical provisions in support of the common heritage principle, the concepts associated with this principle also

[207] Statement by the PrepCom Chairman, LOS/PCN/L.34, 10 April 1986; Statement by the PrepCom Chairman (August 22), LOS/PCN/L.36, 2 September 1986; Statement by the PrepCom Chairman, LOS/PCN/L.41/Rev.1, 11 September 1986. See also Statement by the G77 Chairman, LOS/PCN/L.35, 10 April 1986; UN Press Release SEA/777, 8 September 1986; UN Press Release SEA/KIN/3, 31 March 1987; UN Press Release SEA/821, 27 July 1987.

circumscribed alterations to the LOSC, preventing its complete overhaul on the basis of commercial considerations. Indeed, the continuing normative pull of the common heritage principle even after the need for practical reforms of seabed mining (and its technological non-viability) came to be accepted, illustrates the traction that legal concepts tend to acquire. Evidently, the participants in the Secretary-General's Consultations fully understood this: in crafting the Implementation Agreement they remained keen to state in terms of 'golden principles' those elements of the mining regime for which they could not provide detailed provisions – this was guided by the sense that these golden principles would control how the regime evolved in the future.

Institutional forums

Finally, we come to the institutional forums: the PrepCom and the UN Secretary-General's Consultations. The PrepCom's work may be viewed as an example of the doctrine of approximate application. For, called on by LOSC signatories to implement the pioneer investor regime and by RSR States to remedy the LOSC regime's defects, it took the approach of making minor modifications to the LOSC regime to enable States to resolve overlapping site-claims. It defended these modifications as merely technical in character, and as overcoming practical and political impediments to registering pioneer investors, and thus facilitating effective operation of the LOSC regime (which regime it evidently viewed as operating *in rem*). The PrepCom, in fact, espoused the G77's distinction between effective implementation and illegality, characterising its own actions as the former and the RSR (justified by its own participants as a regime compatible in spirit with the LOSC) as the latter. The PrepCom's actions had no punitive rationale.

Reading the PrepCom's approach as an example of 'approximate application' allows its defence against criticisms that the PrepCom overstepped its mandate in making creative modifications to the pioneer investor regime. It also allows us to use the criteria associated with that doctrine to evaluate the modifications made.

Moreover, comparing the PrepCom's actions to 'approximate application' also helps unveil the limitations of that doctrine itself. Indeed, we might argue that these defects lie in the very criteria that constitute the conditions for its application, because they permit only incremental modifications – they assume that the regime cannot be substantially reassessed. This may have been appropriate in the particular case in which Lauterpacht outlined the doctrine, and, from the perspective of many developing States, was also appropriate in the case of the LOSC. But it cannot always be appropriate for an institution administering a regime to merely uphold it to the extent possible, and to regard acts of opposition as impediments to be overcome. Even with respect to the LOSC regime, it is possible to argue that the PrepCom's approach did not sufficiently remedy its unrealistic and cumbersome institutional framework and could proceed only by bracketing all hard-core issues. Indeed, this led to the shift towards the UN Secretary-General's Consultations, which proved to be the more influential forum despite its more limited participation and informal procedures.

The point is that the core assumption underlying approximate application may be questioned on grounds both of legitimacy and effectiveness, since it can be upheld only in particular contexts (and, even then, perhaps only from particular points of view). Likening the PrepCom's work to approximate application makes explicit the constitutional analogies - that certain treaties possess fundamental features that courts and other international bodies should strive to preserve - that the doctrine relies upon.

However, as Chapter 3 pointed out, Lauterpacht and Rosenne's discussion made another point in favour of an institution's application of the doctrine which we could also apply to the PrepCom. They asserted that, above all, what an institution does through this doctrine is to maintain a *legal* discourse that draws in all stake-holders. Here, the PrepCom's process was instrumental in fostering such a discourse, and this discourse did keep most parties engaged with the LOSC, and further, had a lasting effect on the outcomes deemed acceptable. The PrepCom's work is thus a good example of how approximate application, though it certainly favours incremental over transformational change, indeed mediates stability and change in treaty relations.

The UN Secretary-General's Consultations were different in approach. For all the claims that they lacked the mandate to re-open negotiations, they did not accept the rigid distinction between treaty-making and implementation that characterises approximate application. Of the models of institutional action discussed in Chapter 3, the Consultations were most akin to regime interaction. I will return to regime interaction in Chapter 6, so only a brief discussion is offered here.

To start with, they are a good example of a forum constituting itself as central to a dispute: of course the UN Secretary-General had formal authority to oversee the implementation of the LOSC, but here he took recourse to a process which was expressly described as informal, and thus limited to only some of the UNCLOS III participants, and to the RSR States. Moreover, despite the avowals of a limited mandate, the Consultations sought a substantial transformation of the LOSC regime in order to accommodate concerns expressed through the RSR, but they also extended some key concepts associated with the common heritage principles to the RSR States – mutual learning between regimes, without concern for parallel membership, was thus the leading element of the Consultations.

These Consultations may thus be reviewed according to the standards outlined for regime interaction in Chapter 3: the 'process', in particular, is important. And, indeed, we saw that, as the first round of these Consultations was criticised for limited participation, with each round and phase the participation was broadened. The format of deliberations, too, evolved to permit various States to express their views. Questions of transparency remained (after all, who were the authors of the influential Boat Paper?), but, in the end, as a number of States signed the Implementation Agreement, the Consultations passed the political test.

Conclusion

This chapter's account of the conflict between the LOSC and the RSR shows that the existence of a treaty conflict is a matter of practice, not definition. Moreover, it suggests that rules of thumb for allocating priority between treaties based on the time of their conclusion, or the speciality of their subject-matter, may be less relevant than the record of their actual implementation. Indeed, the conceptual resolution of a treaty conflict – as could be found, in this case, in assertions of the RSR's interim character – does not imply its practical resolution. In fact, arguments as to the lack of a real conflict and the use of interpretative techniques were here used strategically by RSR States to re-modulate the LOSC regime.

Further, the chapter shows that not just the RSR States, but also LOSC signatories and the PrepCom, made instrumental resort to legal discourse and forms to bolster their claims, and to effectively implement their regimes. Indeed, the law subsumed other types of claims, and other information as to the economics and technology of seabed mining. However, the turn to law also had a moderating effect, as neither side could simply deny the regime that conflicted with its own. The turn to law allowed both a *modus vivendi* between the competing regimes and, later, a substantial amendment of the LOSC regime, which were girded by the common heritage principle. Perhaps we may say that the material indeterminacy of this principle made it capable of being expressed through varied institutional frameworks.[208] But, here, material indeterminacy did not amount to complete fluidity; the core concepts with which the principle was associated since the 1970 Declaration had a lasting normative influence: they permitted variation in institutional frameworks but also limited the changes that could be made to the LOSC regime. And these remain part of the amended LOSC regime today.

The recent ISA Technical Study restates these core concepts as guiding principles for the exploitation regime, mentioning non-appropriation, equal sharing of benefits, equal participation and sustainability. It suggests that these principles must combine with the aim of commercial viability, as fleshed out via the Implementation Agreement.[209]

Of course, whether the principles will continue to exercise a regulative effect on commercial aims can only be determined once there is greater practice of seabed mining – in the ISA's newly buoyant expectations, a matter for the short term. Reporting these expectations, the ISA's recent (and otherwise dry) press release extracted from its President's remarks a charmingly existential quote:

> Before it took note of the Secretary-General's note, the President of the Council, Tobias Pierlings (Germany) echoed Jamaica's earlier assertion that the exploitation of the mineral resources of the deep seabed was 'the reason we are here'.[210]

What a strange reason it would have seemed, only a few years ago.

[208] On this point, see Koskenniemi and Lehto, 'The Privilege of Universality', 554.
[209] Clark *et al.*, 'Towards the Development of a Regulatory Framework', 13.
[210] 'Council Considers Secretariat's Note on Regulatory Framework for Nodules Exploitation', Press Release SB/19/14, 22 July 2013, www.isa.org.jm/files/documents/EN/Press/Press13/SB-19-14.pdf.

5 Courting the United States? The International Criminal Court and Article 98 agreements

> We don't want to be party to legitimizing the ICC.
>
> US Ambassador for War Crimes Issues (Pierre-Richard Prosper), January 2005[1]

> We will work closely with our allies and friends ... to strengthen the ICC, to make it the kind of institution that can be effective in investigating, prosecuting, and trying those responsible for ... [international] crimes.
>
> US Ambassador for War Crimes Issues (Stephen J. Rapp), May 2011[2]

Introduction

On 26 February 2011, a few days into the Arab Spring, the UN Security Council referred the situation in Libya 'since 15 February 2011 to the Prosecutor of the International Criminal Court'.[3] Libya was not a party to the Rome Statute of the International Criminal Court (ICC, or 'Court').[4] This was the second time that the Council had referred a situation to the Court, but – as the United States noted – the first time that the Council did so unanimously.[5] On the previous occasion, when the Council referred the situation in Darfur, Sudan, to the Court in 2005, the United States had abstained from voting.[6] Moreover, at the time, the

[1] Human Rights Watch, 'US Fiddles over ICC While Darfur Burns: UN Security Council Should Reject US Scheme for Ad Hoc Court', 30 January 2005, www.hrw.org/news/2005/01/31/us-fiddles-over-icc-while-darfur-burns.

[2] 'Where Can the Victims of Atrocities Find Justice?', Remarks, Forum Hosted by the Women of Ateneo, Makati, Philippines, 10 May 2011, www.state.gov/j/gcj/us_releases/remarks/2011/165257.htm.

[3] UNSC Res. 1970 (26 February 2011).

[4] 2187 UNTS 90, adopted 17 July 1998, entered into force 01/07/2002.

[5] Provisional Verbatim Record, UNSC 6491st Mtg, S/PV.6491, 26 February 2011, 3.

[6] UNSC Res. 1593 (31 March 2005).

United States had offered a lengthy explanation of its abstention to clarify that it did not, in general, support the view that the Court could exercise jurisdiction over States not party to the Rome Statute. On the present occasion, it added no such qualifications in its statement to the Council.

The role of interpolating qualifications, instead, was assumed by India, which pointed out that, as a non-party to the Rome Statute, it was in the company of many other States, particularly 'five of the 15 members of the Council, including 3 permanent members'.[7] India called attention to a paragraph in Resolution 1970 which confirmed that nationals of States not party to the Statute (Libya excepted) would be subject to the exclusive jurisdiction of their home States. India also asserted that it would have 'preferred a calibrated and gradual approach'. Nevertheless, it was persuaded to vote for the Resolution because

> several members of the Council, including our colleagues from Africa and the Middle East, believe that referral to the Court would have the effect of an immediate cessation of violence and the restoration of calm and stability. The letter from the Permanent Representative of Libya of 26 February addressed to you, Madame President, has called for such a referral and strengthened this view. We have therefore gone along with the consensus in the Council.[8]

There are several remarkable features to Resolution 1970. One is the rapidity with which the situation was placed before the ICC Office of the Prosecutor (OTP) – this took place in the initial phase of the Libyan conflict. The United States' affirmative vote and India's explanation that States, including African and Middle Eastern ones, expected the referral to check the ongoing violence, project an image of the Court that has significantly evolved since its initial period of uncertainty, when it was severely challenged by US hostility and many expected it to fail altogether. The referral suggests that the Court has become a crucial element of the political calculus of States responding to grave situations of conflict and human rights abuses.

But not all has changed. The Resolution noted several restrictions upon the Court. The provision relating to non-parties, that India mentioned, is one of these. The Resolution's preamble recalls the Security Council's authority to defer investigations and prosecutions before

[7] S/PV.6491, 2011, 2. [8] *Ibid.*

the Court. Moreover, the Resolution includes the usual caveat that 'none of the expenses incurred in connection with the referral, including expenses related to investigations or prosecutions ... shall be borne by the United Nations and that such costs shall be borne by the parties to the Rome Statute and those States that wish to contribute voluntarily'.[9] Though apparently willing to confer the authority to investigate and prosecute cases from an incendiary political situation upon the OTP, the United States and other non-parties have still not been persuaded to loosen their purse-strings to assist the Court's budget.

Following the adoption of the Resolution, the revolutionary government in Libya, which took over from the Gaddafi government (and whose leadership initially favoured the referral), has been involved in a jurisdictional tussle with the Court, seeking to prosecute Saif al-Islam Gaddafi and Abdullah al-Senussi via its domestic justice system.[10] On 31 May 2013, the Court's Pre-Trial Chamber (PTC) rejected the claim that the Court should cede jurisdiction to the Libyan domestic process in the case of Gaddafi.[11] The decision is under appeal. With respect to al-Senussi, the PTC has decided in favour of the admissibility challenge, finding that Libya is able and willing genuinely to try him under its domestic justice system.[12] That decision, delivered on 11 October 2013, has also been appealed.

On the whole, the Libya referral, and following it the opening of investigations into Côte d'Ivoire and Mali, reinforce that, over time, the Court's business has moved from the exceptional to the routine, at least in some respects. Its docket boasts of eighteen cases in eight situations. A ninth, relating to Israel's actions against the *MV Mavi Marmara* (a ship that had formed part of the 2010 'Gaza Freedom

[9] UNSC Res. 1970, para. 8.

[10] *Prosecutor* v. *Saif Al-Islam Gaddafi and Abdullah Al-Senussi*, Application on Behalf of the Government of Libya Pursuant to Article 19 of the ICC Statute, ICC-01/11-01/11, 1 May 2012, www.icc-cpi.int/iccdocs/doc/doc1405819.pdf. See also *Prosecutor* v. *Saif Al-Islam Gaddafi and Abdullah Al-Senussi*, Application on Behalf of the Government of Libya Relating to Abdullah Al-Senussi pursuant to Article 19 of the ICC Statute, ICC-01/11-01/11, 2 April 2013, www.icc-cpi.int/iccdocs/doc/doc1575650.pdf.

[11] *Prosecutor* v. *Saif Al-Islam Gaddafi and Abdullah Al-Senussi*, Decision on the Admissibility of the Case Against Saif Al-Islam Gaddafi, ICC-01/11-01/11-344-Red, 31 May 2013, www.icc-cpi.int/iccdocs/doc/doc1599307.pdf.

[12] *Prosecutor* v. *Saif Al-Islam Gaddafi and Abdullah Al-Senussi*, Decision on the Admissibility of the Case Against Abdullah Al-Senussi, ICC-01/11-01/11-466-Red, 11 October 2013, www.icc-cpi.int/iccdocs/doc/doc1663102.pdf.

Flotilla') has been referred to it by the Comoros.[13] It is conducting preliminary examinations into a number of other situations. It has issued its first conviction,[14] as well as its first acquittal.[15] By all yardsticks, it is a functional institution, albeit one that still invites controversy.

This was not always foreseeable: the Court in its early years, while earnestly supported by some States, was vigorously opposed by the United States and several others. For some time, it did not seem that the Court would enter into operation; rumours of its imminent failure abounded. The United States concluded more than 100 so-called 'bilateral immunity agreements' (BIAs) with other States, parties and non-parties to the Rome Statute, in several instances by threatening to withdraw economic and military aid from them. These agreements stipulated non-surrender of persons to the Court, and non-cooperation with other requests. Backed by US legislation and – as this chapter will argue – in conflict with the Rome Statute, these Agreements were the most visible element of the US 'campaign' against the ICC: they brought numerous other States into the equation, providing a *legal* – and not only political, or economic – bar to their cooperation with the Court. On a generous reading, the BIAs were meant to restrict the categories of persons over whom the Court could exercise jurisdiction; a more critical interpretation suggests that they sought to altogether undermine the Court. The BIAs were evidently an example of a State using the strategy of treaty conflict to challenge a legal regime: deploying legal form against legal form. Coupled with a shortage of funding (the United States ensured that no UN funds would be given to the Court), and even of public visibility (reportedly, the United States used to ensure deletion of all references to the ICC in UN records in the early years, and sought to force the discussion of the ICC's annual report into the Sixth Committee of the General Assembly, rather than in the Plenary[16]), these agreements made the prospects for the Court's effective functioning seem bleak.

[13] 'Referral under Articles 14 and 12(2)(a) of the Rome Statute Arising from the 31 May 2010, Gaza Freedom Flotilla Situation', submitted by the Union of the Comoros, 14 May 2013, www.icc-cpi.int/iccdocs/otp/Referral-from-Comoros.pdf.

[14] *Prosecutor* v. *Thomas Lubanga Dyilo*, Judgment Pursuant to Article 74 of the Statute, ICC-01/04-1/06-2842, 14 March 2012, www.icc-cpi.int/iccdocs/doc/doc1379838.pdf.

[15] *Prosecutor* v. *Mathieu Ngudjolo Chui*, Judgment Pursuant to Article 74 of the Statute, ICC-01/04-2/12-3, www.icc-cpi.int/iccdocs/doc/doc1529535.pdf.

[16] Anonymous comment, 2010 (on file with the author).

This chapter will trace the change from that situation, into one where the Court indeed functions routinely and even receives (qualified) support from the United States. Focusing on the period from July 2002, when the ICC became operational, up to the Review Conference, in May–June 2010, in which the United States took part (having made its debut at the ICC Assembly of States Parties (ASP) only some months before, in November 2009), the chapter will explain the strategically created treaty conflict that formed the central element of the US challenge to the Court and show the gradual evolution of the United States–ICC relationship, from engagement to hostility, hostility to cautious engagement, and cautious engagement to qualified support. It will make the point that, important among the factors relevant to this evolution is the approach taken by the various Court organs, and especially the OTP, to overcome the hindrances threatened by the BIAs–Rome Statute conflict.

To provide a crude timeline of the United States–ICC relationship: in the years up to the adoption of the Rome Statute establishing the ICC in 1998, and the initial years of the functioning of the ICC Preparatory Commission (ICC PrepCom), which operated from 1999 to 2002, the United States remained engaged with the process of establishment of the ICC. This changed during the last months of the ICC PrepCom's operation. From early 2001 up to mid-2005, the United States was not only completely disengaged from the ICC but also hostile to it – this was the period in which it concluded most of its BIAs. In mid-2005, however, when the Security Council referred the situation in Darfur to the ICC, the United States chose to abstain from – but not veto – the resolution. The thaw in the United States' attitude towards the ICC continued over the next several months. In November 2009, for the first time in eight years, the new Obama Administration sent a delegation to the annual meeting of the ASP (at which ICC organs report the Court's progress and outline their future agenda). In May–June 2010, the United States attended the Review Conference held as mandated in Article 123 of the Rome Statute. The United States remains a non-party to the Rome Statute, but its relationship with the ICC may now fairly be described as one of strategic engagement, and even occasional support.

The change in the United States–ICC relationship is often attributed to the shifts in US domestic politics. While those shifts were certainly relevant, the role played by the Court's organs was equally, if not more, important. As this chapter will describe, the OTP in particular took several creative policy decisions in order to bring the Court into effective operation. Its work in the early years, before the referral of the Darfur situation, combined assuaging (US) concerns that it would intrude upon State sovereignty with securing some self-referrals that would allow it to begin functioning. In the years following the Sudan referral (and in keeping with the United States' strong position against the Sudanese government), the OTP departed from its previous cautious approach, requesting an open warrant for the Sudanese head of State and taking a firmer position that peace processes could not be an excuse for stalling the ICC's process. The gradual thaw in US opposition also allowed the OTP the space to address criticisms from other quarters – particularly from African States, which were understandably disturbed by its exclusive focus on that region, and by its failure to open investigations elsewhere in the world. The chapter will trace these two phases of the OTP's work, highlighting the ways in which its approach diverged from what may have been expected based on the text and purpose of the Rome Statute. It will comment upon, as relevant, the approach taken by the Court's Chambers. The chapter will also trace the shifts in the rhetoric employed by the OTP, and by the Presidency and Registry. It will make the point that, following the discussion in Chapter 3, the ICC organs, particularly the OTP, may be understood as embracing something of a managerial approach to bring the Court into effective operation.

The chapter is organised as follows: it next traces events up to, and immediately following, the Rome Statute's entry into force. It focuses on the United States' mistrust, and the means by which this was expressed. The sections following examine the conflict between the Rome Statute and the BIAs, and review the developments through which the ICC became fully functional, including the United States' renewal of engagement. The chapter then examines how the OTP contributed to this renewal, and charts the rhetoric of the ICC organs. Finally, it offers a review of the OTP's 'managerial' role.

The United States' mistrust of the ICC: background and manifestations

The United States, a key participant in the UN Diplomatic Conference of Plenipotentiaries that had been convened to review and finalise the Statute of the International Criminal Court, was unhappy with the text finally adopted by vote on 17 July 1998. On this date, it refused to sign the Rome Statute. Later, it also expressed the view that the ICC PrepCom, which had been established by the UN Diplomatic Conference in order to 'prepare proposals for practical arrangements for the establishment and coming into operation of the Court', including its rules of procedure and evidence, and definitions of the elements of the crimes over which the ICC was to have jurisdiction, had failed to meet the United States' concerns.[17]

US President Bill Clinton did finally authorise signature of the Rome Statute on 31 December 2000, which was the last possible date for signature without ratification (and just twenty days before he was to hand power over to his successor, George W. Bush). However, he claimed that the signature did not indicate the withdrawal of the United States' objections to the Statute; rather, the Statute was signed to enable the United States to exercise greater control over the Court's development than it could as a non-party. Clinton recommended that Bush not 'submit the Treaty to the Senate for advice and consent until our fundamental concerns are satisfied'.[18] On 6 May 2002, the Bush Administration took the step that is popularly referred to as the 'unsigning' of the Rome Statute.[19] It sent a note to UN Secretary-General Kofi Annan, stating that the United States did not intend to become a party to the Statute, and had no legal obligations towards it.[20] From that time, in the (now dated) words of one commentator, 'the Bush Administration ... [ran] an aggressive, mendacious and ill-informed campaign to undermine the ICC'.[21]

The United States' major concern was to protect its nationals from prosecution before the ICC, for it considered the Court lacking in adequate procedural and evidentiary standards. It worried also about the possibility of malicious and politically driven prosecutions, suggesting that these would particularly affect the United States because it

[17] The PrepCom was established by Resolution F of the Final Act of the UN Diplomatic Conference on the Establishment of an International Criminal Court, A/CONF.183/10, 17 July 1998.

[18] Associated Press, 'Clinton's Words: "The Right Action"', *New York Times*, 1 January 2001.

[19] However, as the ASIL Taskforce has pointed out, there is no provision in the Rome Statute for a State to 'unsign' it: 'US Policy Towards the ICC: Furthering Positive Engagement', Report of an Independent Task Force convened by the American Society of International Law, March 2009, www.asil.org/icc-task-force.cfm.

[20] 'US Letter to UN Secretary-General Kofi Annan', CNN, 5 June 2002.

[21] P. Sands, *Lawless World: America and the Making and Breaking of Global Rules* (London, Penguin 2005) 48.

'shoulders responsibilities worldwide that no other nation comes even close to undertaking'.[22]

According to the United States, its concerns were borne out by several features of the Rome Statute.[23] In the United States' view, first of all, the Court enjoyed very broad bases for its jurisdiction: under Article 12, it could take up cases where an alleged perpetrator's home State *or* a State where an international crime was committed was party to the Statute. Moreover, under Article 15, the Statute conferred a vast autonomy upon the ICC Prosecutor, including the capacity to initiate investigations *proprio motu*. Next, the Statute offered highly disparate protections to States parties and non-parties: it shielded parties from ICC jurisdiction in certain circumstances that did not extend to non-parties. Thus, under Article 121(5), a State party could opt not to agree to amended definitions of international crimes, whereupon these definitions would not be applied to its nationals or its territory, but non-parties could not make such an election. And under Article 124, a provision that James Crawford describes as 'bizarre',[24] a State party could refuse to accept the ICC's jurisdiction over war crimes for a seven-year period following its ratification (or entry into force) of the Rome Statute, but a non-party could not similarly limit the Court's jurisdiction over its nationals or (following a Security Council referral) territory.

Many other States recognised these objections as having merit, and cooperated to address them during the drafting of the Rome Statute, as well as subsequent to its adoption.[25] During the drafting of the Statute, Articles 17–19 on admissibility, and Article 16's conferral of the power to defer prosecutions upon the Security Council, introduced limits on the Court's exercise of jurisdiction. Afterwards, PrepCom negotiations on Rules for Procedure and Evidence created a network of safeguards to ensure the proper exercise of prosecutorial discretion and the observance of due process standards. Indeed, Clinton's signing statement indicates that, at the time it signed the Statute, the United States

[22] D. Scheffer, 'Staying the Course with the International Criminal Court' (2001) 35 *Cornell International Law Journal* 47. Scheffer was the chairman of the US delegation to the UN Diplomatic Conference, and later its delegate to the PrepCom. It was Scheffer who signed the Rome Statute upon Clinton's authorisation.

[23] The US arguments are well summarised in Scheffer, 'Staying the Course with the ICC', 74–86.

[24] J. Crawford, 'The Drafting of the Rome Statute', in P. Sands (ed.), *From Nuremberg to the Hague: The Future of International Criminal Justice* (Oxford University Press 2003) 109, 150.

[25] See Scheffer, 'Staying the Course with the ICC', 72–86.

recognised that it could consolidate diplomatic and legal safeguards to protect the rights of its nationals within the framework of the Statute.

But the United States' end-vision for the ICC was at variance with that of other States, including several NATO members who were committed to realising a strong and independent Court. These States were unwilling to accept amendments that would allow States in general, or particular States, to control the Court's functioning. For the United States, however, the launch of its war on terror made immunity of its nationals from ICC trials an inflexible goal. The United States thus began to retreat from its engagement with the ICC. Whereas it had remained an active participant in negotiations on the 'Rules of Procedure and Evidence' and the 'Elements of Crimes' right up to its signature on 31 December 2000, by the end of 2001 its engagement trickled to a close and in May 2002 it 'unsigned' the treaty. The United States' withdrawal from the ICC was accompanied by increased political muscle-flexing. Starting with attempts to secure blanket immunity for its nationals engaged in peacekeeping operations, in 2002, the United States was able to obtain a Security Council resolution that requested the Court to defer commencement of any investigation or prosecution of UN peacekeeping personnel sent by a non-party, for a period of twelve months.[26] The resolution was renewable for additional twelve-month periods, and was renewed once in 2003,[27] but subsequent attempts at renewal proved unsuccessful (following revelations of torture of Iraqis by the United States and the United Kingdom's soldiers at Abu Ghraib). In 2002, the United States also enacted the American Servicemembers' Protection Act (ASPA),[28] colloquially known as the 'Hague Invasion Act'. ASPA section 2004 stated that the United States would not cooperate with the ICC, would not surrender nationals to it and would limit assistance to other States that cooperated with the ICC. Section 2005 affirmed that the United States would not participate in peacekeeping without a guarantee that its armed forces would not be surrendered to the ICC. Then, in sections 2007 and 2008, followed two provisions that were particularly controversial: section 2007 provided that, except for NATO members and some allies, the United States would not provide military assistance to a State party to the Rome Statute, though it would exempt

[26] UNSC Res. 1422 (12 July 2002). On this, and subsequent resolutions, see N. Jain, 'A Separate Law for Peacekeepers: The Clash between the Security Council and the International Criminal Court' (2005) 16 *European Journal of International Law* 239.

[27] UNSC Res. 1487 (12 June 2003).

[28] Public Law 107–206, 2 August 2002.

States that agreed to the BIAs. Section 2008 authorised the US President to use all means necessary and appropriate to release nationals of the United States or its allies detained by or on the behalf of the ICC. This possibly referred only to the provision of legal assistance to such persons, as was spelt out in subsection 2008(c), but raised the spectre of US forces storming into The Hague, or (more facetiously) into States like the United Kingdom that had offered to house prisoners convicted by the ICC.[29]

The most visible aspect of the United States' campaign against the Court was its conclusion of more than 100 BIAs, providing for non-surrender of its nationals to the ICC. These agreements, once described by Amnesty International as 'impunity' agreements,[30] were concluded with ICC parties and non-parties, with the ASPA being used to coerce agreement. In 2004, the United States also adopted the Nethercutt Amendment, which prohibited assistance from the US Economic Support Fund to any State party to the Rome Statute, unless such State concluded a BIA with the United States, or was otherwise exempted.[31] The BIAs were in conflict with States' commitments under the Rome Statute, and they represented a challenge to the Statute's defining object of ending impunity for international crimes.

Conflict

To grasp the ways in which the BIAs conflicted with the Rome Statute, it is important to understand first the scheme of States' obligations under the Statute and under the BIAs. The next two sections will outline, in turn, the obligations under these instruments.

The Rome Statute regime for investigation and prosecution

The Rome Statute is, for the most part, a constitutional document outlining the powers and duties of the Court, its organs and agents. Part IX, however, speaks directly to States parties, providing for obligations to cooperate with, and render judicial assistance to, the ICC. While the language used is of 'cooperation' by States and 'requests' by the Court,

[29] J. Rozenberg, 'Will Bush Invade Cambridgeshire?', *The Telegraph*, 4 September 2002.
[30] See Amnesty International, Letter to the EU Presidency, 30 August 2002, www.amnesty.eu/en/press-releases/human-rights-in-the-eu/police-and-judicial-co-operation/u-s-agreements-violate-international-court-treaty-0075.
[31] Public Law 108–447, 8 December 2004.

the Statute clearly imposes obligations.[32] Indeed, the script slips into the language of compliance at crucial points, such as Article 86 ('States shall . . . cooperate fully'), Article 87 ('the Court shall have the authority to make requests') and Article 89 ('States parties shall . . . comply with requests for arrest and surrender').

Part IX begins, in Article 86, with a general duty of States parties 'in accordance with the provisions of this Statute, [to] cooperate fully with the Court in its investigation and prosecution of crimes within [its] jurisdiction'. The contours of this duty are elaborated in other provisions of the Statute. States are required to cooperate in arrest, provisional arrest,[33] and surrender of persons upon their territory, whether or not nationals;[34] to cooperate with other States in order to effect surrender by allowing transportation of persons through their territory;[35] and to assist in investigation and prosecution, through taking evidence, interrogations, service of documents, execution of searches and seizures, and protection of witnesses.[36] In almost every case, the provision outlining the obligation specifies that parties will comply in accordance with procedures under their national law. However, Article 88 demands that States 'shall ensure that there are procedures available under their national law for all of the forms of cooperation . . . specified under Part [IX]'. Two other provisions also entail changes to national law: Article 70(4) requires States to penalise offences, such as false testimony, bribery and forging evidence, against the ICC's administration of justice by their nationals or on their territory; and Article 109 requires States to give effect to fines or forfeitures ordered as penalties by the ICC.

Even so, and unlike many other international criminal tribunals, the Rome Statute pays high regard to State sovereignty.[37] The Statute prescribes States' obligations as precisely as possible, and provisions in and outside Part IX carefully take into account various situations in which States may be unable to cooperate with ICC requests. Article 90 addresses situations where a State party is faced with competing

[32] For a review of the drafters' discussions on the language to be used in the text of the Rome Statute, see P. Mochochoko, 'International Cooperation and Judicial Assistance', in R. S. Lee (ed.), *The International Criminal Court: The Making of the Rome Statute* (The Hague, Kluwer 1999) 305, 306–10.

[33] Article 92. [34] Article 89(1). [35] Article 89(3). [36] Article 93(1).

[37] For a comparison, see B. Swart, 'International Cooperation and Judicial Assistance: General Problems', in A. Cassese *et al.* (eds.), *The Rome Statute of the International Criminal Court: A Commentary* (Oxford University Press 2002) 1589–1605.

requests for surrender of a person from the ICC and from another State. Article 93 recognises situations where a State cannot execute the ICC's request because prohibited by a fundamental principle of general application. Article 98 limits the ICC from pressing for assistance or surrender when this would require a State to act inconsistently with its obligations under international law, or with 'international agreements pursuant to which the consent of a sending State is required to surrender a person of that State to the Court'. Appendix 4 of this book discusses these provisions in more detail.

The Rome Statute's matrix of obligations and exceptions, consultation procedures and rule of speciality,[38] suggest a real attempt was made to balance sovereignty with the necessary perquisites of an effective international court. Of course, this still left many uncertainties, including that over who decides if a State is justified in not cooperating with the Court – the Court, or the State? Part IX suggests a two-pronged formula: in general, the Court itself may decide whether to pursue a request, taking into account factors like complementarity, that is, a State's exercise of its domestic jurisdiction; however, in some situations a State may exercise discretion. As discussed in Appendix 4, one such situation may be where the State faces a competing request from another State to which it owes a legal duty. Moreover, in some cases, where there is dispute between States on interpretation of the Statute, including the obligation to cooperate, they may approach the ASP to settle the dispute or to recommend a referral to the International Court of Justice.[39]

Other uncertainties that remained related to, among other issues, the factors (apart from trials) that the Court could deem fit to take into account in deciding the admissibility of cases – for instance, would it take note of truth and reconciliation commissions or national amnesties – and what the status of non-parties 'invited' to assist the Court would be.[40] With respect to non-parties, relevant questions included: whether non-parties could demand the application to them of Articles 121(5) and 124 (discussed above) in situations where they would receive the same treatment as parties; and what would be the consequences of non-cooperation

[38] On consultations: Article 97; on postponement: Articles 93(9), 94 & 95; on the rule of speciality: Article 101.

[39] Article 119(b).

[40] For more on this topic, see: G. Nesi, 'The Obligation to Cooperate with the International Criminal Court and States Not Party to the Statute', in M. Politi and G. Nesi (eds.), *The Rome Statute of the International Criminal Court: A Challenge to Impunity* (Aldershot, Ashgate 2001) 221–3.

for States parties and non-parties. As to the last, the Rome Statute provides that, upon a non-party's failure to cooperate, the Court may *inform* the ASP or, where appropriate, the Security Council (Article 87(5)(b)), while, in the case of non-cooperation by a State party, the Court may make a *finding* and *refer* the matter to the ASP and the Security Council (Article 87(7)). Despite the difference in language, neither procedure throws light on the practical implications for the non cooperating State. These matters are left to be addressed by the practice of the Court.

Bilateral immunity agreements

The BIAs set out a comparatively simple scheme of obligations, though this scheme differs slightly depending on whether or not the United States' co-signatory is a party to the Rome Statute.

A sample BIA (see Appendix 5 of this book) contains two, typically reciprocal, obligations.[41] The first obligation states that one State's (State A's) persons, that is, current or former officials, employees including contractors, military persons or nationals, found in the territory of another State (State B) shall not be surrendered to the ICC without State A's express consent. The second obligation states that, when State B transfers State A's person to a third State, State C, it shall not agree to the surrender of that person to the ICC without the consent of State A.

In a few agreements signed with parties to the Rome Statute, these non-surrender obligations are not stated in a reciprocal way, that is, provision is made only for the non-surrender of the United States' persons without its consent. But non-surrender obligations are stated in a reciprocal way in many agreements signed with States party to the Rome Statute.

In BIAs signed with non-parties, there is an additional provision that, subject to their international obligations, States will not knowingly facilitate, consent to, or cooperate with efforts by any third State to surrender or transfer either State's persons to the ICC.[42] This may include disallowing the transport of such persons through their territory.

41 Georgetown Law Library hosts a database of BIAs. A model BIA is included in J. Crawford *et al.*, Joint Opinion in the Matter of the Statute of the International Criminal Court and in the Matter of Bilateral Agreements sought by the United States under Article 98(2) of the Rome Statute, 2003, www.amicc.org/docs/Art98-14une03FINAL.pdf.

42 See, for instance, Agreement between USA and India Regarding the Surrender of Persons to the International Tribunals, 26 December 2002, www.law.georgetown.edu/library/research/guides/upload/India04-115.pdf; Agreement between USA and Nicaragua Regarding the Surrender of Persons to the International Criminal Court,

Several agreements refer to Article 98 (often more specifically Article 98(2)), and pay lip-service to complementarity, providing in their preambles that 'the parties have each expressed their intention to investigate and prosecute where appropriate acts within the jurisdiction of the ICC [committed by their persons]'.[43] This paragraph is absent in some agreements, especially those signed with other non-parties.[44]

Finally, in some agreements the coercive effect of the ASPA is evident: the United States–Colombia BIA, for instance, notes that Colombia can now be exempted from the ASPA's prohibition of military assistance.[45]

Conflict between the Rome Statute and the BIAs

This section will underscore the point made in Chapter 1, that attempts to define when treaty conflicts 'truly' exist may be red herrings because such true/false classifications are often without relevance to the implications of treaty conflicts, particularly for the effective operation of treaty regimes. It will argue, first, that attempts to play down a conflict by claiming there is only a 'divergence' which may be overcome by a harmonious reading of the treaties (a strategy that scholars often support) may only reflect the determination of parties to one of the treaties to restrict the scope of operation of the other. Next, it will show that the above strategy may divert attention from the actual implications of the treaty conflict.

Reconciling the Rome Statute and BIAs

Prima facie, Rome Statute obligations are those of cooperation with the ICC, while BIAs provide obligations of non-cooperation. On this simple

4 June 2003, www.law.georgetown.edu/library/research/guides/upload/Nicaragua03-126.pdf; Agreement between USA and Singapore Regarding the Surrender of Persons to the International Criminal Court, by Exchange of Notes, 17 October 2003, www.law.georgetown.edu/library/research/guides/upload/Singapore03-145.pdf; Agreement between USA and Tunisia Regarding the Surrender of Persons to the International Criminal Court, by Exchange of Notes, 5 June 2003, www.law.georgetown.edu/library/research/guides/upload/Tunisia04-31.pdf.

43 For instance, the USA–India BIA, *ibid.*; USA–Nicaragua BIA, *ibid.*; USA–Singapore BIA, *ibid.*

44 See, for instance, Agreement between USA and Egypt Regarding the Surrender of Persons to the International Criminal Court, 26 February 2003, www.law.georgetown.edu/library/research/guides/upload/Egypt03-33.pdf; and Extension Agreement, 21 February 2007, www.law.georgetown.edu/library/research/guides/upload/Egyptextendingagreement07-58.pdf.

45 Agreement between USA and Colombia Regarding the Surrender of Persons to the International Tribunals, 17 September 2003, www.law.georgetown.edu/library/research/guides/upload/Colombia03-128_000.pdf.

reading, they are not compatible. However, the agreements are not easily reduced to simple sentences: the Statute makes many concessions to non-cooperation, and most BIAs claim the authority of one of these concessions. Article 98(2) provides:

> The Court may not proceed with a request for surrender which would require the requested State to act inconsistently with its obligations under international agreements pursuant to which the consent of a sending State is required to surrender a person of that State to the Court, unless the Court can first obtain the cooperation of the sending State for the giving of consent for the surrender.

ICC personnel are amongst those who downplay the challenge posed by BIAs to the Court. Their stand is that, as BIAs claim to fall under Article 98(2), they must be read in accordance with the scope of this provision, which is to be determined by the Court itself when faced with the question of whether or not to proceed with a request for surrender involving a party to a BIA.[46] So far, the ICC has not faced this question.

While ICC personnel decline to speculate on how the Court might read Article 98(2), commentaries offer varied interpretations, ranging from a highly specific to quite broad remit. Obviously, a specific remit for Article 98(2) offers smaller scope for BIAs to effectively impede cooperation, while a broad remit permits a range of immunity agreements to be effective against ICC requests for surrender.

Some commentators, notably (now ICC judge) Hans-Peter Kaul and Claus Kress, claim that the Rome Statute's drafting history suggests that Article 98(2) primarily covers Status of Forces Agreements (SOFAs) concluded in advance of deployment of national troops in foreign jurisdictions.[47] These SOFAs exclude military personnel and accompanying civilians 'sent' by one State to the other from the jurisdiction of foreign courts, but not that State's nationals making private journeys. However, Article 98(2) does not expressly limit itself to SOFAs; it speaks more broadly of situations in which a State has 'sent' personnel, not necessarily military, to another State. A government-commissioned photographer could be a 'sent' person, much as relief workers or serving staff at diplomatic missions may be.

[46] Interview with an official from the Office of the Prosecutor, 12 April 2010 (on file); Interview with G. Bassu, Special Advisor on External Relations and Cooperation, Office of the Registrar, 8 April 2010 (on file).

[47] H.-P. Kaul and C. Kress, 'Jurisdiction and Cooperation in the Statute of the International Criminal Court: Principles and Compromises' (1999) 2 *Yearbook of International Humanitarian Law* 143, 165.

There is some confusion over whether extradited persons can fall within Article 98(2), that is, whether a State may refuse to transfer persons sent to its jurisdiction by another State. Kaul and Kress suggest the term 'sending State' is not appropriate to describe the extraditing State.[48] However, many extradition agreements do employ the terminology of 'sending State' and 'sent persons'.[49] This may be another issue to be determined by the Court's practice.

In any event, the reference to a 'sending State' in Article 98(2) excludes persons who happen to be in the territory of another State in their private capacity. Thus, BIAs which include the category of nationals who are not officially 'sent' fall outside this provision.

Some commentators also read Article 98(2) as setting out other limiting criteria for BIAs, such as that they may only cover agreements prior to the Rome Statute;[50] that they must include alternative provisions for investigation and trial of persons whose surrender is requested by the ICC; and even that they may not at all cover nationals of States party to the Statute.[51] However, the text of Article 98(2) does not support these criteria.[52]

It is possible that BIAs can also claim the authority of other provisions of the Rome Statute. One such provision may be Article 98(1); indeed, some BIAs do refer to Article '98' rather than '98(2)'. Article 98(1) provides:

> The Court may not proceed with a request for surrender or assistance which would require the requested State to act inconsistently with its obligations under international law with respect to the State or diplomatic immunity of a person or property of a third State ...

This provision may encompass persons who have personal immunity due to their official status. They carry their immunity even on personal

[48] *Ibid.*

[49] Prost and Schlunk claim such agreements are covered by Article 98(2): K. Prost and A. Schlunk, 'Article 98', in O. Triffterer (ed.), *Commentary on the Rome Statute of the International Criminal Court – Observers' Notes Article by Article* (Baden-Baden, Nomos Verlagsgesellschaft 1999) 1131, 1132.

[50] Kaul and Kress, 'Jurisdiction and Cooperation in the Statute of the ICC', 165, claim that this was intended at the time of drafting. Scheffer, 'Staying the Course with the ICC', disagrees.

[51] D. Akande, 'International Law Immunities and the International Criminal Court' (2004) 98 *American Journal of International Law* 407, 428. But, in footnote 134, Akande notes that 'it is more difficult to interpret the wording of Article 98(2) as applying only to agreements concluded by non parties'.

[52] See Crawford *et al.*, Joint Opinion, for a detailed assessment of the scope of Article 98(2) and the compatibility of BIAs with it.

visits, that is, they do not have to be 'sent' persons. Thus, because of the operation of Article 98(1), a State may refuse to surrender persons of another State who are entitled to personal immunity. However, on a narrower reading, Article 98(1) does not recognise personal immunity with respect to persons of States party to the Rome Statute. For, Article 27(2) of the Statute expressly provides that immunities attached to the official capacity of a person cannot bar ICC jurisdiction. This may be taken to suggest that States party to the Statute have waived such immunity for their nationals.[53] Thus, a State requested to surrender a person of a State party to the Statute might be entitled to assume that the ICC's request overrides such individual's personal immunity. On this reading, Article 98(1) is restricted to a State's obligation to respect personal immunity of non-party nationals.

But even narrower readings of Article 98(1) have been suggested: Akande, for instance, has made the argument that personal immunities do not apply to non-parties like Sudan (or Libya) who have been referred to the Court by the UN Security Council, for the effect of such a referral is to make the Rome Statute binding upon them.[54] Most recently, the Court itself has adopted a reading that all but dispenses with Article 98(1), finding that

> the principle in international law is that immunity of either former or sitting Heads of State can not be invoked to oppose a prosecution by an international court . . .[55] [C]ustomary international law creates an exception to Head of State immunity when international courts seek a Head of State's arrest for the commission of international crimes.[56]

[53] Akande, 'International Law Immunities and the ICC', 419–28.

[54] D. Akande, 'The Legal Nature of Security Council Referrals to the ICC and its Impact on al Bashir's Immunities' (2009) 7(2) *Journal of International Criminal Justice* 333; see also P. Gaeta, 'Does President al Bashir enjoy Immunity from Arrest?' (2009) 7(2) *Journal of International Criminal Justice* 315; R. Rastan, 'The Emerging Jurisprudence of the International Criminal Court – Legal Issues Arising from the First Case Law', in Ling Yan (ed.), *Making Peace through Justice: Essays on the New Development of International Criminal Law* (Beijing, World Affairs Press 2009) Chapter 2.

[55] See *Prosecutor* v. *Omar Hassan Ahmed al-Bashir*, Decision on the Failure by the Republic of Malawi to Comply with the Cooperation Requests Issued by the Court (PTC), ICC-02/05-1/09, 12 December 2011, 17–18, para. 36; *Prosecutor* v. *Omar Hassan Ahmed al-Bashir*, Décision concernant le refus de la République du Tchad d'accéder aux demandes de coopération délivrées par la Cour (PTC), ICC-02/05-1/09, 13 December 2011, 7, para. 13.

[56] *Ibid.* (Malawi), 20, para. 43.

This is an exaggerated view of the sweep of international courts' jurisdiction,[57] but indicates that Article 98(1) may not assist in reconciling the BIAs and the Rome Statute.

In limited circumstances, Article 90 may be a more relevant provision, in a practical sense. It suggests that a State may give primacy to extradition agreements signed with a non-party where such non-party has put forward a competing extradition request; but, if the competing request is from a party to the Rome Statute, the ICC's request must get priority. Article 90 gives effect to BIAs that favour extradition from Rome Statute parties to non-parties under two conditions: first, the non-party should have requested extradition (though perhaps it *may* be acceptable for a BIA to provide that such request be 'deemed' in the event of a request by the ICC); and, second, the non-party should have undertaken to investigate and prosecute the extradited persons. This follows because Article 90 only comes into play where there are competing requests for the surrender of a person for the same crime.

In any event, it is possible to read the BIAs in a manner compatible with the Rome Statute by giving either a narrow reading to their provisions, or a broad reading to Article 98(2): we saw that, for most commentators, BIAs are more compatible when less effective – that is, when they cover a limited category of persons. But the language used in the BIAs themselves seeks to exclude all manner of persons, including all nationals of signatory States, from the jurisdiction of the Rome Statute. A 'harmonious' reading is thus only shorthand for crystallising a limited remit for one or the other treaty involved in this conflict.

Conflict in context

The text of the BIAs, together with the manner in which they were concluded, clarify that they were intended to fulfil practical as well as symbolic purposes. Their practical purpose was to guard against the surrender of US nationals (and 'sent' persons) to the ICC, but it may be noted that BIAs are superfluous to this purpose. Not only could the Court simply take a narrow view of Article 98(2) (like it has taken of article 98(1)), but also, the principle of complementarity makes it unlikely that the ICC would ever actually assert jurisdiction over US nationals. For, under the complementarity principle, the Court

[57] On which point, see also D. Akande, 'ICC Issues Detailed Decision on Bashir's Immunity (. . . at Long Last . . .) But Gets the Law Wrong', *European Journal of International Law: Talk!*, 15 December 2011.

concedes primary jurisdiction to States willing and able to investigate and prosecute international crimes. Even so, from the date of adoption of the Statute, the United States chose to consider its persons vulnerable to malicious prosecution by the ICC – and its BIAs were the symbol of its dissatisfaction with the Court. Through the BIAs, the United States expressed doubts about the autonomy of the ICC organs, and about the ICC's credibility as a judicial institution. The spirit that animated the BIAs was one that denied legitimacy to the Court, and this could hardly be addressed by 'harmonious' readings of these treaties and the Rome Statute.

Commentators consider SOFAs as reconcilable in spirit with the Rome Statute because their focus is not on restricting the ICC's access to alleged criminals, but on determining which State would have the right to primary exercise of jurisdiction. In 2002, the European Union suggested that the BIAs should incorporate elements which would also reflect a similar purpose, by including 'appropriate operative provisions ensuring that persons who have committed crimes falling within the jurisdiction of the Court do not enjoy impunity'. It further noted that '[s]uch provisions should ensure appropriate investigation and – where there is sufficient evidence – prosecution by national jurisdictions concerning persons requested by the ICC ... [and moreover] should only cover persons who are not nationals of an ICC State Party'.[58]

Most BIAs, however, pay little or no attention to combating impunity (and reciprocal ones may extend this disregard to nationals of State parties). At the most, some BIAs concluded between the United States and States parties to the Rome Statute carry the preambular statement that 'the parties have each expressed their intention to investigate and prosecute where appropriate acts within [ICC jurisdiction ... committed by their persons]'.[59] This is merely an abstract statement of intent, not equivalent to 'operative provisions ensuring that persons who have committed crimes falling within the jurisdiction of the Court do not enjoy impunity'. The statement falls far short of what should be the standard – reference to concrete processes for investigation and prosecution by the State.[60]

[58] See EU Guiding Principles concerning Arrangements between a State Party to the Rome Statute and the United States Regarding the Conditions to Surrender of Persons to the Court, 2002.

[59] For instance, the Agreement between USA and Nicaragua, 4 June 2003.

[60] On this, see Crawford *et al.*, Joint Opinion, 21–3.

Consider the message implicit in the omission of such credible assurances against impunity. The ICC is the progeny of a repeatedly aborted, decades-old effort. Even in 1992, the International Law Commission, commissioned to prepare a draft Statute, could not envisage that States would be ready to establish anything more intrusive upon their sovereignty than a procedural surrogate for national, or *ad hoc* international, systems of criminal justice.[61] The Statute as finally adopted, bringing into existence 'an essentially autonomous international criminal justice system, with its own institutions and rules, essentially distinct from national systems and dependent on them only for cooperation and enforcement',[62] was a resounding triumph of multilateralism. Contrary to past practice of selective and *ex post facto* establishment of criminal tribunals, the ICC could exercise jurisdiction generally (once universally ratified) and upon its own prerogative. But the BIAs stood in opposition to this very advance; indeed, in seeking to shield persons from the Court's reach without offering alternatives, the BIAs seemed to imply that the Court – rather than impunity – was the real villain to be resisted.

Despite their (ironic!) reference to Article 98, the BIAs were an outright challenge to the ICC's credibility, and to the integrity of the Rome Statute as its constitutional document. And apparently – if we disregard the frequently coercive process through which BIAs were concluded and look only at their sheer numbers – many States shared the United States' view. Indeed, coercion alone cannot satisfactorily explain why some States concluded reciprocal BIAs, that is, BIAs stipulating that their persons, too, should not be surrendered to the Court. Perhaps the United States may have preferred reciprocal agreements as a further symbolic reflection of the doubts about the Court's credibility, but there is no evidence that it actually pressured States to this end. The ASPA, and other US domestic legislation, did not require reciprocal BIAs. Moreover, the United States signed non-reciprocal BIAs with several States similarly threatened by the ASPA,[63] both before and after it concluded reciprocal BIAs. Perhaps, then, some States may have demanded reciprocal terms as a means of asserting formal equality with the United States? But, given the coercive context in which many States concluded these agreements (occasionally despite their Rome

[61] Crawford, 'The Drafting of the Rome Statute', 145. [62] *Ibid.*, 136.

[63] Agreement between USA and Colombia, 17 September 2003; Agreement between USA and Swaziland Regarding the Surrender of Persons to the International Criminal Court, 10 May 2006, www.law.georgetown.edu/library/research/guides/upload/Swaziland06-253.pdf.

Statute obligations[64]), an assertion of formal equality in the form of reciprocal terms, rather than a salutary reaffirmation of ICC membership symbolised by non-reciprocal terms, seems a curious choice.

The Court in its infancy was hardly more robust than the 'delicate mosaic' of the shared heritage of peoples that it hoped to support.[65] The possibility of its failure was a foreseeable one.[66] Though the impact of BIAs should not be overstated given that they were opposed by several States, including most of the United States' NATO allies, they did contribute to this concern. They offered a legal basis for States to refuse cooperation with the Court. Reciprocal BIAs, in particular, seemed to portend that the Court would have difficulty in achieving an active docket – which put pressure upon the Court to obtain its first referral. As this chapter will show, this consideration influenced the OTP's early policy choices.

Practical relevance of the conflict

ICC personnel point out that BIAs have never been invoked in practice as a basis for non-cooperation with the Court. They also argue that, if a situation involving a BIA did arise, it would not limit the obligations to cooperate of States parties to the Rome Statute.[67] But, so far, the OTP has not taken up any situation in which it may have to investigate US nationals or 'sent' persons, and no requests have been made to the United States for surrender of nationals or 'sent' persons of any other State that has signed a reciprocal BIA with it.

Afghanistan, under preliminary examination by the OTP, opens up this prospect, since Afghanistan has been a party to the Rome Statute since 2003 and a United States–Afghanistan BIA has been in existence since 2002. However, Afghanistan has remained under preliminary examination for more than seven years. Having received more than

[64] For instance, Agreement between USA and Panama Regarding the Surrender of Persons to the International Criminal Court, 23 June 2003, www.law.georgetown.edu/library/research/guides/upload/Panama04-4_000.pdf. Panama ratified the Rome Statute on 21 March 2002.

[65] Preamble, recital 1, Rome Statute.

[66] Interview with W. Schabas, 26 March 2009, http://iccobservers.files.wordpress.com/2009/03/schabas_interview_official.pdf; Interview with T. Ginsburg, 15 March 2009, http://iccobservers.files.wordpress.com/2009/03/icc_observers_ginsburg_interview.pdf; Interview with N. Grono, Deputy President, International Crisis Group, 6 March 2009, http://iccobservers.files.wordpress.com/2009/03/icc_observers_nick_grono_interview1.pdf.

[67] Bassu, personal interview (on file).

ninety-two communications on the situation in Afghanistan between 1 June 2006 and 1 June 2013, the OTP merely expects to reach a determination in 'the near future'. An interview with the legal advisor to the Coalition for the ICC (CICC) clarified that the OTP has been impeded by limited cooperation from Afghanistan's government: it has received no information on crimes allegedly committed by the US-led forces, but has received information about crimes allegedly committed by the Taliban.[68]

Meanwhile, the United States' policy on BIAs has changed, symbolising a change of attitude towards the ICC: it no longer seeks to conclude BIAs. Indeed, its efforts have been in decline since mid-2005 – a majority of the 102 BIAs were concluded before May 2005. Between May 2005 and December 2006, only two BIAs were concluded, and no fresh agreements have been concluded since this date (though the BIA with Egypt was extended in 2007). From 2005 onwards, the United States also issued waivers exempting States which had not concluded BIAs from sanctions under the ASPA and the Nethercutt Amendment. These statutes have also been modified to limit or abrogate their prohibitions.[69]

However, the United States has not officially abandoned its BIAs – in the words of the US Ambassador for War Crimes Issues, the change in approach has been 'quiet', with '[n]o statement that policy was changing, and certainly no admission that the initial approach to the ICC was in any way wrong'.[70] Thus, there is no uniform understanding of the legal or political significance of BIAs. During research, anonymous sources related anecdotes to illustrate the lingering impact of BIAs upon States' attitudes. Bangladesh, in submitting its ratification of the Rome Statute in March 2010, was apprehensive about the impact on its relationship with the United States; the Philippines delayed its ratification (completed in August 2011) assuming that the BIAs reflected the continued hostility of the United States to the Court. Moreover, in one particularly strange instance, much after mid-2005, a US representative, unaware that a policy shift had taken place within the US Administration, was discovered to be pressuring an unnamed State to conclude a BIA.

[68] Interview with S. Pal, Legal Advisor, Coalition for the International Criminal Court, 14 April 2010 (on file).

[69] See Report of the ASIL Taskforce, 13.

[70] C. Williamson, US Ambassador at Large for War Crimes Issues, Remarks at the Century Foundation on 'Reassessing the International Criminal Court: Ten Years Past', Rome, 13 January 2009.

The Court in practice, 2002–10

By the time of the Review Conference of June 2010, the Court was quite swamped with work. It had received four referrals (all between December 2003 and March 2005). Three of these were self-referrals by Uganda, the Democratic Republic of the Congo (DRC) and the Central African Republic (CAR). These referrals were an innovative application of Article 14 of the Rome Statute, which was commonly understood to suggest that States could refer situations in *other* States.[71] Moreover, each of the three States had earlier concluded reciprocal BIAs with the United States. The Security Council made the fourth referral, of the situation in Darfur, Sudan. Only a few weeks before the Review Conference, in March 2010, the OTP opened its fifth investigation, in Kenya, by exercise of its *proprio motu* power.

Since then, the OTP has also opened investigations into Libya (by referral from the Security Council, in February 2011), Côte D'Ivoire (by exercise of its *proprio motu* power, in October 2011) and Mali (by self-referral, in July 2012). Most recently, on 14 May 2013, the OTP received a referral from the Comoros, relating to Israel's raid on the *MV Mavi Marmara*, a ship registered in the Comoros, which was part of the 'Freedom Flotilla' sent to Gaza in May 2010. The referral also mentions attacks on two other vessels that were registered in Greece and Cambodia, both, like the Comoros, parties to the Rome Statute. The OTP has not yet determined whether it will open an investigation into this situation.

The OTP has also received communications relating to other situations. It has dealt with some of these: by the time of the Review Conference, it had rejected communications on Iraq and Venezuela. In April 2012, it rejected opening an investigation in Palestine on the basis that it was not a State. According to the Court's website, the OTP is currently reviewing situations in Colombia, Georgia, Guinea and Nigeria (for admissibility), and Afghanistan, Honduras and South Korea (for subject-matter jurisdiction).[72]

This section briefly reviews the developments concerning the first four situations, which were substantially investigated before the Review

[71] See J. Kleffner, 'Auto-Referrals and the Complementary Nature of the ICC', in C. Stahn and G. Sluiter (eds.), *The Emerging Practice of the International Criminal Court* (Leiden, Martinus Nijhoff 2009) 41–53.

[72] Office of the Prosecutor, Report on Preliminary Examination Activities 2013, November 2013, http://www.icc-cpi.int/en_menus/icc/press%20and%20media/press%20releases/Documents/OTP%20Preliminary%20Examinations/OTP%20-%20Report%20%20Preliminary%20Examination%20Activities%202013.PDF.

Conference. The discussion in the following section will also address some of the other situations.

Self-referrals by Uganda, the DRC and the CAR

Uganda

Uganda ratified the Rome Statute on 14 June 2002. On 12 June 2003, it signed a reciprocal BIA with the United States. The BIA was ratified on 23 October 2003, and was to remain in force for one year after either party notified its intention to terminate. Uganda's decision to sign the BIA was clearly due to the ASPA's coercive influence: just days after Uganda's signature, on 1 July 2003, the United States issued a six-month ASPA waiver for Uganda.[73] The waiver was indefinitely extended on 1 November 2003, following ratification of the BIA.

The European Union termed Uganda's decision to sign a BIA a 'regrettable' action weakening the ICC.[74] Yet, only a few months later, on 16 December 2003, Uganda provided the ICC with its first referral – that is, its first opportunity to become operational. In this sense, Uganda's self-referral was an early triumph for the Court. However, it was soon perceived as a qualified triumph, for the terms of the referral and the position later taken by the Ugandan government both suggested that Uganda took a wholly instrumental view of the Court.

The text of Uganda's referral only mentioned ICC investigation and prosecution of the leaders of the Lord's Resistance Army (LRA), a rebel group engaged in guerrilla warfare against the government, particularly in northern Uganda.[75] The LRA, led by Joseph Kony, has allegedly committed international crimes including the abduction of children for use as soldiers and sex slaves. The organisation's leadership is thought to be limited to only a few individuals, with the cadres made up of child-soldiers.[76] The referral excluded the cadres, who were included within a

[73] Summary Information on BIAs, 2006, www.iccnow.org/documents/BIAdb_Current.pdf.

[74] *Ibid.* See also EU Presidency, Declaration by the EU on the Position of the US Towards the International Criminal Court, 13 May 2002, para. 5, www.amicc.org/docs/EUdec5_13_02.pdf.

[75] 'President of Uganda Refers Situation Concerning the Lord's Resistance Army to the ICC', ICC-20040129-44, www.icc-cpi.int/Menus/ICC/Situations+and+Cases/Situations/Situation+ICC+0204.

[76] P. Akhavan, 'The Lord's Resistance Army Case: Uganda's Submission of the First State Referral to the International Criminal Court' (2005) 99 *American Journal of International Law* 403.

national amnesty law.[77] Problematically, the referral also seemed to exclude Uganda's national army, the Ugandan People's Defense Forces (UPDF), which too has allegedly committed war crimes and crimes against humanity. In mentioning only the LRA, the government appeared to be attempting to harness the ICC's might against its political opponents. In a testimony to the power of appearances in the evaluation of justice (recalling the famous principle of natural justice that 'justice must be *seen to be done*'), this perception was exacerbated by a photograph of Prosecutor Luis Moreno-Ocampo's smiling handshake with Ugandan President Yoweri Museveni as he submitted the self-referral.[78]

In fairness, the OTP immediately clarified that any referral must concern an entire 'situation' and not just a few actors. It informed the Ugandan government that the Prosecutor would reinterpret the referral to include the UPDF, and relied on a BBC interview of Museveni[79] and on a government report to the Ugandan Parliament,[80] for the understanding that this reinterpretation was accepted by Uganda.

Indeed, too much should not be made of the referral's wording: it is understandable that a government will be reluctant to appear to accuse its army and, as Payam Akhavan notes, it is a reasonable inference that Uganda understood that the referral, whatever its wording, would expose the army to the OTP's scrutiny.[81]

However, the OTP's practice itself has been more problematic: even as it clarified that it would conduct an impartial investigation, it only sought arrest warrants against five LRA leaders and declared the UPDF's crimes as not of comparable gravity.[82] As William Schabas observes,

77 Uganda Amnesty Act 2000, www.c-r.org/our-work/accord/northern-uganda/documents/2000_Jan_The_Amnesty_Act.doc.

78 'Forgotten Voices: A Population-Based Survey of Attitudes about Peace and Justice in Northern Uganda', International Centre for Transitional Justice, New York and Human Rights Centre, University of California at Berkeley, July 2005, www.ictj.org/images/content/1/2/127.pdf.

79 Prosecutor (L. Moreno-Ocampo), Remarks at the 27th Meeting of the Committee of Legal Advisers on Public International Law (Cadhi), Strasburg, 18–19 March 2004, www.iccnow.org/documents/ICCProsecutor/CADHI18Mar04.pdf (quoting Museveni: 'I am ready to be investigated for war crimes ... [I]f any of our people were involved in any crimes, we will give him up to be tried by the ICC ... [I]n any case, if such cases are brought to our attention, we will try them ourselves.').

80 Prosecutor (L. Moreno-Ocampo), Statement on Uganda Arrest Warrants, 14 October 2005, www.icc-cpi.int/NR/rdonlyres/AF169689-AFC941B9-8A3E-222F07DA42AD/143834/LMO_20051014_English1.pdf.

81 Akhavan, 'The Lord's Resistance Army Case', 411.

82 Prosecutor, Statement on Uganda Arrest Warrants, 2005, 3.

most people 'would find it far more threatening that the government is committing crimes, even if the outlaws commit more, because outlaws are supposed to commit crimes and governments aren't'.[83] The OTP's justification to exclude the UPDF thus does not persuade.

A second controversy followed Uganda's attempt to withdraw its referral. Initially, following the referral, the LRA leaders agreed to negotiate with the government, to cease hostilities and to submit to domestic trials, if exempted from ICC investigation and trial.[84] The Ugandan government accordingly claimed it would withdraw its referral and try LRA leaders in its national courts or through traditional justice mechanisms.

The Rome Statute does not provide for withdrawals and the OTP discouraged Uganda from taking this route. It suggested that the LRA could instead bring an admissibility challenge on the ground of complementarity before the PTC.[85] In one report, the OTP noted that there would always be interplay between the ICC processes and local conflict-resolution initiatives including local justice mechanisms, but, 'in order to preserve its impartiality, [the OTP] cannot be a component of these initiatives'.[86] Prosecutor Moreno-Ocampo stated that the only concession made to Uganda was the OTP pursuing its investigations in a low-key way so as to not interfere with the peace process.[87]

In 2008, in a PTC-initiated admissibility review, the LRA's defence did make a challenge based on Uganda's domestic process. The PTC however ruled that the cases were admissible;[88] which was confirmed by the Appeals Chamber.[89] By this time, the government had failed to

83 Schabas, ICC Observers Project Interview.

84 K. P. Apuuli, 'The ICC's Possible Deferral of the LRA Case to Uganda' (2008) 6 *Journal of International Criminal Justice* 801; Human Rights Watch, 'Benchmarks for Justice for Serious Crimes in Northern Uganda', Memoranda on Justice Standards and the Juba Peace Talks, May 2007–February 2008, www.hrw.org/legacy/pub/2008/ij/uganda_memos_cover.pdf.

85 Office of the Prosecutor, Statement on Uganda, The Hague, 4 March 2008, www.icc-cpi.int/NR/rdonlyres/945119F8-7107-4FC1-8026-CD03ECCA5BB1/0/ICCOTPST20080304ENG.pdf.

86 Office of the Prosecutor, Report on the Activities Performed in the First Three Years (June 2003–June 2006), 12 September 2006, para. 32.

87 Prosecutor (L. Moreno-Ocampo), 'Keynote Address: Integrating the Work of the ICC into Local Justice Initiatives' (2006) 21 *American University International Law Review* 497, 499.

88 *Prosecutor* v. *Kony, Otti, Odhiambo, Ongwen*, Decision (PTC), ICC-02/04-1/05, 10 March 2009.

89 *Prosecutor* v. *Kony et al.*, Judgment (Appeals), ICC-02/04-1/05 OA 3, 16 September 2009.

arrive at a settlement with the LRA – Kony did not show up at the meetings organised – and again took the position that the five LRA leaders should be tried by the ICC.[90]

In March 2010, galvanised by the fact that it was to host the Rome Statute Review Conference within a few weeks,[91] Uganda passed the International Criminal Court Act to give force to the Rome Statute.[92] The Act incorporates international crimes into domestic law and provides for cooperation with the ICC. Amongst other penalties is a prison sentence of up to seven years for 'conspiracy to defeat justice in ICC'.[93] The Act also contains a number of provisions instructing the government on the procedures for responding to requests for cooperation and surrender of persons issued by the Court.[94] The Act does not, however, operate retroactively: the first LRA member to be tried under Uganda's newly established International Crimes Division was not charged under the Act.[95]

Some commentators have argued that Uganda's self-referral was a brilliant strategic move on the part of its government.[96] For, prior to the referral, the government had been unable to engage the LRA leaders in constructive dialogue. Though Uganda had a functioning judicial system, it seemed that it could only achieve a breakthrough with LRA leaders by granting them amnesty and other concessions. The referral dramatically altered the government's bargaining position. The Court's warrants against Kony and others possibly motivated them to engage with the government on altered terms.

Uganda's efforts to withdraw its referral were equally strategic, but to some, such as Goldstone, they were 'fatally damaging to the credibility of the Court'.[97] This claim may appear mystifying: after all, the Rome Statute seeks to prevent impunity, not secure the primacy of the ICC's

[90] Registrar, Report on the Execution of the Request to the Republic of Uganda for Observations on the Initiation of Proceedings pursuant to Article 19 of the Rome Statute, Annex 2, ICC-02/04-1/05-354-Anx2, 18 November 2008, www.icc-cpi.int/iccdocs/doc/doc589480.PDF.

[91] See S. Nouwen, *Complementarity in the Line of Fire: The Catalysing Effect of the International Criminal Court in Uganda and Sudan* (Cambridge University Press 2013) 198. Nouwen also offers a detailed analysis of the Court's impact on Uganda's domestic justice processes (141–233).

[92] Act 11 of 2010, *Uganda Gazette*, No. 39, Vol. 103, 25 June 2010.

[93] Section 15, ICC Act. [94] Parts III–VI, ICC Act.

[95] Nouwen, *Complementarity in the Line of Fire*, 205–6.

[96] For instance, Akhavan, 'The Lord's Resistance Army Case', 416.

[97] Per R. Goldstone: see C. McGreal, 'Museveni Refuses to Hand Over Rebel Leaders to the War Crimes Court', *Guardian*, 13 March 2008.

jurisdiction, and Uganda's efforts to prosecute LRA leaders would seem to be in keeping with the concept of complementarity. But, as Michael Reisman and Mahnoush Arsanjani point out, the overall manner of Uganda's engagement – first the terms of its initial referral, then its attempts at withdrawal – lent weight to the perception that it was able to use the Court as a political instrument. Uganda showed little respect for the ICC's process, and disregarded the OTP's human and financial investment in preparing for trial.[98] Moreover, Prosecutor Moreno-Ocampo noted that Uganda also represented the ICC's involvement as destroying its chances of peace.[99] Indeed, going by the PTC's decision on the admissibility of the Uganda cases, it seemed that Uganda sought a withdrawal without even providing adequate alternative mechanisms for domestic justice.[100]

Whatever the merits of the view that Uganda made instrumental use of the Court, the perception of the Court's political vulnerability was perhaps burnished by the OTP's and PTC's resistance to Uganda's attempts to withdraw the case – the Court seemed to demonstrate more concern than was justified at the prospect of letting go of the first situation that had come to its hand. We see a similar insistence on keeping hold of a case *vis-à-vis* the situation in the DRC.

The DRC and the CAR

The DRC ratified the Rome Statute on 11 April 2002; and signed a reciprocal BIA on 18 March 2003, which entered into force on 22 July 2003. As with Uganda, the ASPA's influence was apparent.[101] On 19 April 2004, the DRC referred all international crimes committed on its territory to the ICC.[102] To date, the OTP has selected 6 cases, with mixed outcomes. Two of these, against Thomas Lubanga Dyilo and Mathieu Ngudjolo

[98] M. Arsanjani and M. Reisman, 'The Law-in-Action of the International Criminal Court' (2005) 99 *American Journal of International Law* 385.

[99] Prosecutor, 'Keynote Address: Integrating the Work of the ICC into Local Justice Initiatives' (2006) 21 *American University International Law Review* 497, 499. See also J. Amutuhaire, 'Uganda: ICC Urged to Support Local Justice to Promote Peace', Communicating Justice, BBC World Service, 23 April 2008.

[100] *Prosecutor* v. *Kony et al.*, Decision (PTC), ICC-02/04-1/05, para. 52.

[101] The United States waived ASPA on 1 July 2003 until 1 November, 2003. It extended the waiver on 24 September 2003 as the BIA had come into force: Summary Information on BIAs, 2006.

[102] 'Prosecutor Receives Referral of the Situation in the DRC', ICC Press Release, ICC-OTP-20040419-50, www.icc-cpi.int/Menus/ICC/Situations+and+Cases/Situations/Situation+ICC+0104.

Chui have been completed, with the former convicted and the latter acquitted. The trial proceedings have concluded in a third case, against Germain Katanga, while the PTC has declined to confirm the charges in the fourth, against Callixite Mbarushimana. The final two cases, against Bosco Ntaganda and Sylvestre Mudacumura are ongoing. Ntaganda has been surrendered to the Court; the warrant against Mudacumura, the alleged leader of the Forces Démocratiques pour la Libération du Rwanda, remains outstanding. Lubanga was accused of conscripting child soldiers; the others, in addition (except Mudacumura who is not accused of conscripting child soldiers), of various other war crimes and crimes against humanity including directing attacks against civilians, destroying property and sexual violence.

The *Lubanga* case was the first to go under trial at the ICC. This case has led to much criticism of the OTP, particularly of Prosecutor Moreno-Ocampo. The criticism was initially triggered by his decision to focus only on the recruitment of child soldiers to the exclusion of other crimes.[103] More criticism followed from how he handled evidence in this case, particularly his refusal to disclose potentially exculpatory material to the defence, by relying upon provisions of the Rome Statute and of the Rules of Procedure and Evidence that allow refusal of such disclosure under certain circumstances. One commentator noted that, in doing so, the Prosecutor invoked exceptional grounds in a routine situation, denying Lubanga the right to a fair trial.[104] In the event, the Trial Chamber,[105] confirmed by the Appeals Chamber,[106] decided that the defendant must receive all exculpatory material, and stayed the trial to allow the defence to review this material.[107] Subsequently, the Prosecutor represented this episode as proof that the Court would ensure due process even at the cost of delaying its

[103] For instance, 'Statement on the Prosecutions by the International Criminal Court', by Women's Rights and Human Rights NGOs from the DRC, Beni, 16 September 2006, www.iccwomen.org/publications/resources/docs/statements_by_womans_rights_human_rights_ngos.pdf.

[104] H. Stuart, 'The ICC in Trouble' (2008) 6 *Journal of International Criminal Justice* 409, 411.

[105] *Prosecutor* v. *Lubanga*, Decision on Consequences of Non-Disclosure of Exculpatory Materials (Trial Chamber), ICC-01/04-01/06, 13 June 2008.

[106] *Prosecutor* v. *Lubanga*, Judgment on Appeal by Prosecutor against Trial Chamber Decision (Appeals), ICC-01/04-01/06 OA 13, 21 October 2008.

[107] *Prosecutor* v. *Lubanga*, ICC-01/04-01/06, Status Conference Transcript, 18 November 2008, 3–4.

objective of the expedient conclusion of its first few trials.[108] The trial began on 26 January 2009; Lubanga was convicted on 14 March 2012 and sentenced to fourteen years of imprisonment in July 2012. Since the time Lubanga spent in the custody of the ICC is to be deducted from the total period, Lubanga's effective imprisonment will continue up to July 2020.

The CAR ratified the Rome Statute on 3 October 2001. On 13 January 2004 it signed a reciprocal BIA, in circumstances suggestive of coercion by the ASPA.[109] On 22 December 2004, it made a self-referral to the Court for international crimes committed anywhere on its territory.[110] The OTP decided to open investigation in May 2007. In June 2009, the PTC confirmed charges against Jean Pierre Bemba Gombo, the alleged president and commander-in-chief of the Mouvement de Libération du Congo, for war crimes and crimes against humanity, in particular murder, pillaging and sexual violence committed by forces under his control.[111] Bemba's trial began in November 2010. In November 2013, the Court issued arrest warrants against four of Bemba's lawyers and associates, charging them with offences against the administration of justice, including falsifying evidence and corrupting witnesses in the *Bemba* case.[112] All four have been arrested, and three have made their first appearances before the Court.[113]

108 Prosecutor (L. Moreno-Ocampo), Address, Council for Foreign Relations, Washington DC, 4 February 2010, www.icc-cpi.int/NR/rdonlyres/A80CDDDD-8A9A-432E-97CE-F6EAD700B5AE/281527/100204ProsecutorsspeechforCFR.pdf; see also S. Anoushirvani, 'The Future of the International Criminal Court: The Long Road to Legitimacy begins with the Trial of Thomas Lubanga Dyilo' (2010) 22 *Pace International Law Review* 213.

109 On 1 July 2003, the United States declared CAR ineligible for military assistance. In 2004, it reportedly suspended aid of US$150,000. Following the BIA, the United States exempted CAR from the prohibition on military assistance while its BIA was in force. Summary Information on BIAs, 2006.

110 'Prosecutor Receives Referral Concerning CAR', ICC Press Release, ICC-OTP-20050107-86, www.icc-cpi.int/Menus/ICC/Situations+and+Cases/Situations/Situation+ICC+0105.

111 *Prosecutor* v. *Jean Pierre Bemba Gombo*, Decision on Charges (PTC), ICC-01/05-01/08, 15 June 2009.

112 *Prosecutor* v. *Jean-Pierre Bemba Gombo, Aimé Kilolo Musamba, Jean-Jacques Mangenda Kabongo, Fidèle Babala Wandu and Narcisse Arido*, Warrants of Arrest (PTC), ICC-01/05-01/13, 20 November 2013.

113 'Jean-Jacques Mangenda Kabongo Makes First Appearance Before ICC', ICC Press Release, ICC-CPI-20131205-PR969, 5 December 2013, www.icc-cpi.int/en_menus/icc/press%20and%20media/press%20releases/Pages/pr969.aspx; 'Aimé Kilolo Musamba, Fidèle Babala Wandu, and Jean-Pierre Bemba Gombo make first appearance before ICC', ICC Press Release, ICC-CPI-20131127-PR966, 27 November 2013, www.icc-cpi.int/en_menus/icc/press%20and%20media/press%20releases/Pages/966.aspx.

Significance of these referrals

None of these self-referrals directly implicated these States' obligations under their BIAs with the United States. However, they did have significance *vis-à-vis* the symbolic challenge that the BIAs posed to the ICC. The previous section referred to the different connotations of reciprocal and non-reciprocal BIAs as to their signatories' attitudes towards the Court; and these three States had signed reciprocal agreements, all of which were book-ended by non-reciprocal agreements signed by other States. If their decision to sign reciprocal BIAs signalled a denial of the ICC's credibility, their referrals seemed to be conduct reaffirming the ICC's legitimacy (which indeed explains the Court's tenacity in holding on to the cases arising from these referrals). If the United States was perceived as seeking to prevent the ICC from becoming fully operational, these referrals gave the ICC the chance to commence its work. However, as this chapter will discuss, the OTP made several missteps in its handling of these referrals.

Sudan's referral by the Security Council and a shift in US policy

The UN Security Council referred the situation in Darfur, Sudan, to the ICC on 31 March 2005, via Resolution 1593. The Resolution was supported by eleven States including the United Kingdom, France and Russia, while China, the United States, Brazil and Algeria abstained.[114]

The referral was encouraged by the International Commission of Inquiry that had been established in September 2004 by the Security Council in order to investigate whether crimes of genocide had occurred in Darfur.[115] The Commission's Report noted the failure of the Sudanese justice system to investigate and prosecute the crime. It also considered alternative mechanisms, like an *ad hoc* tribunal or mixed court, 'inadvisable'. Even so, for a time the United States lobbied the Security Council to create a 'Sudan tribunal' jointly with the African Union,[116] but it could not convince other Council members. Finally, following the drafting of a Resolution that accommodated its concerns, the United States withdrew its opposition to the referral.

[114] UN Press Release SC/8351, 31 March 2005, www.un.org/News/Press/docs/2005/sc8351.doc.htm.

[115] Report of the International Commission of Inquiry on Darfur, 25 January 2005, 146–8, www.un.org/news/dh/sudan/com_inq_darfur.pdf. The Commission was established by UNSC Res. 1564 (18 September 2004).

[116] J. Cerone, 'Dynamic Equilibrium: The Evolution of US Attitudes towards International Courts and Tribunals' (2007) 18 *European Journal of International Law* 277, 300.

Resolution 1593 is a messy compromise. It empowers the Prosecutor to investigate crimes in Sudan – a non-party – and calls on the Sudanese government to cooperate fully with the investigation, but in the same sentence asserts that States not party to the Rome Statute have no obligation under it. This odd textual juxtaposition is meant to reaffirm that the United States, China and other non-parties remain outside the Court's jurisdiction. The Resolution 'invites' the African Union to discuss practical arrangements with the ICC, but at the same time bars financial contributions from the United Nations. Moreover, even though it gives the Prosecutor the mandate to investigate the entire 'situation in Darfur', it 'decides' that all persons (nationals, current or former officials and personnel) belonging to any non-party State and participating in operations authorised by the Security Council or the African Union will be subject to the exclusive jurisdiction of that State.

Finally, the preamble to the Resolution '[t]ake[s] note of the existence of agreements referred to in Article 98–2 of the Rome Statute'. This statement seems superfluous: Sudan itself has not signed a BIA, and the Resolution does not, as such, mandate cooperation from other States. Even if the Resolution did mandate cooperation from other States, merely taking note of Article 98(2) would not limit its operation – the Resolution does not say that cooperation with the ICC must be *subject to* Article 98(2). Indeed, the phrase 'takes note' was probably agreed upon because the statement in question was recognised to have no practical implications in the Darfur context: speaking during the explanation of votes on the Resolution, the Danish delegate claimed that the reference to Article 98(2) was purely factual.[117]

The United States offered a lengthy explanation of its vote (to abstain),[118] emphasising that it 'continued to fundamentally object to the view that the Court should be able to exercise jurisdiction over the nationals, including government officials, of States not party to the Rome Statute'. The provision exempting persons of non-party States in the Sudan from the ICC prosecution was included at the United States' behest; the United States was particularly concerned for personnel sent on peacekeeping and humanitarian missions. Moreover, going beyond the ambit of the Resolution (and contrary to the Rome Statute), it argued that '[i]n the future ... absent consent of the State involved, any

[117] UN Press Release SC/8351, 31 March 2005.

[118] United States Explanation of Vote on Security Council Resolution 1593, 31 March 2005, www.iccnow.org/documents/US.Statement.SCreferralDarfurICC_31March05.pdf.

investigation or prosecutions of nationals of non-Party States should come only pursuant to a decision by the Security Council'. It also indicated that it would continue to block financial support to the ICC from the United Nations or other organisations to which it contributed, noting that contributions to the ICC from these organisations 'could result in our withholding funding or taking other action in response'. It further noted that it had already concluded ninety-nine BIAs, and would continue to pursue such agreements. Finally, it desired the Security Council to maintain 'firm political oversight' over the OTP's discharge of this referral.

Despite these caveats, the United States' abstention, rather than veto, 'to help promote effective accountability' indicated that its opposition had been scaled back from that expressed only a few weeks previously in an official's blunt declaration that '[w]e don't want to be party to legitimizing the ICC'.[119]

The United States' attitude towards the ICC continued to evolve in a positive direction. Despite the avowed determination to continue pursuing more BIAs, it concluded only three more, and waived sanctions against many States which had refused these agreements. The United States also made affirmative statements about cooperating with the ICC on Darfur.[120] When in July 2008 the OTP made its controversial application for a warrant against Sudan's President, Omar al-Bashir,[121] the Arab League, the Organization of the Islamic Conference and the Non-Aligned Movement were all extremely critical.[122] It was the United States which offered support. The United States even criticised the Security Council's decision not to respond at all when the AU entreated it to exercise its power (under Article 16 of the Rome Statute) to suspend the OTP's activities in Darfur. Instead, a Security Council resolution merely 'took note' of the AU's request.[123]

[119] Human Rights Watch, 'US Fiddles over ICC while Darfur Burns'.

[120] See, for instance, 'State Department Legal Adviser Describes US Views on International Law, Suggests Possible Cooperation with International Criminal Court on Darfur', Contemporary Practice of the United States relating to International Law (compiled by J. R. Crook) (2007) 101 *American Journal of International Law* 636.

[121] *Prosecutor* v. *Omar al-Bashir*, Prosecution's Article 58 Application, ICC-02/05-157-AnxA, 14 July 2008.

[122] 'Security Council Decides to Extend Mandate of African Union–United Nations', UN Press Release SC/9412, 31 July 2008. See also A. Ciampi, 'The Proceedings against President Al Bashir and the Prospect of their Surrender under Article 16 ICC Statute' (2008) 6 *Journal of International Criminal Justice* 885, 886.

[123] UNSC Res. 1828 (31 July 2008).

The United States felt that the Council's silence 'would send the wrong message to [Bashir] and undermine efforts to bring him and others to justice'.[124] This time, it abstained *in support of* (the continuation of) investigations by the OTP. The United States, with the United Kingdom and France, also refused to exercise the Security Council's power of deferral of the investigation,[125] with the result that the PTC issued a warrant for Bashir on 4 March 2009,[126] followed by a revised warrant on 12 July 2010, containing the Court's first charges of genocide.[127]

The thaw that began in the later years of the Bush Administration continued under President Barack Obama's tenure, which has expressly endorsed the ICC's credibility. The US Ambassador to the United Nations stated that the ICC 'looks to become an important and credible instrument for trying to hold accountable the senior leadership responsible for atrocities committed in the Congo, Uganda, and Darfur'.[128] The United States also led the call to move the prosecution of Charles Taylor from Sierra Leone to the ICC premises.[129] In November 2009, the United States attended the annual meeting of the ASP, and in May–June 2010, the Review Conference. The United States has also affirmed its willingness to support in specific ways 'the particular prosecutions that [are] already underway in [the DRC], Sudan, [the CAR], and Uganda'.[130]

Given that at one time the United States attacked the ICC's legitimacy even through petty means like removing references to the ICC from resolutions and documents of international organisations, this represents a major shift in approach. But the United States' engagement remains qualified: it has not acceded to the Rome Statute and maintains its arrangements to exclude its nationals and 'sent' persons from the ICC's jurisdiction.

124 UN Press Release SC/9412, 31 July 2008.

125 L. Charbonneau, 'US, France, UK Oppose Suspending Bashir Darfur Case', Reuters, 13 February 2009.

126 *Prosecutor* v. *Omar al-Bashir*, Warrant of Arrest, ICC-02/05-01/09, 4 March 2009.

127 *Prosecutor* v. *Omar al-Bashir*, Second Warrant of Arrest, ICC-02/05-01/09, 12 July 2010.

128 S. Rice, US Permanent Representative, Statement in the Security Council, 29 January 2009, www.usunnewyork.usmission.gov/press_releases/20090129_020.html.

129 Cerone, 'Dynamic Equilibrium', 302–3.

130 H. Koh, US Department of State Legal Advisor, Keynote Address, ASIL Annual Meeting, Washington DC, 25 March 2010, www.state.gov/s/l/releases/remarks/139119.htm.

The OTP and managerialism

What explains the changes in the United States–ICC relationship? Many accounts focus on the United States' domestic politics – the change of Administration in 2008 and, even prior to that, turnover of key personnel within the government. John Cerone, for instance, offers a succinct summary: 'Rumsfeld has resigned. Delay has left Congress. Helms has died. Bolton failed to win the Congressional support necessary to retain his appointment as US Representative to the United Nations'.[131]

David Caron, in an edited symposium, offers a complex framework to explain the dynamics of State–international court relationships.[132] He argues that an international court's operation may be understood in terms of strategic interactions between various actors, within and outside the framework of its constitutional instrument. One essay in this symposium applies Caron's theory to the ICC, but only looks at the strategic interactions between the United States and the Security Council, and the strategic actions of the United States *vis-à-vis* the ICC.[133] It does not explore the strategies that the ICC organs may have adopted to deal with the United States' challenge. Neither does Caron address the role of the prosecutor, who in the ICC's case, at least initially, was the most pertinent strategic actor – though he notes that adjudicators and the secretariat are important strategic actors. However, Caron does make the point that international courts may be usefully analysed as dynamic institutions, less stable than is conventionally assumed, and shaped by political contests between internal and external actors. To the extent that there has been a taboo on this sort of irreverent analysis, Caron shows why breaking it may be in order.

This chapter builds on that point to evaluate the OTP's work as an example of the compliance-management approach outlined in Chapter 3. Chapter 3 discussed Abram Chayes and Antonia Chayes' work on the role of treaty bodies in implementing multilateral treaties and obtaining compliance with their terms. It noted that this could be accomplished, *inter alia*, by defining an appropriate standard of compliance or making adjustments to the relevant treaty (that is, without formal amendment).

131 Cerone, 'Dynamic Equilibrium', 304.

132 D. Caron, 'Towards a Political Theory of International Courts and Tribunals' (2006) 24 *Berkeley Journal of International Law* 401.

133 C. Heyder, 'The UN Security Council's Referral of the Crimes in Darfur to the International Criminal Court in Light of US Opposition to the Court: Implications for the International Criminal Court's Functions and Status' (2006) 24 Berkeley Journal of International Law 650.

Chayes and Chayes regard such measures as legitimate because some treaty bodies enjoy the necessary competence for this purpose, and, more generally, when such measures are routed through a legal discourse. Chayes and Chayes use the terminology of 'managerialism', but their discussion clarifies that they rely on assumptions that are more administrative than managerial.

Chapter 3 also noted that, where a multilateral treaty is challenged by treaty conflict involving non-parties, a treaty body may be in a tricky position, because its work may be riven by dichotomous priorities. For, while its managerial actions are explained on the basis that it operates by facilitating legal discourse between treaty parties, such conflicts may require it to respond to the challenges raised by non-parties.

This corresponds to the present case: the OTP is a treaty body of the Rome Statute, and an assessment of the 'managerial' or 'administrative' character of its actions would ideally focus on how it has implemented the Rome Statute. This, of course, calls for analysis of its work in the situations before it. But analysis in this section reveals that the OTP consistently seemed under pressure to respond to the challenges levelled by the United States, shaping its policies and public discourse to this end, even though there was little direct communication between it and the United States. The question is whether the OTP has successfully balanced this pressure with its responsibilities as outlined in the Statute, towards the Court, States and individuals – both victims and accused. An adherence to the spirit as well as the letter of these responsibilities is important. If, in attempting to mitigate the challenges posed by the Rome Statute–BIAs treaty conflict, the OTP is found to use the letter of the law to undermine its spirit, then its actions can only be criticised.

It is not common to speak of the OTP as engaged in a managerial role. Yet, it has carried the burden of 'implementing' the Rome Statute through the early years. While other organs – notably the Presidency and the Registry – have contributed towards concretising the presence of the Court particularly through sustained measures of external communication, it was the OTP that, by opening its first investigation, made the Court functional. The OTP proactively sought the referrals that enabled it to commence work, and produced the policy innovations and decisions that allowed it to fill the Court's docket. It also maintained a rigorous programme of communications on the ICC.

This section will show that it is rewarding to analyse the OTP's work in terms of efforts to address challenges to the ICC's legitimacy and its own – doing so explains some of its positions that are frankly puzzling otherwise. The section also reveals the distortions that crept in as the OTP's push to mitigate such challenges seemingly overrode other considerations. What follows is a critique of the OTP's work, which may also serve as the basis for a critique of compliance management.

The section discusses the OTP's work in the context of two phases: an early phase that ran from the Rome Statute's entry into force up to some time after the Security Council referral of Sudan, and a second phase which continued to the Review Conference.

The early phase

The early phase was marked by the United States' extensive pursuit of BIAs and fears that the Court would fail to become operational. The OTP's role was of primary importance in overcoming these fears. In this phase, it adopted a cautious approach exemplified by twin desires: to fill the Court's docket, and to avoid the perception that it may be challenging sovereign States.

Non-exercise of proprio motu powers

One element of the OTP's cautious approach was to encourage States to provide self-referrals, rather than commencing investigations on the basis of the Prosecutor's *proprio motu* powers. The DRC,[134] and Uganda,[135] made self-referrals on the basis of this encouragement. In inviting these self-referrals, the OTP used an innovative interpretation of Article 14 of the Rome Statute. That provision only mentions 'referrals' by States; as mentioned earlier, it was expected to be invoked in terms of one State making a referral of another.

The possibility of self-referrals was, however, suggested in an 'informal expert paper' that the OTP commissioned in April 2003. The paper noted that States had a duty to exercise domestic jurisdiction, which amounted to a duty to prosecute or extradite (*aut dedere aut judicare*). This being the case, a State would be acting consistently with the Rome Statute in choosing not to exercise its domestic jurisdiction in favour of prosecution

[134] Prosecutor (L. Moreno-Ocampo), Report to the Second Assembly of States Parties, 8 September 2003 www.icc-cpi.int/NR/rdonlyres/C073586C-7D46-4CBE-B901-0672908E8639/143656/LMO_20030908_En.pdf; Prosecutor (L. Moreno-Ocampo), Statement to Diplomatic Corps, 12 February 2004 www.icc-cpi.int/NR/rdonlyres/0F999F00-A609-4516A91A80467BC432D3/143670/LOM_20040212_En.pdf.

[135] Prosecutor (L. Moreno-Ocampo), Fourth Report to the Security Council pursuant to UNSC Res. 1593 (2005), 14 December 2006, www.icc-cpi.int/NR/rdonlyres/8903D205-6272-4498-8E83-258F9C99611A/0/OTP_ReportUNSC4Darfur_English.pdf.

before the ICC.[136] In fact, the OTP and the State in question could agree to a consensual division of labour as being in the best interests of justice – this could be 'where a conflict-torn State is unable to carry out effective proceedings against persons most responsible'.[137] The OTP echoed these points, and noted that, in situations of self-referral by a State,

> the Prosecutor has the advantage of knowing that that State has the political will to provide his Office with all the cooperation within the country that it is required to give under the Statute ... [T]he Prosecutor can be confident that the national authorities will assist the investigation, will accord the privileges and immunities necessary ... and will be anxious to provide if possible and appropriate the necessary level of protection to investigators and witnesses.[138]

It is now accepted in principle and practice that self-referrals may be a means to trigger the Court's jurisdiction. But self-referrals do not align well with complementarity or the overall scheme of the Rome Statute.[139] The Statute accords primary jurisdiction to States, and therefore the Court is only supposed to step in when there is an absence of national proceedings because the State in question lacks the requisite ability or will to investigate and prosecute. It is expected, and indeed has been asserted by ICC organs in the case of Colombia,[140] that States will be spurred on to activate their domestic justice processes by the knowledge that the OTP was preparing to open an investigation. In fact, the OTP has claimed as its ideal a situation where the Court's docket is empty because domestic systems are operating effectively.[141] However, to some extent, self-referrals run contrary to these expectations, for through them a State simply cedes jurisdiction rather than activating its domestic process. At the simplest level, this may be an unnecessary application of the Court's resources. More critically, a government may make a self-referral for strategic reasons: in order to use the Court against its political opponents, or to show that it is doing 'something'. Such motives have, after all, been attributed to Uganda.

[136] Informal Experts, 'The Principle of Complementarity in Practice', 2003, www.icc-cpi.int/iccdocs/doc/doc654724.PDF, 19 and n. 24. See also W. Schabas, 'Prosecutorial Discretion and Gravity', in C. Stahn and G. Sluiter (eds.), *The Emerging Practice of the International Criminal Court* (Leiden, Martinus Nijhoff 2009) 229, 235–8.

[137] Informal Experts, 'The Principle of Complementarity in Practice', 4.

[138] Paper on Some Policy Issues before the Office of the Prosecutor, September 2003, www.icc-cpi.int/NR/rdonlyres/1FA7C4C6-DE5F-42B7-8B25-60AA962ED8B6/143594/030905_Policy_Paper.pdf.

[139] For more, see Kleffner, 'Auto-Referrals and the Complementary Nature of the ICC'.

[140] OTP official, personal interview (on file).

[141] Paper on Some Policy Issues, 4.

That such charges of the instrumental use of the Court are plausible suggests that the OTP must be careful in its acceptance of self-referrals, and in how it proceeds following the same. The OTP seemed to recognise this in the case of Uganda's referral, where it immediately notified the government of its intention to interpret the referral as applicable to Uganda as a whole, and not just to the leaders of the LRA. Moreover, it asserted (as it did in the case of the other two referrals) that it would make its own assessment of the admissibility of proceedings arising from the referral. Even so, it subsequently only identified cases against rebels, considering their crimes to be more serious than the UPDF's. It did the same in case of the DRC and the CAR. Since in each of the three situations there was no doubting the involvement of the national armed forces in the international crimes under investigation, the OTP's selection of cases has invited concerns about its impartiality. At the least, it puts in question the OTP's claim that self-referrals would indicate the full cooperation of governments – seemingly, in the first three self-referred situations, it was only able to collect evidence of rebels' crimes.

Of course, the OTP would not have received any greater cooperation from these States had it chosen to exercise its *proprio motu* powers to open investigation rather than waiting for self-referrals. But there would be less reason to be concerned that it had compromised its impartiality for the sake of other objectives: perhaps to signal that the Prosecutor would act with restraint even where convinced that opening an investigation was appropriate; and certainly to immediately commence work. This also provides the requisite gloss upon arguments made by OTP personnel that the Prosecutor did make constructive use of his *proprio motu* power, because, by raising the possibility of its exercise, he encouraged the referrals.[142] For the supposedly subtle use of the *proprio motu* power only contributed to the view that the OTP privileged the perception of acting in cooperation with States over the perception of acting impartially.

Exercise of prosecutorial discretion: the OTP's focus on Africa

If self-referrals allowed the Prosecutor not to exercise his *proprio motu* powers, the provisions of the Rome Statute pertaining to opening investigations into situations and cases demanded exercise of his other

[142] R. Rastan, 'The Responsibility to Enforce: Connecting Justice with Unity', in C. Stahn and G. Sluiter (eds.), *The Emerging Practice of the International Criminal Court* (Leiden, Martinus Nijhoff 2009) 163, 172 and n. 27.

discretionary powers. But, in using these powers, too, the OTP demonstrated a cautious approach. A long-standing criticism of the OTP has been that it has focused on situations in African States since its presence in these situations runs no risk of antagonising the United States and other powerful States.

There are two bases for criticism here: the first is that the OTP has been insistent upon investigating situations in some African States even at the cost of other considerations. For instance, it rejected Uganda's argument that it should be allowed to withdraw its referral in order to facilitate its peace process with the LRA. The second basis for criticism is that it has simply avoided investigating situations in other parts of the world.

In its response, the OTP evidently prefers to focus on the first prong of the criticism, which it has continued to attack with a degree of rhetorical flair. For instance, in November 2009, at a symposium hosted by South Africa's Institute for Security Studies, Prosecutor Moreno-Ocampo stated:

> There are 14 accused, all of them are Africans. There are more than 5 million African victims displaced, more than 40,000 African victims killed, thousands of African victims raped. Hundreds of thousands of African children transformed into killers or rapists. 100% of the victims are Africans. 100% of the accused are African. As Desmond Tutu said: Choose your side. Do you associate with the victims or the perpetrators? I am on the victims' side. I will not apologize for that.[143]

The Prosecutor further claimed that 'misperceptions' about the ICC were promoted by two groups: political leaders like Bashir and Gaddafi, or 'Western "experts"'. Indeed, he accused Bashir of knowing 'how to divide groups to follow his goals' which is rather ironic since the same has been claimed about the OTP's own strategy *vis-à-vis* Uganda and Sudan.[144]

Of course, the Prosecutor is correct in stating that all the situations taken up in its early phase were appropriate for investigation. However, there are reasons to challenge the manner in which the OTP has selected cases for prosecution.

[143] Prosecutor (L. Moreno-Ocampo), 'Working with Africa: The View from the ICC Prosecutor's Office', ISS Symposium, Cape Winelands, 9 November 2009, 3, www.icc-cpi.int/NR/rdonlyres/1229900D-B581-42AE-A078-918550C372FB/281385/south_africa_nov_09_3finalfordistribution.pdf.

[144] S. Nouwen and W. Werner, 'Doing Justice to the Political: The International Criminal Court in Uganda and Sudan' (2011) 21 *European Journal of International Law* 941.

Selecting cases from Africa

Let us begin with a brief review of the Rome Statute's directions for the exercise of prosecutorial discretion. Article 53 provides that the Prosecutor must undertake a three-part test to determine whether to open an investigation, and to select cases for prosecution: they must find that crimes within the Court's jurisdiction have been committed; that investigation and prosecution are not barred by complementarity or gravity; and that the investigation or prosecution is not contrary to the interests of justice. The second and third elements allow significant prosecutorial discretion – while the Statute offers some criteria to guide the application of the complementarity principle, it provides very few for the gravity principle, and minimal guidance on evaluating the interests of justice.

One criticism pertaining to the OTP's selection of cases has been with respect to its application of the complementarity principle, first seen in the *Lubanga* case. The *Lubanga* case, much like the OTP's response to Uganda's attempts to withdraw its referral, has been seen by some critics as demonstrating too much eagerness on the OTP's (and indeed the Court's) part to maintain an active docket at the cost of other considerations.[145] The OTP's decision to prosecute Lubanga for recruitment and use of child soldiers alone was striking because Lubanga already stood accused of other serious crimes, including genocide, in domestic proceedings in the DRC. However, the Prosecutor maintained that the case was admissible, arguing that the national judicial system was 'unable' in the sense required by the complementarity principle. The PTC disagreed with this submission, noting that it 'does not wholly correspond to reality any longer', but decided to grant a warrant because the domestic proceedings against Lubanga did not encompass the exact charges levelled by the Prosecutor.[146] The PTC's reasoning may be a possible way of interpreting Article 17, but it is by no means the most appropriate way.[147]

[145] See W. Schabas, *An Introduction to the International Criminal Court* (3rd edn, Cambridge University Press 2007) 36.

[146] *Prosecutor* v. *Lubanga*, Decision Concerning Arrest Warrant, 24 February 2006, ICC-01/04-01/06, paras. 36–9.

[147] On this, see also Nouwen, *Complementarity in the Line of Fire*, 51–9; R. Rastan, 'What Is a Case for the Purpose of the Rome Statute' (2008) 19 *Criminal Law Forum* 435, 439–40 (asserting the difference between policy considerations and legal interpretation).

This lack in the PTC's reasoning is evident from the rationale of the complementarity principle, which is to give primacy to national proceedings. The Court was meant to assume jurisdiction only where national proceedings did not exist, or did not reflect a genuine will or ability on the part of a State to bring an accused person to justice, in keeping with the Rome Statute's overall purpose of preventing impunity for international crimes. The drafters of the Rome Statute had recommended high standards for this assessment, the critical test being 'whether there was a defect in the approach taken by the State which inevitably, if left to its conclusion, would result in a travesty of justice'.[148] Article 17(2) provides that, to determine the absence of genuine will, the Court must examine whether the domestic proceedings were conducted to shield the person from criminal responsibility, were unjustifiably delayed so as to be inconsistent with the intent to bring a person to justice, or were not conducted independently or impartially. Article 17(3) provides that, to determine the absence of genuine ability to prosecute, the Court is to consider whether there has been a substantial collapse of the relevant national judicial system, due to which the State is unable to obtain the accused or the necessary evidence, or otherwise unable to carry out its proceedings. Evidently, none of these conditions was found to hold *vis-à-vis* the proceedings against Lubanga.

The PTC's focus upon the difference between the exact charges brought by the OTP and Congo's domestic prosecutors is contrary to the *telos* of the Rome Statute, and of the complementarity principle. Indeed, it is remarkable that the PTC took the view that the ICC can exercise jurisdiction if there is a difference in the charges levied by the OTP and in domestic proceedings, for in mass crimes it is likely that any prosecutor will take a selective approach – the ICC Prosecutor himself did so in charging Lubanga only with the recruitment and use of child soldiers. Moreover, to select a person already under trial hardly seems consonant with filling the 'impunity gap'. While the crimes alleged by the OTP are certainly grievous, one cannot but agree with Schabas that

> perhaps the Prosecutor would agree that if the Congolese justice system is working, then it would be better for Lubanga to stand trial at home for genocide

[148] J. Holmes, 'Complementarity: National Courts versus the ICC', in A. Cassese *et al.* (eds.), *The Rome Statute of the International Criminal Court: A Commentary* (Oxford University Press 2002) 667, 674.

and crimes against humanity than to stand trial in The Hague for recruitment of child soldiers ... Lubanga himself ... must be delighted to find himself in The Hague.[149]

However, the PTC's test of admissibility has been used repeatedly by the OTP – it was applied in selecting cases in the Darfur situation,[150] ironically, with the justification that this permitted the OTP to avoid passing judgment on the Sudanese justice system as a whole.[151] But this test is in fact far more intrusive upon State sovereignty, since it disregards a State's own proceedings simply on the basis that they do not encompass exactly the same charges.

Another criticism of the OTP's selection of cases has already been mentioned – that it has only acted against rebels in the three self-referred situations. The Prosecutor simply argued that the crimes committed by the rebels were of sufficient gravity as to merit prosecution by the Court, though, with respect to Uganda, he also stated that the LRA's crimes were graver than those committed by the UPDF. Of course, this assessment has been perceived as dubious, not only because the UPDF had reportedly committed similar crimes but also because it did so in its capacity as the national military of Uganda: State-sponsored crimes should give rise to greater concern than crimes committed by outlaws.

In exercising prosecutorial discretion in selecting cases from African situations, the OTP has seemingly misapplied both the principle of complementarity and – more tangentially – the principle of gravity. The misapplication of the latter principle is more evident in the OTP's response to communication in other situations.

Dealing with non-African situations

The OTP responded to the charge that it had avoided substantial scrutiny of non-African situations by emphasising that four of its five (now four of eight) African situations were self-referred, and by citing its review of situations in Colombia, Georgia, Afghanistan, *et cetera*. But its explanation for its refusal to open investigation into Iraq – the one instance where it applied its discretion not to do so in its early phase – has failed to persuade.

[149] Schabas, 'Prosecutorial Discretion and Gravity', 242.

[150] Prosecutor, Fourth Report to the Security Council, 2006.

[151] Prosecutor (L. Moreno-Ocampo), Seventh Report to the Security Council pursuant to UNSC Res. 1593 (2005), 5 June 2008, para. 20, www.icc-cpi.int/NR/rdonlyres/D6F9DF4F-FB9D-4323-B945-784ED2332BB3/276869/UNSC_2008_En.pdf.

The OTP issued its responses to communications on Iraq and Venezuela on the same day, in February 2006. In the case of Venezuela, its assessment was simply that the alleged crimes did not satisfy the elements of 'crimes within the Court's jurisdiction'.[152] But, in the case of Iraq, while finding that war crimes of wilful killing of civilians and mistreatment of detainees had been committed against Iraqis by UK and US nationals, it declared the situation itself as one of insufficient gravity.[153] (The OTP made only a cursory reference to complementarity, noting that some national proceedings had been initiated.)

The outstanding feature of the OTP's gravity assessment was that it looked at the relative gravity of the *situation*, particularly at the number of crimes committed by UK nationals in Iraq (since Iraq, too, was not party to the Rome Statute, the OTP lacked basis to investigate crimes by Iraqi and US nationals). The OTP claimed that the evidence did not suggest that these crimes were committed as part of 'a plan or policy or as part of a large-scale commission of such crimes', and, moreover

> [t]he number of potential victims of crimes within the jurisdiction of the Court in this situation - 4 to 12 victims of wilful killing and a limited number of victims of inhuman treatment - was of a different order than the number of victims found in other situations under investigation or analysis.[154]

But the Statute may be read to suggest two different assessments of gravity, one for deciding whether the OTP should open an investigation into a situation, the second for selecting cases from it.[155] In the first instance, to determine whether a situation calls for investigation, the Prosecutor should merely assess if there exist within that situation cases of *threshold* gravity to activate the Court's jurisdiction. Such cases include all crimes contemplated by the Statute, though it may be permissible to apply a *de minimis* evaluation to exclude limited categories of war crimes.[156] In the case of Iraq, the Prosecutor did find cases of

152 Office of the Prosecutor, Response to Communications received concerning Venezuela, 9 February 2006, www.icc-cpi.int/Menus/ICC/Structure+of+the+Court/Office+of+the+Prosecutor/Comm+and+Ref/Venezuela.

153 Office of the Prosecutor, Response to Communications received concerning Iraq, 9 February 2006, www.icc-cpi.int/Menus/ICC/Structure+of+the+Court/Office+of+the+Prosecutor/Comm+and+Ref/Iraq.

154 *Ibid.*

155 See M. deGuzman, 'Gravity and the Legitimacy of the International Criminal Court' (2009) 32 *Fordham International Law Journal* 1400, esp. 1432–4 (on Iraq).

156 *Ibid.*, 1457–8.

threshold gravity, and thus could have opened an investigation into the situation. Instead, the Prosecutor simply focused on *relative gravity*, a quality that may assist in selecting cases for further investigation and possible prosecution because, in making such selections, the Prosecutor must act within the constraints of feasibility.

Initially, the OTP justified applying the test of relative gravity to the situation in Iraq. Some weeks prior to the Iraq decision, Prosecutor Moreno-Ocampo insisted that resource constraints, as also a proper appreciation of the Court's strategic role, required him to select between situations that merited investigation by the OTP.[157] He explained that the OTP did not have the resources to investigate all situations; if it accepted all, it would not be able to provide 'steady and predictable budgetary projections, since future resource needs would depend on external circumstances'.[158] He further cautioned that accepting less grave situations and increasing demands for State cooperation 'might lead to ICC "fatigue" and a diminishing of support'. Finally, he noted that the ICC was expected to respect national processes, which might operate more efficiently in less grave situations. Therefore, 'situations involving hundreds of crimes, such as killings and rapes, may have to be set aside in the interest of focusing on a competing situation involving thousands of killings and rapes'.[159]

The Prosecutor did not explain why – even accepting that he would have to decide between situations – he would have to do so purely on the basis of the number of victims of crimes within the ICC's jurisdiction. It seems reasonable that factors such as the nature of the crimes, the context and manner of their commission, their impact, their commission by States rather than outlaw groups, are all relevant to its assessment.[160] Indeed, in considering later submissions, the OTP used both qualitative and quantitative factors. For instance, it noted in its application for a warrant against Abu Garda (Sudan):

> [C]onsistent with the Appeals Chamber ruling that Article 8 Chapeau requirement 'in particular when committed as part of a plan or policy or as part of a

157 Prosecutor (L. Moreno-Ocampo), Statement at informal meeting of Legal Advisors of Ministries of Foreign Affairs, New York, 24 October 2005, www.icc-cpi.int/NR/rdonlyres/9D70039E-4BEC-4F32-9D4A-CEA8B6799E37/143836/LMO_20051024_English.pdf.

158 *Ibid.*, 8. 159 *Ibid.*, 9.

160 See deGuzman, 'Gravity and the Legitimacy of the ICC', 1449–1456; K. J. Heller, 'Situational Gravity under the Rome Statute', in C. Stahn and L. van den Herik (eds.), *Future Perspectives on International Criminal Justice* (The Hague, TMC Asser Press 2010) 227–53.

large-scale commission of such crimes' should not be construed narrowly, the issues of the nature, manner and impact of the attack are critical... [The] gravity of the crimes is not in the instant case related to the number of casualties but to the quality, as peacekeepers, of the personnel attacked ... The gravity of the offence also relates to the intentional directing of such an unlawful attack, which in addition, was on such a large scale, involving one thousand rebel combatants ... [A]ttacks were in effect directed or committed against the international community.[161]

Similarly, in its request to open an investigation into Kenya, the OTP referred to both qualitative and quantitative factors.[162] In its decisions on Abu Garda[163] and Kenya,[164] the PTC too agreed that gravity comprises qualitative and quantitative dimensions and recalled the OTP's arguments for taking the scale, nature, manner of commission and impact into consideration.[165]

The OTP's position on gravity, thus, has evolved. Not only does it make a qualitative and quantitative assessment of gravity, its personnel also confirm that it has abandoned examination of the relative gravity of situations to focus on the gravity of cases within each situation – and rightly so.[166]

Schabas is perhaps the leading critic of the OTP's application of the gravity principle *vis-à-vis* Iraq. He notes the principle's sudden rise to prominence in the Prosecutor's speeches as he was called upon to explain his selection of situations and cases; presumably because this principle permitted him substantial discretion.[167] Even as some scholars have viewed the OTP's initial focus on the numbers of victims as more straightforward than the assessment of qualitative factors,[168] Schabas underlines

[161] *Prosecutor* v. *Abu Garda*, Prosecutor's Application Filed on Request of PTC I, 20 May 2009, ICC-02/05, 41.

[162] *Situation in Kenya*, Prosecutor's Request for Authorisation of Investigation Pursuant to Article 15, 26 November 2009, ICC-01/09.

[163] *Prosecutor* v. *Abu Garda*, Decision on the Confirmation of Charges (PTC), 8 February 2010, ICC-02/05-02/09, paras. 30–4.

[164] *Situation in Kenya*, Decision Pursuant to Article 15 on Authorization of Investigation, 31 March 2010, ICC-01/09, paras. 57–62.

[165] OTP official, personal interview (on file), confirmed that OTP now takes into account qualitative and quantitative factors to evaluate gravity, and that the PTC has endorsed these factors.

[166] Anonymous comment, 2010, on file with the author.

[167] See Schabas, 'Prosecutorial Discretion and Gravity', esp. 231–4.

[168] M. Osiel, 'When Law Expresses More Than It Cares to Admit', in C. Stahn and L. van den Herik (eds.), *Future Perspectives on International Criminal Justice* (The Hague, TMC Asser Press 2010) 254, 256.

that the OTP only maintained this approach when convenient, to enable it to avoid dealing with a highly testing situation. He also notes the distortions in how the OTP applied numerical criteria:

> The methodology of the comparison seems flawed. The Prosecutor could not have been comparing the total number of deaths in Iraq with the total in the [DRC] or Uganda, because he would then have concluded that Iraq was more serious. Nor could he have been comparing the total number of deaths resulting from the crimes attributed to Lubanga with those blamed on the British troops in Iraq, because Lubanga was not charged with killing anybody. Thus the quantitative analysis of gravity . . . appears to get totally muddled in imprecise comparisons.[169]

The OTP might have explained that it was comparing the numbers of victims whose deaths could be directly attributed to actors within the ICC's jurisdiction. But this would only be an ex-post qualification – indeed that all of the OTP's choices might be later justified through such distinctions only highlights that there is nothing 'purely numerical' about deciding which statistics are relevant.

It is hard to avoid the conclusion that, at least in its early phase, the OTP applied the gravity principle with an eye to its impact upon the perception of the ICC amongst powerful States and, most of all, by the United States. While Prosecutor Moreno-Ocampo claimed to reject 'situations which may fail to reflect the concern of the international community as a whole',[170] his decisions often used exactly the opposite criteria. Mass crimes in the context of domestic/regional conflicts did not implicate the interests of powerful States, while Iraq did. Perhaps, given the United States' virulence in the early phase, the OTP did not have the luxury of attending to challenges to its legitimacy from other quarters. This began to gradually change from the time of Sudan's referral.

Post the Sudan referral

Sudan's March 2005 referral to the Court by the UN Security Council offered the OTP an opportunity to act with greater boldness, and, not least, to investigate actors across the spectrum, from the government to its challengers. Indeed, its investigation of the government was encouraged – the United Nations' International Commission of Inquiry had

[169] Schabas, 'Prosecutorial Discretion and Gravity', 245.
[170] Prosecutor, Statement at informal meeting of Legal Advisors of Ministries of Foreign Affairs, 2005, 8.

already concluded that the government was responsible for crimes against humanity.[171] The United States considered it responsible also for genocide in Darfur.[172] And, even though Sudan was not party to the Rome Statute and thus had no obligations under it, the Security Council had applied its Chapter VII mandatory powers in directing Sudan to extend full cooperation to the ICC.[173]

From prudence to publicity

Initially, the OTP continued its cautious approach, demonstrating – as Antonio Cassese dryly observed in 2006 – an 'exceedingly prudent attitude'.[174] Cassese, *inter alia*, had been a member of the UN International Commission of Inquiry and he expressed disappointment in the tenor of the OTP's investigation into Sudan, including its failure to take some simple strategic steps to enlist UN Security Council assistance in eliciting Sudan's cooperation. For Sudan had publicly rejected the referral, and members of the government had declared that they would not allow the ICC to investigate Darfur.[175]

Cassese noted that the OTP should have countered Sudan's actions by making a formal general request for cooperation to Sudan:

> Had the Prosecutor, immediately after his decision to open investigations (on 1 June 2005), squarely requested Sudan's authorization to enter the country and conduct investigations, he would have met with a blunt refusal. Upon receiving such a refusal he could have reported the matter to the Security Council ... he could have at least asked the Council seriously to take into account such refusal to cooperate and envisage appropriate measures designed to secure cooperation.[176]

However, absent a formal request, the OTP could not claim the government of Sudan had actually refused to cooperate. Instead, the OTP

[171] Report of the International Commission of Inquiry on Darfur.

[172] C. Powell, US Secretary of State, Hearing before the US Senate Committee on Foreign Relations on 'The Current Situation in Sudan and the Prospects for Peace', 108th Congress, 2nd Sess., 9 September 2004.

[173] UNSC Res. 1593 (31 March 2005).

[174] A. Cassese, 'Editorial Comment: Is the ICC Still Having Teething Problems?' (2006) 4 *Journal of International Criminal Justice* 434.

[175] But see Nouwen, *Complementarity in the Line of Fire*, 249–50: Nouwen notes that, despite its public rejection, the government of Sudan did for a time extend cooperation to the OTP – until the OTP issued warrants of arrest against Minister of State for Humanitarian Affairs Ahmad Harun, and militia leader Ali Kushayb. Indeed, as discussed in this section, for a time the Prosecutor expressed a fair degree of satisfaction with the cooperation received from Sudan.

[176] Cassese, 'Is the ICC Still Having Teething Problems?', 439.

simply restricted its investigation to sources outside Sudan, making only a few specific cooperation requests to Sudan – Cassese expresses mystification over the Prosecutor not even requesting Sudan 'to allow his investigators to enter its territory and discharge their duties'.[177]

Cassese also noted the OTP's failure to invoke 'command responsibility' to charge major actors. He pointed out that, by charging senior leaders, the OTP could have accomplished many ends: dramatising the conflict, making international pariahs of those who had committed international crimes, perhaps even facilitating a settlement in Darfur by breaking the deadlock created by China and Russia's support for the government.[178] He noted that the warrants issued by the International Criminal Tribunal for the former Yugoslavia against Ratko Mladic and Radovan Karadzic had achieved similar results. As we will see, the OTP took this advice, but carried it too far in charging Sudan's sitting President.

At first, the OTP concentrated on building a cooperative relationship with the Sudanese government, spending months making its own review of whether it was appropriate to open an investigation into Sudan, and on the admissibility of cases from Darfur.[179] One paper describes the OTP's approach as handling the government with 'velvet gloves'.[180] However, once the OTP turned its gaze on senior government members, the cooperative relationship came to an end. The change is apparent in the reports made by the OTP to the Security Council. In its fourth report, in December 2006, the OTP was satisfied with the cooperation received from the government.[181] In its fifth report, in June 2007, the OTP stated that, while a degree of cooperation was forthcoming, a number of specific requests made in November and January (in relation to the permission to question senior government members

[177] *Ibid.*

[178] *Ibid.*, 439–40. Cassese repeated these observations even at a later date: A. Cassese, 'The International Criminal Court Five Years On: Andante or Moderato?', in C. Stahn and G. Sluiter (eds.), *The Emerging Practice of the International Criminal Court* (Leiden, Martinus Nijhoff 2009) 21, 26–9.

[179] Prosecutor, Fourth Report of the Prosecutor to the Security Council, 2006. Ohlin argues that the Prosecutor acted misguidedly in making his own determination of the reasonableness of investigation into a situation referred by the Security Council: J. D. Ohlin, 'Peace, Security and Prosecutorial Discretion', in C. Stahn and G. Sluiter (eds.), *The Emerging Practice of the International Criminal Court* (Leiden, Martinus Nijhoff 2009) 185–208.

[180] Nouwen and Werner, 'Doing Justice to the Political', 958.

[181] Prosecutor, Fourth Report to the Security Council, 2006.

Ahmed Harun and Ali Kushayb) remained outstanding.[182] In the sixth report, in December 2007, Moreno-Ocampo stated:

> [T]he Government ... has not complied with its legal obligations. [It] has not complied with Resolution 1593. [It] is not cooperating with my Office, or the Court. Ahmad Harun and Ali Kushayb have not been arrested and surrendered. While the Sudan continues to publicly insist that it is willing and able to prosecute those responsible for serious crimes, they have done nothing. While the Sudan has known the nature of the case against Ahmad Harun and Ali Kushayb for ten months, they have done nothing. They have taken no steps to prosecute them domestically, or to arrest and transfer them to The Hague.[183]

Simultaneously with the OTP's change in approach towards the Sudanese government, the United States' attitude towards the Court also showed a change. Between 2005 and 2007, the United States modified several policies targeting the Court: it stopped concluding BIAs and introduced modifications to the ASPA and the Nethercutt Amendment. It also offered vocal support for the OTP's efforts in Darfur - while normally OTP reports to the Security Council were followed by closed-door discussion, an open discussion followed the sixth report. At this discussion, the United States stated it was

> particularly troubled by the Prosecutor's report that the Government of the Sudan is still not cooperating and has taken no steps to arrest and surrender the two individuals that are subject to the ICC arrest warrants, namely, Ahmad Muhammad Harun, current Minister of State for Humanitarian Affairs, and the Janjaweed leader known as Ali Kushayb. We call on the Sudanese Government to cooperate fully with the ICC, as required by resolution 1593 (2005).
>
> As we noted following the Prosecutor's last briefing to the Council on Darfur, [the United States] has imposed targeted economic sanctions against certain individuals responsible for the violence, a transport company that has moved weapons to the Janjaweed militia and Government forces, and companies owned or controlled by the Government of the Sudan.[184]

182 Prosecutor (L. Moreno-Ocampo), Fifth Report to the Security Council pursuant to UNSC Res. 1593 (2005), 7 June 2007, 10, www.icc-cpi.int/NR/rdonlyres/65732689-4A7B-467E-9821-BF53F11465D0/0/OTP_ReportUNSC 5Darfur_English.pdf.

183 Prosecutor (L. Moreno-Ocampo), Statement to the Security Council, 5 December 2007, www.icc-cpi.int/NR/rdonlyres/6A4AF1FE-9A86-41C6-9D38-327408612F6F/281542/ProsecutorsStateUNSCDec07EN.pdf. See also Prosecutor (L. Moreno-Ocampo), Sixth Report to the Security Council pursuant to UNSC Res. 1593 (2005), 5 December 2007, www.icc-cpi.int/NR/rdonlyres/19A83943-DF47-4DC0-9EB1-1A84CF862290/281540/ProsecutorsReportUNSCDec07EN.pdf.

184 Provisional Verbatim Record, UNSC 5789th Mtg, S/PV.5789, 5 December 2007, 12.

As has already been discussed in the previous section, the United States' support grew more marked in the wake of the critiques that followed the OTP's decision to apply for a warrant of arrest against Sudanese President Bashir, charging him, among other things, with three counts of genocide. This was in keeping with the United States' own assessment of the violence in Darfur as amounting to genocide, a view not shared by the International Commission of Inquiry.

The Prosecutor's decision to make a public announcement of his request to the Court to issue a warrant against Bashir met with the scepticism that it was mere political grandstanding and would not lead to an arrest.[185] Nor, according to Cassese, would it produce the very outcomes he had earlier hoped for in recommending that the OTP pursue some major actors. In a blog post in July 2008, Cassese noted:

> The arrest warrant, assuming that the ICC issues it, seems unlikely to produce the extra-judicial effects – the political and moral delegitimization of the accused – that sometimes follow. This happened in the case of former Bosnian Serb leader Radovan Karadzic, who, although never arrested, has been removed both from power and the international arena as a result of his indictment in 1995.
>
> Instead, Moreno-Ocampo's request may have negative political repercussions by creating much disarray in international relations. It may harden the Sudanese government's position, endanger the survival of the peacekeeping forces in Darfur, and even induce al-Bashir to take revenge by stopping or making even more difficult the flow of international humanitarian assistance to the two million displaced persons in Darfur. On top of that, Moreno-Ocampo's request might further alienate the Great Powers (China, Russia, and the United States) that are currently hostile to the ICC.[186]

Cassese's assessment was not an about-turn from his suggestions of 2006, but rather a reminder that manoeuvring political outcomes is a chancy affair, calling for a much more sophisticated understanding of politics than the ICC Prosecutor displayed in this case. Indeed, more than four years after the warrant was issued, Bashir – re-elected to the presidency in 2010[187] – remains at large. The public warrant (as opposed to a sealed warrant) has put him on notice leading him to cancel some of

[185] T. Kavulla, 'A Dangerous Grandstand Play', *National Review Online*, 3 March 2009; J. Flint, 'Ocampo's Great Gamble', *Guardian*, 15 July 2008; A. de Waal and J. Flint, 'Case Closed: A Prosecutor Without Borders', *World Affairs*, Spring 2009.

[186] A. Cassese, 'Flawed International Justice for Sudan', *Project Syndicate*, 15 July 2008.

[187] Nouwen, *Complementarity in the Line of Fire*, 251.

his foreign travels,[188] but he has also visited several other States party to the Rome Statute, such as Kenya, Chad, Djibouti, Malawi and Nigeria, which have made no attempt to surrender him to the ICC.[189]

The OTP defended its approach as a strategy to marginalise Bashir and undermine political support for him.[190] Irrespective of the (dubious) merits of this defence, this also marks a change from the OTP's previous claims that it does not pursue political goals. The OTP is now seen as attempting regime change in Sudan; and also as acting in 'revenge' against Bashir for his refusal to surrender other government officials.[191] At the very least, the OTP's announcement of a warrant seems an attention-grabbing tactic to prove its willingness to take bold measures.[192] For this, after all, was the one situation where its actions against senior government officials had the support of other States, most notably the United States – for all its other political miscalculations, the OTP (unlike Cassese) correctly predicted that its warrant against Bashir would not antagonise the US government.

Shifts in public stance

The OTP's decision to proceed against Bashir also reflects two other important changes in its public stance. First, its rhetoric began to include reference to political considerations. Following his application

[188] *Daily News Egypt* reported that Bashir cancelled visits to South Africa and Turkey to avoid arrest: 'Sudan's President Says Ready to Go to War', *Daily News Egypt*, 20 August 2008.

[189] 'Sudan's President Bashir defies arrest warrant in Chad', BBC News, 21 July 2010; 'Court Worry at Omar Al-Bashir's Kenya Trip', BBC News, 28 August 2010; D. Akande, 'ICC Reports Kenya and Chad to the UN Security Council over Bashir's Visits', *European Journal of International Law: Talk!*, 28 August 2010; 'ICC Urges U.N. Action on Bashir Visit to Djibouti', Reuters, 12 May 2011; 'ICC Refers Malawi to UN Over Sudan's Bashir', BBC News, 13 December 2011; 'Sudan's President Bashir Leaves AU Summit in Nigeria', BBC News, 16 July 2013.

[190] Prosecutor (L. Moreno-Ocampo), Speech to the Eighth Session of the Assembly of States Parties, 18 November 2009; www.icc-cpi.int/NR/rdonlyres/CDF496C7-7BA7-4AA3-B670-1EE85BC3E3E8/281268/20091118ASPspeech.pdf; Prosecutor (L. Moreno-Ocampo), Tenth Statement to the Security Council on the Situation in Darfur pursuant to UNSC Res. 1593 (2005), 4 December 2009, www.icc-cpi.int/NR/rdonlyres/BA525867-5B58-4CDD-B6CF-8105181658D6/281343/UNSecurityCouncilStateFINAL1.pdf.

[191] See Nouwen and Werner, 'Doing Justice to the Political'.

[192] In 2009, African States decided not to cooperate with the ICC's request for Bashir's arrest and spoke of the 'publicity seeking approach of the Prosecutor': see 'Decision on the Meeting of African States Parties to the Rome Statute', African Union Press Release, Addis Ababa, 14 July 2009, www.africa-union.org/root/au/Conferences/2009/july/Press%20Release%20-%20ICC.doc.

for a warrant against Bashir, Prosecutor Moreno-Ocampo gave several speeches in which he said such warrants must be executed for reasons both of justice and *realpolitik*. He noted that arrests

> not only serve the interests of justice; they can help alleviate the humanitarian situation, facilitate the deployment and operation of UNAMID and reach lasting political agreements'.[193]

Moreover,

> [f]or almost one year, the first arrest warrant, issued against Harun, was ignored by mediators and political leaders in their discussions on Darfur. They discussed a three track approach: political negotiation, peacekeepers deployment and humanitarian assistance. They ignored the Court's decision, and they ignored the facts . . .
>
> Ignoring the arrest warrants was not an oversight. It was a decision based on the idea to sequence peace and justice. Peace first then Justice. As a consequence there was neither peace nor justice. So let us not repeat history . . .
>
> [P]eace and justice have to work hand in hand.[194]

In contrast, in its early phase, the OTP simply noted that:

> [T]here is a difference between the concepts of the interests of justice and the interests of peace and that the latter falls within the mandate of institutions other than [the OTP].[195]

Indeed, the OTP's later rhetoric is in line with claims that, in its case against Bashir, it used 'judicial diplomacy' to change the political calculus of various States.[196]

The second change in the OTP's public stance was that it began to pay greater attention to legitimacy challenges from quarters other than the United States. For instance, it began to make more effort to respond to the charges of neo-colonialism and targeting of African States. In contrast to

193 Prosecutor (L. Moreno-Ocampo), Keynote Address, Council for Foreign Relations Symposium, New York, 17 October 2008, www.icc-cpi.int/NR/rdonlyres/B8A3B99C-C9CC-4151-8BA6-35C2868BF60F/278840/CFRS2008.pdf; Prosecutor (L. Moreno-Ocampo), 'Combating Genocide and Other Massive Crimes – The International Criminal Court's Contribution', Address, The Hague, 7 December 2008, www.icc-cpi.int/NR/rdonlyres/E82DE594-5DB1-4870-BAB7-B8C71D2CCC13/279611/ICCOTPSTLMO20081207ENG.pdf.

194 Prosecutor (L. Moreno-Ocampo), Keynote Address, Yale University, New Haven, 6 February 2009, 8, www.icc-cpi.int/NR/rdonlyres/F04CB063-1C1E-463E-B8FB-5ECE076FB1E0/279792/090206_ProsecutorskeynoteaddressinYale.pdf.

195 Office of the Prosecutor, Policy Paper on the Interests of Justice, September 2007, 1, www.icc-cpi.int/NR/rdonlyres/772C95C9-F54D-4321-BF09-73422BB23528/143640/ICCOTPInterestsOfJustice.pdf.

196 Ginsburg, ICC Observers Project Interview.

previous summary dismissals of this charge – 'regional balance is not a criterion for situation selection under the Statute'[197] – the OTP presented a more detailed perspective on its relationship with Africa.

In the months following the warrant against Bashir and up to the Review Conference, Prosecutor Moreno-Ocampo and his then Deputy (now successor), Fatou Bensouda, addressed several meetings on the ICC's relationship with Africa.[198] They argued that African States were among the Court's greatest and most numerous supporters and that the rhetoric of 'neo-colonialism' did not correspond with the reality of that support. They denied any desire to bring about regime change in Sudan. They claimed that the Court should be viewed as an overdue response to the general disregard of African conflicts. Moreover, even as the OTP decided to open an investigation in Kenya, and was conducting preliminary examinations of situations in some other African States, they stressed the OTP's review of several non-African situations. They also indicated that the OTP would shortly produce a more detailed policy response to the charge of neo-colonialism in the form of a paper on 'appeasement or justice' (such a paper does not appear on the OTP's web pages). In addition, they expressed a desire for a dialogue with the African Union and the Rome Statute's African States parties.[199]

It is thus observable that, in the second phase of its work, the OTP's policies and public stance underwent a change, from caution to what some have called grandstanding. And, while it may have received criticism from some quarters, from the United States it received more support than at any point before, giving it the space to focus upon its reception by other audiences. These shifts in stance can also be traced through the changes in the OTP's approach to external communications.

A strategy for external communications

The Court's organs – the Presidency, the OTP and the Registry – recognised from early on that external communications, that is, publicising

[197] OTP, Report on Activities in the First Three Years, 2006, 7.

[198] Prosecutor, 'Working with Africa', ISS Symposium, 2009; Prosecutor (L. Moreno-Ocampo), 'The Role of International Judicial Bodies in Administering the Rule of Law', Qatar Law Forum, Doha, 30 May 2009, www.icc-cpi.int/NR/rdonlyres/10F9092D-4376-4E0B-84E1-DEBD55FA183B/280466/300509_QatarLawForum.pdf; Deputy Prosecutor (F. Bensouda), 'Africa's Involvement with the ICC', International Bar Association, 14 April 2009, www.icc-cpi.int/NR/rdonlyres/214816FF-DD8F-4908-97CF-B315C33F24FE/280279/20090414/FatouRomeStatute.pdf.

[199] Moreno-Ocampo, 'Working with Africa', ISS Symposium, 2009.

the purpose, goals and priorities of the Court to various audiences, would be important to secure support for the Court's work. They initially followed a coordinated approach, with a carefully worked out message crystallised into an 'Integrated Strategy for External Communications, Public Information, and Outreach' in July 2005. The Strategy itself is an internal Court document, but a summary may be found on the ICC website.[200]

The summary identifies 'message themes' that project the Court as 'judicial; impartial; effective; efficient; mindful of context; responsive to victims'.[201] The summary notes that, in the Strategy document, 'key messages are provided to elaborate upon the [six themes]'.[202] It directs that:

> Messages must reflect the core message themes; be responsive to the diversity of audiences and hence reflect an inclusive international perspective; manage expectations and explain the need for support and cooperation; and situate the ICC as a global institution and part of a broader international justice movement.
>
> ... Messages must be accurate yet simple to reach a non-specialist audience. Because of complexity of procedural and legal concepts, context should be explained (for example, in background sections of press releases). Where different roles of organs require different messages, the roles should be explained.[203]

Conversations with ICC personnel on the subject of the External Communications Strategy suggest that three themes predominated (some of these continue to be apparent). The first was reference to the Court's moral purpose, as a response to the 'impunity gap' in the international system. The second was its legal-normative authority, based on a close adherence to its constitutional document and other principles of international law, its structural probity and the legal credentials of its staff. The third was its systemic impact, not only in terms of its own investigations and prosecutions but also its effect on the domestic justice processes within States.

Different ICC organs emphasised these themes to different extents: this was in keeping with the Strategy, which did not exhaustively define the contents of their external statements and also permitted the formulation of additional communications strategies to address specific

[200] International Criminal Court, Summary of Integrated Strategy for External Relations, Public Information and Outreach, July 2005, www.icc-cpi.int/NR/rdonlyres/425E80BA-1EBC-4423-85C6-D4F2B93C7506/185049/ICCPIDSWBOR0307070402_IS_En.pdf.
[201] *Ibid.*, 4. [202] *Ibid.* [203] *Ibid.*, 4–5.

situations. The Strategy allocated primary authority for external communications to the Presidency; the OTP was to be responsible for specific external communications relevant to its mandate; and the Registry for administering the ICC's outreach to affected populations. Over the years, these organs began to depart from the Integrated Strategy, and differences may be observed between the communications of the Presidency and Registry, and those of the OTP in its second phase.

Let us examine some of the 'messages' delivered by the OTP, as well as other ICC organs, to see how these have changed with time.

'An idea whose time has come'[204]

In its early years, organs of the Court often stressed its moral purpose of combating impunity, emphasising – in the words of the ICC President – that, in this endeavour, 'we cannot afford to fail'.[205] Both President and Prosecutor pointed out that the Court's work was crucial to security and justice for millions of victims of international crimes around the world.

This remained a common theme even as the rest of the narrative about the Court was adjusted slightly to cater to the perceptions held by different audiences. Court officials would employ two kinds of narrative about the Court's founding.[206] The first would describe the Court as the inheritor of the Nuremberg legacy (though with improvements).[207] The second, deployed before audiences that had been

[204] Summary of Integrated Strategy for External Relations, section IV(5).

[205] President (P. Kirsch), Address to the General Assembly, 8 November 2005, www.icc-cpi.int/NR/rdonlyres/CC2EE876-18C6-4182-8A08-C5155B85802A/146328/PK_20051108_English1.pdf. See also President (P. Kirsch), Address at the Third Session of the ASP, 6 September 2004, www.icc-cpi.int/NR/rdonlyres/E49847E6-B414-4ADB-B8E1-70DC819BE40B/146333/PK_20040906_En.pdf; President (P. Kirsch), 'Applying the Principles of Nuremberg in the ICC', Keynote Address, Washington University, 19 November 2005, www.icc-cpi.int/NR/rdonlyres/ED2F5177-9F9B-4D66-9386-5C5BF45D052C/146323/PK_20060930_English.pdf.

[206] Koller, formerly in charge of the Court's External Communications Strategy, confirmed this: Koller personal interview (on file).

[207] President (P. Kirsch), 'From Nuremberg to The Hague', Nuremberg, 19 November 2005, www.icc-cpi.int/NR/rdonlyres/08AB9F8F-53A2-4533-BCE0-887419726332/143894/PK_20051119_En.pdf. See also President (P. Kirsch), 'La voie canadienne vers la CPI: tous les chemins mènent à Rome – Les enjeux et défis de la mise en œuvre de la CPI', Colloque organisé par les Journées Maximilien-Caron 2003 et l'Institut canadien d'Administration de la Justice, 5 February 2003, www.icc-cpi.int/en_menus/icc/structure%20of%20the%20court/presidency/statements/Pages/index.aspx; President (P. Kirsch), 'La Cour pénale internationale au carrefour du droit international et des relations internationals', University of Quebec, Montreal, 6 May 2003, www.icc-cpi.int/iccdocs/presidency/PK_20030506_Fr.pdf; President (P. Kirsch), 'Independence in the

sceptical of the Nuremberg and Tokyo trials (considering them, rather, examples of victor's justice), would insist on the Court as the product of 'a new and entirely different approach' followed in Rome in 1998.[208]

In its early years, the Court's moral function was asserted to encourage non parties to ratify the Rome Statute.[209] But this had evidently proved to be a delicate matter for the Court, as much of the fierce opposition to it was on the basis that it should exert no pressure on non parties. During conversations with ICC officials, both perspectives were advanced: on the one hand, that Court organs do actively seek ratifications (for instance, persuading Bangladesh to become the first South Asian State to ratify the ICC Statute in March 2010);[210] on the other hand that the Court recognised that non parties owed it no obligations and did not consider it morally incumbent upon States to ratify the Statute.[211] It was also noted that over the years the Court had made the shift away from relying on its moral purpose and on claims that it was 'an idea whose time has come' – though the founding narratives were used occasionally to promote specific initiatives like reparations for victims.[212] Instead, the Court's organs robustly asserted its legal-normative authority. This was evident in Prosecutor Moreno-Ocampo's speeches:

International Justice . . . became an institution.

The Rome Statute created a comprehensive and global criminal justice system:

- Substantial law has been codified in one detailed text . . . elements of crimes have been meticulously defined . . .
- Different legal and procedural traditions have been integrated into a new international model; victims have been given the right to participate in proceedings . . .
- The decision of States to give the Prosecutor the ability to trigger the Jurisdiction of the Court . . . creates a new autonomous actor on the

Context of Interdependence', Frederick K. Cox Lecture in Global Legal Reform, Case Western Reserve University School of Law, Cleveland, 7 November 2005, www.icc-cpi.int/NR/rdonlyres/777C9300-BD47-4EAE-B9A2-8465959772ED/143893/PK_20051107_En.pdf.

208 See, for instance, Prosecutor (L. Moreno-Ocampo), 'Building a Future on Peace and Justice', Address, Nuremberg, 24/25 June 2007, www.icc-cpi.int/NR/rdonlyres/4E466EDB-2B38-4BAF-AF5F-005461711149/143825/LMO_nuremberg_20070625_English.pdf.

209 See, for instance, President (P. Kirsch), 'Protecting the Integrity of the International Criminal Court', Strategy Meeting, Parliamentarians for Global Action, United Nations, New York, 22 April 2003, www.icc-cpi.int/en_menus/icc/structure%20of%20the%20court/presidency/statements/Pages/index.aspx.

210 Bassu, personal interview (on file).

211 Koller, personal interview (on file).

212 *Ibid.*

> international scene ... [and] ensures that the requirements of justice will prevail over any political decision.
>
> ... [T]he Rome Treaty ... is a strong and consistent body of law; the drafters were well aware that rendering justice in the context of conflict or peace negotiations would present particular difficulties and they prepared our institution well to meet those challenges. Careful decisions were made: a high threshold of gravity ... a system of complementarity ... and the UN Security Council was given a role in cases of threats to peace and security ...
>
> It is the new law.
>
> The issue is no longer about whether we agree or disagree with the pursuit of justice in moral or practical terms.
>
> It is the law.[213]

While asserting that the Rome Statue had created a new legal situation, the ICC organs also began to refine their stance on the claim that the Court was a political actor.

'A judicial institution operating in a highly political environment'[214]

The Court's organs make a strong case for its structural legitimacy. Indeed, the Strategic Plan for the Court, developed in 2006, stated that amongst its primary goals was being a 'model of public administration'.[215] The Plan specified that the Court should seek to achieve 'desired results with minimal resources through streamlined structures and processes while maintaining flexibility, guaranteeing accountability and drawing upon sufficient qualified and motivated staff within a caring environment and a non-bureaucratic culture'.[216] This was entirely in keeping with previous statements by the ICC President and Prosecutor directing attention towards the ICC's well-organised institutional structure, which divided responsibilities amongst various organs, and clearly demarcated offices within each organ;[217] and towards the qualifications of its personnel, particularly the excellence

213 Prosecutor, 'Building a Future on Peace and Justice', Nuremberg, 2007; see also Prosecutor, 'Combating Genocide and Other Massive Crimes'.

214 See Prosecutor, Address, Council for Foreign Relations, 2010 (quoting President S.-H. Song).

215 Strategic Plan of the International Criminal Court, ICC-ASP/5/6, 4 August 2006, 5, www.icc-cpi.int/NR/rdonlyres/D6B4058F-2C5D-415E-A85F-64A305C81DF0/0/ICCASP56_English.pdf.

216 *Ibid.*, 5.

217 See, for instance, Prosecutor (L. Moreno-Ocampo), Address at the Third Assembly of States Parties, 6 September 2004, www.icc-cpi.int/NR/rdonlyres/1E4656AC-32D9-483D-9D2A-DE74F2FD8415/0/LMO_20040906_En.pdf.

of its judges.[218] The Prosecutor also took pains to describe the multi-stage processes by which his office reached decisions to investigate and prosecute. The claims of structural legitimacy were particularly significant in the initial phase when the ICC was a completely new organisation with a limited record of actual operation.

As the OTP commenced its first few investigations and prosecutions, the ICC organs continued to rely on the tight separation of functions between the OTP and the Chambers. They insisted that, although the Chambers were called upon to evaluate factors – such as the 'interests of justice' or whether a State is 'unwilling or unable' to investigate or prosecute – that bordered on the political, and though the Presidency played a proactive role in mobilising support for the Court, ICC judges were well able to 'conduct fair, effective and expeditious public proceedings in accordance with the Rome Statute and with high legal standards, ensuring full exercise of the rights of all participants'.[219] Indeed, the controversy surrounding the *Lubanga* case, in which the Trial Chamber was forced to stay the trial because the Prosecutor had failed to disclose exculpatory material to the defence, was relied upon by the Prosecutor himself as an illustration of the Court's judicial probity.[220]

Over the years, the OTP also offered a more nuanced description of its own role. While the Prosecutor continued to insist that he was 'not involved in political considerations' and that his decisions were guided by the legal limits imposed by the Rome Statute and based upon set policies explained in publicly available documents,[221] the OTP began to expressly acknowledge that its work was carried out in a political context. One aspect of this acknowledgment, mentioned earlier, was that the Prosecutor took an express position on the 'peace versus justice' debate. Though earlier he had simply denied the debate by stressing

[218] See, for instance, President (P. Kirsch), Statement at the Inaugural Meeting of the Judges, 11 March 2003, www.icc-cpi.int/NR/rdonlyres/48D76A79-7315-49C2-A16F-86D7CFAAE721/143846/PK_20030311_En.pdf.

[219] Strategic Plan of the ICC, 2006. See also President, Applying the Principles of Nuremberg in the ICC, Washington University, 2005; President (P. Kirsch), Address to the General Assembly, 1 November 2007, www.icc-cpi.int/NR/rdonlyres/B3B8B89D-B9E5-441E-A3D5-EA9E91B22142/277274/PK_20071101_ENG1.pdf; and President (P. Kirsch), Address to the General Assembly, 30 October 2008, www.icc-cpi.int/NR/rdonlyres/86BD12FB-F92F-44B3-89D8-DE376A9EB989/279062/PK_20081030_ENG.pdf ('[the] Court is impartial and enduring . . . [and] stands as a bulwark against the temptation, no matter how well-intentioned, to bargain away justice').

[220] Prosecutor, Address, Council for Foreign Relations, 2010. [221] *Ibid.*

that his mandate was not concerned with issues of peace-making, he now began to stress that justice was an integral component of peace – there could be no peace without justice. This was part of a strategy to press for arrests of Sudanese officials, and the OTP even justified its open warrant for Bashir as a strategy of political marginalisation. Other organs of the ICC too have since spoken on the peace versus justice issue: in one recent speech, the Vice President even quoted an empirical study to argue that trials do not impede peace processes.[222]

'No longer a theoretical construct, but a tangible court'[223]

A consistent element of the ICC organs' external communications has been the assertion, right from the early months of the Court's operation, that the Court was already an essential part of the international system. The President and the Prosecutor pointed to its expanding docket, and its outreach programmes and 'positive' complementarity. They also described the Court as exercising a deterrent effect on the commission of international crimes, citing not only the indirect impact of the Rome Statute on the drafting of national legislation,[224] but also actual instances where persons were encouraged not to commit crimes for fear of being hauled up before the ICC.[225] Moreover, they noted the Court's impact on domestic justice systems, with references to Colombia as an instance where the possibility of an ICC investigation triggered domestic trials.[226]

The emphasis on the complementary nature of the Court's jurisdiction was important also to the management of expectations about its performance. With only a small number of actual trials, the ICC organs insisted that evaluations of the Court must be done using a variety of

222 Vice-President (H.-P. Kaul), 'Peace through Justice? The International Criminal Court in the Hague', National Military History Museum of the Armed Forces of Germany, 2 November 2009, www.icc-cpi.int/NR/rdonlyres/B7BC9709-394D-4449-AA08-4182A98C567B/281395/JudgeKaulSpeech.pdf.

223 President, 'Protecting the Integrity of the ICC', Parliamentarians for Global Action, Strategy Meeting, 2003.

224 Prosecutor, 'Building a Future on Peace and Justice', Nuremberg, 2007.

225 Prosecutor, 'The role of International Judicial Bodies in Administering the Rule of Law', Qatar Law Forum, 2009 ('In 2003 an Australian military pilot conducting operations in Iraq realized that if he executed the order received, he could be prosecuted in accordance with the Rome Statute. He returned to his base without dropping the bombs.').

226 Prosecutor, 'Building a Future on Peace and Justice', Nuremberg, 2007; Address, Council for Foreign Relations, 2010; OTP official, personal interview (on file).

metrics.[227] The OTP asserted that 'the effectiveness of [the ICC] should not be measured only by the number of cases that reach the Court. On the contrary, the absence of trials by the ICC, as a consequence of the effective functioning of national systems, would be a major success.'[228] The Prosecutorial Strategy described 'positive complementarity' as a fundamental element of its approach – this extended to 'encouraging genuine national proceedings', providing information to national judiciaries, involving 'officials, experts and lawyers from situation countries' in the OTP's work, providing information to political mediators, and 'acting as a catalyst with development organisations and donors' conferences to promote support for relevant accountability efforts'.[229] In this context, the Legal Advisor to the CICC made the interesting observation that a focus on 'positive complementarity' had allowed the Court organs to focus on the shortcomings of the domestic justice systems in developing States, rather than on many developed States' omission to implement the Rome Statute through appropriate domestic legislation incorporating international crimes and stipulating cooperation with the ICC.[230] In recent years, the OTP has also stressed the impact of the Court in terms of a concept of law and economics: 'the shadow of the Court', which it claims 'extends to at least 110 States which are Parties to the Rome Statute and even beyond to reach non States Parties'.[231] This concept was articulated by Kornhauser and Mnookin based on a study of divorce cases. They found that judicial decisions on previous divorce cases influenced the bargaining

[227] President, 'Independence in the Context of Interdependence', Cox Lecture, Case Western Reserve University, 2005; President (P. Kirsch), Opening Remarks at the Fifth Session of the ASP, 23 November 2006, www.icc-cpi.int/NR/rdonlyres/3EEF266E-E4B1-486C-9B05-DD0D87CDBEEB/143883/PK_20061123_en1.pdf; President (P. Kirsch), 'ICC Marks Five Years since Entry into Force of Rome Statute', Statement, The Hague, 26 June 2007, www.icc-cpi.int/NR/rdonlyres/C307EC9D-B735-47D6-BA5C-508D0A5D8C71/143884/PK_20070627_en.pdf.

[228] Informal Experts, 'The Principle of Complementarity in Practice'. See also Prosecutor (L. Moreno-Ocampo), Ceremony for the Solemn Undertaking of the Prosecutor, Statement, The Hague, 16 June 2003, www.icc-cpi.int/NR/rdonlyres/D7572226-264A-4B6B-85E3-2673648B4896/143585/030616_moreno_ocampo_english.pdf.

[229] Office of the Prosecutor, Report on Prosecutorial Strategy for 2006–2009, 14 September 2006, 5, www.icc-cpi.int/NR/rdonlyres/D673DD8C-D427-4547-BC69-2D363E07274B/143708/ProsecutorialStrategy20060914_English.pdf; Office of the Prosecutor, Report on Prosecutorial Strategy for 2009–2012, 1 February 2010, 4–6, www.icc-cpi.int/NR/rdonlyres/66A8DCDC-3650-4514-AA62-D229D1128F65/281506/OTPProsecutorialStrategy20092013.pdf.

[230] Pal, personal interview (on file).

[231] Prosecutor, Address, Council for Foreign Relations, 2010.

behaviour of parties even when they were negotiating outside the judicial process.[232] The OTP argues that the ICC has similarly altered the playing field for States and potential criminals.

The ICC organs also managed expectations about the Court's performance by placing the onus for its successful functioning upon 'key partners and audiences'.[233] They emphasised the Court's dependence upon State cooperation, UN support and support from other organisations, and reiterated that the Court was both 'independent and interdependent' with other actors.[234] Stressing the Court's interdependence, the President and Prosecutor, whenever they have appeared before a congregation of States, have offered detailed information on the extent to which the ICC receives cooperation.[235] In addition to presenting a brief scorecard, they have provided suggestions for bolstering State cooperation. The Court organs have also actively nursed civil society support, lacing their policy documents and speeches with management-speak, including that States and civil society should 'take ownership of the Court';[236] the aim to build a 'network of relationships' with national authorities, multilateral institutions, NGOs and other entities; the OTP's aim of 'maximizing the impact' of its activities;[237] and the description of complementarity as a 'consensual division of labour'.[238]

In sum, the message was delivered that, in order to evaluate the Court, one should look not only at the investigations and trials before it, but also all around – at other actors, and how they may have contributed to the Court, or otherwise been impacted by it. For, to see the Court as a part of the calculations of various actors and embedded within 'a network of relationships' is to see it as an integral, immovable part of the landscape of the international legal system – taking it beyond the initial fragility of its position.

232 R. Mnookin and L. Kornhauser, 'Bargaining in the Shadow of the Law: The Case of Divorce' (1987) 88 *Yale Law Journal* 950, 968.

233 A list of 'key partners and audiences' is provided in the Summary of Integrated Strategy for External Relations, Public Information and Outreach 2005.

234 President, Statement at the Inaugural Meeting of the Judges, 2003; President, 'Independence in the Context of Interdependence', Cox Lecture, Case Western Reserve University, 2005; Prosecutor, Statement, Ceremony for the Solemn Undertaking of the Prosecutor, 2003.

235 Prosecutor, Remarks at Meeting of the Committee of Legal Advisers, Strasburg, 2004; President, 'Protecting the Integrity of the ICC', Parliamentarians for Global Action, Strategy Meeting, 2003.

236 Informal Experts, 'The Principle of Complementarity in Practice'.

237 See OTP, Report on Prosecutorial Strategy for 2006–2009.

238 *Ibid.*

A review of the OTP's activities from 2002 to 2010

It is possible and useful to explore the role of international law in mediating the United States–ICC relationship, and to illustrate the OTP's work as that of compliance management by focusing upon three elements of the model suggested by Chayes and Chayes, who had argued that a treaty body would promote compliance by persuading States, as well as by requiring them to publicly explain refusals to comply with generally accepted norms. Moreover, they had claimed that a treaty body could set an appropriate level of compliance *inter alia* by modifying norms – this would be justified where the treaty body was authorised for this purpose, or where the modifications were worked out through a legal discourse involving relevant actors, and following due process. They had asserted that a legal discourse was the most appropriate for weighing and resolving differences between actors.[239] This model may be stated in terms of three elements relevant to the OTP's work: whether it has promoted a culture of compliance with the Rome Statute; its role in fleshing out important elements of the Statute; and the turn to arguments of 'law' in the discourse on international criminal justice.

Compliance with the Court

To begin with, the OTP undoubtedly played the key role in 'realising' the Court. Had the OTP not commenced investigations, the Court might simply have remained an idea on paper. The OTP was pro-active in obtaining referrals from States, using both persuasion and threats (that the Prosecutor would use his *proprio motu* power) to this end. It was also expeditious in identifying cases that it could bring to trial within a short time, allowing for early commencement of the Court's process. And it was assiduous in keeping hold of cases, once these had been identified. In short, it was active in bringing some States within the ordinary process of the Court.

Apart from this, it is not possible – on the basis of the sources used for this chapter – to state definitively whether, or to what extent, the OTP has promoted a culture of compliance with the Rome Statute. The chapter has not investigated the role, if any, that the OTP may have played in encouraging States to ratify the Statute, nor whether there obtains a culture of compliance within the ICC States parties. However,

[239] See the section on 'Compliance management' in Chapter 3 of this book.

it is worth noting that the OTP claims successes for itself in terms that amount to embedding compliance amongst States, groups and individuals. In public speeches, Prosecutor Moreno-Ocampo has referred to specific individuals and States who moderated their behaviour out of respect – or fear – of the ICC and its prosecutorial process, and has asserted the 'shadow of the Court'. The OTP also refers to the 'positive complementarity' effects of the Court on domestic criminal justice systems.

There are, however, also several countervailing indications, with States and even international organisations refusing to comply with demands from the Court, often as the result of the OTP's own policy choices. For instance, Uganda sought to withdraw its referral. Kenya has been seeking to withdraw its ratification of the Rome Statute[240] – and has reportedly encouraged other African Union States to do so too.[241] The African Union, the Arab League and others requested the UN Security Council to 'stay' the OTP's investigations into Sudan, and have criticised its charges against Kenya's top leadership.[242] Previously, the African Union had decided not to cooperate with the Court's request to arrest Sudan's President Bashir. Several States, among them Chad, China, Djibouti, Egypt, Eritrea, Ethiopia, Iran, Iraq, Kenya, Libya, Malawi, Nigeria, Qatar, Saudi Arabia and South Sudan, have hosted Bashir despite the ICC warrant for his arrest.[243] Among these, Chad, Djibouti, Kenya, Malawi and Nigeria are parties to the Rome Statute – they simply ignored the Court's requests, although reports suggest that Malawi has since changed its stance.[244] Overall, there were (and remain) complaints about the Court's Africa focus, and the costs this has had both for peace processes in some of these States as well as for their domestic justice systems.[245] These factors suggest a need to critically evaluate the role that the OTP has played in seeking to bring the Court into effective operation.

[240] See 'Kenya Parliament Calls Urgent Debate on ICC Membership', BBC News, 3 September 2013; K. J. Heller, 'Kenya Moves Closer to Withdrawing from the ICC', *Opinio Juris*, 23 December 2010.

[241] See D. Akande, 'Is Kenya Pushing for a Mass Withdrawal from the ICC', *European Journal of International Law: Talk!*, 14 January 2011.

[242] J. Vaughan and A. Genet, 'Africa Closes Ranks to Condemn "Racist" ICC on Kenya Cases', AFP, 27 May 2013.

[243] The details on Bashir's travels to these countries may be obtained from http://bashirwatch.org.

[244] 'Malawi Not to Host Summit After Row Over Sudan Leader', BBC News, 8 June 2012.

[245] For instance, 'African Union Accuses ICC of "Hunting" Africans', BBC News, 27 May 2013.

The OTP's implementation of the Rome Statute

The debate on the OTP's role in implementing the Rome Statute is usually in terms of whether or not it can be described as a 'political' one. In its contribution to this debate, the OTP has claimed that it does not act politically. Only recently has it slightly altered its stance to acknowledge that there is a political context to its work, as opposed to earlier claims of complete insulation from politics. In several speeches, former Prosecutor Moreno-Ocampo claimed that his decisions on whether to open an investigation into a situation, and which cases to select, were solely guided by 'the law'. On this basis, he also refused for the most part to engage in the peace/justice debate, claiming that peace was not within the Court's mandate, only justice was. Again, the OTP stance on this issue has shifted slightly, to the claim that justice and peace go hand-in-hand.

But the OTP's efforts to claim that its role is an apolitical one have only rendered it vulnerable to criticism. Commentators have found it easy to highlight the vast discretion allowed to the Prosecutor by the Statute, and to argue that this discretion has been exercised in a biased way.[246] This, together with accusations of grandstanding and pursuing regime change, have come together into a narrative of a political body, undermining the OTP's claims to credibility based on the implementation of the law 'without fear or favour'.[247]

It must be noted here that the claim that the OTP acts in a political way is not in itself a damning one – indeed too much may have been made (even by the OTP itself) of the law versus politics distinction. It is not remarkable that the OTP has acted politically – the problem, as the charges enumerated by the OTP's critics indicate, is that its politics have been incoherent. That the OTP cannot exercise the same capacities with respect to the United States and some African States is not surprising, but simply the unfortunate implication of the political context in which the Court must operate. Indeed, the design of the Rome Statute accommodates this context: its admissibility provisions, outlining complementarity, gravity and the interests of justice as relevant factors, allow the OTP to balance its investigation against the political conditions

[246] Commentaries that assert the political character of the OTP's work include: Nouwen and Werner, 'Doing Justice to the Political'; Schabas, 'Prosecutorial Discretion and Gravity'; de Waal and Flint, 'Case Closed: A Prosecutor Without Borders'; and several other scholarly articles and news reports cited in this chapter.

[247] Prosecutor, Keynote Address, Yale, 2009, 3.

prevailing in different States. However, the OTP has failed to follow a coherent or considered policy – its decision-making has been inconsistent, and often at odds with its own narrative of the ICC's proper role. This chapter has offered several examples of the OTP's *ad hoc* justifications and policy avowals: its specious and limited-term embrace of a situational gravity threshold in the case of Iraq; its interpretation of complementarity to apply only where the same person is being tried for exactly the same conduct in the domestic State, though this might only short-circuit an ongoing domestic proceeding, as in *Lubanga*; its refusal to consider the relations of investigations to peace processes; its claim that the UPDF's crimes in Uganda were less serious than the LRA's; its lack of progress in seven years in conducting its preliminary investigation into Afghanistan – these are ill-advised positions legally *and* politically.

As discussed in this chapter, the OTP perhaps felt compelled to take these positions as a response to the dual challenges that it was faced with: on the one hand, effectively implementing the Rome Statute, and on the other, responding to the measures taken by the United States, a non-party. A treaty body may often find itself in this situation when responding to the difficulties posed by conflicts involving treaties with non-identical parties. The OTP's response provides the relevant gloss upon the Chayes and Chayes claim that treaty bodies are able to 'manage' such situations, and promote adherence to its affiliated treaty. For all the difficulties it faced, the OTP offers the picture, not of a politically aware body that (within the limitations of its context) coherently and determinedly implements the Rome Statute; but of a constantly politicking body which is unable to align its long-term and immediate goals, and keeps changing its stance in response to the most organised challenge at the time. The OTP's policies seem reactive, not principled, and it is this – rather than embracing a political role – that hurts its credibility.

The turn to 'the law'

Yet, despite the critique, the OTP (and to some extent other ICC organs) did influence the dynamics of the United States–ICC relationship, overcoming some of the early challenges faced by the Court. And here the ways in which it co-opted the idea and practices of 'the law' were indeed significant. On the basis that it was simply following the law, the OTP was able to avoid answering pointed questions about the practical implications of the Court. The Prosecutor could simply note:

With the entry into force of the Rome Statute, a new legal framework has emerged and this framework necessarily impacts on conflict management efforts. The issue is no longer about whether we agree or disagree with the pursuit of justice in moral or practical terms: it is the law. Any political or security initiative must be compatible with the new legal framework insofar as it involves parties bound by the Rome Statute.[248]

This statement may reflect almost too categorical an agenda, given the types of situations the ICC was expected to be concerned with. However, the stance it represented also allowed the OTP to compile an empire of 'paper truths' that responded to that created by the United States in opposition to the Court.[249] For, the US strategy against the Court had taken the form of (what Chapter 4 calls) document-rattling – through BIAs and associated legislation, the United States sought to limit the Court's capacity for effective operation; by deleting references from inter-governmental documents and similar measures, it also sought to avoid giving recognition to the 'concrete' presence of the Court – to prevent the Court from taking hold, so to speak. Against this, the OTP produced its own trail of documents that proved that the Court was – in the words of its President – 'no longer a theoretical construct, but a tangible court'.[250] It produced not only policy papers to explain its procedures, but also secured referrals, charge-sheets, warrants, and trial documents that, as formal acts, were compelling evidence that the Court was already part of the landscape of the international system. These documents unsettled the consensus against the Court that the United States was seeking to project, even as they made it evident that the OTP would not take a directly confrontational stance against the United States.

Moreover, while the OTP's stance of treating all difficult policy questions as simply matters of interpretation of the Rome Statute has resulted in questionable choices on complementarity, gravity, self-referrals and non-disclosure, it was also successful in re-describing the conflict between the Statute and the BIAs from a politically charged affair into a routine issue of construing the former's cooperation provisions. The OTP, together with other ICC organs and 'friends of the Court'

[248] OTP, Policy Paper on the Interests of Justice, 4. See also Prosecutor, 'Working with Africa', ISS Symposium, 2009.

[249] The phrase 'paper truths' is from E. Tarlo, *Unsettling Memories: Narratives of the Emergency in Delhi* (Berkeley, University of California Press 2003) 10, 62 *et seq.*

[250] President, 'Protecting the Integrity of the ICC', Parliamentarians for Global Action, Strategy Meeting, 2003.

thus represented the lynchpin of the US opposition to the Court as a legal question of the appropriate remit of Article 98 and who may authoritatively pronounce upon the same. The Court's personnel built on this to insist that the BIAs cannot be taken as a serious challenge to the Court, because the Court itself will decide what effect they have when the occasion arises. The CICC commissioned a legal 'opinion' on the compatibility of the BIAs with Article 98.[251] The European Union issued its own opinion, providing Guidelines as to the proper scope of the BIAs. The United States too seemed influenced by this legal turn, with the US State Department adding a bracketed qualification to a draft provision of its Uganda BIA:

> 5. [This paragraph is used only in agreements with states that are not parties or signatories to the Rome Statute]. Each Party agrees, subject to its international legal obligations, not to knowingly facilitate, consent to, or cooperate with efforts by any third party or country to effect the extradition, surrender, or transfer of a person of the other Party to the International Criminal Court.[252]

This paragraph was not included in the agreement finally concluded between these two States.

The OTP has responded to the cooperation challenges following its decision to charge Sudan's President Bashir with an insistence upon Statute-prescribed legal processes. Even as it has publicised instances in which Bashir has had to cancel foreign visits to avoid arrest, it has not commented upon the politics underlying the African Union and some States' decisions not to cooperate on this issue. Instead, it has simply referred States which have not cooperated despite being parties to the Statute to the Security Council. The PTC, meanwhile, has ruled that Bashir does not enjoy personal immunity. These actions have not had any spectacular result, but one State at least - Malawi - seems to have been persuaded by them to change its stance *vis-à-vis* arresting Bashir. Previously, the OTP had also dealt with Uganda's attempts to withdraw its referrals in the same way - by steering it towards the Court's admissibility procedure.

The turn to 'the law' in the OTP's approach has also introduced constraints on some of its own most dubious policy choices. As the *Lubanga* case showed, the Court rejected the OTP's claim on non-disclosure of exculpatory evidence. Of course, the Court's oversight only extends up to a point: in particular, decisions *not* to select

[251] Crawford *et al.*, Joint Opinion. [252] www.amicc.org/docs/UgandaBIA.pdf.

situations or cases are hard to assess judicially. While academic commentary may assist – the OTP giving up its test of 'situational gravity' was surely owed, at least in part, to critiques that this was a bad interpretation of the Statute – there is no standard way for the OTP to proceed in different situations. For instance, the OTP is evidently 'going slow' on some examinations, such as Afghanistan, but there is no legal way to expedite its work – the Statute permits the Security Council to defer investigations, but to nudge the OTP onwards remains a matter for diplomacy and politics.

It is fair to say – and this may be the best indicator of the success of the strategy of 'the law' adopted by the OTP, as also by other ICC organs – that the Court's work has foregrounded issues of individual criminal responsibility in assessments of key political developments. Discussions on the Arab Spring were in terms of violations of international criminal law – the question of referral to the ICC was mooted in the case of Egypt, Syria and Bahrain. While these referrals seem unlikely, we saw that the Security Council resolution to refer Libya to the ICC a very short time after the uprising commenced (the resolution was voted on 26 February 2011; it referred to the situation in Libya since February 15) was not at all controversial, and passed with all affirmative votes – including the United States'. In contrast the Darfur referral, six years previously, had followed a long process of negotiation.

In short, much has changed in the years since the Statute was adopted – it was once unimaginable that all sorts of political upheavals would be routinely discussed in terms of international criminal law. While the OTP directs attention to the Court's impact upon the updating of national legislations, national initiatives to investigate and prosecute crimes, and the prevention of crimes, this change in how events are perceived, even at the popular level, is perhaps the strongest evidence of the growing 'shadow of the Court'.

The evolving Court

This chapter has used the lens of treaty conflict to explain the ICC's evolution in the previous decade. It has focused on the OTP, comparing its role to Chayes and Chayes' model of compliance management of treaties by treaty bodies. The chapter shows that the OTP's role cannot be usefully discussed in terms of whether it is or should be guided by 'the law' alone or also by 'politics', for it is necessarily guided by both. Indeed, it is for the OTP to accept the politics of its work and to bring into these the values of consistency, principled interpretation, impartial application, procedural rigour and transparent reasoning that are associated with the law. While these elements have indeed been present in the actual trials conducted by the ICC, they have not been so consistently in the early choices that the OTP is required to make in each situation examined by it.

However, we must not lose sight of the remarkable success of the OTP and the other ICC organs in infusing ideas of law and criminal responsibility into how we perceive and respond to situations of violence, political upheavals and ethnic conflicts, even at a popular level. Concepts of law and responsibility were not previously missing from our vocabulary, but were not dominant aspects of how any such situations were assessed and responded to – today, as we see with respect to the Arab Spring, they are in the forefront. It is the OTP's difficult and perhaps thankless job to continue to emphasise these concepts, even as it fully embraces that the politics of its involvement in various situations requires it not to reduce these concepts to mere legalisms.

A study of the OTP's practice over several years provides excellent insight into what it means for a treaty body to play a 'managerial' role to effectively implement a treaty challenged by organised opposition from a few States. Here, the US-led BIAs sought to limit the cooperation provisions of the Rome Statute and in a broader sense were a challenge to the ICC's credibility as a judicial institution. The OTP had to simultaneously object to limits on the Court's right to determine the scope of cooperation provisions and avoid a practical confrontation between a State and the Court on this issue; and reassure fears about excessive prosecutorial discretion but also preserve an active docket for the Court. This chapter shows that these objectives are more incoherent than may at first appear. And this is probably true of all treaty bodies that face the task of reconciling their affiliated multilateral treaty with challenges posed through legal devices such as conflicting treaties.

This task is anything but 'managerial' in the sense of being apolitical, and even following 'the law' may be quite an empty claim. However, even as an empty claim, it offers – as it did in the present case – a platform for a sustained constructive critique, suggesting prospects for reform. In the case of the OTP, its recent departures in policy and rhetoric suggest that such reform is underway.

6 Fissions in the nuclear order: the India–US Nuclear Deal and the nuclear-governance regime

> It would be a milestone, timely for ongoing efforts to consolidate the non-proliferation regime, combat nuclear terrorism and strengthen nuclear safety.
>
> Mohammed ElBaradei on the India–US Nuclear Deal[1]

> [Y]ou have consistently argued for universal approaches to addressing the dangers posed by nuclear weapons and against perpetuating double standards governing nuclear weapon haves and have nots. Creating far-reaching exemptions to international rules for India betrays these two principles.
>
> Letter to Mohammed ElBaradei[2]

Introduction

International nuclear policy, no less than nuclear physics, is built on contradiction. It seeks to limit the spread of nuclear weapons at the same time as encouraging States to use nuclear energy for peaceful purposes. Yet, the scientific process for the two overlaps to a great extent, so that States pursuing advanced civil nuclear technology are the ones that might most easily acquire nuclear weapons, should they put their mind to it.

India illustrated this contradiction in 1974, when it detonated a nuclear device at its military range in Pokhran, Rajasthan. Code-named the 'Smiling Buddha', the explosion was described at the time

[1] 'IAEA Director General Welcomes US and India Nuclear Deal', IAEA Press Release 2006/05, 2 March 2006, www.iaea.org/NewsCenter/PressReleases/2006/prn200605.html.

[2] D. Kimball *et al.*, 'An Open Letter to Mohammed ElBaradei from Twelve Nuclear Experts', 24 July 2006, www.armscontrol.org/pdf/20060724_Ltr_ElBaradei_India.pdf.

by Indian authorities as a 'peaceful' one.[3] The *Times of India* observed that India was the first country to 'forswear the military uses of nuclear energy simultaneously with its entry into the select [nuclear] club'.[4] 'India's renunciation of military use, even after attaining nuclear capability', the newspaper continued,

> has confronted the global community with a new situation which the forthcoming conference to review the non-proliferation treaty will have to take notice of. Hitherto there have only been nuclear powers and non-nuclear powers, India has created a new category, which may have considerable relevance to discussions on disarmament . . . and [peaceful explosions].[5]

But, for all India's claims of renunciation, other States worried that India's nuclear test marked an advance of its nuclear weapons programme, facilitated by its diversion of a Canadian-supplied nuclear reactor – 'CIRUS' – from civilian to military use.[6] And, indeed, India continued to develop nuclear weapons, though it waited until 1998 to conduct the five further tests that overtly proclaimed its possession of them.

States have relied upon the nuclear-governance regime to reconcile the contradiction between promoting the use of nuclear energy for peaceful purposes and non-proliferation. This regime is underpinned by the 1968 Treaty on the Non-Proliferation of Nuclear Weapons (NPT),[7] to which all States, except for India, Israel and Pakistan, are parties. The NPT addresses both the possession and proliferation of nuclear weapons and the development and use of nuclear energy for peaceful purposes. It is supported by more narrowly tailored treaties on non-proliferation,[8] nuclear safety[9] and

[3] See 'Blast with a Difference', *Times of India*, 20 May 1974; S. Laxman, 'And We Had a Blast', *Times of India*, 16 May 1999.

[4] 'India Joins Nuclear Club: Successful Underground Test Explosion', *Times of India*, 19 May 1974. 'China', the article continued, 'when it detonated its first atomic bomb in 1964, said it would not be the first to use nuclear weapons, but hold them in reserve for a counter-attack.'

[5] *ibid.*

[6] A summary of international reactions to India's nuclear explosion may be found in G. Perkovich, *India's Nuclear Bomb: The Impact on Global Proliferation* (Berkeley, University of California Press 1999) 183–7.

[7] 729 UNTS 161.

[8] The Comprehensive Nuclear Test Ban Treaty, 1996, 35 ILM 1439; Treaty Banning Nuclear Weapon Tests in the Atmosphere, Outer Space and Under Water, 1963, 480 UNTS 43.

[9] Convention on Physical Protection of Nuclear Material, 1979, 18 ILM 1419; Convention on Nuclear Safety, 1994, 33 ILM 1514.

nuclear disarmament.[10] A principal feature of the NPT is its system of safeguards – arrangements for third-party inspections of nuclear facilities – to prevent diversion of nuclear materials and technology from civilian use to weapons production. These safeguards are administered by the International Atomic Energy Agency (IAEA).[11] In addition, export-control networks such as the Nuclear Suppliers Group (NSG) and the Zangger Committee provide guidelines regulating transfers of nuclear material between States. The NSG was established as a response to India's 1974 nuclear test.

Until 2005, the cumulative practice of States participating in the nuclear-governance regime was to limit, and (following 1998) entirely cease, nuclear supplies to India. This, arguably, was not simply a matter of policy preference, but also dictated by their legal commitments under the NPT and related documents (such as NSG Guidelines). For, while India itself is not party to the NPT, its acquisition of nuclear weapons is contrary to the NPT specification of only five States – the United States, the United Kingdom, France, Russia and China – as *de jure* nuclear weapons States (NWS), implying that all other States must necessarily be non nuclear weapons States (NNWS) (a classification that India regards as discriminatory). The NPT also prohibits direct or indirect assistance or encouragement to NNWS to develop nuclear weapons. While the treaty provides for the inalienable right of such States to develop their peaceful nuclear programmes and enjoins States with advanced civil nuclear capabilities (including, of course, the NWS) to assist the NNWS to this end, this is by way of a bargain offered to NNWS – to forgo nuclear weapons in return for energy assistance, security guarantees and disarmament measures by NWS; a bargain which India rejected both in form and in substance.

In 2005, during the July visit of US President George Bush to India, and following several months of discussions, came the announcement that the two States had agreed upon 'full civil nuclear energy cooperation'.[12] Under the 'Nuclear Deal', India would receive nuclear material and technology from the United States. The United States would 'work

[10] These treaties are often regional in scope: for instance, the Treaty for the Prohibition of Nuclear Weapons in Latin America (Treaty of Tlatelolco), 1967, 634 UNTS 326; African Nuclear-Weapon-Free Zone Treaty (Treaty of Pelindaba), 1996, 35 ILM 698; South Pacific Nuclear-Free Zone Treaty (Treaty of Rarotonga), 1985, 24 ILM 1442.

[11] Established by the Statute of the International Atomic Energy Agency, 1956, 276 UNTS 3.

[12] India–United States Joint Statement, 18 July 2005, www.dae.gov.in/jtstmt.htm.

with friends and allies to adjust international regimes' to enable this cooperation. For its part, India agreed to place many of its nuclear facilities under IAEA safeguards, maintain a moratorium on nuclear testing, adopt strict export-control measures and undertake some other measures so as to 'assume the same responsibilities and practices and acquire the same benefits and advantages as other leading countries with advanced nuclear technology, such as the United States'.[13]

As the quotes cited at the start of this chapter suggest, announcement of the Nuclear Deal evoked mixed reactions. Some, such as the IAEA's Director General, viewed it as a welcome development to consolidate the non-proliferation regime as well as to cater to India's energy needs.[14] But others considered that it violated the rules of this regime, particularly NPT provisions, and feared that it would only encourage nuclear proliferation from India and other States.

The terms of the Deal were written into a bilateral treaty, signed in March 2006, though publicly unveiled only many months later in August 2007. Crystallising the US commitments made in the July 2005 Joint Statement, though arguably narrowing India's, the bilateral agreement also recorded the US promise to 'work with friends and allies to adjust the practices of the Nuclear Suppliers Group to create the necessary conditions for India to obtain full access to the international fuel market'.[15] The commitment to adjust 'international regimes' thus became, in the bilateral agreement, the commitment to adjust NSG practices.

In short, not only did the US initially promise to bring about changes in the international legal landscape on nuclear issues to implement its understanding with India, but via this bilateral agreement also recognised only NSG practices as the relevant regime to be adjusted. There was no reference to the NPT, even though by implication the Deal revised the NPT bargain.

Moreover, the Deal came at a time when the United States had undertaken several other measures that decentred the NPT bargain as the primary basis of the nuclear-governance regime. William Walker

13 *ibid.*

14 See also M. ElBaradei, 'Rethinking Nuclear Safeguards', *Washington Post*, 14 June 2006; M. ElBaradei, *The Age of Deception: Nuclear Diplomacy in Treacherous Times* (London, Bloomsbury 2011) 224–8.

15 Article 5(6), Agreement for Cooperation between the Government of the United States of America and the Government of India concerning Peaceful Uses of Nuclear Energy, 3 August 2007, USA Department of State Media Note 2007/658, http://merln.ndu.edu/archivepdf/india/State/90157.pdf.

refers to the early and mid-2000s as the United States' nuclear 'counter-enlightenment',[16] marked by a growing sense that IAEA verification was unreliable, and that deterrence was futile against 'rogue States' and non-State terrorist groups if they acquired control of nuclear weapons. Especially following the 11 September 2001 terrorist attacks, the United States shifted focus from disarmament and non-proliferation to '*counter*terrorism' and '*counter*proliferation'.[17] This new focus manifested in the United States repudiating specific States' rights to develop a civil nuclear fuel cycle (even though this was permissible under the NPT's guarantee of 'the inalienable right of all the Parties ... to develop research, production and use of nuclear energy for peaceful purposes without discrimination'); and back-pedalling on the disarmament commitments specified in the final documents of the 1995 and 2000 NPT Review Conferences.[18] At the same time, it viewed '"proliferation as inevitable and not necessarily a bad thing" if it involved friendly states such as India'.[19] The widely perceived failure of the 2005 NPT Conference followed from this shift in the US stance and the corresponding reactions of other States.[20]

As part of its shift, the United States also launched the 'Proliferation Security Initiative' (PSI) in September 2003 and the 'Global Nuclear

[16] According to Walker, 'the attempt in the second half of the twentieth century to create an international order which would limit the ... dangers [of nuclear weapons], while exploiting in controlled ways their capacities to discourage war, itself came to possess hallmarks of a grand enlightenment project. It was permeated by assumptions of – and expressions of faith in – a ubiquitous rationality and commitment to reason; the attainability of justice in the face of obvious inequalities of power and opportunity; the possibility of achieving trust among states on the basis of international law; the ability of organizations to exercise control over complex technological activities; and the feasibility of progress in escaping a nuclear-armed chaos and realizing nuclear energy's economic potential': W. Walker, 'Nuclear Enlightenment and Counter Enlightenment' (2007) 83(3) *International Affairs* 431.

[17] *ibid.*, 444. For an excellent and comprehensive analysis of the revisionist stance adopted by the United States between 1998 and 2008, that prioritised non-proliferation, limited the inalienable right to peaceful uses of energy confirmed in the NPT, and diluted disarmament commitments, see D. Joyner, *Interpreting the Nuclear Non-Proliferation Treaty* (Oxford University Press 2011) 35–108. See also S. Ranganathan, 'Book Review of D. Joyner, Interpreting the Nuclear Non-Proliferation Treaty' (2011) 82 *British Yearbook of International Law* 532.

[18] Walker, 'Nuclear Enlightenment and Counter Enlightenment', 446.

[19] *ibid.*, 449.

[20] For a record and analysis of the 2005 conference, see R. Johnson, 'Politics and Protection: Why the 2005 NPT Review Conference Failed', ACRONYM Institute for Disarmament Diplomacy, 1 November 2005, www.acronym.org.uk/dd/dd80/80npt.htm.

Energy Partnership' (GNEP) in February 2006. The PSI calls upon participant States to 'interdict . . . the transfer or transport of [weapons of mass destruction], their delivery systems, and related materials to and from states and non-state actors of proliferation concern'.[21] The GNEP (reconstituted as the International Framework for Nuclear Energy Cooperation in 2010[22]) aimed to limit NNWS' access to enrichment and reprocessing technology in return for supplies of nuclear fuel.[23] While both measures were aimed at preventing nuclear proliferation, they may be criticised on various grounds. The PSI may be charged with non-transparency, possible violations of the law of the sea, and, most importantly, with operating outside the auspices of the United Nations – leaving it to the PSI participants to establish which States pose a proliferation risk and thus can be subjected to interdiction.[24] The GNEP can be criticised for having sought to broaden the technology gap between States – permitting the NWS and some other States to consolidate their privileged position in the nuclear-governance regime at the same time as it imposed constraints on the rights of other States to develop civil nuclear energy programmes.[25] Neither initiative contravened the NPT as such, but both have operated in disregard of its priorities.

While the NPT is notably a treaty that provides for unequal treatment of (NWS and NNWS) States, the imbalance of the rights accorded to these two categories of States is mitigated by the bargain between them, which equally emphasises three goals: non-proliferation, energy assistance, and disarmament. The treaty, moreover, does not suggest that distinctions may be drawn between different types of

[21] Principle 1, Interdiction Principles for the Proliferation Security Initiative, 2003. The PSI principles were set out in a White house Fact Sheet of September 2003, www.state.gov/t/isn/c27726.htm.

[22] www.ifnec.org.

[23] See the Global Nuclear Energy Partnership Strategic Plan, US Department of Energy, January 2007, www.fas.org/programs/ssp/_docs/GNEPStratPlanJan07.pdf; see also GNEP Steering Group Action Plan, 13 December 2007.

[24] For a sample of assessments of the PSI between 2003 and 2013, see 'The Proliferation Security Initiative: The Legal Challenge', Bipartisan Security Group Policy Brief, September 2003; D. Joyner, *International Law and the Proliferation of Weapons of Mass Destruction* (Oxford University Press 2009) 321–31; A. Dunne, 'The Proliferation Security Initiative: Legal Considerations and Operational Realities', SIPRI Policy Paper No. 36, May 2013, esp. 38–42.

[25] ElBaradei notes that the GNEP was perceived to widen the technology gap between nuclear haves and have nots and met with resistance from various NNWS: ElBaradei, *Age of Deception*, 124.

NNWS. The US initiatives not only ignored the NPT bargain but also drew distinctions between 'friendly' and 'rogue' NNWS. As this chapter will discuss, the Deal with India exemplified both trends.

But, if the Deal appeared at first as one of the United States' legal moves to modify the architecture of the nuclear-governance regime (and displace the NPT bargain as its fulcrum), its trajectory gave it a more complex role. The Deal was conditioned on India's conclusion of a safeguards agreement acceptable to the IAEA, and on NSG approval. These were important not only in order for the United States to successfully amend its domestic legislation (which at the time barred nuclear cooperation with States like India), but also in order for India to enter into similar cooperation with other States. And, during these processes, the Deal changed in significant ways, arguably becoming more securely tied to the NPT-based framework. Additionally, its passage encouraged initiatives by States to reaffirm the NPT's central place in the nuclear-governance regime.

This chapter describes the Deal's trajectory between July 2005 and September 2008 as one of 'accommodation' with the NPT-based regime under the aegis of formal and informal institutions. Drawing on the framework of regime interaction discussed in Chapter 3, it analyses how various actors, including India, the United States, other States and the IAEA Director General, employed and were constrained by legal forms and discourse; and evaluates the benefits and disadvantages of such a process. The chapter opens with short introductions to the NPT regime and the Deal. The sections following explore the conflict between the two, and the consequent implications of the Deal for nuclear governance. After this, the chapter turns to the process of accommodation between the Deal and the NPT.

The nuclear-governance regime

The NPT underpins the nuclear-governance regime, and is supported by the IAEA, the NSG and other export-control groups. The following overview of this regime focuses on aspects of this regime relevant to the Deal.[26]

[26] For more detailed accounts, see Joyner, *International Law and the Proliferation of Weapons of Mass Destruction*, 1–77; V. Lamm, *The Utilization of Nuclear Energy and International Law* (Budapest, Akadémiai Kiadó 1984); I. Anthony *et al.*, 'Reforming Nuclear Export Controls: The Future of the Nuclear Suppliers Group', SIPRI Research Report No. 22, 2007.

Non-proliferation

The NPT was negotiated over a three-year period by the Eighteen Nation Committee on Disarmament (ENDC), which had been commissioned by the UN General Assembly to draft a treaty in line with the following principles: (a) exclusion of loopholes that would permit nuclear or non-nuclear Powers to proliferate, directly or indirectly; (b) embodying an acceptable balance of mutual responsibilities and obligations of nuclear and non-nuclear powers; (c) representing an advance towards general and complete disarmament; (d) inclusion of acceptable and workable provisions to ensure its effectiveness; and (e) not adversely affecting a State's right to conclude regional treaties for nuclear-weapons-free zones.[27] The General Assembly adopted the NPT on 12 June 1968;[28] it entered into force on 5 March 1970.

Though later extended indefinitely,[29] the NPT was drafted as an interim measure to limit the spread of nuclear weapons pending complete nuclear disarmament. Perhaps for this reason, its provisions address horizontal proliferation, that is, the acquisition of nuclear weapons capability by the NNWS, far more comprehensively than vertical proliferation, that is, the enhancement of the nuclear arsenals of the NWS.[30] Article I enjoins the NWS not to transfer nuclear weapons, or control over them, to other States and not to encourage, assist or induce the NNWS to manufacture or acquire nuclear weapons. Article II carries a corresponding obligation upon the NNWS not to receive, manufacture or otherwise acquire nuclear weapons. Under Article IV, however, the NPT permits the NNWS to pursue peaceful uses of nuclear energy.

Article IX(2) defines the NWS as States which had manufactured and exploded a nuclear weapon or other nuclear explosive device prior to 1 January 1967; the NNWS are not defined at all. India was unhappy with this distinction between the NWS and the NNWS, and considered the cut-off date, which allowed NWS status to the five permanent members of the Security Council but excluded India (which at the time was developing a weapons programme) extremely unfair. It refused to sign the NPT in 1968, and today remains one of the three non parties to it, along with Pakistan and Israel.

[27] UNGA Res. 2028 (19 November 1965). [28] UNGA Res. 2373 (12 June 1968).

[29] Decision 3, 'Extension of the Treaty on the Non-Proliferation of Nuclear Weapons', NPT Review and Extension Conference 1995, NPT/CONF.1995/32 (Part I) Annex.

[30] See Statement of the US Representative, ENDC/PV. 369, 22 February 1968, 15, para. 50.

Safeguards

NPT provisions

Article III(1) of the NPT requires the NNWS to accept IAEA-prescribed safeguards upon all 'source and special fissionable material' (hereinafter simply referred to as 'nuclear material') in all peaceful nuclear activities within their jurisdiction. Article III(2) prohibits States from supplying nuclear material, or equipment, or material designed to produce, process or use nuclear material, to the NNWS where such supplies are not subject to IAEA-prescribed safeguards.

There is a fine distinction between these two provisions. Article III(1) expressly provides for 'comprehensive safeguards', that is, safeguards on all peaceful nuclear activities of the NNWS. Because NNWS are not expected to pursue non-peaceful nuclear activities, an agreement for comprehensive safeguards presupposes that safeguards will be applied to all nuclear activities; it assumes that there will be no other, unsafeguarded, nuclear activities. Article III(2), directed at NWS, however, provides for safeguards to be applied only to materials or equipment transferred to NNWS; it does not demand that the recipient NNWS must have accepted comprehensive safeguards. This reading suggests that *vis-à-vis* States that are not party to the NPT (that is, India, Pakistan and Israel) the NPT only requires that IAEA safeguards cover all nuclear material and equipment imported from NPT parties; in other words, it does not require comprehensive safeguards.

However, there are suggestions that Article III(2) has been modified by the NPT practice, such that it conditions all nuclear supplies to NPT parties and non parties upon comprehensive safeguards. Ahlström, for instance, draws attention to the 'Principles and Objectives for Nuclear Non-Proliferation and Disarmament', a consensus document adopted at the 1995 NPT Review and Extension Conference,[31] which states in paragraph 12:

> New supply arrangements for the transfer of source and/or special fissionable material or equipment or material especially designed or prepared for the processing, use or production of special fissionable material to non-nuclear-weapon States *should require, as a necessary precondition, acceptance of IAEA full-scope*

[31] C. Ahlström, 'Legal Aspects of the Indian–US Civil Nuclear Cooperation Initiative', Armaments, Disarmament and International Security, *SIPRI Yearbook*, 2006, www.sipri.org/yearbook/2006/13/13B.

safeguards and internationally legally binding commitments not to acquire nuclear weapons or other nuclear explosive devices.[32]

NPT parties reaffirmed this requirement at the 2000 Review Conference. Ahlström convincingly argues that, as directed by Article 31(3) of the Vienna Convention on the Law of Treaties (VCLT),[33] these documents should be viewed as subsequent agreements, or as practice that dictates the interpretation of Article III(2) of the NPT.[34] While it is not clear why the above-cited paragraph 12 refers to 'full-scope' rather than the 'comprehensive' safeguards referred to in previous paragraphs of the same document, there is no substantive difference between the two. The scope of these safeguards is discussed below.

The IAEA safeguards system

IAEA information circular INFCIRC/153 details the essential elements of the comprehensive safeguards agreement to be undertaken by NNWS pursuant to the NPT.[35] IAEA information circulars are published in order to 'bring matters of general interest to the attention of its Member States';[36] they are not legal documents, but as official IAEA publications convey authentic versions of legal texts, guidelines, unilateral declarations and other information. While INFCIRC/153 encapsulates the IAEA's legal understanding of the core elements that must form part of every comprehensive safeguards agreement to be concluded with NPT-member NNWS, the obligation to rely upon INFCIRC/153 as a model safeguards agreement flows from NPT Article III and not from INFCIRC/153 itself.

INFCIRC/153 requires the NNWS to keep detailed records of nuclear material used in their peaceful nuclear activities and provide information on all facilities in which such materials are kept. These States must allow IAEA inspectors to access all such facilities, conduct regular verification of the location and handling of nuclear materials and environmental sampling to confirm non-diversion of materials to nuclear weapons

[32] Decision 2, 'Principles and Objectives for Nuclear Non-Proliferation and Disarmament', NPT Review and Extension Conference 1995, NPT/CONF.1995/32 (Part I) Annex (emphasis added).
[33] 1969, 8 ILM 679.
[34] Ahlström, 'Legal Aspects of the Indian-US Civil Nuclear Cooperation Initiative'.
[35] 'The Structure and Content of Agreements between the Agency and States Required in Connection with the Treaty on the Non-Proliferation of Nuclear Weapons', INFCIRC/153 (corr.), 1972.
[36] 'Information Circulars', www.iaea.org/Publications/Documents/Infcircs/index.html.

programmes. However, INFCIRC/153 permits IAEA inspectors to access only strategic points within nuclear facilities; this is perhaps in fulfilment of the NPT Article III(3) requirement that safeguards should be implemented in a manner that avoids hampering peaceful nuclear programmes, technological development and peaceful nuclear cooperation.

In 1997, following discovery of a clandestine nuclear weapons programme in Iraq, the IAEA Board of Governors adopted a Model Additional Protocol to supplement INFCIRC/153.[37] The Protocol demands detailed information on all research and activities related to the nuclear fuel cycle, not just on activities involving use of nuclear material. It permits IAEA inspectors to access 'any place' on the site of a declared nuclear facility; and any site on which there is information relating to possible nuclear activities (including research). The Protocol also allows IAEA inspectors to demand access to additional locations to conduct environmental monitoring, and to make an inspection at only twenty-four hours' notice.[38] The NPT does not require member States to conclude an Additional Protocol, but many have chosen to do so.

Export-control guidelines

Groups such as the Zangger Committee and the NSG also regulate export of nuclear materials and technology. The NSG, in particular, is an informal consultative group comprising States that are the main exporters of nuclear materials and technology. It was created in 1975, following India's nuclear explosion, to strengthen and harmonise domestic export-control regimes.[39] In 1976, it adopted 'Guidelines on Nuclear Transfers', which were substantially modified in 1992 and published as INFCIRC/254 Part I ('Part I Guidelines').[40] These Guidelines are based on the 'non-proliferation' principle: that suppliers should authorise transfer of (listed) nuclear items only when satisfied that such transfers would not contribute to the proliferation of nuclear weapons or be diverted to acts of nuclear terrorism. The Part I Guidelines apply to items especially

[37] IAEA 'Safeguards Factsheet', www.iaea.org/Publications/Factsheets/English/S1_Safeguards.pdf.

[38] See also Joyner, *International Law and the Proliferation of Weapons of Mass Destruction*, 19–23.

[39] See 'The Nuclear Suppliers Group: Its Origins, Role and Activities', Background document prepared by the Nuclear Suppliers Group, INFCIRC/539/Rev.3, 2005.

[40] The most recent version is 'Guidelines for Nuclear Transfers', INFCIRC/254/Rev.11 Part I, 2012. This chapter will refer to the earlier version of the Part I Guidelines, which was current during the NSG discussions of the Deal.

designed for nuclear use, including material, reactors and equipment; and to equipment for reprocessing, enrichment and conversion of nuclear material, fuel fabrication and heavy water production. They require that supplier States transfer such items to NNWS only if these States have undertaken comprehensive safeguards.

In 1992, in addition to revising the Part I Guidelines, the NSG also adopted Guidelines for transfers of nuclear-related dual-use equipment, material and technology that could significantly contribute to an unsafeguarded nuclear fuel cycle or nuclear explosive activity. These Guidelines were published as INFCIRC/254 Part II ('Part II Guidelines').[41] They provide that suppliers, in considering whether to authorise transfers, should take into account factors such as the recipient State being party to the NPT, or, if not a party, having nuclear facilities that are not under IAEA safeguards; the possibility of the transfer feeding into research or development of any nuclear reprocessing or enrichment facility; and the recipient's past record of proliferation.

While the Part I Guidelines require that recipient States must have in place comprehensive safeguards on all their peaceful nuclear activities, the Part II Guidelines mention the existence of unsafeguarded nuclear activities only as a relevant consideration (that is, not as a necessary condition) for States making nuclear transfers. Of course, neither Part is binding upon members. However, in practice, they have been taken as highly authoritative; in 2000, Russia was criticised for violating its NSG *commitments*.[42] The NSG Guidelines, particularly Part II, are broader in scope than NPT Article III, but, following VCLT Article 31(3), they may be viewed as subsequent practice, or as relevant rules of international law which flesh out the provisions of NPT Article III.[43]

Nuclear energy

NPT Article IV declares that it is the 'inalienable right of all the Parties to the Treaty to develop research, production and use of nuclear energy for peaceful purposes without discrimination and in conformity with

[41] The most recent version is 'Guidelines for Transfer of Nuclear-Related Dual Use Equipment, Materials, Software, and Related Technology', INFCIRC/254/Rev.8 Part II, 2010. This chapter will refer to the earlier version of the Part II Guidelines, which was current during the NSG discussions of the Deal.

[42] US Department of State Deputy Spokesman (P. T. Reeker), Statement, 16 February 2001, www.fas.org/nuke/control/nsg/news/treaty-nsg-010216.htm.

[43] See Joyner, *International Law and the Proliferation of Weapons of Mass Destruction*, 33–6.

Articles I and II'. It enjoins States parties to contribute to the development 'of the applications of nuclear energy for peaceful purposes, especially in the territories of non-nuclear-weapon States Party to the Treaty, with due consideration for the needs of the developing areas of the world'.

The article was one of the concessions that had been offered to the NNWS during the NPT negotiations, in return for a commitment not to develop nuclear weapons. Its scope and application must be interpreted in this context. In fact, some commentators have argued that the benefits of civil nuclear cooperation must be limited solely to NNWS parties to the NPT, and in any case not offered to *de facto* weapons States like India.[44] As discussed below, this is not entirely accurate, but, while Article IV does not bar cooperation with India, its compensatory aspect is in tension with the *terms* of the India–US Nuclear Deal.

Disarmament

NPT Article VI, on disarmament, was a second concession in the bargain offered to the NNWS during NPT negotiations. It provides for an undertaking

> to pursue negotiations in good faith on effective measures relating to cessation of the nuclear arms race at an early date and to nuclear disarmament, and on a treaty on general and complete disarmament under strict and effective international control.

The scope of this undertaking is ambiguous, for Article VI does not clearly direct the NWS to disarm or to set any time frame for reduction of their nuclear weapons. However, in its Advisory Opinion in the *Legality of the Threat or Use of Nuclear Weapons*, the International Court of Justice (the 'Court') clarified that

> [t]he legal import of that obligation goes beyond a mere obligation of conduct; the obligation involved here is an obligation to achieve a precise result – nuclear disarmament in all its aspects – by adopting a particular course of conduct, namely, the pursuit of negotiations on the matter in good faith.[45]

The Court added that '[t]he obligation expressed in Article VI includes its fulfilment in accordance with the basic principle of good faith'. It cited Security Council Resolution 984 as reaffirming 'the need for all States Parties to the [NPT] to comply fully with all their obligations', and

[44] *ibid.*, 49. [45] (1996) ICJ Rep 226, 264–5, paras. 101–3.

urging 'all States, as provided for in Article VI, to pursue negotiations in good faith on effective measures relating to nuclear disarmament'. It also took note of the final document of the 1995 NPT Review and Extension Conference, which 'reaffirmed the importance of fulfilling the obligation expressed in Article VI'.[46]

Indeed, at the 1995 Conference, States agreed to undertake concrete disarmament measures including concluding the Comprehensive Test Ban Treaty (CTBT) by 1996; concluding a Fissile Materials Cut-off Treaty (FMCT) soon after, and making systematic and progressive efforts to reduce nuclear weapons globally.[47] Then, at the 2000 NPT Review Conference, States committed to thirteen 'practical steps' for nuclear disarmament.[48] While these documents do not provide a timeframe within which complete nuclear disarmament must be achieved, and are often criticised as having no practical import for the weapons programmes of any State,[49] they do suggest that Article VI must be interpreted as a commitment to make concrete efforts towards disarmament. It certainly bars actions that encourage the nuclear weapons programmes of any State.

As is frequently pointed out, the NPT is essentially a bargain between the NWS and the NNWS, in which the latter have committed to not pursuing nuclear weapons programmes in return for energy cooperation and other concessions and the former have committed to disarmament. This 'package deal' nature of the NPT is critical to interpreting the scope of the commitments outlined in it, and to testing the coherence of the Nuclear Deal with its provisions.[50]

The India–US Nuclear Deal

The 2005 Joint Statement: a break from the past

The Nuclear Deal was announced in a joint statement by President Bush of the United States and Prime Minister Manmohan Singh of India, on

[46] *ibid.*, 265, para. 103.

[47] Decision 2, NPT Review and Extension Conference 1995, para. 4.

[48] Final Document, NPT Review Conference 2000, NPT/CONF.2000/28 (Parts I and II), 14–15, para. 15.

[49] Interview with Y. Tyagi, Jawaharlal Nehru University, New Delhi, 16–17 November 2009 (personal interview, on file).

[50] On 'package deals', see H. Caminos and M. Molitor, 'Progressive Development of International Law and the Package Deal' (1985) 79 *American Journal of International Law* 871.

18 July 2005. The statement outlined plans for bilateral engagement on several issues such as the economy, energy and environment, democracy, development, non-proliferation, high technology, and space exploration.[51] However, it was the following sentences on civil nuclear cooperation that became the focus of global attention:

> The President told the Prime Minister that he will work to achieve full civil nuclear energy cooperation with India as it realizes its goals of promoting nuclear power and achieving energy security. The President would also seek agreement from Congress to adjust US laws and policies, and the United States will work with friends and allies to adjust international regimes to enable full civil nuclear energy cooperation and trade with India, including but not limited to expeditious consideration of fuel supplies for safeguarded nuclear reactors at Tarapur.

The reference to Tarapur highlights why this particular issue excited so much attention. Tarapur, in the Indian state of Maharashtra, houses a nuclear reactor that has struggled to acquire fuel after the United States cut off its supplies in the late 1970s, in response to India's 'peaceful' nuclear explosion of 1974.[52] India was suspected of having diverted supplies intended for its civil nuclear programme towards developing nuclear weapons, and, in particular, of converting the Canadian-supplied CIRUS reactor to this purpose.[53] The NPT does not include India in the 'NWS' category, and its explosion was an early indicator of the problem that now worries some States in relation to Iran: pursuit of nuclear weapons under the guise of developing civil nuclear capabilities. In 1974, India became a 'nuclear pariah' denied nuclear cooperation, although France, China and Russia provided occasional supplies of nuclear fuel for Tarapur.[54] India's subsequent nuclear weapons tests in 1998 heightened international opprobrium and it was subjected to

[51] India–United States Joint Statement, 2005.

[52] See D. Kux, *India and the United States: Estranged Democracies 1941–1991* (Washington DC, National Defense University Press 1993) 356–66, 371–3. The Tarapur supplies cut-off was repeatedly cited by Indian left-wing parties in their criticism of the Deal. See Press Trust of India, 'Walk Out of N-Deal, CPI(M) Tells PM', *Business Standard*, 17 September 2008; *Left Stand on the Nuclear Deal: Notes Exchanged in the UPA–Left Committee on India–US Civil Nuclear Cooperation* (New Delhi, Hari Singh Kang 2008).

[53] See Perkovich, *India's Nuclear Bomb*, 27–28. CIRUS was for some time a sticking point in the negotiations over the Deal. On 31 December 2010, it was permanently shut down.

[54] For a timeline, see 'India Nuclear Milestones: 1945–2009', Wisconsin Project on Nuclear Arms Control (2010) 16(1) *The Risk Report*, www.wisconsinproject.org/countries/india/india-nuclear-miles.html.

heavy sanctions.[55] For the first time, Russia was forced to explain its decision to provide nuclear fuel to Tarapur, and was condemned as violating its NSG commitments.[56] After 1998, nuclear cooperation with India was considered inconsistent with the NPT-based nuclear-governance regime; UN Security Council Resolution 1172 came close to explicitly stating as much and urged India to accede to the NPT and the CTBT without conditions and without delay.[57]

Prior to 1998, the United States had made attempts to engage India on nuclear issues, and to discourage it from developing nuclear weapons capability. In particular, in 1994, it had asked India and Pakistan to take a number of measures, including banning unsafeguarded production of fissile material, acting to reduce the risk of a regional missile race, and participating in an international conference with the United Kingdom, Russia, China, France, Germany and Japan to consider issues of regional and global arms control and disarmament measures.[58] It did not explicitly demand that either State should roll back its strategic nuclear weapons programme: it could pursue a more subtle approach because India and Pakistan were not declared nuclear powers. Nevertheless, the US proposals were accompanied by strengthened non-proliferation legislation – the 1994 Nuclear Proliferation Prevention Act promised to cut off all financial assistance and impose heavy sanctions if these States detonated a nuclear explosive device.[59]

After 1998, the United States asked for much more. With respect to India, even though it soon withdrew its initial demand that India accede to the NPT, the United States required India to sign the CTBT, strengthen export controls and collaborate on the FMCT. India was also asked to stop development of nuclear weapons and delivery programmes, resolve the Kashmir dispute and improve relations with Pakistan. Only then would the United States suspend its sanctions; the US

[55] See D. Rennack, 'India and Pakistan: Current US Economic Sanctions', Report for Congress by the US Congressional Research Service, 12 October 2001, http://fpc.state.gov/documents/organization/6202.pdf.

[56] US State Department Deputy Spokesman, Statement, 2001. Russia claimed that its supplies fell under the safety exception in the NSG Guidelines, i.e. were permitted in the absence of full-scope safeguards because they were indispensable for the safe operation of a nuclear power plant. However, in 2004, citing international criticism and NSG obligations, Russia decided not to renew its supply: A. Baruah and R. Ramachandran, 'Russian Fuel for Tarapur Ruled Out', *The Hindu*, 5 December 2004.

[57] UNSC Res. 1172 (6 June 1998).

[58] For a discussion of this initiative, see Perkovich, *India's Nuclear Bomb* 340–6.

[59] Public Law 103-236, 30 April 1994.

government was categorical that it would not accord recognition to India's NWS status.[60] India did not sign any of these treaties, though it took steps towards strengthening its export controls.

The possibility of civil nuclear assistance from the United States to India was first mentioned in January 2004, within the framework of the 'Next Steps in Strategic Partnership' (NSSP), a bilateral diplomatic initiative between the two States launched in 2001.[61] The Indian Prime Minister, AB. Vajpayee, made a commitment to strengthening Indian laws and increasing bilateral and international cooperation in order to prevent proliferation of weapons of mass destruction.[62] In September 2004 - now dealing with a new Indian government led by Prime Minister Singh - the United States declared the first phase of the NSSP complete. At this time, it offered a presumptive approval for export of dual-use items not controlled by the NSG to safeguarded nuclear facilities in India.[63] Though India was already aiming for deeper cooperation,[64] the United States' engagement remained cautious. It did not offer full civil nuclear cooperation of the sort outlined in the 2005 Joint Statement.

The 2005 Statement thus represented a novel development. The Deal, as outlined in this Statement, was not only for full civil nuclear cooperation but also spoke of altering international regimes to permit such cooperation. Its critics consider it dominated by commercial considerations, and India's non-proliferation commitments mere sops.[65] The Indian commitments were not negligible, but India appeared to obtain much while giving up little. In return for full civil nuclear cooperation, India undertook to assume 'the same responsibilities and practices and

[60] S. Talbott, *Engaging India: Diplomacy, Democracy and the Bomb* (Washington DC, Brookings Institution Press 2006); J. Singh, *A Call to Honour: In Service of Emergent India* (New Delhi, Rupa 2006); C. Rajamohan, 'Impossible Allies': *Nuclear India, United States and Global Order* (New Delhi, India Research Press 2006) 27–52.

[61] See US President (G. W. Bush), 'Statement on Next Steps in Strategic Partnership with India', 12 January 2004, www.gpo.gov/fdsys/pkg/WCPD-2004-01-19/pdf/WCPD-2004-01-19-Pg61-2.pdf.

[62] Indian Prime Minister (A. B. Vajpayee), 'Next Steps in Strategic Partnership with USA', Statement, New Delhi, 13 January 2004, www.outlookindia.com/article.aspx?222620.

[63] US Department of Commerce, Bureau of Industry and Security, 'Announcement on USA–India Next Steps in Strategic Partnership', September 2004 (the webpage is no longer available).

[64] See Rajamohan, 'Impossible Allies', 27–52.

[65] See S. Ghoshroy, 'The US–India Nuclear Deal: Triumph of the Business Lobby', *The Audit of Conventional Wisdom*, MIT Center for International Studies, September 2006, http://mit.edu/cis/pdf/Audit_09_14_Ghoshroy.pdf.

acquire the same benefits and advantages as other leading countries with advanced nuclear technology such as [the United States]'. It would: separate its military and civilian facilities and 'voluntarily' place the latter under IAEA safeguards;[66] sign an Additional Protocol; continue its unilateral moratorium on nuclear testing; work with the United States to conclude an FMCT; refrain from transferring enrichment and reprocessing technologies to States that do not have them; tighten export controls; and adhere to the Missile Technology Control Regime (MTCR) and NSG Guidelines. Except for undertaking to 'adhere to' rather than being allowed to 'participate in' the MTCR and NSG, India's commitments were similar to those undertaken by all the NWS. Meanwhile, it would receive nuclear materials, equipment and technology from the United States. In short, the Joint Statement seemed to indicate that, despite having firmly opposed the NPT, India would now receive the benefits accorded under this treaty to the NNWS, even as it took on no more than the burden carried by the NWS. Naturally, this generated controversy.

The 123 Agreement: terms of the Deal crystallised

Several months of intense negotiation followed the Joint Statement, resulting in the bilateral '123 Agreement'. This was so called after section 123 of the United States' 1954 Atomic Energy Act, which provides the basis for all US civil nuclear agreements.[67] The India–US 123 Agreement was concluded on 2 March 2006, unveiled publicly on 3 August 2007, and ratified on 10 October 2008.

The terms of this agreement, for 'full civil nuclear cooperation', permit Indian entities to receive assistance in 'activities covering nuclear reactors and aspects of the associated nuclear fuel cycle including technology transfer on an industrial or commercial scale', and to access fuel supplies including for development of a strategic reserve to ensure uninterrupted supply to nuclear reactors.[68] India may also receive supplies of nuclear material for the benefit of third States;[69] but Article 7(2) contains standard provisions restricting the retransfer of materials. The Agreement recognises India's rights to enrich (up to 20 per cent) and reprocess fuel.[70] Finally, it permits 'controlled thermonuclear

[66] The term 'voluntarily' is normally applied to safeguards undertaken by *de jure* nuclear weapons states.

[67] Public Law 83-703, 30 August 1954.

[68] Article 2(2)(d) and (e), 123 Agreement.

[69] Article 2(2)(g), 123 Agreement.

[70] Article 6, 123 Agreement.

fusions'.[71] Significantly, the Agreement also offers obvious (but not explicit) recognition to India's nuclear programme.[72]

In return, India is asked to open up its civil nuclear facilities to inspection.[73] Since no mention is made of its military programme, it is clear that India does not undertake comprehensive safeguards. India is permitted to continue production of fissile material. It is an open

[71] Articles 2(j) and 3(1)(h), 123 Agreement. *Inter alia*, this provides for India's participation in research on the international thermonuclear experimental reactor (ITER).

[72] For instance, the preamble provides, in part:

> Wishing to develop such cooperation on the basis of mutual respect for sovereignty, non-interference in each other's internal affairs, equality, mutual benefit, reciprocity and with due respect for each other's nuclear programmes . . . Affirming that cooperation under this Agreement is between two States possessing advanced nuclear technology, both Parties having the same benefits and advantages . . .

Article 2 ('Scope of Cooperation') provides, in part:

> 4. The Parties affirm that the purpose of this Agreement is to provide for peaceful nuclear cooperation and not to affect the unsafeguarded nuclear activities of either Party. Accordingly, nothing in this Agreement shall be interpreted as affecting the rights of the Parties to use for their own purposes nuclear material, non-nuclear material, equipment, components, information or technology produced, acquired or developed by them independent of any nuclear material, non-nuclear material, equipment, components, information or technology transferred to them pursuant to this Agreement. This Agreement shall be implemented in a manner so as not to hinder or otherwise interfere with any other activities involving the use of nuclear material, non-nuclear material, equipment, components, information or technology and military nuclear facilities produced, acquired or developed by them independent of this Agreement for their own purposes.

Article 12 ('Implementation of the Agreement') provides:

> 1. This Agreement shall be implemented in a manner designed: a) to avoid hampering or delaying the nuclear activities in the territory of either Party; b) to avoid interference in such activities . . .

Article 13 ('Consultations') provides:

> 1. The Parties undertake to consult at the request of either Party regarding the implementation of this Agreement and the development of further cooperation in the field of peaceful uses of nuclear energy on a stable, reliable and predictable basis. The Parties recognize that such consultations are between two States with advanced nuclear technology, which have agreed to assume the same responsibilities and practices and acquire the same benefits and advantages as other leading countries with advanced nuclear technology.

[73] Already, under a previous agreement with the IAEA, India allowed inspections of 6 sites. See 'Agreement with the Government of India for the Application of Safeguards to All Nuclear Material Subject to Agency Safeguards under INFCIRC/154, Part I and under the Agreement between India and the IAEA contained in Exchanges of Letters dated 1 October and 1 December 1993', INFCIRC/433, 1994.

question what would happen if India were to conduct a nuclear test, but there is much in the agreement to suggest that fuel supplies would not be abruptly cut off even if the US decided to terminate the agreement. Article 14(8) states: 'It is not the purpose of the provisions of this Article regarding cessation of cooperation and right of return to derogate from the rights of the Parties under Article 5(6).' In Article 5(6), the United States offers four fuel supply guarantees to India. First, a commitment to create the necessary conditions for India to have an uninterrupted supply of nuclear fuel and to adjust for this purpose the US domestic legislation,[74] and NSG practice. Second, a commitment to support India's negotiation of an India-specific safeguards agreement with the IAEA, which would provide for 'corrective measures that India may take to ensure uninterrupted operation of its civilian nuclear reactors in the event of disruption of foreign fuel supplies'. Third, a commitment to support India's effort to develop a strategic reserve of nuclear fuel. Fourth, in case of a disruption of fuel supplies, a commitment to jointly convene with India a group of friendly supplier countries including Russia, France and the United Kingdom to pursue measures that would restore India's fuel supply.

Only the following commitments from the 2005 Joint Statement find formal expression in the 123 Agreement: that India will place its civil nuclear facilities under IAEA safeguards,[75] and will not divert nuclear supplies made under this agreement to weapons production.[76] India's commitment to separating its civil and military nuclear programmes is implicit.[77] There is reference to an Additional Protocol but no formal obligation to conclude one.[78] India's moratorium on nuclear testing

[74] That is, section 123, Atomic Energy Act. The United States amended this Act via the Henry J. Hyde United States–India Peaceful Atomic Energy Cooperation Act 2006, Public Law 109–401, 18 December 2006.

[75] Article 5.6(c), 123 Agreement. This safeguards agreement is reported as the 'Agreement between the Government of India and the International Atomic Energy Agency for the Application of Safeguards to Civilian Nuclear Facilities Information Circulars', INFCIRC/754, 2009.

[76] Article 9, 123 Agreement.

[77] This was expressly stated in the India–US Joint Statement 2005, and is reiterated in INFCIRC/754, 2009.

[78] An apparently 'India-specific' Additional Protocol has been signed by India and approved by the IAEA Board of Governors, but is not in force: IAEA, 'Conclusion of Additional Protocols: Status as of 15 July 2013', www.iaea.org/safeguards/documents/AP_status_list.pdf. The text of this Additional Protocol is not in the public domain, though preliminary analysis has appeared in the press and elsewhere: see S. Varadarajan, 'India and the Additional Protocol', *The Hindu*, 7 March 2009; P. Crail,

does not find mention, although Article 14, on 'Termination and Cessation of Cooperation', implicitly recognises that a nuclear test might be a basis for cessation of cooperation.[79] There is no mention of the FMCT, or of any obligation to refrain from transfer of enrichment and reprocessing technologies, although there is a reference to tightened export controls. No formal commitment to adhere to MTCR or NSG Guidelines is provided.

Of course, the 123 Agreement is a framework agreement, intended to be fleshed out by additional rules and by specific contractual terms accompanying each supply of nuclear material. One might argue that the 2005 Joint Statement must also be considered a necessary supplement to the Agreement, although this argument would be of doubtful merit given the 123 agreement's status of being later-in-time and of a more specific character. Even so, the omissions described are significant. They suggest that, between 2005 and 2007, India retreated from a stance of greater willingness to undertake various non-proliferation commitments, to one where it sought to avoid giving formal expression to such commitments. Indeed, a comparison of India's 123 Agreement with those that the United States signed with China, Japan, the United Arab Emirates and the European Atomic Energy Community (Euratom), indicates that India's rights and obligations are fewer than those of Japan, the UAE and the NNWS party to Euratom, and are at least comparable to China's. Appendix 6 of this book and its accompanying table provide the details.

Treaty conflict

As discussed in Chapters 1 and 5, 'strict' and 'liberal' definitions of treaty conflict are not helpful in predicting which conflicts offer a greater challenge to the effective operation of the treaties concerned. The following discussion underscores this point by showing that it is possible to avoid reading the NPT and the 123 Agreement as in conflict, but only at the cost of ignoring how the latter threatens the bargain embodied in the former.

'IAEA Approves India Additional Protocol', Arms Control Association, April 2009, www.armscontrol.org/act/2009_04/IndiaProtocol.

[79] It states: 'The Parties agree to consider carefully the circumstances that may lead to termination or cessation of cooperation. They further agree to take into account whether the circumstances that may lead to termination or cessation resulted from a Party's serious concern about a changed security environment or as a response to similar actions by other States which could impact national security.'

To begin with, Article 2(1) of the 123 Agreement avoids a conflict with the NPT, providing: 'Each Party shall implement this Agreement in accordance with its respective applicable treaties ... concerning the use of nuclear energy for peaceful purposes.' This provision thus offers a basis for interpreting the 123 Agreement in conformity with the NPT, to which the United States is a party.

Moreover, on a preliminary reading, the NPT also appears to support the Deal. Article IV(2) permits NPT parties to engage in peaceful nuclear cooperation with other States, whether they be NPT parties or not. Indeed, it provides for a positive obligation, on States 'in a position to do so', to

> co-operate in contributing alone or together with other States or international organisations to the further development of the applications of nuclear energy for peaceful purposes, especially in the territories of non-nuclear-weapon States Party to the Treaty, with due consideration for the needs of the developing areas of the world.

This provision *prima facie* completely supports the United States' collaboration with India, a developing country. However, a closer reading of this provision, together with Article IV(1), suggests three conditions which should guide such cooperation.

The first condition is stated in Article IV(1), which provides for the inalienable right of all the NPT parties to develop research, production and use of nuclear energy for peaceful purposes '*in conformity with Articles I and II*'. Article I, enjoins the NWS not to assist or encourage the NNWS to develop or acquire nuclear weapons, or to transfer the same to them. India already possesses an active nuclear weapons programme and the Deal was perceived as effectively freeing India's indigenous nuclear fuel resources for military application. Even so, it is possible, if the issue is that of avoiding the *appearance* of a treaty conflict, to show that, despite fears of India's nuclear proliferation, Article I does not bar the Deal.

This argument for the compatibility of the Deal with Article I may be constructed as follows. Article I provides for two different undertakings by NWS: first, not to transfer 'to any recipient whatsoever' nuclear weapons or explosive devices; second, not to assist, encourage, or induce 'any non-nuclear-weapon State' to manufacture or otherwise acquire nuclear weapons or other nuclear explosive devices. Therefore, under Article I, NWS are not prevented from assisting, encouraging or inducing States that are not NNWS to manufacture or otherwise acquire nuclear weapons.

The important question, then, is: is India an NNWS? While the NPT does not recognise India as an NWS, it also provides no definition for an NNWS, unlike its previous drafts (which did).[80] It is also evident from the NPT's drafting history that the categories of NWS and NNWS were not seen as fully representative: Alva Myrdal, the Swedish delegate to the ENDC, had suggested a four-part categorisation into nuclear superpowers, other nuclear powers, States with potential nuclear weapons capabilities, and definitely non-nuclear weapons States.[81] She recognised however that the drafters would be unable to agree on a text addressing all these categories, and the categories were narrowed to two. It may be argued that the NPT completely divides the world into *de jure* NWS and NNWS; that is, 'NNWS' is a catch-all category for States not expressly recognised as 'NWS'. Yet, logically, in the absence of a legal definition confirming this, a State which is in overt possession of nuclear weapons can hardly be classified as an NNWS. India is in the ambiguous position of a *de facto* weapons State.

Now, this argument may appear too technical. It may be argued also that Article I must be read in light of the overall purpose of preventing nuclear proliferation. But, a perusal of the drafting history of the NPT demonstrates that Articles I and II were in fact expected to operate only within a limited sphere, preventing horizontal proliferation among NNWS parties to the NPT.[82] Article I was carefully drafted to retain a loophole, to enable the United States to assist the nuclear weapons programme of the United Kingdom (another NWS).[83] At the time, India and Brazil specifically criticised this loophole, noting that Article I permitted one NWS to assist another NWS, whether or not the latter was party to the NPT.[84] In response, the US delegate, probably referring to the Cold War, stated: 'We all know why it is not possible to include in this treaty actual limitations on the nuclear arms of the nuclear-weapons States.'[85] The draft was not modified. Similarly, the delegate of the United Arab Republic pointed out that the language of

[80] M. Shaker, The Nuclear Non-Proliferation Treaty: Origin and Implementation 1959–1979 (London, Oceana Publications 1980)195.

[81] Statement of the Swedish Representative, ENDC/PV. 333, 26 September 1967, 8.

[82] See Shaker, *The Nuclear Non-Proliferation Treaty*, 260.

[83] US Senate Committee for Foreign Relations, Testimony of A. Fisher, Hearing on the Non-Proliferation Treaty, 1969, cited from Shaker, *The Nuclear Non-Proliferation Treaty*, 260; see also US Statement, ENDC/PV. 369 (1968) para. 51.

[84] For instance, Statement of the Indian Representative, ENDC/PV. 334, 28 September 1967, para. 28.

[85] US Statement, ENDC/PV. 369 (1968) para. 51.

Articles I and II in effect allowed NNWS parties to the NPT to assist nuclear weapons programmes of States not party to the NPT.[86] His proposed amendment to remove this loophole, too, was not incorporated into the text. Obviously, if the NPT may be read to permit an NNWS to assist a non-party's nuclear weapons programme, then it is an odd claim that it bars similar assistance from an NWS. Thus, the first condition may be read as not barring the Deal.

Similarly, it may be argued that the second and third conditions for nuclear energy assistance, indicated in NPT Articles IV and V, also do not prohibit US cooperation with India. The condition under Article IV is that energy cooperation should aim at development of nuclear energy 'especially in the territories of [NNWS] Party to the [NPT]'. On a textual reading, it is clear that Article IV does not limit civil nuclear cooperation only to NPT parties, though it expresses a preference in their favour.[87] Article V provides that 'the benefits from any peaceful applications of nuclear explosions' should be made available to any NNWS party to the NPT 'without discrimination'. While *prima facie* this may imply a restriction to NPT parties only, the first NPT Review Conference clarified that the benefits could be extended to NNWS not party to the Treaty.[88]

Therefore, while it may be argued that there is no conflict in the strict sense between the 123 Agreement and the conditions in Articles IV and V of the NPT, it is important to consider the two conditions in relation to the context in which the NPT was formulated. This context is indicated in UN General Assembly Resolution 2028 and subsequent *travaux préparatoires*, which emphasised that the NPT 'should embody an acceptable balance of mutual responsibilities and obligations of the nuclear and non-nuclear powers'. Each NPT provision was therefore an element of a bargain, the aim of which was to persuade all States besides the five *de jure* NWS (the United States, the United Kingdom, Russia, China and France) to give up nuclear weapons ambitions in return for certain commitments made by the NWS. One such commitment was in the form of positive and

86 Statement of the United Arab Republic Representative, ENDC/PV. 340, 19 October 1967, para. 5.

87 Many, however, take a contrary view: for instance, Joyner, *International Law and the Proliferation of Weapons of Mass Destruction*, 49.

88 Final Declaration, 'Review of Article V', NPT Review Conference 1975, NPT/Conf/35/I Annex 1 ('any potential benefits could be made available to non nuclear weapons States not Party to the Treaty by way of nuclear explosion services provided by nuclear weapons States, as defined by the Treaty, and conducted under the appropriate international observation and international procedures called for in Article V and other applicable international obligations').

negative security assurances provided via UN Security Council Resolution 255.[89] Another was the expectation enshrined in Article VI that the NWS would gradually disarm. A significant component was the promise of civil nuclear cooperation from NWS and other States with advanced nuclear technology to the NNWS, to develop their capabilities for peaceful application of nuclear power.[90] Thus, if taken as provisions intended to *compensate* the NNWS, neither Article IV nor Article V can be read as sanctioning civil nuclear cooperation with *de facto* NWS in every case. Their compensatory effect would lose value if the *de facto* NWS obtained the same benefits without making the same commitments.[91] While this does not foreclose civil nuclear cooperation with a *de facto* NWS altogether, an appropriate reading would require that cooperation be in return for strong non-proliferation commitments by that State. Indeed, it could be required to cap and roll back its nuclear weapons programme.

Further, the Deal also appears contrary to NPT Article VI on disarmament. As discussed, this provision demands that States not encourage or facilitate nuclear weapons programmes of other States. However, the Deal thrusts the goal of nuclear disarmament into further obscurity.

It is also possible to argue that there is conflict between the requirement of limited safeguards under the 123 Agreement, and NPT Article III(2) as modified by subsequent practice, such that it now conditions nuclear supplies on a recipient State's undertaking of comprehensive safeguards. NSG Guidelines, too, support this requirement for comprehensive safeguards; it was in this context that the 2005 Joint Statement spoke of the need to adjust 'international regimes', and the 123 Agreement more specifically of the need to adjust 'NSG practice'. But, if Article III(2) is considered modified in practice, adjustment of NSG practice does not remove the conflict between this provision and the 123 Agreement.

Implications of the Deal

If we interpret Article IV (and Article V) in the context of a bargain between NWS and NNWS, it is possible to argue that the Deal is indeed

[89] UNSC Res. 255 (19 June 1968).

[90] Shaker, *The Nuclear Non-Proliferation Treaty*, 320–1, 375; P. van Ham, Managing Non-Proliferation Regimes in the 1990s: Power, Politics and Policies (London, Pinter 1993) 43.

[91] See Shaker, *The Nuclear Non-Proliferation Treaty*, 375, 411.

in breach of the United States' obligations under the NPT. Moreover, in contrast to the previous argument to the contrary, a good-faith reading of Article I suggests that the Deal is impermissible under that provision, as may a good-faith reading of Article VI. And, as discussed, Article III (2) may be interpreted as having been modified, in later practice, to a requirement of comprehensive safeguards. At the very least, whether or not they amount to a breach of the United States' NPT obligations, these provisions do cumulatively suggest that the Deal, as represented in the 123 Agreement, is in conflict with the NPT.

What are the legal implications of this treaty conflict? This conflict evidently is one involving treaties with non-identical parties, for India is not party to the NPT. VCLT Article 30(5) (which, however, neither the United States nor India has ratified) suggests that the United States could incur responsibility for breaching its NPT commitments, such as being required to make reparations, and perhaps even to cancel or modify the Deal.[92] Moreover, the United States' breach may permit other NPT parties to terminate their own treaty obligations (though this is likely to be discouraged in practice), for, under VCLT Article 60(2)(c),

> [a] material breach of a multilateral treaty by one of the parties entitles any party other than the defaulting State to invoke the breach as a ground for suspending the operation of the treaty in whole or in part with respect to itself if the treaty is of such a character that a material breach of its provisions by one party radically changes the position of every party with respect to the further performance of its obligations under the treaty.

VCLT Article 60 also provides that a material breach consists in 'the violation of a provision essential to the accomplishment of the object or purpose of the treaty', and it may be argued that the Deal, in undermining the basic bargain of the NPT represents such a material breach. Moreover, the NPT may be regarded as a treaty of such a character that a material breach of its provisions by one party radically changes the position of every party: disarmament treaties have indeed been regarded as the classic example of this type of treaty.[93]

[92] See Arts. 34–37, Articles on Responsibility of States for Internationally Wrongful Acts, 2001, annexed to UNGA Res. 56/83 (12 December 2001). Of course, these consequences would not be binding upon India.

[93] See ILC, Third Report on the Law of Treaties by G. Fitzmaurice, Special Rapporteur, A/CN.4/101 (1958) *ILC Yearbook*, Vol. II, 44, para. 91. See also Joyner, *International Law and the Proliferation of Weapons of Mass Destruction*, 9–10.

These improbable (and unrealised) legal consequences do not properly comprehend the ways in which the Deal was expected to impact upon the nuclear-governance regime. The Deal was seen to threaten nuclear governance in three ways: encouraging proliferation by India (vertical as well as horizontal); impacting upon the nuclear postures of other States; and undermining the coherence of the NPT-based non-proliferation regime. These threats could not have been argued away simply by showing that it was *possible* to read the two treaties as not in conflict (indeed, the interpretations of the NPT that would have to be embraced to make that argument could only further weaken the NPT). Nor could these threats be addressed by terminating the NPT. The United States was moved to take steps towards modifying the Deal – which did address some of these threats and linked the Deal more closely to the NPT-based regime – but it did so for motives other than resolving the Deal's conflict with the NPT. While the amendments to the Deal were not explicitly in response to the NPT, the Deal served as a catalyst for other States to reconsider (and reaffirm) NPT provisions. These points will be developed in this section and the section that follows.

Threat 1: vertical proliferation by India

An immediately perceived threat of the Deal was that it would boost both the morale of India's nuclear weapons programme and the material available to it: the former by offering tacit recognition to this programme; the latter because the possibility of importing nuclear fuel for energy-generation freed India's indigenous fuel resources for nuclear weapons production.[94]

However, though it is correct to say that the Deal did offer tacit recognition to India's nuclear weapons programme – *inter alia*, in Article 2(4) of the 123 Agreement, the United States pledged not to interfere with India's programme – it is a dubious conclusion that this would serve as a morale boost to that programme. As several studies have argued, India's development of nuclear weapons was not deterred by international disapprobation.[95] In fact, its nuclear weapons programme was partly a gesture of defiance against international pressure

[94] US Senate Committee on Foreign Relations, Testimony of R. J. Einhorn, Senior Advisor, Center for Strategic and International Studies, Hearing on USA–India Atomic Energy Cooperation: Strategic and Non-Proliferation Implications, 26 April 2006.

[95] Perkovich, *India's Nuclear Bomb*; K. Frey, *India's Nuclear Bomb and National Security* (London, Routledge 2006); I. Abraham, *The Making of the Indian Atomic Bomb: Science, Secrecy and the Postcolonial State* (London, Zed Books 1998).

and a discriminatory nuclear order; partly driven by political desire for recognition as a great power; and partly the outcome of scientific ambitions of indigenously creating a nuclear bomb.[96] These accounts also argue that the programme was not led by (cross-border) security concerns – these were only invoked as *post facto* justification of the 1998 tests; they did not trigger these tests.[97] Given the combination of factors that have driven India's nuclear weapons programme, implicit encouragement from the United States would likely have been of limited consequence.

The material encouragement was more significant, because India has limited reserves of nuclear fuel. Indeed, the Indian science establishment publicly celebrated the new availability of these indigenous reserves for weapons production.[98] Even so, to accurately evaluate the change in fuel availability promised by the Deal, it must be remembered that even earlier, and despite its outcast status, India had obtained occasional supplies of fuel for safeguarded reactors from France and Russia. Its domestic resources had thus always been supplemented by imports. Moreover, until the Deal, India's civil and military programmes had not been separated, allowing easier diversion of imports to weapons production. But, again, most importantly, India's nuclear proliferation was less a consequence of the availability of materials than of political will. And the Deal had the potential to reduce the Indian political establishment's incentives for pursuing an isolated nuclear weapons posture, and thus lead to better regulation of its nuclear weapons production.

Threat 2: horizontal proliferation by India

In addition to the concern of vertical proliferation was the fear that,

> if fully implemented, [the Deal] could catapult India into a position as a major supplier of both nuclear and nuclear-related materials, equipment, and technology. With a weak and poorly enforced export control system, Indian

[96] A former chairman of the Indian Atomic Energy Commission (the principal scientific body in charge of the strategic programme), M. R. Srinivasan, wrote in an op-ed in *The Hindu* (7 December 1995): 'Can anyone really believe that India would have sought US help in so important a matter as nuclear weapon capability . . . India would never have contemplated, nor will it in the future, to acquire status and power by riding piggyback on anyone' (cited from Frey, *India's Nuclear Bomb and National Security*, 68).

[97] *ibid.*

[98] For instance, K. Subrahmanyam, 'India and the Nuclear Deal', *Times of India*, 12 December 2005.

companies could become major suppliers to the nuclear weapon programs of adversaries of [the United States], in some cases possibly using technology which [the United States] originally provided.[99]

But this threat, too, must be evaluated contextually. As the notorious episode of nuclear smuggling between Pakistan, Iran, Libya and North Korea by the A. Q. Khan network shows, horizontal proliferation is not hindered merely by the absence of formal nuclear cooperation with an NWS. And the Deal, on the other hand, was from the outset conditioned on measures to strengthen India's export-control regime.

Under Article 7(2) of the 123 Agreement, India committed not to retransfer nuclear materials, equipment, or information to unauthorised persons or beyond its territorial jurisdiction. Under Articles 6(iii), 7(1) and 8, India undertook to maintain high standards of physical protection for transferred nuclear material and equipment. Article 8(2) specified that these standards must at least be equivalent to recommendations in INFCIRC/225/Rev.4 and subsequent revisions thereof, and to provisions of the 1980 Convention on the Physical Protection of Nuclear Material. Shortly before the Joint Statement of 2005, India also enacted new export-control legislation, the 2005 Weapons of Mass Destruction and Their Delivery Systems (Prohibition of Unlawful Activities) Act.[100]

In the Joint Statement, too, India had committed not to assist nuclear proliferation by other States, and especially not to transfer enrichment and reprocessing technologies to States that do not have them. While the success (or otherwise) of India's export controls remains a matter of ongoing practice, India has also asserted that strategically it is not in favour of acquisition of nuclear weapons by other States.[101]

Threat 3: impact on the programmes and postures of other States

A third concern was that the Deal would have a negative impact on the nuclear postures of other States, giving especially Pakistan, North Korea and Iran reason to accelerate their nuclear weapons programmes, or to retract from their NPT commitments. Specifically, it was feared that the

[99] US House Committee on International Relations, Testimony by D. Albright, President, Institute for Science and International Security, Hearing on the USA–India 'Global Partnership' and its Impact on Non-Proliferation, 26 October 2005.

[100] Act No. 21 of 2005, *The Gazette of India Extraordinary*, No. 24, Part II, 6 June 2005.

[101] See, for instance, Indian Foreign Secretary (S. Saran), 'Transforming US–India Relations: Forging a Strategic Partnership', Address to the Carnegie Endowment for International Peace, 21 December 2005, http://carnegieendowment.org/2005/12/21/transforming-u.s.-india-relations-forging-strategic-partnership/37k.

Deal would lead to a nuclear race between India and Pakistan; induce North Korea to mimic India's moral stance on nuclear weapons; and give fodder to Iran's charge of discriminatory application against the nuclear-governance regime.

In Pakistan, the Deal was viewed as both a threat to security and a cause for resentment. Its leading daily newspaper, *Dawn*, editorialised on a possible regional arms race.[102] Pakistan also raised concerns about equal treatment, and demanded similar civil nuclear cooperation from the United States,[103] claiming that the Deal set a 'precedent' for such cooperation.[104] China supported this claim, arguing at an NSG meeting for a criteria-based approach that would address the aspirations of 'other States' as well as India.[105] There have been several reports of nuclear trade between Pakistan and China.[106] Pakistan has also sought to convince other States to supply nuclear fuel and technology to it;[107] among other things, it has sought to play down the reach and influence of the A. Q. Khan network.[108] Pakistan has concluded several item-specific safeguards agreements with the IAEA, the most recent one in April 2011 placing two Chinese-supplied nuclear power stations under IAEA safeguards.[109]

North Korea, in the course of its withdrawal from the NPT in 2003 and since, adopted India's arguments about the discriminatory nuclear order and unacceptable restrictions posed on its sovereignty by IAEA

[102] Editorial, 'US–India Nuclear Deal', *Dawn*, 22 July 2005.

[103] 'Pakistan Wants India-Like Nuclear Deal with US: Karamat', *Pakistan Times*, 13 September 2005.

[104] S. Varadarajan, 'As Pakistan Hails "Precedent," Other IAEA Members Express Doubts, Fears', *The Hindu*, 2 August 2008.

[105] Press Trust of India, 'NSG Should Address "Aspirations" of Others Too: China', *The Hindu*, 6 September 2008.

[106] Editorial, 'The President's Plans', *Dawn*, 10 September 2008; J. Perlez, 'Pakistan Pulls Closer to a Reluctant China', *New York Times*, 6 October 2011; 'Commitment for New Pakistan Nuclear Reactors', *World Nuclear News*, 11 July 2013, www.world-nuclear-news.org/NN_Commitment_for_new_Pakistan_reactors_1106131.html. See also J. M. Smith, 'China and Pakistan's Nuclear Collusion', *Wall Street Journal*, 2 April 2013; G. Balachandran, 'China–Pakistan Nuclear Cooperation: Unclear Facts', Institute for Defense Studies and Analysis (IDSA) Comment, 18 April 2013, http://idsa.in/idsacomments/ChinaPakistanNuclearCooperation_gbalachandran_180413.

[107] Editorial, 'French Nuclear "Offer"', *Dawn*, 18 May 2009.

[108] C. Almeida, 'A. Q. Khan in the News Again', *Dawn*, 25 September 2009.

[109] 'Agreement between the International Atomic Energy Agency and the Government of the Islamic Republic of Pakistan for the Application of Safeguards in Connection with the Supply of two Nuclear Power Stations from the People's Republic of China', INFCIRC/816, 2011.

safeguards.[110] In 2007, it responded to attempts at diplomatic engagement following its alleged nuclear test of 2006 with the claim that the United States should treat North Korea the way it treats India.[111] Its alleged tests of 2006, 2009 and 2013 were condemned in Security Council Resolutions 1718,[112] 1874[113] and 2094,[114] which asked North Korea to retract its NPT withdrawal, comply with NPT obligations and abandon its nuclear weapons programme, and imposed a number of financial sanctions. Since 2003, a diplomatic initiative for 'six-party talks' – North Korea, South Korea, the United States, China, Japan and Russia – has operated sporadically, with talks often breaking down under intensified tensions between North and South Korea, or for other reasons.[115] In 2009, and again in 2013, North Korea has conditioned its return to the six-party talks, and to other disarmament measures, upon being given the opportunity for bilateral dialogue with the United States.[116]

The Deal further complicates the issue of Iran's enrichment of nuclear fuel. Iran is party to the NPT and had accepted full-scope safeguards in December 1974.[117] It has also signed an Additional Protocol in December 2003, but this is not in force.[118] However, since the 2002 revelation of a secret nuclear enrichment facility in the Iranian city of Natanz, various States and the IAEA have remained suspicious of Iran's nuclear weapons ambitions. In February 2006, even though IAEA inspectors confirmed that Iran's enrichment programme did not produce weapons-grade fuel, and could not detect evidence of a nuclear weapons programme,[119] the IAEA Board of Governors voted to report to the Security Council that the agency was unable to conclude that there were no undeclared nuclear materials or

[110] Frey, *India's Nuclear Bomb and National Security*, 189.

[111] M. Schuster, 'North Korea Slows Down Pace of Nuclear Talks', NPR, 30 March 2007, http://m.npr.org/story/9237343#menu.

[112] UNSC Res. 1718 (14 October 2006). [113] UNSC Res. 1874 (12 June 2009).

[114] UNSC Res. 2094 (7 March 2013).

[115] For a detailed chronology, see 'Chronology of US–North Korea Nuclear and Missile Diplomacy', Arms Control Association, www.armscontrol.org/factsheets/dprkchron#2013 (last updated April 2013).

[116] 'N Korean and US Envoys Meet in NY', BBC, 24 October 2009; Choe Sang-Hun, 'North Korea Proposes High Level Talks with US', *New York Times*, 15 June 2013.

[117] 'The Text of the Agreement between Iran and the Agency for Application of Safeguards in Connection with the Treaty on Non-Proliferation of Nuclear Weapons', INFCIRC/214, 1974.

[118] IAEA, Conclusion of Additional Protocols: Status as of 15 July 2013.

[119] *ibid*. See also IAEA, 'Implementation of the NPT Safeguards Agreement in the Islamic Republic of Iran', Report by the Director General, GOV/2006/15, 27 February 2006.

activities in Iran.[120] India voted in favour of this referral, a move seen as linked to its then ongoing negotiations with the United States on the Deal.[121] The Security Council adopted Resolution 1696 demanding that Iran suspend all enrichment and reprocessing activities.[122] Iran refused to comply, claiming its right to pursue nuclear energy, and was subjected to sanctions via Resolution 1737[123] (supplemented by further Resolutions 1747,[124] 1803[125] and 1929[126]). Several attempts at diplomatic mediation have followed, complicated by the further revelation, on 24 September 2009, of another nuclear enrichment facility at Qom.[127] The IAEA continues to verify that there has been no diversion of Iran's enriched fuel; but is 'unable to provide credible assurance about the absence of undeclared nuclear material and activities in Iran, and therefore to conclude that all nuclear material in Iran is in peaceful activities'.[128] The United States and the European Union have imposed stringent unilateral sanctions in addition to those mandated by the UN Security Council,[129] even as a 'P5+1' (Germany) diplomatic initiative continues in fits and starts – Iran's offer to export some portion of its enriched fuel to Turkey or Brazil,[130] and Russia's suggestion of an action plan,[131] have not been acceptable to the US and the EU

[120] IAEA, Implementation of the NPT Safeguards Agreement in the Islamic Republic of Iran, Resolution Adopted by the Board of Governors, GOV/2006/14, 4 February 2006.

[121] S. Varadarajan, 'India Submits to the Bush Doctrine?', *The Hindu*, 28 October 2005. Prakash Karat, the General Secretary of the Communist Party of India (Marxist), a party in the Indian coalition government, described India's vote as a 'betrayal of Iran', and as 'unconscionable' and a 'defection' from the stance taken by other members of the Non-Aligned Movement which upheld Iran's inalienable right to pursue nuclear energy for peaceful purposes: P. Karat, 'Betrayal on Iran: Costs of India–US Partnership', in *Subordinate Ally: The Nuclear Deal and India–US Strategic Relations* (New Delhi, Leftword Books 2007) 46–51 (first published in *People's Democracy*, 2 October 2005).

[122] UNSC Res. 1696 (31 July 2006).

[123] UNSC Res. 1737 (27 December 2006).

[124] UNSC Res. 1747 (24 March 2007).

[125] UNSC Res. 1803 (3 March 2008).

[126] UNSC Res. 1929 (9 June 2010).

[127] 'Director General and Iranian Officials Discuss Enrichment Plant Visit', IAEA Staff Report, 5 October 2009.

[128] 'Implementation of the NPT Safeguards Agreement and Relevant Provisions of Security Council Resolutions in the Islamic Republic of Iran', Report by the IAEA Director General, GOV/2013/27, 22 May 2013, 2–3, 13.

[129] See 'Iran Sanctions', US Department of State, www.state.gov/e/eb/tfs/spi/iran/index.htm.

[130] See 'Nuclear Fuel Declaration by Iran, Turkey and Brazil', BBC News, 17 May 2010; A. Gamboa, 'UN Rift Widens over Brazil–Turkey Deal with Iran', AFP, 27 May 2010.

[131] See 'Russia Proposes "Phased" Resolution of Iran Nuclear Standoff, Nuclear Threat Initiative', Global Security Newswire, 14 July 2011; S. Gutterman and L. Kelly, 'Russia

States;[132] but recently they have agreed to an 'interim deal' under which Iran will dilute its stocks of enriched uranium in return for the easing of some sanctions.[133] Whatever the eventual resolution of this situation, its prominent feature has been international censure of Iran's enrichment programme, and the imposition of severe sanctions even without a finding of breach of a substantive non-proliferation obligation. This is in obvious contrast to the treatment India has received. For its part, Iran has naturally criticised the Deal as reflecting the United States' double standards in its treatment of India and Iran.[134]

Apart from its implications for the nuclear ambitions of the so-called 'rogue States', there was also concern over the Deal's impact on the nuclear postures of many other NPT members. One expert, Ashton Carter, testified before the US Senate Committee on Foreign Relations that several States, including South Africa, Argentina and Brazil, the post-Soviet States of Ukraine, Kazakhstan and Belarus, South Korea, Taiwan and Libya had all forsaken nuclear weapons ambitions, *inter alia* motivated by the threat of lasting international ostracism if they stood outside the NPT regime.[135] However, the Deal gave cause to these States to re-evaluate their postures, and also the depth of their commitment to the NPT regime. Henry Sokolski noted that, following the Deal, 'Brazilian officials and nuclear experts privately expressed the view that neither Brazil or Argentina will ever ratify the additional protocol', being

Hopes Its Proposal Can Revive Iran Nuclear Talk', Reuters, 17 August 2011. See also 'ISIS Analysis of Russian Proposal: Ask Iran to Come Clean on Nuclear Weaponization before Removing Sanctions', Institute for Science and International Security Report, 4 August 2011; D. Albright *et al.*, 'Preventing Iran from Getting Nuclear Weapons: Constraining its Future Nuclear Options', Institute for Science and International Security Report, 5 March 2012, 37–8, 41 (analysing the proposal and reporting that, by end 2011, Iran too remained non-committal on it).

132 See 'Country Profiles – Iran – Nuclear', Nuclear Threat Initiative, www.nti.org/country-profiles/iran/nuclear (last updated June 2013); 'History of Official Proposals on the Iranian Nuclear Issue', Arms Control Association, www.armscontrol.org/factsheets/Iran_Nuclear_Proposals (last updated August 2013).

133 'Iran Nuclear Deal to Enter Into Force on 20 January', BBC News, 12 January 2014.

134 S. Tisdall, 'Tehran Accuses US of Nuclear Double Standard', *Guardian*, 28 July 2005; S. Varadarajan, 'As Pakistan Hails "Precedent," Other IAEA Members Express Doubts, Fears', *The Hindu*, 2 August 2008; S. Roy, 'India Upset over Iran's Poser on US Nuclear Transfer', *Indian Express*, 28 May 2013.

135 US Senate Committee on Foreign Relations, Testimony of A. B. Carter, Co-Director, Preventive Defense Project, John F. Kennedy School of Government, Harvard University, Hearing on USA–India Atomic Energy Cooperation: Strategic and Non-Proliferation Implications, 26 April 2006. See also 'The Nuclear Non-Proliferation Regime: The Importance of An Integrated and Multilateral Approach', Netherlands Advisory Council on International Affairs, No. 47, January 2006.

unwilling to undertake more stringent obligations than India.[136] Another prominent expert observed that, even if these States decided to emulate India's pursuit of nuclear weapons, it would be difficult to argue that they should not receive the same concessions as India.[137]

Threat 4: erosion of the NPT-based nuclear-governance regime

The Deal was perceived as undermining the NPT-based nuclear-governance regime not only by providing fodder for arguments about its unequal implementation *vis-à-vis* different States, but also by creating confusion about the standards that States were expected to conform to in relation to non-proliferation and disarmament. The 123 Agreement specified few non-proliferation commitments by India; and was repeatedly justified upon a thin account of India's 'good' record of non-proliferation.[138] Since India had evidently developed nuclear weapons by diverting civil supplies, the evaluation of its record as 'good' naturally calls into question the standards required by non-proliferation norms. Similarly, while an ordinary interpretation of NPT Article VI would preclude recognition of India's possession of nuclear weapons, and even indirect assistance to its weapons programme, the 123 Agreement runs counter to this expectation.

The potential effect of this may be understood by reference to Thomas Franck's theory of compliance – Franck argues that international legal rules exert compliance-pull when perceived as legitimate, that is, as adopted and implemented in accordance with generally accepted principles of right process.[139] He asserts that a legitimate rule has four characteristics: *determinacy*; *coherence* with other rules; *adherence* to the secondary framework of rule making and recognition; and *symbolic validation*. The conclusion of the Deal in conflict with the NPT creates doubts about the determinacy and coherence of the NPT provisions, undermining the legitimacy of the NPT and the nuclear-governance regime underpinned by it.

[136] H. Sokolski, 'Towards an NPT-Restrained World That Makes Economic Sense' (2007) 83:3 *International Affairs* 531, 543.

[137] US Senate Committee on Foreign Relations, Testimony of R. Gallucci, Dean of the Edmund A. Walsh School of Foreign Service, Georgetown University, Hearing on USA–India Atomic Energy Cooperation: Strategic and Non-Proliferation Implications, 26 April 2006.

[138] US Senate Committee on Foreign Relations, Opening Remarks of US Secretary of State (C. Rice), 5 April 2006.

[139] T. Franck, *The Power of Legitimacy Among Nations* (Oxford University Press 1990) 24, 41–194.

From conflict to accommodation

Despite the challenges that the Deal posed to the nuclear-governance regime at the outset, its subsequent trajectory was a complex one. The implementation of the Deal required a number of approvals following the conclusion of the 123 Agreement. These included: the IAEA's approval of an India-Specific Safeguards Agreement with India; the NSG's waiver of the requirement, in its Part I Guidelines, for the undertaking of comprehensive safeguards by the recipient State; and ratification of the Deal by the US Congress. In India, as it turned out, the Congress-led governing coalition was also subjected to a vote of confidence, after the left-wing parties broke away from the coalition due to their opposition to the Deal.

It took about three years from the time of the Deal's inception for it to even come before the IAEA and the NSG – for long periods, partly due to opposition from non-proliferation lobbies, but most of all because of domestic opposition by Indian and US lawmakers, the Deal seemed unlikely to be realised. In comparison, the process of approvals from the IAEA and the NSG took little time – both were obtained between July and September 2008 (that is to say, the IAEA Board approved of India's safeguards agreement in a short time; the process of finalising the text of this agreement between India and the IAEA Secretariat had taken longer). However, the process had an impact upon the terms of the Deal. The IAEA safeguards agreement and NSG waiver expanded and clarified the range of India's non-proliferation commitments that were conditions for its receiving civil nuclear cooperation from the United States and other States; the NSG waiver also expressly tied the Deal to the NPT's objects and purposes. This section explores the alterations wrought at both forums.

The section also explores the rhetoric deployed during the three years by the United States and India to justify and explain the Deal. It draws attention to the contrast between arguments used before international and US domestic audiences, and those used before Indian audiences during the phase when the Indian government was subjected to a confidence vote in the Parliament. The contrast reveals not only the diversity of interpretations that were given to the Deal but also allows appreciation of the modifications achieved by the IAEA and NSG. Moreover, a perusal of their rhetoric suggests that the United States and India were ultimately constrained by their own justifications of the Deal's compatibility with the purposes and principles of the nuclear-governance regime.

Finally, the Deal's passage also provided fresh impetus for a reconsideration of the scope of the NPT's non-proliferation, energy assistance, and disarmament commitments by many States, which *inter alia* found expression in the outcome document of the 2010 NPT Review Conference. This section explores this document, as well as other ways in which States reaffirmed their commitment to the NPT.

The process of implementation

From the beginning, the United States and India had recognised that there were inconsistencies between US commitments under the NPT and the Deal. The 2005 Joint Statement specifically provided that 'the United States will work with friends and allies to adjust international regimes to enable full civil nuclear energy cooperation and trade with India'.[140] The 123 Agreement defined in a specific and restrictive way the regimes that would need to be so adjusted – it made reference only to adjusting NSG practices to 'create the necessary conditions for India to obtain full access to the international fuel market, including reliable, uninterrupted and continual access to fuel supplies from firms in several nations'.[141] It also required India to negotiate 'an appropriate safeguards agreement with the IAEA'.[142] Notably, its text did not refer to the need for approval from all the NPT parties.

Even so, routing the Deal's implementation through the NSG and the IAEA was instrumental not only for securing acceptance for the Deal but for crystallising its terms so as to prevent erosion of the NPT. In the process, the original bilateral agreement was 'internationalised' in order to confirm the scope of its provisions, explain its rationale, highlight its exceptional, non-precedent-creating character and anchor it more securely to various non-proliferation goals.

IAEA: giving concrete shape to India's commitments, de-emphasising peculiarities

The first relevant step in the process of implementing the Deal was the IAEA's conclusion of an appropriate safeguards agreement with India. This was from the outset a challenging task. While, in general, the Agency follows the INFCIRC/153 model in its dealings with NNWS, it

[140] India–US Joint Statement 2005. [141] Article 5(6)(a), 123 Agreement.

[142] Article 5(6)(c); Article 10(2), 123 Agreement, makes it clear that transfer of nuclear fuel and materials under the nuclear deal is conditioned on there being in force an India-Specific Safeguards Agreement negotiated between India and the IAEA.

does this on the basis that the NPT commits all its NNWS parties to comprehensive safeguards. But India as a non party was not obliged to undertake comprehensive safeguards, and prior to the Deal had only permitted the IAEA to inspect 6 of its civil nuclear facilities. It was willing to add to this number, but would not on any account permit access to its military programme. On the other hand, NPT practice had developed so as to require all NPT parties to condition nuclear exports to NNWS on the acceptance of comprehensive safeguards by those States: the United States was thus under pressure to demand the same from India. The India-Specific Safeguards Agreement (ISSA)[143] had to reconcile India's exceptional position with the need to assure other States that the Deal was compatible with the basic principles of the NPT regime.

India initially took the position that a satisfactory safeguards agreement would be one mirroring the voluntary-offer arrangements concluded by *de jure* NWS. Voluntary-offer arrangements are used by the IAEA

(i) to test innovative safeguards methods, or to give the Agency experience that it might not otherwise gain in safeguarding advanced nuclear fuel cycle facilities; and
(ii) to fulfil expectations of non-nuclear-weapon States that some facilities in nuclear-weapon States are subject to safeguards'.[144]

India interpreted the 2005 Joint Statement as requiring it to conclude only such a voluntary-offer agreement.[145] The Statement had provided that India would 'place voluntarily its civilian nuclear facilities under IAEA safeguards'. It had also provided, as did the 123 Agreement, that India would assume the 'same responsibilities and practices . . . as other leading countries with advanced nuclear technology, such as the United States'.[146]

However, other States were unwilling to accept a voluntary-offer arrangement for India, arguing that it was 'integral to the integrity of the global regime that India not be granted "*de jure*" or "*de facto*" status as a [NWS] under the NPT'.[147] Ultimately, while the phrase that India

[143] INFCIRC/754, 2009.
[144] IAEA, 'The Safeguards System of the International Atomic Energy Agency', 3, www.iaea.org/safeguards/documents/safeg_system.pdf.
[145] The Indian position is elaborately described in Rajamohan, 'Impossible Allies', 247–51.
[146] India–US Joint Statement 2005.
[147] Rajamohan, 'Impossible Allies', 250.

'voluntarily places' its facilities under safeguards finds mention in the ISSA too,[148] India's obligations do, in fact, go beyond those undertaken by NWS under voluntary-offer arrangements.

The ISSA is based on a third template (besides comprehensive or voluntary-offer arrangements) that was already available to the IAEA: INFCIRC/66 on 'item-specific safeguards'.[149] The key distinctions between these three arrangements are of scope and purpose. Comprehensive safeguards apply 'on all source or special fissionable material in all peaceful nuclear activities within [a State's] territory, under its jurisdiction or carried out under its control anywhere, for the exclusive purpose of verifying that such material is not diverted to nuclear weapons or other nuclear explosive devices'.[150] Item-specific safeguards apply 'at the request of the parties, to any bilateral or multilateral arrangement, or at the request of a State, to any of that State's activities in the field of atomic energy'. Their purpose is to ensure that 'materials, services, equipment, facilities, and information made available ... are not used in such a way as to further any military purpose'.[151] This is expressly stated as the ISSA's purpose too. In contrast, the primary purpose of voluntary-offer arrangements is not that of verifying the non-diversion of nuclear material from peaceful uses.

Another contrast between comprehensive, item-specific and voluntary-offer agreements is in their provisions on the termination of safeguards. A voluntary-offer agreement may be terminated at will by the State in question.[152] Under a comprehensive agreement, it is for the IAEA to determine that it is appropriate to terminate safeguards because nuclear material has been 'consumed, or has been diluted in such a way that it is no longer usable for any nuclear activity relevant from the point of view of safeguards, or has become practicably irrecoverable'.[153] Item-specific safeguards may be terminated on this basis, and also when 'the conditions specified in the safeguards agreement, pursuant to which [nuclear material] was subject to Agency safeguards, no longer apply'.[154] For instance, termination of a bilateral or multilateral

[148] References may be found in the preamble and in para. 13, INFCIRC/754, 2009.

[149] 'The Agency's Safeguards System (1965, as Provisionally Extended in 1966 and 1968)', INFCIRC/66/Rev.2, 1968.

[150] Paras. 1 and 2, INFCIRC/153 (corr.), 1972. [151] *ibid.*

[152] See, for instance, Article 26, 'The Text of the Agreement of 18 November 1977 between the United States of America and the Agency for the Application of Safeguards in the United States of America', INFCIRC/288, 1981.

[153] Para. 11, INFCIRC/153 (corr.), 1972. [154] Para. 26(f), INFCIRC/66/Rev.2, 1968.

arrangement pursuant to which safeguards were undertaken is a ground for termination of the safeguards also. This termination clause of INFCIRC/66 is reproduced in the ISSA.[155]

There has been much debate on whether the ISSA conforms to the requirement stated in the 123 Agreement that India undertake 'safeguards in perpetuity'.[156] The word 'perpetuity' could be taken to imply that India could not in the future withdraw civil nuclear facilities from safeguards. However, neither INFCIRC/66 nor INFCIRC/153 envisages that a State will be unable to withdraw from safeguards in all cases. Under INFCIRC/66, safeguards may be withdrawn where the conditions on the basis of which they were undertaken no longer hold, for instance where a facility no longer receives a supply of nuclear material or equipment, nor possesses any previously supplied. The conditions under INFCIRC/153 are more stringent, but also do not support the most expansive reading of perpetuity as precluding termination in all cases.

The ISSA does not include measures of exceptional treatment for India that were envisaged in the 123 Agreement, and that would represent modification of INFCIRC/66. Article 5(6)(c) of the 123 Agreement had stated that India's safeguards agreement may 'provid[e] for corrective measures that India may take to ensure uninterrupted operation of its civilian nuclear reactors in the event of disruption of foreign fuel supplies'. Such measures could have included withdrawal from safeguards of facilities containing previously supplied material or those established through foreign collaboration. However, the ISSA does not flesh out the concept of 'corrective measures' in this manner.[157] Despite reports that India sought an elaborate provision on corrective measures, only the ISSA preamble includes a reference that India may take corrective measures.[158]

155 Paras. 30 and 32, INFCIRC/754, 2009.

156 Phrase used in Article 5(6)(c), 123 Agreement.

157 R. Ramachandran, 'Inching Closer', *Frontline*, 16–29 August 2008, reported that 'Vilmos Cserveny, the chief IAEA negotiator for the Safeguards Agreement, made it clear that "corrective measures" should not be confused with termination of safeguards, which were ... standard'.

158 The ISSA preamble provides, in part:

> Whereas the Statute authorizes the Agency to apply safeguards, at the request of the parties, to any bilateral or multilateral arrangement, or at the request of a State to any of the State's activities in the field of atomic energy and, in this context ...
>
> Noting also for the purposes of this Agreement that:
>
> An essential basis of India's concurrence to accept Agency safeguards ... is the conclusion of international cooperation arrangements creating the necessary conditions

Moreover, in one respect the ISSA can even be seen as extending beyond the scope of the template's item-specific safeguards to embrace a wider scope more akin to comprehensive safeguards. Under INFCIRC/153, the IAEA is permitted to verify not only that declared nuclear material has not been diverted to non-peaceful uses, but also that all material required to be declared has in fact been declared. In other words, it must satisfy itself that the declaration made by a State is not only correct, but also complete, and that no undeclared sites of nuclear activity exist within that State. Of course, the reliability of the IAEA's conclusions on completeness depends on whether it is equipped to detect undeclared nuclear material or activity in a particular State; in the absence of an Additional Protocol, it would largely rely upon the State itself to make a complete declaration. The template for item-specific safeguards, INFCIRC/66, limits the application of safeguards to listed materials and facilities and it is not for the IAEA to inquire into the 'completeness' of the declaration of a State's nuclear activities. However, it is possible to argue that, under the ISSA, India has provided the IAEA with general criteria through which it can verify the completeness of India's declaration as far as its peaceful nuclear activities are concerned. Paragraph 11(b) provides:

> The items subject to this agreement shall be ... [a]ny nuclear material, non-nuclear material, equipment and components supplied to India which are required to be safeguarded pursuant to a bilateral or multilateral arrangement to which India is a party ...

In contrast, previous safeguards agreements with India were limited to specifically listed materials.[159] It is possible to interpret paragraph 11(b) as demanding that India undertake safeguards on all its nuclear imports, unless sourced from Pakistan or Israel.[160] This is because,

for India to obtain access to the international fuel market, including reliable, uninterrupted and continuous access to fuel supplies from companies in several nations, as well as support for an Indian effort to develop a strategic reserve of nuclear fuel to guard against any disruption of supply over the lifetime of India's reactors; and

India may take corrective measures to ensure uninterrupted operation of its civilian nuclear reactors in the event of disruption of foreign fuel supplies.

See also S. Varadarajan, 'Parsing the India-Specific Safeguards Agreement', *The Hindu*, 12 July 2008.

[159] See, for instance, the Annex to India's 1994 Safeguards Agreement, INFCIRC/433, 1994.

[160] Para. 11(b) is supported by paras. 11(a), 11(f), 14(b) and 15. Together, these paragraphs require India to notify the IAEA of all nuclear supplies received by it, and all facilities in which it stores or uses such supplies:

since the NPT permits nuclear exports on the condition that the recipient State has undertaken appropriate safeguards, any nuclear cooperation agreement concluded between an NPT member State and India would impliedly, if not expressly, require supplies to India to be placed under safeguards.

The ISSA was presented before the IAEA Board of Governors on 1 August 2008, and, despite initial criticism, was ultimately adopted by consensus. The proceedings at this IAEA meeting are discussed in the next section.

NSG: from clean waiver to conditional waiver

The second step in implementing the Deal was securing approval from the NSG, specifically in the form of a 'waiver' from NSG Guidelines. While the 2005 Joint Statement did not refer expressly to the NSG as the regime whose practices would have to be adjusted, the 123 Agreement did. Commentaries on the Deal have rarely questioned why the NSG *alone* was the multilateral forum from which the two States sought approval for the Deal (this is discussed in the next section). But, certainly, the NSG was one of the relevant forums, for the terms of the Deal were inconsistent with its practice.

As discussed, the NSG is an informal network of States, including the United States, that are among the principal nuclear suppliers in the world and have come together to set specific Guidelines to regulate

11. The items subject to this Agreement shall be:

(a) Any facility listed in the Annex to this Agreement, as notified by India pursuant to paragraph 14(a) of this Agreement;

...

(f) Any facility other than a facility identified in paragraph 11(a) above, or any other location in India, while producing, processing, using, fabricating or storing any nuclear material, non-nuclear material, equipment or components referred to in paragraph 11(b), (c), (d) or (e) of this Agreement, as notified by India pursuant to paragraph 14(b) of this Agreement.

14 ...

(b) Should India, on the basis of its sole determination, decide to import or transfer any nuclear material, non-nuclear material, equipment or components subject to this Agreement to any facility or other location in India provided for in paragraph 11(f) of this Agreement, it shall so notify the Agency. Any such facility or location so notified by India pursuant to this sub-paragraph shall become subject to this Agreement as of the date of receipt by the Agency of such written notification from India.

15. India shall notify the Agency of the receipt of any nuclear material, non-nuclear material, equipment and components referred to in paragraph 11(b) of this Agreement within four weeks of the arrival in India of such nuclear material, non-nuclear material, equipment and components.

their nuclear supplies. The NSG Guidelines, specifically Part I on 'Nuclear Transfers', demand that recipient States undertake comprehensive safeguards (which India was unwilling to do); it was thus clear from the first that the Deal was not compatible with them. At the same time, NSG Guidelines are not binding *per se*, and the United States, had it wished to, could have disregarded these Guidelines without breaching a legal obligation.[161] However, the NSG is a US-led initiative, and thus unlikely to be overtly disregarded by the United States. Indeed, the United States was also unwilling to promote a limited interpretation of the NSG Guidelines, a possibility that is suggested by the language used in these Guidelines.

For Part I Guidelines provide that a recipient State must have 'safeguards on all source and special fissionable material in its current and future peaceful activities',[162] referring to 'peaceful' nuclear activities rather than 'all nuclear activities' on the presumption that an NNWS cannot conduct any other type of activity. However, the following sentence envisages continued nuclear cooperation where such safeguards are terminated. It states that the recipient must provide assurance that, if an agreement for safeguards on all peaceful nuclear activities is terminated,

> the recipient will bring into force an agreement with the IAEA based on existing IAEA model safeguards agreements requiring the application of safeguards on all trigger list items or related technology transferred by the supplier or processed, or produced or used in connection with such transfers.[163]

[161] Even as negotiations at the NSG were underway, a former Indian diplomat recommended that India should put out a 'strong and clear message regarding India's determination to go ahead with its nuclear programme regardless of the NSG decision'. According to him, '[t]he NSG is, in reality, the key component of a discriminatory nuclear technology regime, and its role and functioning need reassessment ... [I]t is important to note that the NSG is a voluntary group, and its decisions are not legally binding on its members. Thus, it would be possible for a member state that is fully convinced of India's *bona fide* civilian nuclear needs, to engage in nuclear commerce with India. This would be a rather extreme step, but would seem reasonable if it becomes clear that some NSG members ... are adopting an obstructionist approach ... Russia, for example has, in the past, gone ahead with nuclear cooperation despite the NSG. China also extended civil nuclear co-operation to Pakistan despite the NSG, though later it tried to justify the deal by backdating it before its entry into the NSG.' Moreover, he considered that India's choosing to go ahead despite the NSG would only weaken the NSG regime: B. Balakrishnan, 'India's Nuclear Deal: A Bridge Too Far?', *Hindu Business Line*, 3 September 2008.

[162] Para. 4(a), INFCIRC/254 Part I (Rev.9), November 2007. This has not changed in the most recent version (Rev.11) of the Guidelines.

[163] *ibid.*

This is a reference to INFCIRC/66 item-specific safeguards. From here, it is not much of a stretch to argue that item-specific safeguards should suffice *ab initio*.

The Part II Guidelines state a more diluted requirement. Paragraph 2 provides: 'Suppliers should not authorise transfers of equipment, materials, software, or related technology identified in [the Guidelines] for use in a non-nuclear-weapon State in . . . an unsafeguarded nuclear fuel-cycle activity.'[164] Paragraph 4 provides:

> In considering whether to authorise transfers, suppliers should . . . take relevant factors into account, including:
> 1. Whether the recipient State is a party to [the NPT] or . . . similar international legally binding nuclear non-proliferation agreement, and has an IAEA safeguards agreement in force applicable to all its peaceful nuclear activities;
> 2. Whether any recipient State that is not party to [the NPT] . . . or a similar international legally binding nuclear non-proliferation agreement has any facilities . . . that are not, or will not be, subject to IAEA safeguards . . .

Paragraph 4 does not specifically condition nuclear supplies on the adoption of comprehensive safeguards.

The United States could have interpreted the NSG Guidelines as permitting nuclear transfers on the basis of item-specific safeguards, though by doing so it would have seriously altered the NSG practice of considering comprehensive safeguards a prerequisite for nuclear transfers. Such interpretation would have the effect, similar to that of invoking the non-binding nature of NSG Guidelines, of gravely limiting the NSG's normative authority. And this was not desirable to the United States.[165]

Additionally, both the United States and India were keen to obtain NSG approval. The NSG, as an informal, deliberative, fairly close-knit consultative group, was one from which the two States could expect to secure approval of the Deal. Moreover, despite its limited membership of forty-five States, its decisions connote significant multilateral

[164] Again, there is no change between the language used in the version that was in place during the NSG negotiations on the Deal (Rev.7, March 2006) and the current version (Rev.8).

[165] Interview with P. S. Das, Vice-Admiral (retd), New Delhi, 29 November 2009 (personal interview, on file). Das, a participant in an Aspen Institute-hosted Track 2 US–India Strategic Dialogue, notes that, as the principal force behind the creation of the NSG, the United States was interested in preserving the authority of the NSG Guidelines and wished to undertake no action that would undermine them.

support, as these forty-five States are among the most significant nuclear suppliers, and they operate by consensus. For the United States, the NSG was an ideal forum at which to shape the Deal to limit the effect on the nuclear-governance regime of the exception made for India. At the NSG, the United States could affirm its NPT commitments, justify an exception for India, and ensure (and assure other States) that this exception was yet embedded within a larger objective of non-proliferation.[166] It could also clarify that the reasons for which this exception was promoted made it an unsuitable precedent for other States. The NSG provided the opportunity to pre-empt concerns relating to horizontal and vertical non-proliferation, and corrosion of other States' commitments under the NPT. For India, the NSG provided means for creating a general India-specific practice that permitted all States to supply nuclear materials to India without requiring India to undertake comprehensive safeguards;[167] and also for precluding the likelihood of other States being offered similar concessions – a priority *vis-à-vis* Pakistan.

The final text of the NSG waiver indicates that efforts were made both to downplay the Deal's incompatibility with the NPT, and to redefine

[166] Varadarajan notes that, by routing the Deal through the NSG, the United States would not only enhance the Deal's legitimacy, but also secure several non-proliferation commitments from India. In general, the non-proliferation and strategic relations aspects of the Deal cut against each other, and the NSG could provide the conduit for securing the former: Interview with S. Varadarajan, Editor, *The Hindu*, 9 December 2009 (personal interview, on file). Varadarajan (then Deputy Editor of *The Hindu*) received the Ramnath Goenka Memorial Award for Excellence in Journalism for his reportage on the Deal in July–October 2008. This chapter makes references to a number of his news reports. Incidentally, the name '*The Hindu*' should not be taken to indicate a communal agenda – the name dates back to the newspaper's founding in 1878, when it was set up as an Indian nationalist alternative to the British-owned newspapers of that time. *The Hindu* leans to the left in Indian politics, not the right.

[167] Indeed, the desire for NSG approval might have prompted India's decision to conclude the Deal. Varadarajan recalls that a nuclear deal was first discussed by India and France in 1998, but France was firm that the Deal could not be implemented without NSG permission, and suggested that India approach Russia. Soon after this, India conducted its nuclear tests, which for a time made a nuclear deal with any State unlikely. Four years after the tests, Russia too was willing to resume civil nuclear cooperation with India, but suggested that India first approach the United States, which could obtain the necessary waiver for India from the NSG: Varadarajan, *ibid.* A similar background story was recounted in conversation by an official from the UK's Foreign and Commonwealth Office, who noted that the impetus for the Deal came from the United Kingdom and France, who were keen to tap into India's nuclear energy market but felt inhibited by their NPT and NSG commitments, and approached the United States to secure the necessary exception for India: Anonymous comment, 2009.

the Deal in terms that would prevent conduct most inimical to the NPT-based regime.[168]

The first paragraph of the waiver presents five factors as the basis of the NSG's decision; the first four relate to non-proliferation. The first refers to NSG members' '[d]esire to contribute to the effectiveness and integrity of the global non-proliferation regime, and to the widest possible implementation of the provisions and objectives of the Treaty on the Non-Proliferation of Nuclear Weapons'; the third to their '[w]ish to pursue mechanisms to affect positively the non-proliferation commitments and actions of all States'.[169] Read together, these two factors appear to suggest that the waiver was based on the perception that the Deal offers a creative way to engage India's cooperation on non-proliferation issues.

The second and third paragraphs of this five-paragraph document then refer to India's non-proliferation commitments. The second paragraph outlines various commitments and actions that India had already undertaken, including separating its civil and military nuclear programmes and submitting the former to IAEA safeguards; concluding the ISSA and committing to an Additional Protocol; refraining from the transfer of enrichment and reprocessing facilities to States that do not already have them; instituting export controls and adhering to NSG Guidelines; and maintaining a unilateral moratorium on testing and support for the FMCT. The third paragraph refers to a statement issued by the Indian External Affairs Minister during the course of NSG negotiations,[170] in which he reiterated India's commitments on non-proliferation, including its moratorium on nuclear testing. That statement and the commitments and actions stated in paragraph 2 are described as a key basis for waiver.

Paragraph 3 outlines the core elements of the waiver, which in substance exempt India from the application of comprehensive safeguards. In all other respects, however, NSG members are to continue to adhere to the NSG Guidelines when dealing with India. In particular, paragraph 3 states that transfers of sensitive exports must be consistent with paragraphs 6 and 7 of the NSG Part I Guidelines – these, in effect, require

[168] NSG, 'Statement on Civil Nuclear Cooperation with India', 7 September 2008.
[169] The second factor is that NSG members '[s]eek to avert the further spread of nuclear weapons'; and the fourth is that they '[s]eek to promote the fundamental principles of safeguards and export controls for nuclear transfers for peaceful purposes'. The fifth alone notes 'the energy needs of India'.
[170] Indian External Affairs Minister, Statement on the Civil Nuclear Initiative, 2008.

NSG members to exercise restraint in transfer of enrichment and reprocessing technologies to India.

The waiver also requires all NSG members to notify each other of transfers to India of certain types of nuclear material, and to consult with regard to matters connected to the implementation of the waiver.[171] There is provision also for extraordinary consultations '[i]n the event that one or more [NSG members] consider that circumstances have arisen that require consultations'. In such a case, NSG members 'will meet, and then act in accordance with paragraph 16 of the [NSG Part I] Guidelines'.[172] Paragraph 16 of the Part I Guidelines refers to the explosion of a nuclear device, or a violation of IAEA safeguards, as a basis for extra-ordinary consultations. It provides for an immediate suspension of supplies, pending the conclusion of such consultations.

There is no direct reference in the waiver to India's nuclear weapons, only the provision that the waiver is applicable with respect to 'the IAEA-safeguarded civil nuclear program'.[173] The waiver notes India's commitment to adhere to the NSG, and provides that the NSG Chair will consult with India regarding changes to NSG Guidelines, in order 'to facilitate their effective implementation by India'.[174] That is, India is expected to remain current in its implementation of NSG Guidelines.

The text of the NSG waiver was the outcome of much discussion, for, according to news reports, many NSG members were not, initially, in favour of the terms proposed by the United States. There is little 'official' material available on NSG proceedings, so the following account of the NSG proceedings relies heavily on news reports and personal memoirs.

The story runs as follows. On the basis of early negotiations with India, the United States had prepared a draft waiver in 2006, providing simply that a State could transfer nuclear materials or technology covered under NSG Part I Guidelines to safeguarded nuclear facilities in India notwithstanding paragraph 4 of the Guidelines (which referred to comprehensive safeguards), as long as such State was satisfied that India continued to meet its non-proliferation and safeguards agreements and other requirements of the NSG Guidelines.[175] The 2006 draft thus suggested that States could subjectively evaluate India's fulfilment of its commitments. This

[171] NSG, Statement on Civil Nuclear Cooperation with India, 2008, para. 3(c) and (e).
[172] *ibid.*, para. 3(e). [173] *ibid.*, para. 3. [174] *ibid.*, para. 4.
[175] 'US NSG India Proposal', Arms Control Wonk, March 2006, www.armscontrolwonk.com/1009/us-nsg-india-proposal.

was heavily criticised by various non-proliferation lobbies and was diluted in the final text of 2008, which based the waiver on specific commitments undertaken by India, 'without prejudice to national positions thereon'.[176] Unlike the final text, the 2006 draft made no reference to specific restraints, such as those on enrichment and reprocessing technologies. The 2006 draft also paid more regard to India's non-NPT status, as 'a State not party, and never having been a party, to the NPT', and expressed, in paragraph 1, a '[w]ish to pursue mechanisms to affect positively the conduct of those outside the [NPT]'. In contrast the 2008 waiver avoided language suggesting India's position was mainly defined by hostility towards the NPT.

Paragraph 2 of each document outlines India's non-proliferation commitments and actions. However, the text of the 2008 waiver is more specific; for instance, it refers to the actual plan for the separation of civil and nuclear facilities ('Separation Plan'[177]) and the safeguards agreement (ISSA) concluded by India. The commitments mentioned are also bolstered by the incorporated reference to the statement by the Indian External Affairs Minister. The 2006 draft was not linked to these documents and commitments. Moreover, it did not include a reference to ordinary or extra-ordinary consultations, or sharing of information between NSG members on the implementation of the waiver. Nor did it indicate that India was to keep pace with changes to NSG Guidelines.

The 2006 draft, in short, put forth the concrete terms of a 'clean waiver' sought by the United States for India. The draft intended the waiver to be without conditions. Initially, in their bilateral discussions with NSG members and communications to the NSG, both India and the United States appeared to make an effort to secure such a clean waiver. However, the United States' consultations with other NSG members revealed that such terms would not do; consequently by August 2008, it had begun to claim there was a distinction between a 'clean' waiver and an 'unconditional' one, indicating that its new draft would condition the NSG waiver upon India's implementation of non-proliferation commitments.[178]

[176] NSG, Statement on Civil Nuclear Cooperation with India, 2008, para. 3.

[177] The Indian separation plan is reported as 'Implementation of the India–United States Joint Statement of 18 July 2005: India's Separation Plan', INFCIRC/731, 25 July 2008. The Plan was agreed upon by the United States and India in March 2006, and tabled in the Indian Parliament on 11 May 2006.

[178] For instance, Ramachandran, 'Inching Closer', reports remarks of US Ambassador to India, David Mulford.

At the NSG annual meeting on 21–23 August 2008, the United States presented a fresh text that represented an advance in this direction. But other NSG members wanted to include additional conditions, and negotiations collapsed when they outlined about fifty amendments to align the waiver to the existing nuclear-governance regime.[179] Reportedly, New Zealand, Ireland, Austria and the Netherlands were the most insistent that the waiver should include terms proscribing nuclear tests by India under threat of termination of nuclear supplies; restricting transfer of enrichment and reprocessing technology to India; and providing for a review of the waiver based on regular monitoring of India's fulfilment of non-proliferation commitments.[180] These countries also wished the text to state that all States should accede to the NPT. Such terms were not acceptable to India.

A follow-up meeting was scheduled for 5–7 September 2008. In the interim, the United States worked with India and other States to reframe some of these proposed conditions in terms that were acceptable to all, leading to the inclusion of many of the key elements of the final text.[181] However, even with a modified draft, it took two days of intensive negotiations at the September meeting to secure the waiver.[182] The United States expended immense diplomatic resources

179 See NSG, 'Public Statement', Extraordinary Plenary Meeting, Vienna, 21–22 August 2008. This is a dry, two-line statement issued by the NSG following the plenary, which is reflective of the collapse: 'Participating Governments exchanged views in a constructive manner, and agreed to meet again in the near future to continue their deliberations.' The following news stories provide a substantial account of the meeting: P. D. Samanta, 'To US Draft, NSG Sceptics Want to Add Fine Print', *Indian Express*, 21 August 2008; S. Varadarajan, 'NSG Critics Focus on Non-Proliferation Benchmarks', *The Hindu*, 22 August 2008; S. Varadarajan, 'Conditions Mooted for Indian Nuclear Waiver', *The Hindu*, 23 August 2008; S. Varadarajan, 'India Says NSG Clearance Is US Responsibility', *The Hindu*, 23 August 2008.

180 S. Varadarajan, 'Conditions Mooted for Indian Nuclear Waiver', *The Hindu*, 23 August 2008.

181 S. Varadarajan, 'India, US Agree on Amended NSG Draft Waiver', *The Hindu*, 31 August 2008; P. D. Samanta, 'India Agrees to More Tweaks in NSG Draft', *Indian Express*, 2 September 2008.

182 For an account of the NSG deliberations during the September plenary, see: S. Varadarajan, 'As NSG Members Mull New US Draft, Fate of India Deal Hangs in Balance', *The Hindu*, 3 September 2008; S. Varadarajan, 'New NSG Draft Has Small But Significant Changes', *The Hindu*, 5 September 2008; S. Varadarajan, 'NSG Hopeful of Consensus Soon', *The Hindu*, 5 September 2008; S. Varadarajan, 'As NSG Members Take "Political" Call, Differences Narrow', *The Hindu*, 5 September 2008; S. Varadarajan, 'Individual Governments Should Decide', *The Hindu*, 5 September 2008; S. Varadarajan, 'Nuclear Deal Staring at NSG Dead-End', *The Hindu*, 6 September 2008; S. Varadarajan, 'Last-Ditch Talks on to Avert NSG Dead-End', *The Hindu*,

persuading and, some have argued, coercing other States to agree to the waiver.[183] India issued assurances on nuclear testing and disarmament via its External Affairs Minister. Finally, consensus was achieved on the additional basis of a side agreement between NSG members not to 'sell sensitive technologies to India in the "foreseeable future"'.[184]

Several NSG members subsequently issued statements, principally to reiterate that the waiver complied with the requirements of the NPT-based nuclear-governance regime.[185] Indeed, the final text of the waiver states the concession for India in narrower terms and embeds the same in a welter of non-proliferation commitments. The waiver is also 'India-specific'; the NSG did not take on board China's suggestion that it be criteria-based, and applicable to other States. China had stated that it hoped NSG could 'equally address the aspirations of all parties for the peaceful use of nuclear power',[186] but the waiver's text and other NSG

6 September 2008; V. Kumar, '"India Will Not Be a Source of Proliferation", Says Pranab', *The Hindu*, 6 September 2008; S. Varadarajan, 'NSG Lifts Sanctions on India', *The Hindu*, 7 September 2008; S. Varadarajan, 'Waiver Enables Member States to Provide India Full Civil Nuclear Cooperation', *The Hindu*, 7 September 2008. See also P. D. Samanta, 'Beijing Says Why the Hurry as Vienna Moves Closer to a Deal', *Indian Express*, 4 September 2008.

183 S. Varadarajan, 'Waiver Enables Member States to Provide India Full Civil Nuclear Cooperation', *The Hindu*, 7 September 2008; C. Rajghatta, 'US Shows the Way at NSG', *Times of India*, 7 September 2008. In her memoir, former US Secretary of State, Condoleezza Rice, recalls that 'there was significant resistance from the Austrians, the Irish, and the Nordic countries, all of which considered themselves guardians of the non-proliferation regime . . . Jonas Gahr Støre, the Norwegian foreign minister, tried to help, writing language that I approved to bring the recalcitrant States along. I . . . stayed up all night making phone calls. (They were in addition to the more than twenty I'd made before leaving Washington.) Finally it came down to the Austrian foreign minister, Ursula Plassnik, who was at the European Council meeting in Brussels. I asked German Foreign Minister Frank-Walter Steinmeier to track her down and get her agreement. She apparently didn't want to be found. But Frank-Walter persisted, and she instructed her negotiator to agree.' C. Rice, *No Higher Honour: A Memoir of My Years in Washington* (London, Simon & Schuster 2011) 697–8.

184 'NSG Agreed Not to Sell Sensitive Technologies to India', *The Hindu*, 12 September 2008; 'NSG Not to Sell Sensitive Technologies to India', *Times of India*, 11 September 2008.

185 See, for instance, 'Canada Welcomes Exception for India from Nuclear Suppliers Group Guidelines', Canadian Department of Foreign Affairs and International Trade News Release 198, 6 September 2008; 'India Gets NSG Waiver', *Hindu Business Line*, 6 September 2008; V. Radyuhin, 'Russia Welcomes NSG Waiver for India', *The Hindu*, 9 September 2008; S. Varadarajan, 'Waiver Enables Member States to Provide India Full Civil Nuclear Cooperation', *The Hindu*, 7 September 2008.

186 P. Aiyar, 'China Says It Played a Responsible Role at NSG Meet', The Hindu, 10 September 2008.

members' statements do not provide much scope for regarding it as a precedent for other States.

Rhetoric of accommodation

The process of implementation of the Deal was accompanied throughout by a discourse led by the US and Indian governments and assisted by the IAEA Director General that, for the most part, sought to dispel claims that the Deal was incompatible with the NPT-based nuclear-governance regime, and to tie it to India's developmental needs. The two governments and the IAEA Director General also used India's long-held opposition to the NPT as a factor in favour of the Deal rather than against it.

Their arguments on the Deal can be sorted into three phases: an early phase, from the time of the announcement of the Deal up to the public release of the 123 Agreement (July 2005–July 2007); a middle sluggish phase during which the Deal remained mired within Indian domestic politics (August 2007–June 2008); and a final 'fast-track' phase in which the Deal was ushered through the IAEA, the NSG and then the US Congress in quick succession (July 2008–October 2008). The discourse of the second phase was markedly different from that of the first phase; in the third phase, arguments of the first phase were rehearsed, but in more concrete terms.

To map this discourse, I rely on public (or highly publicised) speeches and opinions of members of the US and Indian governments and of the IAEA and on news reports noting the advance of this discourse.

Phase I: July 2005–July 2007

The United States' priority, in the early period, was to secure the consent of its Congress for the Deal (via passage of the Hyde Act[187]) and to build broad international consensus in its favour. In this phase, two main narratives, aimed at domestic and international audiences, underpinned all its major communications. These were at work, for instance, in US Secretary of State Condoleezza Rice's April 2006 speech to the US Senate Committee on Foreign Relations.[188]

The first narrative was of energy security: Rice highlighted India's large population condemned to underdevelopment because of the short supply of energy, shifting attention to the needs of India's people and

[187] See footnote 74 above.
[188] US Secretary of State, Remarks, Senate Committee on Foreign Relations, 2006.

away from the question of the Indian State's entitlement to nuclear cooperation. She also cited the Deal's benefits for the environment and for international commerce, arguing that nuclear energy, though relatively clean and plentiful, had remained underutilised due to concerns over its safe application, but now technologies had advanced to the point where States, India amongst them, were prepared to experiment with harnessing nuclear power, leading to reduced reliance on fossil fuels. Indeed, India with its growing energy needs was a particularly important consumer. Moreover, Rice pointed out, nuclear energy, unlike fossil fuels, was linked to a geo-political framework favourable to the United States – the uranium- and technology-rich States were the developed nations of the West, not the Middle East. These Western States already collaborated in a multilateral export-control regime defining the terms under which nuclear materials may be supplied. They could use nuclear energy diplomacy to secure desirable (to them) foreign-policy outcomes. For instance, the Deal would remove the need for India to purchase fossil fuels from Iran.

The second narrative contested claims that the Deal would weaken the nuclear-governance regime. Four arguments shaped this narrative. First, the need to take a 'realistic' account of the major threats to nuclear non-proliferation: these were from non-State terrorists groups and 'rogue' States; thus, it was the actor possessing nuclear weapons rather than the act of possession that deserved scrutiny.[189] States like India, Rice noted, which were open democracies adhering to the rule of law, were not threats.[190] Furthermore, India's assistance was essential to respond comprehensively to threats posed by non-State actors and rogue States. 'In fact', stated Rice, 'India is increasingly doing its part to support the international community's efforts to curb the dangerous nuclear ambitions of Iran.'

Second, the Deal did not 'seek to renegotiate or amend the NPT', but, by requiring India to undertake several non-proliferation commitments, it brought it into the non-proliferation framework and thus strengthened the regime.[191] India would separate its military and civil programmes and accept perpetual IAEA safeguards on the latter; conclude an Additional Protocol; continue its unilateral moratorium on

[189] See, for instance, D. E. Sanger, 'Reshaping Nuclear Rules', *New York Times*, 15 March 2005.

[190] See also R. Haas, 'A blinkered view of the Third "I"', *Indian Express*, 15 May 2006.

[191] US Secretary of State, Remarks, Senate Committee on Foreign Relations, 2006.

nuclear testing; work with the United States to conclude the FMCT; tighten its export controls; adhere to MTCR and NSG Guidelines; and refrain from transferring enrichment and reprocessing technologies to States that did not have them. These were all 'gains for nuclear non-proliferation'.[192] Indeed, India's then Foreign Secretary, Shyam Saran, argued:

> If we go by the NPT concepts and objectives rather than this littler text, then it is difficult to make a case against the July 18 agreement. Bringing India into the fold is not only a gain for international nonproliferation efforts, but indispensable for the emergence of a new global consensus on nonproliferation in response to current challenges.[193]

The third argument was that there was no necessary link between nuclear weapons and access to nuclear energy. Both India and the United States were quick to emphasise that the Deal was not in any way connected with India's nuclear weapons programme, and should be evaluated on its own merits.[194]

The fourth argument was of India's 'excellent' non-proliferation record. India's refusal to become party to any multilateral nuclear instrument on non-proliferation, such as the NPT and the CTBT, was now used in its favour, to claim that India had never violated a non-proliferation commitment that it had actually undertaken. In consistently maintaining a position outside of multilateral non-proliferation treaties, India had always been an exceptional case. Moreover, despite not being under formal obligation not to supply nuclear weapons or technologies to other States or actors, India had maintained a restrained regime of nuclear exports.

Based on these four arguments, it was claimed that India was uniquely suited for accommodation within the nuclear-governance regime.[195]

[192] See also Associated Press, 'Bush Okays N-Bill, Says It's Important for Entire World', *Indian Express*, 18 December 2006; United States–Russia Joint Statement by President George Bush and President Vladimir Putin, G8 Summit, 15 July 2006; Group of 8, 'Statement on Non-Proliferation', G8 Summit, L'Aquila, 8 July 2006.

[193] Indian Foreign Secretary, 'Transforming US–India Relations', Carnegie Endowment for International Peace, 2005.

[194] *ibid.*

[195] See, for instance, S. R. Weisman, 'US to Broaden India's Access to Nuclear-Power Technology', *New York Times*, 19 July 2005 (reporting official statements that 'the United States would continue to press Iran and North Korea to give up their suspected nuclear weapons programs on the grounds that they had signed various agreements and then cheated on them, while India had an "impeccable" record of not sharing its

Phase II: August 2007–June 2008

The early period was followed by an intermediate, sluggish phase of little international activity. In this phase, the 123 Agreement became public (on 3 August 2007), and this, together with the terms of the Hyde Act, provided scope for major challenges from political parties in India. The most trenchant criticisms came from left-wing parties, then in an uneasy coalition with the Congress-led government headed by Prime Minister Singh.

The Left, suspicious of the US's motives for the Deal, was concerned that India had signed away its sovereignty over its nuclear programme and foreign policy.[196] They argued that, read with the Hyde Act, the 123 Agreement constrained India to act in line with the United States' foreign policy goals and curbed India's right to conduct further nuclear tests. They were particularly apprehensive of a provision in the Hyde Act which suggested that, in case the 123 Agreement was terminated, the United States would work with the NSG to block all fuel and other supplies to India (contrary to its fuel supply guarantees under Article 5(6) of the 123 Agreement). India, meanwhile, would remain bound to IAEA safeguards on its civil nuclear programme. The Left also highlighted that the 123 Agreement continued to block India's access to nuclear enrichment and reprocessing technologies, and that the Hyde Act further constrained India's access even to dual-use technologies that could be used for these purposes. Finally, they pointed out that, via the Deal, India had in effect subscribed to the unequal global order it previously criticised, and had abandoned its commitment to universal disarmament.

The Indian government adjusted its arguments to respond to these domestic criticisms.[197] In a striking shift of rhetoric, it now highlighted the very fact that it had earlier sought to downplay: in contrast to other States, India would receive nuclear energy without committing to the NPT. The United States, too, carefully avoided making any statement that would undercut the perception that India had secured an

weapons technology with other countries'); 'Rice Rebuts Critics on the Hill, Point by Point', *Indian Express*, 6 April 2006 (reporting that, 'when [Senator] Kerry suggested that China could undermine the Indo-US nuclear deal by threatening a similar deal with Pakistan, Rice said, "We've been very clear – publicly, privately – with China, with Pakistan itself, that Pakistan is not an appropriate state for this kind of an exception. It's just a different history."').

196 *Left Stand on the Nuclear Deal*, 9–15.

197 See *ibid.*, 31–46, 66–81, 110–21, 157–70, 180–90, for the Indian government's responses to the criticisms made by India's left-wing parties.

extraordinarily favourable bargain. To its domestic audience, the Indian government stressed the non-applicability of the Hyde Act to India, and the overriding character of the bilateral agreement as an international obligation of the United States. It emphasised that both the 123 Agreement and the Hyde Act gave implicit recognition to India's strategic programme. It asserted that India would not undertake obligations that would hamper its military or civil nuclear programmes. It claimed that 'enshrined in the Agreement is India's freedom to develop strategic reserves of nuclear fuel to guard against any disruption of supply ... and to take corrective measures to ensure uninterrupted operation of its civilian nuclear reactors in case of disruption of foreign fuel supply'.[198] It claimed that its acceptance of safeguards was conditioned on this provision. It also argued that many provisions of the Indian 123 Agreement offered more favourable terms to India than the United States offered to other States. It dismissed concerns that India had waived its right to resume nuclear testing. It also dismissed objections relating to restrictions on the supply of enrichment and reprocessing technology, stating that these were unnecessary for India, but in any case not excluded under the 123 Agreement. It also underlined that a principal advantage of the 123 Agreement lay in its potential to catalyse nuclear cooperation with other States. Finally, it repeatedly stressed India's energy needs.[199] This phase, from August 2007 to June 2008, characterised by sluggish international developments and heated domestic debate, culminated in the failure of a no-confidence motion tabled in the Indian Parliament by the Left. With this, the Deal moved into its final phase.

Phase III: July 2008–October 2008

The final phase was one of rapid activity. In three months, various approvals necessary for the Deal's implementation were secured. These included the IAEA's approval of the ISSA, the NSG waiver and also the US Congress' approval of the 123 Agreement. The rhetoric during this phase was overwhelmingly internationalist: it focused on promoting the Deal as primarily a measure furthering nuclear non-proliferation, while permitting nuclear commerce with India. As in

198 'Above Noise from Left and Right, PM Is Loud and Clear: Deal Is Historic', *Indian Express*, 13 August 2007.

199 'PM Spells N-Deal Out Again: It's Energy, Growth, Security', *Indian Express*, 1 September 2007.

the first phase, the need to adjust current rules was acknowledged, but the extent of divergence between the Deal and the current architecture of the nuclear-governance regime was again deemphasised. For instance, at a meeting of the IAEA Board of Directors to review the ISSA, Director General ElBaradei made two points.[200] First, that, though 'India-specific', the agreement was modelled on an IAEA template, the INFCIRC/66 model for item-specific safeguards. While not full-scope, argued Baradei, the ISSA 'maintain[ed] all the Agency's legal requirements'. Second, that the agreement was not an eccentric bargain between India and the IAEA; the approach taken towards India's safeguards would also serve as a model for safeguards agreements with other States. The US Ambassador, too, emphasised the conformity of the ISSA to standard practices of the IAEA.[201]

Moreover, in various ways, other States were assured that the seemingly broad concessions made in the 123 Agreement would be narrowed in implementation. For instance, a few days prior to the NSG waiver and in the days between the unsuccessful August NSG session and the follow-up September session, a confidential letter from the US State Department to the chairperson of the US House Foreign Relations Committee was revealed to the press.[202] *Inter alia*, this letter confirmed that, if India conducted a nuclear test, nuclear cooperation would be terminated as would all fuel supply assurances. Kept confidential during the tricky period of domestic discord in India,[203] this letter now allayed fears amongst NSG members that 'Washington was being too soft on India'.[204] The NSG received further assurance that the Deal

[200] 'Introductory Statement to the Board of Governors', IAEA Director General (Dr Mohamed ElBaradei), Vienna, 1 August 2008.

[201] See Ramachandran, 'Inching Closer'.

[202] See Letter from Assistant Secretary, US Department of State (J. T. Bergner) to Chairman, Committee on Foreign Affairs, US House of Representatives (T. Lantos) responding to 'Questions for the record submitted to Assistant Secretary Bergner by Chairman Lantos on October 5, 2007', 16 January 2008, http://media.washingtonpost.com/wp-srv/world/documents/Lantos_Letter.pdf. The letter was made public on 2 September 2008 by the new Chairman of the Committee on Foreign affairs, Howard Berman, and was published by the *Washington Post*: see G. Kessler, 'In Secret Letter, Tough US Line on India Nuclear Deal', *Washington Post*, 3 September 2008.

[203] Kessler, *ibid.*, notes that '[t]he answers were considered so sensitive, particularly because debate over the agreement in India could have toppled the government of Prime Minister Manmohan Singh, that the State Department requested they remain secret even though they were not classified'.

[204] S. Varadarajan, 'As NSG Members Take "Political" Call, Differences Narrow', *The Hindu*, 5 September 2008.

would bind India to non-proliferation obligations from a statement issued by the Indian External Affairs Minister during the NSG negotiations.[205] This statement reiterated India's various commitments on non-proliferation including its moratorium on nuclear testing and support for the FMCT. It also stressed India's efforts to strengthen its nuclear export-control regime, and assured that India would not transfer sensitive technologies to States that did not already possess the same. It underscored also India's high regard for, and cooperation with, the IAEA. This letter was mentioned in the NSG waiver as a key basis on which the waiver was granted.[206]

Attempts to reaffirm the NPT

In addition to insisting that the Deal did not undermine the NPT, the United States and several other States also reaffirmed the NPT on several occasions during the process of the Deal's implementation and subsequently.

First, at various forums, States restated their own NPT commitments and expressed their desire for its universal application. The NSG waiver itself referred to NSG members' '[d]esire to contribute to the effectiveness and integrity of the global non-proliferation regime, and to the widest possible implementation of the *provisions and objectives* of the [NPT]',[207] while previous drafts had referred only to implementation of the *objectives* of the NPT. The reference to provisions was an expression of support for its universal ratification.[208] Subsequently, at the preparatory conference for the 2010 NPT Review Conference, the United States clarified that India's accession to the NPT 'remains a fundamental objective of [the United States]'.[209]

[205] Indian External Affairs Minister, Statement on the Civil Nuclear Initiative, 2008.

[206] NSG, Statement on Civil Nuclear Cooperation with India, 2008: 'Based on the commitments and actions . . . as reiterated by India September 5, 2008 . . . Participating Governments have adopted and will adopt the following policy on civil nuclear cooperation by Participating Governments with the IAEA-safeguarded Indian civil nuclear program . . .'

[207] *ibid.*, para. 1(a).

[208] Compare NSG, *ibid.*, with NSG, Draft of US Proposal on India, 2006. See also S. Varadarajan, 'New NSG Draft Has Small But Significant Changes', *The Hindu*, 5 September 2008.

[209] Summary Record of 3rd Mtg, NPT Preparatory Committee for the 2010 Review Conference, New York, 4–15 May 2009, NPT/CONF.2010/PC.III/SR.3, para. 17. See also S. Varadarajan, 'Obama Administration Wants India to Sign the NPT', The Hindu, 7 May 2009.

Second, following the NSG waiver, several NSG members chose to limit the extent of their civil nuclear cooperation with India because it had remained a non-party to the NPT. Australia, for instance, claimed that it would not supply uranium to India, because of its 'well-known' policy of not engaging in nuclear trade with non-NPT States.[210] The United States, too, attempted to dilute the concessions made in the 123 Agreement: following the NSG waiver but prior to US Congressional approval (and perhaps for the sake of that approval) President Bush claimed that Article 5(6)'s fuel supply assurances were not legally binding upon the United States.[211] NSG members also agreed *inter se* not to transfer enrichment and reprocessing technologies to India.[212] There was also a move within the NSG to adopt a requirement of NPT membership for supply of such technologies.[213] At the July 2009 Group of 8 (G8) summit, the United States, now under a new government, reportedly convinced other G8 countries to adopt such a policy on a national basis, pending its approval at the NSG. As a result, paragraph 8 of the G8 Statement on Non-Proliferation states:

> [W]e welcome the progress that continues to be made by [the NSG] on mechanisms to strengthen controls on transfers of such enrichment and reprocessing items and technology. While noting that the NSG has not yet reached consensus on this issue, we agree that the NSG discussions have yielded useful and constructive proposals contained in the NSG's 'clean text' developed at the 20 November 2008 Consultative Group meeting. Pending completion of work in the NSG, we agree to implement this text on a national basis in the next year.[214]

[210] S. Roy, 'No Sale of Uranium to India, Says Australian Minister', *Indian Express*, 11 September 2008. However, in October 2012, Australia indicated that it was willing to sell uranium to India, and in January 2013 Australia and India decided to launch consultations on a civil nuclear Deal: S. Dikshit, 'First-Ever Talks on Nuclear Partnership with Australia Soon', *The Hindu*, 22 January 2013. For a brief analysis of Australia's change in position, see G. Hiscock, 'Australia and the Great Indian Uranium Sale Debate', *CNN Special Report*, 20 August 2013.

[211] See S. Varadarajan, 'End of the Road for the 123 Agreement', *The Hindu*, 16 September 2008; S. Varadarajan, 'Bush Signing Statement on 123 Leaves Flaws Intact', *The Hindu*, 10 October 2008.

[212] 'NSG Agreed Not to Sell Sensitive Technologies to India', *The Hindu*, 12 September 2008; 'NSG Not to Sell Sensitive Technologies to India', *Times of India*, 11 September 2008.

[213] S. Varadarajan, 'G8 Blocks "Full" Nuclear Trade with India', *The Hindu*, 11 July 2009; S. Varadarajan, 'NSG Ends India's "Clean" Waiver', *The Hindu*, 25 June 2011.

[214] G8, Statement on Non-Proliferation, 2009.

In July 2011, the NSG amended its Part I Guidelines, adding to its previous requirement of 'restraint' in the export of sensitive technologies that

> [s]uppliers should exercise a policy of restraint in the transfer of sensitive facilities, equipment, technology and material usable for nuclear weapons or other nuclear explosive devices . . .
> (a) . . . suppliers should not authorise the transfer of enrichment and reprocessing facilities, and equipment and technology therefor, if the recipient does not meet, at least, all of the following criteria:
> (i) is a Party to the Treaty on the Non-Proliferation of Nuclear Weapons and is in full compliance with its obligations under the Treaty . . .[215]

Third, as Indian policy experts had predicted,[216] the 2010 NPT Review Conference affirmed the NPT 'bargain'. Of course, the Deal was only one of the issues that the NPT parties had to consider; others, concerning North Korea, Iran and the Middle East Nuclear Weapons-Free Zone were more prominent. However, some portions of the Final Outcome document can be attributed to the Deal. In a report prepared for the United States Institute for Peace, Jayantha Dhanapala, the former UN Under-Secretary-General for Disarmament and Chairman of the 1995 Review Conference, claims that, at the 2010 Conference, NNWS challenged the NSG waiver, calling it a violation of Article I of the NPT. While they 'acknowledged that the Deal could not be undone, they were quite firm that no more exceptions should be made'. With this object,

> paragraph 13 [of the Final Outcome] recalled paragraph 12 of Decision II in the 1995 NPT Review and Extension Conference whereby new supply arrangements had to align with nonproliferation obligations and comprehensive IAEA safeguards . . . [And] In the action part of the declaration (paragraph 35), all parties are urged 'to ensure that their nuclear-related exports do not directly or indirectly assist the development of nuclear weapons or other nuclear explosive devices' and that such exports comply with the NPT and the 1995 NPT Review and Extension Conference decisions.[217]

Three other elements whose inclusion, too, may be read at least partly as a response to the Deal's challenge to the NPT are: the reminders in

[215] See paras. 6 and 7, INFCIRC/254/Rev.10 Part I, 26 July 2011 (compare with paras. 6 and 7 in the earlier, Rev.9, version of these Guidelines).

[216] Interview with M. Sethi, Centre for Air Power Studies, 2 December 2009 (personal interview, on file).

[217] J. Dhanapala, 'Evaluating the 2010 NPT Review Conference', Special Report of the United States Institute for Peace, October 2010, 7–8, www.usip.org/files/resources/SR258%20-%20Evaluating%20the%202010%20NPT%20Review%20Conference.pdf.

paragraph 30 and Action 50 of the Final Outcome that, 'in all activities designed to promote the peaceful uses of nuclear energy, preferential treatment be given to the [NNWS] parties to [the NPT]'; the call, in paragraphs 107 and 114, for India and Pakistan (and Israel, too, in paragraph 114) to accede to the NPT as NNWS and place all their nuclear facilities under comprehensive IAEA safeguards; and the stronger statement of disarmament commitments of the NWS.[218] While the Deal was only lightly debated at the Conference, the above portions of the Final Outcome make it clear that it infused vigour into the discussions on nuclear energy cooperation and disarmament.[219]

Accommodation and international law

The above-described accommodation between the Deal and the NPT regime, in terms of both rhetoric and practice, may be compared to the regime interaction framework described in Chapter 3. In particular, as suggested by Margaret Young, the NPT and related instruments provided benchmarks for India's commitments; whereas the deliberations on the Deal catalysed decisions to restrict enrichment and reprocessing technologies, strengthen export controls and reaffirm the NPT. The IAEA and the NSG served as international institutions that brought the two conflicting treaty regimes into conversation.

As Chapter 3 also discusses, the legal justification for regime interaction slips between several factors - institutional authority, process, and outcome - which together provide evidence of the quality of the accommodation achieved. This section considers these factors with particular reference to the competence and procedures of the two forums and the role of legal forms and discourse in shaping the outcome. It highlights the benefits and disadvantages of accommodation as revealed in this particular instance.

'Multilateralising' the Deal: the sanction of international forums

The IAEA and the NSG were the two institutions involved in the passage of the Deal. The specific documents sought from them - an India-specific safeguards agreement from the IAEA, and a waiver of the requirement for comprehensive safeguards from the NSG - were

[218] Final Document, 2010 NPT Review Conference, NPT/CONF.2010/50 (Vol. I)*.

[219] Dhanapala, 'Evaluating the 2010 NPT Review Conference', 7; Sethi, personal interview (on file).

to facilitate not only India–US nuclear cooperation, but also nuclear deals between India and other States. These two institutions thus acted as gatekeepers for India's inclusion into the nuclear-governance regime despite its refusal to take the normal course of accession to the NPT.

Various treaties, including the NPT, identify the IAEA as the principal institution responsible for promoting non-proliferation, disarmament and peaceful uses of nuclear energy. While membership of the IAEA is not co-extensive with the NPT, there is significant overlap. The IAEA Secretariat, presided over by the Director General, maintains safeguards programmes in all IAEA member States, oversees NPT members' compliance with NPT obligations, and reports their failures to the IAEA Board of Governors (the 'Board'). The approval of Board members is also required for amendment of the NPT.[220] The Board comprises thirty-five States – elected annually by the IAEA General Conference – but the criteria for Board membership virtually guarantee permanent membership for the NWS and for several 'Western' States.[221] While these criteria are meant to secure the representation of all States with advanced nuclear technology, a two-thirds majority voting rule coupled with the Board's treatment of Iran suggests that its decision-making lacks independence from Western foreign policy interests. Even so, with respect to the Deal, the Secretariat and Board were competent, respectively, to conclude and approve the ISSA. Moreover, the final safeguards agreement recommended by the Secretariat for the Board's approval represented an advance over the terms that the United States and India had agreed to in the 123 Agreement and to some extent even over the INFCIRC/66 model for item-specific safeguards. The Secretariat indicated that it was satisfied that the terms permitted it to maintain an effective safeguards regime.[222] The Board's approval, by consensus, followed after the implications for nuclear proliferation were reviewed by a diverse group of States that included Asian nuclear powers Pakistan and China; two States most opposed to the Deal, Austria and Ireland; and Brazil and Argentina, States that, scholars had earlier claimed, were unhappy with concessions offered to India while they were expected to faithfully comply with intrusive safeguards regimes.[223]

220 Article 8, NPT. 221 Article VI(A), IAEA Statute.

222 IAEA Director General, Introductory Statement to the Board of Governors, 2008.

223 'IAEA Board Approves India-Specific Safeguards Agreement', 1 August 2008, www.iaea.org/newscenter/news/2008/board010808.html.

Given the above, it is possible to claim that the IAEA's involvement not only resulted in an expanded commitment by India, but also facilitated multilateral acceptance of nuclear trade with India despite its non-membership of the NPT. In some sense, the United States did make this claim – ElBaradei recalls that the United States made full use of his endorsement of the Deal: 'in the case of the US–India nuclear agreement, they referred to me freely as "the custodian of the NPT".'[224] However, we should remember that the task before the IAEA Secretariat and the Board was a limited one. While the Deal did provide the context for their work, they were asked to consider only the safeguards appropriate for India. Given India's lack of NPT membership, they had neither the power nor the obligation to insist upon comprehensive safeguards. Indeed, it has been suggested that several Board members, while expressing criticism, decided to reserve their opposition to the Deal for the NSG meeting to be held later that month.[225] It is therefore also possible to argue that the IAEA's approval of the ISSA not so much marked multilateral acceptance for the Deal as was demarcated from it.

The NSG, on the other hand, was asked for a document that would squarely reflect multilateral support for the Deal and for other States' nuclear trade with India. As mentioned earlier, though the NSG was an attractive forum for the United States and India, it was not – considered in terms of formal competences – the most compelling option. While the routing of the Deal through the NSG demonstrates that the NSG is accorded great respect in practice, we might query the basis for the authority it enjoys. For, despite including forty-five leading exporters of nuclear materials and technology, it is after all an informal club of limited membership, with opaque procedures. Moreover, while NSG members have at the NPT Conferences of Parties emphasised the relevance of NSG Guidelines to all States[226] and the increased transparency of the NSG's process,[227] the decisions adopted at these Conferences have made no specific reference to its work. The most these decisions suggest is that States 'make use of multilaterally negotiated and agreed guidelines and understandings' to strengthen their export-control

[224] ElBaradei, *Age of Deception*, 254. [225] Ramachandran, 'Inching Closer'.

[226] NSG, Statement by H. E. Ambassador Györgyi Martin Zanathy, Delegation of the Republic of Hungary, 2010 NPT Review Conference, Main Committee II, New York, 13 May 2010, www.nuclearsuppliersgroup.org/Leng/PDF/NSG-H-statement.pdf.

[227] NSG, Report by the Representative of Italy, Ambassador Giuseppe Balboni Acqua on NSG Transparency, 2000 NPT Review Conference, Main Committee III, New York 27 April 2000, www.nuclearsuppliersgroup.org/Leng/PDF/NPT_2000_Report_by_NSG_1.pdf.

regimes.[228] Thus, the NSG is not formally competent to determine how the NPT regime can accommodate the Deal, nor should it be taken as representative of the interests of all NPT members.

Nevertheless, routing the Deal through the NSG brought it within the purview of a consultative process that involved several key actors in the nuclear-governance regime. The NSG's requirement for consensus in decision-making enables – in theory at least – the effective participation of all States and indicates significant multilateral support for decisions made. This was indeed illustrated by the NSG practice in connection with the Deal: while there were reports of the United States' and India's massive leveraging of political influence to secure the NSG waiver, the text finally adopted was more limited than the draft first circulated by the United States. Formally competent or not, the NSG promoted accommodation between the Deal and the NPT-based nuclear-governance regime.

Under the NSG, and prior to that the IAEA, the Deal evolved in significant ways. Outside the framework of these bodies, bilateral negotiations between the US and India had spawned an understanding that was considerably more expansive in the benefits that it offered India and more limited in the commitments it demanded in return. The bitter criticism, in fact, was that all that the United States seemed to have extracted by way of concessions from India was an agreement to supply mangoes. In early 2006, one member of the US Congress summed up the 'nukes for mangoes' Deal as follows:

> India walked away from the negotiating table with unsafeguarded nuclear facilities, a free pass into the world of nuclear weapons states and the blessing of the United States, and the president went home with an IOU for mangoes.[229]

The 123 Agreement, with its even narrower statement of India's obligations, was seen as a further blow to the NPT-based non-proliferation regime.[230] But the trade-offs agreed during bilateral negotiations

[228] Action 36, Final Document, 2010 NPT Review Conference.

[229] Per US House of Representatives member, Ed Markey, reported in 'White House Bombs Critics', Reuters, 9 March 2006; see also A. Kamen, 'Mired in Diplo-Gobbledygook', *Washington Post*, 24 March 2006.

[230] For instance, Editorial, 'A Bad Deal Gets Worse', *New York Times*, 5 August 2007; M. Krepon, 'The US–India 123 Agreement: From Bad to Worse', *Spotlight*, Stimson Center, 23 August 2007; D. G. Kimball and F. McGoldrick, 'US–Indian Nuclear Agreement: A Bad Deal Gets Worse', Background Memo, Arms Control Association, 3 August 2007, www.armscontrol.org/pressroom/2007/20070803_IndiaUS; E. J. Markey, 'US–India Nuclear Deal', Federation of American Scientists Press Event, 18 October 2007: Markey (member of the US House of Representatives) summed up the

evidently did not satisfy within the NSG and the IAEA, and – as discussed in the previous section – India and the United States both agreed to the inclusion of terms (and, for India, also the elision of other terms) that were consonant with their claims that the Deal would not undermine the non-proliferation regime.

Even so, we might consider whether approval for the Deal should have been sought also from a conference of NPT parties. Of course, there are procedural hurdles to this: the NPT only provides for a conference to be called by request of a majority of parties, every five years, to review the NPT's implementation; or, by request of one-third of the NPT's parties, to consider a proposed amendment.[231] Neither context was applicable here – the 2005 NPT Review conference had concluded in May and the next conference was not due until 2010, and the United States was clear that it was not attempting an amendment of the NPT.[232] Nevertheless, NPT parties do come together on other occasions: at the Preparatory Conferences prior to each Review Conference. The Deal could have been discussed at one of the three Preparatory Conferences that took place in 2007, 2008 and 2009. NGO coalitions suggested, and attempted, as much.[233] However, while some States referred to the Deal directly or indirectly at the Preparatory Conferences, there was no sustained debate.[234] The United States did not mention the Deal even once in its working papers or statements at these conferences.[235] Its clearest implied reference was to note in one working paper that '[i]t also has a separate agreement with IAEA that permits [transfers of material and equipment] to IAEA members that are prepared to meet [the United States'] legal and policy requirements for such cooperation'.[236]

Agreement as avoiding 'even fig-leaf non proliferation conditions', arguing that 'the Bush Administration negotiated a deal with India which is universally recognized as blowing an enormous hole in the nonproliferation regime by granting unprecedented concessions to India'.

231 Article VIII, NPT.

232 US Secretary of State, Remarks, Senate Committee on Foreign Relations, 2006.

233 See D. G. Kimball, 'The US–Indian Nuclear Deal: Round II', *News in Review*, No. 4, 3 May 2007, 2, www.reachingcriticalwill.org/legal/NPT/NIR2007/day4.pdf; P. White, 'US–India Nuclear Agreement: Bad for Nuclear Nonproliferation, Bad for Nuclear Disarmament', *News in Review* No. 3, 30 April 2008, 2, www.reachingcriticalwill.org/legal/NPT/NIR2008/No.3.pdf.

234 White, *ibid.*

235 United States Working Papers and Statements at Meetings of Preparatory Committee for the 2010 NPT Review Conference, www.un.org/NPT2010/documents.html.

236 'Promoting Expanded and Responsible Peaceful Uses of Nuclear Energy', Working paper submitted by the United States to the Preparatory Committee for the 2010

Evidently, the impediments to more sustained discussion were strategic, not procedural: obviously it would have been harder to convince all the NPT parties to approve the Deal; possibly the United States wished to avoid a discussion of the compatibility of its commitments under both treaties; and, most certainly, India did not view the NPT as a forum that was entitled to deliberate on the Deal. Thus, ultimately, the multilateral institutions that the Deal went through were one institution of limited mandate (the IAEA), and another of limited membership and no formal competence (the NSG).

Legal forms and discourse

The present case, unlike the two discussed in the previous chapters, was not marked by a process of document-rattling between States in support of one or other of the conflicting treaties. Though the United States did launch several initiatives to decentre the NPT in the nuclear-governance regime, and the Deal could be perceived as amongst these initiatives, its crystallisation in the 123 Agreement was not followed by further documents seeking to challenge the NPT. Nor were there moves by NPT parties or at NPT Review and Preparatory Conferences to deny the legitimacy or legality of the Deal - even the efforts to 'tighten' the NPT regime were made after the Deal.

Instead, the process of producing legal and quasi-legal documents relevant to the implementation of the Deal - the ISSA, the NSG waiver and India's Separation Plan - provided opportunities for tying it closer to the NPT-based regime. These documents linked the interpretation and operation of the Deal to a general framework of non-proliferation commitments and actions, based on the NPT and related instruments. They clarified, for instance, the consequences of an Indian nuclear test and the conditions for the application and termination of IAEA safeguards. They both constrained India in terms supported by the NPT-based regime and provided a basis for it to enter into civil nuclear cooperation with all other States; that is, they crystallised its position within the nuclear-governance regime.

In addition, arguments of law were central to the outcomes reached. The United States and India sought to counter arguments that the Deal undermined nuclear governance, asserting that it was a legally justified undertaking, in line with the aims of nuclear governance. But these very

Review Conference of the Parties to the Treaty on the Non-Proliferation of Nuclear Weapons, NPT/CONF.2010/PC.I/WP.23, 3 May 2007.

claims of the Deal's legality pushed them towards accepting additional terms that more closely aligned the Deal with the NPT-based regime.

For its part, India discussed the Deal in terms of the core principles of reciprocity, non-discrimination and sovereign equality that underlie the international legal system.[237] Thus, it defended its non-membership of the NPT as the rejection of a discriminatory treaty. It also insisted that the NPT supporters should view the Deal as an advance upon India's previous commitments to non-proliferation compatible with 'the NPT concepts and objectives rather than [its] littler text'.[238] But this was ultimately also the basis on which NPT members (at the NSG) rejected India's demands, insisting upon more expansive non-proliferation commitments, and limitation of the benefits to be accorded to India.

The United States justified nuclear cooperation with India on the basis that India had not violated any non-proliferation commitments that it had undertaken, and (like India and the IAEA Director General) represented the Deal as an expansion of India's non-proliferation commitments. Consistency with this stance had led it to route the Deal through the NSG, and, in the process of securing a waiver for India, the United States was pushed to retreat from its promise of a clean waiver, to acceptance of a conditional one.

This point may be reinforced also with reference to India's Separation Plan. Given that one of the main justifications in favour of the Deal was that it would lead India to accept safeguards on its civil nuclear facilities, the United States also placed heavy emphasis on the need for India to produce a credible plan for separating its civil and military nuclear facilities, that would be defensible from a non-proliferation perspective: a US Congressional Research Service report noted that 'officials acknowledge the importance of a credible separation plan to ensuring that the United States complies with its Article I obligations under the Nuclear Nonproliferation Treaty'.[239] The United States pushed India to add many more reactors and sites to the civilian list, and insisted that the plan would be the initial step in the implementation of the Deal – passage of the Deal through the IAEA and the NSG would follow. C. Rajamohan notes that India had initially objected to this sequential

[237] Rajamohan, 'Impossible Allies', 245–56.

[238] Indian Foreign Secretary, 'Transforming US–India Relations', Carnegie Endowment for International Peace, 2005.

[239] See S. Squassoni, 'India's Nuclear Separation Plan: Issues and Views', CRS Report for Congress, 22 December 2006, i.

approach, wishing to separate its military and civil facilities in a phased manner, but ultimately agreed to this approach.[240]

The influence of the argument of the Deal's legality may also be seen in the discussion before the IAEA Board, where the IAEA Director General ElBaradei, for long a proponent of the Deal,[241] used such arguments both to justify and secure approval of the ISSA and to clarify the limits upon the exceptional privileges accorded to India.

ElBaradei's opening speech at the IAEA August 2008 Board Meeting underlined that the Deal was 'based on the Agency's standard safeguards practices and procedures'.[242] Moreover, the ISSA was 'an "umbrella agreement", which provides for any facility notified by India to the Agency in the future to become subject to safeguards'. As such it represented an improvement over previous agreements: '[t]he "umbrella" nature of this agreement provides a more efficient mechanism for ensuring that safeguards requirements can be met. It satisfies India's needs while maintaining all the Agency's legal requirements.' He noted that the same approach could also be followed in other cases where INFCIRC/66-type agreements were concluded. Here, then, the point made was that the ISSA did not represent an erratic exception for India, but rather a model that not only fulfilled all legal requirements, but could also be generalised to other states. The Director General added to these remarks in response to comments from Board members, by asserting that the agreement was 'lawful'; it violated no legal obligations undertaken by India; and 'as a lawyer' he saw no problems with the text.[243]

ElBaradei also justified the omission and inclusion of specific terms by reference to their force (or lack thereof) under international law. He argued that the absence of a specific commitment by India in the ISSA to undertake safeguards 'in perpetuity' (as had been promised in the 123 Agreement) was immaterial, because these terms could not, under

[240] Rajamohan, 'Impossible Allies', 231. See also P. Bidwai, 'Snags Surface in India–US Nuclear Deal', *Inter Press Service*, 6 February 2006; P. Bagla, 'US Shifting the Goalpost on N-Deal: Atomic Energy Chief', *Indian Express*, 6 February 2006.

[241] 'Director General Welcomes US and India Nuclear Deal', IAEA Press Release, 2006. In his memoirs, ElBaradei writes that he 'viewed the agreement as a win-win situation, good for development and good for arms control . . . Although the Deal would not bring India into the NPT, it would draw the country closer to the nuclear nonproliferation regime': ElBaradei, *The Age of Deception*, 225.

[242] IAEA Director General, Introductory Statement to the Board of Governors, 2008.

[243] S. Varadarajan, 'As Pakistan Hails "Precedent," Other IAEA Members Express Doubts, Fears', *The Hindu*, 2 August 2008.

international law, bind a State: 'Perpetuity is a misnomer. There is no such thing in international law.'[244] He referred to the principle of *rebus sic stantibus to underline that* treaty law itself provided for termination of obligations if the fundamental conditions of an agreement changed.

At the same time, he quelled concerns over the novel inclusion of a reference to 'corrective measures' by India in the event of a disruption of foreign fuel supplies in the agreement's preamble. To States that were worried that this suggested the possibility that India might withdraw facilities from IAEA safeguards, he clarified that, as per 'the general rules of international law ... the agreement should be read as an integral whole. The preamble provides for contextual background and safeguards are implemented in accordance with the terms of the agreement.'[245] And the terms of the agreement, he insisted, expressly and exhaustively stated the conditions for the discontinuation of safeguards.

Some implications of accommodation

The above discussion demonstrates two aspects of the process of accommodation of the Deal: first, the strategic motives underlying recourse to multilateral forums and discourse, forms and practices of law; second, the impact of this recourse upon the final shape of the Deal, which was to bring the Deal closer to the purposes and principles of the nuclear-governance regime, and mediate its conflict with – and implications for – the NPT-based framework of this regime. A balanced evaluation of the Deal requires appreciation of both aspects. This section outlines some additional implications of routing the Deal via the NSG (but avoiding altogether its discussion at a formal NPT Conference).

One implication was that the Deal was discussed in a piecemeal way. At the IAEA, the issue seemed to have been narrowly defined as having to do only with India's safeguards obligations. Even though the Board's discussion and approval clearly took place in the context of the Deal, there was little express reference made to it – and none at all in the Director General's remarks. The broader ramifications of India's limited safeguards were apparently postponed to the NSG, which did debate them. But the NSG's opaque procedures make it impossible to evaluate the quality of the debate. Indeed, some reports indicate that several States simply took a political call to approve the Deal, based on their

[244] *ibid.* [245] *ibid.*

relationship with India.[246] It also appears that the NSG members' scrutiny of India's safeguards commitments was discouraged on the basis that this matter had already been discussed, and closed, at the IAEA. The focus, instead, was placed on the consequences of a fresh nuclear test by India. In sum, a distinction appears to have been made between the technical competence of the one, and the political competence of the other forum, such that each was precluded from considering matters supposedly on the agenda of the other. This may have permitted expeditious passage of the Deal, but it is worth considering that it may have also short-circuited important discussion on the advisability of the Deal.

Second, neither India nor the United States offered any public explanation of the shifts in rhetoric during the conclusion of the Deal. India's shifts were apparent, with the government avowing and disavowing the scope of its commitments under the Deal; the United States' shifts were more implicit, marked by a studied silence during the period where the Deal was mired in Indian domestic politics. But these were discussed neither at the IAEA, presumably because the issue was narrowly defined; nor, apparently, at the NSG, where India was not present during the negotiations. While the shifts may be explained as the two governments' responses to their most immediate challenges in each phase, that explanation does not offer reliable guidance on how they actually intended to interpret their commitments. Where a government makes contrary claims before its parliament and before international audiences, then it should at least be asked to explain why – as some governments would be. There is something disquieting about a club-like atmosphere of negotiations where it is not apparent that such matters were even raised.

Moreover, at the NSG, reliance was placed on evidence that could have little value in more formal settings. Important examples include a secret letter between two US officials revealed in a newspaper, and a public statement posted on the Indian External Affairs Ministry's website. Of the two, the latter had greater merit for it was a public statement and could perhaps qualify as a unilateral declaration. But its substance was nothing new, being a reiteration of commitments India had avowed

[246] S. Varadarajan, 'As NSG Members Take "Political" Call, Differences Narrow', *The Hindu*, 5 September 2008. ('"At the end of the day, I think the logic that is prevailing here is what your foreign secretary, Mr [Shiv Shankar] Menon told us here last month, that NSG members had to take a political call because the proposal was really about what kind of relationship they wished to have with India", a European diplomat told *The Hindu*.').

in the 2005 Joint Statement and the first and third phases of the Deal (but had suppressed mention of in the middle phase). That it was referred to as a 'turning point' by a European diplomat suggests that, by the end, NSG members were simply looking for a plausible justification for the waiver they had granted India.[247] And, even here, reports suggest that India initially resisted the NSG's attempts to incorporate this statement in the operative part of the waiver, and thus as a compromise the reference to it was made in the chapeau of paragraph 3.[248]

It is not that there was little discussion on the Deal, within or outside these multilateral forums; Siddharth Varadarajan, whose award-winning reportage of the final phase of the Deal provides much of the raw material for the analysis in this chapter, recalls that the process by which the Deal was finalised was almost 'tiresomely deliberative'.[249] However, the quality of this discussion, its representativeness and its breadth and depth are harder to evaluate. After all, what was the participation of the NNWS outside the NSG, of non-governmental actors, of advocates of complete nuclear disarmament, of campaigns for safe use of nuclear energy, of the local communities where nuclear power plants would be built? Their exclusion pushed a number of issues into the background. In particular, two issues barely got an airing: health, safety and livelihood concerns of residents in areas earmarked as nuclear sites; and an appropriate liability regime for nuclear accidents and damages. These omissions may seem odd given, especially, India's experience of the 1984 Bhopal tragedy (in which a leakage of more than forty tonnes of the highly toxic methyl iso-cyanate killed more than 15,000 people and caused injuries, respiratory disorders and genetic mutations in more than 500,000 others) and its subsequent failure to recover adequate compensation from Union Carbide, the US parent company of the plant operator. But the omissions follow from the fact that the constituencies representing these interests formed no part of the discussions on the Deal. Yet, today these issues are strong impediments to the actual implementation of the Deal (see the next section).

The above analysis of the Deal-making process is a comment on the very turn to accommodation via regime interaction, for it is hard to design a template for the process it must take, the views it must include, and issues it must address. Ultimately, these depend upon the

[247] S. Varadarajan, 'Waiver Enables Member States to Provide India Full Civil Nuclear Cooperation', *The Hindu*, 7 September 2008.

[248] *ibid.* [249] Varadarajan, personal interview, 2009 (on file).

preferences of the actors who take the lead in a given context, and the impact of the surrounding critiques.

Finally, it is relevant to consider whether routing the Deal via the NSG, though it may have brought the Deal into closer alignment with the NPT-based regime, may not have also crystallised the *NSG* as the central arbiter of this regime.[250] It was, after all, the NSG's approval that made the Deal an accepted fact, and opened the way for other States also to enter into nuclear cooperation with India. Yet, the NSG remains an exclusive club and there are cogent reasons why it should not have the status of institutional gatekeeper of the non-proliferation regime. In this respect, it is interesting that at the 2010 NPT Review Conference, NNWS reportedly made it a point to challenge the NSG waiver as a violation of Article I of the NPT, and argued that no further exceptions should be made; and moreover that this argument found expression in various conclusions and recommendations of the outcome document.[251] Nor did the 2010 outcome document change the practice of omitting specific reference to the NSG. Thus, while the Deal may have cemented the NSG's importance in the nuclear-governance regime, it has not served to establish it as the only relevant institutional gatekeeper of that regime.

Conclusion, and afterword on the Deal

This chapter describes the dynamics of implementing the India–US Nuclear Deal as a process of accommodation with the NPT-based nuclear-governance regime, under the aegis of the IAEA and the NSG and through the exertions of a range of actors, including the two principal States, other States, the IAEA Director General and Secretariat, and various critics of the Deal. It also explores the role of legal forms and arguments in this process. It is true that, once the United States and India forged a common intention to conclude the Deal, the question of its 'legality' or 'illegality' *vis-à-vis* the existing architecture of the nuclear-governance regime may not have precluded its implementation. But both States were keen to secure multilateral acceptance for the Deal, not least because this would afford a

[250] For such a reading of the NSG, and a parallel one of the IAEA, see S. Ranganathan, 'The Value of Narratives: The India–USA Nuclear Deal in Terms of Fragmentation, Pluralism, Constitutionalisation and Global Administrative Law' (2012) 6(1) *Erasmus Law Review* 16.

[251] See Dhanapala, 'Evaluating the 2010 NPT Review Conference', 7, 8.

general basis for India to enter into nuclear cooperation with various other States. Hence legal discourse, practices and forms played a significant role. Significantly, they served not only to justify the Deal, but also to shape its terms, tying it more closely with the NPT-based regime. There still remains reason to see the Deal as in conflict with the NPT, and India still remains a non-party to that treaty, but the two agreements can now be seen as part of a common framework with aligned purposes.

The chapter also notes that, for all their influence upon the Deal, neither the IAEA nor the NSG can substitute for approval from a conference of NPT parties. The Deal may well have taken a different shape had it been routed through one of the NPT's Preparatory or Review Conferences. But this would have been an unlikely step both for the United States and (even more so) for India. Given this, the basis for evaluating the Deal is a matter of choosing between reference points: should we focus on the efforts that *were* made to conclude and implement it in a legitimate way, or on the ways in which inconvenient procedures were ignored in favour of more congenial ones? Should we focus on the benefits of India's expanded participation in the nuclear-governance regime, and of nuclear trade, or on the unfairness of the exception made for India, and the many uneasy questions that arise in connection with the use of nuclear energy? And what to make of the many exclusions from the ranks of those whose approval was sought?

Ultimately, these are the choices that will arise in any situation of regime interaction: once we shift away from issues of legal competence, the bases upon which we might endorse or critique the involvement of particular institutions, the process followed and outcomes reached become less clear. That is, once 'accommodation' is accepted as the relevant framework, there is no linking it to a template; the decisions and choices that are made in its name can only be evaluated according to context in which they were made. Moreover, accommodation implies that some decisions and choices (say, rejection of one of the conflicting treaties) are no longer available. This does not, however, mean that the process and outcomes of accommodation cannot be evaluated at all; in fact they are perhaps all the more vulnerable to individual perception and critique than would be a formal process of treaty conflict resolution.

As to the Deal itself, today, five years later, the first US–India nuclear exchange is still to take place, with trade stalled due to differences between the two States on an appropriate nuclear liability regime.

India passed the Civil Liability for Nuclear Damage Act in 2010,[252] which provides for no-fault, but limited, liability for the operator of a nuclear facility.[253] It also under certain conditions allows the operator to recover the compensation paid from the supplier of the nuclear equipment in question: if there is a contract to this effect, if the supplier acted (or omitted to act) with intent to cause damage, and if defects in the material, equipment or services supplied had led to the damage.[254] The provisions - particularly those related to defective equipment - have had a chilling effect on corporate suppliers in Russia and France as well as the United States. Recently, having aired the possibility of contractually *waiving* its right to recourse, India has announced an agreement with American company Westinghouse, but, as two nuclear physicists note:

> The details of this agreement - reportedly worth just $16 million - are more modest than Mr Obama's rosy language might suggest. Some propriety information will be transferred from Westinghouse to the public-sector Indian Nuclear Power Corporation, but the signing of a reactor contract remains a long distance away.[255]

Agreements with Russia and France too, though announced earlier, and envisaging more substantial cooperation, are yet to be finalised, again partly due to differences over nuclear liability. Moreover, in the aftermath of the Fukushima nuclear disaster of 2011, these have become the subject of protest from local residents in the areas in which the plants are proposed to be built. The previously excluded issues are now in the forefront, and for good reason.

252 Act No. 38 of 2010, *The Gazette of India Extraordinary*, No. 47, Part II, 21 September 2010.

253 See Articles 4(4), 5 and 6.

254 Article 17.

255 M. V. Ramana and S. Raju, 'The Impasse over Liability Clause in the Indo-US Nuclear Deal', India Ink (*New York Times* blog), 15 October 2013.

Conclusion

7 The politics of international law

Two inquiries in one

The book began with a few empirical observations: that treaty conflicts were not only the result of inadvertence, but in fact often seemed created for strategic ends. Strategically created treaty conflicts could challenge or change legal regimes and often conformed to two patterns, that of a small treaty/large treaty dynamic – that is, States' use of bilateral or small-group agreements against multilateral treaty regimes – and of non-parties being included in the conflicting treaty (AB/AC conflicts). My aim, initially, was to examine the possible means of legally regulating such conflicts, for they seemed both to typify practice and to require a different approach from that taken in legal doctrine towards inadvertent conflicts. But this examination segued into a larger inquiry into international law's role and limits in international affairs.

AB/AC conflicts are difficult to resolve through legal means, for standard techniques of reconciliation and priority may contravene the *pacta tertiis* principle. The same principle may also limit judicial remedies, and though State responsibility may be triggered in the case of conflicts resulting in the breach of a specific treaty obligation, there are several practical hurdles to securing its application. Moreover, when such conflicts are strategically created, the actors involved may not even seek judicial solutions; or such solutions may not be suited to addressing such conflicts' implications for the effective operation of treaty regimes. Indeed, techniques for legal resolution seem to complement the strategy of creating treaty conflict by ensuring that any new treaty, even if deliberately created in conflict with an existing one, is taken into account for determining the scope of the existing treaty.

These early findings indicated a summary conclusion to the book: of the limits to legal resolution of AB/AC conflicts – a conclusion comprehensively explained by Jan Klabbers and by the International Law Commission (ILC)[1] – and even more so where such conflicts were deliberately created.

But it seemed unsatisfying to leave matters there. The reason for extensive legal scholarship on treaty conflicts is that legal scholars – while recognising such conflicts as productive of change and development in international law – consider it essential that such conflicts be amenable to principled legal solutions. For, in the absence of principles governing the relationship between treaties (and other norms), it may be argued – as H. L. A. Hart had argued[2] – that international law does not constitute a legal system. And yet, here was my research emphasising that the very principles of international treaty law limited the application of legal solutions to certain kinds (strategic, AB/AC) of treaty conflict. My early research could then be taken to support the view that international law was merely contingent to politics, or perhaps even complicit in them, but did not regulate politics in any way. This seemed to run contrary to other works that, while writing of the politics of international law, also highlighted that international law's rules and principles limited politics in their turn.[3]

Prima facie, the incidence of strategically created treaty conflicts appeared to support either, or both, of two critiques of international law: first, as Jack Goldsmith and Eric Posner propose, that international law is simply epiphenomenal to politics, in particular to the political preferences of powerful States;[4] second, as David Kennedy argues, that it is a mode of politics, or *lawfare*.[5] In the lawfare thesis, international law is a powerful legitimating force in international relations and so is

[1] J. Klabbers, *Treaty Conflicts and the European Union* (Cambridge University Press 2009) 3–112; 'Fragmentation of International Law: Difficulties Arising from the Diversification and Expansion of International Law', Report of the Study Group of the International Law Commission (chaired by M. Koskenniemi), A/CN.4/L.682 (2006), 7–20, 115–65.

[2] H. L. A. Hart, *The Concept of Law* (2nd edn, Oxford University Press 1994) 213–37.

[3] For instance, M. Byers, *Custom, Power and the Power of Rules* (Cambridge University Press, 1999).

[4] *The Limits of International Law* (Oxford University Press, 2005).

[5] It must be noted here that the concept of 'lawfare' has been previously outlined in works by John and Jean Comaroff, and US General Charles Dunlap. The Comaroffs, researching colonialism in Africa, described lawfare as a 'mode of warfare . . . the effort to conquer and control indigenous peoples by the coercive use of legal means', and 'the resort to legal instruments, to the violence inherent in the law, to commit acts of political coercion, even erasure': see J. L. Comaroff, 'Colonialism, Culture and the Law: A Foreword'

invoked strategically by all actors, but in an *allsorts* way so as to gradually undermine the concept of law and lead all to view it as purely instrumental. Both critiques, rising into prominence in the 2000s, had some resonance. Without digressing into autobiography, their influence was all the greater upon an Indian lawyer, receiving training in the post 9/11 United States, and already taught to be mildly suspicious of international law's politics and pathologies.

Perhaps, then, it was the move to Cambridge, and its investment in the forms and practices of international law that motivated further inquiry into a number of questions, starting with the relative merits of the epiphenomenality and lawfare theses: Which was more apposite? Did strategically created treaty conflicts reveal treaties as no more than contingent to State power and interests? Or, was the greater significance to be attached to the use of a legal act – a treaty – to challenge another? Most importantly, which conception of law was the more appropriate: the doctrinal conception of international law as formal legal rules, both derided in and embraced by the epiphenomenality thesis; or the lawfare conception of international law as an allsorts discourse? Further questions resulted from curiosity about the reasons so many scholars had for so long reposed faith in international law. I was not persuaded by suggestions that they did not 'see' the politics of international law and so were content with black-letter analysis.[6] An alternative explanation was that they collectively bought into a 'functionalist' attitude towards international law, which allowed for flexible, purpose-driven acts and claims of 'legality'. But this too had problems: a large portion of legal scholarship did not espouse a purely functional attitude. Strategically created treaty conflicts provided context in which

(2011) 26 *Law and Social Inquiry* 305, 306; J. L. Comaroff and J. Comaroff, '*Law and Disorder in the Postcolony*: An Introduction', in J. L. Comaroff and J. Comaroff (eds.), Law and Disorder in the Postcolony (University of Chicago Press 2006) 1, 30. Dunlap, referred to in Kennedy's book, stated that '[l]awfare describes a method of warfare where law is used as a means of realizing a military objective', and, later, '[a]lthough I've tinkered with the definition over the years, I now define "lawfare" as the strategy of using – or misusing – law as a substitute for traditional military means to achieve an operational objective': see C. Dunlap, 'Law and Military Interventions: Preserving Humanitarian Values in 21st Century Conflicts', paper presented at the Humanitarian Challenges in Military Intervention Conference, Carr Center for Human Rights Policy, Kennedy School of Government, Harvard University, Washington DC, 29 November 2011, http://people.duke.edu/~pfeaver/dunlap.pdf; C. Dunlap, 'Lawfare Today: A Perspective' (2008) 3 *Yale Journal of Foreign Affairs* 146. The book, however, focuses on Kennedy's work, since it stands apart in tracing the implications of lawfare for (the fate of) international law.

6 See, amongst others, J. Goldsmith and E. Posner, *The Limits of International Law* (Oxford University Press 2005), 15.

I could explore these questions and, in doing so, could reflect upon the role and limits of international law.

The book therefore delves into legal thought and practice relating to treaty conflict. My study of 'mainstream' legal thought reveals that this thought expounds a common conception of international law that seeks a balance between formalism and functionalism and is informed by liberal and constructivist assumptions. My studies of practice focus on three instances of strategically created treaty conflicts. These studies identify the ways in which the 'legal' was manifested, in specific forms and claims, and how these forms and claims perpetuated and shaped conflict dynamics. The studies support the lawfare thesis to a significant extent, noting that: States and others use law instrumentally; strategic uses of international law leverage its normative authority; and international law manifests as a broadly conceived discursive practice that includes invocations of legal rules, processes, forms and practices, and more. Yet, though the concept of legality itself is contested and constructed in multiple ways, its value is not in doubt. Nor does it appear all that open-textured. Instead, it seems to foreclose many types of pleas. For these reasons, strategically created treaty conflicts – though of course successful when backed by powerful States and well-orchestrated practices – may yet be shaped, mediated and (the treaties) susceptible to unpredicted afterlives.

Treaty conflict in thought and practice

This section elaborates on the specific arguments made in the book, building upon which, the next section will offer some reflections on how we might think about international law, and strategically created treaty conflicts.

A reading of legal thought

The book discusses several strands of legal thought in Chapters 2 and 3, and suggests that, for all their differences, these strands reflect three common perspectives: they perceive international law as a broadly conceived legal discourse, and embrace liberal and constructivist assumptions as to its role and path of development.

Chapter 1 introduces these three perspectives. It argues that a discourse may go beyond a doctrinal exposition of legal rules as well as the trappings of formal legal procedures but still be identified as distinctively one of 'law'. Indeed, critiques of particular legal rules and procedures are immanent to international law. I explain by reference to Friedrich Kratochwil and Martti Koskenniemi's work (particularly the latter) that scholars associate 'legal' argument with a distinctive style, the hallmarks of which are: justification of actions by reference to independent standards, generalisability of these justifications, and attentiveness to the procedural conditions that determine who gets to offer and be offered these justifications. A discourse that combines these is unlikely to represent the vanishing point of international law: indeed, based on liberal and constructivist assumptions, mainstream legal scholars foresee, rather, the opposite outcome. The liberal assumption, in a range of works, consists in the expectation that a legal discourse regulates, and is not reducible to, immediate politics: legal forms and arguments must be produced according to specific criteria and conform to requirements stemming from accumulated thought and practice; legal discourse thus constrains even as it is instrumentalised. The constructivist assumption lies in the understanding of international law as a thing and as a process – constituting and being constituted by, shaping and being shaped by, States and other actors. In such a case, the more actors use international law, the more deeply it becomes entrenched as the medium for their interactions. The constructivist assumption does not entail that States must ultimately comply with specific legal norms, but that they conform to a practice of debating, challenging and justifying norms, in the legal 'style'.

Chapter 2 examines the work of the ILC in drafting the Vienna Convention on the Law of Treaties (VCLT). The 1950s and 1960s, during which the VCLT was drafted, were years of both expectation and anxiety for ILC members, concerned with realising law-governed international relations. And, as discussed, treaty conflicts, unless regulated by law, raise questions about the very possibility of an international legal system. ILC members recognised the role of deliberation in creating treaty conflicts and the difficulties of finding an appropriate conflict rule especially for AB/AC conflicts, but could not simply omit the issue from the VCLT – that would amount to conceding a limited remit for law in international relations (and accepting States' use of treaties as 'conflicting makeshifts of political expediency').[7] They sought to

[7] H. Lauterpacht, 'The Covenant as Higher Law' (1936) 17 *British Yearbook of International Law* 54, 64.

draft appropriate conflict rules that would neither invite States' rejection nor prejudice justice in actual cases. By various routes, they came to the view that the best rules would be those that enabled and encouraged States' resort to legal discourse to settle their claims, for such discourse would lead to more appropriate outcomes in specific cases and strengthen the respect for international law. The formula adopted in Article 30, especially paragraph (4)(b) on AB/AC conflicts, was considered well suited to this purpose.

Chapter 3 explores three proposals for institutional implementation of multilateral treaties that encompass altering, if necessary, their specific provisions. These proposals address a core challenge presented by treaty conflict: maintaining the effective operation of treaty regimes (and not merely the enforcement of specific rights of States). However, the proposals also raise the issue of the basis upon which institutions may *suo moto* make adjustments to treaty regimes, rather than seeking direction from (a conference of) States parties to those treaties. They do address this issue as well, offering various initial justifications, and a common ultimate one. As to the initial justifications, Hersch Lauterpacht explains that a court may employ the doctrine of approximate application as a species of the principle of effective interpretation; Abram and Antonia Chayes focus on the formal competence of treaty bodies associated with a multilateral treaty to adopt a managerial approach for the sake of promoting compliance with it; and Margaret Young, and Rüdiger Wolfrum and Nele Matz consider that institutions may facilitate treaty coordination/regime interaction due to their functional competences, and because this would promote mutual learning between and enrichment of those treaties/regimes. Ultimately, recognising the limits of these justifications, the proposals fall back upon the idea that, even if the relevant institutions exceed their competences, their interventions are justified where they promote legal discourse between actors.

These three perspectives – international law as a broadly conceived discourse and liberal and constructivist assumptions – may of course be subjected to normative and factual critiques. However, the point made in the first three chapters is that they are pervasive in legal scholarship that is otherwise spread across time and academic traditions. These perspectives add up to a 'mainstream' view, of international law and its role and path of progress through international relations, that cannot be slotted into simple categories of doctrinalism or managerialism. Typically, it traverses and co-opts these categories.

Three studies of practice

While Chapters 1 to 3 present the mainstream view of international law as a broadly conceived legal discourse, Chapters 4 to 6 offer further insight into the practices that make up this discourse, and examine how they both enable and constrain various actors in pursuing their interests. Based on three studies of treaty conflicts on seabed mining, the International Criminal Court (ICC or Court), and nuclear governance, the chapters highlight, in particular, practices of document-rattling and making of legality claims.

Briefly, document-rattling refers to the production of documents as a matter of strategy and tactic. In the three studies, document-rattling served various ends. In the seabed mining dispute, formal and quasi-formal documents were consequential acts: triggering a chain of responses – verbal and actual – by each 'side', aimed at the production of yet other documents to redeem their position. The documents produced also served as 'unlocking' devices, calling forth sharp responses including dramatic changes of position by various parties. Even an informal document, the Boat Paper, presented in the style of a formal one, had an agenda-setting effect. Comprising drafts of the relevant General Assembly resolution and the Implementation Agreement for Part XI, it led to a rapid closure of consultations on the modification of the UN seabed mining regime.

In the case of the ICC, the Court's organs, particularly the Office of the Prosecutor (OTP), responded to US attempts to undermine the Court by producing a trail of documents that substantiated the claim that the Court was 'no longer a theoretical construct, but a tangible court'.[8] The OTP produced policy papers, secured referrals, and prepared charge-sheets, warrants and trial documents. These formal acts were compelling evidence that the Court was already in operation. They responded to the US challenge even as they clarified that the OTP would avoid direct confrontation with the United States.

In the case of the India–US Nuclear Deal, the two States linked the legitimacy of the Deal to three documents – India's Separation Plan, an International Atomic Energy Agency (IAEA) approved safeguards agreement, and the Nuclear Suppliers Group (NSG) waiver – and de-linked it

[8] President (P. Kirsch), 'Protecting the Integrity of the International Criminal Court', Strategy Meeting, Parliamentarians for Global Action, United Nations, New York, 22 April 2003, www.icc-cpi.int/en_menus/icc/structure%20of%20the%20court/presidency/statements/Pages/index.aspx.

from the United States' NPT commitments. The process of producing these documents provided opportunities for tying the Deal closer to the NPT regime.

Legality claims were made by various actors, both State and institutional, to justify or challenge the production and use of various documents, as being in compliance (or not) with legal and quasi-legal requirements. Such claims were front and centre in each of the exchanges. In the case of the seabed mining dispute, we saw that initial ideology-based claims were overtaken by legality claims, and, moreover, these legality claims took specific forms. There were claims as to: (i) the validity and scope of both regimes; (ii) the categories of States entitled to have their claims to mining sites considered by the Preparatory Commission and by each other, and to participate in efforts to resolve overlapping site claims or make alterations to the UN Convention on the Law of the Sea (LOSC) regime; and (iii) the distinction between justified 'technical' adjustments in the implementation of the LOSC regime and unjustified 'political' changes to it.

The OTP also drew a distinction between 'the law' and considerations of politics and policy in the conflict concerning the ICC. The Prosecutor rejected questions about the practical implications of the Court on the basis that '[t]he issue is no longer about whether we agree or disagree with the pursuit of justice in moral or practical terms: *it is the law*',[9] and the OTP justified its positions on complementarity, gravity, self-referrals and non-disclosure on the basis that those positions represented valid interpretations of the Rome Statute. In making these claims, the OTP opened the way for scrutiny of its legal interpretations, and its positions with respect to gravity and non-disclosure have changed since they were first aired. The OTP also recruited legality claims in order to re-describe the challenge posed by the bilateral immunity agreements as a routine legal issue of construing the Rome Statute's cooperation provisions and not a political matter. In this, it was supported by the European Union and NGOs such as the Coalition for the ICC.

In the case of the India–US Nuclear Deal, legality claims were entailed by the very object underlying the Deal's conclusion, which was to enable India's return to the nuclear market in order that various

[9] Office of the Prosecutor, Policy Paper on the Interests of Justice, September 2007, www.icc-cpi.int/NR/rdonlyres/772C95C9-F54D-4321-BF09-73422BB23528/143640/ICCOTPInterestsOfJustice.pdf (emphasis added).

States could conclude trading arrangements with it. US, Indian, and even IAEA, officials justified the Deal as 'legal' and a step forward for the nuclear-governance regime. The IAEA Director General claimed that it would 'consolidate the non-proliferation regime';[10] the Indian foreign Secretary argued '[i]f we go by the NPT concepts and objectives rather than this littler text, then it is difficult to make a case against the … agreement'.[11] But, in initiating such legality claims, the two States also came to accept limits to the Deal, including non-supply of enrichment and reprocessing technologies to India; and a ban on Indian nuclear testing. India's claim that it could take 'corrective measures' upon disruptions in supply of nuclear fuel to it also received limited expression in its safeguards agreement.

The chapters discuss these and other legality claims and counter-claims. Some of these claims may be seen as only quasi- or soft-legal, scaffolded by principles associated with 'law' but not crystallised in doctrine. Moreover, the claims were often made in a broad discursive context, and only partly filtered through formal bodies. Even so, they relied precisely on points such as the verifiability and proper interpretation of cited standards, the generalisability of their application, the competence of specific States or other actors to participate, or have their views considered, procedures followed, and implications for the claim-maker itself. Arguments of policy, justice and expedience were relevant and provided a basis to challenge particular legal positions, but were filtered through these legality claims.

The three chapters also review the roles played by different types of institutions, noting that their modes of action map on to the proposals identified in Chapter 3. In each case, the institutions' interventions could be, and were, justified on the basis of the specific competences of the relevant bodies and also because they propagated (and operated through) legal discourse to protect effective operation of the relevant legal regimes. Each institution could moreover be criticised on various grounds: the Preparatory Commission's approach, directed at making minute alterations to the pioneer investor regime, was unable to engage with 'hard-core' issues relating to the LOSC regime; the OTP, perhaps

10 'IAEA Director General Welcomes US and India Nuclear Deal', IAEA Press Release 2006/05, 2 March 2006, www.iaea.org/NewsCenter/PressReleases/2006/prn200605.html.

11 Indian Foreign Secretary (S. Saran), 'Transforming US–India Relations: Forging a Strategic Partnership', Address to the Carnegie Endowment for International Peace, 21 December 2005, http://carnegieendowment.org/2005/12/21/transforming-u.s.-india-relations-forging-strategic-partnership/37k.

too heavily influenced by the need to respond to external stimuli (US challenges), acted in a manner that generated hostility in other quarters (African States); and the routing of the implementation of the Nuclear Deal through the IAEA and the NSG meant that one formal body of limited mandate and one informal club were given sole authority to pronounce upon the Deal, to the exclusion of various interests and viewpoints. The same critiques may be applied more generally to the three modes of institutional action discussed in Chapter 3.[12]

As a whole, Chapters 4 to 6 provide some understanding of the practices that constitute a legal discourse between States and institutions in three quite different contexts. The chapters do not advance any single idea of this discourse, or of international law's role. But they do illuminate the liberal and constructivist assumptions highlighted in Chapters 1 to 3 in two respects. First, while they do not show (nor try to show) that over time States develop a preference for complying with legal rules, they show that States routinely and heavily rely upon 'legality', which is constructed in multiple, but delimited ways, with the existing accumulation of doctrine and practice providing reference points. Second, for this reason, though reliance upon legality may only be for instrumental reasons, it imposes some constraints on all actors, since legal documents and claims must follow established modes of production and application. It is worth keeping in mind of course that the constraints may be weak – aimed at procedures and preconditions for producing documents, and at the plausibility of interpretations – and differentiated. They may work for good or bad; this book offers a variety of evaluations. But, recognising them is essential to a full appreciation of the role of international law and its influence upon different actors.

Implications and further questions

This book does not support any specific rule to resolve treaty conflicts; the analysis carried out recommends, rather, attention to the reasons

[12] That is to say, approximate application limits itself to incremental modifications to a given treaty, and may distract from discussion on whether more comprehensive changes are called for; the managerial approach may be too concerned with responding to dissidents and opponents of a treaty regime, and in tailoring its provisions to induce their compliance may disregard interests of other actors within the regime; regime interaction is not linked to any particular template, and though seemingly pluralist, may exclude various interests.

that underlie the creation of a conflict, and to the uses of international law in perpetuating and mediating it. In several cases, where the progress of a treaty conflict depends upon inter-State dynamics, international law may regulate only indirectly. That is, international law may not determine the 'solution' to a conflict, but even its instrumental use by States and institutions may constrain the processes followed and outcomes reached.

A study of strategically created treaty conflicts thus reveals multiple dimensions to international law's relationship with politics. Such conflicts confirm that law is contingent upon politics, as asserted by the epiphenomenality thesis. They also evidence the ways in which States and other actors may use law, and legality, as a strategic asset in advancing their interests by coding those interests into legal regimes.[13] But, in addition, they also indicate the regulative effects of legal practices of making and using legal documents and asserting legal claims. Such practices are in themselves a certain kind of politics, privileging criteria and conditions for invoking international law that are drawn from the accumulated weight of thought and practice as to the appropriate ways of doing so. In other words, innovative and specific moves have to be validated by linking them back to general ideas of interpretation, processes and forms associated with the international legal system. This, in effect, makes the practice of international law more routine and incremental than is recognised in presentations of its indeterminacy and political instrumentality.

With these points, the book may finally be summed up in terms of the modes of thought about international law and its relationship with politics that it advances, and those that it does not engage with.

First, the book offers support for a transactional view of international law. This view was summed up in Vaughan Lowe's remarks at a conference to commemorate the seventy-fifth anniversary of the publication

[13] Political science research in international law offers several analyses of the reasons for which international law and legality may exert power, including coercion by States, agenda-setting by states and international institutions; influence of norms and ideas upon underlying interests, wants and beliefs of (elites within) States and institutions, the role of norm entrepreneurs, persuasion, acculturation, mimicry, socialisation *et cetera*. For a review, see E. M. Hafner-Burton, D. G. Victor and Y. Lupu, 'Political Science Research on International Law: The State of the Field' (2012) 106 *American Journal of International Law* 47–97. Disentangling these types of power is analytically interesting, but this book does not attempt that task. It focuses on the modes in which international law and legality are overtly asserted between actors and used to define contexts as those of conflict or cooperation, not reasons for which these assertions prove effective.

of Lauterpacht's *The Function of Law in the International Community*. Lowe observed that it was inconceivable in the twenty-first century that anyone would write a monograph of the same title and scope as *Function*, which dealt with

> the potential of international law rather than its achievements, with a focus on courts and the question of justiciability. The current focus would be on the transactional features of international law rather than on the settlement of disputes. International law has become a method for doing things more than a method for settling disputes ... As a result, the framework of analysis as presented in [*Function*] would no longer be acceptable.[14]

Lowe's remarks were made in the course of a discussion initiated by Koskenniemi, who located the book within the trend of the German academy, at the time occupied with the question of the appropriate relationship between legal and political sovereignty. One side argued that politics was the ultimate arbiter of the law, and the other argued that all political disputes were capable of being settled by the application of law. In this debate, *legal* was equated with *judicial*.[15] Lowe's remarks point to a shift away from that equation. This book suggests, additionally, that the transactional view has a longer genealogy. Its

[14] 'The Function of Law in the International Community: Opening Plenary Session', in J. Crawford and M. Young (eds.), *The Function of Law in the International Community: An Anniversary Symposium* (2008), Proceedings of the 25th Anniversary Conference of the Lauterpacht Centre for International Law, http://moot.law.cam.ac.uk/Media/25_anniversary/Opening_Plenary_discussion.pdf.

[15] Koskenniemi points out that the key question was of exercise of emergency powers under the Weimar Constitution – while Hans Kelsen claimed that law regulated the limits of its own validity so that the appropriate use of emergency powers was a matter of legal interpretation by a court, Carl Schmitt argued that it was ultimately the executive's decision to follow the Constitution or not. This debate also spilled-over into international affairs: Hans Morgenthau's doctoral thesis argued that international conflicts were either 'disputes' that could be settled through legal mechanisms or 'tensions' that implied a wider political antagonism that could not be usefully submitted to legal mechanisms. There was no general rule by which the two could be identified and the 'political' nature of a problem depended simply on how intensely a State felt about it; where the intensity was high enough, a legal procedure would be not only useless but quite harmful. Law was thus delimited by politics. Lauterpacht's *Function* countered that, while indeed there was no general rule to distinguish legal from political conflicts, this did not mean that all conflicts were political. In fact, irrespective of their gravity, or the intensity of a state's feeling, all were 'capable of an answer by the application of legal rules', and would be so answered where, in recognition of the rule of law, they were taken to a court: M. Koskenniemi, 'The Function of Law in the International Community: 75 Years After' (2008) 79 *British Yearbook of International Law* 353, 353–9.

presence may be detected even in the work of *Function*'s author, as in other strands of legal thought on treaty conflict.

Related to the above, the book suggests that, for international law to maintain its influence on international relations, it must *combine* integrity and instrumentality; the two qualities are complementary, not antithetical. A too-rigid body of rules would invite rejection or disregard by States, but international law would also lose authority if seen as entirely without formal integrity and completely instrumental to particular interests. Kennedy's lawfare thesis and writings on international law's 'deformalisation'[16] and 'managerial' turn[17] offer warnings of the latter. But, in practice, integrity and instrumentality may and do work together; international law as a broadly conceived legal discourse between various actors accommodates more than just formal rules and procedures, but retains a distinctively legal style, marked by specific practices of document production and claim-making. The formal concept of international law, as elaborated in an accumulation of thought and practice, provides the reference points for these practices.

In this context, a further point may be made about Goldsmith and Posner's criticism of the mainstream 'research agenda, which is that of doctrinalism: identifying the "black letter of international law" in any domain, independent of actual behaviours'.[18] It has already been discussed that the mainstream research agenda is not limited to doctrinal work. But, it follows from the view of international law as a set of discursive practices that there is value to doctrinal work: it consolidates thought and practice, and contributes material for key moves of legal discourse. Indeed, if doctrinal work was disregarded, legal discourse would lose one of its central anchors, just as, in the absence of critical or normative scholarship, it loses out on other voices that enrich and expand it. The healthy subsistence of all these forms of engagement with international law further suggests that, in accepting a more expansive notion of international law as a broadly conceived legal discourse, we need not feel undue alarm about reaching a point where international law and its imposters become indistinguishable.

[16] For instance, J. d'Aspremont, 'The Politics of Deformalization of International Law' (2011) 3 *Goettingen Journal of International* Law, 503. D'Aspremont focuses on the move away from formal criteria to ascertain legal rules.

[17] For instance, M. Koskenniemi, 'International Law: Constitutionalism, Managerialism and the Ethos of Legal Education' (2007) 1 *European Journal of Legal Studies* 1.

[18] Goldsmith and Posner, *The Limits of International Law*, 15.

Instead – as the empirical studies in this book evidence – we should perhaps worry that international legal practices operate in an exclusionary way, giving voice only to specific actors (some States, some international organisations), privileging only certain forms and claims as properly legal or adequately 'law-like', and accepting only certain types of claims as relevant to the assessment of legality.

To end then, with a face to the future. I believe this book opens up several directions for research. First, to seek after a comprehensive theory of legal practices and categories of the same, for such a theory may substantially answer questions about what makes international law distinctive even when it extends beyond formal rules and processes. Second, to undertake research into yet other contexts of international legal discourse, including those theatres and interactions that entail the 'translation' or 'vernacularisation' of legal rules and processes into domestic/local equivalents,[19] for in such cases it is necessary to think further whether there are distinctive modes and practices of using international law, and what they may be. Third, with respect to the contexts studied in this book, to focus upon cases such as the Bogotá Declaration (Chapter 1) in which less powerful States have tried to use strategically created conflicts to change the legal *status quo*, for in such cases we may find further limits to leveraging clashing legalities and further illumination of the role of international legal practices.

[19] See, for instance, P. Levitt and S. Merry, 'Vernacularization on the Ground: Local Uses of Global Women's Rights in Peru, China, India and the United States' (2009) 9(4) *Global Networks* 441–61.

Appendices

Appendix 1 Seabed mining policies of LOSC, Part XI, Annexes III and IV

Part XI and the two annexes set out the following policies in relation to seabed mining.

PARALLEL SYSTEM AND SITE-BANKING

The ISA would regulate mining, and could also conduct mining through an organ called the Enterprise, and enter into contracts enabling private and State ventures to acquire mining rights.[1] An applicant would have to identify two areas of equal estimated commercial value; the ISA would allocate one to the applicant and reserve the other for exploitation by the Enterprise or by developing States.[2]

FINANCIAL AND TECHNOLOGICAL AID TO THE ENTERPRISE

The LOSC sought to enable the Enterprise to compete with private and developed State ventures.[3] States, particularly developed States, would provide funds to the ISA, which could transfer a portion to the Enterprise in its early years.[4] They would also pay heavy licence fees and annual fees to the ISA, and, following commencement of commercial production, a production charge.[5] At the ISA's request, a contractor would transfer to the Enterprise technology used in the activities specified in its contract.[6] Where not legally entitled to

[1] Art. 153, LOSC. [2] *ibid.*, Annex III Arts. 8, 9.

[3] *ibid.*, Annex IV Art. 11 provides a detailed scheme of financial support.

[4] Art. 173(2), LOSC Art. 160(2)(e), LOSC, provides for assessed contributions based on the scale used for UN contributions.

[5] *ibid.*, Annex III Art. 13. [6] *ibid.*, Annex III Art. 5.

transfer, the contractor would obtain assurance from the owner of the technology to make it available to the Enterprise.[7] Under certain conditions, it would take the same steps in favour of developing States.[8]

PRODUCTION POLICIES

Part XI imposed production ceilings via an elaborate formula based on projected annual increases in global demand for nickel. Of the permitted amount, a certain portion was reserved for exclusive production by the Enterprise.[9] It also envisaged compensation to land-based producers and other economic adjustment assistance.[10]

QUALIFICATIONS OF APPLICANTS

Applications for licences to explore and exploit the seabed could only be made by State parties or, under their sponsorship, by (i) State enterprises; (ii) natural or juridical nationals; or (iii) persons under their effective control.[11] Applicants would have to meet qualification standards, relating to financial or technical capabilities and performance under previous ISA contracts.[12]

REVIEW

Part XI provided for a regular five-yearly review of the seabed mining regime by the ISA Assembly[13] and a more detailed review following a fifteen-year period.[14]

MEMBERSHIP OF THE ISA COUNCIL

LOSC Article 161 provided for thirty-six members of the ISA Council, selected on the basis of criteria such as large investments in seabed mining and heavy consumption of minerals produced. A provision for membership of the largest consumer implied *de facto* permanent membership to the United States.[15] A few places were reserved for developing States, and eighteen seats were to be distributed to ensure an equitable geographical representation.

Article 161 provides as follows:

[7] *ibid.*, Annex III Art. 5(3). [8] *ibid.*, Annex III Art. 5(3)(e). [9] Art. 151, LOSC.
[10] *ibid.*, Art. 151(10). [11] *ibid.*, Art. 153(2)(b), Annex III Art. 4(1).
[12] *ibid.*, Annex III Art. 4(2) and (6). [13] Art. 154, LOSC. [14] *ibid.*, Art. 155.
[15] *ibid.*, Art. 161(1)(a).

Article 161 Composition, procedure and voting

1. The Council shall consist of 36 members of the Authority elected by the Assembly in the following order:
   (a) four members from among those States Parties which, during the last five years for which statistics are available, have either consumed more than 2 per cent of total world consumption or have had net imports of more than 2 per cent of total world imports of the commodities produced from the categories of minerals to be derived from the Area, and in any case one State from the Eastern European (Socialist) region, as well as the largest consumer;
   (b) four members from among the eight States Parties which have the largest investments in preparation for and in the conduct of activities in the Area, either directly or through their nationals, including at least one State from the Eastern European (Socialist) region;
   (c) four members from among States Parties which on the basis of production in areas under their jurisdiction are major net exporters of the categories of minerals to be derived from the Area, including at least two developing States whose exports of such minerals have a substantial bearing upon their economies;
   (d) six members from among developing States Parties, representing special interests. The special interests to be represented shall include those of States with large populations, States which are land-locked or geographically disadvantaged, States which are major importers of the categories of minerals to be derived from the Area, States which are potential producers of such minerals, and least developed States;
   (e) eighteen members elected according to the principle of ensuring an equitable geographical distribution of seats in the Council as a whole, provided that each geographical region shall have at least one member elected under this subparagraph. For this purpose, the geographical regions shall be Africa, Asia, Eastern European (Socialist), Latin America and Western European and Others.
2. In electing the members of the Council in accordance with paragraph 1, the Assembly shall ensure that:
   (a) land-locked and geographically disadvantaged States are represented to a degree which is reasonably proportionate to their representation in the Assembly;
   (b) coastal States, especially developing States, which do not qualify under paragraph 1(a), (b), (c) or (d) are represented to a degree which is reasonably proportionate to their representation in the Assembly;
   (c) each group of States Parties to be represented on the Council is represented by those members, if any, which are nominated by that group.

Appendix 2 Pioneer investor provisions of Resolution II

QUALIFICATIONS

Resolution II names eight pioneer investors, in two categories. In the first: France, India, Japan and the USSR, or some duly certified entity from each;[1] in the second: four consortia composed of entities from Belgium, Canada, Germany, Italy, Japan, the Netherlands, the UK and the USA.[2] The PrepCom could register applicants as pioneer investors if they had expended at least US$30 million in pioneer activities before 1 January 1983, and at least 10 per cent of that amount in prospecting a certain site; and if the relevant certifying State had signed the LOSC. Any developing state signatory to the LOSC, or its entity, could also apply to be registered as a pioneer investor if it had made the same investment prior to 1 January 1985.[3]

ALLOCATION OF MINE SITES

Resolution II provided maximum-area specifications for pioneer mining sites, and requires progressive relinquishment of slices of such sites over several years.[4] It followed the site-banking provisions of Part XI; in applying for registration as a pioneer investor, an entity was to provide coordinates of two comparable sites to the PrepCom, one of which would be reserved for use by the Enterprise or a developing State.[5] Prior to registration, the certifying States would have to ensure that the sites applied for did not overlap with other sites already allocated, or under application.[6] Following the entry into force of the LOSC, a registered pioneer investor would have to submit its plan of work to the ISA within six months; at this stage, the certifying state must have become

[1] Res. II, para. 1(a)(i), LOSC. [2] *ibid.*, para. 1(a)(ii). [3] *ibid.*, para. 1(a)(iii).
[4] *ibid.*, para. 1(e). [5] *ibid.*, para. 3. [6] *ibid.*, para. 5.

party to the LOSC.[7] Authorisations for commercial production could be granted by the ISA alone. In granting such authorisations, it would give priority to pioneer investors.[8] This was the key benefit of pioneer investor status.

RIGHTS AND OBLIGATIONS

Prior to the entry into force of the LOSC, a pioneer investor would have exclusive right to conduct exploratory activities short of commercial production in the site allotted to it.[9] Pioneer investors would have to pay both a licence fee and annual fees, and, following commencement of production, a production charge.[10] Pioneer investors were also expected to maintain investments in their sites at levels prescribed by the PrepCom.[11] The PrepCom could also require them to explore one of the sites reserved for the Enterprise or a developing State, on a 'costs plus 10 per cent' basis, to train personnel, and to perform their technology-transfer obligations prior to the entry into force of the LOSC.[12] Certifying States were also obliged to ensure that funds were available to the Enterprise to enable it to commence its activities following the LOSC's entry into force.[13]

[7] *ibid.*, para. 8. [8] *ibid.*, para. 9(a). [9] *ibid.*, para. 6. [10] *ibid.*, para. 7(a) and (b).
[11] *ibid.*, para. 7(c). [12] *ibid.*, para. 12(a). [13] *ibid.*, para. 12(b).

Appendix 3 Alterations made by the 1994 Implementation Agreement

The Implementation Agreement entered into force on July 28, 1996. For the months between its adoption (16 November 1994) and entry into force, Article 7 provided for its provisional application by States which had established their consent to be bound by it, or which had notified the depositary of their consent to its provisional application.

It introduced the following alterations to the LOSC Part XI regime.

REDUCED FINANCIAL OBLIGATIONS TO THE ISA

The Agreement reduced the costs that developed States would incur in undertaking seabed mining. It moderated the size and scope of the ISA providing for an 'evolutionary approach' to setting up its organs.[1] It limited the ISA to a budget, which from 1998 would be met solely from assessed contributions of its members and funds generated by the Enterprise; though prior to this it could draw upon UN funds.[2] The ISA could no longer exercise the power to borrow funds that had been granted under LOSC Article 174(1).

ALTERED FINANCIAL TERMS OF CONTRACTS

The Agreement deleted the LOSC terms,[3] instead providing a flexible, revisable system of payments.[4] It states that the system of payments from contractors to the ISA should be fair to both,[5] and not impose a competitive disadvantage either on contractors or land-based producers.[6] Its structure should be determined by the ISA Council.[7] An

[1] Annex Section 1, paras. (2) and (3), Implementation Agreement. [2] *ibid.*, para. (14).
[3] *ibid.*, Annex Section 8, para. (2). [4] *ibid.*, para. 1(e). [5] *ibid.*, para. 1(a).
[6] *ibid.*, para. 1(b). [7] *ibid.*, para. 1(c).

annual fixed fee could be payable, if not credited against other payments based on royalties or profits;[8] the sum would be determined by the ISA Council, unlike the LOSC which provided for a US$1 million fee. The initial application fee (fixed at US$500,000 by the LOSC) was altered to US$250,000 for plans of work limited to either exploration or exploitation.[9]

REDUCED SUPPORT TO THE ENTERPRISE

The Agreement provides that States would no longer have to finance a mining venture of the Enterprise as provided in LOSC Annex IV Article 11(3).[10] The Enterprise will now have to conduct mining through joint ventures, and, from the time of commencement of its first joint venture, or approval of any contractors' plan of work for exploitation, it will have to function independently from the ISA Secretariat.[11] It will have to assume all obligations applicable to contractors; its plans of work will be in the form of contracts with the ISA.[12] In each case in which it decides to enter into a joint venture in a reserved mine site, the Enterprise will have to offer first right of refusal to the contractor which had contributed that mine site.[13] If it did not submit a plan of work with respect to a reserved site within fifteen years of its reservation, or of its commencing to function independently (whichever is later), the contractor could apply for a licence if it offered to include the Enterprise as a joint-venture partner.

GREATER CONTROL OVER DECISION-MAKING

The Agreement has reduced the scope of discretionary exercise of power by the Assembly, providing that it must act on the Council's recommendation on all matters for which the Council also has competence, or any administrative, budgetary or financial matters.[14]

Moreover, in the absence of consensus, the Council will follow a system of chambered voting. Each chamber will have to establish that a majority of its members favours the decision made.[15] The following groups of States will each represent a chamber: (i) four States which consumed or imported more than 2 per cent of the total value of world consumption or imports, including the state with the largest GDP in

[8] *ibid.*, para. 1(d). [9] *ibid.*, para. (3). [10] *ibid.*, Annex Section 2, para. (3).
[11] *ibid.*, para. (2). [12] *ibid.*, para. (4). [13] *ibid.*, para. (5).
[14] *ibid.*, Annex Section 3, para. (4). [15] *ibid.*, para. (5).

Eastern Europe, and the State with the largest GDP in the world on the date of entry into force of the LOSC, that is, the United States; (ii) four States from among the eight States which had made the largest investment in mining activities; (iii) four States which were major net exporters of seabed minerals including two developing States; and (iv) twenty-four States, including (a) six developing States representing special interests of large population, island States, landlocked or geographically disadvantaged location, importers of seabed minerals, producers of such minerals, and least developed States; and (b) eighteen States selected for equitable geographical representation from Africa, Asia, Eastern Europe, Latin America, the Caribbean, Western Europe and Others.[16] This ensures that developed States will have significant ability to block undesirable decisions.

The Agreement also established a Finance Committee to make recommendations on financial and budgetary management, including assessment of contributions from States Parties,[17] an administrative budget[18] and equitable sharing of financial and other economic benefits from seabed mining.[19] Members of the Finance Committee will be drawn from each group of States mentioned above;[20] and, until the Authority has amassed sufficient funds from sources other than assessed contributions to meet its administrative expenses, members would include representatives from the five largest financial contributors to the administrative budget (that is, five representatives from developed States).[21]

NO MANDATORY TRANSFER OF TECHNOLOGY

The Agreement provides that ordinarily the Enterprise and developing States will have to seek seabed mining technology on the open market or through joint-venture arrangements.[22] If they cannot obtain it through these means, the ISA may request contractors and their sponsoring States to provide such technology to the Enterprise or developing state, but consistently with the effective protection of intellectual property rights.[23] This is quite different from the technology-transfer provisions of the LOSC, which disregarded intellectual property rights in demanding mandatory transfer of technology to the Enterprise and to developing States.

16 *ibid.*, paras. 9(a) and (15). 17 *ibid.*, Annex Section 9, para. 7(b). 18 *ibid.*, para. 7(d).
19 *ibid.*, para. 7(f). 20 *ibid.*, para. 3. 21 *ibid.* 22 *ibid.*, Annex Section 5, para. 1(a).
23 *ibid.*, para. 1(b).

NO PRODUCTION CEILINGS OR SUBSIDIES

The Agreement underlines that seabed resources should be developed in accordance with commercial principles,[24] rather than the principles of equity and no-harm incorporated in the LOSC. Trade in seabed minerals will be governed by the GATT;[25] and there will be no discrimination between seabed minerals and those derived from other sources.[26] Mineral production will not be subsidised except as permitted by the GATT.[27] Production ceilings and other policies specified in LOSC Articles 151(1)–(7), (9) and related provisions would no longer apply.[28] The ISA can, however, provide assistance to developing countries which were severely affected by loss of earnings from mineral exports due to their production via seabed mining.[29] Funds for such assistance will have to be drawn from payments received from contractors and voluntary contributions; but assessed contributions from States parties cannot be diverted for this purpose.[30]

MISCELLANEOUS

The Agreement also scrapped the Review Conference, and provides that the Assembly may undertake a review of the matters prescribed in LOSC Article 155(1) at any time, but on a recommendation of the Council.[31] Pioneer investors were allowed a window of three years within which to submit a plan of work for exploration to the ISA following the entry into force of the LOSC; this was a much longer timeframe as compared to the six-month period prescribed in Resolution II.[32] Moreover, since the overall application fee is now reduced, the fee paid for registration as a pioneer investor will be deemed to be the application fee relating to the plan of work for exploration.[33]

[24] *ibid.*, Annex Section 6, para. 1(a). [25] *ibid.*, para. 1(b). [26] *ibid.*, para. 1(d).
[27] *ibid.*, para. 1(c). [28] *ibid.*, para. 7. [29] *ibid.*, Annex Section 7, para. 1(a). [30] *ibid.*
[31] *ibid.*, Annex Section 4. [32] *ibid.*, Annex Section 1, para. 6(a)(ii). [33] *ibid.*

Appendix 4 Limits to the Rome Statute's obligation to cooperate

ARTICLE 90

Article 90 addresses situations where a party is faced with competing requests – from the ICC and from another State – for surrender of the same person for the same or different offenses. In such cases, the ICC can press for surrender only after it has taken into account the investigation or prosecution in the competing state, and has determined the surrender admissible under Articles 18 and 19 of the Rome Statute.[1] To the extent that the competing state is also a party to the Rome Statute, or, if not a party, is not owed an obligation of surrender by the requested state, the requested state must give priority to the request made by the ICC.[2] But, if the requested state is under a legal obligation of surrender to the competing state, then it is entitled to decide which of the two requests it will honour, taking into account the criteria specified in Article 90(6) and, as applicable, Article 90(7).[3] Here, it might consult with the ICC and the competing state to determine if it is possible to fulfil both requests, perhaps by postponing one.[4]

ARTICLE 93

Article 93 takes note of situations where a State cannot execute a request made by the ICC because such execution is prohibited by a fundamental principle of general application. The State must then consult with the ICC, to determine if it is possible to fulfil the request in another manner, perhaps subject to certain conditions. If the matter cannot be resolved, then the ICC must modify its request. A State may also deny a request that concerns the production of any documents or

[1] Article 90(2), Rome Statute. [2] *Ibid.*, Article 90(4). [3] *ibid.*, Article 90(6).
[4] *ibid.*, Article 93(9).

disclosure of evidence which relates to its national security. However, in doing so, it must give due regard to whether it is possible to fulfil the request subject to specified conditions.

ARTICLE 98

The Rome Statute also limits the Court from pressing a State for assistance or surrender, when this would require the State to act inconsistently with its obligations under international law, and particularly towards the diplomatic immunity of a person or property of a third State.[5] Related to this, the Court may not press a request for surrender which would require the requested State 'to act inconsistently with obligations under international agreements pursuant to which the consent of a sending State is required to surrender a person of that State to the Court'. This article, Article 98(2), is the key to construing the relationship between the Rome Statute and a bilateral immunity agreement. In any event, with respect to both these situations, the Court must endeavour to obtain the consent (to surrender) of the third state before pressing its request on the requested State.

[5] *ibid.*, Article 98(1).

Appendix 5 Sample bilateral investment agreement[1]

Reaffirming the importance of bringing to justice those who commit genocide, crimes against humanity and war crimes,

Recalling that the Rome Statute of the International Criminal Court done at Rome on July 17, 1998 by the United Nations Diplomatic Conference of Plenipotentiaries on the Establishment of an International Criminal Court is intended to complement and not supplant national criminal jurisdiction,

Considering that the Government of the United States of America has expressed its intention to investigate and to prosecute where appropriate acts within the jurisdiction of the International Criminal Court alleged to have been committed by its officials, employees, military personnel, or other nationals,

Bearing in mind Article 98 of the Rome Statute,

Hereby agree as follows:

1. For purposes of this agreement, 'persons' are current or former Government officials, employees (including contractors), or military personnel or nationals of one Party.
2. Persons of one Party present in the territory of the other shall not, absent the expressed consent of the first Party,
   (a) be surrendered or transferred by any means to the International Criminal Court for any purpose, or
   (b) be surrendered or transferred by any means to any other entity or third country, or expelled to a third country, for the purpose of surrender to or transfer to the International Criminal Court.

[1] J. Crawford *et al.*, Joint Opinion in the Matter of the Statute of the International Criminal Court and in the Matter of Bilateral Agreements sought by the United States under Article 98(2) of the Rome Statute, 5 June 2003, www.amicc.org/docs/Art98-14une03 FINAL.pdf.

3. [This paragraph is included only in reciprocal agreements.] When the United States extradites, surrenders, or otherwise transfers a person of the other Party to a third country, the United States will not agree to the surrender or transfer of that person to the International Criminal Court by the third country, absent the expressed consent of the Government of X.
4. When the Government of X extradites, surrenders, or otherwise transfers a person of the United States of America to a third country, the Government of X will not agree to the surrender or transfer of that person to the International Criminal Court by a third country, absent the expressed consent of the Government of the United States.
5. [This paragraph is used only in agreements with States that are not parties or signatories to the Rome Statute.] Each Party agrees, subject to its international legal obligations, not to knowingly facilitate, consent to, or cooperate with efforts by any third party or country to effect the extradition, surrender, or transfer of a person of the other Party to the International Criminal Court.
6. This Agreement shall enter into force upon an exchange of notes confirming that each Party has completed the necessary domestic legal requirements to bring the Agreement into force. It will remain in force until one year after the date on which one Party notifies the other of its intent to terminate this Agreement. The provisions of this Agreement shall continue to apply with respect to any act occurring, or any allegation arising, before the effective date of termination.

Appendix 6 The 123 Agreement compared with other agreements for civil nuclear cooperation

The key features of the US–India 123 Agreement may be compared with four other agreements for nuclear cooperation entered into by the US, namely, those with the United Arab Emirates, Japan, China and the European Atomic Energy Community (Euratom). Admittedly, the text of an agreement does not always provide sufficient indication of how it will be implemented in practice, as illustrated in the case of the US–China agreement. And the five agreements under consideration here represent a diverse range of legal and political contexts in which nuclear cooperation was initiated. Even so, a comparison is not futile. A structural examination clearly shows that the agreements are similarly modelled. In each case the terms of the earlier agreements appear to have been rigorously parsed, with narrow variations introduced to tailor later texts to the interests of the negotiating parties. The variations are suggestive of the different initial bargains concluded between the US and the other States (and Euratom). It is therefore plausible to claim, for instance, that the Indian agreement carries a more generous provision on reprocessing than the US agreement with UAE. In terms of indicia of comparison, the following features of the agreements are particularly appropriate: (i) reference to full civil nuclear cooperation; (ii) enrichment and reprocessing rights; (iii) retransfer provisions; (iv) safeguards requirements; (v) other non-proliferation obligations; (vi) fuel supply guarantees; (vii) conditions for cessation of cooperation and (viii) dispute settlement provisions.

Table 1 at the end of this appendix provides a comprehensive overview of the key elements of these agreements.

US–UAE 123 AGREEMENT

The US–UAE agreement was concluded on 20 May 2009.[1] Even though the UAE is party to the NPT, the agreement is not for 'full civil nuclear cooperation'.[2] While the Agreed Minute claims that the terms of cooperation are to be no less favourable in scope or effect than those accorded 'to any [NNWS] in the Middle East in a peaceful nuclear cooperation agreement', the terms are less favourable than those accorded to India. An obvious distinction relates to enrichment and reprocessing rights. The UAE has none in the first instance. Article 6(1) provides that 'material transferred ... shall not be reprocessed unless the Parties so agree'. Article 6(3) contains a similar bar against enrichment. Article 7 further bars the UAE from possessing sensitive nuclear facilities upon its territory for enrichment, reprocessing or other alteration in form or content of nuclear material. Article 10 demands confirmation of this in the form of an obligation upon the UAE to maintain full-scope safeguards. While there is only a brief reference to an 'Additional Protocol when it is in force' in Article 10, the Agreed Minute clarifies that exports shall not be licensed until the UAE brings it into force.

The preamble indicates that the agreement was meant to provide an incentive to UAE to renounce enrichment and reprocessing capabilities in favour of secure external fuel supplies. Yet, the US fuel supply guarantee is ambiguously worded. Article 4 only provides that the US shall 'endeavor to take such actions as are necessary and feasible to ensure a reliable supply of nuclear fuel' to the UAE. There is none of the detailed attention to the 'what if' situations that accompanies a crisply stated 'commitment to the reliable supply of fuel to India' that is present in the Indian agreement. And Article 13(2) explicitly mentions the US right to terminate cooperation if the UAE 'detonates a nuclear explosion device'. As in the Indian agreement, there are clear provisions restricting retransfers of nuclear material or equipment. Article 5 provides that these shall not be transferred to unauthorised persons or, without agreement, beyond the recipient party's territorial jurisdiction.

US–EURATOM 123 AGREEMENT

US cooperation with Euratom is long-standing. The first agreement dates back to 1958. The US has also had long-standing bilateral

[1] Agreement for Cooperation between the United Arab Emirates and the United States of America Concerning Peaceful Uses of Nuclear Energy, 20 May 2009.

[2] *Ibid.*, Article 2(1).

agreements with several member States of Euratom. The US and Euratom cooperation agreement of 1995[3] provides for 'full civil cooperation'. Both Parties also contribute to the activities of the international thermonuclear experimental reactor (ITER). Under the Deal, India too has been able to participate in this programme.[4]

The US–Euratom agreement refers to 'fullest possible exchange of equipment, materials and scientific and technological information for the peaceful uses of nuclear energy'.[5] It contains expansive provisions on nuclear trade, allowing for transfers and retransfers to third States.[6] The agreement does not call for full-scope safeguards. The provisions on safeguards are complicated of necessity, because Euratom members include NWS as well as NNWS. There is reference to coverage as required by the NPT, and it is stated that safeguards may be revised and replaced to keep abreast of NPT provisions;[7] the Agreed Minute also indicates that all Euratom members and the US are bound to adhere to the more recently revised version of NSG Part I Guidelines. In practice, Euratom's NNWS members have undertaken comprehensive safeguards; and the UK and France have concluded voluntary safeguards agreements. All Euratom States have concluded Additional Protocols (as has Euratom). Euratom also operates its own safeguards regime 'enabling the IAEA to deploy an inspection effort less than that applied under other safeguards agreements'.[8]

Article 8 provides for enrichment, reprocessing and other alteration in the form or content of transferred nuclear material. Reprocessing and alteration must be carried out in facilities that are part of delineated peaceful nuclear programmes of Euratom members and the US. To this extent there is similarity with the Indian agreement. However, the Agreed Minute introduces the possibility of termination of these activities by a party where the other party determines 'that their continuation would entail a serious threat to the security of either Party or of a Member State of the Community, or a significant increase in the risk of a nuclear proliferation'. This includes situations where an NNWS member of Euratom detonates a nuclear device, or where the UK, France or the US detonates a nuclear device using any item subject to the 123 Agreement; where either party or any member of Euratom violates

[3] Agreement for Cooperation in the Peaceful Uses of Nuclear Energy between the European Atomic Energy Community and the United States of America, 1995.
[4] India was accepted in ITER on 6 December 2005, www.iter-india.org.
[5] Article 3, US–Euratom Agreement. [6] *ibid.*, Article 5. [7] *ibid.*, Article 6(1).
[8] *ibid.*, Article 6(3)(b).

or declares itself not bound by the NPT, relevant safeguards agreements, or INFCIRC/254 Part 1; and where any State retransfers an item to any NNWS which has not concluded a full-scope safeguards agreement with the IAEA. In case of a nuclear detonation by an NNWS, or detonation using a transferred item by an NWS, the other party may also demand return of all transferred material. In contrast, the Indian agreement avoids explicit mention of nuclear detonations.

Similarly to the Indian agreement, the Euratom agreement requires that consultations shall precede termination of cooperation; the Euratom agreement also provides for the applicability of all means of dispute settlement including arbitration.[9] Both agreements seek to assure the unlikelihood of termination of cooperation; the Euratom agreement states that the demand for suspension of Article 8 activities shall be made only in the 'most extreme circumstances of exceptional concern from a non-proliferation or security point of view' and for the 'minimum time necessary'.[10] There is no parallel provision in the Indian agreement. It is more clearly stated for the Euratom agreement that Parties recognise that it is 'extremely unlikely that actions would be taken by the Community, its Member States or the US which would cause the other Party to invoke the rights specified in Article 13', that is, terminate cooperation and demand a return of all material transferred.[11] There is similar, but less confident, language about India's likely actions in the Indian agreement. In India's case, the US commits to taking into consideration 'whether the circumstances that may lead to termination or cessation resulted from a Party's serious concern about a changed security environment or as a response to similar actions by other States which could impact national security'.[12] The provisions of the Euratom agreement are comparable to those in the Indian agreement; indeed, Euratom members' non-proliferation commitments exceed those made by India. Certainly, fewer commitments are *formally* stated by India.

US–JAPAN 123 AGREEMENT

Left-wing Indian political parties have described the 1987 US–Japan 123 Agreement[13] as containing more favourable terms of

[9] *ibid.*, Article 12. [10] *ibid.*, Agreed Minute, para. 12.
[11] *ibid.*, Agreed Minute, para. 16. [12] Article 14 (2), 123 Agreement.
[13] Agreement for Cooperation between the United States of America and Japan Concerning Peaceful Uses of Nuclear Energy, 4 November 1987.

cooperation.[14] The context of the Japanese agreement was naturally different. The changes to the NPT regime, such as the adoption of full-scope safeguards requirements by NSG and by the NPT parties at the 1995 Review Conference had not occurred; nor had the Model Additional Protocol been formulated. NSG Part II Guidelines were not adopted. The danger of weapons proliferation by States under the guise of nuclear energy programmes was not yet salient. The 1987 agreement moreover succeeded a previous agreement of 1968.

Even so, the agreement requires Japan to accept comprehensive IAEA safeguards, 'with respect to all nuclear material in all nuclear activities' within Japan's jurisdiction.[15] The agreement contains the standard retransfer clause.[16] It permits enrichment up to less than 20 per cent.[17] In addition, Article 6 mentions the possibility of further enrichment (20 per cent or more) if the Parties agree. Reprocessing also requires further agreement between the Parties.[18] Article 12 expressly states that a nuclear detonation by Japan is a basis for termination of cooperation; the Agreed Minute clarifies that the Parties will not differentiate between a 'peaceful' nuclear explosion and a non-peaceful one. Of course, as with the Indian agreement, termination will not be automatic. There is a requirement for consultation and a provision for arbitration.[19] The Agreed Minute provides a US fuel supply guarantee, that the US 'will take such actions as may be necessary and feasible to ensure a reliable supply of nuclear fuel to Japan'. Unlike the Indian agreement, the guarantee does not continue beyond the termination of the agreement.

US–CHINA 123 AGREEMENT

The US–China 123 Agreement was finalised in 1985, but remained in a suspended state until 1998.[20] At the time of its conclusion, China was not a party to the NPT. Of course, NPT provisions allowed China to accede as an NWS in 1992. In 1985, however, China was still criticising the NPT as a discriminatory treaty, though perhaps no longer as 'a

[14] See *Left Stand on the Nuclear Deal: Notes Exchanged in the UPA–Left Committee on India–US Civil Nuclear Cooperation*, (New Delhi, Hari Singh Kang 2008) 20, 50–1, 101. In particular, the Indian left-wing parties cite the arbitration clause in the Japan 123 Agreement as evidence of its more favourable terms.

[15] Article 2, US-Japan Agreement. [16] *ibid.*, Article 4. [17] *ibid.*, Article 6.

[18] *ibid.*, Article 5(1). [19] *ibid.*, Article 14.

[20] Agreement for Cooperation between the United States of America and the People's Republic of China concerning Peaceful Uses of Nuclear Energy, 23 July 1985.

conspiracy concocted by the USSR and the US to maintain their nuclear monopoly'.[21] China's nuclear relations with the US were just beginning to improve. China became a member of the IAEA in 1984, and agreed to condition its exports upon acceptance of international safeguards by its recipients, in order to demonstrate that it did not encourage nuclear proliferation.[22] The US was seeking to engage China on non-proliferation, as it has, post-1998, sought to engage India.

Owing to China's *de jure* NWS status, the US–China agreement imposes few restrictions upon China. Article 8 of the agreement clearly states that the cooperation is between two NWSs and that bilateral safeguards are not required. The retransfer provision is less restrictive than in the Indian agreement; the China agreement does not restrict retransfer of special nuclear material produced through use of transferred material. This is tempered, however, by the assertion, in Article 5(2), that:

> [n]either party has any plans to change locations for storage of plutonium, uranium 233 ... or high enriched uranium transferred pursuant to this agreement or used in or produced through the use of any material or facility so transferred. In the event that a party would like at some future time to undertake such activities, the parties will promptly hold consultations to agree on a mutually acceptable arrangement.

Detonation is not mentioned as a reason for cessation of cooperation. The provision on cessation only states that each party 'shall endeavor to avoid taking any actions that affect cooperation under this agreement'.[23] There is less emphasis on using consultations to resolve matters, and there is no language indicating that ceasing cooperation would be a matter of grave concern. Article 7 provides simply that, while 'parties shall promptly hold consultations on the problem', it is 'understood that the other party shall have the rights to cease further cooperation under this agreement'. There is also a similarly ambiguous restriction on enrichment and reprocessing. Article 5 states that

[21] This was how China described the NPT in a document submitted to the UN in 1978: see M. Zhu, 'The Evolution of China's Nuclear Non-Proliferation Policy' (1997) 4 *Nonproliferation Review* 40.

[22] Announced during China's First Address to the IAEA Conference in September 1984. See S. Kan and M. Holt, 'USA-China Nuclear Cooperation Agreement', US Congressional Research Service Report for Congress, 5 December 2005, 5. This is also expressly stated in the IAEA safeguards agreement with China, 1989: 'Agreement of 20 September 1988 between the People's Republic of China and the International Atomic Energy Agency for the Application of Safeguards in China', INFCIRC/369, 1989.

[23] Article 7(1), US–China Agreement.

'[n]either party has any plans to enrich to twenty percent or greater, reprocess, or alter in form or content material transferred pursuant to this agreement or material used in or produced through the use of any material or facility so transferred'. If a party would like to undertake these activities, it must consult with the other party to create an acceptable arrangement; the other party will consider such activities favourably. The agreement does not carry fuel supply assurances of the sort found in the Indian agreement.

Article 2(1) is also ambiguously worded. It incorporates 'with respect to the observance of this agreement, the principle of international law that ... a party may not invoke the provisions of its internal law as justification for its failure to perform a treaty'. The left-wing Indian political parties, suspicious of the impact of US domestic laws on implementation of the Indian agreement, have argued that an explicit statement of this principle provides greater assurance of US cooperation with China.[24] Acting Chairman Roberts of the US Nuclear Regulatory Commission was also concerned that this statement would 'expressly qualify the authority of the [US] Congress to enact subsequent legislation affecting the activities covered by the Agreement'.[25] In fact, a US Congressional requirement for Presidential certification prevented implementation of the China agreement for thirteen years. The President was to certify that: there was effective verification to ensure peaceful use of US exports; that China did not encourage nuclear proliferation; and that US decision-making would not be prejudiced by Article 5(2) of the agreement to favourably consider China's wish to undertake enrichment and reprocessing.[26] In 1990, following the Tiananmen Square episode, the US Congress demanded further certifications, that China was not assisting any NNWS to acquire nuclear explosives; and it had made progress in political reform, or it was in

[24] *Left Stand on the Nuclear Deal: Notes Exchanged in the UPA–Left Committee on India–US Civil Nuclear Cooperation*, 18–9, 50–1.

[25] Roberts also wanted a more clearly stated restriction on enrichment and reprocessing. Reminiscent of US conduct in relation to the Indian agreement, the US government preferred to avoid these issues. President Reagan focused on the fact that the China agreement was the first peaceful nuclear cooperation agreement with a Communist country and would have a significant, positive impact on overall US-China relations, and bring economic benefits to the US: see Kan and Holt, 'USA–China Nuclear Cooperation Agreement', 7.

[26] Joint Resolution of Congress, relating to the approval and implementation of the proposed agreement for nuclear cooperation between the United States and the People's Republic of China 1985, Public Law 99-183 (SJ Res. 238), 16 December 1985.

the US national interest to cooperate with China.[27] By the time President Clinton made the required certifications, China had concluded a voluntary-offer safeguards agreement with the IAEA, acceded to the NPT, joined the Zangger Committee and promised not to begin nuclear projects with Iran.[28] The US and China had also concluded a Memorandum of Understanding on arrangements for visits and exchange of information that would permit the monitoring of sales and use of transferred equipment.[29] Transfers were allowed on a case-by-case basis.[30] The agreement was fully 'operationalised' (that is, export licences were issued and transfers authorised) in September 2004.[31] By this time, China's Additional Protocol was in force, and China had joined the NSG, besides offering written non-proliferation assurances to the US.[32]

Table 1 provides a summary of the key elements.

[27] Section 902(a)(6), Foreign Relations Authorization Act for Fiscal Years 1990 and 1991, Public Law 101-246.

[28] China's voluntary safeguards agreement entered into force on 18 October 1989. China acceded to the NPT in 1992, and joined the Zangger Committee in 1997. The promise not to begin new projects with Iran came in a letter to US Secretary of State Madeleine Albright: Kan and Holt, 'USA-China Nuclear Cooperation Agreement', 16. See also US Department of State, 'Daily Press Briefing', 30 October 1997, www.fas.org/news/usa/1997/10/971030db.html.

[29] *ibid.*

[30] *ibid.* See also US Department of State, 'Daily Press Briefing', 2 September 2004, http://usinfo.org/wf-archive/2004/040902/epf401.htm.

[31] Kan and Holt, 'USA-China Nuclear Cooperation Agreement', 20.

[32] China's Additional Protocol was concluded on 31 December 1998, and entered into force on 28 March 2002: 'Protocol Additional to the Agreement between the People's Republic of China and the International Atomic Energy Agency for the Application of Safeguards in China', INFCIRC 369/Add. 1, 2002. China's participation was approved by the NSG on 28 May 2004: NSG, Press Release, Plenary Meeting, Göteborg, Sweden, 27–28 May 2004 www.nuclearsuppliersgroup.org/Leng/PRESS/2004-05-goteborg.pdf. Its non-proliferation assurances were acknowledged in the US Department of State, Press Briefing, 2 September 2004. See also Kan and Holt, 'USA-China Nuclear Cooperation Agreement', 20.

Table 1 A comparative overview of US agreements on civil nuclear cooperation

	India	UAE	Euratom	Japan	China
Date	2007	2009	1995	1987	1985
NPT status	Non-party.	Party.	All EU Member States are party to the NPT. The UK and France are NWS States.	Party.	Party since 1992.
Reference to full civil nuclear cooperation.	Stated.	Not stated.	Stated.	Not stated.	Not stated.
Enrichment and reprocessing of supplied fuel, or fuel produced using supplied material	Allowed. Enrichment up to 20 per cent.	Not allowed. Moreover, UAE may not possess any enrichment or reprocessing facility on its territory.	Allowed. Enrichment up to 20 per cent. More than 20 per cent if parties agree.	Partly allowed. Enrichment to less than 20 per cent. 20 per cent or more if parties agree. Reprocessing if parties agree.	Not allowed (for transferred material) without agreement of the parties. But, request to enrich or reprocess will be considered favourably.
Retransfer of nuclear supplies, or material produced using supplied material	Standard, not allowed without agreement of parties.	Standard, not allowed without agreement of parties.	Allowed.	Standard, not allowed without agreement of parties.	Standard, except no bar on retransfer of special nuclear material produced through use of transferred material.

Safeguards requirements	Item-specific safeguards (covering supplied materials).	Comprehensive safeguards.	Reference to safeguards as required by the NPT; should be revised to keep abreast of the NPT.	Comprehensive safeguards.	No requirement.
Other non-proliferation commitments	For reprocessing: India will establish a new facility under IAEA safeguards. India will separate civil and military nuclear programmes.	Additional Protocol required in order for US to license exports.	Adherence to NSG Part I Guidelines. Agreement also takes note of Euratom's own safeguards system. Also refers to delineation of civil and military components of nuclear programmes.	–	Agreement was not operationalised until China joined the NPT, the Zangger Committee and the NSG; concluded a voluntary-offer safeguards agreement with IAEA; brought into force an Additional Protocol and offered other non-proliferation assurances, in writing, to US.

Table 1 (cont.)

	India	UAE	Euratom	Japan	China
Fuel supply guarantees	Affirmatively stated. Continue beyond termination of the agreement.	Weak and vaguely stated: US shall 'endeavor to take such actions as are necessary and feasible to ensure a reliable supply of nuclear fuel.'	Not included.	Affirmatively stated: 'US will take such actions as may be necessary and feasible to ensure a reliable supply of nuclear fuel to Japan.' Do not continue beyond termination of agreement.	Not included.
Conditions for cessation of cooperation	None expressly stated.	Nuclear test. Possession of enrichment or reprocessing facility; enrichment or reprocessing of transferred material. Retransfers, other actions contrary to the provisions of the agreement.	Nuclear test by an NNWS, or nuclear test using supplied material by an NWS. If either party or any member of Euratom violates or declares itself not bound by the NPT, relevant safeguards agreements, or NSG Part 1 Guidelines.	Nuclear test. Violation or termination of safeguards agreement. Action contrary to provisions of the Agreement.	No express reason. Each party 'shall endeavor to avoid taking any actions that affect cooperation under this agreement'.

		Termination or violation of IAEA safeguards agreement.	If any State retransfers an item to any NNWS which has not concluded a full-scope safeguards agreement with the IAEA.		
Dispute settlement provisions	Consultation, negotiation.	Negotiation, diplomatic consultation or. other means of peaceful dispute resolution. Inquiry by expert bodies such as the IAEA.	Consultations, followed by application of all other means of dispute settlement, including arbitration.	Consultations and arbitration.	Consultations, but each party 'shall have the rights to cease further cooperation under this agreement'.

Bibliography

ARTICLES, BOOKS AND COMMENTS

Abraham, I., *The Making of the Indian Atomic Bomb: Science, Secrecy and the Postcolonial State* (London, Zed Books 1998)

Adler, E., 'Seizing the Middle Ground: Constructivism in World Politics' (1997) 3 *European Journal of International Relations* 319

Adler, E., and Pouliot, V., *International Practices* (Cambridge University Press 2011)

Ahlström, C., 'Legal Aspects of the Indian–US Civil Nuclear Cooperation Initiative', Armaments, Disarmament and International Security, *SIPRI Yearbook* 2006, www.sipri.org/yearbook/2006/13/13B

Akande, D., 'ICC Issues Detailed Decision on Bashir's Immunity (. . . at Long Last . . .) But Gets the Law Wrong', *European Journal of International Law: Talk!*, 15 December 2011

'ICC Reports Kenya and Chad to the UN Security Council over Bashir's Visits', *European Journal of International Law: Talk!*, 28 August 2010

'International Law Immunities and the International Criminal Court' (2004) 98 *American Journal of International Law* 407

'Is Kenya Pushing for a Mass Withdrawal from the ICC', *European Journal of International Law: Talk!*, 14 January 2011

'The Legal Nature of Security Council Referrals to the ICC and its Impact on Al Bashir's Immunities' (2009) 7(2) *Journal of International Criminal Justice* 333

Akhavan, P., 'The Lord's Resistance Army Case: Uganda's Submission of the first State Referral to the International Criminal Court' (2005) 99 *American Journal of International Law* 403

Albright, D., *et al.*, 'Preventing Iran from Getting Nuclear Weapons: Constraining Its Future Nuclear Options', Institute for Science and International Security Report, 5 March 2012

Allott, P., 'The Concept of International Law' (1999) 10 *European Journal of International Law* 31

Alter, K., and Meunier, S., 'The Politics of International Regime Complexity', Framing Paper, Conference on the Politics of International Regime

Complexity, Princeton University, 1 March 2007, www.princeton.edu/~smeunier/AlterMeunierFramingPiece2.pdf
Alvarez, J., 'Foreword, Why Nations Behave: A Symposium on Implementation, Compliance and Effectiveness' (1998) 19 *Michigan Journal of International Law* 303
Amnesty International, Letter to the EU Presidency, 30 August 2002, www.amnesty.eu/en/press-releases/human-rights-in-the-eu/police-and-judicial-co-operation/u-s-agreements-violate-international-court-treaty-0075
Anand, R. P., '*Common Heritage of Mankind: Mutilation of an Ideal*', in *Studies in International Law and History: An Asian Perspective* (Leiden, Martinus Nijhoff 2004) 180
Anderson, D. H., 'British Accession to the UN Convention on the Law of the Sea' (1997) 46 *International and Comparative Law Quarterly* 761
'Efforts to Achieve Universal Participation in the UN Convention on the Law of the Sea' (1993) 42 *International and Comparative Law Quarterly* 644
Anoushirvani, S., 'The Future of the International Criminal Court: The Long Road to Legitimacy begins with the Trial of Thomas Lubanga Dyilo' (2010) 22 *Pace International Law Review* 213
Anthony, I., *et al.*, 'Reforming Nuclear Export Controls: The Future of the Nuclear Suppliers Group', SIPRI Research Report No. 22, 2007
Apuuli, K. P., 'The ICC's Possible Deferral of the LRA Case to Uganda' (2008) 6 *Journal of International Criminal Justice* 801
Arato, J., 'Subsequent Practice and Evolutive Interpretation: Techniques of Treaty Interpretation over Time and Their Diverse Consequences' (2010) 9 *The Law and Practice of International Courts and Tribunals* 443
Arend, A. C., 'Do Legal Rules Matter? International Law and International Politics' (1998) 38 *Virginia Journal of International Law* 107
Legal Rules and International Society (Oxford University Press 1999)
Arms Control Association, Chronology of US–North Korea Nuclear and Missile Diplomacy, www.armscontrol.org/factsheets/dprkchron@2013
'History of Official Proposals on the Iranian Nuclear Issue', www.armscontrol.org/factsheets/Iran_Nuclear_Proposals (last updated August 2013)
Arms Control Wonk, 'US NSG India Proposal', March 2006, www.armscontrolwonk.com/1009/us-nsg-india-proposal
Arnsperger, C., and Picavet, E., 'More Than Modus Vivendi, Less Than Overlapping Consensus: Towards a Political Theory of Social Compromise' (2004) 43(2) *Social Science Information* 167
Arsanjani, M., and Reisman, M., 'The Law-in-Action of the International Criminal Court' (2005) 99 *American Journal of International Law* 385
Aufricht, H., 'Supersession of Treaties in International Law' (1951–2) 37 *Cornell Legal Quarterly* 698
Balachandran, G., 'China–Pakistan Nuclear Cooperation: Unclear Facts', Institute for Defense Studies and Analysis (IDSA) Comment, 18 April 2013, http://idsa.in/idsacomments/ChinaPakistanNuclearCooperation_gbalachandran_180413
Barnett, M., and Finnemore, M., 'The Politics, Power, and Pathologies of International Organizations' (1999) 53 *International Organization* 699

Bartoš, M., *Medjunarodno javno pravo* Vol. 1 (Beograd, Cultura 1954)

Bassu, G., Special Advisor on External Relations and Cooperation, Office of the Registrar, Personal Interview, 8 April 2010 (on file)

Bedjaoui, M., *Towards a New International Economic Order* (London, Holmes and Meier 1979)

Benvenisti, E., and Downs, G., 'The Empire's New Clothes: Political Economy and the Fragmentation of International Law' (2007) 60 *Stanford Law Review* 595

Berman, P. S., 'Review Essay: Seeing Beyond the Limits of International Law' (2006) 84 *Texas Law Review* 1265

Binder, G., *Treaty Conflict and Political Contradiction: The Dialectic of Duplicity* (New York, Praeger 1989)

Bipartisan Security Group Policy Brief, 'The Proliferation Security Initiative: The Legal Challenge', September 2003

Borgen, C., 'Resolving Treaty Conflicts' (2005) 37 *George Washington International Law Review* 573

'*Treaty Conflicts and Normative Fragmentation*', in D. B. Hollis, *The Oxford Guide to Treaties* (Oxford University Press 2012) 448–70

Brennan, K., 'The United Nations Conference on the Law of the Sea' (1982) 76 *ASIL Proceedings* 107

Brierly, J. L., 'The Codification of International Law' (1948–9) 47 *Michigan Law Review* 2

Broomhall, B., *International Justice and the International Criminal Court: Between Sovereignty and the Rule of Law* (Oxford University Press 2003)

Brown, E. D., *Seabed Energy and Minerals: The International Legal Regime* Vols. 1–3 (The Hague, Martinus Nijhoff 2001)

The International Law of the Sea (Aldershot, Dartmouth 1994)

Brunnée, J., and Toope, S., *Legitimacy and Legality in International Law: An Interactional Account* (Cambridge University Press 2010)

Byers, M., *Custom, Power and the Power of Rules* (Cambridge University Press 1999)

Caminos, H., and Molitor, M., 'Progressive Development of International Law and the Package Deal' (1985) 79 *American Journal of International Law* 871

Caron, D., 'Towards a Political Theory of International Courts and Tribunals' (2006) 24 *Berkeley Journal of International Law* 401

Cassese, A., 'Editorial Comment: Is the ICC Still Having Teething Problems?' (2006) 4 *Journal of International Criminal Justice* 434

'Flawed International Justice for Sudan', *Project Syndicate*, 15 July 2008

'*The International Criminal Court Five Years on: Andante or Moderato?*', in C. Stahn and G. Sluiter (eds.), *The Emerging Practice of the International Criminal Court* (Leiden, Martinus Nijhoff 2009) 21

Cerone, J. P., 'Dynamic Equilibrium: The Evolution of US Attitudes towards International Courts and Tribunals' (2007) 18 *European Journal of International Law* 277

Charney, J., 'International Law and Multiple International Tribunals' (1998) 271 *Recueil des Cours* 145
Charnovitz, S., 'WTO Cosmopolitics' (2002) 34 *NYU Journal of International Law and Politics* 299
Chayes, A., *The Cuban Missile Crisis: International Crises and the Role of Law* (Oxford University Press 1974)
Chayes, A., and Chayes, A. H., *The New Sovereignty: Compliance with International Regulatory Agreements* (Harvard University Press 1998)
Chimni, B. S., 'Cooption and Resistance: Two Faces of Global Administrative Law' (2006) 37 *NYU Journal of International Law and Politics* 799
'Imperialism All the Way' (1982) 17 *Economic and Political Weekly* 407
'International Law Scholarship in Post-Colonial India: Coping with Dualism' (2010) 23 *Leiden Journal of International Law* 23
'Law of the Sea: Winners Are Losers' (1982) 17 *Economic and Political Weekly* 987
Churchill, R. R., and Lowe, A. V., *Law of the Sea* (3rd edn, Manchester University Press 1999)
Ciampi, A., 'The Proceedings against President Al Bashir and the Prospect of their Surrender under Article 16 ICC Statute' (2008) 6 *Journal of International Criminal Justice* 885
Comaroff, J. L., 'Colonialism, Culture and the Law: A Foreword' (2011) 26 *Law and Social Inquiry* 305
Comaroff, J. L., and Comaroff, J., *'Law and Disorder in the Postcolony: An Introduction'*, in J. L. Comaroff and J. Comaroff (eds.), *Law and Disorder in the Postcolony* (University of Chicago Press 2006) 1
Crail, P., 'IAEA Approves India Additional Protocol', Arms Control Association, April 2009, www.armscontrol.org/act/2009_04/IndiaProtocol
Crawford, J., 'Chance, Order, Change: The Course of International Law', General Course on Public International Law (2013) 365 *Recueil des Cours* 9–382
'Responsibility to the International Community as a Whole' (2001) 8 *Indiana Journal of Global Legal Studies* 303
'The Drafting of the Rome Statute', in P. Sands (ed.), *From Nuremberg to The Hague: The Future of International Criminal Justice* (Oxford University Press 2003) 109
The International Law Commission's Articles on State Responsibility: Introduction, Text and Commentaries (Cambridge University Press 2002)
Crawford, J., *et al.*, Joint Opinion in the Matter of the Statute of the International Criminal Court and in the Matter of Bilateral Agreements Sought by the United States under Article 98 (2) of the Rome Statute, 5 June 2003, www.amicc.org/docs/Art98-14une03FINAL.pdf
Crook, J. R. (ed.), 'Contemporary Practice of the United States Relating to International Law' (2007) 101 *American Journal of International Law* 636
Cryer, R., 'Déjà Vu in International Law' (2002) 65 *Modern Law Review* 931
Czaplinski, W., and Danilenko, G., 'Conflicts of Norms in International Law' (1990) 21 *Netherlands Yearbook of International Law* 12
D'Amato, A., Editorial Comment: 'An Alternative to the Law of the Sea Convention' (1983) 77 *American Journal of International Law* 281

Danish, K., 'Book Review: The New Sovereignty' (1997) 37 *Virginia Journal of International Law* 789
Das, P. S., Vice-Admiral (retd), New Delhi, Personal Interview, 29 November 2009
d'Aspremont, J., 'The Politics of Deformalization of International Law' (2011) 3 *Goettingen Journal of International Law* 503
de Certeau, M., *The Practice of Everyday Life* (S. Randall (trans.), University of California Press 1984)
de Visscher, C., *Theory and Reality in International Law* (Princeton University Press 1957)
de Waal, A., and Flint, J., 'Case Closed: A Prosecutor Without Borders', *World Affairs*, Spring 2009
deGuzman, M., 'Gravity and the Legitimacy of the International Criminal Court' (2009) 32 *Fordham International Law Journal* 1400
Dhanapala, J., 'Evaluating the 2010 NPT Review Conference', Special Report of the United States Institute for Peace, October 2010, www.usip.org/files/resources/SR258%20-%20Evaluating%20the%202010%20NPT%20Review%20Conference.pdf
Downs, G., *et al.*, 'Is the Good News about Compliance Good News about Cooperation?' (1996) 50 *International Organization* 379
Duff, J., 'The United States and the Law of the Sea Convention: Sliding Back from Accession and Ratification' (2006) 11 *Ocean and Coastal Law Journal* 1
Dunlap, C., 'Law and Military Interventions: Preserving Humanitarian Values in 21st Century Conflicts', paper presented at the Humanitarian Challenges in Military Intervention Conference, Carr Centre for Human Rights Policy, Kennedy School of Government, Harvard University, Washington DC, 29 November 2011, http://people.duke.edu/~pfeaver/dunlap.pdf
'Lawfare Today: A Perspective' (2008) 3 *Yale Journal of Foreign Affairs* 146
Dunne, A., 'The Proliferation Security Initiative: Legal Considerations and Operational Realities', SIPRI Policy Paper No. 36, May 2013
Dupuy, P.-M., '*On the "Doctrine" of Approximate Application of Treaties in International Law*', in G. Hafner *et al.* (eds.), *Liber Amicorum: Ignaz Siedl-Hohenveldern – In Honour of His 80th Birthday* (The Hague, Kluwer 1998) 97
Egede, E., *Africa and the Deep Seabed Regime: Politics and International Law of the Common Heritage of Mankind* (London, Springer 2011)
ElBaradei, M., *The Age of Deception: Nuclear Diplomacy in Treacherous Times* (London, Bloomsbury 2011)
Fitzmaurice, G., 'The Foundations of Authority of International Law and the Problem of Enforcement' (1956) 19 *Modern Law Review* 1
'The General Principles of International Law considered from the Standpoint of the Rule of Law' (1957) 92[II] *Recueil des Cours* 5
Fitzmaurice, M., '*Dynamic (Evolutive) Interpretation of Treaties and the European Court of Human Rights*', in A. Orakhelashvili and S. Williams (eds.), *Forty Years of the Vienna Convention on the Law of Treaties* (London, BIICL 2010) 55
Fitzmaurice, M., and Elias, O., *Contemporary Issues in the Law of Treaties* (Utrecht, Eleven International Publishing 2005)

Fox, G., 'International Organizations: Conflicts of International Law' (2001) 95 *ASIL Proceedings* 183

Franck, T. M., *Fairness in International Law and International Institutions* (Oxford, Clarendon Press 1995)

'Fairness in the International Legal and Institutional System', General Course on Public International Law (1993) 240 *Recueil des Cours* 9

Recourse to Force: State Action against Threats and Armed Attacks (Cambridge University Press 2002)

'Remarks: In What Sense is International Law Law', (2009) 103 ASIL Proceedings 161.

The Power of Legitimacy Among Nations (Oxford University Press 1990)

Franck, T. M., and ElBaradei, M., 'The Codification and Progressive Development of International Law: A UNITAR Study of the Role and Use of the International Law Commission' (1982) 76 *American Journal of International Law* 630

Frey, K., *India's Nuclear Bomb and National Security* (London, Routledge 2006)

Fuller, L., 'Positivism and Fidelity to Law' (1957) 71 *Harvard Law Review* 630

The Morality of Law (revised edn, Yale University Press 1969)

Gaeta, P., 'Does President Al Bashir enjoy Immunity from Arrest?' (2009) 7(2) *Journal of International Criminal Justice* 315

Garner, J., 'Harvard Research in International Law: Draft Convention on the Law of Treaties' (1935) 29 *American Journal of International Law Supplement* 1024

Ghoshroy, S., 'The US-India Nuclear Deal: Triumph of the Business Lobby', *The Audit of Conventional Wisdom*, MIT Center for International Studies, September 2006, http://mit.edu/cis/pdf/Audit_09_14_Ghoshroy.pdf

Ginsburg, T., ICC Observers Interview, 15 March 2009, http://iccobservers.files.wordpress.com/2009/03/icc_observers_ginsburg_interview.pdf

Goldsmith, J., 'Mea Culpa: Lawfare', *Lawfare*, 8 September 2011

Goldsmith, J., and Posner, E., *The Limits of International Law* (Oxford University Press 2005)

Golove, D. M., 'Leaving Customary International Law Where It Is: Goldsmith and Posner's The Limits of International Law' (2005–6) 34 *Georgia Journal of International and Comparative Law* 333

Goodman, R., and Jinks, D., 'How to Influence States: Socialization and International Human Rights Law' (2004) 54 *Duke Law Journal* 621

Gray, J., 'Where Plurals and Liberals Part Company' (1998) 6(1) *International Journal of Philosophical Studies* 17

Grono, N., Deputy President, International Crisis Group, ICC Observers Interview, 6 March 2009, http://iccobservers.files.wordpress.com/2009/03/icc_observers_nick_grono_interview1.pdf

Habermas, J., *Between Facts and Norms: Contributions to a Discourse Theory of Law and Democracy* (W. Rehg (trans.), MIT Press 1996)

Hafner-Burton, E. M., *et al.*, 'Political Science Research on International Law: The State of the Field' (2012) 106 *American Journal of International Law* 47–97

Harrison, J., *Making the Law of the Sea: A Study in the Development of International Law* (Cambridge University Press 2011)

Hart, H. L. A., *The Concept of Law* (2nd edn, Oxford University Press 1994)

Hegel, G. W. F., *Hegel's Philosophy of Right* (T. Knox (trans.), Oxford University Press 1967)

Helfer, L., 'Regime Shifting: The TRIPs Agreement and the New Dynamics of Intellectual Property Lawmaking' (2004) 29 *Yale Journal of International Law* 1

Heller, K. J., 'Kenya Moves Closer to Withdrawing from the ICC', *Opinio Juris*, 23 December 2010

'*Situational Gravity under the Rome Statute*', in C. Stahn and L. van den Herik (eds.), *Future Perspectives on International Criminal Justice* (The Hague, TMC Asser Press 2010) 227

Henkin, L., *How Nations Behave* (2nd edn, Columbia University Press 1979)

Heyder, C., 'The UN Security Council's Referral of the Crimes in Darfur to the International Criminal Court in Light of US Opposition to the Court: Implications for the International Criminal Court's Functions and Status' (2006) 24 *Berkeley Journal of International Law* 650

Hicks, B. L., 'Comment: Treaty Congestion in International Environmental Law: The Need for Greater International Coordination' (1998–9) 32 *University of Richmond Law Review* 1643

Higgins, R., 'International Law and the Avoidance, Containment and Resolution of Disputes', General Course on Public International Law (1991) 230 *Recueil des Cours* 9–342

'Policy Considerations and the International Judicial Process' (1968) 17 *International and Comparative Law Quarterly* 58

Problems and Process: International Law and How We Use It (Oxford, Clarendon Press 1994)

Holmes, J., '*Complementarity: National Courts versus the ICC*', in A. Cassese *et al.* (eds.), *The Rome Statute of the International Criminal Court: A Commentary* (Oxford University Press 2002) 667

Horton, J., 'John Gray and the Political Theory of Modus Vivendi' (2006) 9(2) *Critical Review of Internatonal Social and Political Philosophy* 155

Human Rights Watch, 'Benchmarks for Justice for Serious Crimes in Northern Uganda', Memoranda on Justice Standards and the Juba Peace Talks, May 2007–February 2008, www.hrw.org/legacy/pub/2008/ij/uganda_memos_cover.pdf

'US Fiddles Over ICC While Darfur Burns: UN Security Council Should Reject US Scheme for Ad Hoc Court', 30 January 2005, www.hrw.org/news/2005/01/31/us-fiddles-over-icc-while-darfur-burns

Hurst, C., 'A Plea for the Codification of International Law on New Lines' (1946) 32 *Transactions of the Grotius Society* 135

Independent Task Force convened by the American Society of International Law, 'US policy towards the ICC: Furthering Positive Engagement', Report, March 2009, www.asil.org/icc-task-force.cfm

Indian Foreign Secretary (S. Saran), 'Transforming US–India Relations: Forging a Strategic Partnership', Address to the Carnegie Endowment for International Peace, 21 December 2005

Institute for Science and International Security, 'ISIS Analysis of Russian Proposal: Ask Iran to Come Clean on Nuclear Weaponization Before Removing Sanctions', Report, 4 August 2011

International Centre for Transitional Justice, New York and Human Rights Centre, University of California at Berkeley, 'Forgotten Voices: A Population-Based Survey of Attitudes about Peace and Justice in Northern Uganda', July 2005, www.ictj.org/images/content/1/2/127.pdf

Jain, N., 'A Separate Law for Peacekeepers: The Clash between the Security Council and the International Criminal Court' (2005) 16 *European Journal of International Law* 239

Jenks, C. W., 'The Conflict of Law-Making Treaties' (1953) 30 *British Yearbook of International Law* 401

Jennings, R. Y., 'The Progressive Development of International Law and its Codification' (1947) 24 *British Yearbook of International Law* 301

Johns, F., *Non-Legality in International Law: Unruly Law* (Cambridge University Press 2013)

Johnson, R., 'Politics and Protection: Why the 2005 NPT Review Conference Failed', ACRONYM Institute for Disarmament Diplomacy, 1 November 2005, www.acronym.org.uk/dd/dd80/80npt.htm

Jolls, C., *et al.*, *'A Behavioural Approach to Law and Economics'*, in C. Sunstein (ed.), *Behavioural Law and Economics* (Cambridge University Press 2000) 13

Joyner, C., *International Law in the 21st Century: Rules for Global Governance* (Lanham, MD, Rowman and Littlefield 2005)

Joyner, D., *International Law and the Proliferation of Weapons of Mass Destruction* (Oxford University Press 2009)

Interpreting the Nuclear Non-Proliferation Treaty (Oxford University Press 2011)

Jütersonke, O., *Morgenthau, Law and Realism* (Cambridge University Press 2010)

Kan, S., and Holt, M., 'USA–China Nuclear Cooperation Agreement', Report for Congress by the US Congressional Research Service, 15 December 2005, www.au.af.mil/au/awc/awcgate/crs/rl33192.pdf

Karat, P., *'Betrayal on Iran: Costs of India–US Partnership'*, in *Subordinate Ally: The Nuclear Deal and India–US Strategic Relations* (New Delhi, Leftword Books 2007) 46

Karl, W., 'Conflicts between Treaties', in R. Bernhardt (ed.), *Encyclopedia of Public International Law*, Vol. VII (1984) 468

Kaul, H.-P., and Kress, C., 'Jurisdiction and Cooperation in the Statute of the International Criminal Court: Principles and Compromises' (1999) 2 *Yearbook of International Humanitarian Law* 143

Kavulla, T., 'A Dangerous Grandstand Play', *National Review Online*, 3 March 2009

Kelsen, H., *Pure Theory of Law* (M. Knight (trans.), University of California Press 1967)

Kennedy, D., *Of War and Law* (Princeton University Press 2006)

'Tom Franck and the Manhattan School' (2003) 35 *NYU Journal of International Law and Politics* 397

'Lawyers and Warfare', in J. Crawford and M. Koskenniemi (eds.), *The Cambridge Companion to International Law* (Cambridge University Press 2012) 158

Keohane, R., and Martin, L., 'The Promise of Institutionalist Theory' (1995) 20 *International Security* 39
Keohane, R., and Nye, J., 'Transgovernmental Relations and International Organizations' (1974) 27 *World Politics* 39
Kimball, D. G., 'The US–Indian Nuclear Deal: Round II', *News in Review*, No. 4, 3 May 2007, www.reachingcriticalwill.org/legal/NPT/NIR2007/day4.pdf
Kimball, D. G. and F. McGoldrick, 'US–Indian Nuclear Agreement: A Bad Deal Gets Worse', Background Memo, Arms Control Association, 3 August 2007, www.armscontrol.org/pressroom/2007/20070803_IndiaUS
Kimball, D. G., *et al.*, 'An Open Letter to Mohammed ElBaradei from Twelve Nuclear Experts', 24 July 2006, www.armscontrol.org/pdf/20060724_Ltr_ElBaradei_India.pdf
Kimball, L., 'Introductory Note on the Midnight Agreement' (1987) 26 ILM 1502
Kingsbury, B., '*International Law as Inter-Public Law*', in Henry Richardson and Melissa Williams (eds.), *Nomos XLIX: Moral Universalism and Pluralism* (New York University Press 2009) 167
'The Concept of Compliance as a Function of Competing Conceptions of International Law' (1998) 19 *Michigan Journal of International Law* 345
Kingsbury, B., and Donaldson, M., 'From Bilateralism to Publicness in International Law', NYU IILJ Public Law and Legal Theory Research Paper, No. 11–07 (January 2011) 79
Kingsbury, B., *et al.*, 'The Emergence of Global Administrative Law' (2005) 68 *Law and Contemporary Problems* 15
Klabbers, J., *Treaty Conflicts and the European Union* (Cambridge University Press 2009)
Kleffner, J., '*Auto-Referrals and the Complementary Nature of the ICC*', in C. Stahn and G. Sluiter (eds.), *The Emerging Practice of the International Criminal Court* (Leiden, Martinus Nijhoff 2009) 41–53
Klein, N., *Dispute Settlement in the International Law of the Sea* (Cambridge University Press 2005)
Koh, H., 'Bringing International Law Home: The Frankel Lecture' (1998) 35 *Houston Law Review* 623
'Review Essay: Why Do Nations Obey International Law?' (1997) 106 *Yale Law Journal* 2599
'Transnational Legal Process' (1996) 75 *Nebraska Law Review* 181
Koller, D., Legal Officer, Appeals Division, ICC, Personal Interview, 6 April 2010 (on file)
Koskenniemi, M., *From Apology to Utopia: The Structure of International Legal Argument* (reissue with new epilogue, Cambridge University Press 2005)
'International Law: Constitutionalism, Managerialism and the Ethos of Legal Education' (2007) 1 *European Journal of Legal Studies* 1
'Letter to the Editors of the Symposium', Symposium on Method in International Law (1999) 93 *American Journal of International Law* 351
'The Fate of Public International Law: Between Technique and Politics' (2007) 70 *Modern Law Review* 1

'The Function of Law in the International Community: 75 Years After' (2008) 79 *British Yearbook of International Law* 353

The Gentle Civilizer of Nations: The Rise and Fall of International Law 1870–1960 (Cambridge University Press 2001)

'The Lauterpacht Tradition and Its Successors: Towards Theory?', in J. Crawford and M. Young (eds.), *The Function of Law in the International Community: An Anniversary Symposium* (2008), Proceedings of the 25th Anniversary Conference of the Lauterpacht Centre for International Law, http://moot.law.cam.ac.uk/Media/25_anniversary/Lauterpacht_Tradition_paper.pdf

'The Politics of International Law – 20 Years Later' (2009) 20 *European Journal of International Law* 7

Koskenniemi, M., and Lehto, M., 'The Privilege of Universality: International Law, Economic Ideology and Seabed Resources' (1996) *Nordic Journal of International Law* 533

Koskenniemi, M., and Leino, P., 'Fragmentation of International Law? Postmodern Anxieties' (2002) 15 *Leiden Journal of International Law* 553

Kratochwil, F., *Rules, Norms and Decisions: On the Concept of Practical and Legal Reasoning in International Relations and Domestic Affairs* (Cambridge University Press 1999)

Krepon, M., 'The US–India 123 Agreement: From Bad to Worse', *Spotlight*, Stimson Center, 23 August 2007

Krisch, N., 'International Law in Times of Hegemony' (2004) 16 *European Journal of International Law* 369

'The Pluralism of Global Administrative Law' (2006) 17 *European Journal of International Law* 247

Kronmiller, T. G., *The Lawfulness of Deep Seabed Mining*, Vol. I (London, Oceana Publications 1980)

Kux, D., *India and the United States: Estranged Democracies 1941–1991* (Washington DC, National Defense University Press 1993)

Lamm, V., *The Utilization of Nuclear Energy and International Law* (Budapest, Akadémiai Kiadó 1984)

Lange, F., 'Conference Report – The Intellectual History of International Law as a Research Field – "Lauterpacht and Beyond: Jewish/German Authorship and the History of International Law"' (2012) 13(6) *German Law Journal* 793

Lauterpacht, H., 'Codification and Development of International Law' (1955) 49 *American Journal of International Law* 16

'The Covenant as Higher Law' (1936) 17 *British Yearbook of International Law* 54

The Function of Law in the International Community (Oxford University Press 2011 [1933])

'*The International Community and the Universality of International Law*', in E. Lauterpacht (ed.), *International Law: Being the Collected Papers of Hersch Lauterpacht*, Vol.1 (Cambridge University Press 1970)

'The Oscar Chinn Case' (1935) 16 *British Yearbook of International Law* 164

Lee, R., *Law and Regulation of Commercial Mining of Minerals in Outer Space* (London, Springer 2012)

Left Stand on the Nuclear Deal: Notes Exchanged in the UPA–Left Committee on India–US Civil Nuclear Cooperation (New Delhi, Hari Singh Kang 2008)

Leonard, E., ICC Observers Interview, 14 April 2009, http://iccobservers.files.wordpress.com/2009/04/leonard_interview_official.pdf

Levitt, P., and Merry, S. E., 'Vernacularization on the Ground: Local Uses of Global Women's Rights in Peru, China, India and the United States' (2009) 9(4) *Global Networks* 441–61

Lindroos, A., 'Conflicts in a Fragmented Legal System: The Doctrine of Lex Specialis' (2005) 74 *Nordic Journal of International Law* 30

Malone, J., 'The United States and the Law of the Sea after UNCLOS III' (1983) 46(2) *Law and Contemporary Problems* 29

Markey, E. J., 'US–India Nuclear Deal', Federation of American Scientists Press Event, 18 October 2007

Marks, S., 'Naming Global Administrative Law' (2005) 37 *NYU Journal of International Law and Politics* 995

McNair, A. D., *Law of Treaties* (Oxford, Clarendon Press 1961)

Miéville, C., *Between Equal Rights: A Marxist Theory of International Law* (Leiden and Boston, Brill 2005)

Mnookin, R. M., and Kornhauser, L., 'Bargaining in the Shadow of the Law: The Case of Divorce' (1987) 88 *Yale Law Journal* 950

Mochochoko, P., '*International Cooperation and Judicial Assistance*', in Roy S. Lee (ed.), *The International Criminal Court: The Making of the Rome Statute* (The Hague, Kluwer 1999) 305

Moravcsik, A., 'Taking Preferences Seriously: A Liberal Theory of International Politics' (1997) 51 *International Organization* 513

Morell, J., *The Law of the Sea: The 1982 Treaty and its Rejection by the United States* (Jefferson, NC, McFarland 1992)

Morgenthau, H., 'Positivism, Functionalism and International Law' (1940) 34 *American Journal of International Law* 260

Mus, J., 'Conflicts between Treaties in International Law' (1998) 15 *Netherlands International Law Review* 214

Nesi, G., '*The Obligation to Cooperate with the International Criminal Court and States Not Party to the Statute*', in M. Politi and G. Nesi (eds.) *The Rome Statute of the International Criminal Court: A Challenge to Impunity* (Aldershot, Ashgate 2001) 221

Netherlands Advisory Council on International Affairs, 'The Nuclear Non-Proliferation Regime: The Importance of an Integrated and Multilateral Approach', No. 47, January 2006

Nouwen, S., *Complementarity in the Line of Fire: The Catalysing Effect of the International Criminal Court in Uganda and Sudan* (Cambridge University Press 2013)

Nouwen, S., and Werner, W., 'Doing Justice to the Political: The International Criminal Court in Uganda and Sudan' (2011) 21 *European Journal of International Law* 941

Noyes, J., 'US Policy and the UN Convention on the Law of the Sea' (2007) 39 *George Washington International Law Review* 621

Nuclear Threat Initiative, 'Country profiles - Iran - Nuclear', www.nti.org/country-profiles/iran/nuclear (last updated June 2013)

Ohlin, J. D., '*Peace, Security and Prosecutorial Discretion*', in C. Stahn and G. Sluiter (eds.), *The Emerging Practice of the International Criminal Court* (Leiden, Martinus Nijhoff 2009) 185

Okafor, O., 'Newness, Imperialism, and International Legal Reform in Our Time: A TWAIL Perspective' (2005) 43 *Osgoode Hall Law Journal* 171

Okowa, P., 'Case Concerning the Gabcikovo-Nagymaros Project (Hungary/Slovakia) (Unreported, 1997) (ICJ)' (1998) 47 (3) *International and Comparative Law Quarterly* 688

Onuf, N., '*Constructivism: A User's Manual*', in V. Kubálková *et al.* (eds.), *International Relations in a Constructed World* (New York, M. E. Sharpe 1998)

'The Constitution of International Society' (1994) 5 *European Journal of International Law* 1

World of Our Making: Rules and Rule in Social Theory and International Relations (University of South Carolina Press 1989)

Osiel, M., '*When Law Expresses More Than It Cares to Admit*', in C. Stahn and L. van den Herik (eds.), *Future Perspectives on International Criminal Justice* (The Hague, TMC Asser Press 2010) 254

Oxman, B. H., 'The Third United Nations Conference on the Law of the Sea, The Tenth Session (1981)' (1982) 76 *American Journal of International Law* 1

Pahuja, S., '*Conserving the world's resources?*', in J. Crawford and M. Koskenniemi (eds.), *The Cambridge Companion to International Law* (Cambridge University Press 2012) 398

Pal, S., Legal Advisor, Coalition for the International Criminal Court, Personal Interview, 14 April 2010 (on file)

Pardo, A., 'Before and After' (1983) 46 *Law and Contemporary Problems* 95

Pauwelyn, J., *Conflict of Norms in Public International Law: How WTO Law Relates to Other Rules of International Law* (Cambridge University Press 2003)

Perelman, C., and Olbrechts-Tyteca, L., *The New Rhetoric: A Treatise on Argumentation* (University of Notre Dame Press 1968)

Perkovich, G., *India's Nuclear Bomb: The Impact on Global Proliferation* (University of California Press 1999)

Pogge, T., '*From Modus Vivendi to Value Overlap*', in *Realizing Rawls* (Cornell University Press 1989) 218

Prost, K., and Schlunk, A., '*Article 98*', in O. Triffterer (ed.), *Commentary on the Rome Statute of the International Criminal Court - Observers' Notes Article by Article* (Baden-Baden, Nomos Verlagsgesellschaft 1999) 1131

Rajagopal, B., 'Martti Koskenniemi's From Apology to Utopia: A Reflection' (2006) 7(12) *German Law Journal* 1089

Rajamohan, C., *Impossible Allies: Nuclear India, United States and Global Order* (New Delhi, India Research Press 2006)

Ramana, M. V., and Raju, S., 'The Impasse over Liability Clause in the Indo-US Nuclear Deal', India Ink (*New York Times* blog), 15 October 2013

Ranganathan, S., 'Between Philosophy and Anxiety? The Early International Law Commission, Treaty Conflict and the Project of International Law' (2012) 83 *British Yearbook of International Law* 82

'Book Review of D. Joyner, Interpreting the Nuclear Non-Proliferation Treaty' (2011) 82 *British Yearbook of International Law* 532

'Responding to Deliberately-Created Treaty Conflicts', in C. Tams *et al.* (eds.), *Research Handbook on the Law of Treaties* (Cheltenham, Edward Elgar 2014) Chapter 15

'The Value of Narratives: The India–USA Nuclear Deal in terms of Fragmentation, Pluralism, Constitutionalisation and Global Administrative Law' (2012) 6(1) *Erasmus Law Review* 16

'Visions of International Law: Lessons from the 123 Agreement', Special Issue on India, the 123 Agreement, and Nuclear Energy: Issues of International Law (2011) 51 (2) *Indian Journal of International Law* 146

Rastan, R., '*The Emerging Jurisprudence of the International Criminal Court – Legal Issues Arising from the First Case-law*', in L. Yan (ed.), *Making Peace Through Justice: Essays on the New Development of International Criminal Law* (Beijing, World Affairs Press 2009)

'*The Responsibility to Enforce: Connecting Justice with Unity*', in C. Stahn and G. Sluiter (eds.), *The Emerging Practice of the International Criminal Court* (Leiden, Martinus Nijhoff 2009) 163

'What Is a Case for the Purpose of the Rome Statute' (2008) 19 *Criminal Law Forum* 435

Raustiala, K., 'Refining the Limits of International Law' (2006) 34 *Georgia Journal of International and Comparative Law* 423

Rawls, J., 'The Idea of Overlapping Consensus' (1987) 7(1) *Oxford Journal of Legal Studies* 1

Reichert-Facilides, D., 'Down the Danube: The Vienna Convention on the Law of Treaties and the Case Concerning the Gabcikovo–Nagymaros Project' (1998) 47(4) *International and Comparative Law Quarterly* 837

Rennack, D., 'India and Pakistan: Current US Economic Sanctions', Report for Congress by the US Congressional Research Service, 12 October 2001, http://fpc.state.gov/documents/organization/6202.pdf

'Report of the International Commission of Inquiry on Darfur', 25 January 2005, www.un.org/news/dh/sudan/com_inq_darfur.pdf

Rice, C., *No Higher Honour: A Memoir of My Years in Washington* (London, Simon & Schuster 2011)

Riddell-Dixon, E., 'Individual Leadership and Structural Power' (1997) 30 *Canadian Journal of Political Science* 257

Rieff, D., *A Bed for the Night: Humanitarianism in Crisis* (London, Vintage 2002) 15

Risse, T., 'Let's Argue!: Communicative Action in World Politics' (2000) 54 *International Organization* 1

Rosenne, S., *Breach of Treaty* (Cambridge, Grotius 1985)

'The International Law Commission, 1949–59' (1960) 36 *British Yearbook of International Law* 104

Rousseau, C., 'De la compatibilité des normes juridiques contradictoires dans l'ordre international' (1932) 39 *Revue Générale de Droit International Public* 153
Ruggie, J. G., 'What Makes the World Hang Together? Neo-Utilitarianism and the Social Constructivist Challenge' (1998) 52 *International Organization* 855
Sadat-Akhavi, S. A., *Methods of Resolving Conflict between Treaties* (Leiden, Martinus Nijhoff 2003)
Safrin, S., 'Treaties in Collision? The Biosafety Protocol and the World Trade Organization' (2002) 56 *American Journal of International Law* 606
Sands, P., *Lawless World: America and the Making and Breaking of Global Rules* (London, Penguin 2005)
Sanger, C., *Ordering the Oceans: The Making of the Law of the Sea* (University of Toronto Press 1987)
Schabas, W., *An Introduction to the International Criminal Court* (3rd edn, Cambridge University Press 2007)
ICC Observers Interview, 26 March 2009, http://iccobservers.files.wordpress.com/2009/03/schabas_interview_official.pdf
'*Prosecutorial Discretion and Gravity*', in C. Stahn and G. Sluiter (eds.), *The Emerging Practice of the International Criminal Court* (Leiden, Martinus Nijhoff 2009) 229
Scheffer, D., 'Staying the Course with the International Criminal Court' (2001) 35 *Cornell International Law Journal* 47
Schimdt, M. G., *Common Heritage or Common Burden* (Oxford, Clarendon Press 1989)
Scobbie, I., 'Tom Franck's Fairness' (2002) 13 *European Journal of International Law* 909
Setala, M., 'Rhetoric and Deliberative Democracy', *Redescriptions: Yearbook of Political Thought, Conceptual History and Feminist Theory* (2009) 61
Setear, J., 'An Iterative Perspective on Treaties: A Synthesis of International Relations Theory and International Law' (1996) 37 *Harvard International Law Journal* 139
Sethi, M., Centre for Air Power Studies, Personal Interview, 2 December 2009
Shaker, M., *The Nuclear Non-Proliferation Treaty: Origin and Implementation 1959–1979* (London, Oceana Publications 1980)
Sinclair, A., *International Relations Theory and International Law: A Critical Approach* (Cambridge University Press 2010)
Sinclair, I., *The Vienna Convention on the Law of Treaties* (Manchester University Press 1984)
Singh, J., *A Call to Honour: In Service of Emergent India* (New Delhi, Rupa 2006)
Slaughter, A.-M., *A New World Order* (Princeton University Press 2004)
'Sovereignty and Power in a Networked World Order' (2004) 40 *Stanford Journal of International Law* 283
Sohn, L. B., 'International Law Implications of the 1994 Agreement' (1994) 88 *American Journal of International Law* 696
Sokolski, H., 'Towards an NPT-Restrained World That Makes Economic Sense' (2007) 83(3) *International Affairs* 531

Squassoni, S., 'India's Nuclear Separation Plan: Issues and Views', CRS Report for Congress, 22 December 2006

Stone, J., 'On the Vocation of the International Law Commission' (1957) 57 *Columbia Law Review* 16

Stuart, H. V., 'The ICC in Trouble' (2008) 6 *Journal of International Criminal Justice* 409

Sunstein, C., *Infotopia* (Oxford University Press 2006)

Swart, B., '*International Cooperation and Judicial Assistance: General Problems*', in A. Cassese *et al.* (eds.), *The Rome Statute of the International Criminal Court: A Commentary* (Oxford University Press 2002) 1589

Talbott, S., *Engaging India: Diplomacy, Democracy and the Bomb* (Washington DC, Brookings Institution Press 2006)

Tarlo, E., *Unsettling Memories: Narratives of the Emergency in Delhi* (University of California Press 2003)

'*The Function of Law in the International Community: Opening Plenary Session*', in J. Crawford and M. Young (eds.), *The Function of Law in the International Community: An Anniversary Symposium* (2008), Proceedings of the 25th Anniversary Conference of the Lauterpacht Centre for International Law, http://moot.law.cam.ac.uk/Media/25_anniversary/Opening_Plenary_discussion.pdf

Thompson, E. P., *Whigs and Hunters: The Origin of the Black Act* (London, Allen Lane 1975)

Treves, T., '*The Agreement Completing the UN Law of the Sea Convention: Formal and Procedural Aspects*', in M. H. Nordquist and J. N. Moore (eds.), *Entry into Force of the Law of the Sea Convention: Rhodes Papers* (Leiden, Martinus Nijhoff 1994) 99

'*The Role of Universal International Organizations in Implementing the 1982 UN Law of the Sea Convention*', in A. H. A. Soons (ed.), *Implementation of the Law of the Sea Convention through International Institutions* (Honolulu, The Law of the Sea Institute 1989)

Tyagi, Y., Jawaharlal Nehru University, New Delhi, Personal Interview, November 16–17, 2009 (on file)

Tzanakopoulos, A., 'Legality of Veto to NATO Accession: The ICJ's Decision in the Dispute between FYR Macedonia and Greece', *European Journal of International Law: Talk!*, 7 December 2011

United States Ambassador at Large for War Crimes Issues (C. Williamson), Remarks at the Century Foundation on 'Reassessing the International Criminal Court: Ten Years Past', Rome, 13 January 2009

United States Ambassador at Large for War Crimes Issues (S. J. Rapp), 'Where Can the Victims of Atrocities Find Justice?', Remarks, Forum Hosted by the Women of Ateneo, Makati, Philippines, 10 May 2011

United States Department of State Legal Advisor (H. Koh), Keynote Address, ASIL Annual Meeting, Washington DC, 25 March 2010, www.state.gov/s/l/releases/remarks/139119.htm

Valle, H., '*Adjustments to Part XI: United Nations Efforts (The Negotiation Process)*', in M. H. Nordquist and J. N. Moore (eds.), *Entry into Force of the Law of the Sea Convention: Rhodes Papers* (Leiden, Martinus Nijhoff 1994) 47

van Aaken, A., 'To Do Away with International Law? Some Limits to "The Limits of International Law"' (2006) 17 *European Journal of International Law* 289
van Ham, P., *Managing Non-Proliferation Regimes in the 1990s: Power, Politics and Policies* (London, Pinter 1993)
Varadarajan, S., Editor, *The Hindu*, Personal Interview, 9 December 2009 (on file)
Waldock, H., 'General Course on Public International Law' (1962) 106[II] *Recueil des Cours* 5
Walker, W., 'Nuclear Enlightenment and Counter Enlightenment' (2007) 83(3) *International Affairs* 431
Weil, P., 'Non Liquet Revisited' (1998) 36 *Columbia Journal of Transnational Law* 109
Wendt, A., *Social Theory of International Politics* (Cambridge University Press 1998)
White, P., 'US–India Nuclear Agreement: Bad for Nuclear Nonproliferation, Bad for Nuclear Disarmament', *News in Review*, No. 3, 30 April 2008, www.reachingcriticalwill.org/legal/NPT/NIR2008/No.3.pdf
Wisconsin Project on Nuclear Arms Control, 'India Nuclear Milestones: 1945–2009' (2010) 16(1) *The Risk Report*, www.wisconsinproject.org/countries/india/india-nuclear-miles.html
Wolfrum, R., and Matz, N., *Conflicts in International Environmental Law* (London, Springer 2003)
Women's Rights and Human Rights NGOs from the DRC, 'Statement on the Prosecutions by the International Criminal Court', Beni, 16 September 2006, www.iccwomen.org/publications/resources/docs/statements_by_womans_rights_human_rights_ngos.pdf
Wright, Q., 'Conflicts between International Law and Treaties' (1917) 11 *American Journal of International Law* 566
Young, M., '*Regime Interaction in Creating, Implementing and Enforcing International Law*', in Margaret Young (ed.), *Regime Interaction in International Law: Facing Fragmentation* (Cambridge University Press 2012)
Trading Fish, Saving Fish: The Interaction between Regimes in International Law (Cambridge University Press 2011)
Zuleeg, M., 'Vertragskonkurrenz in Völkerrecht. Teil I: Verträge zwischen souveränen Staaten' (1977) 20 *German Yearbook of International Law* 246

DOCUMENTS OF INTERNATIONAL CONFERENCES

Vienna Conference on the Law of Treaties

Summary Record of the 31st Mtg of the Committee of the Whole, A/CONF.39/C.1/SR.31 (19 April 1968)
Summary Record of the 85th Mtg of the Committee of the Whole, A/CONF.39/C.1/SR.85 (10 April 1969)
Summary Record of the 91st Mtg of the Committee of the Whole, A/CONF.39/C.1/SR.91 (19 April 1969)
Summary Record of the 13th Mtg of the Plenary, A/CONF.39/SR.13 (6 May 1969)

Third United Nations Conference on the Law of the Sea

Second Session, Caracas, 19th Plenary Meeting, A/Conf.62/SR.19, 27 June 1974
Letter from the Representative of Sierra Leone to the President of UNCLOS III, A/Conf.62/L.146, 29 April 1982

Eighteen Nation Committee on Disarmament Conference

Statement of the Swedish Representative, ENDC/PV. 333, 26 September 1967
Statement of the Indian Representative, ENDC/PV. 334, 28 September 1967
Statement of the United Arab Republic Representative, ENDC/PV. 340, 19 October 1967
Statement of the US Representative, ENDC/PV. 369, 22 February 1968

NPT Review Conferences

Final Declaration, 'Review of Article V', NPT Review Conference 1975, NPT/Conf/35/I Annex 1
Decision 2, 'Principles and Objectives for Nuclear Non-Proliferation and Disarmament', NPT Review and Extension Conference 1995, NPT/CONF.1995/32 (Part I) Annex
Decision 3, 'Extension of the Treaty on the Non-Proliferation of Nuclear Weapons', NPT Review and Extension Conference 1995, NPT/CONF.1995/32 (Part I) Annex
Final Document, NPT Review Conference 2000, NPT/CONF.2000/28 (Parts I and II)
'Promoting Expanded and Responsible Peaceful Uses of Nuclear Energy', Working paper submitted by the United States to the Preparatory Committee for the 2010 Review Conference of the Parties to the Treaty on the Non-Proliferation of Nuclear Weapons, NPT/CONF.2010/PC.I/WP.23, 3 May 2007
Summary Record of 3rd Mtg, NPT Preparatory Committee for the 2010 Review Conference, New York, 4–15 May 2009, NPT/CONF.2010/PC.III/SR.3, 11 June 2009
Final Document, NPT Review Conference 2010, NPT/CONF.2010/50 (Vol. I)*

DOCUMENTS OF INTERNATIONAL ORGANISATIONS

UN General Assembly resolutions

UNGA Res. 749A (28 November 1953), 'Question of South West Africa'
UNGA Res. 2028 (19 November 1965), 'Non-proliferation of Nuclear Weapons'
UNGA Res. 2166 (XXI) (5 December 1966), 'International Conference of Plenipotentiaries on the Law of Treaties'
UNGA Res. 2287 (XXII) (6 December 1967), 'United Nations Conference on the Law of Treaties'
UNGA Res. 22/2340 (18 December 1967), 'Examination of the Question of the Reservation Exclusively for Peaceful Purposes of the Seabed and the Ocean

Floor, and the Subsoil Thereof, Underlying the High Seas Beyond the Limits of Present National Jurisdiction, and the Use of Their Resources in the Interests of Mankind'

UNGA Res. 2373 (12 June 1968), 'Treaty on the Non-Proliferation of Nuclear Weapons'

UNGA Res. 23/2467 (21 December 1968), 'Examination of the Question of the Reservation Exclusively for Peaceful Purposes of the Seabed and the Ocean Floor, and the Subsoil Thereof, Underlying the High Seas Beyond the Limits of Present National Jurisdiction, and the Use of Their Resources in the Interests of Mankind'

UNGA Res. 24/2574 (15 December 1969), 'Moratorium Resolution'

UNGA Res. 25/2749 (17 December 1970), 'Declaration of Principles Governing the Seabed and the Ocean Floor, and the Subsoil Thereof, Beyond the Limits of National Jurisdiction'

UNGA Res. S-6/3201 (1 May 1974), 'Declaration on the Establishment of a New International Economic Order'

UNGA Res. S-6/3202 (1 May 1974), 'Programme of Action on the Establishment of a New International Economic Order'

UNGA Res. 29/3281 (12 December 1974), 'Charter on Economic Rights and Duties of States'

UNGA Res. 43/18 (1 November 1988), 'Law of the Sea'

UNGA Res. 44/26 (20 November 1989), 'Law of the Sea'

UNGA Res. 56/83, 'Articles on the Responsibility of States for Internationally Wrongful Acts (2001), 12 December 2001, Annex and A/56/49(Vol. I)/Corr.4'

UN Security Council resolutions

UNSC Res. 255 (19 June 1968), 'Question Relating to the Measures to Safeguard Non-Nuclear Weapons States Parties to the Treaty on the Non-Proliferation of Nuclear Weapons'

UNSC Res. 1172 (6 June 1998), 'International Peace and Security'

UNSC Res. 1422 (12 July 2002), 'United Nations Peacekeeping'

UNSC Res. 1487 (12 June 2003), 'United Nations Peacekeeping'

UNSC Res. 1564 (18 September 2004), 'Report of the Secretary-General on the Sudan'

UNSC Res. 1593 (31 March 2005), 'Reports of the Secretary-General on the Sudan'

UNSC Res. 1696 (31 July 2006), 'Non-Proliferation'

UNSC Res. 1718 (14 October 2006), 'Non-Proliferation/Democratic People's Republic of Korea'

UNSC Res. 1737 (27 December 2006), 'Non-Proliferation'

UNSC Res. 1747 (24 March 2007), 'Non-Proliferation'

UNSC Res. 1803 (3 March 2008), 'Non-Proliferation'

UNSC Res. 1828 (31 July 2008), 'Reports of the Secretary-General on the Sudan'

UNSC Res. 1874 (12 June 2009), 'Non-Proliferation/Democratic People's Republic of Korea'
UNSC Res. 1929 (9 June 2010), 'Non-Proliferation'
UNSC Res. 1970 (26 February 2011), 'Peace and Security in Africa'
UNSC Res. 2094 (7 March 2013), 'Non-Proliferation/Democratic People's Republic of Korea'

Records of UN meetings

UNGA Provisional Verbatim Record, UNGA 44th Sess., 61st Mtg (November 20), A/44/PV.61, 28 November 1989
UNGA Provisional Verbatim Record, UNGA 44th Sess., 62nd Mtg (November 20), A/44/PV.61, 1 December 1989
UNSC Provisional Verbatim Record, UNSC 5789th Mtg, S/PV.5789, 5 December 2007
UNSC Provisional Verbatim Record, UNSC 6491st Mtg, S/PV.6491, 26 February 2011
Maltese Ambassador (A Pardo), Address to the General Assembly, UN GAOR 22nd Sess., First Committee, 1515th and 1516th meetings, General Debate, 1 November 1967, UN Doc. A/C.1/PV. 1515 and A/C.1/PV. 1516 (1967)
Malta Note Verbale of 17/8/1967 to UN Secretary General, UN GAOR, 22nd Sess., UN Doc. A/6695 (1967)
UN Press Release SC/8351, 31 March 2005, 'Security Council Refers Situation in Darfur, Sudan, to Prosecutor'
UN Press Release SC/9412, 31 July 2008, 'Security Council Decides to Extend Mandate of African Union–United Nations'
United States Explanation of Vote on Security Council Resolution 1593, 31 March 2005, www.iccnow.org/documents/US.Statement.SCreferralDarfurICC_31March05.pdf
United States Permanent Representative to the United Nations (S. Rice), Statement in the Security Council, 29 January 2009, http://usun.state.gov/briefing/statements/2009/january/127018.htm

European Union

EU Guiding Principles Concerning Arrangements between a State Party to the Rome Statute and the United States Regarding the Conditions to Surrender of Persons to the Court, 2002
EU Presidency, Declaration by the EU on the Position of the US Towards the International Criminal Court, 13 May 2002, www.amicc.org/docs/EUdec5_13_02.pdf
European Council Conclusions on the International Criminal Court, 30 September 2002, www.consilium.europa.eu/uedocs/cmsUpload/ICC34EN.pdf

African Union

'Decision on the Meeting of African States parties to the Rome Statute', African Union Press Release, Addis Ababa, 14 July 2009

International Atomic Energy Agency

'Conclusion of Additional Protocols: Status as of 15 July 2013', www.iaea.org/safeguards/documents/AP_status_list.pdf

'Director General and Iranian Officials Discuss Enrichment Plant Visit', IAEA Staff Report, 5 October 2009

'IAEA Board Approves India-Specific Safeguards Agreement', 1 August 2008, www.iaea.org/newscenter/news/2008/board010808.html

'IAEA Director General Welcomes US and India Nuclear Deal', IAEA Press Release 2006/05, 2 March 2006, www.iaea.org/NewsCenter/PressReleases/2006/prn200605.html

'Implementation of the India–United States Joint Statement of 18 July 2005: India's Separation Plan', INFCIRC/731, 25 July 2008

'Implementation of the NPT Safeguards Agreement and Relevant provisions of Security Council resolutions in the Islamic Republic of Iran', Report by the IAEA Director General, GOV/2013/27, 22 May 2013

'Implementation of the NPT Safeguards Agreement in the Islamic Republic of Iran', Report by the Director General, GOV/2006/15, 27 February 2006

'Implementation of the NPT Safeguards Agreement in the Islamic Republic of Iran', Resolution adopted by the Board of Governors, GOV/2006/14, 4 February 2006

'Information Circulars', www.iaea.org/Publications/Documents/Infcircs/index.html

'Introductory Statement to the Board of Governors', Director-General (Dr Mohamed ElBaradei), Vienna, 1 August 2008

'Latest Status of Safeguards Agreements and Additional Protocols' (as of 6 October 2009) www.iaea.org/OurWork/SV/Safeguards/sir_table.pdf

'Safeguards Factsheet', www.iaea.org/Publications/Factsheets/English/S1_Safeguards.pdf

'The Agency's Safeguards System (1965, as Provisionally Extended in 1966 and 1968)', INFCIRC/66/Rev.2, 1968

'The Safeguards System of the International Atomic Energy Agency', www.iaea.org/safeguards/documents/safeg_system.pdf

'The Structure and Content of Agreements between the Agency and States Required in Connection with the Treaty on the Non-Proliferation of Nuclear Weapons', INFCIRC/153 (corr.), 1972

'Transcript of IAEA Director General's Remarks at Joint Press Conference with Atomic Energy Organization of Iran', 4 October 2009, www.iaea.org/NewsCenter/Transcripts/2009/transcript051009.pdf

International Criminal Court

'Aimé Kilolo Musamba, Fidèle Babala Wandu, and Jean-Pierre Bemba Gombo Make First Appearance before ICC', ICC Press Release, ICC-CPI-20131127-PR966, 27 November 2013, www.icc-cpi.int/en_menus/icc/press%20and%20media/press%20releases/Pages/966.aspx

Deputy Prosecutor (F. Bensouda), 'Africa's Involvement with the ICC', International Bar Association, 14 April 2009, www.icc-cpi.int/NR/rdonlyres/214816FF-DD8F-4908-97CF-B315C33F24FE/280279/20090414FatouRome Statute.pdf

Informal Experts, 'The Principle of Complementarity in Practice', 2003, www.icc-cpi.int/iccdocs/doc/doc654724.PDF

'Jean-Jacques Mangenda Kabongo Makes First Appearance before ICC', ICC Press Release, ICC-CPI-20131205-PR969, 5 December 2013, www.icc-cpi.int/en_menus/icc/press%20and%20media/press%20releases/Pages/pr969.aspx

Office of the Prosecutor, Paper on Some Policy Issues September 2003, www.icc-cpi.int/NR/rdonlyres/1FA7C4C6-DE5F-42B7-8B25-60AA962ED8B6/143594/030905_Policy_Paper.pdf

Office of the Prosecutor, Policy Paper on the Interests of Justice, September 2007, www.icc-cpi.int/NR/rdonlyres/772C95C9-F54D-4321-BF09-73422BB23528/143640/ICCOTPInterestsOfJustice.pdf

Office of the Prosecutor, Report on Preliminary Examination Activities 2013, November 2013, http://www.icc-cpi.int/en_menus/icc/press%20and%20media/press%20releases/Documents/OTP%20Preliminary%20Examinations/OTP%20-%20Report%20%20Preliminary%20Examination%20Activities%202013.PDF

Office of the Prosecutor, Report on Prosecutorial Strategy for 2006–2009, 14 September 2006, www.icc-cpi.int/NR/rdonlyres/D673DD8C-D427-4547-BC69-2D363E07274B/143708/ProsecutorialStrategy20060914_English.pdf

Office of the Prosecutor, Report on Prosecutorial Strategy for 2009–2012, 1 February 2010, www.icc-cpi.int/NR/rdonlyres/66A8DCDC-3650-4514-AA62-D229D1128F65/281506/OTPProsecutorialStrategy20092013.pdf

Office of the Prosecutor, Report on the Activities Performed in the First Three Years (June 2003–June 2006), 12 September 2006

Office of the Prosecutor, Response to Communications received Concerning Venezuela, 9 February 2006, www.icc-cpi.int/Menus/ICC/Structure+of+the+Court/Office+of+the+Prosecutor/Comm+and+Ref/Venezuela

Office of the Prosecutor, Response to Communications received Concerning Iraq, 9 February 2006, www.icc-cpi.int/Menus/ICC/Structure+of+the+Court/Office+of+the+Prosecutor/Comm+and+Ref/Iraq

Office of the Prosecutor, Statement on Uganda, The Hague, 4 March 2008, www.icc-cpi.int/NR/rdonlyres/945119F8-7107-4FC1-8026-CD03ECCA5BB1/0/ICCOTPST20080304ENG.pdf

President (P. Kirsch), Address at the Third Session of the ASP, 6 September 2004, www.icc-cpi.int/NR/rdonlyres/E49847E6-B414-4ADB-B8E1-70DC819BE40B/146333/PK_20040906_En.pdf

President (P. Kirsch), Address to the General Assembly, 1 November 2007, www.icc-cpi.int/NR/rdonlyres/B3B8B89D-B9E5-441E-A3D5-EA9E91B22142/277274/PK_20071101_ENG1.pdf

President (P. Kirsch), Address to the General Assembly, 30 October 2008, www.icc-cpi.int/NR/rdonlyres/86BD12FB-F92F-44B3-89D8-DE376A9EB989/279062/PK_20081030_ENG.pdf

President (P. Kirsch), Address to the General Assembly, 8 November 2005, www.icc-cpi.int/NR/rdonlyres/CC2EE876-18C6-4182-8A08-C5155B85802A/146328/PK_20051108_English1.pdf

President (P. Kirsch), 'Applying the Principles of Nuremberg in the ICC', Keynote Address, Washington University, 19 November 2005, www.icc-cpi.int/NR/rdonlyres/ED2F5177-9F9B-4D66-9386-5C5BF45D052C/146323/PK_20060930_English.pdf

President (P. Kirsch), 'From Nuremberg to The Hague', Nuremberg, 19 November 2005, www.icc-cpi.int/NR/rdonlyres/08AB9F8F-53A2-4533-BCE0-887419726332/143894/PK_20051119_En.pdf

President (P. Kirsch), 'ICC Marks Five Years since Entry into Force of Rome Statute', Statement, The Hague, 26 June 2007, www.icc-cpi.int/NR/rdonlyres/C307EC9D-B735-47D6-BA5C-508D0A5D8C71/143884/PK_20070627_en.pdf

President (P. Kirsch), 'Independence in the Context of Interdependence', Frederick K. Cox Lecture in Global Legal Reform, Case Western Reserve University School of Law, Cleveland, 7 November 2005, www.icc-cpi.int/NR/rdonlyres/777C9300-BD47-4EAE-B9A2-8465959772ED/143893/PK_20051107_En.pdf

President (P. Kirsch), 'La Cour pénale internationale au carrefour du droit international et des relations internationals', University of Quebec, Montreal, 6 May 2003, www.icc-cpi.int/iccdocs/presidency/PK_20030506_Fr.pdf

President (P. Kirsch), 'La voie canadienne vers la CPI: tous les chemins mènent à Rome – Les enjeux et défis de la mise en œuvre de la CPI', Colloque organisé par les Journées Maximilien-Caron 2003 et l'Institut canadien d'Administration de la Justice, 5 February 2003, www.icc-cpi.int/en_menus/icc/structure%20of%20the%20court/presidency/statements/Pages/index.aspx

President (P. Kirsch), Opening Remarks at the Fifth Session of the ASP, 23 November 2006, www.icc-cpi.int/NR/rdonlyres/3EEF266E-E4B1-486C-9B05-DD0D87CDBEEB/143883/PK_20061123_en1.pdf

President (P. Kirsch), 'Protecting the Integrity of the International Criminal Court', Strategy Meeting, Parliamentarians for Global Action, United Nations, New York, 22 April 2003, www.icc-cpi.int/en_menus/icc/structure%20of%20the%20court/presidency/statements/Pages/index.aspx

President (P. Kirsch), Statement at the Inaugural Meeting of the Judges, 11 March 2003, www.icc-cpi.int/NR/rdonlyres/48D76A79-7315-49C2-A16F-86D7CFAAE721/143846/PK_20030311_En.pdf

'President of Uganda Refers Situation Concerning the Lord's Resistance Army to the ICC', 29 January 2004, ICC-20040129-44, www.icc-cpi.int/Menus/ICC/Situations+and+Cases/Situations/Situation+ICC+0204

Prosecutor (L. Moreno-Ocampo), Address at the Third Assembly of States Parties, 6 September 2004, www.icc-cpi.int/NR/rdonlyres/1E4656AC-32D9-483D-9D2A-DE74F2FD8415/0/LMO_20040906_En.pdf

Prosecutor (L. Moreno-Ocampo), Address, Council for Foreign Relations, Washington DC, 4 February 2010, www.icc-cpi.int/NR/rdonlyres/A80CDDDD-8A9A-432E-97CE-F6EAD700B5AE/281527/100204Prosecutors speech forCFR.pdf

Prosecutor (L. Moreno-Ocampo), 'Building a Future on Peace and Justice', Address, Nuremberg, 24/25 June 2007, www.icc-cpi.int/NR/rdonlyres/4E466EDB-2B38-4BAF-AF5F-005461711149/143825/LMO_nuremberg_20070625_English.pdf

Prosecutor (L. Moreno-Ocampo), Ceremony for the Solemn Undertaking of the Prosecutor, Statement, The Hague, 16 June 2003, www.icc-cpi.int/NR/rdonlyres/D7572226-264A-4B6B-85E3-2673648B4896/143585/030616_moreno_ocampo_english.pdf

Prosecutor (L. Moreno-Ocampo), 'Combating Genocide and Other Massive Crimes – The International Criminal Court's contribution', Address, The Hague, 7 December 2008, www.icc-cpi.int/NR/rdonlyres/E82DE594-5DB1-4870-BAB7-B8C71D2CCC13/279611/ICCOTPSTLMO20081207ENG.pdf

Prosecutor (L. Moreno-Ocampo), Fifth Report to the Security Council pursuant to UNSC Res. 1593 (2005), 7 June 2007, www.icc-cpi.int/NR/rdonlyres/65732689-4A7B-467E-9821-BF53F11465D0/0/OTP_ReportUNSC5Darfur_English.pdf

Prosecutor (L. Moreno-Ocampo), Fourth Report to the Security Council pursuant to UNSC Res. 1593 (2005), 14 December 2006, www.icc-cpi.int/NR/rdonlyres/8903D205-6272-4498-8E83-258F9C99611A/0/OTP_ReportUNSC4Darfur_English.pdf

Prosecutor (L. Moreno-Ocampo), Keynote Address, Council for Foreign Relations Symposium, New York, 17 October 2008, www.icc-cpi.int/NR/rdonlyres/B8A3B99C-C9CC-4151-8BA6-35C2868BF60F/278840/CFRS2008.pdf

Prosecutor (L. Moreno-Ocampo), Keynote Address, Yale University, New Haven, 6 February 2009, www.icc-cpi.int/NR/rdonlyres/F04CB063-1C1E-463E-B8FB-5ECE076FB1E0/279792/090206_Prosecutorskeynoteaddressin Yale.pdf

Prosecutor (L. Moreno-Ocampo), 'Keynote Address: Integrating the Work of the ICC into Local Justice Initiatives' (2006) 21 *American University International Law Review* 497

Prosecutor (L. Moreno-Ocampo), Remarks at the 27th Meeting of the Committee of Legal Advisers on Public International Law (Cadhi), Strasburg, March 18–19, 2004, www.iccnow.org/documents/ICCProsecutorCADHI18Mar04.pdf

Prosecutor (L. Moreno-Ocampo), Report to the Second Assembly of States Parties, 8 September 2003, www.icc-cpi.int/NR/rdonlyres/C073586C-7D46-4CBE-B901-0672908E8639/143656/LMO_20030908_En.pdf

Prosecutor (L. Moreno-Ocampo), Seventh Report to the Security Council pursuant to UNSC Res. 1593 (2005), 5 June 2008, www.icc-cpi.int/NR/

rdonlyres/D6F9DF4F-FB9D-4323-B945-784ED2332BB3/276869/UNSC_2008_En.pdf
Prosecutor (L. Moreno-Ocampo), Sixth Report to the Security Council pursuant to UNSC Res. 1593 (2005), 5 December 2007, www.icc-cpi.int/NR/rdonlyres/19A83943-DF47-4DC0-9EB1-1A84CF862290/281540/ProsecutorsReportUNSCDec07EN.pdf
Prosecutor (L. Moreno-Ocampo), Speech to the Eighth Session of the Assembly of States Parties, 18 November 2009, www.icc-cpi.int/NR/rdonlyres/CDF496C7-7BA7-4AA3-B670-1EE85BC3E3E8/281268/20091118ASPspeech.pdf
Prosecutor (L. Moreno-Ocampo), Statement at informal meeting of Legal Advisors of Ministries of Foreign Affairs, New York, 24 October 2005, www.icc-cpi.int/NR/rdonlyres/9D70039E-4BEC-4F32-9D4A-CEA8B6799E37/143836/LMO_20051024_English.pdf
Prosecutor (L. Moreno-Ocampo), Statement on Uganda Arrest Warrants, 14 October 2005, www.icc-cpi.int/NR/rdonlyres/AF169689-AFC9-41B9-8A3E-222F07DA42AD/143834/LMO_20051014_English1.pdf
Prosecutor (L. Moreno-Ocampo), Statement to Diplomatic Corps, 12 February 2004, www.icc-cpi.int/NR/rdonlyres/0F999F00-A609-4516A91A80467BC432D3/143670/LOM_20040212_En.pdf
Prosecutor (L. Moreno-Ocampo), Statement to the Security Council, 5 December 2007, www.icc-cpi.int/NR/rdonlyres/6A4AF1FE-9A86-41C6-9D38-327408612F6F/281542/ProsecutorsStateUNSCDec07EN.pdf
Prosecutor (L. Moreno-Ocampo), Tenth Statement to the Security Council on the Situation in Darfur pursuant to UNSC Res. 1593 (2005), 4 December 2009, www.icc-cpi.int/NR/rdonlyres/BA525867-5B58-4CDD-B6CF-8105181658D6/281343/UNSecurityCouncilStateFINAL1.pdf
Prosecutor (L. Moreno-Ocampo), 'The Role of International Judicial Bodies in Administering the Rule of Law', Qatar Law Forum, Doha, 30 May 2009, www.icc-cpi.int/NR/rdonlyres/10F9092D-4376-4E0B-84E1-DEBD55FA183B/280466/300509_QatarLawForum.pdf
Prosecutor (L. Moreno-Ocampo), 'Working with Africa: The View from the ICC Prosecutor's Office', ISS Symposium, Cape Winelands, 9 November 2009, www.icc-cpi.int/NR/rdonlyres/1229900D-B581-42AE-A078-918550C372FB/281385/south_africa_nov_09_3finalfordistribution.pdf
'Prosecutor Receives Referral Concerning CAR', ICC Press Release, ICC-OTP-20050107-86, 7 January 2005, www.icc-cpi.int/Menus/ICC/Situations+and+Cases/Situations/Situation+ICC+0105
'Prosecutor Receives Referral of the Situation in the DRC', ICC Press Release, ICC-OTP-20040419-50, 19 April 2004, www.icc-cpi.int/Menus/ICC/Situations+and+Cases/Situations/Situation+ICC+0104
'Referral Under Articles 14 and 12(2)(a) of the Rome Statute Arising from the 31 May 2010, Gaza Freedom Flotilla Situation', Submitted by the Union of the Comoros, 14 May 2013, www.icc-cpi.int/iccdocs/otp/Referral-from-Comoros.pdf

Registrar, Report on the Execution of the Request to Uganda for Observations on the Initiation of Proceedings pursuant to Article 19 of the Rome Statute, Annex 2, ICC-02/04-01/05-354-Anx2, 18 November 2008, www.icc-cpi.int/iccdocs/doc/doc589480.PDF

Strategic Plan of the International Criminal Court, ICC-ASP/5/6, 4 August 2006, www.icc-cpi.int/NR/rdonlyres/D6B4058F-2C5D-415E-A85F-64A305C81DF0/0/ICCASP56_English.pdf

Summary of Integrated Strategy for External Relations, Public Information and Outreach, July 2005, www.icc-cpi.int/NR/rdonlyres/425E80BA-1EBC-4423-85C6-D4F2B93C7506/185049/ICCPIDSWBOR0307070402_IS_En.pdf

Vice-President (H.-P. Kaul), 'Peace through Justice? The International Criminal Court in the Hague', National Military History Museum of the Armed Forces of Germany, 2 November 2009, www.icc-cpi.int/NR/rdonlyres/B7BC9709-394D-4449-AA08-4182A98C567B/281395/JudgeKaulSpeech.pdf

TREATY BODIES AND OTHER INTERGOVERNMENTAL FORUMS

International Law Commission

'Survey of International Law in Relation to the Work of Codification of the International Law Commission: Preparatory Work within the Purview of Article 18, Paragraph 1, of the Statute of the International Law Commission', Memorandum submitted by the UN Secretary-General, A/CN.4/1/Rev.1, 1949

First Report on the Law of Treaties by H. Lauterpacht, Special Rapporteur, A/CN.4/63 (1953) *ILC Yearbook*, Vol. II, 90

Second Report on the Law of Treaties by H. Lauterpacht, Special Rapporteur, A/CN.4/87 and Corr.1 (1954) *ILC Yearbook*, Vol. II, 123

First Report on the Law of Treaties by G. Fitzmaurice, Special Rapporteur, A/CN.4/101 (1956) *ILC Yearbook*, Vol. II, 105

Third Report on the Law of Treaties by G. Fitzmaurice, Special Rapporteur, A/CN.4/101 (1958) *ILC Yearbook*, Vol. II, 21

Second Report on the Law of Treaties by H. Waldock, Special Rapporteur, A/CN.4/156 and Add.1–3 (1963) *ILC Yearbook*, Vol. II, 36

Third Report on the Law of Treaties by H. Waldock, Special Rapporteur, A/CN.4/167 and Add.1–3 (1964) *ILC Yearbook*, Vol. II, 6

Report to the UN General Assembly on the Law of Treaties, A/5809 (1964) *ILC Yearbook*, Vol. II, 177

Draft Articles on the Law of Treaties with Commentaries, (1966) *ILC Yearbook*, Vol.II, 187

Third Report on State Responsibility by J. Crawford, Special Rapporteur, UN Doc. A/CN.4/507, 10 March 2000

'Fragmentation of International Law: Difficulties arising from the Diversification and Expansion of International Law', Report of the ILC Study Group compiled by M. Koskenniemi, Chairman of the Study Group, A/CN.4/L.682, 2006

Summary Record of the 685th Mtg of the ILC, A/CN.4/SR.685 (22 May 1963)
Summary Record of the 687th Mtg of the ILC, A/CN.4/SR.687 (27 May 1963)
Summary Record of the 703rd Mtg of the ILC, A/CN.4/SR.703 (19 June 1963)
Summary Record of the 742nd Mtg of the ILC, A/CN.4/SR.742 (10 June 1964)
Summary Record of the 743rd Mtg of the ILC, A/CN.4/SR.743 (11 June 1964)
Summary Record of the 755th Mtg of the ILC, A/CN.4/SR.755 (30 June 1964)
Summary Record of the 857th Mtg of the ILC, A/CN.4/SR.857 (24 May 1966)
Summary Record of the 858th Mtg of the ILC, A/CN.4/SR.858 (25 May 1966)
Summary Record of the 875th Mtg of the ILC, A/CN.4/SR.875 (22 June 1966)
Summary Record of the 893rd Mtg of the ILC, A/CN.4/SR.893 (18 July 1966)

Law of the Sea, International Seabed Authority

A. Clark *et al.*, 'Towards the Development of a Regulatory Framework for Polymetallic Nodule Exploitation in the Area', ISA Technical Study No. 11, 26 February 2013, www.isa.org.jm/files/documents/EN/Pubs/TStudy11.pdf

'Towards the Development of a Regulatory Framework for Polymetallic Nodule Exploitation in the Area', Note by the ISA Secretariat, ISBA/19/C/5, 25 March 2013, www.isa.org.jm/files/documents/EN/19Sess/Council/ISBA-19C-5.pdf

'Council Considers Secretariat's Note on Regulatory Framework for Nodules Exploitation', Press Release SB/19/14, 22 July 2013, www.isa.org.jm/files/documents/EN/Press/Press13/SB-19-14.pdf

Law of the Sea, Secretary General's Informal Consultations

'Boat Paper (August 3, 1993)' (1993) 9 *International Organizations and the Law of the Sea Documentary Yearbook* 440

'Boat Paper (Amended), Report of the Secretary-General, UN Doc. A/48/950 (June 9, 1994), Annex II: "Draft Resolution and Draft Agreement Relating to the Implementation of Part XI of the United Nations Convention on the Law of the Sea of 10 December 1982"' (1994) 10 *International Organizations and the Law of the Sea Documentary Yearbook* 76

'Consultations of the Secretary General on Outstanding Issues: Report of the UN Secretary General (9 June 1992)' (1994) 10 *International Organizations and the Law of the Sea Documentary Yearbook* 76

'Information Note Concerning the Secretary General's Informal Consultations (December 10, 1992)' (1992) 8 *International Organizations and the Law of the Sea Documentary Yearbook* 246

'Information Note Concerning the Secretary General's Informal Consultations (April 8, 1993)' (1993) 9 *International Organizations and the Law of the Sea Documentary Yearbook* 431

Report of the UN Secretary-General, 'Law of the Sea', Addendum, A/48/527/Add.1, 30 November 1993, (1993) 9 *International Organizations and the Law of the Sea Documentary Yearbook* 79

Law of the Sea, PrepCom

'Current Status of Deep Seabed Exploration and Mining Technology', Paper Prepared by PrepCom Secretariat, LOS/PCN/L.56, 23 February 1988

Decision of the General Committee of the PrepCom on the Application of France for Registration as a Pioneer Investor under Resolution II (December 17), LOS/PCN/97, 6 January 1988

Decision of the General Committee of the PrepCom on the Application of Japan for Registration as a Pioneer Investor under Resolution II (December 17), LOS/PCN/98, 6 January 1988

Decision of the General Committee of the PrepCom on the Application of the USSR for Registration as a Pioneer Investor under Resolution II (December 17), LOS/PCN/99, 6 January 1988

Decision of the General Committee on the Application of India for Registration as a Pioneer Investor under Resolution II, LOS/PCN/94, 9 October 1987

Declaration adopted by the Preparatory Commission (August 30), LOS/PCN/72, 2 September 1985

Declaration of the Group of 77, LOS/PCN/5, 11 April 1983

'Economic Viability of Deep Seabed Mining of Polymetallic Nodules', Working Paper submitted by Australia, LOS/PCN/SCN.2/WP.10, 14 January 1986

Letter from France, Japan and the USSR addressed to the Chairman of the Preparatory Commission (February 28), LOS/PCN/56, 12 March 1985

Letter from Japan addressed to the Chairman of the Preparatory Commission, LOS/PCN/45, 16 August 1984

Letters from the Acting Permanent Representative of the USSR addressed to the Chairman of the Preparatory Commission (June 28), LOS/PCN/65–66, 8 July 1985

Letters from the Acting Permanent Representative of the USSR (June 10), LOS/PCN/64, 1 July 1985 and LOS/PCN/76, 27 March 1986

Letter from the Alternate Representative of the Delegation of Canada addressed to the Chairman of the Preparatory Commission (April 11), LOS/PCN/40, 11 April 1984

Letter from the Chairman of the Delegation of Belgium addressed to the Chairman of the Preparatory Commission (April 2), LOS/PCN/61, 26 April 1985

Letter from the Chairman of the Delegation of Canada addressed to the Chairman of the Preparatory Commission (April 3), LOS/PCN/63, 26 April 1985

Letter from the Chairman of the Delegation of China addressed to the Chairman of the Preparatory Commission (August 15), LOS/PCN/71, 20 August 1985

Letter from the Chairman of the Delegation of Federal Republic of Germany addressed to the Chairman of the Preparatory Commission (April 6), LOS/PCN/37, 6 April 1984

Letter from the Chairman of the Delegation of Federal Republic of Germany addressed to the Acting Chairman of the Preparatory Commission (August 6), LOS/PCN/93, 6 August 1987

Letter from the Chairman of the Delegation of France addressed to the Chairman of the Preparatory Commission (April 2), LOS/PCN/35, 2 April 1984
Letter from the Chairman of the Delegation of France addressed to the Chairman of the Preparatory Commission (April 12), LOS/PCN/44, 12 April 1984
Letters from the Chairman of the Delegation of France addressed to the Chairman of the Preparatory Commission (July 31), LOS/PCN/67–70, 16 August 1985
Letter from the Chairman of the Delegation of Italy addressed to the Chairman of the Preparatory Commission (April 2), LOS/PCN/62, 26 April 1985
Letter from the Chairman of the Delegation of Japan addressed to the Chairman of the Preparatory Commission (March 29), LOS/PCN/34, 29 March 1984
Letter from the Chairman of the Delegation of Japan addressed to the Chairman of the Preparatory Commission (April 12), LOS/PCN/42, 12 April 1984
Letter from the Chairman of the Delegation of the Federal Republic of Germany addressed to the Chairman of the Preparatory Commission (October 25), LOS/PCN/73, 9 January 1986
Letter from the Chairman of the Delegation of the Netherlands addressed to the Chairman of the Preparatory Commission (March 28), LOS/PCN/60, 26 April 1985
Letter from the Chairman of the Delegation of the United Kingdom addressed to the Chairman of the Preparatory Commission (September 4), LOS/PCN/54, 24 September 1984
Letter from the Chairman of the Delegation of the United Kingdom addressed to the Chairman of the Preparatory Commission (November 4), LOS/PCN/74, 9 January 1986
Letter from the Chairman of the Delegation of the United Kingdom addressed to the Acting Chairman of the Preparatory Commission (August 5), LOS/PCN/92, 6 August 1987
Letter from the Chairman of the Delegation of the USSR addressed to the Chairman of the Preparatory Commission (March 27), LOS/PCN/76, 27 March 1986
Letter from the Chairman of the Delegation of France to the PrepCom Chairman (August 3), LOS/PCN/47, 16 August 1984
Letter from the Chairman of the USSR Delegation addressed to the Chairman of the Preparatory Commission (April 3), LOS/PCN/36, 5 April 1984
Letter from the Chairman of the USSR Delegation addressed to the Preparatory Commission (April 6), LOS/PCN/4, 8 April 1983
Letter from the Chairman of the USSR Delegation addressed to the Preparatory Commission (April 9), LOS/PCN/38, 10 April 1984
Letter from the Delegation of the USSR addressed to the Chairman of the Preparatory Commission (March 19), LOS/PCN/81, 24 March 1987
Letter from the Delegations of France, India, Japan and the USSR addressed to the Chairman of the Preparatory Commission (March 19), LOS/PCN/82, 24 March 1987

Letter from the Government of the Netherlands to the PrepCom Chairman (August 3), LOS/PCN/46, 16 August 1984

Letter from the Head of Bulgarian Delegation and Chairman of the Group of Eastern European Socialist Countries (August 21), LOS/PCN/L.7/Rev.1, 21 August 1984

Letter from the Permanent Representative of Belgium to the United Nations addressed to the Chairman of the Preparatory Commission (April 27), LOS/PCN/14, 29 April 1983

Letter from the Permanent Representative of Canada to the United Nations addressed to the Chairman of the Preparatory Commission (April 28), LOS/PCN/15, 29 April 1983

Letter from the Permanent Representative of France to the United Nations addressed to the Chairman of the Preparatory Commission (April 27), LOS/PCN/8, 27 April 1983

Letter from the Permanent Representative of Italy to the United Nations addressed to the Chairman of the Preparatory Commission (April 28), LOS/PCN/10, 28 April 1983

Letter from the Permanent Representative of Japan to the United Nations addressed to the Chairman of the Preparatory Commission (April 28), LOS/PCN/11, 28 April 1983

Letter from the Permanent Representative of the Netherlands to the United Nations addressed to the Chairman of the Preparatory Commission (April 27), LOS/PCN/18, 3 May 1983

Letter from the Permanent Representative of the USSR to the United Nations addressed to the Chairman of the Preparatory Commission (July 20), LOS/PCN/30, 24 October 1983

Letter from the Representative of the United Kingdom addressed to the Chairman of the Preparatory Commission (April 27), LOS/PCN/13, 29 April 1983

Letter from the Representatives of the Delegations of Belgium, Canada, Italy, and the Netherlands addressed to the Chairman of the Preparatory Commission (March 30), LOS/PCN/83, 30 March 1987

Letter from the Representatives of the Delegations of Belgium, Canada, Italy, the Netherlands and the USSR addressed to the Chairman of the Preparatory Commission (August 3), LOS/PCN/90, 3 August 1987

Letter from the Representatives of the Delegations of Belgium, France, the Federal Republic of Germany, Italy, Japan, the Netherlands and the United Kingdom addressed to the Chairman of the Preparatory Commission (April 12), LOS/PCN/41, 12 April 1984

Letter from the USSR, LOS/PCN/17, 2 May 1983

Note Verbale from the Permanent Representative of India to the United Nations addressed to the Chairman of the Preparatory Commission (April 24), LOS/PCN/7, 26 April 1983

Note Verbale from the Permanent Representative of the Federal Republic of Germany to the United Nations addressed to the Chairman of the Preparatory Commission (April 27), LOS/PCN/9, 28 April 1983

'PrepCom Agrees on Formula on Registration of Pioneer Investors; Decides to Hold Next Session in March/April at Kingston', Press Release SEA/777, 8 September 1986

PrepCom Declaration, LOS/PCN/78, 21 April 1986

'PrepCom Hears Calls for Early Finalization of Work', Press Release SEA/KIN/32, 13 March 1992

'PrepCom Hears Calls for Resolution of "Hard Core" Issues, Statement by Thailand on Behalf of the G77', Press Release SEA/1285, 30 August 1991

'PrepCom Hears Statements on Registration of Pioneer Investors; Clarifications Requested by Speakers', Press Release SEA/KIN/3, 31 March 1987

'PrepCom to Begin First Session at Kingston', Press Release SEA/515, 9 March 1983

Progress Report by the PrepCom Chairman, LOS/PCN/L.103, 7 July 1992

Receipt of a Revised Application from France for Registration as a Pioneer Investor under Resolution II of UNCLOS III, LOS/PCN/89, 23 July 1987

Receipt of a Revised Application from India for Registration as a Pioneer Investor under Resolution II of UNCLOS III, LOS/PCN/87, 23 July 1987

Receipt of a Revised Application from Japan for Registration of the Japanese Enterprise 'Deep Ocean Resources Development Co. Ltd' as a Pioneer Investor under Resolution II of UNCLOS III, LOS/PCN/86, 23 July 1987

Receipt of a Revised Application from the USSR for Registration of the Soviet Enterprise 'Yuhzmorgeologia' as a Pioneer Investor, LOS/PCN/88, 23 July 1987

Receipt of Application from France for Registration of AFERNOD as a Pioneer Investor under Resolution II of UNCLOS III, LOS/PCN/51, 23 August 1984

Receipt of Application from India for Registration as a Pioneer Investor under Resolution II of UNCLOS III, LOS/PCN/32, 14 February 1984

Receipt of Application from Japan for Registration of the Japanese Enterprise 'Deep Ocean Resources Development Co., Ltd.' as a Pioneer Investor under Resolution II of UNCLOS III, LOS/PCN/50, 22 August 1984

Report by the PrepCom Chairman regarding the Resolution of Conflicts among Applicants for Registration as Pioneer Investors, LOS/PCN/L.28, 21 March 1986

'Seabed Authority Preparatory Commission Resumes Session, Hears Soviet Appeal for Immediate Registration of Pioneer Investors', Press Release SEA/821, 27 July 1987

'Secretary-General's Statement to the Law of the Sea Preparatory Commission on Settlement Reached Concerning Deep Seabed Mine Site Claims', Press Release SEA/845, 6 August 1987

'Special Commission on Mining Code Discusses Obligations of Contractors to Transfer Technology to Enterprise', Press Release SEA/KIN/37, 29 March 1988

Statement by PrepCom Chairman, LOS/PCN/L.13, 4 September 1984

Statement by PrepCom Chairman, LOS/PCN/L.62, 7 April 1988

Statement by PrepCom Chairman, LOS/PCN/L.67, 1 September 1988

Statement by PrepCom Chairman, LOS/PCN/L.87, 30 August 1990
Statement by PrepCom Chairman, LOS/PCN/L.102, 13 March 1992
Statement by PrepCom Chairman, LOS/PCN/L.108, 20 August 1992
Statement by the Acting Chairman of the PrepCom, LOS/PCN/L.34, 10 April 1986
Statement by the Chairman of the Group of 77, LOS/PCN/L.5, 20 March 1985
Statement by the Chairman of the Group of East European Socialist Countries (August 13), LOS/PCN/49, 17 August 1984
Statement by the G77 Chairman delivered to the Preparatory Commission (August 13), LOS/PCN/48, 16 August 1984
Statement by the G77 Chairman delivered to the Preparatory Commission (March 11), LOS/PCN/L.15, 20 March 1985
Statement by the G77 Chairman, LOS/PCN/L.35, 10 April 1986
Statement by the Netherlands, on behalf of Belgium, France, Germany, Italy, Japan and the United Kingdom (August 14), LOS/PCN/52, 24 August 1984
Statement by the PrepCom Chairman (August 22), LOS/PCN/L.36, 2 September 1986
Statement made by the Acting Chairman of the PrepCom, LOS/PCN/L.41, 5 September 1986
Statement made by the Acting Chairman of the PrepCom, LOS/PCN/L.41/Rev.1, 11 September 1986
Statement of PrepCom Chairman regarding the Understanding on Resolution of Conflicts among Applicants for Registration as Pioneer Investors, LOS/PCN/L.8, 31 August 1984
Statement of Understanding on the Implementation of Resolution II made by PrepCom Chairman (April 10), LOS/PCN/L.43/Rev.1, 15 April 1987
Statements by Denmark on behalf of the Friends of the Group of Eleven, France on behalf of the European Economic Community, Bulgaria on behalf of the Group of Eastern European States, Italy on behalf of the Group of Six (UK, the Netherlands, Belgium, Japan, Italy, and Germany), and Canada on behalf of Potential Applicants (1 September 1989), 15 *Law of the Sea Bulletin*, May 1990
Statements by the Representative from Jamaica, and France on behalf of India, Japan and the USSR reported in Press Release SEA/1193, 31 August 1990
Statement by Zambia on behalf of the G77 (1 September 1989), 15 *Law of the Sea Bulletin*, May 1990
Suggestions from the PrepCom Chairman adopted at the 5th Plenary Meeting of the PrepCom (September 8), LOS/PCN/27, 8 September 1983

Nuclear Suppliers Group

Plenary Meeting Press Release, Göteborg, Sweden, 27–28 May 2004, NSG_GOT/PRESS/FINAL, www.nuclearsuppliersgroup.org/Leng/PRESS/2004-05-goteborg.pdf
'Public Statement', Extraordinary Plenary Meeting, Vienna, 21–22 August 2008

Report by the Representative of Italy, Ambassador Giuseppe Balboni Acqua, on NSG Transparency, 2000 NPT Review Conference, Main Committee III, New York 27 April 2000, www.nuclearsuppliersgroup.org/Leng/PDF/NPT_2000_Report_by_NSG_1.pdf

Statement by HE Ambassador Györgyi Martin Zanathy, Delegation of the Republic of Hungary, 2010 NPT Review Conference, Main Committee II, New York, 13 May 2010, www.nuclearsuppliersgroup.org/Leng/PDF/NSG-H-statement.pdf

'The Nuclear Suppliers Group: Its Origins, Role and Activities', Background document prepared by the Nuclear Suppliers Group, INFCIRC/539/Rev.3, 2005

US Draft of NSG waiver for India, 2006, www.armscontrolwonk.com/1009/us-nsg-india-proposal

GOVERNMENT DOCUMENTS

Legislation

France: Law on the Exploration and Exploitation of the Mineral Resources of the Deep Sea-bed, 1981, 21 ILM 808

Germany (FRG): Act of Interim Regulation of Deep Seabed Mining, 1980, 20 ILM 393 (amended 1982, 21 ILM 832)

India: Weapons of Mass Destruction and Their Delivery Systems (Prohibition of Unlawful Activities) Act, Act No. 21 of 2005, *The Gazette of India Extraordinary*, Part II, 6 June 2005

India: Civil Liability for Nuclear Damage Act, Act No. 38 of 2010, *The Gazette of India Extraordinary*, No. 47, Part II, 21 September 2010

Italy: Regulations on the Exploration and Exploitation of the Mineral Resources of the Deep Sea-bed, 1985, 24 ILM 983

Japan: Law on Interim Measures for Deep Sea-bed Mining, 1982, 22 ILM 102

Uganda: International Criminal Court Act, 2010, *Uganda Gazette*, No. 39, Vol. 103, 25 June 2010

Uganda: Amnesty Act, 2000, *Uganda Gazette*, No. 5, Vol. 103, 21 January 2000

UK: Deep Sea Mining (Temporary Provisions) Act, 1981, 20 ILM 1217

UK: International Seabed Authority (Immunities and Privileges) Order 1996

US: American Service-Members' Protection Act, Public Law 107-206, 2 August 2002

US: Atomic Energy Act, Public Law 83-703, 30 August 1954

US: Deep Seabed Hard Mineral Resources Act, 1980, Public Law 96-283, 19 ILM 1003 (1980)

US: Foreign Relations Authorization Act for Fiscal Years 1990 and 1991 (1990), Public Law 101-246, 16 February 1990

US: Henry J. Hyde United States–India Peaceful Atomic Energy Cooperation Act 2006, Public Law 109-401, 18 December 2006

US: Joint Resolution of Congress, Relating to the approval and implementation of the proposed agreement for nuclear cooperation between the United

States and the People's Republic of China, 1985, Public Law 99-183 (SJ Res. 238), 16 December 1985
US: Nethercutt Amendment, Public Law 108-447, 8 December 2004
US: Nuclear Proliferation Prevention Act, Public Law 103-236, 30 April 1994
USSR: Edict on Provisional Measures to Regulate Soviet Enterprises for the Exploration and Exploitation of Mineral Resources, 1982, 21 ILM 551

Other documents

Canada: Department of Foreign Affairs and International Trade 'Canada Welcomes Exception for India from Nuclear Suppliers Group Guidelines', News Release 198, 6 September 2008
India: External Affairs Minister, 'Statement on the Civil Nuclear Initiative', 5 September 2008
India: Prime Minister (A. B. Vajpayee), 'Next Steps in Strategic Partnership with USA', Statement, New Delhi, 13 January 2004
US: Department of Commerce, Bureau of Industry and Security, 'Announcement on USA–India Next Steps in Strategic Partnership', September 2004
US: Department of Energy, Global Nuclear Energy Partnership Strategic Plan, January 2007, www.fas.org/programs/ssp/_docs/GNEPStratPlanJan07.pdf
US: Department of State Assistant Secretary (J. T. Bergner), Letter to Chairman, Committee on Foreign Affairs, US House of Representatives (T. Lantos) responding to 'Questions for the record submitted to Assistant Secretary Bergner by Chairman Lantos on October 5, 2007', 16 January 2008, http://media.washingtonpost.com/wp-srv/world/documents/Lantos_Letter.pdf
US: Department of State Deputy Spokesman (P. T. Reeker), Statement, 16 February 2001, www.fas.org/nuke/control/nsg/news/treaty-nsg-010216.htm
US: Department of State, 'Iran Sanctions', www.state.gov/e/eb/tfs/spi/iran/index.htm
US: Department of State, Daily Press Briefing, 30 October 1997, www.fas.org/news/usa/1997/10/971030db.html
US: Department of State, Daily Press Briefing, 2 September 2004, http://usinfo.org/wf-archive/2004/040902/epf401.htm
US: Department of State, Press Release, 2 March 1981
US: House Committee on International Relations, Testimony by D. Albright, President, Institute for Science and International Security, Hearing on the USA–India 'Global Partnership' and Its Impact on Non-Proliferation, 26 October 2005
US: National Oceanic and Atmospheric Administration, 'Deep Seabed Mining Report to the US Congress in compliance with Section 309 of the Deep Seabed Hard Mineral Resources Act (PL 96-283)', December 1989, www.gc.noaa.gov/documents/gcil_dsm_89_20110607085546.pdf

US: President (G. W. Bush), 'Statement on Next Steps in Strategic Partnership with India', 12 January 2004, www.gpo.gov/fdsys/pkg/WCPD-2004-01-19/pdf/WCPD-2004-01-19-Pg61-2.pdf

US: Secretary of State (C. Powell), Hearing before the US Senate Committee on Foreign Relations on 'The Current Situation in Sudan and the Prospects for Peace', 108th Congress, 2nd Sess., 9 September 2004

US: Secretary of State (C. Rice), Opening Remarks before the US Senate Committee on Foreign Relations, 5 April 2006

US: Senate Committee on Foreign Relations, Testimony of A. B. Carter, Co-Director, Preventive Defense Project, John F. Kennedy School of Government, Harvard University, Hearing on USA–India Atomic Energy Cooperation: Strategic and Non-Proliferation Implications, 26 April 2006

US: Senate Committee on Foreign Relations, Testimony of R. Gallucci, Dean of the Edmund A. Walsh School of Foreign Service, Georgetown University, Hearing on USA–India Atomic Energy Cooperation: Strategic and Non-Proliferation Implications, 26 April 2006

US: Senate Committee on Foreign Relations, Testimony of R. J. Einhorn, Senior Advisor, Center for Strategic and International Studies, Hearing on USA–India Atomic Energy Cooperation: Strategic and Non-Proliferation Implications, 26 April 2006

US: Working Papers and Statements at Meetings of Preparatory Committee for the 2010 NPT Review Conference, www.un.org/NPT2010/documents.html

Index

CAMBRIDGE STUDIES IN INTERNATIONAL AND COMPARATIVE LAW

Books in the series

Strategically Created Treaty Conflicts and the Politics of International Law
Surabhi Ranganathan

Investment Treaty Arbitration as Public International Law: Procedural Aspects and Implications
Eric De Brabandere

The New Entrants Problem in International Fisheries Law
Andrew Serdy

Substantive Protection under Investment Treaties: A Legal and Economic Analysis
Jonathan Bonnitcha

Popular Governance of Post-Conflict Reconstruction: The Role of International Law
Matthew Saul

Evolution of International Environmental Regimes: The Case of Climate Change
Simone Schiele

Judges, Law and War: The Judicial Development of International Humanitarian Law
Shane Darcy

Religious Offence and Human Rights: The Implications of Defamation of Religions
Lorenz Langer

Forum Shopping in International Adjudication: The Role of Preliminary Objections
Luiz Eduardo Ribeiro Salles

International Law and the Arctic
Michael Byers

Cooperation in the Law of Transboundary Water Resources
Christina Leb

Underwater Cultural Heritage and International Law
Sarah Dromgoole

State Responsibility: The General Part
James Crawford

The Origins of International Investment Law
Kate Miles

The Crime of Aggression under the Rome Statute of the International Criminal Court
Carrie McDougall

Crimes against Peace and International Law
Kirsten Sellars

The Non-Legal in International Law
Fleur Johns

Armed Conflict and Displacement: The Protection of Refugees and Displaced Persons under International Humanitarian Law
Mélanie Jacques

Foreign Investment and the Environment in International Law
Jorge Viñuales

The Human Rights Treaty Obligations of Peacekeepers
Kjetil Larsen

Cyberwarfare and the Laws of War
Heather Harrison Dinniss

The Right to Reparation in International Law for Victims of Armed Conflict
Christine Evans

Global Public Interest in International Investment Law
Andreas Kulick

State Immunity in International Law
Xiaodong Yang

Reparations and Victim Support in the International Criminal Court
Conor McCarthy

Reducing Genocide to Law: Definition, Meaning, and the Ultimate Crime
Payam Akhavan

Decolonizing International Law: Development, Economic Growth and the Politics of Universality
Sundhya Pahuja

Complicity and the Law of State Responsibility
Helmut Philipp Aust

State Control over Private Military and Security Companies in Armed Conflict
Hannah Tonkin

'Fair and Equitable Treatment' in International Investment Law
Roland Kläger

The UN and Human Rights: Who Guards the Guardians?
Guglielmo Verdirame

Sovereign Defaults before International Courts and Tribunals
Michael Waibel

Making the Law of the Sea: A Study in the Development of International Law
James Harrison

Science and the Precautionary Principle in International Courts and Tribunals: Expert Evidence, Burden of Proof and Finality
Caroline E. Foster

Transition from Illegal Regimes in International Law
Yaël Ronen

Access to Asylum: International Refugee Law and the Globalisation of Migration Control
Thomas Gammeltoft-Hansen

Trading Fish, Saving Fish: The Interaction between Regimes in International Law
Margaret Young

The Individual in the International Legal System: Continuity and Change in International Law
Kate Parlett

The Participation of States in International Organisations: The Role of Human Rights and Democracy
Alison Duxbury

'Armed Attack' and Article 51 of the UN Charter: Evolutions in Customary Law and Practice
Tom Ruys

Science and Risk Regulation in International Law
Jacqueline Peel

Theatre of the Rule of Law: Transnational Legal Intervention in Theory and Practice
Stephen Humphreys

The Public International Law Theory of Hans Kelsen: Believing in Universal Law
Jochen von Bernstorff

Vicarious Liability in Tort: A Comparative Perspective
Paula Giliker

Legal Personality in International Law
Roland Portmann

Legitimacy and Legality in International Law: An Interactional Account
Jutta Brunnée and Stephen J. Toope

The Concept of Non-International Armed Conflict in International Humanitarian Law
Anthony Cullen

The Challenge of Child Labour in International Law
Franziska Humbert

Shipping Interdiction and the Law of the Sea
Douglas Guilfoyle

International Courts and Environmental Protection
Tim Stephens

Legal Principles in WTO Disputes
Andrew D. Mitchell

War Crimes in Internal Armed Conflicts
Eve La Haye

Humanitarian Occupation
Gregory H. Fox

The International Law of Environmental Impact Assessment: Process, Substance and Integration
Neil Craik

The Law and Practice of International Territorial Administration: Versailles to Iraq and Beyond
Carsten Stahn

Cultural Products and the World Trade Organization
Tania Voon

United Nations Sanctions and the Rule of Law
Jeremy Farrall

National Law in WTO Law: Effectiveness and Good Governance in the World Trading System
Sharif Bhuiyan

The Threat of Force in International Law
Nikolas Stürchler

Indigenous Rights and United Nations Standards
Alexandra Xanthaki

International Refugee Law and Socio-Economic Rights
Michelle Foster

The Protection of Cultural Property in Armed Conflict
Roger O'Keefe

Interpretation and Revision of International Boundary Decisions
Kaiyan Homi Kaikobad

Multinationals and Corporate Social Responsibility: Limitations and Opportunities in International Law
Jennifer A. Zerk

Judiciaries within Europe: A Comparative Review
John Bell

Law in Times of Crisis: Emergency Powers in Theory and Practice
Oren Gross and Fionnuala Ní Aoláin

Vessel-Source Marine Pollution:The Law and Politics of International Regulation
Alan Tan

Enforcing Obligations Erga Omnes *in International Law*
Christian J. Tams

Non-Governmental Organisations in International Law
Anna-Karin Lindblom

Democracy, Minorities and International Law
Steven Wheatley

Prosecuting International Crimes: Selectivity and the International Law Regime
Robert Cryer

Compensation for Personal Injury in English, German and Italian Law: A Comparative Outline
Basil Markesinis, Michael Coester, Guido Alpa, Augustus Ullstein

Dispute Settlement in the UN Convention on the Law of the Sea
Natalie Klein

The International Protection of Internally Displaced Persons
Catherine Phuong

Imperialism, Sovereignty and the Making of International Law
Antony Anghie

Necessity, Proportionality and the Use of Force by States
Judith Gardam

International Legal Argument in the Permanent Court of International Justice: The Rise of the International Judiciary
Ole Spiermann

Great Powers and Outlaw States: Unequal Sovereigns in the International Legal Order
Gerry Simpson

Local Remedies in International Law
C.F. Amerasinghe

Reading Humanitarian Intervention:Human Rights and the Use of Force in International Law
Anne Orford

Conflict of Norms in Public International Law: How WTO Law Relates to Other Rules of International Law
Joost Pauwelyn

Transboundary Damage in International Law
Hanqin Xue

European Criminal Procedures
Edited by Mireille Delmas-Marty and John Spencer

The Accountability of Armed Opposition Groups in International Law
Liesbeth Zegveld

Sharing Transboundary Resources: International Law and Optimal Resource Use
Eyal Benvenisti

International Human Rights and Humanitarian Law
René Provost

Remedies Against International Organisations
Karel Wellens

Diversity and Self-Determination in International Law
Karen Knop

The Law of Internal Armed Conflict
Lindsay Moir

International Commercial Arbitration and African States: Practice, Participation and Institutional Development
Amazu A. Asouzu

The Enforceability of Promises in European Contract Law
James Gordley

International Law in Antiquity
David J. Bederman

Money Laundering: A New International Law Enforcement Model
Guy Stessens

Good Faith in European Contract Law
Reinhard Zimmermann and Simon Whittaker

On Civil Procedure
J.A. Jolowicz

Trusts: A Comparative Study
Maurizio Lupoi

The Right to Property in Commonwealth Constitutions
Tom Allen

International Organizations Before National Courts
August Reinisch

The Changing International Law of High Seas Fisheries
Francisco Orrego Vicuña

Trade and the Environment: A Comparative Study of EC and US Law
Damien Geradin

Unjust Enrichment: A Study of Private Law and Public Values
Hanoch Dagan

Religious Liberty and International Law in Europe
Malcolm D. Evans

Ethics and Authority in International Law
Alfred P. Rubin

Sovereignty Over Natural Resources: Balancing Rights and Duties
Nico Schrijver

The Polar Regions and the Development of International Law
Donald R. Rothwell

Fragmentation and the International Relations of Micro-States: Self-determination and Statehood
Jorri Duursma

Principles of the Institutional Law of International Organizations
C.F. Amerasinghe

Lightning Source UK Ltd.
Milton Keynes UK
UKOW04n0614250816

281437UK00005B/117/P

9 781107 043305